ACCA

S T U D Y   T E X T

PAPER P2

CORPORATE REPORTING (INTERNATIONAL)

In this new syllabus third edition approved by ACCA

- We **discuss** the **best strategies** for studying for ACCA exams
- We **highlight** the **most important elements** in the syllabus and the **key skills** you will need
- We **signpost** how each chapter links to the syllabus and the study guide
- We **provide** lots of **exam focus points** demonstrating what the examiner will want you to do
- We emphasise key points in regular **fast forward summaries**
- We **test your knowledge** of what you've studied in **quick quizzes**
- We **examine your understanding** in our **exam question bank**
- We **reference all the important topics** in our **full index**
- Fully up to date for all examinable documents.

BPP's **i-Learn** and **i-Pass** products also support this paper.

FOR EXAMS IN DECEMBER 2009 AND JUNE 2010

LEARNING MEDIA

First edition 2007

Third edition June 2009

ISBN 9780 7517 6376 8
(Previous ISBN 9780 7517 4735 5)

British Library Cataloguing-in-Publication Data
A catalogue record for this book
is available from the British Library

Published by

BPP Learning Media Ltd
BPP House, Aldine Place
London W12 8AA

www.bpp.com/learningmedia

Printed in the United Kingdom

We are grateful to the Association of Chartered Certified
Accountants for permission to reproduce past
examination questions. The suggested solutions in the
exam answer bank have been prepared by BPP Learning
Media Ltd, except where otherwise stated.

Your learning materials, published by BPP
Learning Media Ltd, are printed on paper
sourced from sustainable, managed forests.

Contents

A note about copyright

Dear Customer

What does the little © mean and why does it matter?

Your market-leading BPP books, course materials and e-learning materials do not write and update themselves. People write them: on their own behalf or as employees of an organisation that invests in this activity. Copyright law protects their livelihoods. It does so by creating rights over the use of the content.

Breach of copyright is a form of theft – as well as being a criminal offence in some jurisdictions, it is potentially a serious breach of professional ethics.

With current technology, things might seem a bit hazy but, basically, without the express permission of BPP Learning Media:

- Photocopying our materials is a breach of copyright
- Scanning, ripcasting or conversion of our digital materials into different file formats, uploading them to facebook or emailing them to your friends is a breach of copyright

You can, of course, sell your books, in the form in which you have bought them – once you have finished with them. (Is this fair to your fellow students? We update for a reason.) But the e-products are sold on a single user licence basis: we do not supply 'unlock' codes to people who have bought them second-hand.

And what about outside the UK? BPP Learning Media strives to make our materials available at prices students can afford by local printing arrangements, pricing policies and partnerships which are clearly listed on our website. A tiny minority ignore this and indulge in criminal activity by illegally photocopying our material or supporting organisations that do. If they act illegally and unethically in one area, can you really trust them?

How the BPP ACCA-approved Study Text can help you pass your exams – AND help you with your Practical Experience Requirement!

NEW FEATURE – the PER alert!

Before you can qualify as an ACCA member, you do not only have to pass all your exams but also fulfil a three year **practical experience requirement** (PER). To help you to recognise areas of the syllabus that you might be able to apply in the workplace to achieve different performance objectives, we have introduced the '**PER alert**' feature. You will find this feature throughout the Study Text to remind you that what you are **learning to pass** your ACCA exams is **equally useful to the fulfilment of the PER requirement**.

Tackling studying

Studying can be a daunting prospect, particularly when you have lots of other commitments. The **different features** of the text, the **purposes** of which are explained fully on the **Chapter features** page, will help you whilst studying and improve your chances of **exam success**.

Developing exam awareness

Our Texts are completely **focused** on helping you pass your exam.

Our advice on **Studying P4** outlines the **content** of the paper, the **necessary skills** the examiner expects you to demonstrate and any **brought forward knowledge** you are expected to have.

Exam focus points are included within the chapters to highlight when and how specific topics were examined, or how they might be examined in the future.

Using the Syllabus and Study Guide

You can find the syllabus, Study Guide and other useful resources for P4 on the ACCA web site:

www.accaglobal.com/students/study_exams/qualifications/acca_choose/acca/professional/afm/

The Study Text covers **all aspects** of the syllabus to ensure you are as fully prepared for the exam as possible.

Testing what you can do

Testing yourself helps you develop the skills you need to pass the exam and also confirms that you can recall what you have learnt.

We include **Questions** – lots of them - both within chapters and in the **Exam Question Bank**, as well as **Quick Quizzes** at the end of each chapter to test your knowledge of the chapter content.

Chapter features

Each chapter contains a number of helpful features to guide you through each topic.

Topic list

Topic list	Syllabus reference

Tells you what you will be studying in this chapter and the relevant section numbers, together the ACCA syllabus references.

Introduction

Puts the chapter content in the context of the syllabus as a whole.

Study Guide

Links the chapter content with ACCA guidance.

Exam Guide

Highlights how examinable the chapter content is likely to be and the ways in which it could be examined.

Knowledge brought forward from earlier studies

What you are assumed to know from previous studies/exams.

FAST FORWARD 〉〉

Summarises the content of main chapter headings, allowing you to preview and review each section easily.

Examples

Demonstrate how to apply key knowledge and techniques.

Key terms

Definitions of important concepts that can often earn you easy marks in exams.

Exam focus points

Tell you when and how specific topics were examined, or how they may be examined in the future.

Formula to learn

Formulae that are not given in the exam but which have to be learnt.

PER alert

This is a new feature that gives you a useful indication of syllabus areas that closely relate to performance objectives in your Practical Experience Requirement (PER).

Question

Give you essential practice of techniques covered in the chapter.

Case Study

Provide real world examples of theories and techniques.

Chapter Roundup

A full list of the Fast Forwards included in the chapter, providing an easy source of review.

Quick Quiz

A quick test of your knowledge of the main topics in the chapter.

Exam Question Bank

Found at the back of the Study Text with more comprehensive chapter questions. Cross referenced for easy navigation.

Studying P2

Paper P2 Corporate Reporting is a demanding paper, reflecting the demands that will be made upon the professional accountant in his or her working life. At the Fundamentals level, you will have studied the essentials of financial statement preparation and analysis, including those of group accounts. At the Professional level, these essentials will be assumed knowledge. You will be required to apply them, assuming the role of a professional adviser and analyst to the management as well as the shareholders and other stakeholders.

What is the paper about?

The P2 syllabus comprises eight main areas:

A   The professional and ethical duty of the accountant
B   The financial reporting framework
C   Reporting the financial performance of entities
D   Financial statements of groups of entities
E   Specialised entities
F   Implications of changes in accounting regulation on financial reporting
G   The appraisal of financial performance and position of entities
H   Current developments

There is, of course, some overlap between these areas. For example, if you are discussing current developments (H), you might be talking about the proposed changes to accounting for business combinations (D) and considering the implications of changes in accounting regulation (F) and perhaps even the ethical duty of the accountant to report those changes fairly and accurately (A).

What skills must you demonstrate?

At the Fundamentals level, or in your earlier studies, the questions would be more easily categorised into syllabus areas. However, at this level you may need to demonstrate knowledge, skills and thinking from outside the syllabus area that the question seems to be about on the surface. The examiner has stated:

> Students should be capable of relating professional issues to relevant concepts and practical situations. The evaluation of alternative accounting practices and the identification and prioritisation of issues will be a key element of the paper. Professional and ethical judgement will need to be exercised, together with the integration of technical knowledge when addressing corporate reporting issues in a business context.

So the paper is not predictable. That said, clear guidance has been given. The compulsory Section A question, worth 50 marks, will always be on group accounts. It will also deal with issues in financial reporting and will be case study based. In Section B, questions could be on any area of they syllabus, but we have been told that two questions will be scenario based and one question will be an essay. You have a choice of two from three.

Exam technique for P2

Do not be needlessly intimidated

There is no shortcut to passing this exam. It looks very difficult indeed, and many students wonder if they will ever pass. But many do. Why is this?

Easy marks

All the questions are demanding, but there are many easy marks to be gained. Suppose, for example, you had a consolidated cash flow statement with a disposal, some foreign exchange complications and an impairment calculation. There will be easy marks available simply for the basic cash flow aspects, setting out the proforma, setting up your workings, presenting your work neatly. If you recognise, as you should, that the disposal needs to be taken into account, of course you will get marks for that, even if you make a mistake in the arithmetic. If you get the foreign exchange right, so much the better, but you could pass the question comfortably omitting this altogether. If you're short of time, this is what you should do.

Be ruthless in ignoring the complications

Look at the question. Within reason, if there are complications – often only worth a few marks – that you know you will not have time or knowledge to do, cross them out. It will make you feel better. Than tackle the bits you can do. This is how people pass a seemingly impossible paper.

Be ruthless in allocating your time

At BPP, we have seen how very intelligent students do one almost perfect question, one averagely good and one sketchy. For a fifty mark question, the first twenty marks are the easiest to get. Then you have to push it up to what you think is thirty to get yourself a clear pass. For a twenty-five mark question, the first eight to ten marks are the easiest to get, and then you must try to push it up to fifteen.

Do your best question either first or second, and the compulsory question either first or second. The compulsory question, being on groups, will always have some easy marks available for consolidation techniques.

The exam paper

The paper will comprise two sections.

		Number of marks
Section A:	1 compulsory case study	50
Section B:	Choice of 2 from 3 questions (25 marks each)	50
		100

Section A will consist of one scenario based question worth 50 marks. It will deal with the preparation of consolidated financial statements including group cash flow statements and with issues in financial reporting.

Students will be required to answer two out of three questions in Section B, which will normally comprise two questions which will be scenario or case-study based and one question which will be an essay. Section B could deal with any aspects of the syllabus.

Analysis of past papers – by sitting

December 2008

Section A

1   Group statement of cash flows with adjustments and interpretation; ethics

Section B

2   Changes to accounting for business combinations
3   Tangibles, intangibles and revenue recognition
4   Accounting standards and disclosure

June 2008

Section A

1   Groups with a foreign subsidiary, other adjustments and the remainder on ethical issues

Section B

2   Segment reporting and revenue recognition in a specialised industry
3   Retirement benefits and financial instruments
4   Transition to IFRS

December 2007

Section A

1   Piecemeal acquisition; factored receivables; environmental provision and report; ethical and social attitudes

Section B

2   Employee benefits; provisions
3   Discontinued operations; deferred tax; impairment; lease
4   Conceptual framework

Pilot paper

Section A

1 Statement of cash flows; criteria for consolidation; ethical behaviour

Section B

2 Environmental provision; leasing; EABRP; share-based payment
3 Deferred tax with pension scheme and financial instruments
4 Adoption of IFRS; proposals on business combinations

Analysis of past papers – by syllabus topic

The table below provides details of when each element of the syllabus has been examined and the question number and section in which each element appeared. Further details can be found in the Exam Focus Points in the relevant chapters.

Covered in Text chapter		Pilot Paper	Dec 2007	June 2008	Dec 2008
3	**THE PROFESSIONAL AND ETHICAL DUTY OF THE ACCOUNTANT**				
3	Professional behaviour and compliance with accounting standards			Q1(c)	Q1(c)
3	Ethical requirements of corporate reporting and the consequences of unethical behaviour	Q1(c)	Q1(c)		Q1(c)
	Social responsibility		Q1(c)		
	THE FINANCIAL REPORTING FRAMEWORK				
1	The contribution and limitations of financial statement in meeting users' and capital markets' needs				Q4(c)
1	The applications, strengths and weaknesses of an accounting framework				
1	Critical evaluation of principles and practices – Revenue recognition – Substance over form issues	Q2 Q1(b)		Q2(b)	Q3
	REPORTING THE FINANCIAL PERFORMANCE OF ENTITIES				
	Performance reporting				
4	Non-current assets – Property, plant ad equipment – Intangible assets – Impairment – Investment properties – Government grants – Borrowing costs		Q1(a), Q3(c)	Q1(b) Q2(b)	Q3 Q2,Q3 Q1(a), Q3
7	Financial instruments	Q3	Q1(a)	Q1(b), Q3	Q1(a), Q2
11	Leases	Q2	Q1(a), Q3(d)		Q3
18	Segment reporting			Q2(a)	
5	Employee benefits	Q1(a), Q3	Q2(a)	Q1(b), Q3(b)	Q1(a)
6	Income taxes	Q3	Q3(b)		
9	Provisions, contingencies and events after the reporting period – Provisions, contingency liabilities and contingent assets – Events after the reporting period	Q2 Q2	Q1(a), Q2(b)	Q3	Q1(a), Q2
10	Related parties				
8	Share-based payment	Q2	Q1(a)	Q1(b)	Q2

Covered in Text chapter		Pilot Paper	Dec 2007	June 2008	Dec 2008
	FINANCIAL STATEMENTS OF GROUPS OF ENTITIES				
12, 13, 17	Group accounting including statements of cash flow			Q3(c)	
	– Complex groups				
	– Associates				Q1(a), Q2
	– Joint ventures				
	– Group statements of cash flows	Q1(a)			Q1(a)
13	Continuing and discontinued interests				
	– Discontinued operations				
	– Non-current assets held for sale		Q3(a)		
14	Changes in group structure				
	– Mid year acquisitions				
	– Disposals				Q2
	– Business combinations achieved in stages		Q1(a)		Q2
16	Foreign transactions and entities				
	– Foreign currency transactions		Q1(a)	Q1(b)	Q1(a)
	– Foreign subsidiaries			Q1(a), (b)	
	SPECIALISED ENTITIES				
20	Financial reporting in specialised, not-for-profit and public sector entities	Q2		Q2	
20	Reporting requirements for small- and medium-sized entities (SMEs)				
	IMPLICATIONS OF CHANGES IN ACCOUNTING REGULATION ON FINANCIAL REPORTING				
21	The effect of changes in accounting standards on accounting systems			Q4(a)	
12	Proposed changes to accounting standards				
	– Business combinations Exposure Draft	Q4(b)			
	THE APPRAISAL OF FINANCIAL PERFORMANCE AND POSITION ENTITIES				
18	The creation of suitable accounting policies			Q2(b), Q3	
18	Analysis and interpretation of financial information and measurement of performance				Q1(b)
	CURRENT DEVELOPMENTS				
19	Environmental and social reporting		Q1(b)		
19	Convergence between national and international reporting standards	Q4(a)		Q4(a)	
19	Comparison of national reporting requirements			Q4(b)	
1, 6, 19	Current reporting issues		Q4		
	– Conceptual framework Discussion Paper				
	– Fair value measurement Discussion Paper				
	– Management commentary Discussion Paper				
	– Pensions Discussion Paper				

Regulatory and ethical framework

Financial reporting framework

Topic list	Syllabus reference
1 International Financial Reporting Standards (IFRSs)	A1
2 Corporate governance	C1
3 Conceptual framework	B2
4 Revenue recognition	A2, B1

Introduction

Welcome to the Corporate Reporting paper using International Financial
Reporting Standards (IFRS). This paper is about thinking and applying your
knowledge of the IFRS. Most of the standards and topics have been covered in
your earlier studies. However, at the professional level, you need to think
critically about them and show an understanding of topical issues. In the exam,
you will need to put yourself in the role of an adviser to a business entity, using
your knowledge to give practical advice.

In the exam, you will often be required to consider the impact of proposed
changes to IFRS. Any such proposals are dealt with in this Study Text within
the topic to which they relate.

Important notice

IAS 1 *Presentation of financial statements* has been revised. Changes are
detailed in Chapter 18. For now, note that 'balance sheet' is generally termed
'statement of financial position' and 'income statement ' is also called
'statement of comprehensive income'.

Study guide

		Intellectual level
A1	**Professional behaviour and compliance with accounting standards**	
(a)	Appraise the ethical and professional issues in advising on corporate reporting	3
(b)	Assess the relevance and importance of ethical and professional issues in complying with accounting standards	3
C1	**Performance reporting**	
(a)	Prepare reports relating to corporate performance for external stakeholders	3
B2	**The applications, strength and weaknesses of an accounting framework**	
(a)	Evaluate the 'position statement' and fair value models adopted by standard setters.	3
(b)	Discuss the use of the IASB *Framework* in the production of accounting standards.	3
(c)	Assess the success of the IASB *Framework* in introducing rigorous and consistent accounting standards.	3

Exam guide

This chapter is partly background knowledge to set the scene about the reporting framework before you look at ethical issues. It also discusses the Management Commentary and the conceptual framework.

The examiner has stated that revenue recognition is important.

1 International Financial Reporting Standards (IFRSs)

One of the competences you need to fulfil Objective 10 of the Practical Experience Requirement (PER) is to recognise and apply the external legal and professional framework and regulations to financial reporting. You can apply the knowledge you obtain from this section of the text to demonstrate this competence.

To date the IASB has been in existence for approximately three years and it has the following standards in issue.

1.1 Current accounting standards and documents examinable at P2

The documents listed as being examinable are the latest that were issued prior to 30 September 2008, and will be examinable in December 2009. At the time of writing (June 2009) we have not received guidance on which new documents will be examinable in June 2010, so you should check *Student Accountant* magazine, and the ACCA's website (www.accaglobal.com/students) for up to date information. Any documents examinable in June 2010 not covered in this text will be covered in the Current Issues section of the BPP 2010 Practice & Revision Kit.

Knowledge of new examinable regulations issued by 30 September will be required in examination sessions being held in the following calendar year. Documents may be examinable even if the effective date is in the future.

The study guide offers more detail guidance on the depth and level at which the examinable documents will be examined. The study guide should be read in conjunction with the examinable documents list.

	Title	Date issued
	International Accounting Standards (IASs)/International Financial Reporting Standards (IFRSs)	
IAS 1	Presentation of financial statements	Dec 03, revised Sept 07
IAS 2	Inventories	Dec 03
IAS 7	Statement of cash flows	Dec 92
IAS 8	Accounting policies, changes in accounting estimates and errors	Dec 03
IAS 10	Events after the reporting period	Dec 03
IAS 11	Construction contracts	Dec 93
IAS 12	Income taxes	Nov 00
IAS 16	Property, plant and equipment	Dec 03
IAS 17	Leases	Dec 03
IAS 18	Revenue	Dec 93
IAS 19	Employee benefits	Nov 00
IAS 20	Accounting for government grants and disclosure of government assistance	Jan 95
IAS 21	The effects of changes in foreign exchange rates	Dec 03
IAS 23	Borrowing costs	Dec 93
IAS 24	Related party disclosures	Dec 03
IAS 27	Consolidated and separate financial statements	Dec 03
IAS 28	Investments in associates	Dec 03
IAS 29	Financial reporting in hyperinflationary economies	Jan 95
IAS 31	Interests in joint ventures	Dec 03
IAS 32	Financial Instruments: presentation	Dec 03
IAS 33	Earnings per share	Dec 03
IAS 34	Interim financial reporting	Feb 98
IAS 36	Impairment of assets	June 98
IAS 37	Provisions, contingent liabilities and contingent assets	Sept 98
IAS 38	Intangible assets	Sept 98
IAS 39	Financial Instruments: recognition and measurement	Dec 03
IAS 40	Investment property	Dec 03
IAS 41	Agriculture	Feb 01
IFRS 1	First-time adoption of international financial reporting standards	June 03
IFRS 2	Share-based payment	Feb 04
IFRS 3	Business combinations	Mar 04, revised Jan 08
IFRS 5	Non-current assets held for sale and discontinued operations	Mar 04
IFRS 7	Financial instruments: disclosures	Aug 05
IFRS 8	Operating segments	Nov 06

Other Statements			
	Framework for the Preparation and Presentation of Financial Statements		
Interpretations of the International Financial Reporting Interpretations Committee (IFRIC)			
SIC-12	Consolidation – special purpose entities
SIC-13	Jointly controlled entities – non monetary contributions by venturers
SIC-15	Operating leases – incentives
SIC-21	Income taxes – recovery of revalued non-depreciable assets
SIC-27	Evaluating the substance of transactions in the legal form of a lease
SIC-32	Intangible assets – website costs
IFRIC 1	Changes in existing decommissioning, restoration and similar liabilities
IFRIC 4	Determining whether an arrangement contains a lease
IFRIC 5	Rights to interests from decommissioning restoration and environmental rehabilitation funds
IFRIC 7	Applying the restatement approach under IAS 29 Financial reporting in hyperinflationary economies
IFRIC 8	Scope of IFRS 2
IFRIC 9	Reassessment of embedded derivatives
IFRIC 10	Interim financial reporting and impairment
IFRIC 11	IFRS 2: group and treasury share transactions
IFRIC 12	Service concession arrangements
IFRIC 13	Customer loyalty programmes
EDs, Discussion Papers and Other Documents	
ED	IFRS for small and medium-sized entities
ED	Simplifying earnings per share: Proposed amendments to IAS 33
ED	Improvements to IFRS 5
ED	An improved conceptual framework for financial reporting. Chapters 1 and 2
DP	Management commentary
DP	Fair value measurements
DP	Preliminary views on amendments to IAS 19 Employee benefits

2 Corporate governance

Corporate governance has been important in recent years and in the current syllabus it is important in the context of ethical behaviour.

One of the major business debates recently is about corporate governance, particularly in the UK and the USA.

Key term | **Corporate governance** is the system by which companies are directed and controlled. *(Cadbury Report)*

The trigger for this debate was the **collapse** of major international companies during the 1980s, including Maxwell, BCCI and Polly Peck. These collapses were often unexpected, and dubious (or even fraudulent) activities were sometimes attributed to their owners and managers. These events represented a nasty shock for countries, such as the UK and the USA, that felt they had well-regulated markets and strong company legislation. It became obvious, however, that part of the problem was the way in which regulation was spread between **different national authorities** for these global conglomerates, so that no one national authority had the whole picture of the affairs of such companies, nor full powers over the whole of the business.

Individual countries began to develop **better guidelines** for the corporate governance, and efforts have been made to produce an international standard on corporate governance.

3 Conceptual framework   12/07

3.1 The search for a conceptual framework

The financial reporting process is concerned with providing information that is useful in the business and economic decision-making process. Therefore a conceptual framework will form the theoretical basis for determining which events should be accounted for, how they should be measured and how they should be communicated to the user.

Although it is theoretical in nature, a conceptual framework for financial reporting has highly practical final aims.

The **danger of not having a conceptual framework** is demonstrated in the way some countries' standards have developed over recent years; standards tend to be produced in a **haphazard and fire-fighting approach**. Where an agreed framework exists, the standard-setting body act as an architect or designer, rather than a fire-fighter, building accounting rules on the foundation of sound, agreed basic principles.

The lack of a conceptual framework also means that fundamental principles are tackled more than once in different standards, thereby producing contradictions and inconsistencies in basic concepts, such as those of prudence and matching. This leads to ambiguity and it affects the true and fair concept of financial reporting.

Another problem with the lack of a conceptual framework has become apparent in the USA. The large number of highly detailed standards produced by the Financial Accounting Standards Board (FASB) has created a financial reporting environment governed by specific rules rather than general principles. This would be avoided if a cohesive set of principles were in place.

A conceptual framework can also bolster standard setters against political pressure from various 'lobby groups' and interested parties. Such pressure would only prevail if it was acceptable under the conceptual framework.

3.2 Advantages and disadvantages of a conceptual framework

The **advantages** arising from using a conceptual framework may be summarised as follows.

(a)   The situation is **avoided** whereby standards are being developed on a **patchwork** basis, where a particular accounting problem is recognised as having emerged, and resources were then channelled into standardising accounting practice in that area, without regard to whether that particular issue was necessarily the most important issue remaining at that time without standardisation.

(b) As stated above, the development of certain standards (particularly national standards) have been subject to considerable political interference from interested parties. Where there is a conflict of interest between user groups on which policies to choose, policies deriving from a conceptual framework will be **less open** to criticism that the standard-setter buckled to **external pressure**.

(c) Some standards may concentrate on the statement of comprehensive income (income statement) whereas some may concentrate on the valuation of net assets (statement of financial position).

3.3 Counter-argument

A counter-argument might be as follows.

(a) Financial statements are intended for a variety of users, and it is not certain that a single conceptual framework can be devised which will suit all users.

(b) Given the diversity of user requirements, there may be a need for a variety of accounting standards, each produced for a different purpose (and with different concepts as a basis).

(c) It is not clear that a conceptual framework makes the task of preparing and then implementing standards any easier than without a framework.

Before we look at the IASB's attempt to produce a conceptual framework, we need to consider another term of importance to this debate: generally accepted accounting principles; or GAAP.

3.4 Generally Accepted Accounting Principles (GAAP)

This term has sprung up in recent years and its signifies all the rules, from whatever source, which govern accounting. In individual countries this is seen primarily as a combination of:

* National corporate law
* National accounting standards
* Local stock exchange requirements

Although those sources are the basis for the GAAP of individual countries, the concept also includes the effects of non-mandatory sources such as:

* International accounting standards
* Statutory requirements in other countries

In the many countries, like the UK, GAAP does not have any statutory or regulatory authority or definition, unlike other countries, such as the USA. The term is mentioned rarely in legislation, and only then in fairly limited terms.

There are different views of GAAP in different countries. The UK position can be explained in the following extracts from *UK GAAP* (Davies, Paterson & Wilson, Ernst & Young).

> 'Our view is that GAAP is a dynamic concept which requires constant review, adaptation and reaction to changing circumstances. We believe that use of the term "principle" gives GAAP an unjustified and inappropriate degree of permanence. GAAP changes in response to changing business and economic needs and developments. As circumstances alter, accounting practices are modified or developed accordingly..... We believe that GAAP goes far beyond mere rules and principles, and encompasses contemporary permissible accounting practice.'

> 'It is often argued that the term "generally accepted" implies that there must exist a high degree of practical application of a particular accounting practice. However, this interpretation raises certain practical difficulties. For example, what about new areas of accounting which have not, as yet, been generally applied? What about different accounting treatments for similar items – are they all generally accepted?

> 'It is our view that "generally accepted" does not mean "generally adopted or used". We believe that, in the UK context, GAAP refers to accounting practices which are regarded as permissible by the accounting profession. The extent to which a particular practice has been adopted is, in our

opinion, not the overriding consideration. Any accounting practice which is legitimate in the circumstances under which it has been applied should be regarded as GAAP. The decision as to whether or not a particular practice is permissible or legitimate would depend on one or more of the following factors:

(a)   Is the practice addressed either in the accounting standards, statute or other official pronouncements?

(b)   If the practice is not addressed in UK accounting standards, is it dealt with in International Accounting Standards, or the standards of other countries such as the US?

(c)   Is the practice consistent with the needs of users and the objectives of financial reporting?

(d)   Does the practice have authoritative support in the accounting literature?

(e)   Is the practice being applied by other companies in similar situations?

(f)   Is the practice consistent with the fundamental concept of "true and fair"?'

This view is not held in all countries, however. In the USA particularly, the equivalent of a 'true and fair view' is 'fair presentation in accordance with GAAP'. Generally accepted accounting principles are defined as those principles which have 'substantial authoritative support'. Therefore accounts prepared in accordance with accounting principles for which there is not substantial authoritative support are presumed to be misleading or inaccurate.

The effect here is that 'new' or 'different' accounting principles are not acceptable unless they have been adopted by the mainstream accounting profession, usually the standard-setting bodies and/or professional accountancy bodies. This is much more rigid than the UK view expressed above.

3.5 GAAP and a conceptual framework

A conceptual framework for financial reporting can be defined as an attempt to codify existing GAAP in order to reappraise current accounting standards and to produce new standards.

3.6 The IASB'S Framework

In July 1989 the IASB produced a document, *Framework for the Preparation and Presentation of Financial Statements* ('Framework'). The *Framework* is, in effect, the **conceptual** framework upon which all IASs are based and hence which determines how financial statements are prepared and the information they contain.

The *Framework* consists of several sections or chapters, following on after a preface and introduction. These chapters are as follows.

- The objective of financial statements.
- Underlying assumptions
- Qualitative characteristics of financial statements
- The elements of financial statements
- Recognition of the elements of financial statements
- Measurement of the elements of financial statements
- Concepts of capital and capital maintenance

Exam focus point

The IASB *Framework* has been discussed in detail in your earlier studies and in Chapter 11 as regards off balance sheet finance.

3.7 Exposure Draft: An Improved Conceptual Framework for Financial Reporting

In July 2006, the IASB produced a Discussion Paper, Preliminary views on an improved conceptual framework for financial reporting. Responses to this were considered in and taken account of in the Exposure Draft of the same name, issued in May 2008.

3.7.1 Background

This Exposure Draft is part of a series of publications being developed jointly by FASB and the IASB as part of a joint project to develop a common Conceptual Framework for Financial Reporting.

The aim is to provide the best common foundation for developing principles-based and converged standards.

The Paper covers the **first two chapters** of a proposed Conceptual Framework:

- Chapter 1: The objective of financial reporting
- Chapter 2: Qualitative characteristics of decision-useful financial reporting information.

The ED also includes the draft chapters themselves.

3.7.2 Objective

The proposed objective of general purpose external financial reporting is 'to provide information that is useful to present and potential equity investors, lenders and other creditors in making decisions in their capacity as capital providers'. The **focus therefore is on the capital markets**.

To accomplish the objective, financial reports should communicate information about:

- An entity's economic resources
- Claims on those resources
- Transactions and other events that change them

The extent to which that financial information is useful will depend on it its qualitative characteristics.

3.7.3 Qualitative characteristics

Like the current *Framework*, the proposed chapter considers the users of the financial statements, their abilities and their needs. Qualitative characteristics are attributes that make financial reporting useful.

The proposed chapter distinguishes between **fundamental** and **enhancing** qualitative characteristics, for analysis purposes. Fundamental qualitative characteristics distinguish useful financial reporting information from information that is not useful or misleading. Enhancing qualitative characteristics distinguish more useful information from less useful information.

Fundamental qualitative characteristics are:

(a) **Relevance**: predictive value or confirmatory value

(b) **Faithful representation**: information must be complete, neutral and free from material error (replacing 'reliability')

Enhancing qualitative characteristics are:

(a) **Comparability**: achieved by consistency in use of the same accounting policies

(b) **Verifiability**: credibility, assurance that information faithfully represents the economic phenomena

(c) **Timeliness**: information is provided before it loses the capacity to influence decisions

(d) **Understandability**: for users who have a reasonable knowledge of business and economic activities and who are able to read a financial report; information should not be excluded on the grounds that it may be too complex/difficult for some users to understand. Enhanced when information is classified, characterised and presented clearly and concisely.

Constraints of financial reporting

(a) **Materiality**: all material information included; not cluttered with immaterial information (information is material if its omission or misstatement could influence users' decisions).

(b) **Cost**: the benefits of financial information should justify the costs.

3.8 Discussion Paper on an Improved Conceptual Framework: The Reporting Entity

This Paper was issued in May 2008. It presents the IASB's consideration of issues in the development of a reporting entity concept for inclusion in the *Conceptual Framework for Financial Reporting.* There are four sections.

3.8.1 Section 1: The reporting entity concept

This deals with general issues relating to the reporting entity concept. For example, it considers whether a precise definition of a reporting entity is necessary and whether w reporting entity must be a legal entity.

The Board's conclusion at this stage is that the conceptual framework should broadly describe rather than precisely define a reporting entity **as a circumscribed area of business activity of interest to present and potential equity investors, lenders and other capital providers.**

Examples of reporting entities include a sole trader, corporation, trust, partnership, association and group.

3.8.2 Section 2: Group reporting entity

This section considers matters relating to a group reporting entity, that is a reporting entity that comprises two or more entities that are presented as a single unit. It considers the **meaning of control** in the context of one entity having control over another. Its preliminary conclusions are as follows:

(a)   All the existing facts and circumstances should be considered when assessing whether an entity has control over another entity.

(b)   Control includes situations in which control currently exists but might be temporary.

(c)   The control concept should not be limited to circumstances in which the entity has majority voting rights or other legal rights (sometimes referred to as de facto or effective control).

(d)   In some cases, an entity holds enough options over voting rights that exercise of those options would give the entity control over a second entity. That fact is not sufficient, in itself, to establish that the first entity currently controls the second entity.

(e)   Power must be held by one entity only.

3.8.3 Section 3: Parent entity financial reporting

This section considers two issues:

(a)   The **parent company approach** to consolidated financial statements

(b)   **Parent-only financial statements** and consolidated financial statements – which set meets the objectives of financial reporting, and do we need both?

The IASB's preliminary conclusion is (a) **that consolidated financial statements should be presented from the perspective of the group reporting entity**, not the parent company's shareholders, and (b) that consolidated financial statements meet the objective of financial reporting, but that **parent-only financial statements may be presented** provided they are included in the same financial report as consolidated financial statements.

3.8.4 Section 4: Control issues

This section considers **other issues relating to the control concept**, such as latent control and the treatment of options over voting rights.

3.9 Potential problems

The UK's Accounting Standards Board (ASB) has highlighted a number of potential objections that may be made to the proposals.

(a) **Users.** The ASB is concerned about the proposal that the objective of financial reporting should focus only on decision-usefulness, with stewardship being subsumed within this rather than being referred to as a specific part of the objective, or a separate objective. The ASB believes that stewardship should be a separate objective. The ASB is also concerned that the shareholder user perspective is being downplayed.

(b) **Qualitative characteristics: what happens to reliability?** The DP proposes replacing the qualitative characteristic of 'reliability' in the current Framework with 'faithful representation'. The ASB believes that faithful representation is a softer notion which, when combined with a lack of specific identification of substance over form as a principle, could lead to a number of problems.

(c) **Financial reporting or financial statements.** The ASB believes the boundary between financial statements and financial reporting has not been properly considered.

(d) **Limited in scope.** The Discussion Paper is limited to private enterprises, rather than, as the ASB believes it should be, encompassing the not-for profit sector.

(e) **Too theoretical.** This may alienate preparers and auditors of accounts.

(f) **Too piecemeal.** This is likely to lead to internal inconsistency

(g) The **entity perspective is adopted without an in-depth comparison** with other possible perspectives (such as the proprietary perspective, the parent shareholder perspective and other hybrid models).

(h) The differentiation between fundamental and enhancing qualitative characteristics is **artificial.**

(i) The qualitative characteristic of **'verifiability'** is problematic.

(j) In the proposed 'Reporting Entity' chapter, the **entity perspective and the definitions of control have been insufficiently thought through.** In addition, the 'risks and rewards' model is not adopted, thereby losing a useful concept.

3.10 Recent developments

So far the other parts of the *Framework* are still at the **discussion stage.** Below is a **summary of progress** so far (June 2009).

(a) **Objectives and qualitative characteristics** – see above.

(b) **Elements and recognition.** The Board has tentatively agreed that the focus of the definition of an asset should be on a present economic resource rather than on future economic benefits and an assessment of likelihood should be remove from the definition of an asset. The definition should focus on the present rather than on past transactions or events. No definition of a liability has been agreed.

(c) **Measurement.** Various measurement bases have been discussed. They are divided into past present and future. Past bases are:

(i) Past entry price
(ii) Modified past entry amount
(iii) Past exit price

Present bases are:

(i) Current entry price
(ii) Current exit price
(iii) Current equilibrium price
(iv) Value in use

Future bases are:

(i) Future entry price
(ii) Future exit price

(d) **Reporting entity** - see above

(f)   **Purpose and status** – discussions pending

(g)   **Application to not for profit entities** – discussions pending

(h)   **Remaining issues** – discussions pending

The examiner has flagged this topic as important. Keep an eye on future developments by reading *Student Accountant* and http://www.iasplus.com/agenda/framework.htm

4 Revenue recognition   6/08, 12/08

FAST FORWARD

Revenue recognition is straightforward in most business transactions, but some situations are more complicated.

4.1 Introduction

Accruals accounting is based on the **matching of costs with the revenue they generate**. It is crucially important under this convention that we can establish the point at which revenue may be recognised so that the correct treatment can be applied to the related costs. For example, the costs of producing an item of finished goods should be carried as an asset in the statement of financial position until such time as it is sold; they should then be written off as a charge to the trading account. Which of these two treatments should be applied cannot be decided until it is clear at what moment the sale of the item takes place.

The decision has a **direct impact on profit** since under the prudence concept it would be unacceptable to recognise the profit on sale until a sale had taken place in accordance with the criteria of revenue recognition.

Revenue is generally recognised as **earned at the point of sale**, because at that point four criteria will generally have been met.

- The product or service has been **provided to the buyer**.
- The buyer has **recognised his liability** to pay for the goods or services provided. The converse of this is that the seller has recognised that ownership of goods has passed from himself to the buyer.
- The buyer has indicated his **willingness to hand over cash** or other assets in settlement of his liability.
- The **monetary value** of the goods or services has been established.

At earlier points in the business cycle there will not in general be **firm evidence** that the above criteria will be met. Until work on a product is complete, there is a risk that some flaw in the manufacturing process will necessitate its writing off; even when the product is complete there is no guarantee that it will find a buyer.

At later points in the business cycle, for example when cash is received for the sale, the recognition of revenue may occur in a period later than that in which the related costs were charged. Revenue recognition would then depend on fortuitous circumstances, such as the cash flow of a company's customers, and might fluctuate misleadingly from one period to another.

However, there are times when revenue is **recognised at other times than at the completion of a sale**. For example, in the recognition of profit on long-term construction contracts. Under IAS 11 *Construction contracts* contract revenue and contract costs associated with the construction contract should be recognised as revenue and expenses respectively by reference to the stage of completion of the contract activity at the year end.

(a)   Owing to the length of time taken to complete such contracts, to defer taking profit into account until completion may result in the income statement reflecting, not so much a fair view of the activity of the company during the year, but rather the results relating to contracts which have been completed by the year end.

(b)   Revenue in this case is recognised when production on, say, a section of the total contract is complete, even though no sale can be made until the whole is complete.

4.2 IAS 18 *Revenue*

IAS 18 *Revenue* is concerned with the **recognition of revenues** arising from fairly common transactions.

- The sale of goods
- The rendering of services
- The use by others of enterprise assets yielding interest, royalties and dividends

Generally revenue is recognised when the entity has transferred to the buyer the **significant risks and rewards of ownership** and when the revenue can be **measured reliably**.

IAS 18 governs the recognition of revenue in specific (common) types of transaction. Generally, recognition should be when it is probable that **future economic benefits** will flow to the enterprise and when these benefits can be **measured reliably**.

Income, as defined by the IASB's *Framework* document (see above), includes both revenues and gains. Revenue is income arising in the ordinary course of an enterprise's activities and it may be called different names, such as sales, fees, interest, dividends or royalties.

4.3 Scope

IAS 18 covers the revenue from specific types of transaction or events.

- **Sale of goods** (manufactured products and items purchased for resale)
- **Rendering of services**
- Use by others of enterprise assets yielding **interest, royalties and dividends**

Interest, royalties and dividends are included as income because they arise from the use of an entity's assets by other parties.

Key terms

> **Interest** is the charge for the use of cash or cash equivalents or amounts due to the entity.
>
> **Royalties** are charges for the use of non-current assets of the entity, eg patents, computer software and trademarks.
>
> **Dividends** are distributions of profit to holders of equity investments, in proportion with their holdings, of each relevant class of capital.

The standard specifically **excludes** various types of revenue arising from leases, insurance contracts, changes in value of financial instruments or other current assets, natural increases in agricultural assets and mineral ore extraction.

4.4 Definitions

The following definitions are given in the standard.

Key terms

> **Revenue** is the gross inflow of economic benefits during the period arising in the course of the ordinary activities of an enterprise when those inflows result in increases in equity, other than increases relating to contributions from equity participants.
>
> **Fair value** is the amount for which an asset could be exchanged, or a liability settled, between knowledgeable, willing parties in an arm's length transaction.   *(IAS 18)*

Revenue **does not include** sales taxes, value added taxes or goods and service taxes which are only collected for third parties, because these do not represent an economic benefit flowing to the entity. The same is true for revenues collected by an agent on behalf of a principal. Revenue for the agent is only the commission received for acting as agent.

4.5 Measurement of revenue

When a transaction takes place, the amount of revenue is usually decided by the **agreement of the buyer and seller**. The revenue is actually measured, however, as the **fair value of the consideration received**, which will take account of any trade discounts and volume rebates.

4.6 Identification of the transaction

Normally, each transaction can be looked at **as a whole**. Sometimes, however, transactions are more complicated, and it is necessary to break a transaction down into its **component parts**. For example, a sale may include the transfer of goods and the provision of future servicing, the revenue for which should be deferred over the period the service is performed.

At the other end of the scale, **seemingly separate transactions must be considered together** if apart they lose their commercial meaning. An example would be to sell an asset with an agreement to buy it back at a later date. The second transaction cancels the first and so both must be considered together.

4.7 Sale of goods

Revenue from the sale of goods should only be recognised when *all* these conditions are satisfied.

(a)   The entity has transferred the **significant risks and rewards** of ownership of the goods to the buyer

(b)   The entity has **no continuing managerial involvement** to the degree usually associated with ownership, and no longer has effective control over the goods sold

(c)   The amount of revenue can be **measured reliably**

(d)   It is probable that the **economic benefits** associated with the transaction will flow to the enterprise

(e)   The **costs incurred** in respect of the transaction can be measured reliably

The transfer of risks and rewards can only be decided by examining each transaction. Mainly, the transfer occurs at the same time as either the **transfer of legal title**, or the **passing of possession** to the buyer - this is what happens when you buy something in a shop.

If **significant risks and rewards remain with the seller**, then the transaction is *not* a sale and revenue cannot be recognised, for example if the receipt of the revenue from a particular sale depends on the buyer receiving revenue from his own sale of the goods.

It is possible for the seller to retain only an **'insignificant' risk of ownership** and for the sale and revenue to be recognised. The main example here is where the seller retains title only to ensure collection of what is owed on the goods. This is a common commercial situation, and when it arises the revenue should be recognised on the date of sale.

The probability of the enterprise receiving the revenue arising from a transaction must be assessed. It may only become probable that the economic benefits will be received when an uncertainty is removed, for example government permission for funds to be received from another country. Only when the uncertainty is removed should the revenue be recognised. This is in contrast with the situation where revenue has already been recognised but where the **collectability of the cash** is brought into doubt. Where recovery has ceased to be probable, the amount should be recognised as an expense, *not* an adjustment of the revenue previously recognised. These points also refer to services and interest, royalties and dividends below.

Matching should take place, ie the revenue and expenses relating to the same transaction should be recognised at the same time. It is usually easy to estimate expenses at the date of sale (eg warranty costs, shipment costs, etc). Where they cannot be estimated reliably, then revenue cannot be recognised; any consideration which has already been received is treated as a liability.

4.8 Rendering of services

When the outcome of a transaction involving the rendering of services can be estimated reliably, the associated revenue should be recognised by reference to the **stage of completion of the transaction** at the year end. The outcome of a transaction can be estimated reliably when *all* these conditions are satisfied.

(a)   The amount of revenue can be **measured reliably**

(b)   It is probable that the **economic benefits** associated with the transaction will flow to the enterprise

(c)   The **stage of completion** of the transaction at the year end can be measured reliably

(d)   The **costs incurred** for the transaction and the costs to complete the transaction can be measured reliably

The parties to the transaction will normally have to agree the following before an enterprise can make reliable estimates.

(a)   Each party's **enforceable rights** regarding the service to be provided and received by the parties

(b)   The **consideration** to be exchanged

(c)   The **manner and terms of settlement**

There are various methods of determining the stage of completion of a transaction, but for practical purposes, when services are performed by an indeterminate number of acts over a period of time, revenue should be recognised on a **straight line basis** over the period, unless there is evidence for the use of a more appropriate method. If one act is of more significance than the others, then the significant act should be carried out *before* revenue is recognised.

In uncertain situations, when the outcome of the transaction involving the rendering of services cannot be estimated reliably, the standard recommends a **no loss/no gain approach**. Revenue is recognised only to the extent of the expenses recognised that are recoverable.

This is particularly likely during the **early stages of a transaction**, but it is still probable that the enterprise will recover the costs incurred. So the revenue recognised in such a period will be equal to the expenses incurred, with no profit.

Obviously, if the costs are not likely to be reimbursed, then they must be recognised as an expense immediately. **When the uncertainties cease to exist**, revenue should be recognised as laid out in the first paragraph of this section.

4.9 Interest, royalties and dividends

When others use the enterprise's assets yielding interest, royalties and dividends, the revenue should be recognised on the bases set out below when:

(a)   it is probable that the **economic benefits** associated with the transaction will flow to the enterprise; and

(b)   the amount of the revenue can be **measured reliably**.

The revenue is recognised on the following bases.

(a)   **Interest** is recognised on a time proportion basis that takes into account the effective yield on the asset

(b)   **Royalties** are recognised on an accruals basis in accordance with the substance of the relevant agreement

(c)   **Dividends** are recognised when the shareholder's right to receive payment is established

It is unlikely that you would be asked about anything as complex as this in the exam, but you should be aware of the basic requirements of the standard. The **effective yield** on an asset mentioned above is the rate of interest required to discount the stream of future cash receipts expected over the life of the asset to equate to the initial carrying amount of the asset.

Royalties are usually recognised on the same basis that they accrue **under the relevant agreement**. Sometimes the true substance of the agreement may require some other systematic and rational method of recognition.

Once again, the points made above about **probability and collectability** on sale of goods also apply here.

4.10 Disclosure

The following items should be disclosed.

(a) The **accounting policies** adopted for the recognition of revenue, including the methods used to determine the stage of completion of transactions involving the rendering of services

(b) The amount of each **significant category of revenue** recognised during the period including revenue arising from:

    (i)   The sale of goods
    (ii)   The rendering of services
    (iii) Interest
    (iv) Royalties
    (v)   Dividends

(c) The amount of revenue arising from **exchanges of goods or services** included in each significant category of revenue

Any **contingent gains or losses**, such as those relating to warranty costs, claims or penalties should be treated according to IAS 37 *Provisions, contingent liabilities and contingent assets* (covered in your earlier studies).

4.11 Question practice

Exam focus point

> The examiner has recently emphasised that revenue recognition is an important topic, so have a go at the questions below.

Question   Recognition

Given that prudence is the main consideration, discuss under what circumstances, if any, revenue might be recognised at the following stages of a sale.

(a) Goods are acquired by the business which it confidently expects to resell very quickly.
(b) A customer places a firm order for goods.
(c) Goods are delivered to the customer.
(d) The customer is invoiced for goods.
(e) The customer pays for the goods.
(f) The customer's cheque in payment for the goods has been cleared by the bank.

Answer

(a) A sale must never be recognised before the goods have even been ordered by a customer. There is no certainty about the value of the sale, nor when it will take place, even if it is virtually certain that goods will be sold.

(b) A sale must never be recognised when the customer places an order. Even though the order will be for a specific quantity of goods at a specific price, it is not yet certain that the sale transaction will go through. The customer may cancel the order, the supplier might be unable to deliver the goods as ordered or it may be decided that the customer is not a good credit risk.

(c) A sale will be recognised when delivery of the goods is made only when:

(i)   the sale is for cash, and so the cash is received at the same time; or

(ii)   the sale is on credit and the customer accepts delivery (eg by signing a delivery note).

(d)   The critical event for a credit sale is usually the despatch of an invoice to the customer. There is then a legally enforceable debt, payable on specified terms, for a completed sale transaction.

(e)   The critical event for a cash sale is when delivery takes place and when cash is received; both take place at the same time.

It would be too cautious or 'prudent' to await cash payment for a credit sale transaction before recognising the sale, unless the customer is a high credit risk and there is a serious doubt about his ability or intention to pay.

(f)   It would again be over-cautious to wait for clearance of the customer's cheques before recognising sales revenue. Such a precaution would only be justified in cases where there is a very high risk of the bank refusing to honour the cheque.

Question

Revenue recognition

Caravans Deluxe is a retailer of caravans, dormer vans and mobile homes, with a year end of 30 June 20X8. It is having trouble selling one model – the $30,000 Mini-Lux, and so is offering incentives for customers who buy this model before 31 May 20X7:

(a)   Customers buying this model before 31 May 20X7 will receive a period of interest free credit, provided they pay a non-refundable deposit of $3,000, an instalment of $15,000 on 1 August 20X7 and the balance of $12,000 on 1 August 20X9.

(b)   A three-year service plan, normally worth $1,500, is included free in the price of the caravan.

On 1 May 20X7, a customer agrees to buy a Mini-Lux caravan, paying the deposit of $3,000. Delivery is arranged for 1 August 20X7.

As the sale has now been made, the director of Caravans Deluxe wishes to recognise the full sale price of the caravan, $30,000, in the accounts for the year ended 30 June 20X7.

Required

Advise the director of the correct accounting treatment for this transaction. Assume a 10% discount rate. Show the journal entries for this treatment.

Answer

The director wishes to recognise the sale as early as possible. However, following IAS 18 *Revenue*, he cannot recognise revenue from this sale because the risks and rewards of ownership of the caravan have not been transferred. This happens on the date of delivery, which is 1 August 20X7. Accordingly, no revenue can be recognised in the current period.

The receipt of cash in the form of the $3,000 deposit must be recognised. However, while the deposit is termed 'non-refundable', it does create an obligation to complete the contract. The other side of the entry is therefore to deferred income in the statement of financial position.

The journal entries would be as follows:

DEBIT	Cash	$3,000
CREDIT	Deferred income		$3,000

Being deposit received in advance of the sale being recognised.

On 1 August 20X7, when the sale is recognised, this deferred income account will be cleared. In addition:

The revenue from the sale of the caravan will be recognised. Of this, $12,000 is receivable in two years' time, which, with a 10% discount rate, is: $12,000 / 1.1^2 = $9,917. $15,000 is receivable on 1 August 20X7.

The service plan is not really 'free' – nothing is. It is merely a deduction from the cost of the caravan. The $1,500 must be recognised separately. It is deferred income and will be recognised over the three year period.

The sales revenue recognised in respect of the caravan will be a balancing figure.

The journal entries are as follows

DEBIT	Deferred income	$3,000	
DEBIT	Cash (1st instalment)	$15,000	
DEBIT	Receivable (balance discounted)	$9,917	
CREDIT	Deferred income (service plan monies received in advance)		$1,500
CREDIT	Sales (balancing figure)		$26,417

BPP Note. This question is rather fiddly, so do not worry too much if you didn't get all of it right. Read through our solution carefully, going back to first principles where required.

4.12 IFRIC 12 *Service concession arrangements*

4.12.1 What is a service concession arrangement

Service concession arrangements are arrangements whereby a government or other body grants contracts for the supply of public services – such as roads, energy distribution, prisons or hospitals – to private operators. The objective of this project of the IFRIC is to clarify how certain aspects of existing IASB literature are to be applied to service concession arrangements. *(IFRIC 12)*

4.12.2 Two Types of Service Concession Arrangements

IFRIC 12 draws a distinction between two types of service concession arrangement.

(a)   In one, the operator receives a **financial asset**, specifically an unconditional contractual right to receive cash or another financial asset from the government in return for constructing or upgrading the public sector asset.

(b)   In the other, the operator receives an **intangible asset** – a right to charge for use of the public sector asset that it constructs or upgrades. A right to charge users is not an unconditional right to receive cash because the amounts are contingent on the extent to which the public uses the service.

IFRIC 12 allows for the possibility that **both types of arrangement may exist within a single contract**: to the extent that the government has given an unconditional guarantee of payment for the construction of the public sector asset, the operator has a financial asset; to the extent that the operator has to rely on the public using the service in order to obtain payment, the operator has an intangible asset.

4.12.3 Accounting – Financial asset model

The operator recognises a **financial asset** to the extent that it has an unconditional contractual right to receive cash or another financial asset from or at the direction of the grantor for the construction services. The operator has an unconditional right to receive cash if the grantor contractually guarantees to pay the operator

(a)   Specified or determinable amounts or

(b)   The shortfall, if any, between amounts received from users of the public service and specified or determinable amounts, even if payment is contingent on the operator ensuring that the infrastructure meets specified quality or efficiency requirements.

The operator measures the financial asset at fair value.

4.12.4 Accounting – Intangible asset model

The operator recognises an **intangible asset** to the extent that it receives a right (a licence) to charge users of the public service. A right to charge users of the public service is not an unconditional right to receive cash because the amounts are contingent on the extent that the public uses the service.

The operator measures the intangible asset at fair value.

4.12.5 Operating revenue

The operator of a service concession arrangement recognises and measures revenue in accordance with IASs 11 and 18 for the services it performs.

4.13 IFRIC 13 Customer loyalty programmes

4.13.1 The issue

IFRIC 13 *Customer loyalty programmes* addresses accounting by entities that grant loyalty award credits (such as 'points' or travel miles) to customers who buy other goods or services. Specifically, it explains how such entities should account for their obligations to provide free or discounted goods or services ('awards') to customers who redeem award credits.

4.13.2 Key provisions

(a)   An entity that grants loyalty award credits shall allocate some of the proceeds of the initial sale to the award credits as a liability (its obligation to provide the awards). In effect, the award is accounted for as a separate component of the sale transaction.

(b)   The amount of proceeds allocated to the award credits is measured by reference to their fair value, that is, the amount for which the award credits could have been sold separately.

(c)   The entity shall recognise the deferred portion of the proceeds as revenue only when it has fulfilled its obligations. It may fulfil its obligations either by supplying the awards itself or by engaging (and paying) a third party to do so.

(d)   If at any time the expected costs of meeting the obligation exceed the consideration received, the entity has an onerous contract for which IAS 37 would require recognition of a liability.

(e)   If IFRIC 13 causes an entity to change its accounting policy for customer loyalty awards, IAS 8 applies.

4.14 Exposure Draft: Improvements to IFRS: Principal or agent?

IAS 18 currently covers the **accounting treatment** for amounts collected by an agent on behalf of a principal, which is: recognise only the commission as revenue (not the amounts collected on behalf of the principal). However, it **does not give guidance** on determining whether an entity is acting as agent or principal.

In August 2008, the IASB issued an Exposure Draft of improvements to IFRS, most of which are minor. The most significant proposal is the additional guidance in the appendix to IAS 18 *Revenue* on determining whether an entity is acting as an agent or principal. The proposed guidance is as follows:

4.14.1 Acting as principal

An entity is acting as a principal when it is **exposed to the significant risks and rewards** associated with the sale of goods or rendering of services. Features that indicate that an entity is acting as a principal include (individually or in combination):

(a)   **Primary responsibility** for providing goods or services to the customer or for fulfilling the order

(b)   The entity having the **inventory risk** before or after the customer order, during shipping or on return

(c)   **Discretion in establishing prices** (directly or indirectly) eg providing additional goods or services

(d)   The entity bearing the **customer's credit risk**.

4.14.2 Acting as agent

An entity is acting as an agent when it is **not exposed to the significant risks and rewards** associated with the sale of goods or rendering of services. One feature that indicates that an entity is an agent is that the amount the entity earns is **predetermined** eg fixed fee per transaction or percentage of amount billed to the customer.

Chapter Roundup

- **Corporate governance** has been important in recent years and in the current syllabus it is important in the context of ethical behaviour.

- The IASB's *Framework* provides the backbone of the IASB's **conceptual framework**. IASs were based on the IASC (now IASB) *Framework*.

- **Revenue recognition** is straightforward in most business transactions, but some situations are more complicated. It is necessary to determine the **substance of each transaction, rather than the legal form**.

- IAS 18 *Revenue* is concerned with the **recognition of revenues** arising from fairly common transactions.

  - The sale of goods
  - The rendering of services
  - The use by others of enterprise assets yielding interest, royalties and dividends

- Generally revenue is recognised when the entity has transferred to the buyer the **significant risks and rewards of ownership** and when the revenue can be **measured reliably**.

Quick Quiz

1 What is corporate governance?

2 Why is a conceptual framework necessary?

3 What are the disadvantages of a conceptual framework?

4 What are the seven sections of the IASB's *Framework*?

5 Revenue is generally recognised; under IAS 18, as earned at the ………….. ………….. ………….. (fill in the blanks).

6 How is revenue measured?

7 How should revenue be recognised when the transaction involves the rendering of services?

Answers to Quick Quiz

1   Corporate governance is the system by which companies are directed and controlled.

2   To provide a theoretical basis for financial reporting.

3   (a)   A single conceptual framework may not suit all users

        (b)   Different standards, based on a different framework, may be needed to meet the needs of different users

        (c)   It is not clear that a conceptual framework does in fact facilitate the preparation of financial statements

4   (a)   The objective of financial statements

        (b)   Underlying assumptions

        (c)   Qualitative characteristics of financial statements

        (d)   The elements of financial statements

        (e)   Recognition of the elements of financial statements

        (f)   Measurement of the elements of financial statements

        (g)   Concepts of capital and capital maintenance

5   Point of sale.

6   At the fair value of the consideration received.

7   By reference to the stage of completion of the transaction at the year end.

Now try the question below from the Exam Question Bank

Number	Level	Marks	Time
Q1	Introductory	n/a	n/a

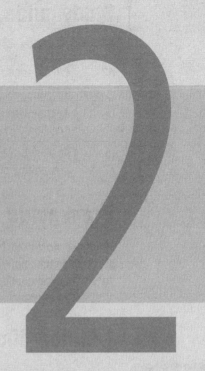

Professional and ethical duty of the accountant

Topic list	Syllabus reference
1 Ethical theories	A2
2 Influences on ethics	A2
3 The social and ethical environment	A2
4 Ethics in organisations	A2
5 Principles and guidance on and professional ethics	A2
6 Practical situations	A2
7 Examination questions: an approach	A2
8 Professional skills: guidance from the ACCA	N/A

Introduction

Ethics are an important aspect of the ACCA qualification. They need to be applied in all aspects of managerial behaviour. An attempt to massage profit figures, or non-disclosure of a close relationship may amount to unethical behaviour. However, it is the nature of ethics to deny easy answers; furthermore, in the context of business, ethical prescriptions have to be practical to be of any use. This chapter focuses on the professional integrity of the accountant and director, but you will also consider ethics in the context of off balance sheet finance.

Study guide

		Intellectual level
A2	**Ethical requirements of corporate reporting and the consequences of unethical behaviour**	
(a)	Appraise the potential ethical implications of professional and managerial decisions in the preparation of corporate reports.	3
(b)	Assess the consequences of not upholding ethical principles in the preparation of corporate reports.	3

Exam guide

Ethics are most likely to be considered in the context of the accountant's role as adviser to the directors. A question on the Pilot Paper asked you to explain why a deliberate misrepresentation in the financial statements was unethical. A scenario question at the end of this Study Text asks for a discussion of why directors might have acted unethically in adopting accounting policies to boost earnings.

1 Ethical theories

FAST FORWARD

A key debate in ethical theory is whether ethics can be determined by **objective**, **universal principles**. How important the **consequences of actions** should be in determining an ethical position is also a significant issue.

1.1 An introduction to ethics

In this chapter you will encounter various philosophical, academic terms. We have to use this terminology as the examiner will use it in questions. However provided that you focus on certain basic issues, you will be able to negotiate this chapter successfully.

1.1.1 Do ethics change over time and place?

One viewpoint is that ethics do vary between time and place. Slavery for example is now regarded as wrong, whereas in Roman times slavery was acceptable. The view that ethics vary between different ages and different communities is known as **ethical relativism** and is discussed in Section 1.3.

The opposing view is that ethics are unchanging over time and place; some courses of action are always right, others are always wrong. A simple example would be saying that it is always wrong to steal. The view that there are certain unchanging ethical rules is known as **ethical absolutism** and is discussed in Section 1.4.

1.1.2 Should you consider the consequences of your actions when making ethical decisions?

One view is that society is best served by everyone following certain ethical rules, and obeying them no matter what the results are. The argument is that people will undermine society if they disobey the ethical rules, even if they do so with the intention of avoiding adverse consequences. This viewpoint, known as **deontological ethics**, was developed by Kant.

The opposing viewpoint is that you cannot divorce an action from its consequences, and when taking ethical decisions you must take account of what the consequences will be. This viewpoint is known as **teleological ethics.** If you take this viewpoint, that implies that you have to define what the best possible consequences are. The different variations of the teleological viewpoint try to do this.

1.1.3 What thought processes do people use when making ethical decisions?

What the theories are aiming to do to complete the following sentence:

'You should act ethically because ...

In Section 2 we shall look at the work of Kohlberg who supplied various examples of thought processes, depending on the degree of ethical development of the individual.

- People who are less ethically developed may think: 'You should act ethically because you'll be punished if you don't.'
- People who have more advanced ethical development may think: 'You should act ethically because your country's laws say you should.'
- People at the highest level of ethical development may think: ' You should act ethically because it's always right to do so, no matter what the consequences and costs are to you personally.'

Question
Ethical issues

Briefly explain the main ethical issues that are involved in the following situations.

(a) Dealing with a repressive authoritarian government abroad
(b) An aggressive advertising campaign
(c) Employee redundancies
(d) Payments or gifts to officials who have the power to help or hinder the payees' operations

Answer

(a) Dealing with unpleasantly authoritarian governments can be supported on the grounds that it **contributes to economic growth and prosperity** and all the benefits they bring to society in both countries concerned. This is a consequentialist argument. It can also be opposed on consequentialist grounds as **contributing to the continuation of the regime,** and on deontological grounds as **fundamentally repugnant**.

(b) Honesty in advertising is an important problem. Many products are promoted exclusively on image. Deliberately creating the impression that purchasing a particular product will enhance the happiness, success and sex-appeal of the buyer can be attacked as **dishonest.** It can be defended on the grounds that the supplier is actually **selling a fantasy or dream** rather than a physical article.

(c) Dealings with employees are coloured by the **opposing views of corporate responsibility and individual rights**. The idea of a job as property to be defended has now disappeared from labour relations in many countries, but corporate decisions that lead to redundancies are still deplored. This is because of the obvious **impact of sudden unemployment on aspirations and living standards**, even when the employment market is buoyant. Nevertheless businesses have to consider the cost of employing labour as well as its productive capacity.

(d) The main problems with payments or gifts to officials are making distinction between those that should never be made, and those that can be made in certain cultural circumstances.

　　(i)　**Extortion**. Foreign officials have been known to threaten companies with the complete closure of their local operations unless suitable payments are made.

　　(ii)　**Bribery**. This is payments for services to which a company is not legally entitled. There are some fine distinctions to be drawn; for example, some managers regard political contributions as bribery.

　　(iii)　**Grease money**. Multinational companies are sometimes unable to obtain services to which they are legally entitled because of deliberate stalling by local officials. Cash payments to the right people may then be enough to oil the machinery of bureaucracy.

(iv) **Gifts**. In some cultures (such as Japan) gifts are regarded as an essential part of civilised negotiation, even in circumstances where to Western eyes they might appear ethically dubious. Managers operating in such a culture may feel at liberty to adopt the local customs.

1.2 Role of ethical theory

Ethics is concerned with right and wrong and how conduct should be judged to be good or bad. It is about how we should live our lives and, in particular, how we should **behave towards other people**. It is therefore relevant to all forms of human activity.

Business life is a fruitful source of ethical dilemmas because its whole purpose is **material gain**, the making of profit. Success in business requires a constant, avid search for potential advantage over others and business people are under pressure to do whatever yields such advantage.

It is important to understand that if ethics is applicable to corporate behaviour at all, it must therefore be a fundamental aspect of **mission**, since everything the organisation does flows from that. Managers responsible for strategic decision making cannot avoid responsibility for their organisation's ethical standing. They should consciously apply ethical rules to all of their decisions in order to filter out potentially undesirable developments. The question is however what ethical rules should be obeyed. Those that always apply or those that hold only in certain circumstances?

Ethical assumptions underpin all business activity as well as guiding behaviour. The continued existence of capitalism makes certain assumptions about the 'good life' and the desirability of private gain, for example. As we shall see in Chapter 10, accountancy is allegedly not a value-neutral profession. It establishes and follows rules for the protection of shareholder wealth and the reporting of the performance of capital investment. Accordingly accounting, especially in the private sector, can be seen as a servant of capital, making the implicit assumptions about morality that capitalism does.

1.3 Ethical relativism and non-cognitivism

> **Relativism** is the view that a **wide variety of acceptable ethical beliefs and practices** exist. The ethics that are most appropriate in a given situation will depend on the conditions at that time.

The relativist approach suggests that all moral statements are essentially subjective and arise from the culture, belief or emotion of the speaker.

Non-cognitivism recognises the differences that exist between the rules of behaviour prevailing in different cultures. The view that right and wrong are culturally determined is called **ethical relativism** or **moral relativism**. Ethical rules will differ in different periods within the same society, and will differ between different societies. Acceptance of ethical relativism implies that a society should not impose moral imperatives strictly, since it accepts that different ethical and belief systems are acceptable.

This is clearly a matter of significance in the context of international business. Managers encountering cultural norms of behaviour that differ significantly from their own may be puzzled to know what rules to follow.

Question   Morality

What can be said about the morality of a society that allows abortion within certain time limits in certain circumstances, or which allows immigration if immigrants fulfil certain requirements (will benefit the local economy)?

The suggested treatment of these issues suggests that the society is a non-cognitivist, ethically relative society. Banning abortion would be one sign of an ethically absolute society.

1.3.1 Strengths of relativism

(a) Relativism highlights our **cognitive bias** in observing with our senses (we see only what we know and understand) and our **notational bias** (what we measure without using our senses is subject to the bias of the measurement methods used).

(b) Relativism also highlights differences in **cultural beliefs**; for example all cultures may say that it is wrong to kill innocents, but different cultures may have different beliefs about who innocents actually are.

(c) The philosopher Bernard Crick argued that differing absolutist beliefs result in **moral conflict** between people; (relativist) ethics should act to resolve such conflicts.

(d) In the global economy, where companies conduct businesses in many different countries and cultures, adopting a relativist approach presumes **more flexibility** and therefore greater success.

1.3.2 Criticisms of relativism

(a) Put simply, strong relativism is a based on a **fundamental contradiction**; the statement that 'All statements are relative' is itself an absolute, non-relative statement. However it is possible to argue that some universal truths (certain laws of physics) exist, but deny other supposedly objective truths.

(b) A common criticism of relativism, particularly by religious leaders, is that it leads to a **philosophy of 'anything goes'**, denying the existence of morality and permitting activities that are harmful to others.

(c) Alternatively some critics have argued for the existence of **natural moral laws** (discussed below). These are not necessarily religious laws; the atheist scientist Richard Dawkins has argued in favour of natural laws.

(d) Ideas such as **objectivity and final truth** do have value – consider for example the ethical principle that we shall discuss later for accountants to be objective.

(e) If it's valid to say that everyone's differing opinions are **right**, then it's equally valid to say that **everyone's differing opinions are wrong**.

1.4 Ethical absolutism and cognitivism

Key term

> **Absolutism** is the view that there is an unchanging set of ethical principles that will apply in all situations, at all times and in all societies.

Absolutist approaches to ethics are built on the principle that **objective, universally applicable moral truths** exist and can be known. There is a set of moral rules that are always true. There are various methods of establishing these:

(a) **Religions** are based on the concept of universally applicable principles.

(b) **Law** can be a source of reference for establishing principles. However, ethics and law are not the same thing. Law must be free from ambiguity. However, unlike law, ethics can quite reasonably be an arena for debate, about both the principles involved and their application in specific rules.

(c) **Natural law** approaches to ethics are based on the idea that a set of objective or 'natural' moral rules exists and we can come to know what they are. In terms of business ethics, the natural law approach deals mostly with **rights and duties**. Where there is a right, there is also a duty to respect that right. For those concerned with business ethics there are undeniable implications for behaviour towards individuals. Unfortunately, the implications about duties can only be as clear as the rights themselves and there are wide areas in which disagreement about rights persists.

(d) **Deontological approaches** (see below).

Many absolutists would accept that some ethical truths may differ between different cultures. However they would also believe in certain basic truths that should be common to all cultures (for example 'thou shall not kill').

1.4.1 Strengths of absolutism

(a) Fundamentally the statement that **absolute truth does not exist** is **flawed**; if it does not exist, then the statement that it does not exist cannot be true.

(b) Absolutism lays down their certain unambiguous rules that people are able to follow, knowing that their **actions are right**.

1.4.2 Criticisms of absolutism

(a) Absolutist ethics takes **no account of evolving norms** within society and the development of 'advances' in morality, for example development of the belief that slavery is wrong.

(b) From **what source** should absolutist ethics be derived? Should it be religion, universal laws, human nature? Whatever source is used, it is then possibly subject to human interpretation with the result that different views may exist on the same issue and there will never be universal agreement.

(c) What happens when **two absolutist positions** appear **incompatible**. For example is it permissible to tell a lie in order to save an innocent life?

(d) A theory can be **true according to a relative framework** as well as true according to an absolute framework; what differs is the nature of the framework and not the truth of the statement.

1.5 Deontological ethics

Key term

> **Deontology** is concerned with the application of absolute, universal ethical principles in order to arrive at rules of conduct, the word deontology being derived from the Greek for 'duty'.

Deontology lays down **criteria** by which actions may be judged in advance, the outcomes of the actions are not relevant. The definitive treatment of deontological ethics is found in the work of the eighteenth century German philosopher, *Immanuel Kant*.

Kant's approach to ethics is based on the idea that facts themselves are neutral: they are what is; they do not give us any indication of what should be. If we make moral judgements about facts, the criteria by which we judge are separate from the facts themselves. Kant suggested that the criteria come from within ourselves and are based on a **sense of what is right**; an intuitive awareness of the nature of good.

Kant spoke of motivation to act in terms of 'imperatives'. A **hypothetical imperative** lays down a course of action to achieve a certain result. For instance, if I wish to pass an examination I must study the syllabus. A **categorical imperative**, however, defines a course of action in terms of acting in accordance with **moral duty** without reference to outcomes, desire or motive. For Kant, moral conduct is defined by categorical imperatives. We must act in certain ways because it is right to do so – right conduct is an **end in itself**.

Kant arrived at three formulations of the categorical imperative.

(a) 'So act that the maxim of your will could hold as a principle establishing universal law.'

This is close to the common sense maxim called the golden rule found in many religious teachings, for example the bible:

In everything do to others what you would have them do to you, for this sums up the Law and the Prophets (Matthew 7:12)

The difference between Kant's views and the golden rule is that under the golden rule, one could inflict harm on others if one was happy for the same harm to be inflicted on oneself. Kant however would argue that certain actions were universally right or wrong, irrespective of the personal, societal or cultural conditions.

Kant went on to suggest that this imperative meant that we have a duty not to act by maxims that result in logical contradictions. Theft of property for examples implies that it is permissible to steal, but also implies the existence of property; however if theft is allowed there can be no property, a logical contradiction. Kant also argued that we should act only by maxims that we believe should be universal maxims. Thus if we only helped others when there was advantage for ourselves, no-one would ever give help to others.

(b)   'Do not treat people simply as means to an end but as an end in themselves.'

The point of this rule is that it distinguishes between **people** and **objects**. We use objects as means to achieve an end: a chair is for sitting on, for instance. People are different.

We regard people differently from the way we regard objects, since they have unique intellects, feelings, motivations and so on of their own: treating them as objects denies their rationality and hence rational action.

Note, however, that this does not preclude us from using people as means to an end as long as we, at the same time, recognise their right to be treated as autonomous beings. Clearly, organisations and even society itself could not function if we could not make use of other people's services.

(c)   'So act as though you were through your maxims a law-making member of the kingdom of ends.'

Autonomous human beings are not subject to any particular interest and are therefore only subject to the universal laws which they make for themselves. However they must regard those laws as binding on others, or they would not be universal and would not be laws at all.

1.5.1 Criticisms of Kant

(a)   Critics have pointed out a dualism in Kant's views; he sees humans as part of nature whose actions can be explained in terms of natural causes. Yet Kant also argues that human beings are **capable of self-determination** with full freedom of action and in particular an ability to act in accordance with the principles of duty. Man is therefore capable in effect of rising above nature, which appears to conflict with the view that man is a natural animal.

(b)   It is argued that you cannot take actions in a vacuum and must have regard for their **consequences**. The Swiss philosopher Benjamin Constant put forward the 'enquiring murderer' argument; if you agree with Kant and hold that Truth telling must be universal, then one must, if asked, tell a known murderer the location of his prey. Kant's response was that lying to a murderer denied the murderer's rationality, and hence denied the possibility of there being free rational action at all. In addition Kant pointed out that we cannot always know what the consequences of our actions would be.

(c)   Kierkegaard argued that, whatever their expectations of others, **people failed to apply Kant's duties** to themselves, either by not exercising morally laws or not punishing themselves if they morally transgressed.

1.6 Teleological or consequentialist ethics: utilitarianism

There are two versions of consequentialist ethics:

- Utilitarianism – what is best for the greatest number
- Egoism – what is best for me

The teleological approach to ethics is to make moral judgements about courses of action by reference to their **outcomes or consequences**. The prefix *telios* is derived from the Greek and refers to issues of ends or outcomes.

Right or wrong becomes a question of **benefit or harm** rather than observance of universal principles.

Utilitarianism is the best-known formulation of this approach and can be summed up in the '**greatest good**' principle – 'greatest happiness of the greatest number'. This says that when deciding on a course of action we should choose the one that is likely to result in the greatest good for the greatest number of people. It therefore contrasts sharply with any absolute or universal notion of morality. The 'right' or 'wring' can **vary between situations and over time** according to the greatest happiness of the greatest number.

Utilitarianism underlies the assumption that the **operation of the free market** produces the **best possible consequences**. Free markets, it is argued, create wealth, this leads to higher tax revenue, this can pay for greater social welfare expenditures.

1.6.1 Problems with utilitarianism

There is an immediate problem here, which is how we are to define what is good for people. Bentham, a philosopher who wrote on utilitarianism, considered that **happiness** was the measure of good and that actions should therefore be judged in terms of their potential for promoting happiness or relieving unhappiness. Others have suggested that longer lists of harmful and beneficial things should be applied.

Case Study

A connected problem lies in outcomes that may in fact be beneficial but are not recognised as such. The **structural adjustment programmes** provided by the International Monetary Fund are a case in point. They are designed to align a country's economic incentives so that, by improving trade and public finances, to meet an objective, such as debt repayment. The IMF might argue, therefore, that the pain and dislocation suffered are short-term difficulties for long-term well-being. Critics of IMF structural adjustment programmes might suggest the opposite: that they are designed to remove money from the very poorest. The rights of the poor are more important than those of bondholders and to insist on repayment is unethical.

The utilitarian approach may also be questioned for its potential effect upon minorities. A situation in which a large majority achieved great happiness at the expense of creating misery among a small minority would satisfy the 'greatest good' principle. It could not, however, be regarded as ethically desirable.

However, utilitarianism can be a useful guide to conduct. It has been used to derive wide ranging rules and can be applied to help us make judgements about individual, unique problems.

Exam focus point

> The Pilot paper asked for the consequentialist and deontological approaches to ethics to be contrasted.

1.7 Teleological or consequentialist ethics: egoism

Key term

> **Egoism** states that an act is ethically justified if decision-makers freely decide to pursue their own short-term desires or their long-term interests. The subject to all ethical decisions is the self.

Adam Smith argued that an egoistic pursuit of individual self-interest produced a desired outcome for society through **free competition and perfect information** operating in the marketplace. Producers of goods for example have to offer value-for-money, since competition means that customers will buy from competitors if they don't. Egoism can also link in with enlightened self-interest; a business investing in good facilities for its workforce to keep them content and hence maintain their loyalty.

1.7.1 Criticisms of egoism

One criticism of pure egoism is that it makes short-term selfish desires equivalent to longer-term, more beneficial, interests. A modified view would give most validity to exercising those short-term desires that were in long-term interests. A more serious criticism has been that the markets do not function perfectly, and that some participants can benefit themselves at the expense of others and also the wider environment – hence the debate on sustainability which we shall consider in Chapter 3. Most fundamentally egoism is argued to be the **ethics of the thief** as well as the short-termist.

1.8 Pluralism

Pluralism accepts that different views may exist on morality, but suggests a consensus may be able to be reached in certain situations. A pluralist viewpoint is helpful in business situations where a range of perspectives have to be understood in order to establish a **course of action**. It emphasises the importance of morality as a **social phenomenon**; that some rules and arrangements need to be established for us to live together and we therefore need a good understanding of the different moralities that we will encounter.

However a consensus may not always be possible, and this is a key message of this section of the text. Irreconcilable ethical disputes tend to arise when absolutists argue with relativists, or if you have a deontological viewpoint opposed to a teleological viewpoint . For example during the recent debate in the UK about embryology, deontological arguments on the sanctity of life were opposed to teleological arguments about the scientific benefits of experimentation on embryos.

2 Influences on ethics

FAST FORWARD

Ethical decision making is influenced by **individual and situational factors**.

Individual factors include **age and gender, beliefs, education and employment**, how much **control** individuals believe they have over their own situation and their **personal integrity**.

Kohlberg's framework relates to individuals' degree of **ethical maturity**, the extent to which they can take their own ethical decisions.

Situational factors include **the systems of reward, authority** and **bureaucracy, work roles, organisational factors**, and the **national and cultural contexts**.

2.1 The cultural context of ethics and corporate social responsibility

Models of ethical decision-making divide the cultural factors that influence decision-making into two categories:

- **Individual** – the characteristics of the individual making the decision
- **Situational** – the features of the context which determine whether the individual will make an ethical or unethical decision

The problem with identifying these factors is that it is difficult to break them down individually since many of them are interdependent. Also evidence on the importance of **individual factors** seems to be mainly from the **USA**, whereas information on **situational factors** seems mainly to be from **Europe**. This arguably reflects an American focus on individual economic participants, whereas European attention is more focused on the design of economic institutions and how they function morally and promote moral behaviour in others.

2.2 Individual influences

2.2.1 Age and gender

Although some evidence suggests that the ways in which men and women respond to ethical dilemmas may differ, empirical studies do not clearly show whether men or women can be considered as more ethical. Similarly, although different age groups have been influenced by different experiences, again empirical evidence does not suggest that certain age groups are more moral than others.

2.2.2 National and cultural beliefs

By contrast national and cultural beliefs seem to have a significant effect on ethical beliefs, shaping what individuals regard as acceptable business issues. Hofstede has indicated that significant differences lie in the following four areas:

(a) **Individualism/collectivism** – the extent to which the culture emphasises the autonomous individual as opposed to group and community goals

(b) **Power distance** – how much acceptance there is in the society of the unequal distribution of power, and the perceived gap between juniors and seniors in a society or social structure (eg children/parents, students/teachers, citizens/legislators)

Hickson and Pugh describe power distance as 'how removed subordinates feel from superiors in a social meaning of the word distance. In a high power distance culture, inequality is accepted… in a low power distance culture inequalities and overt status symbols are minimised and subordinates expect to be consulted and to share decisions with approachable managers'.

(c) **Uncertainty avoidance** – individuals' preferences for certainties, rules and absolute truths

(d) **Masculinity/femininity** – or the extent to which money and possessions are valued as against people and relationships

These factors may influence how an individual tackles an ethical problem; alone (in an individualist culture) or in consultation (in a collectivist situation). Other influences might be on how individuals respond to ethically questionable directives from their superiors; in power distance cultures, where hierarchy is respected, commands are less likely to be questioned (I was only obeying orders). Globalisation may weaken the influence of national factors, although there is often a close connection between the local culture and a particular geographical region.

2.2.3 Education and employment

By contrast globalisation might be expected to strengthen the influence of education and employment. There do appear to be some differences in ethical decision-making between those with different educational and professional experiences.

2.2.4 Psychological factors

Psychological factors are concerned with the ways in which people think, and hence **decide what is the morally right or wrong course of action.** Discussion has centred on **cognitive moral development** and **locus of control.**

2.2.5 Locus of control

The locus of control is **how much influence individuals believe** they have over the course of their own lives. Individuals with a high internal locus believe that they can shape their own lives significantly, whereas those with external locus believe that their lives will be shaped by circumstances or luck. This distinction suggests that those with an internal locus will take more responsibility for their actions and are more likely to consider the moral consequences of what they do. Research however does not clearly indicate whether this is true in practice. This may also link into attitudes towards risk and what can be done to deal with risk.

2.2.6 Personal integrity

Integrity can be defined as adhering to moral principles or values. Its ethical consequences are potentially very significant, for example in deciding whether to **whistleblow** on questionable practice at work, despite pressure from colleagues or superiors or negative consequences of doing so. However evidence of its importance is limited because strangely it has not been included in many ethical decision models.

2.2.7 Moral imagination

Moral imagination is the level of awareness individuals have about the variety of moral consequences of what they do, how creatively they reflect on ethical dilemmas. The consequences of having a wide moral imagination could be an ability to see beyond the conventional organisational responses to moral difficulties, and formulate different solutions. Again there is little research on this subject, but differing levels of moral imagination would seem to be a plausible reason why individuals with the same work background view moral problems in different ways.

2.3 Kohlberg's cognitive moral development

Kohlberg's cognitive moral development theories relate to the thought processes people go through when making ethical decisions.

Kohlberg explains the ethical development of individuals in terms of development through three levels of moral development with two stages within each level. Although these levels are meant to relate to an individual's experience, in fact all three levels can be related to ethical behaviour. They show the **reasoning process** of individuals; it is possible that individuals at different levels will make the same moral decisions, but they will do so as a result of different reasoning processes. Kohlberg emphasises **how** the decision is reached, not **what** is decided.

Level 1 Pre-conventional (rewards/punishment/self-interest)

The decisions individuals make on ethical matters will have nothing to do with the ethical issues involved, but instead will depend on the personal advantage or disadvantage to the individual.

Stage 1

Individuals will see ethical decisions in terms of the rewards and punishments that will result:

- How will I be rewarded if I do this?
- What punishment will I suffer if I do this?

Stage 2

Individuals will see ethical decisions in the more complex terms of acting in their own best interests. They will see the decision in terms of the deals they can make and whether these deals are fair for them. For example it can mean helping others when others appear over-worked, but in return expecting others to help them when the situation is reversed.

Level 2 Conventional

Stage 3

This stage can be defined as individuals learning to live up to what is **expected** of them by their **immediate circle** (friends, workmates or even close competitors). This can work both ways in a business context; an individual might feel pressurised into staying out for a long lunch because everybody else in his team does; on the other hand individuals may feel they have to be at work by a certain time because everybody else is, even if it is earlier than their prescribed hours.

Stage 4

Individuals are seen as operating on a higher stage within this level if they operate in line with **social or cultural accord** rather than just the opinion of those around them. This certainly means **complying with the law** as it codifies social accord but it doesn't just mean that. Directors may for example decide to offer better terms to overseas workers because of the activities of pressure groups campaigning against 'sweatshop labour'. Many business managers appear to think with Level 2 reasoning. So do many accountants; arguably Stage 4 reasoning underlies most behaviour by accountants, as they comply with financial reporting and corporate governance requirements.

Level 3 Post-conventional

The most advanced level relates to individual development towards making their **own ethical decisions** in terms of what they believe to be right, not just acquiescing in what others believe to be right.

Stage 5

On the lower stage what individuals believe to be right is in terms of the **basic values** of their society, including ideas of mutual self-interest and the welfare of others. For example, is it is right to charge interest.

Stage 6

On the higher stage, individuals base their decisions on **wider universal ethical principles** such as justice, equity or rights, or Kant's framework. It also means respecting the demands of individuals' consciences. Business decisions made on these grounds could be disclosure on grounds of right-to-know that isn't compelled by law, or stopping purchasing from suppliers who test products on animals, on the grounds that animal rights to be free from suffering should be respected. We must stress here that using Stage 6 reasoning may involve a personal cost, since it may mean failing to comply with existing social norms and regulations as they are seen as unethical.

2.3.1 Criticisms of Kohlberg

Kohlberg argued that the higher the stage, the more ethical a decision was. However Kohlberg's work has been criticised for:

(a) Being **narrowly founded** on the typical abstract principles of American males such as fairness, impartiality, rights, maintenance of rules. Carol Gilligan, one of Kohlberg's former students(!), argued that women tend to use an ethic of care with a focus on empathy, harmony and interdependent relationships.

(b) Basing the **framework on his own value judgements**. Critics argue that the framework values rights and justice above other bases of morality such as basing actions upon social consequences or the need to achieve a peaceful settlement of conflict or problems.

(c) Arguing that the **acceptability of a solution** depends on the method of reasoning; the stage of moral development reached here would also appear to be significant.

(d) Assuming that moral action is **primarily decided by formal reasoning**. Social intuitionists argue that people make moral judgements in real-life without necessarily considering concerns such as fairness, law, human rights and abstract values; the judgements they make to solve a problem in real-life may be different to those if given the same problem as a theoretical problem.

(e) **Assuming individual development.** This is perhaps the most serious criticism of Kohlberg, that individuals do not necessarily progress during their lives, and even if they do progress, it may only be in certain situations; they may use different methods of moral reasoning inside and outside the workplace.

Question	Kohlberg's framework

Lowfloat Airlines has been under pressure from its institutional shareholders to cut costs and boost margins. Its Board issued an internal memo to all budget holders with a demand to 'seek all possible cost reductions'. The memo is strongly worded and amongst other things encourage budget holders 'to push back the boundaries, innovate, and to think the unthinkable'.

Traditionally a major area of cost had been aeroplane maintenance. Aircraft are constructed largely from aluminum, which is notoriously difficult to weld. In order to overcome this problem the manufacturers of aircraft resorted to the use of aluminum composite rivets to hold the super-structure together. However due to the molecular properties of the aluminum used, and the extremes of temperature that planes are exposed to in-flight, these rivets fatigue very quickly. Failure to replace rivets has been attributed as the cause of many of the crashes suffered by Russian airlines in the past few years.

Many aviation authorities lay down strict rules on the replacement of aircraft rivets because the reliability of the aircraft is severely compromised if rivets remain on the aircraft beyond a set number of flying hours.

The rivets are very expensive due to the price of the raw materials and the fact that they must be stored in freezers prior to fitting to maintain the integrity of the composite. As such, all rivets produced by aerospace manufacturers are colour-coded in line with an international agreement so that once a rivet is past its replacement date it can be easily identified and replaced during maintenance checks.

In order to cut costs senior managers in the Engineering department are recommending maintenance staff paint over the heads of rivets that are approaching the end of their recommended life. It is the view of the maintenance managers that rules governing rivet use are too strict and that it is perfectly safe to extend their use by 2–3 years.

At the board meeting the following opinions were expressed:

(a)   We should find out whether and how our competitors are cutting maintenance.

(b)   We shouldn't trade human lives off against shareholder value.

(c)   Passengers travel with us on the assumption that we're providing a safe form of transport.

(d)   We should weigh up the penalties we might suffer if we're discovered against the very high costs of our current maintenance schedule.

(e)   We have an obligation to meet the aircraft industries' regulations.

(f)   We should find out the chances of being grounded if the aviation regulators discover what we've done.

Required

Identify the levels and stages of moral development from Kohlberg's framework that are demonstrated by the six contributions made at the meeting.

Answer

Pre-conventional

Stage 1

(f)   The decision is seen solely in terms of how Lowfloat will be punished if its deception is discovered.

Stage 2

(d)   This shows a more sophisticated view of economic self-interest with the costs of different options being weighed up.

Conventional

Stage 3

(a)   This argument is based on Lowfloat doing what its peers are doing. Peers can include competitors, so the director is arguing that Lowfloat should behave in a way that is normal for the industry.

Stage 4

(e)   This argument grounds ethical compliance as obeying aircraft industry regulations. It differs from Stage 3 in that it sees decisions in terms of best practice as defined by regulation, what Lowfloat and its competitors should be doing rather than what they are doing.

Post-conventional

Stage 5

(c)   This is based on the underlying ideas of how society operates and what is expected of business. Passengers, when paying Lowfloat, have the expectation that Lowfloat will be able to convey them safely; if they do not have that expectation of airlines, then the whole business model would be undermined.

Stage 6

(b)   This is based on the absolute ethical view that it is always wrong to give economic considerations priority over human safety. Lowfloat should spend whatever it takes to ensure that passengers are conveyed safely.

Kohlberg's framework is emphasised significantly in the syllabus, and you therefore will need to consider it when dealing with various ethical situations. For example does the organisation's ethical framework allow people to make up their own minds on ethics, or does it assume (or promote) a lower level of ethical awareness.

You may also need to identify the Kohlberg level that someone is at given that he is behaving in a certain way, and produce arguments for and against operating at certain levels.

2.4 Situational influences

The reason for considering situational influences on moral decision-making is that individuals appear to have 'multiple ethical selves' – they make different decisions in different circumstances. These circumstances might include **issue-related factors** (the nature of the issue and how it is viewed in the organisation) and **context-related factors** (the expectations and demands that will be placed on people working in an organisation).

2.5 Issue-related factors

2.5.1 Moral intensity

Thomas Jones proposed a list of six criteria that decision-makers will use to decide how ethically significant an issue was, and hence what they should do:

- **Magnitude of consequences** – the harms or the benefits that will result
- **Social consequences** – the degree of general agreement about the problem
- **Probability of effect** – the probability of the harms or benefits actually happening
- **Temporal immediacy** – the speed with which the consequences are likely to occur; if they are likely to take years, the moral intensity may be lower
- **Proximity** – the feelings of nearness that the decision-maker has for those who will suffer the impacts of the ethical decision
- **Concentration of effect** – whether some persons will suffer greatly or many people will suffer lightly

Research suggests that moral intensity is significant but has to be seen in the context of how an issue is perceived in an organisation.

2.5.2 Moral framing

Moral framing sets the context for how issues are **perceived** in organisations. Language is very important. Using words such as fairness and honesty is likely to trigger moral thinking. However evidence suggests that many managers are reluctant to frame issues in moral terms seeing it as promoting disharmony, distorting decision-making and suggesting that they are not practical. Instead issues are more likely to be discussed in terms of **rational corporate self-interest**.

2.6 Context-related factors

2.6.1 Systems of reward

Reward mechanisms have obvious potential consequences for ethical behaviour. This works both ways. Basing awards on sales values achieved may encourage questionable selling practices; failing to reward ethical behaviour (or worst still penalising whistleblowers or other staff who act ethically) will not encourage an ethical culture.

Sadly a majority of studies on this area seem to indicate that there is a significant link between the rewarding of unethical behaviour and its continuation.

2.6.2 Authority

There are various ways in which managers may encourage ethical behaviour; by **direct instructions** to subordinates, by setting subordinates **targets** that are so challenging that they can only be achieved through taking unethical shortcuts. Failing to act can be as bad as acting, for example failing to prevent bullying. Studies suggest that many employees perceive their managers as lacking ethical integrity.

2.6.3 Bureaucracy

Key term

> **Bureaucracy** is a system characterised by detailed rules and procedures, impersonal hierarchical relations and a fixed division of tasks.

Bureaucracy underpins the authority and reward system, and may have a number of impacts on individual's reactions to ethical decision-making:

- **Suppression of moral autonomy** – individual ethical beliefs tend to be overridden by the rules and roles of the bureaucracy
- **Instrumental morality** – seeing morality in terms of following procedures rather than focusing on the moral substance of the goals themselves
- **Distancing** individuals from the consequences of what they do
- **Denial of moral status** – that ultimately individuals are resources for carrying out the organisation's will rather than autonomous moral beings

2.6.4 Work roles

Education and experience build up expectations of how people in particular roles will act. Strong evidence suggests that the expectations staff have about the roles that they adopt in work will override the individual ethics that may influence their decisions in other contexts.

2.6.5 Organisational field

Key term

> An **organisational field** is a community of organisations with a common 'meaning system' and whose participants interact more frequently with one another than those outside the field.

Organisations within an organisation field tend to share a common business environment, such as a common system of training or regulation. This means that they tend to cohere round common norms and values.

Within an organisational field a **recipe** is a common set of assumptions about organisational purposes and how to manage organisations. If the recipe is followed, it means that organisations within the organisational field can provide consistent standards for consumers for example. However it can also mean that managers within the field cannot appreciate the lessons that could be learnt from organisations outside the field, and therefore transition outside the field may be difficult.

Case Study

An example would be a private sector manager joining a public service organisation and having to get used to different traditions and mechanisms, for example having to build consensus into the decision-making process.

The result of being in an organisational field can be a desire to achieve **legitimacy** – meeting the **expectations** that those in the same organisational field have in terms of the assumptions, behaviours and strategies that will be pursued.

2.6.6 Organisational culture

Key term

> **Organisational culture** is the 'basic assumptions and beliefs that are shared by members of an organisation, that operate unconsciously and define in a basic taken-for-granted fashion an organisation's view of itself and its environment.'
>
> (Handy)

Organisational culture relates to ways of acting, talking, thinking and evaluating. It can include shared:

*   **Values** that often have 'official' status being connected to the organisation's mission statement but which can be vague (acting in the interests of the community)
*   **Beliefs** that are more specific than assumptions but represent aspects of an organisation that are talked about, for example using 'ethical suppliers'
*   **Behaviours**, the ways in which people within the organisation and the organisation itself operates, including work routines and symbolic gestures
*   **Taken** for **granted assumptions**, which are at the core of the organisation's culture which people find difficult to explain but are central to the organisation. The **paradigm** represents the common assumptions and collective experience that an organisation must have to function meaningfully

Organisational culture may be different to (may conflict with) the official rules of the bureaucracy. Unsurprisingly it has been identified as a key element in decisions of what is morally right or wrong, as employees become conditioned by it into particular attitudes to ethical decision making.

 Case Study

In his memoirs the journalist Hunter Davies related that when he started working on a newspaper in London, he discovered that he was financially rather better off than he thought he would be because of being able to claim expenses. 'This was something that was explained to me on my very first day, not by the management, but by other reporters.' Staff would spend the first working morning of their week filling out their expenses 'for some the hardest part of their week'.

Davies was told what the normal expense claim for his role as a junior reporter was. All he had to do in order to claim that amount was submit bills for lunch or dinner with anyone; it didn't matter who they were so long as he had a piece of paper and could name them as a potential contact. Davies was informed that management knew, that it was an accepted part of national newspaper life and he would undermine the system if he didn't do what everyone else did.

This is a very good example of Level 2 Stage 3 of Kohlberg's framework, doing something because those close to you (colleagues) are doing it.

In addition to the main organisational culture, there may also be **distinct subcultures** often dependent upon the way the organisation is structured, for example function or division subcultures.

2.6.7 National and cultural context

In an organisational context, this is the **nation** in which the ethical decision is made rather than the nationality of the decision-maker. If someone spends a certain length of time working in another country, their views of ethical issues may be shaped by the norms of that other country, for example on sexual harassment. Globalisation may complicate the position on this.

3 The social and ethical environment   12/07, 6/08, 12/08

FAST FORWARD

Firms have to ensure they obey the law: but they also face **ethical concerns**, because their reputations depend on a good image.

Ethics: a set of moral principles to guide behaviour.

Whereas the political environment in which an organisation operates consists of laws, regulations and government agencies, the social environment consists of the customs, attitudes, beliefs and education of society as a whole, or of different groups in society; and the ethical environment consists of a set (or sets) of well-established rules of personal and organisational behaviour.

Social attitudes, such as a belief in the merits of education, progress through science and technology, and fair competition, are significant for the management of a business organisation. Other beliefs have either gained strength or been eroded in recent years:

(a)   There is a growing belief in preserving and improving the quality of life by reducing working hours, reversing the spread of pollution, developing leisure activities and so on. Pressures on organisations to consider the environment are particularly strong because most environmental damage is irreversible and some is fatal to humans and wildlife.

(b)   Many pressure groups have been organised in recent years to protect social minorities and under-privileged groups. Legislation has been passed in an attempt to prevent racial discrimination and discrimination against women and disabled people.

(c)   Issues relating to the environmental consequences of corporate activities are currently debated, and respect for the environment has come to be regarded as an unquestionable good.

The ethical environment refers to justice, respect for the law and a moral code. The conduct of an organisation, its management and employees will be measured against ethical standards by the customers, suppliers and other members of the public with whom they deal.

3.1 Ethical problems facing managers

Managers have a duty (in most entities) to aim for profit. At the same time, modern ethical standards impose a duty to guard, preserve and enhance the value of the entity for the good of all touched by it, including the general public. Large organisations tend to be more often held to account over this than small ones.

In the area of **products and production**, managers have responsibility to ensure that the public and their own employees are protected from danger. Attempts to increase profitability by cutting costs may lead to dangerous working conditions or to inadequate safety standards in products. In the United States, product liability litigation is so common that this legal threat may be a more effective deterrent than general ethical standards. The Consumer Protection Act 1987 and EU legislation generally is beginning to ensure that ethical standards are similarly enforced in the UK.

Another ethical problem concerns **payments by companies to government or municipal officials** who have power to help or hinder the payers' operations. In *The Ethics of Corporate Conduct, Clarence Walton* refers to the fine distinctions which exist in this area.

(a)   **Extortion**. Foreign officials have been known to threaten companies with the complete closure of their local operations unless suitable payments are made.

(b)   **Bribery**. This refers to payments for services to which a company is not legally entitled. There are some fine distinctions to be drawn; for example, some managers regard political contributions as bribery.

(c)   **Grease money**. Multinational companies are sometimes unable to obtain services to which they are legally entitled because of deliberate stalling by local officials. Cash payments to the right people may then be enough to oil the machinery of bureaucracy.

(d)   **Gifts**. In some cultures (such as Japan) gifts are regarded as an essential part of civilised negotiation, even in circumstances where to Western eyes they might appear ethically dubious. Managers operating in such a culture may feel at liberty to adopt the local customs.

Business ethics are also relevant to competitive behaviour. This is because a market can only be free if competition is, in some basic respects, fair. There is a distinction between competing aggressively and competing unethically. The dispute between British Airways and Virgin centred around issues of business ethics.

3.2 Examples of social and ethical objectives

Companies are not passive in the social and ethical environment. Many organisations pursue a variety of social and ethical objectives.

Employees

(a) A minimum wage, perhaps with adequate differentials for skilled labour
(b) Job security (over and above the protection afforded to employees by government legislation)
(c) Good conditions of work (above the legal minima)
(d) Job satisfaction

Customers may be regarded as entitled to receive a produce of good quality at a reasonable price.

Suppliers may be offered regular orders and timely payment in return for reliable delivery and good service.

Society as a whole

(a) Control of pollution
(b) Provision of financial assistance to charities, sports and community activities
(c) Co-operation with government authorities in identifying and preventing health hazards in the products sold

As far as it is possible, social and ethical objectives should be expressed quantitatively, so that actual results can be monitored to ensure that the targets are achieved. This is often easier said than done – more often, they are expressed in the organisation's mission statement which can rarely be reduced to a quantified amount.

Many of the above objectives are commercial ones – for example satisfying customers is necessary to stay in business. The question as to whether it is the business of businesses to be concerned about wider issues of social responsibility *at all* is discussed shortly.

3.3 Social responsibility and businesses

Arguably, institutions like hospitals, schools and so forth exist because health care and education are seen to be desirable social objectives by government at large, if they can be afforded.

However, where does this leave businesses? How far is it reasonable, or even appropriate, for businesses to exercise 'social responsibility' by giving to charities, voluntarily imposing strict environmental objectives on themselves and so forth?

One school of thought would argue that **the management of a business has only one social responsibility, which is to maximise wealth for its shareholders**. There are two reasons to support this argument.

(a) If the business is owned by the shareholders the assets of the company are, ultimately, the shareholders' property. Management has no moral right to dispose of business assets (like cash) on non-business objectives, as this has the effect of reducing the return available to shareholders. The shareholders might, for example, disagree with management's choice of beneficiary. Anyhow, it is for the shareholders to determine how their money should be spent.

(b) A second justification for this view is that management's job is to maximise wealth, as this is the best way that society can benefit from a business's activities.

    (i) Maximising wealth has the effect of increasing the tax revenues available to the state to disburse on socially desirable objectives.

    (ii) Maximising wealth for the few is sometimes held to have a 'trickle down' effect on the disadvantaged members of society.

    (iii) Many company shares are owned by pension funds, whose ultimate beneficiaries may not be the wealthy anyway.

This argument rests on certain assumptions.

(a)   The first assumption is, in effect, the opposite of the stakeholder view. In other words, it is held that the *rights* of legal ownership are paramount over all other *interests* in a business: while other stakeholders have an interest, they have few legal or moral rights over the wealth created.

(b)   The second assumption is that a business's *only* relationship with the wider social environment is an economic one. After all, that is what businesses exist for, and any other activities are the role of the state.

(c)   The defining purpose of business organisations is the maximisation of the wealth of their owners.

4 Ethics in organisations

Ethics is a code of moral principles that people follow with respect to what is right or wrong. Ethical principles are not necessarily enforced by law, although the law incorporates moral judgements (murder is wrong ethically, and is also punishable legally).

Companies have to follow legal standards, or else they will be subject to fines and their officers might face similar charges. Ethics in organisations relates to **social responsibility** and **business practice.**

People that work for organisations bring their own values into work with them. Organisations contain a variety of ethical systems.

(a)   **Personal ethics** (eg deriving from a person's upbringing, religious or non-religious beliefs, political opinions, personality). People have different ethical viewpoints at different stages in their lives. Some will judge situations on 'gut feel'. Some will consciously or unconsciously adopt a general approach to ethical dilemmas, such as 'the end justifies the means'.

(b)   **Professional ethics** (eg ACCA's code of ethics, medical ethics).

(c)   **Organisation cultures** (eg 'customer first'). Culture, in denoting what is normal behaviour, also denotes what is the right behaviour in many cases.

(d)   **Organisation systems**. Ethics might be contained in a formal code, reinforced by the overall statement of values. A problem might be that ethics does not always save money, and there is a real cost to ethical decisions. Besides, the organisation has different ethical duties to different stakeholders. Who sets priorities?

 Case Study

Organisation systems and targets do have ethical implications. The Harvard Business Review reported that the US retailer, Sears, Roebuck was deluged with complaints that customers of its car service centre were being charged for unnecessary work: apparently this was because mechanics had been given targets of the number of car spare parts they should sell.

4.1 Leadership practices and ethics

The role of culture in determining the ethical climate of an organisation can be further explored by a brief reflection on the role of leaders in setting the ethical standard. A culture is partly a collection of symbols and attitudes, embodying certain truths about the organisation. Senior managers are also symbolic managers; inevitably they decide priorities; they set an example, whether they like it or not. Remember, too, that one of the roles of managers, according to Mintzberg is the **ceremonial one**.

There are four types of cultural leadership in organisations. (Note that these should *not* be confused with leadership styles.)

(a)   **Creative**. The culture of an organisation often reflects its founder, and it is therefore reasonable to expect that the founding visionary should set the ethical tone. Such leaders create the ethical style.

(b)   **Protective**. Such leaders sustain, or exemplify, the organisation's culture: for example a company which values customer service may have leaders who are 'heroic' in their efforts to achieve it.

(c) **Integrative**. Other leaders aim to create consensus through people, and perhaps flourish in an involvement culture. The danger is that this can turn to political manipulation; the 'consensus' created should work towards some valued cultural goal.

(d) **Adaptive**. These leaders change an existing culture or set of ethics. (When appointed to run *British Airways, Colin Marshall* changed the sign on his door from Chief Executive to his own name.) However, a leader has to send out the right signals, to ensure that competitive behaviour remains ethical, to avoid bad publicity if nothing else.

4.2 Two approaches to managing ethics

FAST FORWARD

Inside the organisation, a **compliance based approach** highlights conformity with the law. An **integrity based approach** suggests a wider remit, incorporating ethics in the organisation's values and culture.

Organisations sometimes issue **codes of conduct** to employees. Many employees are bound by professional codes of conduct.

Lynne Paine (*Harvard Business Review*, March-April 1994) suggests that ethical decisions are becoming more important as penalties, in the US at least, for companies which break the law become tougher. (This might be contrasted with UK, where a fraudster whose deception ran into millions received a sentence of community service.) Paine suggests that there are two approaches to the management of ethics in organisations.

- Compliance-based
- Integrity-based

4.2.1 Compliance-based approach

A compliance-based approach is primarily designed to ensure that the company acts within the letter of the law, and that violations are prevented, detected and punished. Some organisations, faced with the legal consequences of unethical behaviour take legal precautions such as those below.

- Compliance procedures
- Audits of contracts
- Systems for employees to inform superiors about criminal misconduct without fear of retribution
- Disciplinary procedures

Corporate compliance is limited in that it refers only to the law, but legal compliance is 'not an adequate means for addressing the full range of ethical issues that arise every day'. This is especially the case in the UK, where **voluntary** codes of conduct and self-regulation are perhaps more prevalent than in the US.

An example of the difference between the **legality** and **ethicality** of a practice is the sale in some countries of defective products without appropriate warnings. 'Companies engaged in international business often discover that conduct that infringes on recognised standards of human rights and decency is legally permissible in some jurisdictions.'

The compliance approach also overemphasises the threat of detection and punishment in order to channel appropriate behaviour. Arguably, some employers view compliance programmes as an insurance policy for senior management, who can cover the tracks of their arbitrary management practices. After all, some performance targets are impossible to achieve without cutting corners: managers can escape responsibility by blaming the employee for not following the compliance programme, when to do so would have meant a failure to reach target.

Furthermore, mere compliance with the law is no guide to **exemplary** behaviour.

4.2.2 Integrity-based programmes

'An integrity-based approach combines a concern for the law with an **emphasis on managerial responsibility** for ethical behaviour. Integrity strategies strive to define companies' guiding values, aspirations and patterns of thought and conduct. When integrated into the day-to-day operations of an organisation, such strategies can help prevent damaging ethical lapses, while tapping into powerful human impulses for moral thought and action.

It should be clear to you from this quotation that an integrity-based approach to ethics treats ethics as an issue of organisation culture.

Ethics management has several tasks.

- To define and give life to an organisation's defining values.
- To create an environment that supports ethically sound behaviour
- To instil a sense of shared accountability amongst employees.

The table below indicates some of the differences between the two main approaches.

	Compliance	Integrity
Ethos	Knuckle under to external standards	Choose ethical standards
Objective	Keep to the law	Enable legal and responsible conduct
Originators	Lawyers	Management, with lawyers, HR specialists etc
Methods (both includes education, and audits, controls, penalties)	Reduced employee discretion	Leadership, organisation systems
Behavioural assumptions	People are solitary self-interested beings	People are social beings with values
Standards	The law	Company values, aspirations (including law)
Staffing	Lawyers	Managers and lawyers
Education	The law, compliance system	Values, the law, compliance systems
Activities	Develop standards, train and communicate, handle reports of misconduct, investigate, enforce, oversee compliance	Integrate values *into* company systems, provide guidance and consultation, identify and resolve problems, oversee compliance

In other words, an integrity-based approach **incorporates** ethics into corporate culture and systems.

 Case Study

Charles Hampden-Turner (in his book *Corporate Culture*) notes that attitudes to safety can be part of a corporate *culture*. He quotes the example of a firm called (for reasons of confidentiality) *Western Oil*.

Western Oil had a bad safety record. 'Initially, safety was totally at odds with the main cultural values of productivity (management's interests) and maintenance of a macho image (the worker's culture) ... Western Oil had a culture which put safety in conflict with other corporate values.' In particular, the problem was with its long-distance truck drivers (which in the US have a culture of solitary independence and self reliance) who drove sometimes recklessly with loads large enough to inundate a small town. The company instituted *Operation Integrity* to improve safety, in a lasting way, changing the policies and drawing on the existing features of the culture but using them in a different way.

The culture had five dilemmas.

- **Safety-first vs macho-individualism**. Truckers see themselves as 'fearless pioneers of the unconventional lifestyle ... "Be careful boys!" is hardly a plea likely to go down well with this particular group'. Instead of trying to control the drivers, the firm recommended that they become *road safety consultants* (or design consultants). Their advice was sought on improving the system.

This had the advantage that 'by making drivers critics of the system their roles as outsiders were preserved and promoted'. It tried to tap their heroism as promoters of public safety.

- **Safety everywhere vs safety specialists**. Western Oil could have hired more specialist staff. However, instead, the company promoted cross functional safety teams from existing parts of the business, for example, to help in designing depots and thinking of ways to reduce hazards.

- **Safety as cost vs productivity as benefit**. 'If the drivers raced from station to station to win their bonus, accidents were bound to occur ... . The safety engineers rarely spoke to the line manager in charge of the delivery schedules. The unreconciled dilemma between safety and productivity had been evaded at management level and passed down the hierarchy until drivers were subjected to two incompatible injunctions, work fast and work safely'. To deal with this problem, safety would be built into the reward system.

- **Long-term safety vs short-term steering**. The device of recording 'unsafe' acts in operations enabled them to be monitored by cross-functional teams, so that the causes of accidents could be identified and be reduced.

- **Personal responsibility vs collective protection**. It was felt that if 'safety' was seen as a form of management policing it would never be accepted. The habit of management 'blaming the victim' had to stop. Instead, if an employee reported another to the safety teams, the person who was reported would be free of *official* sanction. Peer presence was seen to be a better enforcer of safety than the management hierarchy.

It has also been suggested that the following institutions can be established.

- An **ethics committee** is a group of executives (perhaps including non-executive directors) appointed to oversee company ethics. It rules on misconduct. It may seek advice from specialists in business ethics.

- An **ethics ombudsperson** is a manager who acts as the corporate conscience.

Accountants can also appeal to their professional body for ethical guidance.

Whistle-blowing is the disclosure by an employee of illegal, immoral or illegitimate practices on the part of the organisation. In theory, the public ought to welcome the public trust: however, confidentiality is very important in the accountants' code of ethics. Whistle-blowing frequently involves **financial loss** for the whistle-blower.

- The whistle-blower may lose his or her job.
- If the whistle-blower is a member of a professional body, he or she cannot, sadly, rely on that body to take a significant interest, or even offer a sympathetic ear. Some professional bodies have narrow interpretations of what is meant by ethical conduct. For many the duties of **commercial confidentiality** are felt to be more important.

Exam focus point

The ethics codes described above can be related to mission, culture and control strategies. A compliance-based approach suggest that bureaucratic control is necessary; an integrity based approach relies on cultural control.

5 Principles and guidance on professional ethics

FAST FORWARD

IFAC's and ACCA's guidance is very similar.

5.1 The public interest

FAST FORWARD

Organisations sometimes issue **codes of conduct** to employees. Many employees are bound by professional codes of conduct.

IFAC's *Code of Ethics* gives the key reason why accountancy bodies produce ethical guidance: the public interest.

> 'A distinguishing mark of the accountancy profession is its acceptance of the responsibility to act in the public interest. Therefore, a professional accountant's responsibility is not exclusively to satisfy the needs of an individual client or employer.
>
> **The public interest** is considered to be the collective well-being of the community of people and institutions the professional accountant serves, including clients, lenders, governments, employers, employees, investors, the business and financial community and others who rely on the work of professional accountants.'

The **key reason** that **accountants need** to have an **ethical code** is that **people rely on them and their expertise**.

Accountants deal with a range of issues on behalf of clients. They often have access to confidential and sensitive information. Auditors claim to give an independent view. It is therefore critical that accountants, and particularly auditors, are, and are seen to be, independent.

As the auditor is required to be, and seen to be, ethical in his dealings with clients, ACCA publishes guidance for its members, the *Code of Ethics and Conduct*. This guidance is given in the form of fundamental principles, specific guidance and explanatory notes.

IFAC also lays down fundamental principles in its *Code of Ethics*. The fundamental principles of the two associations are extremely similar.

5.2 The fundamental principles

ACCA
• **Integrity.** Members should be **straightforward** and **honest** in all professional and business relationships.
• **Objectivity.** Members **should not allow bias, conflict of interest or undue influence of others** to override professional or business judgements.
• **Professional Competence and Due Care**. Members have a continuing duty to maintain professional knowledge and skill at a level required to ensure that a client or employer receives the advantage of competent professional service based on current developments in practice, legislation and techniques. Members should act diligently and in accordance with applicable technical and professional standards when providing professional services.
• **Confidentiality**. Members should respect the confidentiality of information acquired as a result of professional or business relationships **and should not disclose** any such information to third parties without proper and specific authority **unless there is a legal or professional right or duty to disclose**. Confidential information acquired as a result of professional and business relationships should not be used for the personal advantage of the professional accountant or third parties.
• **Professional Behaviour**. Members should **comply with relevant laws and regulations and should avoid any action that discredits the profession.**

5.3 Ethical framework

The ethical guidance discussed above is in the form of a framework. It contains some rules, for example, ACCA prohibits making loans to clients, but in the main it is flexible guidance. It can be seen as being a **framework rather than a set of rules**. There are a number of advantages of a framework over a system of ethical rules. These are outlined in the table below.

Advantages of an ethical framework over a rules based system
A framework of guidance places the onus on the auditor to **actively consider** independence for every given situation, rather than just agreeing a checklist of forbidden items. It also requires him to **demonstrate** that a responsible conclusion has been reached about ethical issues.
The framework **prevents auditors interpreting legalistic requirements narrowly** to get around the ethical requirements. There is an extent to which rules engender deception, whereas principles encourage compliance.
A framework **allows for** the variations that are found in every **individual situation**. Each situation is likely to be different.
A framework can accommodate a **rapidly changing environment**, such as the one that auditors are constantly in.
However, a **framework can contain prohibitions** (as noted above) where these are necessary as safeguards are not feasible.

6 Practical situations

12/07, 6/08, 12/08

FAST FORWARD

Exam questions may ask you to think about what should be done if breaches of laws, regulations or ethical guidelines occur. **Close relationships** between the parties or other **conflicts of interest** are often a complication.

6.1 Examination questions

Examination questions will expect you to be able to apply your understanding of ethical issues to practical problems arising in organisations. Later in this chapter we are going to suggest an approach that you may find helpful in dealing with such questions, but first we are going to take the bare bones of a situation and see how it might be built up into the kind of scenario you will have to face.

6.2 The problem

The exam may present you with a scenario, typically containing an array of detail much of which is potentially relevant. The problem, however, will be one or other of two basic types.

(a)   A wishes B to do C which is in breach of D
       where

       A   =   a situation, person, group of people, institution or the like

       B   =   you/a management accountant, the person with the ethical dilemma

       C   =   acting, or refraining from acting, in a certain way

       D   =   an ethical principle, quite possibly one of the ACCA's fundamental
                 principles

(b)   Alternatively, the problem may be that A has done C, B has become aware of it and D requires
       some kind of response from B.

6.3 Example: the problem

An accountant joined a manufacturing company as its Finance Director. The company had acquired land on which it built industrial units. The Finance Director discovered that, before he had started at the company, one of the units had been sold and the selling price was significantly larger than the amount which appeared in the company's records. The difference had been siphoned off to another company – one in which his boss, the Managing Director, was a major shareholder. Furthermore, the Managing Director had kept his relationship with the second company a secret from the rest of the board.

The Finance Director confronted the Managing Director and asked him to reveal his position to the board. However, the Managing Director refused to disclose his position to anyone else. The secret profits on the sale of the unit had been used, he said, to reward the people who had secured the sale. Without their help, he added, the company would be in a worse position financially.

The Finance Director then told the Managing Director that unless he reported to the board he would have to inform the board members himself. The Managing Director still refused. The Finance Director disclosed the full position to the board.

The problem is of the **second basic type. B** is of course the easiest party to identify. Here it is the **Finance Director. A** is clear, as well: it is the **Managing Director. C** is the **MD's breach of his directorial duties** regarding related party transactions not to obtain any personal advantage from his position of director without the consent of the company for whatever gain or profit he has obtained. **D** is the **principle that requires B not to be a party to an illegal act**. (Note that we distinguish between ethical and legal obligations. B has legal obligations as a director of the company. He has ethical obligations not to ignore his legal obligations. In **this** case the two amount to the same thing.)

6.4 Relationships

You may have a feeling that the resolution of the problem described above is just too easy, and you would be right. This is because A, B, C and D are either people, or else situations involving people, who stand in certain relationships to each other.

- A may be B's boss, B's subordinate, B's equal in the organisational hierarchy, B's husband, B's friend.
- B may be new to the organisation, or well-established and waiting for promotion, or ignorant of some knowledge relevant to the situation that A possesses or that the people affected by C possess.
- C or D, as already indicated, may involve some person(s) with whom B or A have a relationship – for example the action may be to misrepresent something to a senior manager who controls the fate of B or A (or both) in the organisation.

Question	Relationships

Identify the relationships in the scenario above. What are the possible problems arising from these relationships?

Answer	

The MD is the Finance Director's boss. He is also a member of the board and is longer established as such than B the Finance Director.

In outline the problems arising are that **by acting ethically the Finance Director will alienate the MD**. Even if the problem were to be resolved the episode would sour all future dealings between these two parties. Also, **the board may not be sympathetic to the accusations of a newcomer**. The Finance Director may find that he is ignored or even dismissed.

Relationships should never be permitted to affect ethical judgement. If you knew that your best friend at work had committed a major fraud, for example, **integrity** would demand that **in the last resort** you would have to bring it to the attention of somebody in authority. But note that this is only in the last resort. Try to imagine what you would do in practice in this situation.

Surely your **first course** would be to try to **persuade your friend** that what they had done was wrong, and that they themselves had an ethical responsibility to own up. Your **second option**, if this failed, might be to try to get **somebody** (perhaps somebody outside the organisation) that you knew could **exert pressure** on your friend to persuade him or her to own up.

There is obviously a limit to how far you can take this. The important point is that just because you are dealing with a situation that involves ethical issues, this **does not mean that all the normal principles of good human relations and good management have to be suspended**. In fact this is the time when such business principles are most important.

6.5 Consequences

Actions have consequences and the consequences themselves are quite likely to have their own ethical implications.

In the example given above, we can identify the following further issues.

(a) The MD's secret transaction appears to have been made in order to secure the sale of an asset the proceeds of which are helping to prop up the company financially. Disclosure of the truth behind the sale may mean that the company is pursued for compensation by the buyer of the site. The **survival of the company** as a whole may be jeopardised.

(b) If the truth behind the transaction becomes public knowledge this could be highly damaging for the company's **reputation**, even if it can show that only one black sheep was involved.

(c) The board may simply rubber stamp the MD's actions and so the Finance Director may still find that he is expected to be party to dishonesty. (This assumes that the **company as a whole is amoral** in its approach to ethical issues. In fact the MD's refusal to disclose the matter to the board suggests otherwise.)

In the last case we are back to square one. In the first two cases, the Finance Director has to consider the ethicality or otherwise of taking action that could lead to the collapse of the company, extensive redundancies, unpaid creditors and shareholders and so on.

6.6 Actions

In spite of the difficulties, your aim will usually be to reach a satisfactory resolution to the problem. **The actions that you recommend** will often include the following.

- **Informal discussions** with the parties involved.
- **Further investigation** to establish the full facts of the matter. What extra information is needed?
- The **tightening up of controls or the introduction of new ones**, if the situation arose due to laxity in this area. This will often be the case and the principles of professional competence and due care and of technical standards will usually be relevant.
- **Attention to organisational matters** such as changes in the management structure, improving communication channels, attempting to change attitudes.

Question   **Cunning plan**

Your finance director has asked you to join a team planning a takeover of one of your company's suppliers. An old school friend works as an accountant for the company concerned, the finance director knows this, and has asked you to try and find out 'anything that might help the takeover succeed, but it must remain secret'.

Answer

There are three issues here. Firstly you have a **conflict of interest** as the finance director wants you to keep the takeover a secret, but you probably feel that you should tell your friend what is happening as it may affect their job.

Second, the finance director is asking you to deceive your friend. Deception is unprofessional behaviour and will break your ethical guidelines. Therefore the situation is presenting you with **two conflicting demands**. It is worth remembering that no employer can ask you to break your ethical rules.

Finally, the request to break your own ethical guidelines constitutes **unprofessional behaviour** by the finance director. You should consider reporting him to their relevant body.

7 Examination questions: an approach

7.1 Dealing with questions

In a situation involving ethical issues, there are **practical steps** that should be taken.

- Establish the facts of the situation by further investigation and work.
- Consider the alternative options available for action.
- Consider whether any professional guidelines have been breached.
- State the best course of action based on the steps above.

An article in a student magazine contained the following advice for candidates who wish to achieve good marks in ethics questions. (The emphasis is BPP's.)

'The precise question requirements will vary, but in general marks will be awarded for:

- Analysis of the situation
- A recognition of ethical issues
- Explanation if appropriate of relevant part of ethical guidelines, and interpretation of its relevance to the question
- Making clear, logical, and appropriate recommendations for action. Making inconsistent recommendations does not impress examiners
- Justifying recommendations in practical business terms and in ethical terms

As with all scenario based questions there is likely to be **more than one acceptable answer**, and marks will depend on how well the case is argued, rather than for getting the 'right' answer.

However, questions based on ethical issues tend to produce a range of possible solutions which are, on the one hand, consistent with the ethical guidelines and acceptable, and on the other hand, a range of clearly inadmissible answers which are clearly in breach of the ethical guidelines and possibly the law.'

7.2 Step-by-step approach

We suggest, instead, that:

(a) **You use the question format to structure your answer**
(b) **You bear in mind what marks are being awarded for (see above)**
(c) **You adhere to the following list of do's and don'ts. Be sure to read the notes following.**

DO	Note	DON'T
Identify the key facts as briefly as possible (one sentence?)	1	Merely paraphrase the question
Identify the major principle(s) at issue	2	Regurgitate the entire contents of the Ethical Guidelines
Consider alternative actions and their consequences	3	List every single possible action and then explain how all the unsuitable ones can be eliminated
Make a decision and recommend action as appropriate	4	Fail to make a decision or recommend action. Propose actions in breach of the *Ethical Guidelines* or the law
Justify your decision	5	Be feeble. 'This should be done because it is ethical' is not terribly convincing

Notes

1   **One sentence** is an ideal to aim for.

2   (a)   **Use the terminology of the ethical guidelines, but not *ad nauseam*.** 'Integrity' is often more clearly described as 'honesty' (although the two words are not synonymous). Don't forget the words 'fairness', 'bias', and 'influence' when discussing 'objectivity'.

(b) **Don't torture the case study to make it fit a fundamental principle**: if, say, 'justice' is the most persuasive word for a situation don't be afraid of using it.

(c) If the law is involved, don't get carried away – this is **not a law exam**. 'The director has a statutory duty to ...' is sufficient: there is no need to go into legal detail.

3 Useful ways of generating alternatives are:

(a) To **consider the problem from the other side of the fence**: imagine you are the guilty party

(b) To **consider the problem from the point of view of the organisation** and its culture and environment

4 Making a decision is often very hard, but if you cannot do this you are simply not ready to take on the responsibilities of a qualified accountant. There are usually a number of decisions that could be justified, so **don't be afraid of choosing the 'wrong' answer.**

5 This is not actually as hard as you might think.

7.3 Regurgitating the question

Possibly the most **common fault** in students' answers to questions on ethics is that they include large **amounts of unanalysed detail copied out from the question** scenarios in their answers. This earns no marks.

You can very easily avoid the temptation to merely paraphrase the question. Simply **begin your answer by stating that you are referring to 'issues'** (by which you mean all the details contained in the question) **discussed at a previous meeting, or set out in full in 'appended documents'.** If you do this you will be writing your report to someone already in possession of the same facts as you have.

7.4 Justifying your decision

The article quoted above says that **marks will be awarded for 'justifying recommendations in practical business terms and in ethical terms'.** We shall conclude by examining a passage from a model solution to a question on ethics to see how this can be done.

'Perhaps the first thing to do is to **report** the whole matter, **in confidence** and **informally**, to the chief internal auditor with suggestions that a **tactful investigation** is undertaken to **verify as many of the facts** as possible. The fact that the sales manager has already been tackled (informally) about the matter may be a positive advantage as **he/she may be recruited** to assist in the investigation. It could however be a problem as the information needed for further **investigation** may have already been removed. **Tact** is crucial as handling the matter the wrong way could adversely influence the whole situation. An understanding of who participants are and how they are implicated can be used positively to bring about change with the **minimum of disruption**.'

The key to this approach is **using the right language**, and to a large extent you cannot help doing so if you have sensible suggestions to make. The real problem that many students experience with questions of this type is lack of confidence in their own judgement. If you have sound business and managerial sense and you know the ethical guidelines there is every reason to suppose that an answer that you propose will be acceptable, so don't be shy of expressing an opinion.

Exam focus point

In an internal company role, ethical problems could be in the following forms.

- Conflict of duties to different staff superiors
- Discovering an illegal act or fraud perpetrated by the company (ie its directors)
- Discovering a fraud or illegal act perpetrated by another employee
- Pressure from superiors to take certain viewpoints, for example towards budgets (pessimistic/optimistic etc) or not to report unfavourable findings

---

8 Professional Skills – guidance from the ACCA

FAST FORWARD

Marks are awarded for **professional skills**.

Ethics and professionalism are a key part of your ACCA qualification. Accordingly, the ACCA has stated that marks for professional skills will be awarded at the Professional Level. The examiner has provided specific guidance for P2 *Corporate Reporting*.

8.1 Professional Skills – Basis of the award of marks

Marks will be awarded for professional skills in this paper. These skills encompass the creation, analysis, evaluation and synthesis of information, problem solving, decision making and communication skills. More specifically they will be awarded for:

(a)   Developing information and ideas and forming an opinion.

(b)   Developing an understanding of the implications for the entity of the information including the entity's operating environment.

(c)   Analysing information and ideas by identifying:

The purpose of the analysis
The limitations of given information
Bias and underlying assumptions and their impact
Problems of liability and inconsistency

(d)   Identifying the purpose of a computation and whether it meets its purpose.

(e)   Analysing information, drawing conclusions and considerable implications, and any further action required.

(f)   Identifying appropriate action in response to the information/analysis including advice or amendments to the data.

(g)   Considering, discussing and combining ideas and information from diverse sources to arrive at a solution or a broader understanding of the issues.

(h)   Analysing the information in the context of the views and reactions of the stakeholders.

(i)   Identifying solutions to problems or ranking potential solutions, or ways to manage the problem, or recommending a course of action.

(j)   Exercising good judgement and an ethical approach to providing advice in line with:

Relevant standards
Stakeholders interests
The stated objectives

(k)   Communicating effectively and efficiently in producing required documents including:

The intended purpose of the document
Its intended users and their needs
The appropriate type of document
Logical and appropriate structure/format
Nature of background information and technical language
Detail required
Clear, concise and precise presentation

There will be **six marks awarded in each paper for the above professional skills**. Not all skills will be required in each paper.

Chapter Roundup

- A key debate in ethical theory is whether ethics can be determined by **objective**, **universal principles**. How important the **consequences of actions** should be in determining an ethical position is also a significant issue.

- Ethical decision-making is influenced by **individual and situational factors**.

- **Individual factors** include **age and gender, beliefs, education and employment**, how much **control** individuals believe they have over their own situation and their **personal integrity**.

- **Kohlberg's** framework relates to individuals' degree of **ethical maturity**, the extent to which they can take their own ethical decisions.

- **Situational factors** include **the systems of reward**, **authority** and **bureaucracy**, **work roles**, **organisational factors**, and the **national and cultural contexts**.

- Firms have to ensure they obey the law: but they also face **ethical concerns**, because their reputations depend on a good image.

- Inside the organisation, a **compliance based approach** highlights conformity with the law. An **integrity based approach** suggests a wider remit, incorporating ethics in the organisation's values and culture.

- Organisations sometimes issue **codes of conduct** to employees. Many employees are bound by professional codes of conduct.

- Accountants require an **ethical code** because they hold positions of trust, and people rely on them.

- IFAC's and ACCA's guidance is very similar.

- Exam questions may ask you to think about what should be done if breaches of laws, regulations or ethical guidelines occur. **Close relationships** between the parties or other **conflicts of interest** are often a complication.

- In a situation involving ethical issues, there are **practical steps** that should be taken.
    - Establish the facts of the situation by further investigation and work.
    - Consider the alternative options available for action.
    - Consider whether any professional guidelines have been breached.
    - State the best course of action based on the steps above.

- Marks are awarded for **professional skills**.

1   Which view of ethics states that right and wrong are culturally determined?

    A   Ethical relativism   C   Teleological
    B   Cognitivism   D   Deontological

2   Fill in the blank

    The .... approach to ethics is to make moral judgements about courses of action by reference to their outcomes or consequences.

3   In what areas of national and cultural beliefs has Hofstede identified significant differences?

4   What is the significance of the post-conventional stage of an individual's moral development according to Kohlberg?

5   What ethical problems face management?

6   What objectives might a company have in relation to wider society?

7   To whom might management have responsibilities, and what are some of these responsibilities?

8   Why does Mintzberg say that the profit motive is not enough?

9   Describe two approaches to the management of ethics in an organisation.

10   What systems of ethics might you find in an organisation?

11   What is whistle-blowing?

12   Match the fundamental principle to the characteristic.
    (a)   Integrity
    (b)   Objectivity

        (i)   Members should be straightforward and honest in all professional and business relationships.
        (ii)   Members should not allow bias, conflict or interest or undue influence of others to override professional or business judgements.

1   A   Ethical relativism

2   Teleological or consequentialist

3   • Individualism vs collectivism
    • Acceptance of unequal distribution of power and status
    • How much individuals wish to avoid uncertainties
    • Masculinity vs femininity, money and possessions vs people and relationships

4   The post-conventional stage is when individuals make their own ethical decisions in terms of what they believe to be right, not just acquiescing in what others believe to be right.

5   There is a constant tension between the need to achieve current profitability, the need to safeguard the stakeholders' long term investment and the expectations of wider society.

6   Protection of the environment, support for good causes, a responsible attitude to product safety.

7   Managers of businesses are responsible to the owners for economic performance and to wider society for the externalities related to their business operations.

8   Large businesses are rarely controlled by their shareholders; they receive a lot of support from public funds; and their activities have wider consequences.

9   A compliance-based approach aims to remain within the letter of the law by establishing systems of audit and review so that transgressions may be detected and punished. An integrity-based approach tries to promote an ethical culture in which individuals will do the right thing.

10 Personal ethics, professional ethics, organisation culture, organisation systems.

11 Informing outside regulatory agencies about transgressions by one's organisation.

12 (a) (i) (b) (ii).

Now try the question below from the Exam Question Bank

Number	Level	Marks	Time
Q2	Introductory	n/a	n/a

3

Environmental and social reporting

Topic list	Syllabus reference
1 Environmental reporting	A1
2 Sustainability	A3
3 Social responsibility	A3
4 Human resource accounting	A3

Introduction

Environmental issues are very topical. Just because these topics are discursive does not mean that you can 'waffle'. Environmental reporting also comes under current developments as this is an area that is changing.

Study guide

		Intellectual level
A3	**Social responsibility**	
(a)	Discuss the increased demand for transparency in corporate reports and the emergence of non-financial reporting standards	3
(b)	Discuss the progress towards a framework for environmental and sustainability reporting	3
H1	**Environmental and social reporting**	
(a)	Appraise the impact of environmental, social and ethical factors on performance measurement	3
(b)	Evaluate current reporting requirements in this area	3
(c)	Discuss why entities might include disclosures relating to the environment and society.	3

Exam guide

This topic could be tested as a current issue, or as an aspect of the limitations of conventional financial statements, or alternatively in the context of provisions, covered in Chapter 9.

Environmental reporting may be tested under the broader heading of social responsibilities.

1 Environmental reporting   12/07

FAST FORWARD

Although not compulsory, **environmental reports** are becoming increasingly important. You should distinguish

- Items that affect the financial statements (eg IAS 37)
- Items that affect the environmental report

At the end of the 1980s there were perhaps only two or three companies in the world issuing environmental reports. Now most listed companies produce them. Worldwide there are around 20 award schemes for environmental reporting, notably the ACCA's. This section looks at environmental reporting mainly under three headings:

- The effect of environmental matters on management information and accounting
- External reporting and auditing
- Possible future developments

Let us consider the major areas of impact on (any) accountant's job caused by consideration of environmental matters.

(a) **Management accountant**

    (i)   Investment appraisal: evaluation of environmental costs and benefits.

    (ii)   Incorporating new costs, capital expenditure and so on, in to budgets and business plans.

    (iii)   Undertake cost/benefit analysis of any environmental improvements.

(b) **Financial accountant**

    (i)   The effect of revenue costs: site clean up costs, waste disposal or waste treatment costs and so on, which will affect the profit and loss account.

    (ii)   Gauging impacts on the statement of financial position, particularly liabilities, contingencies, provisions *and* valuation of assets.

    (iii)   The effect of environmental matters, and particularly potential liabilities, on a company's relationship with bankers, insurers and major shareholders (institutional shareholders).

    (iv)   Environmental performance evaluation in annual reports.

(c) **Project accountant**

    (i)   Environmental audit of proposed takeovers, mergers and other planning matters.
    (ii)   Investment appraisal.

(d) **Internal auditor**: environmental audit.

(e) **Systems accountant**: effect on, and required changes to management and financial information systems.

1.1 What is environmental accounting?

The following list encompasses the major aspects of environmental accounting.

(a) Recognising and seeking to mitigate the negative environmental effects of conventional accounting practice.

(b) Separately **identifying environmentally related costs and revenues** within the conventional accounting systems.

(c) Devising new forms of financial and non-financial accounting systems, information systems and control systems to **encourage more environmentally benign management decisions.**

(d) Developing new forms of **performance measurement**, reporting and appraisal for both internal and external purposes.

(e) Identifying, examining and seeking to **rectify** areas in which conventional (financial) criteria and environmental criteria are in **conflict**.

(f) Experimenting with ways in which, **sustainability** may be assessed and incorporated into organisational orthodoxy.'

Accounting for the Environment Bob Gary (with Jan Bebbington and Diane Walters)

The whole environmental agenda is **constantly changing** and businesses therefore need to monitor the situation closely. Most businesses, certainly those in the UK, have generally ignored environmental matters in the past. How long will they be able to do so?

1.2 Management information and accounting

The means of codifying a company's attitude towards the environment is often the creation of a published **environmental policy document** or charter. This may be internally generated or it may be adopted from a standard environmental charter, such as the **CERES Principles**

The CERES Principles

We adopt, support and will implement the principles of:

1 Protection of the biosphere
2 Sustainable use of natural resources
3 Reduction and disposal of waste
4 Wise use of energy
5 Risk reduction
6 Marketing of safe products and services
7 Damage compensation
8 Disclosure
9 Environmental directors and managers
10 Assessment and annual audit

The problem here, as with other similar principles or charters, is that the commitment required from companies is generally too high and the fear exists that the principles may have legal status which could have a severe effect on a company's liability. Other documents available which are similar to the *Valdez Principles* are:

- The International Chamber of Commerce Business Charter for Sustainable Developments
- The Chemical Industries Association Responsible Care Programme
- The Confederation of British Industry Agenda for Voluntary Action
- Friends of the Earth Environmental Charter for Local Government

Adopting such a charter is one thing; implementing and monitoring it are more important and generally more difficult to achieve.

1.3 Environmental audit

Environmental auditing is exactly what is says: auditing a business to assess its impact on the environment, or as the CBI expressed it 'the systematic examination of the interactions between any business operation and its surroundings'.

The audit will cover a range of areas and will involve the performance of different types of testing. The scope of the audit must be determined and this will depend on each individual organisation. There are, however, some aspects of the approach to environmental auditing which are worth mentioning.

(a) **Environmental Impact Assessments (EIAs)** are required, under EU directive, for all major projects which require planning permission and have a material effect on the environment. The EIA process can be incorporated into any environmental auditing strategy.

(b) **Environmental surveys** are a good way of starting the audit process, by looking at the organisation as a whole in environmental terms. This helps to identify areas for further development, problems, potential hazards and so forth.

(c) **Environmental SWOT analysis**. A 'strengths, weaknesses, opportunities, threats' analysis is useful as the environmental audit strategy is being developed. This can only be done later in the process, when the organisation has been examined in much more detail.

(d) **Environmental Quality Management (EQM).** This is seen as part of TQM (Total Quality Management) and it should be built in to an environmental management system. Such a strategy has been adopted by companies such as IBM, Dow Chemicals and by the Rhone-Poulenc Environmental Index which has indices for levels of water, air and other waste products.

(e) **Eco-audit**. The European Commission has adopted a proposal for a regulation for a voluntary community environmental auditing scheme, known as the eco-audit scheme. The scheme aims to promote improvements in company environmental performance and to provide the public with information about these improvements. Once registered, a company will have to comply with certain on-going obligations involving disclosure and audit.

(f) **Eco-labelling**. Developed in Germany, this voluntary scheme will indicate those EC products which meet the highest environmental standards, probably as the result of an EQM system. It is suggested that eco-audit *must* come before an eco-label can be given.

(g) **BS 7750 Environmental Management Systems**. BS 7750 also ties in with eco-audits and eco-labelling and with the quality BSI standard BS 5750. Achieving BS 7750 is likely to be a first step in the eco-audit process.

(h) **Supplier audits**, to ensure that goods and services bought in by an organisation meet the standards applied by that organisation.

 Case Study

In June 1999 BP Amoco commissioned KPMG to conduct an independent audit of its greenhouse gas emissions in the first ever environmental audit.

1.4 Financial reporting

There are **no disclosure requirements relating to environmental matters under IASs**, so any disclosures tend to be **voluntary** unless environmental matters happen to fall under standard accounting principles (eg recognising liabilities).

(a) In most cases disclosure is descriptive and unquantified.

(b) There is little motivation to produce environmental information and many reasons for not doing so, including secrecy.

(c) The main factor seems to be apathy on the part of businesses but more particularly on the part of shareholders and investors. The information is not demanded, so it is not provided.

Environmental matters may be reported in the accounts of companies in the following areas.

- Contingent liabilities
- Exceptional charges
- Operating and financial review comments
- Profit and capital expenditure forecasts

The voluntary approach contrasts with the position in the United States, where the SEC/FASB accounting standards are obligatory.

While nothing is compulsory, there are a number of **published guidelines** and **codes of practice**, including:

- The Confederation of British Industry's guideline *Introducing Environmental Reporting*
- The ACCA's *Guide to Environment and Energy Reporting*
- The Coalition of Environmentally Responsible Economies (CERES) formats for environmental reports
- The Friends of the Earth *Environmental Charter for Local Government*
- The Eco Management and Audit Scheme Code of Practice

1.5 Example: environmental liabilities

You have met IAS 37 *Provisions, contingent liabilities and contingent assets* in your earlier studies. IAS 37 deals with the issue of whether environmental liabilities should be provided for. The example below is taken from an article by Alan Pizzey which appeared in the February 1998 edition of *CIMA Student*. Study the example and attempt the question which follows it.

MegaBux Co is a multinational holding company. During the year a number of situations have arisen and the board is to meet soon to determine an appropriate treatment .

Site A

This site is occupied by a small refinery. The site and some adjacent land has been contaminated by chemical spillages. The cost of remedying the contamination is $20m, but under local laws there is no requirement to clean up the site.

Site B

Similar contamination has arisen but the local government, and a neighbouring land owner, require the contamination to be remedied soon. The cost of cleaning up the site is $15m, but an extra $5m could be spent to raise the standard of the operation in line with undertakings given to the local community ten years ago.

Solution

Site A

The mere existence of contamination does not establish an obligation on the part of the company and without an obligation there is no need for a provision.

Site B

An obligation does exist which the local government and a neighbour can prove in court. At least $15m must be provided, but there may be a constructive obligation, wider than a legal obligation, to spend an extra $5m to raise the standard of rectification. Concern for its long term reputation may influence the company to honour its undertaking given to the local community.

Site C

Considerable contamination needs to be remedied, but the managing director is arguing that no provision is required this year since the amount concerned cannot be estimated with accuracy.

Site D

Spillage of chemicals has reduced the value of the site from $25m, its book value, to $10m, its current realisable value. By spending $5m on rectification, the site value will be increased to $20m. The spillage has seeped into a local river and fines of $3m are now payable.

Answer

Site C

Whilst the exact amount of the expenditure may not be known with certainty, it should be possible to arrive at a realistic and prudent estimate. It is not acceptable to omit a liability on the grounds that its amount is not known with certainty – this would be a distortion.

Site D

The fines of $3m are a current cost to be charged to profit or loss. The spillage has impaired the value of the site, which must be written down to its new market value of $20m after rectification. The cost of the write-down ($5m) and the cost of the rectification ($5m) are charged to profit or loss. The site is now carried in the books at its recoverable amount.

1.6 The environmental report and the exam

You may be asked in the exam to interpret an environmental report, though not to prepare one. Your report should distinguish between:

(a)   Transactions that affect the financial statements, for example provisions that need to be made under IAS 37

(b)   Information to be disclosed elsewhere, for example in the operating and financial review, or in a separate environmental report.

Exam focus point

> Have a go at the Pilot Paper question in the Exam Question Bank. This distinguishes between environmental matters that affect the financial statements and those which do not, but are nevertheless important.

1.7 Example: environmental report

A good example of an environmental report is the Boots report for 1999/2000. This was published as a separate report consisting of around 20 pages. Extracts from the report are reproduced below to give you a feel for it. Note that the report is based around 'key performance indicators'. These are monitored against targets. We emphasise that this is not the only possible approach to environmental reporting.

> 'Environmental policy statement
>
> We have a responsibility as a company to take proper care of the environment on behalf of our shareholders, customers, staff and the communities in which we operate. Caring for the environment is an essential part of the way we run our business.

We are committed to managing responsibly the way in which our activities affect the environment by:

- Optimising the use of energy
- Ensuring efficient use of materials
- Encouraging re-use and recycling
- Incorporating the principle of sustainable development.

By integrating environmental considerations into our everyday activities, the environment will be managed alongside other business considerations such as safety, quality and value.

Management

We will set objectives and targets for those activities which significantly affect the environment and we will measure our performance over time. Details of our progress will be published at least annually.

Environmental audits and inspections will be undertaken to monitor our progress against this policy.

Within the individual businesses there is a clear structure of responsibility devolved into each business via an appointed manager with overall environmental responsibility. At a corporate level, the Environmental Affairs team co-ordinates environmental issues for the company through the Environmental Working Party.

The company's significant impacts have been assessed and Key Performance Indicators (KPIs) have been selected to track performance over time. Data to monitor these is generated via environmental management systems that are incorporated into business systems and regularly audited.

Environmental management is integrated into everything we do from product development to the supply chain and staff training.

Key performance indicators 99/00

Energy

In 1999/2000 total company energy use decreased by 5.3 per cent, while energy efficiency improved by 10.2 per cent.

Over the last four years energy efficiency, as measured by kWh per $ thousand turnover, has improved by 12 per cent overall, maintaining a positive trend.

Transport

Commercial transport efficiency improved by 2 per cent.

Alongside the ongoing internal data verification programme, improvements to data management systems have resulted in additional transport data being reported for 1998/99. Transport efficiency over the last three years, as measured by litres of diesel consumed per $ million turnover, maintained a positive trend overall with a 2 per cent improvement recorded over the last year.

The efficiency of inventory delivery, as measured by the volume of inventory delivered per 1000 litres of fuel, reduced by 3.7 per cent at Boots The Chemists. This is due to a combination of factors, including new store openings and the closure of an old warehouse in an urban centre (see Progress against targets). The move to lower sulphur diesel for commercial fleets has also had a negative impact on fuel efficiency. Trials of alternative fuel vehicles have continued.

Carbon dioxide and global warming

In the last year, like-for-like CO_2 emissions decreased by 4.4 per cent.

The main greenhouse gas associated with the company's operations is CO_2 arising primarily from energy use in manufacturing and retailing, and emissions from its transport fleets. Some 84 per cent of total emissions relate to energy consumption. Similarly, around 85 per cent of transport emissions relate to commercial fleets, with around 8 per cent to company cars.

The company's modern combined heat and power (CHP) energy centre on the head office site continues to contribute to a global reduction in annual CO_2 emissions of around 44,000 tonnes compared with purchasing electricity from third party suppliers. This represents a reduction in the company's total CO_2 emissions of around 15 per cent each year. The saving is achieved through the re-use of waste heat from the electricity generation process to generate usable steam.

Waste

Around 26,000 tonnes of waste was recovered through recycling or incineration with heat recovery.

As the business is primarily retailing, the largest proportion of waste (91 per cent) is transit packaging and general office waste that is mainly non-hazardous. Other wastes arise from manufacturing processes, laboratories, garage and pharmacy operations.

Of the 54,000 tonnes of material identified as waste, some 26,000 tonnes (48 per cent) was recovered through recycling or incineration with heat recovery. The majority of the remaining 28,000 tonnes of waste (94 per cent) was disposed to landfill.

Quantifying the weight of non-hazardous waste is difficult due to small quantities of unweighed waste being collected from a large number of retail locations by multiple collection vehicles, and shopping centres amalgamating non-hazardous waste from a number of retailers for bulk collection. Because of this, although the company's data collection systems for waste have continued to improve, it is unlikely that year-on-year comparisons will be meaningful for some time to come.

Packaging

In the last year the company handled some 162,000 tonnes of packaging.

Minimising packaging is a complex business challenge where a number of considerations have to be balanced. These include evaluating the wide variety of roles performed by packaging (from improved keeping qualities for food and medical products to optimal shapes for efficient stacking and transportation) together with aspects such as design, quality, performance, cost and environment.

In addition, several factors mask the performance that can be directly attributed to packaging management. In particular, consumer and business demands in retailing require ongoing changes to the scale of product ranges and the general product mix within stores, which can produce conflicting trends in packaging use.

The issue will remain as a key performance indicator given its perceived environmental impact in the retail and manufacturing sectors, but it is unlikely that a valid, quantitative comparison of company performance will be developed in this area.

Water and effluent

In the last year Boots Contract Manufacturing reduced the effluent load per unit produced by more than 18 per cent.

Centralised monitoring of water consumption continued with substantial effort being put into the development of robust data management systems. This section relates mainly to Boots Contract Manufacturing, but from April 2000 the data available will include all business units and will be comparable across future years. The acquisition of historical water consumption data proved more difficult than expected, so the overall picture for the company is currently incomplete. Information has been included in the data section where meaningful.

Water conservation in Boots Contract Manufacturing, across all production areas, has again been an area of considerable focus. Improvements such as the elimination of 'once-through' water cooling systems have been implemented in key areas. Fitting improved temperature controls to a tempering belt reduced steam demand as well as saving cooling water.

Water use has been benchmarked across departments and factories to enable sharing of best practice in successful conservation strategies. A computerised data reporting system in the main factory on the Nottingham site allows water use profiles to be analysed. This has been a significant factor in bringing about change. For example, over the past four years water consumption in the factory over the Christmas shutdown period has been reduced from 60 per cent to less than 10 per cent of that on a normal working day. This experience has been shared and improved water metering is now being installed at the Airdrie factory.

In other areas external factors, such as the reduced use of preservatives in products and third party customer specifications that predefine equipment-cleaning procedures, resulted in some increased water use. Overall, water use per unit of production was reduced by 2.6 per cent against a target of 3 per cent.

Reducing waste discharged as effluent has been targeted in several key areas. Process changes have brought about material savings at Nottingham and, at Airdrie, a new system for cleaning pipes between product batches has reduced the amount of water required for this operation by 90 per cent. Together, all these initiatives reduced the loss of material to drain by more than 18 per cent (as measured by chemical oxygen demand and solids load per unit 'produced').'

2 Sustainability

2.1 What is sustainability?

Pressure is mounting for companies to **widen** their **scope for corporate public accountability**. Many companies are responding by measuring and disclosing their social impacts.

Examples of social measures include: philanthropic donations, employee satisfaction levels and remuneration issues, community support, and stakeholder consultation information.

The next step beyond environmental and social reporting is sustainability reporting which includes the economic element of sustainability (such as wages, taxes and core financial statistics) and involves integrating environmental, social and economic performance data and measures.

2.2 The Global Reporting Initiative (GRI)

FAST FORWARD

The Global Reporting Initiative arose from the need to **address the failure of the current governance structures to respond to changes in the global economy**.

It is 'a long-term, multi-stakeholder, international undertaking whose mission is to develop and disseminate globally applicable Sustainability Reporting Guidelines for voluntary use by organisations reporting on the economic, environmental and social dimensions of their activities, products and services'.

2.3 GRI Guidelines

The GRI published revised Sustainability Reporting Guidelines ('G3') in 2006.

The Guidelines set out the framework of a sustainability report. It consists of five sections:

	GRI Report content	Detail of GRI requirements
1	Strategy and Analysis	Provides a high-level, strategic view of the organisation's relationship to sustainability in order to provide context for subsequent and more detailed reporting, including a statement from the CEO.
2	Organisational Profile	The organisation's structure including brands, location of operations, geographical markets served and size of operations.
3	Report Parameters	The reporting period, materiality, report boundaries (eg countries), data measurement techniques and a GRI Content Index.
4	Governance, Commitments and Engagement	Governance structure of the organisation, commitments to external initiatives and how the organisation engages the stakeholders in its business.
5	Management Approach and Performance Indicators	Organised by economic, environmental, and social categories. Each category includes a Disclosure on Management Approach and a corresponding set of Core and Additional Performance Indicators.

2.4 Indicators in the GRI framework

GRI structures key performance indicators according to a hierarchy of category, aspect and indicator. Indicators are grouped in terms of the three dimensions of the conventional definition of sustainability – economic, environmental, and social.

	CATEGORY	ASPECT
Economic	Economic	Economic performance
		Market presence
		Indirect economic impacts
Environmental	Environmental	Materials
		Energy
		Water
		Biodiversity
		Emissions, effluents, and waste
		Products and services
		Compliance
		Transport
		Overall
Social	Labour Practices and Decent Work	Employment
		Labour/management relations
		Occupational health and safety
		Training and education
		Diversity and equal opportunity
	Human Rights	Investment and procurement practices
		Non-discrimination
		Freedom of association and collective bargaining
		Child labour
		Forced and compulsory labour
		Security practices
		Indigenous rights
	Society	Community
		Corruption
		Public policy
		Anti-competitive behaviour
		Compliance
	Product Responsibility	Customer health and safety
		Product and service labelling
		Marketing communications
		Customer privacy
		Compliance

2.5 Influence of GRI

There is a trend to report on broader sustainability issues and to include **social and economic information** alongside environmental disclosures.

An increasing number of companies, including BT, Vauxhall Motors Ltd, British Airways and Shell are following the GRI guidelines to some extent in their reporting.

2.6 Example: BT

BT's Social and Environmental Report for the year ended 31 March 2004 complies with the 2002 Global Reporting Initiative Guidelines. To give an overview of the company's social and environmental performance, the report selects 11 non-financial key performance indicators. This performance relates to the 2004 financial year, compared with 2003.

(a) Customer dissatisfaction down 22%

(b) Broadband now available to more than 85% of all UK homes and businesses, up from 67%

(c) People Satisfaction Index increased from 67% to 71%

(d) Increase in the percentage of ethnic minority employees from 8.6% to 8.9% and disabled employees from 2.0% to 2.1%, though the percentage of women declined from 23.6% to 22.7%

(e) Global Warming CO_2 emissions now 42% lower than 1996

(f) Waste to landfill down 10,201 tonnes to 79,677 tonnes, percentage of total waste recycled up from 25% to 26%

(g) Health & Safety significant incident rate down from 113 to 87 per 10,000 full-time employees

(h) Percentage of suppliers stating they have a good working relationship with BT is 94%

(i) Ethical trading risk assessment questionnaires completed by 242 suppliers and 13 on-site assessments undertaken

(j) Awareness of our Statement of Business Practice in the UK up 1% to 84%

(k) Direct community investment of £5.6 million plus £12.4 million in further funding and support in mind.

Question   Indicators

Compare this brief summary with the table above, ticking off performance indicators. If you have time, look for further details and developments on www.globalreporting.org.

3 Social responsibility

FAST FORWARD

The **stakeholder** view holds that there are many groups in society with an interest in the organisation's activities. Some firms have objectives for these issues. Some argue, however, that a business's only objective should be to make money: the state, representing the public interest, can levy taxes to spend on socially desirable projects or can regulate organisational activities.

Not only does the environment have a significant influence on the structure and behaviour of organisations, but also organisations have some influence on their environment.

Since organisations have an effect on their environment, it is arguable that they should act in a way which shows **social awareness and responsibility**.

> 'A society, awakened and vocal with respect to the urgency of social problems, is asking the managers of all kinds of organisations, particularly those at the top, what they are doing to discharge their social responsibilities and why they are not doing more.'

Koontz, O'Donnell and Weihrich

Social responsibility is expected from all types of organisation.

(a) **Local government** is expected to provide services to the local community, and to preserve or improve the character of that community, but at an acceptable cost to the ratepayers.

(b) **Businesses** are expected to provide goods and services, which reflect the needs of users and society as a whole. These needs may not be in harmony – arguably, the development of the Concorde aeroplane and supersonic passenger travel did not contribute to the public interest, and caused considerable inconvenience to residents near airports who suffer from excessive aircraft noise. A business should also be expected to anticipate the future needs of society; examples of socially useful products might be energy-saving devices and alternative sources of power.

(c) **Pollution control** is a particularly important example of social responsibility by industrial organisations, and some progress has been made in the development of commercial processes for re-cycling waste material. British Coal attempts to restore the environment by planting on old slag heaps.

(d) **Universities and schools** are expected to produce students whose abilities and qualifications will prove beneficial to society. A currently popular view of education is that greater emphasis should be placed on vocational training for students.

(e) In some cases, **legislation** may be required to enforce social need, for example to regulate the materials used to make crash helmets for motor cyclists, or to regulate safety standards in motor cars and furniture. Ideally, however, organisations should avoid the need for legislation by taking **earlier self-regulating action**.

3.1 Social responsibility and businesses

Arguably, institutions like hospitals, schools and so forth exist because health care and education are seen to be desirable social objectives by government at large, if they can be afforded.

However, where does this leave businesses? How far is it reasonable, or even appropriate, for businesses to exercise 'social responsibility' by giving to charities, voluntarily imposing strict environmental objectives on themselves and so forth?

One school of thought would argue that **the management of a business has only one social responsibility, which is to maximise wealth for its shareholders**. There are two reasons to support this argument.

(a) If the business is owned by the shareholders the assets of the company are, ultimately, the shareholders' property. Management has no moral right to dispose of business assets (like cash) on non-business objectives, as this has the effect of reducing the return available to shareholders. The shareholders might, for example, disagree with management's choice of beneficiary. Anyhow, it is for the shareholders to determine how their money should be spent.

(b) A second justification for this view is that management's job is to maximise wealth, as this is the best way that society can benefit from a business's activities.

    (i) Maximising wealth has the effect of increasing the tax revenues available to the state to disburse on socially desirable objectives.

    (ii) Maximising wealth for the few is sometimes held to have a 'trickle down' effect on the disadvantaged members of society.

    (iii) Many company shares are owned by pension funds, whose ultimate beneficiaries may not be the wealthy anyway.

This argument rests on certain assumptions.

(a) The first assumption is, in effect, the opposite of the stakeholder view. In other words, it is held that the *rights* of legal ownership are paramount over all other *interests* in a business: while other stakeholders have an interest, they have few legal or moral rights over the wealth created.

(b) The second assumption is that a business's *only* relationship with the wider social environment is an economic one. After all, that is what businesses exist for, and any other activities are the role of the state.

(c) The defining purpose of business organisations is the maximisation of the wealth of their owners.

Henry Mintzberg (in *Power In and Around Organisations*) suggests that simply viewing organisations as vehicles for shareholder investment is inadequate.

(a) In practice, he says, organisations are rarely controlled effectively by shareholders. Most shareholders are passive investors.

(b) Large corporations can manipulate markets. Social responsibility, forced or voluntary, is a way of recognising this.

(c) Moreover, businesses do receive a lot of government support. The public pays for roads, infrastructure, education and health, all of which benefits businesses. Although businesses pay tax, the public ultimately pays, perhaps through higher prices.

(d) Strategic decisions by businesses always have wider social consequences. In other words, says Mintzberg, the firm produces two outputs: **goods and services** and the **social consequences of its activities** (eg pollution).

3.1.1 Externalities

If it is accepted that businesses do not bear the total social cost of their activities, then the exercise of social responsibility is a way of compensating for this.

An example is given by the environment. Industrial pollution is injurious to health: if someone is made ill by industrial pollution, then arguably the polluter should pay the sick person, as damages or in compensation, in the same way as if the business's builders had accidentally bulldozed somebody's house.

In practice, of course, while it is relatively easy to identify statistical relationships between pollution levels and certain illnesses, mapping out the chain of cause and effect from an individual's wheezing cough to the dust particles emitted by Factory X, as opposed to Factory Y, is quite a different matter.

Of course, it could be argued that these external costs are met out of general taxation: but this has the effect of spreading the cost amongst other individuals and businesses. Moreover, the tax revenue may be spent on curing the disease, rather than stopping it at its source. Pollution control equipment may be the fairest way of dealing with this problem. Thus advocates of social responsibility in business would argue that business's responsibilities then do not rest with paying taxes.

However, is there any justification for social responsibility outside remedying the effects of a business's direct activities. For example, should businesses give to charity or sponsor the arts? There are several reasons why they should.

(a) If the **stakeholder concept** of a business is held, then the public is a stakeholder in the business. A business only succeeds because it is part of a wider society. Giving to charity is one way of encouraging a relationship.

(b) Charitable donations and artistic sponsorship are a useful medium of **public relations** and can reflect well on the business. It can be regarded, then, as another form of promotion, which like advertising, serves to enhance consumer awareness of the business, while not encouraging the sale of a particular brand.

The arguments for and against social responsibility of business are complex ones. However, ultimately they can be traced to different assumptions about society and the relationships between the individuals and organisations within it.

Question	Ethics

The Heritage Carpet Company is a London-based retailer which imports carpets from Turkey, Iran and India. The company was founded by two Europeans who travelled independently through these countries in the 1970s. The company is the sole customer for carpets made in a number of villages in each of the source countries. The carpets are hand woven. Indeed, they are so finely woven that the process requires that children be used to do the weaving, thanks to their small fingers. The company believes that it is preserving a 'craft', and the directors believe that this is a justifiable social objective. Recently a UK television company has reported unfavourably on child exploitation in the carpet weaving industry. There were reports of children working twelve hour shifts in poorly lit sheds and cramped conditions, with consequent deterioration in eyesight, muscular disorders and a complete absence of education. The examples cited bear no relation to the Heritage Carpet Company's suppliers although children are used in the labour force, but there has been a spate of media attention. The regions in which the Heritage Carpet Company's supplier villages are found are soon expected to enjoy rapid economic growth.

What boundary management issues are raised for the Heritage Carpet Company?

Many. This is a case partly about boundary management and partly about enlightened self-interest and business ethics. The adverse publicity, although not about the Heritage Carpet Company's own suppliers, could rebound badly. Potential customers might be put off. Economic growth in the area may also mean that parents will prefer to send their children to school. The Heritage Carpet Company as well as promoting itself as preserving a craft could reinvest some of its profits in the villages (eg by funding a school), or by enforcing limits on the hours children worked. It could also pay a decent wage. It could advertise this in a 'code of ethics' so that customers are reassured that the children are not simply being exploited. Alternatively, it could not import child-made carpets at all. (This policy, however, would be unlikely to help communities in which child labour is an economic necessity. Children already living on the margins of subsistence might end up even more exploited, in begging or prostitution.)

4 Human resource accounting

Human resource accounting is an approach which regards **people as assets**.

4.1 Introduction

Human resource accounting has at its core the principle that **employees are assets.** Competitive advantage is largely gained by **effective use of people**.

4.2 Implications of regarding people as organisational assets

(a)   **People are a resource** which needs to be carefully and efficiently managed with overriding concern for organisational objectives.

(b)   The organisation needs to **protect its investment** by retaining, safeguarding and developing its human assets.

(c)   **Deterioration in the attitudes and motivation** of employees, increases in labour turnover (followed by costs of hiring and training replacements) are **costs to the company** – even though a 'liquidation' of human assets, brought about by certain managerial styles, may produce short-term increases in profit.

(d)   A concept developed some time ago was that of **human asset accounting** (the inclusion of human assets in the financial reporting system of the organisation).

 Case Study

There are difficulties in isolating and measuring human resources, and it is also hard to forecast the time period (and area of business) over which benefits will be received from expenditure on human assets. *Texas Instruments* uses a system which identifies potential replacement costs for groups of people, taking into account the learning time required by the replacement, and the individual's salary during that period.

4.3 Intellectual assets

There are **problems in putting a value on people** which traditional accounting has yet to overcome.

Because of the difficulties found in both theory and practice, the concept of **human assets was broadened and became intellectual assets**. Intellectual assets, or 'intellectual capital' as they are sometimes called can be divided into three main types.

(a) **External assets.** These include the reputation of brands and franchises and the strength of customer relationships.

(b) **Internal assets.** These include patents, trademarks and information held in customer databases.

(c) **Competencies.** These reflect the capabilities and skills of individuals.

'Intellectual assets' thus includes 'human assets'.

The value of intellectual assets will continue to rise and will represent an increasing proportion of the value of most companies. Whether or not traditional accounting will be able to measure them, remains to be seen.

Chapter Roundup

- Although not compulsory, **environmental reports** are becoming increasingly important. You should distinguish

  - Items that **affect the financial statements** (eg IAS 37)
  - Items that **affect the environmental report**

- The **stakeholder** view holds that there are many groups in society with an interest in the organisation's activities. Some firms have objectives for these issues. Some argue, however, that a business's only objective should be to make money: the state, representing the public interest, can levy taxes to spend on socially desirable projects or can regulate organisational activities.

- The Global Reporting Initiative arose from the need to **address the failure of the current governance structures to respond to changes in the global economy.**

- **Human resource accounting** is an approach which regards **people as assets.**

- There are **problems in putting a value on people** which traditional accounting has yet to overcome.

Quick Quiz

1 Give an example of a recent environmental audit.

2 Name four areas of company accounts where environmental matters may be reported.

3 If a site is contaminated, a provision must be made.

   True ☐

   False ☐

4 What objectives might a company have in relation to wider society?

5 To whom might management have responsibilities, and what are some of these responsibilities?

6 Why does Mintzberg say that the profit motive is not enough?

7 What is the basic principle of human resource accounting?

8 Give three examples of intellectual assets.

Answers to Quick Quiz

1   In 1999 KPMG conducted an audit of the greenhouse gas emissions of BP Amoco.

2   Contingent liabilities
    Exceptional charges
    Operating and financial review comments
    Profit and capital expenditure forecasts

3   False. an obligation must be established.

4   Protection of the environment, support for good causes, a responsible attitude to product safety.

5   Managers of businesses are responsible to the owners for economic performance and to wider society for the externalities related to their business operations.

6   Large businesses are rarely controlled by their shareholders; they receive a lot of support from public funds; and their activities have wider consequences.

7   Employees are assets.

8   External assets
    Internal assets
    Competencies

Now try the question below from the Exam Question Bank

Number	Level	Marks	Time
Q3	Introductory	n/a	n/a

Accounting standards

Non-current assets

Topic list	Syllabus reference
1 The definition of an asset	C2
2 Revision of IASs 16, 20 and 23	C2
3 IAS 36 *Impairment of assets*	C2
4 IAS 40 *Investment property*	C2
5 IAS 38 *Intangible assets*	C2
6 Goodwill	C2, D1

Introduction

We look again here at the **IASB definition of an asset**, as given in the *Framework* and compare it with the definitions given by other standard setters, particularly FASB in the USA and the ASB in the UK.

You have covered several of the relevant standards relating to non-current assets in your earlier studies. These are straightforward and are revised briefly in Section 2, with some questions for you to try. If you have any problems, **go back to your earlier study material**.

The IASB has a standard covering the **impairment of assets**. This is a controversial topic and you must understand the standard on the topic. **IAS 36** is discussed in depth in Section 3.

In March 2000, a standard on **investment property** was issued. **IAS 40** is discussed in detail in Section 4.

We begin our examination of intangible non-current assets with a discussion of **IAS 38**.

Goodwill and its treatment is a controversial area, as is the accounting for items similar to goodwill, such as brands. Goodwill is very important in **group accounts**.

Important notice

In this chapter, you will come across the term '**non-controlling interest**'. This is the new name for 'minority interest' under the revised IFRS 3, covered in Part C.

Study guide

		Intellectual level
C2	**Non-current assets**	
(a)	Apply and discuss the timing of the recognition of non-current assets and the determination of their carrying amounts, including impairment and revaluations	3
(c)	Apply and discuss accounting treatment of investment properties including classification, recognition and measurement issues.	3

Exam guide

The approach of Paper P2 to accounting standards is very different from your earlier studies. You will need to think critically and deal with controversial issues. Ensure that you visit the IASB website on a regular basis.

On intangibles, you may be given an unusual situation and asked to identify the issues. Is a football player an intangible asset?

1 The definition of an asset

FAST FORWARD

You must learn the IASB *Framework* **definition of an asset**: a resource controlled by the entity as a result of past events and from which future economic benefits are expected to flow to the entity.

This definition ties in closely with the definitions produced by **other standard-setters**, particularly FASB (USA) and ASB (UK).

Assets have been defined in many different ways and for many purposes. The definition of an asset is important because it directly affects the **treatment** of such items. A good definition will prevent abuse or error in the accounting treatment: otherwise some assets might be treated as expenses, and some expenses might be treated as assets.

Let us begin with a simple definition from the CIMA *Official Terminology*.

Key term

> An **asset** is any tangible or intangible possession which has value.

This admirably succinct definition seems to cover the main points: **ownership** and **value**. An asset is so called because it is owned by someone who values it. However, this definition leaves several questions unanswered.

(a)   What determines ownership?
(b)   What determines value?

Such a simple definition is not adequate in the current accounting climate, where complex transactions are carried out daily.

1.1 IASB definition

Remember the definition of a asset in the IASB's *Framework*.

Key term

> **Asset.** A resource controlled by the entity as a result of past events and from which future economic benefits are expected to flow to the entity. *(Framework)*

Let us also look at one or two other definitions from other standard-setters.

1.2 Accounting Standards Board (ASB): UK

In the ASB's *Statement of Principles,* Chapter 3 *The Elements of Financial Statements* assets are defined as follows.

Key term

Assets are rights or other access to future economic benefits controlled by an entity as a result of past transactions or events.

The *Statement* goes on to discuss various aspects of this definition, and it is broadly consistent with the IASB's *Framework.* The *Statement* then goes further in discussing the complimentary nature of assets and liabilities.

1.3 Financial Accounting Standards Board (FASB): USA

The definition given by the FASB in its *Statement of Concepts* is very similar.

Key term

Assets are probable future economic benefits obtained or controlled by a particular entity as a result of past transactions or events.

'Probable' is given in its general meaning merely to reflect the fact that no future outcome can be predicted with total certainty.

1.4 Comparison of definitions

FAST FORWARD

The definition has three important characteristics:

- **Future economic benefit**
- **Control (ownership)**
- **Transaction to acquire has taken place**

It is clear from what we have seen so far that a general consensus seems to exist in the standard setting bodies as to the definition of an asset. That definition encompasses **three important characteristics**.

- Future economic benefit
- Control (ownership)
- The transaction to acquire control has already taken place

1.5 Definition of a non-current asset

Non-current assets may be defined as follows.

Exam focus point

A **non-current asset** is one intended for use on a continuing basis in the company's activities, ie it is not intended for resale.

2 Revision of IASs 16, 20 and 23   12/08

FAST FORWARD

You should already be familiar with many standards relating to **non-current assets** from earlier studies. If not, go back to your earlier study material.

- IAS 16 *Property, plant and equipment*
- IAS 20 *Accounting for government grants and disclosure of government assistance*
- IAS 23 *Borrowing costs*

You have studied these standards for earlier papers, but they are fairly straightforward. Read the summary of knowledge brought forward and try the relevant questions. If you have any difficulty, go back to your earlier study material and re-read it.

IASs studied in earlier papers will probably not be examined in any depth in Paper 2, but you will be expected to know the principles of the standards. In particular, it would not look very good if you mentioned something in the exam which actually contradicted any of these standards.

2.1 IAS 16 Property, plant and equipment

IAS 16 has recently been revised, and the amendments are included where appropriate in the following text.

Knowledge brought forward from earlier studies

IAS 16 *Property, plant and equipment*

Definitions

- **Property, plant and equipment** are tangible assets with the following properties.
    - Held by an entity for use in the production or supply of goods or services, for rental to others, or for administrative purposes
    - Expected to be used during more than one period
- **Cost** is the amount of cash or cash equivalents paid or the fair value of the other consideration given to acquire an asset at the time of its acquisition or construction.
- **Residual value** is the estimated amount that an entity would currently obtain from disposal of the asset, after deducting the estimated costs of disposal, if the asset were already of the age and in the condition expected at the end of its useful life.
- **Fair value** is the amount for which an asset could be exchanged between knowledgeable, willing parties in an arm's length transaction.
- **Carrying amount** is the amount at which an asset is recognised after deducting any accumulated depreciation and accumulated impairment losses.

Accounting treatment

- As with all assets, **recognition** depends on two criteria.
    - It is probable that **future economic benefits** associated with the item will flow to the entity
    - The cost of the item can be **measured reliably**
- These recognition criteria apply to **subsequent expenditure** as well as costs incurred initially (ie, there are no longer separate criteria for recognising subsequent expenditure).
- Once recognised as an asset, items should **initially be measured at cost**.
    - **Purchase price**, less trade discount/rebate
    - **Directly attributable costs** of bringing the asset to working condition for intended use
    - **Initial estimate** of the **costs of dismantling and removing the item** and **restoring the site** on which it is located.

The revised IAS 16 provides additional guidance on directly attributable costs included in the cost of an item of property, plant and equipment.

(a) These costs bring the asset to the location and working condition necessary for it to be capable of operating in the manner intended by management, including those costs to test whether the asset is functioning properly.

(b) These are determined after deducting the net proceeds from selling any items produced when bringing the asset to its location and condition.

The revised standard also states that income and related expenses of operations that are incidental to the construction or development of an item of property, plant and equipment should be recognised in the profit or loss.

The revised IAS 16 specifies that exchanges of items of property, plant and equipment, regardless of whether the assets are similar, are measured at fair value, unless the exchange transaction lacks commercial substance or the fair value of neither of the assets exchanged can be measured reliably. If the acquired item is not measured at fair value, its cost is measured at the carrying amount of the asset given up.

This amends the previous requirement to measure the cost of the asset acquired at the carrying amount of the asset given up in respect of the following exchanges:

- an acquisition of an item of property, plant and equipment in exchange for a similar asset that has a similar use in the same line of business and a similar fair value; and

- a sale of an item of property, plant and equipment in exchange for an equity interest in a similar asset.

- **Expenditure incurred in replacing or renewing a component** of an item of property, plant and equipment shall be **recognised in the carrying amount of the item**. The carrying amount of the replaced or renewed component asset shall be derecognised. A similar approach is also applied when a separate component of an item of property, plant and equipment is identified in respect of a major inspection to enable the continued use of the item.

- **Measurement subsequent to initial recognition**.

  - **Cost model:** carry asset at cost less depreciation and any accumulated impairment losses

  - **Revaluation model:** carry asset at revalued amount, ie fair value less subsequent accumulated depreciation and any accumulated impairment losses. (The revised IAS 16 makes clear that the revaluation model is available only if the fair value of the item can be measured reliably.)

- **Revaluations**.

  - Carry out regularly, depending on volatility
  - Fair value is usually market value, or depreciated replacement cost
  - If one asset is revalued, so must be the whole of the rest of the class at the same time
  - Increase in value is credited to a revaluation surplus (part of owners' equity)
  - Decrease is an expense in profit or loss after cancelling a previous revaluation surplus
  - Additional disclosure required

- **Depreciation and revaluations**.

  - Depreciation is based on the carrying value in the statement of financial position. It must be determined separately for each significant part of an item.

  - Excess over historical cost depreciation can be transferred to realised earnings through reserves

  - The residual value and useful life of an asset, as well as the depreciation method must be reviewed at least at each financial year end, rather than periodically as per the previous version of IAS 16. Changes are changes in accounting estimates and are accounted for prospectively as adjustments to future depreciation.

  - Depreciation of an item does not cease when it becomes temporarily idle or is retired from active use and held for disposal.

- **Retirements and disposals:** gains or losses are calculated by comparing net proceeds with carrying amount of the asset and are recognised as income/expense in profit or loss.

A further point worth emphasising here is the relationship between the accounting treatment of **impairments and revaluations**.

(a)   An **impairment loss** should be treated in the same way as a **revaluation decrease**, ie the decrease should be recognised as an expense. However, a revaluation decrease (or impairment loss) should be charged directly against any related revaluation surplus to the extent that the decrease does not exceed the amount held in the revaluation surplus in respect of that same asset.

(b)   A **reversal of an impairment** loss should be treated in the same way as a **revaluation increase**, ie a revaluation increase should be recognised as income to the extent that it reverses a revaluation decrease or an impairment loss of the same asset previously recognised as an expense.

Question   Depreciation

What are the purposes of providing for depreciation?

Answer

The accounts of a business try to recognise that the cost of a non-current asset is gradually consumed as the asset wears out. This is done by gradually writing off the asset's cost in profit or loss over several accounting periods. This process is known as depreciation, and is an example of the accrual assumption. Depreciation should be allocated on a systematic basis to each accounting period during the useful life of the asset.

With regard to the accrual principle, it is fair that the profits should be reduced by the depreciation charge, this is not an arbitrary exercise. Depreciation is not, as is sometimes supposed, an attempt to set aside funds to purchase new long-term assets when required. Depreciation is not generally provided on freehold land because it does not 'wear out' (unless it is held for mining).

2.1.1 Measurement subsequent to initial recognition

The standard offers two possible treatments here, essentially a choice between keeping an asset recorded at **cost** or revaluing it to **fair value**.

(a)   **Cost model.** Carry the asset at its cost less depreciation and any accumulated impairment loss.

(b)   **Revaluation model.** Carry the asset at a revalued amount, being its fair value at the date of the revaluation less any subsequent accumulated depreciation and subsequent accumulated impairment losses. The revised IAS 16 makes clear that the **revaluation model is available only if the fair value of the item can be measured reliably**.

2.1.2 Revaluations

The **market value** of land and buildings usually represents fair value, assuming existing use and line of business. Such valuations are usually carried out by professionally qualified valuers.

In the case of **plant and equipment**, fair value can also be taken as **market value**. Where a market value is not available, however, depreciated replacement cost should be used. There may be no market value where types of plant and equipment are sold only rarely or because of their specialised nature (ie they would normally only be sold as part of an ongoing business).

The frequency of valuation depends on the **volatility of the fair values** of individual items of property, plant and equipment. The more volatile the fair value, the more frequently revaluations should be carried out. Where the current fair value is very different from the carrying value then a revaluation should be carried out.

Most importantly, when an item of property, plant and equipment is revalued, **the whole class of assets to which it belongs should be revalued.**

All the items within a class should be **revalued at the same time**, to prevent selective revaluation of certain assets and to avoid disclosing a mixture of costs and values from different dates in the financial statements. A rolling basis of revaluation is allowed if the revaluations are kept up to date and the revaluation of the whole class is completed in a short period of time.

How should any **increase in value** be treated when a revaluation takes place? The debit will be the increase in value in the statement of financial position, but what about the credit? IAS 16 requires the increase to be credited to a **revaluation surplus** (ie part of owners' equity), *unless* the increase is reversing a previous decrease which was recognised as an expense. To the extent that this offset is made, the increase is recognised as income; any excess is then taken to the revaluation reserve.

2.1.3 Example: revaluation surplus

Binkie Co has an item of land carried in its books at $13,000. Two years ago a slump in land values led the company to reduce the carrying value from $15,000. This was taken as an expense in profit or loss (the income statement part of the statement of comprehensive income). There has been a surge in land prices in the current year, however, and the land is now worth $20,000.

Account for the revaluation in the current year.

Solution

The double entry is:

DEBIT	Asset value (statement of financial position)	$7,000	
CREDIT	Income statement (profit or loss for year)		$2,000
	Revaluation surplus		$5,000

The case is similar for a **decrease in value** on revaluation. Any decrease should be recognised as an expense, except where it offsets a previous increase taken as a revaluation surplus in owners' equity. Any decrease greater than the previous upwards increase in value must be taken as an expense in profit or loss for the year.

2.1.4 Example: revaluation decrease

Let us simply swap round the example given above. The original cost was $15,000, revalued upwards to $20,000 two years ago. The value has now fallen to $13,000.

Account for the decrease in value.

Solution

The double entry is:

DEBIT	Revaluation surplus	$5,000	
DEBIT	Income statement (profit or loss)	$2,000	
CREDIT	Asset value (statement of financial position)		$7,000

There is a further complication when a **revalued asset is being depreciated**. As we have seen, an upward revaluation means that the depreciation charge will increase. Normally, a revaluation surplus is only realised when the asset is sold, but when it is being depreciated, part of that surplus is being realised as the asset is used. The amount of the surplus realised is the difference between depreciation charged on the revalued amount and the (lower) depreciation which would have been charged on the asset's original cost. **This amount can be transferred to retained (ie realised) earnings but *not* through profit or loss.**

2.1.5 Example: revaluation and depreciation

Crinckle Co bought an asset for $10,000 at the beginning of 20X6. It had a useful life of five years. On 1 January 20X8 the asset was revalued to $12,000. The expected useful life has remained unchanged (ie three years remain).

Account for the revaluation and state the treatment for depreciation from 20X8 onwards.

Solution

On 1 January 20X8 the carrying value of the asset is $10,000 – (2 × $10,000 ÷ 5) = $6,000. For the revaluation:

DEBIT	Asset value (statement of financial disposition)	$6,000	
CREDIT	Revaluation surplus		$6,000

The depreciation for the next three years will be $12,000 ÷ 3 = $4,000, compared to depreciation on cost of $10,000 ÷ 5 = $2,000. So each year, the extra $2,000 can be treated as part of the surplus which has become realised:

DEBIT	Revaluation surplus	$2,000	
CREDIT	Retained earnings		$2,000

This is a movement on owners' equity only, not through profit or loss.

2.1.6 On disposal

When a revalued asset is **disposed** of, any revaluation surplus may be **transferred directly to retained earnings**.

Alternatively, it may be **left in equity** under the heading revaluation surplus.

The transfer to retained earnings **should not be made through profit or loss for the year**. In other words it must not be made as a reclassification adjustment ('recycling').

2.2 IAS 20: Government grants

IAS 20 is very straightforward. The question after the following summary covers the accounting problem it tackled.

Knowledge brought forward from earlier studies

IAS 20 *Accounting for government grants and disclosure of government assistance*

Definitions

- **Government assistance.** Action by government designed to provide an economic benefit specific to an entity or range of entities qualifying under certain criteria.
- **Government grants.** Assistance by government in the form of transfers of resources to an entity in return for past or future compliance with certain conditions relating to the operating activities of the entity. They exclude those forms of government assistance which cannot reasonably have a value placed upon them and transactions with government which cannot be distinguished from the normal trading transactions of the entity.
- **Grants related to assets.** Government grants whose primary condition is that an entity qualifying for them should purchase, construct or otherwise acquire long-term assets. Subsidiary conditions may also be attached restricting the type or location of the assets or the periods during which they are to be acquired or held.
- **Grants related to income.** Government grants other than those related to assets.
- **Forgivable loans.** Loans which the lender undertakes to waive repayment of under certain prescribed conditions.

Accounting treatment

- **Recognise government grants and forgivable loans** once conditions complied with and receipt/waiver is assured.

- Grants are recognised under the **income approach**: recognise grants as income to match them with related costs that they have been received to compensate.
- Use a **systematic basis** of matching over the relevant periods.
- Grants for **depreciable assets** should be recognised as income on the same basis as the asset is depreciated.
- Grants for **non-depreciable assets** should be recognised as income over the periods in which the cost of meeting the obligation is incurred.
- A grant may be **split into parts** and allocated on different bases where there are a series of conditions attached.

Knowledge brought forward from earlier studies (continued)

- Where **related costs have already been incurred**, the grant may be recognised as income in full immediately.
- A grant in the form of a **non-monetary asset** may be valued at fair value or a nominal value.
- **Grants related to assets** may be presented in the statement of financial position *either* as **deferred income** *or* deducted in arriving at the carrying value of the asset.
- **Grants related to income** may be presented in profit or loss (income statement) *either* as a **separate credit** *or* **deducted** from the related expense.
- Repayment of government grants should be accounted for as a **revision of an accounting estimate**.

Disclosure

- **Accounting policy** note.
- **Nature and extent** of government grants and other forms of assistance received.
- **Unfulfilled conditions** and other contingencies attached to recognised government assistance.

Question

Government grants

IAS 20 suggests that there are two approaches to recognising government grants: a capital approach (credit directly to shareholders' interests) and an income approach. IAS 20 requires the use of the income approach, but what are the arguments in support of each method?

Answer

IAS 20 gives the following arguments in support of each method.

Capital approach

(a) The grants are a **financing device**, so should go through the statement of financial position. In the statement of comprehensive income (income statement) they would simply offset the expenses which they are financing. No repayment is expected by the Government, so the grants should be credited directly to shareholders' interests.

(b) Grants are **not earned**, they are incentives without related costs, so it would be wrong to take them to profit or loss.

Income approach

(a) The grants are **not received from shareholders** so should not be credited directly to shareholders' interests.

(b) Grants are **not given or received for nothing**. They are earned by compliance with conditions and by meeting obligations. There are therefore associated costs with which the grant can be matched in the statement of comprehensive income (income statement) as these costs are being compensated by the grant.

(c)   Grants are an extension of **fiscal policies** and so as income and other taxes are charged against income, so grants should be credited to income.

2.3 IAS 23 Borrowing costs

This is another straightforward standard. This time there are two calculation questions to remind you of how IAS 23 is applied.

IAS 23 *Borrowing costs*

- IAS 23 deals with the treatment of borrowing costs, often associated with the construction of **self-constructed assets**, but which can also be applied to an asset purchased that takes time to get ready for use/sale.

Definitions

- **Borrowing costs**. Interest and other costs incurred by an entity in connection with the borrowing of funds.
- **Qualifying asset**. An asset that necessarily takes a substantial period of time to get ready for its intended use or sale.

Accounting treatment

- **Borrowing costs must** be **capitalised** as part of the cost of the asset if they are directly attributable to acquisition/construction/production. **Other borrowing costs must be expensed**.
- **Borrowing costs eligible for capitalisation** are those that would have been avoided otherwise. Use judgement where a range of debt instruments is held for general finance.
- **Amount of borrowing costs available for capitalisation** is actual borrowing costs incurred less any investment income from temporary investment of those borrowings.
- For borrowings obtained generally, apply the **capitalisation rate** to the expenditure on the asset (weighted average borrowing cost). It must not exceed actual borrowing costs.
- **Capitalisation is suspended** if active development is interrupted for extended periods. (Temporary delays or technical/administrative work will not cause suspension.)
- **Capitalisation ceases** (normally) when physical construction of the asset is completed, capitalisation should cease when each stage or part is completed.
- Where the carrying amount of the asset falls below cost, it must be **written down/off**.

Disclosure

- **Accounting policy** note.
- Amount of **borrowing costs capitalised** during the period.
- **Capitalisation rate** used to determine borrowing costs eligible for capitalisation.

Question

Borrowing costs 1

On 1 January 20X6 Rechno Co borrowed $15m to finance the production of two assets, both of which were expected to take a year to build. Production started during 20X8. The loan facility was drawn down on 1 January 20X8, and was utilised as follows, with the remaining funds invested temporarily.

	Asset X	Asset Y
	$m	$m
1 January 20X8	2.5	5.0
1 July 20X8	2.5	5.0

The loan rate was 10% and Rechno Co can invest surplus funds at 8%.

Required

Ignoring compound interest, calculate the borrowing costs which may be capitalised for each of the assets and consequently the cost of each asset as at 31 December 20X8.

Answer

		Asset X $'000	Asset Y $'000
Borrowing costs			
To 30 June 20X8	$2.5m/$5.0m × 10% × 6/12	125	250
To 31 December 20X8	$5.0m/$10m × 10% × 6/12	250	500
		375	750
Less investment income			
To 30 June 20X8	$2.5m/$5.0m × 8% × 6/12	(100)	(200)
		275	550

	$'000	$'000
Cost of assets		
Expenditure incurred	5,000	10,000
Borrowing costs	275	550
	5,275	10,550

Question

Borrowing costs 2

Zenzi Co had the following loans in place at the beginning and end of 20X8.

	1 January 20X8 $m	31 December 20X8 $m
10.0% Bank loan repayable 20Y3	120	120
9.5% Bank loan repayable 20Y1	80	80
8.9% debenture repayable 20Y8	–	150

The 8.9% debenture was issued to fund the construction of a qualifying asset (a piece of mining equipment), construction of which began on 1 July 20X8.

On 1 January 20X8, Zenzi Co began construction of a qualifying asset, a piece of machinery for a hydro-electric plant, using existing borrowings. Expenditure drawn down for the construction was: $30m on 1 January 20X8, $20m on 1 October 20X8.

Required

Calculate the borrowing costs to be capitalised for the hydro-electric plant machine.

Answer

Capitalisation rate = weighted average rate = $(10\% \times \frac{120}{120+80}) + (9.5\% \times \frac{80}{120+80}) = 9.8\%$

Borrowing costs = ($30m × 9.8%) + ($20m × 9.8% × 3/12)
= $3.43m

3 IAS 36 Impairment of assets

12/07

IAS 36 *Impairment of assets* covers a controversial topic and it affects goodwill as well as tangible long-term assets.

There is an established principle that assets should not be carried at above their recoverable amount. An entity should write down the carrying value of an asset to its recoverable amount if the carrying value of an asset is not recoverable in full. It puts in place a detailed methodology for carrying out impairment reviews and related accounting treatments and disclosures.

3.1 Scope

IAS 36 applies to all tangible, intangible and financial assets except inventories, assets arising from construction contracts, deferred tax assets, assets arising under IAS 19 *Employee benefits* and financial assets within the scope of IAS 32 *Financial instruments: presentation*. This is because those IASs already have rules for recognising and measuring impairment. Note also that IAS 36 does not apply to non–current assets held for sale, which are dealt with under IFRS 5 *Non-current assets held for sale and discontinued operations*.

Key terms

> **Impairment**: a fall in the value of an asset, so that its 'recoverable amount' is now less than its carrying value in the balance sheet.
>
> **Carrying amount**: is the net value at which the asset is included in the statement of financial position (ie after deducting accumulated depreciation and any impairment losses). *(IAS 36)*

The basic principle underlying IAS 36 is relatively straightforward. If an asset's value in the accounts is higher than its realistic value, measured as its 'recoverable amount', the asset is judged to have suffered an impairment loss. It should therefore be reduced in value, by the amount of the **impairment loss**. The amount of the impairment loss should be **written off against profit** immediately.

The main accounting issues to consider are therefore as follows.

(a)   How is it possible to **identify when** an impairment loss may have occurred?
(b)   How should the **recoverable amount** of the asset be measured?
(c)   How should an 'impairment loss' be **reported in the accounts**?

3.2 Identifying a potentially impaired asset

An entity should carry out a **review of its assets at each year end**, to assess whether there are any indications of impairment to any assets. The concept of **materiality** applies, and only material impairment needs to be identified.

If there are indications of possible impairment, the entity is required to make a formal estimate of the **recoverable amount** of the assets concerned.

IAS 36 suggests how **indications of a possible impairment** of assets might be recognised. The suggestions are based largely on common sense.

(a)   **External sources of information**
  (i)   A fall in the asset's market value that is more significant than would normally be expected from passage of time over normal use.
  (ii)   A significant change in the technological, market, legal or economic environment of the business in which the assets are employed.
  (iii)   An increase in market interest rates or market rates of return on investments likely to affect the discount rate used in calculating value in use.
  (iv)   The carrying amount of the entity's net assets being more than its market capitalisation.

(b)   **Internal sources of information**: evidence of obsolescence or physical damage, adverse changes in the use to which the asset is put, or the asset's economic performance

Even if there are no indications of impairment, the following assets must **always** be tested for impairment annually.

(a)   An intangible asset with an **indefinite useful life**
(b)   **Goodwill** acquired in a business combination

3.3 Measuring the recoverable amount of the asset

Impairment is determined by comparing the carrying amount of the asset with its **recoverable amount**.
The recoverable amount of an asset is the higher of the asset's **fair value less costs to sell** and **its value in use**.

What is an asset's recoverable amount?

Key term

The **recoverable amount of an asset** should be measured as the *higher value* of:

(a)   the asset's fair value less costs to sell; and
(b)   its value in use.   (IAS 36)

An asset's fair value less costs to sell is the amount net of selling costs that could be obtained from the sale of the asset. Selling costs include sales transaction costs, such as legal expenses.

(a)   If there is **an active market** in the asset, the net selling price should be based on the **market value**, or on the price of recent transactions in similar assets.

(b)   If there is **no active market** in the assets it might be possible to **estimate** a net selling price using best estimates of what 'knowledgeable, willing parties' might pay in an arm's length transaction.

Net selling price **cannot** be reduced, however, by including within selling costs any **restructuring or reorganisation expenses**, or any costs that have already been recognised in the accounts as liabilities.

The concept of 'value in use' is very important.

Key term

The **value in use** of an asset is measured as the present value of estimated future cash flows (inflows minus outflows) generated by the asset, including its estimated net disposal value (if any) at the end of its expected useful life.

The cash flows used in the calculation should be **pre-tax cash flows** and a **pre-tax discount rate** should be applied to calculate the present value.

The calculation of **value in use** must reflect the following.

(a)   An estimate of the **future cash flows** the entity expects to derive from the asset
(b)   Expectations about **possible variations** in the amount and timing of future cash flows
(c)   The **time value of money**
(d)   The price for bearing the **uncertainty** inherent in the asset, and
(e)   **Other factors** that would be reflected in pricing future cash flows from the asset

Calculating a value in use therefore calls for estimates of future cash flows, and the possibility exists that an entity might come up with **over-optimistic estimates** of cash flows. The IAS therefore states the following.

(a)   Cash flow projections should be based on **'reasonable and supportable' assumptions**.

(b)   Projections of cash flows, normally up to a maximum period of five years, should be based on the most **recent budgets or financial forecasts**.

(c)   Cash flow projections beyond this period should be obtained by extrapolating short-term projections, using either a **steady or declining growth rate** for each subsequent year (unless a rising growth rate can be justified). The long term growth rate applied should not exceed the average long term growth rate for the product, market, industry or country, unless a higher growth rate can be justified.

3.3.1 Composition of estimates of future cash flows

These should include the following.

(a)   Projections of **cash inflows** from **continuing use** of the asset

(b)   Projections of **cash outflows** necessarily incurred to **generate the cash inflows** from continuing use of the asset

(c)   **Net cash flows** received/paid on **disposal** of the asset at the end of its useful life

There is an underlying principle that future cash flows should be estimated for the asset in its current condition. Future cash flows relating to restructurings to which the entity is not yet committed, or to future costs to add to, replace part of, or service the asset are excluded.

Estimates of future cash flows should **exclude** the following.

(a)   Cash inflows/ outflows from financing activities
(b)   Income tax receipts/payments

The amount of net cash inflow/outflow on **disposal** of an asset should assume an arm's length transaction.

Foreign currency future cash flows should be forecast in the currency in which they will arise and will be discounted using a rule appropriate for that currency. The resulting figure should then be translated into the reporting currency at the spot rate at the year end.

The **discount rate** should be a current pre-tax rate (or rates) that reflects the current assessment of the time value of money and the risks specific to the asset. The discount should not include a risk weighting if the underlying cash flows have already been adjusted for risk.

3.4 Recognition and measurement of an impairment loss

> When it is not possible to calculate the recoverable amount of a single asset, then that of its **cash generating unit** should be measured instead.

The rule for assets at historical cost is:

Rule to learn

> If the recoverable amount of an asset is lower than the carrying amount, the carrying amount should be reduced by the difference (ie the impairment loss) which should be charged as an expense in profit or loss for the year.

The rule for assets held at a revalued amount (such as property revalued under IAS 16) is:

Rule to learn

> The impairment loss is to be treated as a revaluation decrease under the relevant IAS.

In practice this means:

- To the extent that there is a revaluation surplus held in respect of the asset, the impairment loss should be charged to revaluation surplus.
- Any excess should be charged to profit or loss.

The IAS goes into quite a large amount of detail about the important concept of cash generating units. As a basic rule, the recoverable amount of an asset should be calculated for the **asset individually**. However, there will be occasions when it is not possible to estimate such a value for an individual asset, particularly in the calculation of value in use. This is because cash inflows and outflows cannot be attributed to the individual asset.

If it is not possible to calculate the recoverable amount for an individual asset, the recoverable amount of the asset's cash generating unit should be measured instead.

Key term

> **A cash generating unit** is the smallest identifiable group of assets for which independent cash flows can be identified and measured.

Question   Cash generating unit 1

Can you think of some examples of how a cash generating unit would be identified?

Here are two possibilities.

(a)   A mining company owns a private railway that it uses to transport output from one of its mines. The railway now has no market value other than as scrap, and it is impossible to identify any separate cash inflows with the use of the railway itself. Consequently, if the mining company suspects an impairment in the value of the railway, it should treat the mine as a whole as a cash generating unit, and measure the recoverable amount of the mine as a whole.

(b)   A bus company has an arrangement with a town's authorities to run a bus service on four routes in the town. Separately identifiable assets are allocated to each of the bus routes, and cash inflows and outflows can be attributed to each individual route. Three routes are running at a profit and one is running at a loss. The bus company suspects that there is an impairment of assets on the loss-making route. However, the company will be unable to close the loss-making route, because it is under an obligation to operate all four routes, as part of its contract with the local authority. Consequently, the company should treat all four bus routes together as a cash generating unit, and calculate the recoverable amount for the unit as a whole.

Question

Minimart belongs to a retail store chain Maximart. Minimart makes all its retail purchases through Maximart's purchasing centre. Pricing, marketing, advertising and human resources policies (except for hiring Minimart's cashiers and salesmen) are decided by Maximart. Maximart also owns 5 other stores in the same city as Minimart (although in different neighbourhoods) and 20 other stores in other cities. All stores are managed in the same way as Minimart. Minimart and 4 other stores were purchased 5 years ago and goodwill was recognised.

What is the cash-generating unit for Minimart?

Answer

In identifying Minimart's cash-generating unit, an entity considers whether, for example:

(a)   Internal management reporting is organised to measure performance on a store-by-store basis.
(b)   The business is run on a store-by-store profit basis or on a region/city basis.

All Maximart's stores are in different neighbourhoods and probably have different customer bases. So, although Minimart is managed at a corporate level, Minimart generates cash inflows that are largely independent from those of Maximart's other stores. Therefore, it is likely that Minimart is a cash-generating unit.

Question

Mighty Mag Publishing Co owns 150 magazine titles of which 70 were purchased and 80 were self-created. The price paid for a purchased magazine title is recognised as an intangible asset. The costs of creating magazine titles and maintaining the existing titles are recognised as an expense when incurred. Cash inflows from direct sales and advertising are identifiable for each magazine title. Titles are managed by customer segments. The level of advertising income for a magazine title depends on the range of titles in the customer segment to which the magazine title relates. Management has a policy to abandon old titles before the end of their economic lives and replace them immediately with new titles for the same customer segment.

What is the cash-generating unit for an individual magazine title?

It is likely that the recoverable amount of an individual magazine title can be assessed. Even though the level of advertising income for a title is influenced, to a certain extent, by the other titles in the customer segment, cash inflows from direct sales and advertising are identifiable for each title. In addition, although titles are managed by customer segments, decisions to abandon titles are made on an individual title basis.

Therefore, it is likely that individual magazine titles generate cash inflows that are largely independent one from another and that each magazine title is a separate cash-generating unit.

If an active market exists for the output produced by the asset or a group of assets, this asset or group should be identified as a cash generating unit, even if some or all of the output is used internally.

Cash generating units should be identified consistently from period to period for the same type of asset unless a change is justified.

The group of net assets less liabilities that are considered for impairment should be the same as those considered in the calculation of the recoverable amount. (For the treatment of goodwill and corporate assets see below.)

3.5 Example: Recoverable amount and carrying amount

Fourways Co is made up of four cash generating units. All four units are being tested for impairment.

(a)   Property, plant and equipment and separate intangibles would be allocated to be cash generating units as far as possible.

(b)   Current assets such as inventories, receivables and prepayments would be allocated to the relevant cash generating units.

(c)   Liabilities (eg payables) would be deducted from the net assets of the relevant cash generating units.

(d)   The net figure for each cash generating unit resulting from this exercise would be compared to the relevant recoverable amount, computed on the same basis.

3.6 Goodwill and the impairment of assets

3.6.1 Allocating goodwill to cash-generating units

Goodwill acquired in a business combination does not generate cash flows independently of other assets. It must be **allocated** to each of the acquirer's **cash-generating units** (or groups of cash-generating units) that are expected to benefit from the synergies of the combination. Each unit to which the goodwill is so allocated should:

(a)   Represent the **lowest level** within the entity at which the goodwill is monitored for internal management purposes

(b)   Not be **larger than a reporting segment** determined in accordance with IFRS 8 *Operating segments*

It may be impractical to complete the allocation of goodwill before the first reporting date after a business combination, particularly if the acquirer is accounting for the combination for the first time using provisional values. The initial allocation of goodwill must be completed before the end of the first reporting period after the acquisition date.

3.6.2 Testing cash-generating units with goodwill for impairment

There are two situations to consider.

(a)   Where goodwill has been allocated to a cash-generating unit

(b)   Where it has not been possible to allocate goodwill to a specific cash-generating unit, but only to a group of units

A cash-generating unit to which goodwill has been allocated is tested for impairment annually. The **carrying amount** of the unit, including goodwill, is **compared with the recoverable amount**. If the carrying amount of the unit exceeds the recoverable amount, the entity must recognise an impairment loss.

If there is a **non-controlling (minority) interest** in a cash-generating unit to which goodwill has been allocated, the carrying amount of the goodwill allocated to that unit must be **grossed up** to include the goodwill attributable to the non-controlling interest. This is because the goodwill recognised in a business combination represents only the goodwill owned by the parent, not the amount of goodwill actually controlled by the parent. Part of the recoverable amount of the cash-generating unit is attributable to the non-controlling interest in goodwill.

Where goodwill relates to a cash-generating unit but has not been allocated to that unit, the unit is tested for impairment by **comparing its carrying amount** (excluding goodwill) **with its recoverable amount**. The entity must recognise an impairment loss if the carrying amount exceeds the recoverable amount.

The annual impairment test may be performed at any time during an accounting period, but must be performed at the **same time every year**.

3.7 Example: Non-controlling interest

On 1 January 20X4 a parent acquires an 80% interest in a subsidiary for $1,600,000, when the identifiable net assets of the subsidiary are $1,500,000. The subsidiary is a cash-generating unit.

At 31 December 20X4, the recoverable amount of the subsidiary is $1,000,000. The carrying amount of the subsidiary's identifiable assets is $1,350,000.

Calculate the impairment loss at 31 December 20X4.

Solution

At 31 December 20X4 the cash-generating unit consists of the subsidiary's identifiable net assets (carrying amount $1,350,000) and goodwill of $400,000 (1,600,000 – £80% × 1,500,000)). Goodwill is grossed up to reflect the 20% non-controlling interest.

	Goodwill $	Net assets $	Total $
Carrying amount	400	1,350	1,750
Unrecognised non-controlling interest	100		100
	500	1,350	1,850
Recoverable amount			(1,000)
Impairment loss			850

3.8 Corporate assets

Corporate assets are group or divisional assets such as a head office building, EDP equipment or a research centre. Essentially, corporate assets are assets that do not generate cash inflows independently from other assets, hence their carrying amount cannot be fully attributed to a cash-generating unit under review.

In testing a cash generating unit for impairment, an entity should identify all the corporate assets that relate to the cash-generating unit.

(a)   If a portion of the carrying amount of a corporate asset **can be allocated** to the unit on a reasonable and consistent basis, the entity compares the carrying amount of the unit (including the portion of the asset) with its recoverable amount.

(b) If a portion of the carrying amount of a corporate asset **cannot be allocated** to the unit on a reasonable and consistent basis, the entity:

    (i) Compares the carrying amount of the unit (excluding the asset) with its recoverable amount and recognises any impairment loss

    (ii) Identifies the smallest group of cash-generating units that includes the cash-generating unit to which the asset belongs and to which a portion of the carrying amount of the asset can be allocated on a reasonable and consistent basis

    (iii) Compares the carrying amount of that group of cash-generating units, (including the portion of the asset allocated to the group of units) with the recoverable amount of the group of units and recognises any impairment loss

3.9 Accounting treatment of an impairment loss

If, and only if, the recoverable amount of an asset is less than its carrying amount in the statement of financial position, an impairment loss has occurred. This loss should be **recognised immediately**.

(a) The asset's **carrying amount** should be reduced to its recoverable amount in the statement of financial position.

(b) The **impairment loss** should be recognised immediately in profit or loss (unless the asset has been revalued in which case the loss is treated as a revaluation decrease; see Paragraph 3.4).

After reducing an asset to its recoverable amount, the **depreciation charge** on the asset should then be based on its new carrying amount, its estimated residual value (if any) and its estimated remaining useful life.

An impairment loss should be recognised for a **cash generating unit** if (and only if) the recoverable amount for the cash generating unit is less than the carrying amount in the statement of financial position for all the assets in the unit. When an impairment loss is recognised for a cash generating unit, the loss should be allocated between the assets in the unit in the following order.

(a) First, to the **goodwill** allocated to the cash generating unit

(b) Then to all other assets in the cash-generating unit, on a **pro rata basis**

In allocating an impairment loss, the carrying amount of an asset should not be reduced below the highest of:

(a) Its fair value less costs to sell

(b) Its value in use (if determinable)

(c) Zero

Any remaining amount of an impairment loss should be recognised as a liability if required by other IASs.

3.10 Example 1: Impairment loss

A company that extracts natural gas and oil has a drilling platform in the Caspian Sea. It is required by legislation of the country concerned to remove and dismantle the platform at the end of its useful life. Accordingly, the company has included an amount in its accounts for removal and dismantling costs, and is depreciating this amount over the platform's expected life.

The company is carrying out an exercise to establish whether there has been an impairment of the platform.

(a) Its carrying amount in the statement of financial position is $3m.

(b) The company has received an offer of $2.8m for the platform from another oil company. The bidder would take over the responsibility (and costs) for dismantling and removing the platform at the end of its life.

(c) The present value of the estimated cash flows from the platform's continued use is $3.3m.

(d) The carrying amount in the statement of financial position for the provision for dismantling and removal is currently $0.6m.

What should be the value of the drilling platform in the statement of financial position, and what, if anything, is the impairment loss?

Solution

Fair value less costs to sell	=	$2.8m
Value in use	=	PV of cash flows from use less the carrying amount of the provision/liability = $3.3m – $0.6m = $2.7m
Recoverable amount	=	Higher of these two amounts, ie $2.8m
Carrying value	=	$3m
Impairment loss	=	$0.2m

The carrying value should be reduced to $2.8m

3.11 Example 2: Impairment loss

A company has acquired another business for $4.5m: tangible assets are valued at $4.0m and goodwill at $0.5m.

An asset with a carrying value of $1m is destroyed in a terrorist attack. The asset was not insured. The loss of the asset, without insurance, has prompted the company to estimate whether there has been an impairment of assets in the acquired business and what the amount of any such loss is. The recoverable amount of the business is measured at $3.1m.

Solution

The recoverable amount of the business (a single cash generating unit) is measured as $3.1m. There has consequently been an impairment loss of $1.4m ($4.5m – $3.1m).

The impairment loss will be recognised in profit or loss. The loss will be allocated between the assets in the cash generating unit as follows.

(a) A loss of $1m can be attributed directly to the uninsured asset that has been destroyed.
(b) The remaining loss of $0.4m should be allocated to goodwill.

The carrying value of the assets will now be $3m for tangible assets and $0.1m for goodwill.

3.12 Reversal of an impairment loss

The annual review of assets to determine whether there may have been some impairment should be **applied to all assets**, including assets that have already been impaired in the past.

In some cases, the recoverable amount of an asset that has previously been impaired might turn out to be **higher** than the asset's current carrying value. In other words, there might have been a reversal of some of the previous impairment loss.

(a) The reversal of the impairment loss should be **recognised immediately** as income in profit or loss for the year.
(b) The carrying amount of the asset should be increased to its **new recoverable amount**.

Rule to learn

> An impairment loss recognised for an asset in prior years should be recovered if, and only if, there has been a change in the estimates used to determine the asset's recoverable amount since the last impairment loss was recognised.

The asset cannot be revalued to a carrying amount that is higher than its value would have been if the asset had not been impaired originally, ie its **depreciated carrying value** had the impairment not taken place. Depreciation of the asset should now be based on its new revalued amount, its estimated residual value (if any) and its estimated remaining useful life.

An exception to the rule above is for **goodwill**. An impairment loss for goodwill should not be reversed in a subsequent period.

A cash generating unit comprising a factory, plant and equipment etc and associated purchased goodwill becomes impaired because the product it makes is overtaken by a technologically more advanced model produced by a competitor. The recoverable amount of the cash generating unit falls to $60m, resulting in an impairment loss of $80m, allocated as follows.

	Carrying amounts before impairment $m	Carrying amounts after impairment $m
Goodwill	40	
Patent (with no market value)	20	
Tangible long-term assets	80	60
Total	140	60

After three years, the entity makes a technological breakthrough of its own, and the recoverable amount of the cash generating unit increases to $90m. The carrying amount of the tangible long-term assets had the impairment not occurred would have been $70m.

Required

Calculate the reversal of the impairment loss.

Answer

The reversal of the impairment loss is recognised to the extent that it increases the carrying amount of the tangible non-current assets to what it would have been had the impairment not taken place, ie a reversal of the impairment loss of $10m is recognised and the tangible non-current assets written back to $70m. Reversal of the impairment is not recognised in relation to the goodwill and patent because the effect of the external event that caused the original impairment has not reversed – the original product is still overtaken by a more advanced model.

3.13 Disclosure

IAS 36 calls for substantial disclosure about impairment of assets. The information to be disclosed includes the following.

(a) For each class of assets, the amount of **impairment losses recognised** and the amount of any **impairment losses recovered** (ie reversals of impairment losses)

(b) For each individual asset or cash generating unit that has suffered a **significant impairment loss**, details of the nature of the asset, the amount of the loss, the events that led to recognition of the loss, whether the recoverable amount is fair value price less costs to sell or value in use, and if the recoverable amount is value in use, the basis on which this value was estimated (eg the discount rate applied)

3.14 Section summary

The main aspects of IAS 36 to consider are:

- **Indications** of impairment of assets
- **Measuring recoverable amount**, as net selling price or value in use
- **Measuring value in use**
- **Cash generating units**
- **Accounting treatment** of an impairment loss, for individual assets and cash generating units
- **Reversal** of an impairment loss

4 IAS 40 Investment property

IAS 40 *Investment property* defines investment property as property **held to earn rentals or for capital appreciation** or both, rather than for:

- Use in production or supply of goods or services
- Sale in the ordinary course of business

An entity may own land or a building **as an investment** rather than for use in the business. It may therefore generate cash flows largely independently of other assets which the entity holds.

Consider the following definitions.

Key terms

> **Investment property** is property (land or a building – or part of a building – or both) held (by the owner or by the lessee under a finance lease) to earn rentals or for capital appreciation or both, rather than for:
>
> (a) Use in the production or supply of goods or services or for administrative purposes, or
> (b) Sale in the ordinary course of business
>
> **Owner-occupied property** is property held by the owner (or by the lessee under a finance lease) for use in the production or supply of goods or services or for administrative purposes.
>
> **Fair value** is the amount for which an asset could be exchanged between knowledgeable, willing parties in an arm's length transaction.
>
> **Cost** is the amount of cash or cash equivalents paid or the fair value of other consideration given to acquire an asset at the time of its acquisition or construction.
>
> **Carrying amount** is the amount at which an asset is recognised in the statement of financial position.
>
> A property interest that is held by a lessee under an **operating lease** may be classified and accounted for as an **investment property**, if and only if, the property would otherwise meet the definition of an investment property and the lessee uses the IAS 40 **fair value model**. This classification is available on a property-by-property basis.

Examples of investment property include:

(a) **Land held for long-term capital appreciation** rather than for short-term sale in the ordinary course of business

(b) A **building** owned by the reporting entity (or held by the entity under a finance lease) and **leased out under an operating lease**

Question
Investment property

Rich Co owns a piece of land. The directors have not yet decided whether to build a factory on it for use in its business or to keep it and sell it when its value has risen.

Would this be classified as an investment property under IAS 40?

Answer

Yes. If an entity has not determined that it will use the land either as an owner-occupied property or for short-term sale in the ordinary course of business, the land is considered to be held for capital appreciation.

4.1 IAS 40

IAS 40 *Investment property* was published in 2000 and later revised. Its objective is to prescribe the accounting treatment for investment property and related disclosure requirements.

The standard includes investment property held under a finance lease or leased out under an operating lease. However, the current IAS 40 does not deal with matters covered in IAS 17 *Leases*.

You now know what **is** an investment property under IAS 40. Below are examples of items that are **not investment property**.

Type of non-investment property	Applicable IAS
Property held for sale in the ordinary course of business	IAS 2 *Inventories*
Property being constructed or developed on behalf of third parties	IAS 11 *Construction contracts*
Owner-occupied property	IAS 16 *Property, plant and equipment*
Property being constructed or developed for future use as investment property	IAS 16 until construction or development is complete, then treat as investment property

4.2 Recognition

Investment property should be recognised as an asset when **two conditions** are met.

(a) It is **probable** that the **future economic benefits** that are associated with the investment property will **flow to the entity**.

(b) The **cost** of the investment property can be **measured reliably**.

4.3 Initial measurement

An investment property should be measured initially at its **cost,** including transaction costs.

A property interest held under a lease and classified as an investment property shall be accounted for **as if it were a finance lease**. The asset is recognised at the lower of the fair value of the property and the present value of the minimum lease payments. An equivalent amount is recognised as a liability.

4.4 Measurement subsequent to initial recognition

FAST FORWARD

Entities can choose between:

- A **fair value model**, with changes in fair value being measured
- A **cost model** – the treatment most commonly used under IAS 16

IAS 40 requires an entity to **choose between two models.**

- The fair value model
- The cost model

Whatever policy it chooses should be applied to **all of its investment property**.

Where an entity chooses to classify a property held under an **operating lease** as an investment property, there is **no choice**. The **fair value model must be used** for **all the entity's investment property**, regardless of whether it is owned or leased.

4.4.1 Fair value model

Key term

(a) After initial recognition, an entity that chooses the **fair value model** should measure all of its investment property at fair value, except in the extremely rare cases where this cannot be measured reliably. In such cases it should apply the IAS 16 cost model.

(b) A gain or loss arising from a change in the fair value of an investment property should be recognised in net profit or loss for the period in which it arises.

(c) The fair value of investment property should reflect market conditions at the year end.

This is the first time that the IASB has allowed a fair value model for non-financial assets. This is not the same as a revaluation, where increases in carrying amount above a cost-based measure are recognised as revaluation surplus. Under the fair-value model all changes in fair value are recognised in profit or loss.

The standard elaborates on **issues relating to fair value**.

(a)   Fair value assumes that an arm's length transaction has taken place between '**knowledgeable, willing parties**', ie both buyer and seller are reasonably informed about the nature and characteristics of the investment property.

(b)   A willing buyer is **motivated but not compelled** to buy. A willing seller is neither an over-eager nor a forced seller, nor one prepared to sell at any price or to hold out for a price not considered reasonable in the current market.

(c)   **Fair value is not the same as 'value in use'** as defined in IAS 36 *Impairment of assets*. Value in use reflects factors and knowledge specific to the entity, while fair value reflects factors and knowledge relevant to the market.

(d)   In determining fair value an entity **should not double count assets**. For example, elevators or air conditioning are often an integral part of a building and should be included in the investment property, rather than recognised separately.

(e)   In those rare cases where the **entity cannot determine the fair value of an investment property reliably**, the cost model in **IAS 16** must be applied until the investment property is disposed of. The **residual value must be assumed to be zero**.

4.4.2 Cost model

The cost model is the **cost model in IAS 16**. Investment property should be measured at **depreciated cost, less any accumulated impairment losses**. An entity that chooses the cost model should **disclose the fair value of its investment property**.

4.4.3 Changing models

Once the entity has chosen the fair value or cost model, it should apply it to all its investment property. It **should not change from one model to the other unless the change will result in a more appropriate presentation**. IAS 40 states that it is highly unlikely that a change from the fair value model to the cost model will result in a more appropriate presentation.

4.5 Transfers

Transfers to or from investment property should **only** be made **when there is a change in use**. For example, owner occupation commences so the investment property will be treated under IAS 16 as an owner-occupied property.

When there is a transfer from investment property carried at fair value to owner-occupied property or inventories, the property's cost for subsequent accounting under IAS 16 or IAS 2 should be its fair value at the date of change of use.

Conversely, an owner-occupied property may become an investment property and need to be carried at fair value. An entity should apply IAS 16 up to the date of change of use. It should treat any difference at that date between the carrying amount of the property under IAS 16 and its fair value as a revaluation under IAS 16.

4.6 Disposals

Derecognise (eliminate from the statement of financial position) an investment property on disposal or when it is permanently withdrawn from use and no future economic benefits are expected from its disposal.

Any **gain or loss** on disposal is the difference between the net disposal proceeds and the carrying amount of the asset. It should generally be **recognised as income or expense in profit or loss**.

Compensation from third parties for investment property that was impaired, lost or given up shall be recognised in profit or loss when the compensation becomes receivable.

4.7 Disclosure requirements

These relate to:

- Choice of fair value model or cost model
- Whether property interests held as operating leases are included in investment property
- Criteria for classification as investment property
- Assumptions in determining fair value
- Use of independent professional valuer (encouraged but not required)
- Rental income and expenses
- Any restrictions or obligations

4.7.1 Fair value model – additional disclosures

An entity that adopts this must also disclose a **reconciliation** of the carrying amount of the investment property at the beginning and end of the period.

4.7.2 Cost model – additional disclosures

These relate mainly to the depreciation method. In addition, an entity which adopts the cost model **must disclose the fair value** of the investment property.

4.8 Decision tree

The decision tree below summarises which IAS apply to various kinds of property.

Exam focus point

Learn this decision tree – it will help you tackle most of the problems you are likely to meet in the exam!

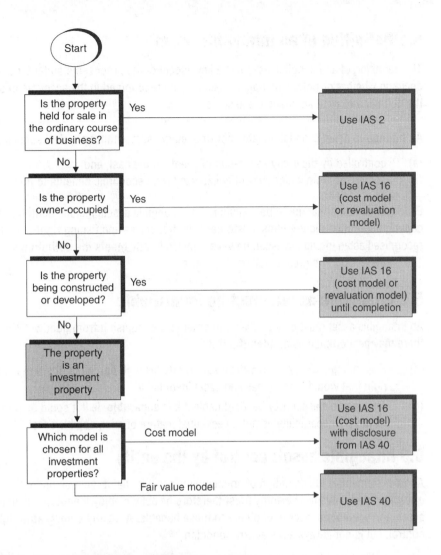

5 IAS 38 Intangible assets

12/08

Intangible assets are defined by **IAS 38** as non-monetary assets without physical substance. They must be:

- **Identifiable**
- **Controlled** as a result of a past event
- Able to provide **future economic benefits**

IAS 38 *Intangible assets* was revised in 2003 to reflect changes introduced by IFRS 3 *Business combinations*.

The objectives of the standard

(a) To establish the criteria for when an intangible assets may or should be **recognised**
(b) To specify how intangible assets should be **measured**
(c) To specify the **disclosure requirements** for intangible assets

It applies to all intangible assets with certain **exceptions**: deferred tax assets (IAS 12), leases that fall within the scope of IAS 17, financial assets, insurance contracts, assets arising from employee benefits (IAS 19) non-current assets held for sale and mineral rights and exploration and extraction costs for minerals etc (although intangible assets used to develop or maintain these rights are covered by the standard). It does *not* apply to goodwill acquired in a business combination, which is dealt with under IFRS 3 *Business combinations.*

5.1 Definition of an intangible asset

The definition of an intangible assets is a key aspect of the proposed standard, because the rules for deciding whether or not an intangible asset may be **recognised** in the accounts of an entity are based on the definition of what an intangible asset is.

> An **intangible asset** is an identifiable non-monetary asset without physical substance The asset must be:
>
> (a)   controlled by the entity as a result of events in the past, and
>
> (b)   something from which the entity expects future economic benefits to flow.

Examples of items that might be considered as intangible assets include computer software, patents, copyrights, motion picture films, customer lists, franchises and fishing rights. An item should not be recognised as an intangible asset, however, unless it **fully meets the definition** in the proposed standard. The guidelines go into great detail on this matter.

5.2 Intangible asset: must be identifiable

An intangible asset must be identifiable in order to distinguish it from goodwill. With non-physical items, there may be a problem with **'identifiability'**.

(a)   If an intangible asset is **acquired separately through purchase**, there may be a transfer of a legal right that would help to make an asset identifiable.

(b)   An intangible asset may be identifiable if it is **separable**, ie if it could be rented or sold separately. However, 'separability' is not an essential feature of an intangible asset.

5.3 Intangible asset: control by the entity

Another element of the definition of an intangible asset is that it must be under the control of the entity as a result of a past event. The entity must therefore be able to enjoy the future economic benefits from the asset, and prevent the access of others to those benefits. A **legally enforceable right** is evidence of such control, but is not always a *necessary* condition.

(a)   Control over **technical knowledge or know-how** only exists if it is protected by a **legal right**.

(b)   The skill of employees, arising out of the benefits of **training costs**, are most unlikely to be recognisable as an intangible asset, because an entity does not control the future actions of its staff.

(c)   Similarly, **market share and customer loyalty** cannot normally be intangible assets, since an entity cannot control the actions of its customers.

5.4 Intangible asset: expected future economic benefits

An item can only be recognised as an intangible asset if economic benefits are expected to flow in the future from ownership of the asset. Economic benefits may come from the **sale** of products or services, or from a **reduction in expenditures** (cost savings).

An intangible asset, when recognised initially, must be measured at **cost**. It should be recognised if, and only if **both** the following occur.

(a)   It is probable that the **future economic benefits** that are attributable to the asset will **flow to the entity**.

(b)   The **cost can be measured reliably.**

Management has to exercise its judgement in assessing the degree of certainty attached to the flow of economic benefits to the entity. External evidence is best.

(a)   If an intangible asset is **acquired separately**, its cost can usually be measured reliably as its purchase price (including incidental costs of purchase such as legal fees, and any costs incurred in getting the asset ready for use).

(b)   When an intangible asset is acquired as **part of a business combination** (ie an acquisition or takeover), the cost of the intangible asset is its fair value at the date of the acquisition.

IFRS 3 explains that the fair value of intangible assets acquired in business combinations can normally be measured with sufficient reliability to be **recognised separately** from goodwill.

Quoted market prices in an active market provide the most reliable estimate of the fair value of an intangible asset. If no active market exists for an intangible asset, its fair value is the amount that the entity would have paid for the asset, at the acquisition date, in an arm's length transaction between knowledgeable and willing parties, on the basis of the best information available. In determining this amount, an entity should consider the outcome of recent transactions for similar assets. There are techniques for estimating the fair values of unique intangible assets (such as brand names) and these may be used to measure an intangible asset acquired in a business combination.

In accordance with IAS 20, intangible assets acquired by way of government grant and the grant itself may be recorded initially either at cost (which may be zero) or fair value.

5.5 Exchanges of assets

If one intangible asset is exchanged for another, the cost of the intangible asset is measured at fair value unless:

(a)　The exchange transaction lacks commercial substance, or
(b)　The fair value of neither the asset received nor the asset given up can be measured reliably.

Otherwise, its cost is measured at the carrying amount of the asset given up.

5.6 Internally generated goodwill

Rule to learn

Internally generated goodwill may **not** be recognised as an **asset**.

The standard deliberately precludes recognition of internally generated goodwill because it requires that, for initial recognition, the cost of the asset rather than its fair value should be capable of being measured reliably and that it should be identifiable and controlled. Thus you do not recognise an asset which is subjective and cannot be measured reliably.

5.7 Research and development costs

5.7.1 Research

Research activities by definition do not meet the criteria for recognition under IAS 38. This is because, at the research stage of a project, it cannot be certain that future economic benefits will probably flow to the entity from the project. There is too much uncertainty about the likely success or otherwise of the project. **Research costs should therefore be written off as an expense as they are incurred**.

Examples of research costs

(a)　Activities aimed at obtaining new knowledge
(b)　The search for, evaluation and final selection of, applications of research findings or other knowledge
(c)　The search for alternatives for materials, devices, products, processes, systems or services
(d)　The formulation, design evaluation and final selection of possible alternatives for new or improved materials, devices, products, systems or services

5.7.2 Development

Development costs **may qualify** for recognition as intangible assets provided that the following **strict criteria** are met.

(a)　The technical feasibility of completing the intangible asset so that it will be available for use or sale.
(b)　Its intention to complete the intangible asset and use or sell it.
(c)　Its ability to use or sell the intangible asset.

(d)   How the intangible asset will generate probable future economic benefits. Among other things, the entity should demonstrate the existence of a market for the output of the intangible asset or the intangible asset itself or, if it is to be used internally, the usefulness of the intangible asset.

(e)   Its ability to measure the expenditure attributable to the intangible asset during its development reliably.

In contrast with research costs development costs are incurred at a later stage in a project, and the probability of success should be more apparent. Examples of development costs include the following.

(a)   The design, construction and testing of pre-production or pre-use prototypes and models

(b)   The design of tools, jigs, moulds and dies involving new technology

(c)   The design, construction and operation of a pilot plant that is not of a scale economically feasible for commercial production

(d)   The design, construction and testing of a chosen alternative for new or improved materials, devices, products, processes, systems or services

5.7.3 Other internally generated intangible assets

The standard **prohibits** the recognition of **internally generated brands**, **mastheads**, **publishing titles and customer lists** and similar items as intangible assets. These all fail to meet one or more (in some cases all) the definition and recognition criteria and in some cases are probably indistinguishable from internally generated goodwill.

5.7.4 Cost of an internally generated intangible asset

The costs allocated to an internally generated intangible asset should be only costs that can be **directly attributed** or allocated on a reasonable and consistent basis to creating, producing or preparing the asset for its intended use. The principles underlying the costs which may or may not be included are similar to those for other than non-current assets and inventory.

The cost of an internally operated intangible asset is the sum of the **expenditure incurred from the date when** the intangible asset first **meets the recognition criteria**. If, as often happens, considerable costs have already been recognised as expenses before management could demonstrate that the criteria have been met, this earlier expenditure should not be retrospectively recognised at a later date as part of the cost of an intangible asset.

5.7.5 Example: computer software and hardware

The treatments can be illustrated by reference to computer software and hardware. The treatment depends on the nature of the asset and its origin.

Asset	Origin	Treatment
Computer software	Purchased	Capitalise
Operating system for hardware	Purchased	Include in hardware cost
Computer software Operating system for hardware (For use or sale)	Internally developed	Charge to expense until 'Development criteria' (para 5.7.2) are met. Amortise over useful life, based on pattern of benefits straight line is default).

Question   Recognition criteria

Doug Co is developing a new production process. During 20X3, expenditure incurred was $100,000, of which $90,000 was incurred before 1 December 20X3 and $10,000 between 1 December 20X3 and 31 December 20X3. Doug Co can demonstrate that, at 1 December 20X3, the production process met the criteria for recognition as an intangible asset. The recoverable amount of the know-how embodied in the process is estimated to be $50,000.

How should the expenditure be treated?

Answer

At the end of 20X3, the production process is recognised as an intangible asset at a cost of $10,000. This is the expenditure incurred since the date when the recognition criteria were met, that is 1 December 20X3. The $90,000 expenditure incurred before 1 December 20X3 is expensed, because the recognition criteria were not met. It will never form part of the cost of the production process recognised in the statement of financial position.

5.8 Recognition of an expense

All expenditure related to an intangible which does not meet the criteria for recognition either as an identifiable intangible asset or as goodwill arising on an acquisition should be **expensed as incurred**. The IAS gives examples of such expenditure.

- Start up costs
- Training costs
- Advertising costs
- Business relocation costs

Prepaid costs for services, for example advertising or marketing costs for campaigns that have been prepared but not launched, can still be recognised as a **prepayment**.

If tangible asset costs have been expensed in previous financial statements, they may not be recognised as part of the cost of the asset.

5.9 Measurement of intangible assets subsequent to initial recognition

> **FAST FORWARD**
>
> Intangible assets should initially be measured at cost, but subsequently they can be carried at **cost or at a fair value**.

The proposed standard allows two methods of valuation for intangible assets after they have been first recognised.

Applying the **cost model**, an intangible asset should be **carried at its cost**, less any accumulated depreciation and less any accumulated impairment losses.

The **revaluation model** allows an intangible asset to be carried at a revalued amount, which is its **fair value** at the date of revaluation, less any subsequent accumulated amortisation and any subsequent accumulated impairment losses.

(a) The fair value must be able to be measured reliably with reference to an **active market** in that type of asset.

(b) The **entire class** of intangible assets of that type must be revalued at the same time (to prevent selective revaluations).

(c) If an intangible asset in a class of revalued intangible assets cannot be revalued because there is **no active market** for this asset, the asset should be carried at its **cost less any accumulated amortisation and impairment losses**.

(d) Revaluations should be made with such **regularity** that the carrying amount does not differ from that which would be determined using fair value at the year end.

Point to note

> This treatment is **not** available for the **initial recognition** of intangible assets. This is because the cost of the asset must be reliably measured.

The guidelines state that there **will not usually be an active market** in an intangible asset; therefore the revaluation model will usually not be available. For example, although copyrights, publishing rights and film right can be sold, each has a unique sale value. In such cases, revaluation to fair value would be inappropriate. A fair value might be obtainable however for assets such as fishing rights or quotas or taxi cab licences.

Where an intangible asset is revalued upwards to a fair value, the amount of the revaluation should be credited directly to equity under the heading of a **revaluation surplus**.

However, if a revaluation surplus is a **reversal of a revaluation decrease** that was previously charged against income, the increase can be recognised as income.

Where the carrying amount of an intangible asset is revalued downwards, the amount of the **downward revaluation** should be charged as an expense against income, unless the asset has previously been revalued upwards. A revaluation decrease should be first charged against any previous revaluation surplus in respect of that asset.

Question
Downward valuation

An intangible asset is measured by a company at fair value. The asset was revalued by $400 in 20X3, and there is a revaluation surplus of $400 in the statement of financial position. At the end of 20X4, the asset is valued again, and a downward valuation of $500 is required.

Required

State the accounting treatment for the downward revaluation.

Answer

In this example, the downward valuation of $500 can first be set against the revaluation surplus of $400. The revaluation surplus will be reduced to 0 and a charge of $100 made as an expense in 20X4.

When the revaluation model is used, and an intangible asset is revalued upwards, the cumulative revaluation **surplus may be transferred to retained earnings** when the surplus is eventually realised. The surplus would be realised when the asset is disposed of. However, the surplus may also be realised over time as the **asset is used** by the entity. The amount of the surplus realised each year is the difference between the amortisation charge for the asset based on the revalued amount of the asset, and the amortisation that would be charged on the basis of the asset's historical cost. The realised surplus in such case should be transferred from revaluation surplus directly to retained earnings, and should not be taken through profit or loss (the income statement).

5.10 Useful life

An entity should **assess** the useful life of an intangible asset, which may be **finite or infinite**. An intangible asset has an indefinite useful life when there is **no foreseeable limit** to the period over which the asset is expected to generate net cash inflows for the entity.

Many factors are considered in determining the useful life of an intangible asset, including: expected usage; typical product life cycles; technical, technological, commercial or other types of obsolescence; the stability of the industry; expected actions by competitors; the level of maintenance expenditure required; and legal or similar limits on the use of the asset, such as the expiry dates of related leases. Computer software and many other intangible assets normally have short lives because they are susceptible to technological obsolescence. However, uncertainty does not justify choosing a life that is unrealistically short.

The useful life of an intangible asset that arises from **contractual or other legal rights** should not exceed the period of the rights, but may be shorter depending on the period over which the entity expects to use the asset.

5.11 Amortisation period and amortisation method

An intangible asset with a finite useful life should be amortised over its **expected useful life**.

(a) Amortisation should start when the asset is **available for use**.

(b) Amortisation should cease at the earlier of the date that the asset is classified **as held for sale** in accordance with IFRS 5 *Non-current assets held for sale and discontinued operations* and the date that the asset is **derecognised**.

(c) The amortisation method used should reflect the **pattern in which the asset's future economic benefits are consumed**. If such a pattern cannot be predicted reliably, the straight-line method should be used.

(d) The amortisation charge for each period should normally be recognised **in profit or loss**.

The **residual value** of an intangible asset with a finite useful life is **assumed to be zero** unless a third party is committed to buying the intangible asset at the end of its useful life or unless there is an active market for that type of asset (so that its expected residual value can be measured) and it is probable that there will be a market for the asset at the end of its useful life.

The amortisation period and the amortisation method used for an intangible asset with a finite useful life should be **reviewed at each financial year-end**.

5.12 Intangible assets with indefinite useful lives

An intangible asset with an indefinite useful life **should not be amortised**. (IAS 36 requires that such an asset is tested for impairment at least annually.)

The useful life of an intangible asset that is not being amortised should be **reviewed each year** to determine whether it is still appropriate to assess its useful life as indefinite. Reassessing the useful life of an intangible asset as finite rather than indefinite is an indicator that the asset may be impaired and therefore it should be tested for impairment.

Question   Useful life

It may be difficult to establish the useful life of an intangible asset, and judgement will be needed. Consider how to determine the useful life of a *purchased* brand name and how to provide evidence that its useful life might in fact exceed 20 years.

Answer

Factors to consider would include the following.

(a) Legal protection of the brand name and the control of the entity over the (illegal) use by others of the brand name (ie control over pirating)

(b) Age of the brand name

(c) Status or position of the brand in its particular market

(d) Ability of the management of the entity to manage the brand name and to measure activities that support the brand name (eg advertising and PR activities)

(e) Stability and geographical spread of the market in which the branded products are sold

(f) Pattern of benefits that the brand name is expected to generate over time

(g) Intention of the entity to use and promote the brand name over time (as evidenced perhaps by a business plan in which there will be substantial expenditure to promote the brand name)

5.13 Disposals/retirements of intangible assets

An intangible asset should be eliminated from the statement of financial position when it is disposed of or when there is no further expected economic benefit from its future use. On disposal the gain or loss arising from the **difference between the net disposal proceeds and the carrying amount** of the asset should be taken to the income statement (profit or loss) as a gain or loss on disposal (ie treated as income or expense).

5.14 Disclosure requirements

The standard has fairly extensive disclosure requirements for intangible assets. The financial statements should disclose the **accounting policies** for intangible assets that have been adopted.

For **each class of intangible assets**, disclosure is required of the following.

- The method of amortisation used
- The useful life of the assets or the amortisation rate used
- The gross carrying amount, the accumulated amortisation and the accumulated impairment losses as at the beginning and the end of the period
- A reconciliation of the carrying amount as at the beginning and at the end of the period (additions, retirements/disposals, revaluations, impairment losses, impairment losses reversed, amortisation charge for the period, net exchange differences, other movements)
- The carrying amount of internally-generated intangible assets

The financial statements should also disclose the following.

- In the case of intangible assets that are assessed as having a indefinite useful life, the carrying amounts and the reasons supporting that assessment
- For intangible assets acquired by way of a **government grant** and initially recognised at fair value, the **fair value initially recognised**, the **carrying amount**, and whether they are carried under the **benchmark or** the **allowed alternative** treatment for subsequent remeasurements
- The carrying amount, nature and remaining amortisation period of any intangible asset that is **material to the financial statements of the entity as a whole**
- The existence (if any) and amounts of intangible assets whose **title is restricted** and of intangible assets that have been **pledged as security** for liabilities
- The amount of any **commitments for the future acquisition of intangible assets**

Where intangible assets are accounted for at revalued amounts, disclosure is required of the following.

- The **effective date of the revaluation** (by class of intangible assets)
- The **carrying amount** of revalued intangible assets
- The carrying amount that would have been shown (by class of assets) **if the cost model had been used**, and the amount of amortisation that would have been charged
- The amount of any **revaluation surplus** on intangible assets, as at the beginning and end of the period, and movements in the surplus during the year (and any restrictions on the distribution of the balance to shareholders)

The financial statements should also disclose the amount of research and development expenditure that have been charged as expenses of the period.

5.15 SIC 32 *Intangible assets – website costs*

5.15.1 The problem

Websites are used for a wide variety of business purposes, including promotion and advertising of products and services; taking orders for products or services; and selling access to information that is contained on the Website. Many companies incur significant costs in developing such Websites.

The costs of developing a Website include:

(a) **Planning costs** – including, for example, the costs of undertaking feasibility studies, determining the objectives and functionalities of the Website, exploring ways of achieving the desired functionalities, identifying appropriate hardware and Web applications and selecting suppliers and consultants.

(b) **Application and infrastructure development costs** – including the costs of obtaining and registering a domain name and of buying or developing hardware and operating software that relate to the functionality of the site (for example, updateable content management systems and e-commerce systems, including encryption software, and interfaces with other IT systems used by the entity).

(c) **Content costs** – expenditure incurred on preparing, accumulating and posting the Website content.

(d) **Operating costs**

5.15.2 SIC 32 treatment

SIC 32 concludes that a website developed by an enterprise using internal expenditure, whether for internal or external access, is an internally generated intangible asset that is subject to the requirements of IAS 38 *Intangible assets*.

Specifically, the treatment is as follows:

(a) **Website planning costs** should be charged as an expense as incurred.

(b) **Application and infrastructure development costs**. Expenditure incurred in these stages should be included in the cost of a website recognised as an intangible asset in accordance with this Interpretation when the expenditure can be directly attributed, or allocated on a reasonable and consistent basis, to preparing the website for its intended use. For example, expenditure on purchasing or creating content (other than content that advertises and promotes an enterprise's own products and services) specifically for a website, or expenditure to enable use of the content (such as a fee for acquiring a licence to reproduce) on the website, should be included in the cost of development when this condition is met. However, in accordance with IAS 38, expenditure on an intangible item that was initially recognised as an expense in previous financial statements should not be recognised as part of the cost of an intangible asset at a later date (for instance, when the costs of a copyright have been fully amortised, and the content is subsequently provided on a website).

(c) **Content Development**. Expenditure incurred in the Content Development stage, to the extent that content is developed to advertise and promote an enterprise's own products and services (such as digital photographs of products) should be recognised as an expense when incurred in accordance with IAS 38. For example, when accounting for expenditure on professional services for taking digital photographs of an enterprise's own products and for enhancing their display, expenditure should be recognised as an expense as the professional services are received during the process, not when the digital photographs are displayed on the website.

(d) **Operating**. The Operating stage begins once development of a website is complete. Expenditure incurred in this stage should be recognised as an expense when it is incurred unless it meets the criteria in IAS 38.

A website that is recognised as an intangible asset under SIC 32 should be measured after initial recognition by applying the requirements of IAS 38. The best estimate of a website's useful life should be short.

5.16 Section summary

- An intangible asset should be recognised if, and only if, it is probable that future economic benefits will flow to the entity and the cost of the asset can be measured reliably.
- An asset is initially recognised at cost and subsequently carried either at cost or revalued amount.
- Costs that do not meet the recognition criteria should be expensed as incurred.
- An intangible asset with a finite useful life should be amortised over its useful life. An intangible asset with an indefinite useful life should not be amortised.

Question

As an aid to your revision, list the examples given in IAS 38 of activities that might be included in either research or development.

Answer

IAS 38 gives these examples.

Research

- Activities aimed at obtaining new knowledge
- The search for applications of research findings or other knowledge
- The search for product or process alternatives
- The formulation and design of possible new or improved product or process alternatives

Development

- The evaluation of product or process alternatives
- The design, construction and testing of pre-production prototypes and models
- The design of tools, jigs, moulds and dies involving new technology
- The design, construction and operation of a pilot plant that is not of a scale economically feasible for commercial production

Question

Forkbender Co develops and manufactures exotic cutlery and has the following projects in hand.

	Project			
	1	2	3	4
	$'000	$'000	$'000	$'000
Deferred development Expenditure b/f 1.1.X8	280	450	–	–
Development expenditure Incurred during the year				
Salaries, wages and so on	35	–	60	20
Overhead costs	2	–	–	3
Materials and services	3	–	11	4
Patents and licences	1	–	–	–
Market research	–	–	2	–

Project 1 was originally expected to be highly profitable but this is now in doubt, since the scientist in charge of the project is now behind schedule, with the result that competitors are gaining ground.

Project 2: commercial production started during the year. Sales were 20,000 units in 20X8 and future sales are expected to be: 20X8 30,000 units; 20X9 60,000 units; 20Y0 40,000 units; 20Y1 30,000 units. There are no sales expected after 20Y1.

Project 3: these costs relate to a new project, which meets the criteria for deferral of expenditure and which is expected to last for three years.

Project 4 is another new project, involving the development of a 'loss leader', expected to raise the level of future sales.

The company's policy is to defer development costs, where permitted by IAS 38. Expenditure carried forward is written off evenly over the expected sales life of projects, starting in the first year of sale.

Required

Show how the above projects should be treated in the accounting statements of Forkbender Co for the year ended 31 December 20X8 in accordance with best accounting practice. Justify your treatment of each project.

Project 1 expenditure, including that relating to previous years, should all be written off in 20X8, as there is now considerable doubt as to the profitability of the project.

Since commercial production has started under project 2 the expenditure previously deferred should now be amortised. This will be done over the estimated life of the product, as stated in the question.

Project 3: the development costs may be deferred.

Since project 4 is not expected to be profitable its development costs should not be deferred.

STATEMENT OF FINANCIAL POSITION AS AT 31 DECEMBER 20X8 (extract)

	$'000
NON-CURRENT ASSETS	
Intangible assets	
Development costs (Note 2)	850

NOTES TO THE ACCOUNTS

1   *Accounting policies*

   Research and development

   Research and development expenditure is written off as incurred, except that development costs incurred on an individual project are carried forward when their future recoverability can be foreseen with reasonable assurance. Any expenditure carried forward is amortised over the period of sales from the related project.

2   *Development costs*

	$'000	$'000
Balance brought forward 1 January 20X8		730
Development expenditure incurred during 20X8	188	
Development expenditure amortised during 20X8	438	
		(250)
Balance carried forward 31 December 20X8		480

Note. IAS 38 would not permit the inclusion of market research in deferred development costs. Market research costs might, however, be carried forward separately under the accruals principle.

Workings

	1	2	3	4	Total
	$'000	$'000	$'000	$'000	$'000
B/F	280	450			730
Salaries etc	35		60	20	115
Overheads	2			3	5
Materials etc	3		11	4	18
Patents etc	1				1
C/F		(360)	(71)		(431)
Written off	321	90		27	438

* *Note.* An alternative basis for amortisation would be:

$$\frac{20}{180} \times 450 = 50$$

The above basis is more prudent, however, in this case.

6 Goodwill

FAST FORWARD

Impairment rules follow **IAS 36**. There are substantial disclosure requirements.

Goodwill is **created by good relationships** between a business and its customers.

(a) By building up a **reputation** (by word of mouth perhaps) for high quality products or high standards of service

(b) By **responding promptly and helpfully** to queries and complaints from customers

(c) Through the **personality of the staff** and their attitudes to customers

The value of goodwill to a business might be **extremely significant**. However, goodwill is not usually valued in the accounts of a business at all, and we should not normally expect to find an amount for goodwill in its statement of financial position. For example, the welcoming smile of the bar staff may contribute more to a bar's profits than the fact that a new electronic cash register has recently been acquired. Even so, whereas the cash register will be recorded in the accounts as a long-term asset, the value of staff would be ignored for accounting purposes.

On reflection, we might agree with this omission of goodwill from the accounts of a business.

(a) The goodwill is **inherent** in the business but it has not been paid for, and it does not have an 'objective' value. We can guess at what such goodwill is worth, but such guesswork would be a matter of individual opinion, and not based on hard facts.

(b) Goodwill **changes** from day to day. One act of bad customer relations might damage goodwill and one act of good relations might improve it. Staff with a favourable personality might retire or leave to find another job, to be replaced by staff who need time to find their feet in the job, etc. Since goodwill is continually changing in value, it cannot realistically be recorded in the accounts of the business.

6.1 Purchased goodwill

FAST FORWARD

If a business has **goodwill**, it means that the value of the business as a going concern is greater than the value of its separate tangible assets. The valuation of goodwill is extremely subjective and fluctuates constantly. For this reason, non-purchased goodwill is **not** shown as an asset in the statement of financial position.

There is one exception to the general rule that goodwill has no objective valuation. This is **when a business is sold**. People wishing to set up in business have a choice of how to do it – they can either buy their own long-term assets and inventory and set up their business from scratch, or they can buy up an existing business from a proprietor willing to sell it. When a buyer purchases an existing business, he will have to purchase not only its long-term assets and inventory (and perhaps take over its accounts payable and receivable too) but also the goodwill of the business.

Purchased goodwill is shown in the statement of financial position because it has been paid for. It has no tangible substance, and so it is an **intangible long-term asset**.

6.2 How is the value of purchased goodwill decided?

FAST FORWARD

When someone **purchases a business** as a going concern the purchaser and vendor will fix an agreed price which includes an element in respect of goodwill. The way in which goodwill is then valued is not an accounting problem, but a matter of agreement between the two parties.

When a business is sold, there is likely to be some purchased goodwill in the selling price. But **how is the amount of this purchased goodwill decided**?

This is not really a problem for accountants, who must simply record the goodwill in the accounts of the new business. The value of the goodwill is a **matter for the purchaser and seller to agree upon in fixing the purchase/sale price**. However, two methods of valuation are worth mentioning here.

(a)   The seller and buyer agree on a price **without specifically quantifying the goodwill.** The purchased goodwill will then be the difference between the price agreed and the value of the tangible assets in the books of the new business.

(b)   However, the calculation of goodwill often precedes the fixing of the purchase price and becomes a **central element of negotiation**. There are many ways of arriving at a value for goodwill and most of them are related to the profit record of the business in question.

No matter how goodwill is calculated within the total agreed purchase price, the goodwill shown by the purchaser in his accounts will be **the difference between the purchase consideration and his own valuation of the tangible net assets acquired**. If A values his tangible net assets at $40,000, goodwill is agreed at $21,000 and B agrees to pay $61,000 for the business but values the tangible net assets at only $38,000, then the goodwill in B's books will be $61,000 – $38,000 = $23,000.

6.3 IFRS 3 (revised) *Business combinations*

FAST FORWARD

Purchased goodwill is then retained in the statement of financial position as an intangible asset under the requirements of **IFRS 3**. It must then be reviewed for impairment annually.

IFRS 3 covers the accounting treatment of goodwill acquired in a business combination.

It is possible to define goodwill in different ways. The IFRS 3 definition of goodwill is different from the more traditional definition and emphasises benefits, rather than the method of calculation.

Key terms

Goodwill. An asset representing the future economic benefits arising from other assets acquired in a **business combination** that are not individually identified and separately recognised.   *(IFRS 3)*

Goodwill recognised in a business combination is **an asset** and is initially measured at **cost**. Cost is the excess of the cost of the combination over the acquirer's interest in the net fair value of the acquiree's identifiable assets, liabilities and contingent liabilities.

After initial recognition goodwill acquired in a business combination is measured **at cost less any accumulated impairment losses**. It is **not amortised**. Instead it is tested for impairment at least annually, in accordance with IAS 36 *Impairment of assets*.

6.3.1 Goodwill and non-controlling interests

The old IFRS 3 looked at goodwill from the point of view of the parent company, ie comparing, consideration transferred with the parent's share of net assets acquired.

IMPORTANT!

The revised IFRS 3 views the **group as an economic entity**. This means that it treats **all provides of equity including non-controlling interests as shareholders in the group**, even if they re not shareholders in the parent.

Thus goodwill attributed to the non-controlling interest needs to be recognised.

We will come back to this point in Chapter 12.

6.3.2 Bargain purchase

A bargain purchase arises when the net of the acquisition-date amounts of the identifiable assets acquired and the liabilities assumed exceeds the consideration transferred (see Chapter 12).

A bargain purchase might happen, for example, in a business combination that is a forced sale in which the seller is acting under compulsion. However, the recognition or measurement exceptions for particular items may also result in recognising a gain (or change the amount of a recognised gain) on a bargain purchase..

Before recognising a gain on a bargain purchase, the acquirer must reassess whether it has correctly identified all of the assets acquired and all of the liabilities assumed and must recognise any additional assets or liabilities that are identified in that review. The acquirer must then review the procedures used to measure the amounts this IFRS requires to be recognised at the acquisition date for all of the following:

(a) The identifiable assets acquired and liabilities assumed

(b) The non-controlling (formerly minority) interest in the accquiree, if any

(c) For a business combination achieved in stages, the acquirer's previously held interest in the acquiree

(d) The consideration transferred

The purpose of this review is to ensure that the measurements appropriately reflect all the available information as at the acquisition date.

Question

Characteristics of goodwill

What are the main characteristics of goodwill which distinguish it from other intangible non-current assets? To what extent do you consider that these characteristics should affect the accounting treatment of goodwill? State your reasons.

Answer

Goodwill may be distinguished from other intangible non-current assets by reference to the following characteristics.

(a) It is incapable of realisation separately from the business as a whole.

(b) Its value has no reliable or predictable relationship to any costs which may have been incurred.

(c) Its value arises from various intangible factors such as skilled employees, effective advertising or a strategic location. These indirect factors cannot be valued.

(d) The value of goodwill may fluctuate widely according to internal and external circumstances over relatively short periods of time.

(e) The assessment of the value of goodwill is highly subjective.

It could be argued that, because goodwill is so different from other intangible non-current assets it does not make sense to account for it in the same way. Thus the capitalisation and amortisation treatment would not be acceptable. Furthermore, because goodwill is so difficult to value, any valuation may be misleading, and it is best eliminated from the statement of financial position altogether. However, there are strong arguments for treating it like any other intangible non-current asset. This issue remains controversial.

Chapter Roundup

- You must learn the IASB *Framework* **definition of an asset**: a resource controlled by the entity as a result of past events and from which future economic benefits are expected to flow to the entity.

- This definition ties in closely with the definitions produced by **other standard-setters**, particularly FASB (USA) and ASB (UK).

- The definition has three important characteristics:

  - **Future economic benefit**
  - **Control (ownership)**
  - **Transaction to acquire has taken place**

- You should already be familiar with many standards relating to **non-current assets** from earlier studies. If not, go back to your earlier study material.

  - IAS 16 *Property, plant and equipment*
  - IAS 20 *Accounting for government grants and disclosure of government assistance*
  - IAS 23 *Borrowing costs*

- **IAS 36 *Impairment of assets*** covers a controversial topic and it affects goodwill as well as tangible long-term assets.

- Impairment is determined by comparing the carrying amount of the asset with its **recoverable amount**.

- The recoverable amount of an asset is the higher of the asset's **fair value less costs to sell** and **its value in use**.

- When it is not possible to calculate the recoverable amount of a single asset, then that of its **cash generating unit** should be measured instead.

- IAS 40 *Investment property* defines investment property as property **held to earn rentals or for capital appreciation** or both, rather than for:

  - Use in production or supply of goods or services
  - Sale in the ordinary course of business

- Entities can choose between:

  - A **fair value model**, with changes in fair value being measured
  - A **cost model** – the treatment most commonly used under IAS 16

- **Intangible assets** are defined by **IAS 38** as non-monetary assets without physical substance. They must be:

  - **Identifiable**
  - **Controlled** as a result of a past event
  - Able to provide **future economic benefits**

- Intangible assets should initially be measured at cost, but subsequently they can be carried at **cost or at a fair value**.

- **Internally-generated goodwill** cannot be recognised as an asset but other internally-generated assets may be, eg R & D.

- **Impairment** rules follow **IAS 36**. There are substantial disclosure requirements.

- If a business has **goodwill**, it means that the value of the business as a going concern is greater than the value of its separate tangible assets. The valuation of goodwill is extremely subjective and fluctuates constantly. For this reason, non-purchased goodwill is **not** shown as an asset in the statement of financial position.

Chapter Roundup (continued)

- When someone **purchases a business** as a going concern the purchaser and vendor will fix an agreed price which includes an element in respect of goodwill. The way in which goodwill is then valued is not an accounting problem, but a matter of agreement between the two parties.

- **Purchased goodwill** is then retained in the statement of financial position as an intangible asset under the requirements of **IFRS 3**. It must then be reviewed for impairment annually.

Quick Quiz

1   How does the IASB *Framework* define an asset?

2   How might a non-current asset be defined?

3   Define an impairment.

4   How is value in use calculated?

5   What is a cash generating unit?

6   What is the correct treatment for property being constructed for future use as investment property?

7   Investment property **must** be valued at fair value. True or false?

8   Internally generated goodwill can be recognised. *True or false*?

9   How should research and development costs be treated under IAS 38?

10 When can a revaluation surplus on intangible assets be transferred to retained earnings?

11 Over what period should an intangible asset normally be amortised?

12 How should the gain or loss on the disposal of an intangible asset be calculated?

13 Why is it unusual to record goodwill as an asset in the accounts?

14 What is purchased goodwill?

15 What method of accounting for purchased goodwill is required by IFRS 3?

16 Over what period should goodwill be amortised?

17 What treatment does IFRS 3 prescribe for a gain on a bargain purchase?

Answers to Quick Quiz

1   A resource controlled by the entity as a result of past events and from which future economic benefits are expected to flow to the entity.

2   One intended for use on a continuing basis in the company's activities.

3   A fall in the value of an asset, so that its recoverable amount is now less than its carrying value.

4   The present value of estimated future cash flows generated by the asset, including its estimated net disposal value (if any).

5   The smallest identifiable group of assets for which independent cash flows can be identified and measured.

6   Use IAS 16 until the construction is complete, then IAS 40.

7   False, it can be valued at cost or fair value.

8   False

9   • Research costs are written off as an expense as they are incurred
     • Development costs may qualify as intangible assets if the criteria in Paragraph 1.18 are met.

10   When the surplus is eventually realised.

11   Over its useful life, which may be finite or indefinite

12   The difference between the net disposal proceeds and the carrying value.

13   The value of goodwill is usually inherent in the business but does not have an 'objective' value.

14   The excess of the purchase price over the value of the net assets.

15   Cost less accumulated impairment losses.

16   Goodwill should not be amortised

17   Before recognising a gain, measurement procedures for assets and liabilities and for consideration must be reviewed.

Now try the questions below from the Exam Question Bank

Number	Level	Marks	Time
Q4	Introductory	n/a	n/a
Q5	Examination	25	45 mins
Q6	Examination	25	45 mins

4: Non-current assets │ Part B Accounting standards

Employee benefits

Topic list	Syllabus reference
1 IAS 19 *Employee benefits*	C6
2 Post-employment benefits	C6
3 Defined contribution plans	C6
4 Defined benefit plans: recognition and measurement	C6
5 Defined benefit plans: other matters	C6
6 Other issues and recent developments	C6, F2

Introduction

An increasing number of companies and other entities now provide a **pension and other employee benefits** as part of their employees' remuneration package. In view of this trend, it is important that there is standard best practice for the way in which employee benefit costs are **recognised, measured, presented and disclosed** in the sponsoring entities' accounts.

Section 6 deals with a proposed amendment to IAS 19.

Study guide

		Intellectual level
C6	**Employee benefits**	
(a)	Apply and discuss the accounting treatment of defined contribution and defined benefit plans.	3
(b)	Account for gains and losses on settlements and curtailments.	2
(c)	Account for the reporting of actuarial gains and losses.	2
(d)	Determine going concern issues arising after the reporting period.	3
F2	**Proposed changes to accounting standards**	
(a)	Identify the issues and deficiencies which have led to a proposed change to an accounting standard.	2
(b)	Apply and discuss the implications of a proposed change to an accounting standard on the performance and position of an entity	2

Exam guide

This topic will be new to you at this level. It may be examined as part of a multi-standard scenario question, or perhaps you will be asked to outline the changes proposed in the ED.

1 IAS 19 Employee benefits   12/07, 6/08

FAST FORWARD

> IAS 19 *Employee benefits* is a long and complex standard covering both short-term and long-term (post-employment) benefits. The complications arise when dealing with **post-employment benefits**.

Exam focus point

> This is a very difficult topic – employee benefit costs are inherently complex and their accounting is both **problematic and controversial**. As such this is a ripe topic for Paper 2 and is highlighted as a key topic by the examiner

IAS 19 (revised) *Employee benefits* has replaced the previous IAS 19 *Retirement benefit costs*. Note the increased scope of the new standard, which covers **all employee benefit costs**, except share-based payment, not only retirement benefit (pension) costs. Before we look at IAS 19, we should consider the nature of employee benefit costs and why there is an accounting problem which must be addressed by a standard.

1.1 The conceptual nature of employee benefit costs

When a company or other entity employs a new worker, that worker will be offered a **package of pay and benefits.** Some of these will be short-term and the employee will receive the benefit at about the same time as he or she earns it, for example basic pay, overtime etc. Other employee benefits are **deferred**, however, the main example being retirement benefits (ie a pension).

The cost of these deferred employee benefits to the employer can be viewed in various ways. They could be described as **deferred salary** to the employee. Alternatively, they are a **deduction** from the employee's true gross salary, used as a tax-efficient means of saving. In some countries, tax efficiency arises on retirement benefit contributions because they are not taxed on the employee, but they are allowed as a deduction from taxable profits of the employer.

1.2 Accounting for employee benefit costs

Accounting for **short-term employee benefit costs** tends to be quite straightforward, because they are simply recognised as an expense in the employer's financial statements of the current period.

Accounting for the cost of **deferred employee benefits** is much more difficult. This is because of the large amounts involved, as well as the long time scale, complicated estimates and uncertainties. In the past, entities accounted for these benefits simply by charging profit or loss (the income statements) of the employing entity on the basis of actual payments made. This led to substantial variations in reported profits of these entities and disclosure of information on these costs was usually sparse.

1.3 IAS 19 Employee benefits

IAS 19 is intended to prescribe the following.

(a)   When the cost of employee benefits should be **recognised as a liability or an expense**
(b)   The **amount** of the liability or expense that should be recognised

As a basic rule, the standard states the following.

(a)   A **liability** should be recognised when an employee has provided a service in exchange for benefits to be received by the employee at some time in the future.

(b)   An **expense** should be recognised when the entity enjoys the economic benefits from a service provided by an employee regardless of when the employee received or will receive the benefits from providing the service.

The basic problem is therefore fairly straightforward. An entity will often enjoy the **economic benefits** from the services provided by its employees in advance of the employees receiving all the employment benefits from the work they have done, for example they will not receive pension benefits until after they retire.

1.4 Categories of employee benefits

The standard recognises five categories of employee benefits, and proposes a different accounting treatment for each. These four categories are as follows.

1   Short-term benefits including:
   - Wages and salaries
   - Social security contributions
   - Paid annual leave
   - Paid sick leave
   - Paid maternity/paternity leave
   - Profit shares and bonuses paid within 12 months of the year end
   - Paid jury service
   - Paid military service
   - Non-monetary benefits, eg medical care, cars, free goods
2   Post-employment benefits, eg pensions and post-employment medical care
3   Other long-term benefits, eg profit shares, bonuses or deferred compensation payable later than 12 months after the year end, sabbatical leave, long-service benefits
4   Termination benefits, eg early retirement payments and redundancy payments

Benefits may be paid to the employees themselves, to their dependants (spouses, children, etc) or to third parties.

1.5 Definitions

IAS 19 uses a great many important definitions. They are grouped together here, but you should refer back to them as necessary as you work through the rest of this chapter.

Employee benefits are all forms of consideration given by an entity in exchange for service rendered by employees.

Short-term employee benefits are employee benefits (other than termination benefits) which fall due wholly within twelve months after the end of the period in which the employees render the related service.

Post-employment benefits are employee benefits (other than termination benefits) which are payable after the completion of employment.

Post-employment benefit plans are formal or informal arrangements under which an entity provides post-employment benefits for one or more employees.

Defined contribution plans are post-employment benefit plans under which an entity pays fixed contributions into a separate entity (a fund) and will have no legal or constructive obligation to pay further contributions if the fund does not hold sufficient assets to pay all employee benefits relating to employee service in the current and prior periods.

Defined benefit plans are post-employment benefit plans other than defined contribution plans.

Multi-employer plans are defined contribution plans (other than state plans) or defined benefit plans (other than state plans) that:

(a)   pool the assets contributed by various entities that are not under common control, and

(b)   use those assets to provide benefits to employees of more than one entity, on the basis that contribution and benefit levels are determined without regard to the identity of the entity that employs the employees concerned.

Other long-term employee benefits are employee benefits (other than post-employment benefits and termination benefits) which do not fall due wholly within twelve months after the end of the period in which the employees render the related service.

Termination benefits are employee benefits payable as a result of either:

(a)   an entity's decision to terminate an employee's employment before the normal retirement date, or

(b)   an employee's decision to accept voluntary redundancy in exchange for those benefits.

Vested employee benefits are employee benefits that are not conditional on future employment.

The **present value of a defined benefit** obligation is the present value, without deducting any plan assets, of expected future payments required to settle the obligation resulting from employee service in the current and prior periods.

Current service cost is the increase in the present value of the defined benefit obligation resulting from employee service in the current period.

Interest cost is the increase during a period in the present value of a defined benefit obligation which arises because the benefits are one period closer to settlement.

Plan assets comprise:

(a)   Assets held by a long-term employee benefit fund; and

(b)   Qualifying insurance policies

The **return on plan assets** is interest, dividends and other revenue derived from the plan assets, together with realised and unrealised gains or losses on the plan assets, less any cost of administering the plan and loess any tax payable by the plan itself.

Actuarial gains and losses comprise:

(a)   Experience adjustments (the effects of differences between the previous actuarial assumptions and what has actually occurred), and

(b)   The effects of changes in actuarial assumptions.

Past service cost is the change in the present value of the defined benefit obligation for employee service in prior periods, resulting in the current period from the introduction of, or changes to, post-employment benefits or other long-term employee benefits. Past service cost may be either positive (when benefits are introduced or changed so that the present value of the defined benefit obligation increases) or negative (when existing benefits are changed so that the present value of the defined benefit obligation decreases).

(IAS 19)

1.6 Asset ceiling test

The revisions to IAS 19 in May 2002 seek to prevent what the IASB regards as a 'counter-intuitive' result produced by the interaction of two aspects of the existing IAS 19.

(a)   Permission to defer recognition of actuarial gains and losses
(b)   Imposition of an upper limit on the amount that can be recognised as an asset (the asset ceiling)

The issue affects only those entities that have, at the beginning or end of the accounting period, a surplus in a defined benefit plan that, based on the current terms of the plan, the entity cannot fully recover through refunds or reductions in future contributions.

The issue is the impact of the wording of the asset ceiling.

(a)   Sometimes a gain is recognised when a pension plan is in surplus only because of the deferring and amortising of an actuarial loss or added past service cost in the current period.
(b)   Conversely, a loss may be recognised because of a deferral of actuarial gains.

The revisions to IAS 19 introduces a limited amendment that would prevent gains (losses) from being recognised solely as a result of past service cost or actuarial losses (gains) arising in the period. No change is currently proposed to the general approach of allowing deferral of actuarial gains and losses. During its deliberations on the amendments to IAS 19, the IASB concluded that there were further conceptual and practical problems with these provisions. The IASB intends to conduct a comprehensive review of these aspects of IAS 19 as part of its work on convergence of accounting standards across the world.

1.7 Section summary

There are **two key issues** or problems to consider.

*   It may be necessary to rely on **actuarial assumptions** about what the future amount of benefits payable will be.
*   If benefits are payable later than 12 months after the end of the accounting period, the future benefits payable should be **discounted** to a present value.

2 Post-employment benefits

There are two types of post-employment benefit plan:

*   Defined contribution plans
*   Defined benefit plans

Defined contribution plans are simple to account for as the benefits are defined by the contributions made.

Defined benefit plans are much more difficult to deal with as the benefits are promised, they define the contributions to be made.

Many employers provide post-employment benefits for their employees after they have stopped working. **Pension schemes** are the most obvious example, but an employer might provide post-employment death benefits to the dependants of former employees, or post-employment medical care.

Post-employment benefit schemes are often referred to as '**plans**'. The 'plan' receives regular contributions from the employer (and sometimes from current employees as well) and the money is invested in assets, such as stocks and shares and other investments. The post-employment benefits are paid out of the income from the plan assets (dividends, interest) or from money from the sale of some plan assets.

There are two types or categories of post-employment benefit plan, as given in the definitions in Section 1 above.

(a)   **Defined contribution plans**. With such plans, the employer (and possibly current employees too) pay regular contributions into the plan of a given or 'defined' amount each year. The contributions are invested, and the size of the post-employment benefits paid to former employees depends on how well or how badly the plan's investments perform. If the investments perform well, the plan will be able to afford higher benefits than if the investments performed less well.

(b) **Defined benefit plans**. With these plans, the size of the post-employment benefits is determined in advance, ie the benefits are 'defined'. The employer (and possibly current employees too) pay contributions into the plan, and the contributions are invested. The size of the contributions is set at an amount that is expected to earn enough investment returns to meet the obligation to pay the post-employment benefits. If, however, it becomes apparent that the assets in the fund are insufficient, the employer will be required to make additional contributions into the plan to make up the expected shortfall. On the other hand, if the fund's assets appear to be larger than they need to be, and in excess of what is required to pay the post-employment benefits, the employer may be allowed to take a 'contribution holiday' (ie stop paying in contributions for a while).

It is important to make a clear distinction between the following.

(a) **Funding** a defined benefit plan, ie paying contributions into the plan
(b) **Accounting for** the cost of funding a defined benefit plan

Before we examine accounting for both these types of scheme, we need to mention a couple of other issues addressed by the standard.

2.1 Multi-employer plans

These were defined above. IAS 19 requires an entity to **classify** such a plan as a defined contribution plan or a defined benefit plan, depending on its terms (including any constructive obligation beyond those terms).

For a multi-employer plan that is a **defined benefit plan**, the entity should account for its proportionate share of the defined benefit obligation, plan assets and cost associated with the plan in the same way as for any other defined benefit plan and make full disclosure.

When there is **insufficient information** to use defined benefit accounting, then the multi-employer plan should be accounted for as a defined contribution plan and additional disclosures made (that the plan is in fact a defined benefit plan and information about any known surplus or deficit).

2.2 Section summary

- There are two categories of **post-retirement benefits**:
  - Defined contribution schemes
  - Defined benefit schemes
- **Defined contribution schemes** provide benefits commensurate with the fund available to produce them.
- **Defined benefit schemes** provide promised benefits and so contributions are based on estimates of how the fund will perform.
- **Defined contribution scheme costs** are easy to account for and this is covered in the next section.
- The rest of the chapter deals with the more difficult question of how **defined benefit scheme costs** are accounted for.

3 Defined contribution plans

Accounting for payments into defined contribution plans is straightforward.

(a) The **obligation** is determined by the amount paid into the plan in each period.
(b) There are no actuarial assumptions to make.
(c) If the obligation is settled in the current period (or at least no later than 12 months after the end of the current period) there is **no requirement for discounting**.

IAS 19 requires the following.

(a) **Contributions** to a defined contribution plan should be recognised as an **expense** in the period they are payable (except to the extent that labour costs may be included within the cost of assets).

(b) Any liability for **unpaid contributions** that are due as at the end of the period should be recognised as a **liability** (accrued expense).

(c) Any **excess contributions** paid should be recognised as an asset (prepaid expense), but only to the extent that the prepayment will lead to, eg a reduction in future payments or a cash refund.

In the (unusual) situation where contributions to a defined contribution plan do not fall due entirely within 12 months after the end of the period in which the employees performed the related service, then these should be **discounted**. The discount rate to be used is discussed below in Paragraphs 5.22 and 5.23.

Disclosure requirements

(a) A **description** of the plan
(b) The amount recognised as an **expense** in the period

4 Defined benefit plans: recognition and measurement

Accounting for defined benefit plans is much more complex. The complexity of accounting for defined benefit plans stems largely from the following factors.

(a) The future benefits (arising from employee service in the current or prior years) **cannot be estimated exactly**, but whatever they are, the employer will have to pay them, and the liability should therefore be recognised now. To estimate these future obligations, it is necessary to use **actuarial assumptions**.

(b) The obligations payable in future years should be valued, by discounting, on a **present value** basis. This is because the obligations may be settled in many years' time.

(c) If actuarial assumptions change, the amount of required contributions to the fund will change, and there may be **actuarial gains or losses**. A contribution into a fund in any period is not necessarily the total for that period, due to actuarial gains or losses.

Most of the definitions given in the standard (shown in Section 1) are to do with defined benefit plans.

4.1 Outline of the method

There is a **six-step method** for accounting for the expenses and liability of a defined benefit pension plan.

An outline of the method used for an employer to account for the expenses and obligation of a defined benefit plan is given below. The stages will be explained in more detail later.

Step 1 **Actuarial assumptions** should be used to make a reliable estimate of the amount of future benefits employees have earned from service in relation to the current and prior years. Assumptions include, for example, assumptions about employee turnover, mortality rates, future increases in salaries (if these will affect the eventual size of future benefits such as pension payments).

Step 2 These **future benefits** should be attributed to service performed by employees in the current period, and in prior periods, using the **Projected Unit Credit Method**. This gives a total present value of future benefit obligations arising from past and current periods of service.

Step 3 The **fair value** of any plan assets should be established.

Step 4 The size of any **actuarial gains or losses** should be determined, and the amount of these that will be recognised.

Step 5 If the benefits payable under the plan have been improved, the **extra cost arising from past service** should be determined.

Step 6   If the **benefits payable** under the plan have been reduced or cancelled, the resulting gain should be determined.

4.2 Constructive obligation

IAS 19 makes it very clear that it is not only its legal obligation under the formal terms of a defined benefit plan that an entity must account for, but also for any **constructive obligation** that it may have. A constructive obligation, which will arise from the entity's informal practices, exist when the entity has no realistic alternative but to pay employee benefits, for example if any change in the informal practices would cause unacceptable damage to employee relationships.

4.3 The Projected Unit Credit Method

With this method, it is assumed that each period of service by an employee gives rise to an **additional unit of future benefits**. The present value of that unit of future benefits can be calculated, and attributed to the period in which the service is given. The units, each measured separately, build up to the overall obligation. The accumulated present value of (discounted) future benefits will incur interest over time, and an interest expense should be recognised.

In practice, the mathematics will be complex and you will not need to go into the detail in the exam.

4.4 Interest cost

The interest cost in the statement of comprehensive income is the **present value of the defined benefit obligation** as at the start of the year multiplied by the discount rate.

Note that the interest charge is *not* the opening statement of financial position liability multiplied by the discount rate, because the liability is stated after deducting the market value of the plan assets and after making certain other adjustments, for example for actuarial gains or losses. Interest is the **obligation** multiplied by the discount rate.

4.5 The statement of financial position

In the statement of financial position, the amount recognised as a **defined benefit liability** (which may be a negative amount, ie an asset) should be the total of the following.

(a)   The **present value of the defined obligation** at the year end, **plus**

(b)   Any **actuarial gains** or minus any **actuarial losses** that have not yet been recognised, **minus**

(c)   Any **past service cost** not yet recognised (if any), **minus**

(d)   The **fair value of the assets of the plan** as at the year end (if there are any) out of which the future obligations to current and past employees will be directly settled

If this total is a **negative amount**, there is an asset in the position statement asset and this should be shown in the balance sheet as the **lower** of (a) and (b) below.

(a)   The figure as calculated above

(b)   The total of the present values of:

(i)   Any unrecognised actuarial losses and past service costs

(ii)   Any refunds expected from the plan

(iii) Any reductions in future contributions to the plan because of the surplus

The determination of a discount rate is covered below.

4.6 The statement of comprehensive income

The **expense** that should be recognised in the statement of comprehensive income (in profit or loss for the year) for post-employment benefits in a defined benefit plan is the total of the following.

(a)   The current service cost

(b) Interest
(c) The expected return on any plan assets
(d) The actuarial gains or losses, to the extent that they are recognised
(e) Past service cost to the extent that it is recognised
(f) The effect of any curtailments or settlements

4.7 Attributing benefit to periods of service

Consider a situation where a defined benefit plan provides for annual pension for former employees on retirement. The size of the pension is 2.5% of the employee's salary in his/her final year, for each full year of service. The pension is payable from the age of 65.

The post-employment benefit for each employee is an annual pension of 2.5% of his/her final year's salary for every full year of service. This annual payment obligation should first be converted to a present 'lump sum' value *as at the retirement date*, using actuarial assumptions. Having established an obligation as at the expected retirement date, the **current service cost** is calculated as the present value of that obligation, ie the present value of monthly pension payments of 2.5% of final salary, multiplied by the number of years of service up to the current year end.

For example, if an employee is expected to earn $10,000 in his final year of employment, and is expected to live for 15 years after retirement, the benefit payable for each year of employment would be calculated as the discounted value, as at retirement date, of $250 per annum for 15 years. This should then be converted to a present value (as at the year end) to determine the current service cost for the year for that employee.

4.8 Probabilities

Probabilities should be taken into consideration in the calculations. Suppose that a benefit of $1,000 for every year of service is payable to employees when they retire at the age of 60, provided that they remain with the employer until they retire (ie that they don't leave to work for someone else). Suppose also that an employee joins the firm at the age of 40, with 20 years to work to retirement.

The benefit attributable to each year of service is $1,000 **multiplied by the probability** that the employee will remain with the employer until he/she is 60. Since the benefit is payable at retirement as a lump sum, it should be discounted to a present value as at the year end to determine the current service cost for a given year. The obligation should be calculated as the present value of $40,000 (40 years × $1,000) **multiplied by the same probability**.

No added obligations arise **after all significant post-employment benefits have vested**; in other words, no extra post-benefit obligations arise after an employee has already done everything necessary to qualify in full for the post-employment benefit. Suppose for example that employees have an entitlement to a lump sum payment on retirement of $2,000 for every year they have worked, up to a maximum of 10 years, ie a maximum lump sum payment of $20,000. The benefit vests after 10 years.

In accounting for this **lump sum benefit on retirement**, a benefit of $2,000 should be attributed to each of the first ten years of an employee's service. The current service cost in each of the ten years should be the present value of $2,000. If an employee has 25 years to go to retirement from the time he/she joins the firm, there should be a service cost in each of the first ten years, and none in the 15 years thereafter (other than the interest cost on the obligation).

Question	Service periods

Under Hibbo Co's plan, all employees are paid a lump sum retirement benefit of $100,000. They must be still employed aged 55 after 20 years' service, *or* still employed at the age of 65, no matter what their length of service.

Required

State how this benefit should be attributed to service periods.

This answer is in three parts.

(a) In the case of those employees joining before age 35, service first leads to benefits under this plan at the age of 35, because an employee could leave at the age of 30 and return at the age of 33, with no effect on the amount/timing of benefits. In addition, service beyond age 55 will lead to no further benefits. Therefore, for these employees Hibbo Co should allocate $100,000 ÷ 20 = $5,000 to each year between the ages of 35 and 55.

(b) In the case of employees joining between the ages of 35 and 45, service beyond 20 years will lead to no further benefit. For these employees, Hibbo Co should allocate $100,000 ÷ 20 = $5,000 to each of the first 20 years.

(c) Employees joining at 55 exactly will receive no further benefit past 65, so Hibbo Co should allocate $100,000 ÷ 10 = $10,000 to each of the first 10 years.

The current service cost and the present value of the obligation for all employees reflect the probability that the employee may not complete the necessary period of service.

4.9 Actuarial assumptions

Actuarial assumptions made should be unbiased and based on market expectations.

Discount rates used should be determined by reference to market yields on high-quality fixed-rate corporate bonds.

Actuarial assumptions are needed **to estimate the size of the future (post-employment) benefits** that will be payable under a defined benefits scheme. The main categories of actuarial assumptions are as follows.

(a) **Demographic assumptions** are about mortality rates before and after retirement, the rate of employee turnover, early retirement, claim rates under medical plans for former employees, and so on.

(b) **Financial assumptions** are the discount rate to apply, the expected return on plan assets, future salary levels (allowing for seniority and promotion as well as inflation) and the future rate of increase in medical costs (not just inflationary cost rises, but also cost rises specific to medical treatments and to medical treatments required given the expectations of longer average life expectancy).

The standard requires actuarial assumptions to be neither too cautious nor too imprudent: they should be **'unbiased'**. They should also be based on **'market expectations'** at the year end, over the period during which the obligations will be settled.

The **discount rate** adopted should be determined by reference to **market yields** (at the year end) on high quality fixed-rate corporate bonds. In the absence of a 'deep' market in such bonds, the yields on comparable government bonds should be used as reference instead. The maturity of the corporate bonds that are used to determine a discount rate should have a term to maturity that is consistent with the expected maturity of the post-employment benefit obligations, although a single weighted average discount rate is sufficient.

The guidelines comment that there may be some difficulty in obtaining a **reliable yield for long-term maturities**, say 30 or 40 years from now. This should not, however, be a significant problem: the present value of obligations payable in many years time will be relatively small and unlikely to be a significant proportion of the total defined benefit obligation. The total obligation is therefore unlikely to be sensitive to errors in the assumption about the discount rate for long-term maturities (beyond the maturities of long-term corporate or government bonds).

4.10 Actuarial gains or losses

Actuarial gains and losses arise for several reasons, but IAS 19 requires only a portion to be recognised, to avoid volatility in the accounts.

Actuarial gains or losses arise because of the following.

- **Actual events** (eg employee turnover, salary increases) differ from the actuarial assumptions that were made to estimate the defined benefit obligations.
- **Actuarial assumptions are revised** (eg a different discount rate is used, or a different assumption is made about future employee turnover, salary rises, mortality rates, and so on)
- **Actual returns on plan assets** differ from expected returns

Since actuarial assumptions are rarely going to be exact, some actuarial gains or losses are inevitable. The proposed standard suggests that, given the inevitability of actuarial gains or losses, they **should not be recognised unless they appear 'significant'**. They are not sufficient to warrant recognition if they fall within a tolerable range or 'corridor'.

The standard requires the following.

(a) An entity should, as a **general rule**, recognise actuarial gains and losses as an item of income or expense (in profit or loss), and as part of the deferred benefit liability (statement of financial position).

(b) However, only a portion of such actuarial gains or losses (as calculated above) should be recognised if the **net cumulative actuarial gains/losses exceed** the *greater* of:

    (i) 10% of the present value of the defined benefit obligation (ie before deducting plan assets), and

    (ii) 10% of the fair value of the plan assets.

A separate calculation should be made for each defined benefit plan: two or more plans should not be aggregated.

The excess calculated under Paragraph 4.10(b) should be **divided by the expected average remaining working lives of participating employees** and this gives the portion of actuarial gains and losses to be recognised.

IAS 19 allows, however, any systematic method to be adopted if it results in **faster recognition** of actuarial gains and losses. The same basis must be applied to both gains and losses and applied consistently between periods.

4.10.1 Immediate recognition – amendment to IAS 19

In December 2004, the IASB issued an amendment to IAS 19. This allows an entity to **recognise actuarial gains and losses immediately** in the period in which it arises, outside profit and loss. These gains and losses need to be presented in the **'other comprehensive income'** section of the statement of comprehensive income. If the entity adopts this approach, it must do so:

- For all of its defined benefits plans
- For all of its actuarial gains and losses

This makes IAS 19 more convergent with the UK standard, FRS 17.

In addition, the amendment requires **improved disclosures**, including many also required by FRS 17, and slightly eases the methods whereby the amounts recognised in the consolidated financial statements have to be allocated to individual group companies for the purposes of their own reporting under IFRSs.

4.11 Past service cost

A past service cost arises when an entity either introduces a defined benefits plan or **improves the benefits payable** under an existing plan. As a result, the entity has taken on additional obligations that it has not hitherto provided for. For example, an employer might decide to introduce a medical benefits scheme for former employees. This will create a new defined benefit obligation, that has not yet been provided for. How should this obligation be accounted for?

A past service cost may be in respect of either **current employees or past employees**. IAS 19 has introduced a different accounting treatment for past service costs, according to whether they relate to **current employees or past employees**.

(a) For **current employees**, the past service cost should be recognised as part of the defined benefit liability in the statement of financial position. For the statement of comprehensive income, the past service cost should be amortised on a straight line basis over the average period until the benefits become vested.

(b) For **past employees** (if the change affects them) the past service cost should be recognised in full immediately the plan is introduced or improved (ie because they are immediately 'vested'), as part of the defined benefit liability and as an expense (in full) to the financial period.

Question   Past service costs

Watkins Co operates a pension plan that provides a pension of 2% of final salary for every year of service and the benefits become vested after five years' service. On 1 January 20X6 Watkins Co improved the pension to 2.5% of final salary for every year of service starting from 1 January 20X2.

At the date of improvement, the present value of the additional benefits for service from 1 January 20X2 to 1 January 20X6 is as follows.

	$m
Employees with more than 5 years' service at 1/11/X6	300
Employees with less than 5 years' service at 1/11/X6 (average period until vesting = 3 years)	240
	540

Required

State the correct accounting treatment for past service costs.

Answer

Watkins Co should recognise $300m immediately, because these benefits are already vested. $240m should be recognised on a straight-line basis over three years from 1 January 20X6.

4.12 Plan assets

The contributions into a plan by the employer (and employees) are invested, and the plan builds up assets in the form of stocks and shares, etc. The **fair value of these plan assets** are deducted from the defined benefits obligation, in calculating the liability in the statement of financial position. This makes sense, because the employer is not liable to the defined benefits scheme to the extent that the assets of the fund are sufficient to meet those obligations.

The standard includes the following specific requirements.

(a) The fair value of the plan assets should be **net of any transaction costs** that would be incurred in selling them.

(b) The plan assets should **exclude any contributions due** from the employer but not yet paid.

4.13 Return on plan assets

FAST FORWARD

The difference between the expected return and actual return on plan assets must be calculated.

It is also necessary to recognise the distinction between:

(a) the **expected return** on the plan assets, which is an actuarial assumption, and

(b) the **actual return** made by the plan assets in a financial period.

The **expected return** on the plan assets is a component element in the income statement (in profit or loss), not the actual returns. The **difference between the expected return and the actual return** may also be included in profit or loss, but within the actuarial gains or losses. This difference will only be reported if the actuarial gains or losses are outside the 10% corridor for these gains or losses, otherwise they will not be included in the expense item because they are not regarded as significant.

4.14 Example: plan assets

At 1 January 20X2 the fair value of the assets of a defined benefit plan were valued at $1m. Net cumulative actuarial gains and losses were $76,000.

On 31 December 20X2, the plan received contributions from the employer of $490,000 and paid out benefits of $190,000.

After these transactions, the fair value of the plan's assets at 31 December 20X2 were $1.5m. The present value of the defined benefit obligation was $1,479,200 and actuarial losses on the obligation for 20X2 were $6,000.

The expected return on the plan assets (net of investment transaction costs) is 8% per annum.

The reporting entity made the following estimates at 1 January 20X2, based on market prices at that date.

	%
Dividend/interest income (after tax payable by fund)	9.25
Realised and unrealised gains (after tax) on plan assets	2.00
Administration costs	(1.00)
	10.25

Required

Calculate the expected and actual return on plan assets, calculate any actuarial gain or loss and state the required accounting.

Solution

The expected and actual return for 20X2 are as follows.

	$
Return on $1m held for 12 months at 10.25%	102,500
Return on $(490,000 – 190,000) = $300,000	
for 6 months at 5% (ie 10.25% annually	
compounded every 6 months)	15,000
Expected return on plan assets	117,500

	$
Fair value of plan assets at 31/12/X2	1,500,000
Less fair value of plan assets at 1/1/X2	(1,000,000)
Less contributions received	(490,000)
Add benefits paid	190,000
Actual return on plan assets	200,000

Actuarial gain = $(200,000 – 117,500) = $82,500.

∴ Cumulative net unrecognised actuarial gains = $(76,000 + 82,500 – 6,000) = $152,500.

The limits of the corridor are set at the *greater* of:

(a)   10% × $1m = $100,000, and
(b)   10% × $1.5m = $150,000.

In 20X3 the entity should recognise an actuarial gain of $(152,500 – 150,000) = $2,500, divided by the expected average remaining working life of the relevant employees.

For 20X3, the expected return on plan assets will be based on market expectations at 1/1/X3 for returns over the entire life of the obligation.

The following accounting treatment is required.

(a)   In the **statement of comprehensive income**, an expected return on fund assets of $117,500 will be recognised, together with an actuarial gain of $2,500 divided by the expected average remaining useful life of the employees.

(b)   In the **statement of financial position**, the defined benefit liability will adjust the defined benefit obligation as at 31 December 20X2. The unrecognised actuarial gain (ie the gain within the 10% corridor) should be added, and the market value of the plan assets as at that date should be subtracted.

4.15 Section summary

The recognition and measurement of defined benefit plan costs are complex issues.

- Learn the **outline method** of accounting (see Paragraph 4.1)
- Learn the calculations for the **Projected Unit Credit Method**
- Learn the recognition method for the:
  - Statement of financial position
  - Statement of comprehensive income

5 Defined benefit plans: other matters

This section looks at the presentation and disclosure of defined benefit plans, but we begin here by looking at the special circumstances of curtailment and settlements.

5.1 Curtailments and settlements

You should know how to deal with **curtailments** and **settlements**.

A **curtailment** occurs when an entity cuts back on the benefits available under a defined benefit scheme, so that there is either a significant reduction in the number of employees eligible for the post-employment benefits (eg because a large number of staff have been made redundant due to a plant closure), or there is a reduction in the post-employment benefits that will be given for the future service of current employees.

A **settlement** occurs either when an employer pays off its post-employment benefit obligations in exchange for making a lump sum payment, or when an employer reduces the size of post-employment benefits payable in the future in respect of **past service**.

A curtailment and settlement might **happen together**, for example when an employer brings a defined benefit plan to an end by settling the obligation with a one-off lump sum payment and then scrapping the plan.

Gains or losses arising from the curtailment or settlement of a defined benefit plan should be **recognised in full in the financial year that they occur**. These gains or losses will comprise the following.

- Any **change in the present value of the future obligations** of the entity as a result of the curtailment or settlement
- Any **change in the fair value of the plan assets** as a consequence of the curtailment or settlement
- Any related **actuarial gains/losses** and **past service cost** that had not previously been recognised

An entity should **remeasure the obligation** (and the related plan assets, if any) using current actuarial assumptions, before determining the effect of a curtailment or settlement.

Hewsan Co discontinues a business segment. Employees of the discontinued segment will earn no further benefits (ie this is a curtailment without a settlement). Using current actuarial assumptions (including current market interest rates and other current market prices) immediately before the curtailment, the Hewsan Co had a defined benefit obligation with a net present value of $500,000, plan assets with a fair value of $410,000 and net cumulative unrecognised actuarial gains of $25,000. The entity had first adopted IAS 19 (revised) one year later. This increased the net liability by $50,000, which the entity chose to recognise over five years (this is permitted under the transitional provisions: see below).

Required

Show the required treatment for the curtailment.

Answer

Of the previously unrecognised actuarial gains and transitional amounts, 10% ($50,000/$500,000) relates to the part of the obligation that was eliminated through the curtailment. Therefore, the effect of the curtailment is as follows.

	Before Curtailment	*Curtailment gain*	*After curtailment*
	$'000	*$'000*	*$'000*
Net present value of obligation	500.0	(50.0)	450.0
Fair value of plan assets	(410.0)	–	(410.0)
	90.0	(50.0)	40.0
Unrecognised actuarial gains	25.0	(2.5)	22.5
Unrecognised transitional amount ($50,000 × 4/5)	(40.0)	4.0	(36.0)
Net liability recognised in statement of financial position	75.0	(43.5)	26.5

5.2 Suggested approach and questions

The suggested approach to defined benefit schemes is to deal with the change in the obligation and asset in the following order, building up the disclosure notes:

Step	Item	Recognition	
1	**Record opening figures:** • asset • obligation • any unrecognised gains and losses		
2	**Interest cost** • Based on discount rate and PV obligation at start of period. • Should also reflect any changes in obligation during period.	DEBIT CREDIT	*Interest cost (I/S)* *(x% × b/d obligation)* *PV defined benefit obligation (B/S)*

Step	Item	Recognition	
3	**Expected return on plan assets** • Based on long-term expectations as advised by actuary and asset value at start of period. • Technically, the expected return is also time apportioned on contributions less benefits paid in the period.	DEBIT CREDIT	*Plan assets (B/S)* *Exp'd return on plan assets (I/S)* *(y% × b/d assets)*
4	**Current service cost** • Increase in the present value of the obligation resulting from employee service in the current period.	DEBIT CREDIT	*Current service cost (I/S)* *PV defined benefit obligation (B/S)*
5	**Contributions** • As advised by actuary.	DEBIT CREDIT	*Plan assets (B/S)* *Company cash*
6	**Benefits** • Actual pension payments made.	DEBIT CREDIT	*PV defined benefit obligation (B/S)* *Plan assets (B/S)*
7	**Past service cost** • Increase in PV obligation as a result of introduction or improvement of benefits. • Past service cost is *vested* when any minimum employment period has been completed.	**Vested benefits:** DEBIT *Past service cost (I/S)* CREDIT *PV defined benefit obligation (B/S)* **Non-vested benefits:** DEBIT *Unrecognised past service cost (B/S)* CREDIT *PV defined benefit obligation (B/S)* The unrecognised past service cost is amortised through profit or loss straight line over the average period until the minimum employment period is completed.	
8	**Actuarial gains and losses** • Arising from annual valuations of obligation and asset. • On obligation, differences between actuarial assumptions and actual experience during the period, or changes in actuarial assumptions. • On assets, differences between expected and actual return.	(a) *(only If using corridor approach):* recognise unrecognised gains/losses b/d outside 10% corridor in profit or loss over average remaining working lives of employees. (b) Calculate carried down actuarial gains/losses from statement of financial position workings. Recognise in: – Unrecognised gains/losses, *or* – Profit or loss directly, *or* – Retained earnings directly according to accounting policy.	
9	**Disclose in accordance with the standard**	See comprehensive question.	

 Question

During the year ended 30 November 20X3, the directors of Pole decided to form a defined benefit pension scheme for the employees of the company and contributed cash of $160 million to it. The following details relate to the scheme at 30 November 20X3:

	$m
Present value of obligation	208
Fair value of plan assets	200
Current service cost	176
Interest cost – scheme liabilities	32
Expected return on pension scheme assets	16

The only entry in the financial statements made to date is in respect of the cash contribution which has been included in trade receivables. The directors have been uncertain as to how to deal with the above pension scheme in the consolidated financial statements because of the significance of the potential increase in the charge to profit or loss (in the income statements) relating to the pension scheme. They wish to recognise any actuarial gain immediately.

Required

Show how the defined benefit pension scheme should be dealt with in the financial statements for the year ended 30 November 20X3.

Answer

The defined benefit pension scheme is treated in accordance with IAS 19 Employee benefits.

The pension scheme has a deficit of liabilities over assets:

	$m
Fair value of plan assets	200
Less: present value of obligation	(208)
	(8)

The deficit is reported as a liability in the statement of financial position.

The statement of comprehensive income for the year includes:

	$m
Current service cost	176
Interest cost	32
Expected return on plan assets	(16)
	192

The company proposes to recognise the $24,000,000 actuarial gain, although under IAS 19 it is not required to do so. IAS 19 requires actuarial gains and losses at the end of the previous accounting period to be recognised using the '10% corridor approach'. Alternatively, they may be recognised more quickly, or immediately. There were no actuarial gains or losses at the start of the current period.

However, recognising the gain provides useful information to users of the financial statements, given that the pension scheme is new and results in a significant additional charge to profit or loss. Under IAS 19 an actuarial gain cannot be recognised in profit or loss, but must be taken to equity (reserves). The statement of changes in equity for the year includes:

	$m
Actuarial gain on defined benefit pension scheme assets	24

Adjustment to the financial statements:

DEBIT	Retained earnings	$168 million
CREDIT	Receivables	$160 million
CREDIT	Defined benefit pension scheme liability	$8 million

Working

	$m
Scheme assets:	
Contributions paid	160
Expected return on plan assets	16
Actuarial gain (balancing figure)	24
Fair value of plan assets	200
Scheme liabilities:	
Current service cost	176
Interest cost	32
Present value of obligation	208
Net pension liability	5

> It would be useful for you to do one last question on accounting for post employment defined benefit schemes. Questions on these are likely in the exam.

Question

Comprehensive

For the sake of simplicity and clarity, all transactions are assumed to occur at the year end.

The following data applies to the post employment defined benefit compensation scheme of an entity.

Expected return on plan assets: 12% (each year)
Discount rate: 10% (each year)
Present value of obligation at start of 20X2: $1m
Market value of plan assets at start of 20X2: $1m

The following figures are relevant.

	20X2	20X3	20X4
	$'000	$'000	$'000
Current service cost	140	150	150
Benefits paid out	120	140	150
Contributions paid by entity	110	120	120
Present value of obligation at year end	1,200	1,600	1,700
Market value of plan assets at year end	1,250	1,450	1,610

Required

Show how the reporting entity should account for this defined benefit plan in each of years 20X2, 20X3 and 20X4. Actuarial gains and losses outside the 10% corridor are to be recognised in full in profit or loss for the year.

Answer

The actuarial gain or loss is established as a balancing figure in the calculations, as follows.

Present value of obligation

	20X2	20X3	20X4
	$'000	$'000	$'000
PV of obligation at start of year	1,000	1,200	1,600
Interest cost (10%)	100	120	160
Current service cost	140	150	150
Benefits paid	(120)	(140)	(150)
Actuarial (gain)/loss on obligation: balancing figure	80	270	(60)
PV of obligation at end of year	1,200	1,600	1,700

Market value of plan assets

	20X2	20X3	20X4
	$'000	$'000	$'000
Market value of plan assets at start of year	1,000	1,250	1,450
Expected return on plan assets (12%)	120	150	174
Contributions	110	120	120
Benefits paid	(120)	(140)	(150)
Actuarial gain/(loss) on plan assets: balancing figure	140	70	16
Market value of plan assets at year end	1,250	1,450	1,610

10% corridor

The next step is to determine whether the actuarial gains or losses exceed the tolerance limit of the 10% corridor. The 10% limit is 10% of the higher amount of the PV of the **opening obligation** (before deducting the plan assets) and the **opening plan assets**.

	20X2 $'000	20X3 $'000	20X4 $'000
Limit of corridor	100	125	160
Unrecognised actuarial gains/(losses) b/fwd	–	60	(140)
Actuarial gain/(loss) for year: obligation	(80)	(270)	60
Actuarial gain/(loss) for year: plan assets	140	70	16
Sub-total	60	(140)	(64)
Actuarial gain/(loss) realised	–	–	–
Unrecognised actuarial gains/(losses) c/fwd	60	(140)	(64)

The actuarial loss recognised in 20X2 is nil. This is because the figure for the cumulative unrecognised actual gains/losses at the start of 20X2 is nil. This is less than the corridor limit of $100,000.

Similarly, the actuarial loss recognised in 20X3 is nil. This is because the figure for cumulative unrecognised actuarial gains brought forward at the **beginning** of the year of $60,000 is less than the corridor limit of $125,000.

In the statement of financial position, the liability that is recognised is calculated as follows.

	20X2 $'000	20X3 $'000	20X4 $'000
Present value of obligation	1,200	1,600	1,700
Market value of plan assets	1,250	1,450	1,610
	(50)	150	90
Unrecognised actuarial gains/(losses)	60	(140)	(64)
Liability/(asset) in statement of financial position	10	10	26

The following will be recognised in profit or loss for the year:

	20X2 $'000	20X3 $'000	20X4 $'000
Current service cost	140	150	150
Interest cost	100	120	160
Expected return on plan assets	(120)	(150)	(174)
Net actuarial (gain)/loss recognised in the year		15	
Expense recognised in profit or loss	120	135	136

6 Other issues and recent developments

6.1 Problems with IAS 19

Accounting for employee benefits, particularly retirement benefits, has been seen as **problematic** in the following respects:

(a) **Income statement (statement of comprehensive income) treatment.** It has been argued that the complexity of the presentation makes the treatment hard to understand and the splitting up of the various components is arbitrary.

(b) **Fair value and volatility.** The fair value of plan assets may be volatile, and values in the statement of financial position may fluctuate. However, not all those fluctuations are recognised in the statement of financial position.

(c) **Fair value and economic reality.** Fair value, normally market value, is used to value plan assets. This may not reflect economic reality, because fair values fluctuate in the short term, while pension scheme assets and liabilities are held for the long term. It could be argued that plan assets should be valued on an actuarial basis instead.

(d) **Problems in determining the discount rate used in measuring the defined benefit obligation.** Guidance is contradictory.

> An ED contains proposals on termination benefits, and a recent Discussion Paper proposes improvements to accounting for employee benefits.

An Exposure Draft issued in June 2005 proposes amendments to IAS 19.

Key term

> **Termination benefits** are defined as employee benefits provided in connection with the termination of an employee's employment. 'Involuntary' termination benefits arise from an entity's decision to terminate an employee's employment, whereas 'voluntary' termination benefits arise from an employee's decision to accept voluntary termination.

6.2 ED proposals

(a) Termination benefits are to be defined as employee benefits provided **in connection with the termination of an employee's employment**.

(b) Termination benefits may be **either 'involuntary'** (provided as a result of an entity's decision to terminate an employee's employment) **or 'voluntary'** (offered for a short period of time in exchange for an employee's decision to accept voluntary termination).

(c) Benefits offered to encourage employees to leave service early are voluntary termination benefits **only if they are offered for a short period.**

(d) **A liability and expense** for **voluntary** termination benefits should be **recognised** when the **employee accepts the entity's offer** to those termination benefits.

(e) A liability and expense **for involuntary termination benefits**, except where provided in exchange for the employees' future services, should be **recognised when the entity has a plan of termination that it has communicated to the employees** and the plan meets the criteria specified in the Standard.

(f) **Involuntary termination benefits** are provided in exchange for employees' future services if they:

   (i) Are **incremental** to what the employees would otherwise be entitled to receive (ie benefits are not provided in accordance with the terms of an ongoing benefit plan)

   (ii) Do not **vest** until the employment is **terminated**

   (iii) Are provided to employees who will be **retained beyond the minimum retention period**. The minimum retention period will normally be the period of notice an entity is required to provide employees in advance of terminating their employment

(g) Where **involuntary** termination benefits are provided in exchange for employees' future service the termination benefits are **recognised as a liability and expense over the period of future service**.

(h) Where termination benefits are provided as an **enhancement** of retirement benefits the liability and expense recognised initially includes **only the value of the additional benefits** that arise from the provision of the termination benefits.

6.3 Discussion Paper

In March 2008, the IASB issued a Discussion Paper *Preliminary Views on Amendments to IAS 19 Employee Benefits.* The purpose of the Discussion Paper is to improve accounting in the short-term for employee benefits in the light of criticisms of the current IAS 19 by users and preparers of financial statements, including the US SEC and the EU's European Financial Reporting Advisory Group (that approves IFRS for use in the EU). In the long term, the IASB intends to produce a common IASB-FASB standard, but recognises that this will take many years to complete.

6.3.1 Scope

Because the Paper is a short-term measure, its **scope is limited to** the following areas.

(a) Deferred recognition of some gains and losses arising from defined benefit plans
(b) Presentation of changes in value of the defined benefit obligation and assets
(c) Accounting for benefits that are based on contributions and a promised return
(d) Accounting for benefit promises with a 'higher of' option.

However, the IASB recognises that the scope **could be expanded** to include items such as:

(a) **Recognition of the obligation based on the 'benefit' formula.** This current approach means that unvested benefits are recognised as a liability which is inconsistent with other IFRSs.

(b) **Measurement of the obligation**. The 'projected unit credit method' (as defined before) is used which is based on expected benefits (including salary increases). Alternative approaches include accumulated benefit, projected benefit, fair value and settlement value.

(c) **Presenting of a net defined benefit obligation**. Defined benefit plan assets and liabilities are currently presented net on the grounds that the fund is not controlled (which would require consolidation of the fund).

(d) **Multi-employer plans.** Current accounting is normally for the entity's proportionate share of the obligation, plan assets and costs as for a single-employer plan, but an exemption is currently provided where sufficient information is not available, and defined contribution accounting can be used instead. Should the exemption be removed?

6.3.2 Preliminary discussions

(a) **Deferred recognition**

   (i) This (ie the corridor method) is to be eliminated. Actuarial gains and losses to be recognised in the period incurred.

   (ii) The actual return on assets would not be divided into expected return and actuarial gain/loss.

   (iii) Past service costs would be recognised in the period of plan amendment.

(b) **Presentation of changes in value of the defined benefit obligation and assets**

Possible options are as follows:

   (i) Show all in profit or loss in the period incurred

   (ii) Include all costs of service in profit or loss, all other changes in other comprehensive income

   (iii) Re-measurements arising from changes in financial assumptions (that is, changes in the discount rate for liabilities and changes in plan assets) in other comprehensive income, all other changes in profit or loss.

(c) **Benefits based on contributions plus a promised return on assets**

   (i) Arguably these are not faithfully represented under current approach

   (ii) It is proposed to measure the liability for contribution-based promises at fair value (as a separate category; as consideration of the projected unit credit method approach to measuring the defined benefit liability itself deferred to a later date)

   (iii) Changes are to be disaggregated into a service cost and other value changes (but both recognised in profit or loss).

(d) **Benefit promises with a 'higher of' option**

   (i) These occur where a plan member will receive the higher of a defined benefit pension or contributions plus a promised return on assets.

(ii)   In substance there is an embedded option/guarantee.

(iii)   The liability may be underestimated under the current IAS 19 approach.

(iv)   It is proposed to separate out the 'higher of' option and separately measure it at fair value
         assuming the terms of the benefit promise do not change (with all changes in the option
         value recognised in profit or loss).

6.3.3 ASB and discount rate

Some of the above issues have been considered in a January 2008 Discussion Paper from the UK
Accounting Standards Board in the context of FRS 17 *Retirement benefits*.

Curently the techniques used to quantify pension liabilities rely on a number of assumptions, including the
return that is expected to be made on assets in the time before the benefit will be paid. The paper notes
that this is not appropriate because it does not reflect the present economic burden of the liability. The
proposal in the Discussion Paper is that the liability should be **quantified** for financial reporting purposes
at an assessment of the cost of settling the benefit, which will typically **reflect all future cash flows**.
Information about the riskiness of the liability would be conveyed by disclosure rather than by adjusting
the liability. According **the cash flows should be discounted at the risk-free rate**.

6.3.4 Ongoing discussions

The publications so far, the discount rate referred to above and at 6.1 and other issues are being
discussed by the Employee Benefits Working Group. Exposure Drafts are to be published later in 2009,
with final standards in 2011.

Chapter Roundup

- IAS 19 *Employee benefits* is a long and complex standard covering both short-term and long-term (post-employment) benefits. The complications arise when dealing with **post-employment benefits**.

- There are **two types of post-employment benefit plan**:
    - Defined contribution plans
    - Defined benefit plans

- **Defined contribution plans** are simple to account for as the benefits are defined by the contributions made.

- **Defined benefit plans** are much more difficult to deal with as the benefits are promised, they define the contributions to be made.

- There is a **six-step method** for accounting for the expenses and liability of a defined benefit pension plan.

- **Actuarial assumptions** made should be unbiased and based on market expectations.

- **Discount rates** used should be determined by reference to market yields on high-quality fixed-rate corporate bonds.

- **Actuarial gains and losses** arise for several reasons, but IAS 19 requires only a portion to be recognised, to avoid volatility in the accounts.

- The difference between the **expected return and actual return on plan assets** must be calculated.

- You should know how to deal with **curtailments** and **settlements**.

- An **ED** contains proposals on **termination benefits,** and a recent **Discussion Paper** proposes **improvements to accounting for employee benefits.**

Quick Quiz

1   What are the five categories of employee benefits given by IAS 19?

2   What is the difference between defined contribution and defined benefit plans?

3   What is a 'constructive obligation' compared to a legal obligation?

4   How should a defined benefit expense be recognised in profit or loss for the year?

5   What causes actuarial gains or losses?

6   How should termination benefits be recognised?

    A   Provided for as part of the costs of employment when incurred
    B   Part of a special provision for future liabilities
    C   Recognised in full as a liability and expense when a future obligation is recognised
    D   Amortised over the period of employment

7   How should equity compensation benefits be treated?

1
- Short-term
- Post-employment
- Other long-term
- Termination
- Equity compensation

2 See Paragraph 3.2

3 A constructive obligation exists when the entity has no realistic alternative than to pay employee benefits.

4 Current service cost + interest + expected return + recognised actuarial gains/losses + past service cost + curtailments or settlements.

5 See Paragraph 5.1

6 C Recognised in full as a liability and an expense in the accounting period when the entity recognises a demonstrable obligation to pay the benefits in the future.

7 Amount held at the beginning and end of the period, and amounts issued to the scheme, or employees, during the period.

Now try the question below from the Exam Question Bank

Number	Level	Marks	Time
Q5	Introductory	17	31 mins

Income taxes

Topic list	Syllabus reference
1 Current tax revised	C7
2 Deferred tax	C7
3 Taxable temporary differences	C7
4 Deductible temporary differences	C7
5 Measurement and recognition of deferred tax	C7
6 Deferred taxation and business combinations	C7

Introduction

In almost all countries entities are taxed on the basis of their trading income. In some countries this may be called corporation or corporate tax, but we will follow the terminology of IAS 12 *Income taxes* and call it **income tax**.

There are two main systems for taxing corporate income: the **classical system** and the **imputation system**: go back to your earlier study material if necessary. For this chapter we will assume a classical system. Of course, each country will be different in its tax legislation and its method of accounting for taxation may reflect this.

There are two aspects of income tax which must be accounted for: **current tax** and **deferred tax**. Current tax is revised briefly in Section 1. The rest of this chapter is concerned with deferred tax, which students invariably find difficult.

Section 6 introduces a new aspect of deferred tax, relating to **business combinations**. This represents one of the most complex areas of deferred tax.

Note. Throughout this chapter we will assume a current corporate income tax rate of 30% and a current personal income tax rate of 20%, unless otherwise stated.

Study guide

		Intellectual level
C7	**Income taxes**	
(a)	Apply and discuss the recognition and measurement of deferred tax liabilities and deferred tax assets	3
(b)	Determine the recognition of tax expenses or income and its inclusion in the financial statements	3

Exam guide

Be prepared for a whole question on deferred tax, as happened on the Pilot Paper, when you were asked to discuss the conceptual basis for its accounting treatment and to calculate the deferred tax provision after making adjustments.

1 Current tax revised

FAST FORWARD

Taxation consists of **two components.**

- Current tax
- Deferred tax

Current tax is ordinarily straightforward. Complexities arise, however, when we consider the future tax consequences of what is going on in the accounts now. This is an aspect of tax called deferred tax, which we will look at in the next section. IAS 12 *Income taxes* covers both current and deferred tax. The parts relating to current tax are fairly brief, because this is the simple and uncontroversial area of tax.

1.1 Definitions

These are some of the definitions given in IAS 12. We will look at the rest later.

Key terms

Accounting profit. Net profit or loss for a period before deducting tax expense.

Taxable profit (tax loss). The profit (loss) for a period, determined in accordance with the rules established by the taxation authorities, upon which income taxes are payable (recoverable).

Tax expense (tax income). The aggregate amount included in the determination of net profit or loss for the period in respect of current tax and deferred tax.

Current tax. The amount of income taxes payable (recoverable) in respect of the taxable profit (tax loss) for a period.   *(IAS 12)*

Remember the difference between current and deferred tax.

(a)   **Current tax** is the amount *actually payable* to the tax authorities in relation to the trading activities of the entity during the period.

(b)   **Deferred tax** is an *accounting measure*, used to match the tax effects of transactions with their accounting impact and thereby produce less distorted results.

1.2 Recognition of current tax liabilities and assets

FAST FORWARD

Current tax is the amount payable to the tax authorities in relation to the trading activities during the period. It is generally straightforward.

IAS 12 requires any **unpaid tax** in respect of the current or prior periods to be recognised as a **liability**.

Conversely, any **excess tax** paid in respect of current or prior periods over what is due should be recognised as an asset.

In 20X8 Darton Co had taxable profits of $120,000. In the previous year (20X7) income tax on 20X7 profits had been estimated as $30,000.

Required

Calculate tax payable and the charge for 20X8 if the tax due on 20X7 profits was subsequently agreed with the tax authorities as:

(a) $35,000
(b) $25,000

Any under or over payments are not settled until the following year's tax payment is due.

Answer

(a)

	$
Tax due on 20X8 profits ($120,000 × 30%)	40,000
Underpayment for 20X7	5,000
Tax charge and liability	45,000

(b)

	$
Tax due on 20X8 profits (as above)	40,000
Overpayment for 20X7	(5,000)
Tax charge and liability	35,000

Alternatively, the rebate due could be shown separately as income in the statement of comprehensive income and as an asset in the statement of financial position. An offset approach like this is, however, most likely.

Taking this a stage further, IAS 12 also requires recognition as an asset of the benefit relating to any tax loss that can be **carried back** to recover current tax of a previous period. This is acceptable because it is probable that the benefit will flow to the entity *and* it can be reliably measured.

1.3 Example: Tax losses carried back

In 20X7 Eramu Co paid $50,000 in tax on its profits. In 20X8 the company made tax losses of $24,000. The local tax authority rules allow losses to be carried back to offset against current tax of prior years.

Required

Show the tax charge and tax liability for 20X8.

Solution

Tax repayment due on tax losses = 30% × $24,000 = $7,200.

The double entry will be:

DEBIT	Tax receivable (statement of financial position)	$7,200	
CREDIT	Tax repayment (statement of comprehensive income)		$7,200

The tax receivable will be shown as an asset until the repayment is received from the tax authorities.

1.4 Measurement

Measurement of current tax liabilities (assets) for the current and prior periods is very simple. They are measured at the **amount expected to be paid to (recovered from) the tax authorities**. The tax rates (and tax laws) used should be those enacted (or substantively enacted) by the year end.

1.5 Recognition of current tax

Normally, current tax is recognised as income or expense and included in the net profit or loss for the period, except in two cases.

(a) Tax arising from a **business combination** which is an acquisition is treated differently (see Section 6 of this chapter).

(b) Tax arising from a transaction or event which is recognised **directly in equity** (in the same or a different period).

The rule in (b) is logical. If a transaction or event is charged or credited directly to equity, rather than to profit or loss, then the related tax should be also. An example of such a situation is where, under IAS 8, an adjustment is made to the **opening balance of retained earnings** due to either a change in accounting policy that is applied retrospectively, or to the correction of a fundamental error.

1.6 Presentation

In the statement of financial position, **tax assets and liabilities** should be shown separately from other assets and liabilities.

Current tax assets and liabilities can be **offset**, but this should happen only when certain conditions apply.

(a) The entity has a **legally enforceable right** to set off the recognised amounts.

(b) The entity intends to settle the amounts on a **net basis**, or to realise the asset and settle the liability at the same time.

The **tax expense (income)** related to the profit or loss from ordinary activities should be shown in the income statement.

2 Deferred tax   12/07

FAST FORWARD

Deferred tax is an accounting measure, used to match the tax effects of transactions with their accounting impact. It is quite complex.

Exam focus point

Students invariably find deferred tax very confusing. It is an inherently difficult topic and as such it likely to appear frequently in its most complicated forms in Paper P2. You *must* understand the contents of the rest of this chapter.

2.1 What is deferred tax?

When a company recognises an asset or liability, it expects to **recover or settle the carrying amount** of that asset or liability. In other words, it expects to sell or use up assets, and to pay off liabilities. What happens if that recovery or settlement is likely to make future tax payments larger (or smaller) than they would otherwise have been if the recovery or settlement had no tax consequences? In these circumstances, IAS 12 requires companies to recognise a **deferred tax liability** (or **deferred tax asset**).

2.2 Definitions

Here are the definitions relating to deferred tax given in IAS 12.

Deferred tax liabilities are the amounts of income taxes payable in future periods in respect of taxable temporary differences.

Deferred tax assets are the amounts of income taxes recoverable in future periods in respect of:

- Deductible temporary differences
- The carryforward of unused tax losses
- The carryforward of unused tax credits

Temporary differences are differences between the carrying amount of an asset or liability in the statement of financial position and its tax base. Temporary differences may be either:

- **Taxable temporary differences**, which are temporary differences that will result in taxable amounts in determining taxable profit (tax loss) of future periods when the carrying amount of the asset or liability is recovered or settled

- **Deductible temporary differences**, which are temporary differences that will result in amounts that are deductible in determining taxable profit (tax loss) of future periods when the carrying amount of the asset or liability is recovered or settled.

The **tax base** of an asset or liability is the amount attributed to that asset or liability for tax purposes.

(IAS 12)

2.3 Tax base

We can expand on the definition given above by stating that the **tax base of an asset** is the amount that will be deductible for tax purposes against any taxable economic benefits that will flow to the entity when it recovers the carrying value of the asset. Where those economic benefits are not taxable, the tax base of the asset is the same as its carrying amount.

Question · Tax base 1

State the tax base of each of the following assets.

(a) A machine cost $10,000. For tax purposes, depreciation of $3,000 has already been deducted in the current and prior periods and the remaining cost will be deductible in future periods, either as depreciation or through a deduction on disposal. Revenue generated by using the machine is taxable, any gain on disposal of the machine will be taxable and any loss on disposal will be deductible for tax purposes.

(b) Interest receivable has a carrying amount of $1,000. The related interest revenue will be taxed on a cash basis.

(c) Trade receivables have a carrying amount of $10,000. The related revenue has already been included in taxable profit (tax loss).

(d) A loan receivable has a carrying amount of $1m. The repayment of the loan will have no tax consequences.

(e) Dividends receivable from a subsidiary have a carrying amount of $5,000. The dividends are not taxable.

Answer

(a) The tax base of the machine is $7,000.
(b) The tax base of the interest receivable is nil.
(c) The tax base of the trade receivables is $10,000.
(d) The tax base of the loan is $1m.
(e) The tax base of the dividend is $5,000.

In the case of (e), in substance the entire carrying amount of the asset is deductible against the economic benefits. There is no taxable temporary difference. An alternative analysis is that the accrued dividends receivable have a tax base of nil and a tax rate of nil is applied to the resulting taxable temporary difference ($5,000). Under both analyses, there is no deferred tax liability.

In the case of a **liability**, the tax base will be its carrying amount, less any amount that will be deducted for tax purposes in relation to the liability in future periods. For revenue received in advance, the tax base of the resulting liability is its carrying amount, less any amount of the revenue that will *not* be taxable in future periods.

State the tax base of each of the following liabilities.

(a)   Current liabilities include accrued expenses with a carrying amount of $1,000. The related expense will be deducted for tax purposes on a cash basis.

(b)   Current liabilities include interest revenue received in advance, with a carrying amount of $10,000. The related interest revenue was taxed on a cash basis.

(c)   Current assets include prepaid expenses with a carrying amount of $2,000. The related expense has already been deducted for tax purposes.

(d)   Current liabilities include accrued fines and penalties with a carrying amount of $100. Fines and penalties are not deductible for tax purposes.

(e)   A loan payable has a carrying amount of $1m. The repayment of the loan will have no tax consequences.

Answer

(a)   The tax base of the accrued expenses is nil.
(b)   The tax base of the interest received in advance is nil.
(c)   The tax base of the accrued expenses is $2,000.
(d)   The tax base of the accrued fines and penalties is $100.
(e)   The tax base of the loan is $1m.

IAS 12 gives the following examples of circumstances in which the carrying amount of an asset or liability will be **equal to its tax base**.

- **Pre-paid expenses** have already been deducted in determining an entity's current tax liability for the current or earlier periods.

- A **loan payable** is measured at the amount originally received and this amount is the same as the amount repayable on final maturity of the loan.

- **Accrued expenses** will never be deductible for tax purposes.

- **Accrued income** will never be taxable.

2.4 Temporary differences

You may have found the definition of temporary differences somewhat confusing. Remember that accounting profits form the basis for computing **taxable profits**, on which the tax liability for the year is calculated. However, accounting profits and taxable profits are different. There are two reasons for the differences.

(a)   **Permanent differences**. These occur when certain items of revenue or expense are excluded from the computation of taxable profits (for example, entertainment expenses may not be allowable for tax purposes).

(b)   **Temporary differences**. These occur when items of revenue or expense are included in both accounting profits and taxable profits, but not for the same accounting period. For example, an expense which is allowable as a deduction in arriving at taxable profits for 20X7 might not be included in the financial accounts until 20X8 or later. In the long run, the total taxable profits and total accounting profits will be the same (except for permanent differences) so that timing differences originate in one period and are capable of reversal in one or more subsequent periods. Deferred tax is the tax attributable to **temporary differences.**

The distinction made in the definition between **taxable temporary differences** and **deductible temporary differences** can be made clearer by looking at the explanations and examples given in the standard and its appendices.

2.5 Section summary

- Deferred tax is an **accounting device**. It does *not* represent tax payable to the tax authorities.
- The **tax base** of an asset or liability is the value of that asset or liability for tax purposes.
- You should understand the difference between **permanent and temporary differences**.
- Deferred tax is the tax attributable to **temporary differences**.

3 Taxable temporary differences

FAST FORWARD

Deferred tax assets and liabilities arise from taxable and deductible temporary differences.

Exam focus point

The rule to remember here is that:

'All taxable temporary differences give rise to a deferred tax liability.'

The following are examples of circumstances that give rise to taxable temporary differences.

3.1 Transactions that affect the statement of comprehensive income

- **Interest revenue** received in arrears and included in accounting profit on the basis of time apportionment. It is included in taxable profit, however, on a cash basis.
- **Sale of goods revenue** is included in accounting profit when the goods are delivered, but only included in taxable profit when cash is received.
- **Depreciation** of an asset is accelerated for tax purposes. When new assets are purchased, allowances may be available against taxable profits which exceed the amount of depreciation chargeable on the assets in the financial accounts for the year of purchase.
- **Development costs** which have been capitalised will be amortised in profit or loss, but they were deducted in full from taxable profit in the period in which they were incurred.
- **Prepaid expenses** have already been deducted on a cash basis in determining the taxable profit of the current or previous periods.

3.2 Transactions that affect the statement of financial position

- **Depreciation of an asset** is not deductible for tax purposes. No deduction will be available for tax purposes when the asset is sold/scrapped.
- A borrower records a **loan** at proceeds received (amount due at maturity) less transaction costs. The carrying amount of the loan is subsequently increased by amortisation of the transaction costs against accounting profit. The transaction costs were, however, deducted for tax purposes in the period when the loan was first recognised.
- A **loan** payable is measured on initial recognition at net proceeds (net of transaction costs). The transaction costs are amortised to accounting profit over the life of the loan. Those transaction costs are not deductible in determining the taxable profit of future, current or prior periods.
- The liability component of a **compound financial instrument** (eg a convertible bond) is measured at a discount to the amount repayable on maturity, after assigning a portion of the cash proceeds to the equity component (see IAS 32). The discount is not deductible in determining taxable profit.

3.3 Fair value adjustments and revaluations

- **Current investments** or financial instruments are carried at fair value. This exceeds cost, but no equivalent adjustment is made for tax purposes.
- Property, plant and equipment is **revalued** by an entity (under IAS 16), but no equivalent adjustment is made for tax purposes. This also applies to long-term investments.

The standard also looks at the deferred tax implications of business combinations and consolidations. We will look at these in Section 7.

Remember the rule we gave you above, that all taxable temporary differences give rise to a deferred tax liability? There are **two circumstances** given in the standards where this does *not* apply.

(a) The deferred tax liability arises from the initial recognition of **goodwill**.

(b) The deferred tax liability arises from the **initial recognition** of an asset or liability in a transaction which:

(i) is *not* a business combination (see Section 6), *and*

(ii) at the time of the transaction affects neither accounting profit nor taxable profit.

Try to **understand the reasoning** behind the recognition of deferred tax liabilities on taxable temporary differences.

(a) When an **asset is recognised**, it is expected that its carrying amount will be recovered in the form of economic benefits that flow to the entity in future periods.

(b) If the carrying amount of the asset is **greater than** its tax base, then taxable economic benefits will also be greater than the amount that will be allowed as a deduction for tax purposes.

(c) The difference is therefore a **taxable temporary difference** and the obligation to pay the resulting income taxes in future periods is a **deferred tax liability**.

(d) As the entity recovers the carrying amount of the asset, the taxable temporary difference will **reverse** and the entity will have taxable profit.

(e) It is then probable that economic benefits will flow from the entity in the form of **tax payments**, and so the recognition of all deferred tax liabilities (except those excluded above) is required by IAS 12.

3.3.1 Example: Taxable temporary differences

A company purchased an asset costing $1,500. At the end of 20X8 the carrying amount is $1,000. The cumulative depreciation for tax purposes is $900 and the current tax rate is 25%.

Required

Calculate the deferred tax liability for the asset.

Solution

Firstly, what is the tax base of the asset? It is $1,500 – $900 = $600.

In order to recover the carrying value of $1,000, the entity must earn taxable income of $1,000, but it will only be able to deduct $600 as a taxable expense. The entity must therefore pay income tax of $400 × 25% = $100 when the carrying value of the asset is recovered.

The entity must therefore recognise a deferred tax liability of $400 × 25% = $100, recognising the difference between the carrying amount of $1,000 and the tax base of $600 as a taxable temporary difference.

3.4 Revalued assets

Under IAS 16 assets may be revalued. If this affects the taxable profit for the current period, the tax base of the asset changes and **no temporary difference** arises.

If, however (as in some countries), the revaluation does *not* affect current taxable profits, the tax base of the asset is not adjusted. Consequently, the taxable flow of economic benefits to the entity as the carrying value of the asset is recovered will differ from the amount that will be deductible for tax purposes. The difference between the carrying amount of a revalued asset and its tax base is a temporary difference and gives rise to a **deferred tax liability or asset**.

3.5 Initial recognition of an asset or liability

A temporary difference can arise on initial recognition of an asset or liability, eg if part or all of the cost of an asset will not be deductible for tax purposes. The **nature of the transaction** which led to the initial recognition of the asset is important in determining the method of accounting for such temporary differences.

If the transaction affects *either* accounting profit or taxable profit, an entity will **recognise any deferred tax liability** or asset. The resulting deferred tax expense or income will be recognised in profit or loss.

Where a transaction affects **neither accounting profit nor taxable profit** it would be normal for an entity to recognise a deferred tax liability or asset and adjust the carrying amount of the asset or liability by the same amount (unless exempted by IAS 12 as under Paragraph 3.6 above). However, IAS 12 does *not* permit this recognition of a deferred tax asset or liability as it would make the financial statements less transparent. This will be the case both on initial recognition and subsequently, nor should any subsequent changes in the unrecognised deferred tax liability or asset as the asset is depreciated be made.

3.6 Example: Initial recognition

As an example of the last paragraph, suppose Petros Co intends to use an asset which cost $10,000 in 20X7 through its useful life of five years. Its residual value will then be nil. The tax rate is 40%. Any capital gain on disposal would not be taxable (and any capital loss not deductible). Depreciation of the asset is not deductible for tax purposes.

Required

State the deferred tax consequences in each of years 20X7 and 20X8.

Solution

As at 20X7, as it recovers the carrying amount of the asset, Petros Co will earn taxable income of $10,000 and pay tax of $4,000. The resulting deferred tax liability of $4,000 would not be recognised because it results from the initial recognition of the asset.

As at 20X8, the carrying value of the asset is now $8,000. In earning taxable income of $8,000, the entity will pay tax of $3,200. Again, the resulting deferred tax liability of $3,200 is not recognised, because it results from the initial recognition of the asset.

The following question on accelerated depreciation should clarify some of the issues and introduce you to the calculations which may be necessary in the exam.

Question   Deferred tax

Jonquil Co buys equipment for $50,000 and depreciates it on a straight line basis over its expected useful life of five years. For tax purposes, the equipment is depreciated at 25% per annum on a straight line basis. Tax losses may be carried back against taxable profit of the previous five years. In year 20X0, the entity's taxable profit was $25,000. The tax rate is 40%.

Required

Assuming nil profits/losses after depreciation in years 20X1 to 20X5 show the current and deferred tax impact in years 20X1 to 20X5 of the acquisition of the equipment.

Jonquil Co will recover the carrying amount of the equipment by using it to manufacture goods for resale. Therefore, the entity's current tax computation is as follows.

	20X1 $	20X2 $	20X3 $	20X4 $	20X5 $
			Year		
Taxable income*	10,000	10,000	10,000	10,000	10,000
Depreciation for tax purposes	12,500	12,500	12,500	12,500	0
Taxable profit (tax loss)	(2,500)	(2,500)	(2,500)	(2,500)	10,000
Current tax expense (income) at 40%	(1,000)	(1,000)	(1,000)	(1,000)	4,000

* ie nil profit plus ($50,000 ÷ 5) depreciation add-back.

The entity recognises a current tax asset at the end of years 20X1 to 20X4 because it recovers the benefit of the tax loss against the taxable profit of year 20X0.

The temporary differences associated with the equipment and the resulting deferred tax asset and liability and deferred tax expense and income are as follows.

	20X1 $	20X2 $	20X3 $	20X4 $	20X5 $
			Year		
Carrying amount	40,000	30,000	20,000	10,000	0
Tax base	37,500	25,000	12,500	0	0
Taxable temporary difference	2,500	5,000	7,500	10,000	0
Opening deferred tax liability	0	1,000	2,000	3,000	4,000
Deferred tax expense (income): bal fig	1,000	1,000	1,000	1,000	(4,000)
Closing deferred tax liability @ 40%	1,000	2,000	3,000	4,000	0

The entity recognises the deferred tax liability in years 20X1 to 20X4 because the reversal of the taxable temporary difference will create taxable income in subsequent years. The entity's income statement is as follows.

	20X1 $	20X2 $	20X3 $	20X4 $	20X5 $
			Year		
Income	10,000	10,000	10,000	10,000	10,000
Depreciation	10,000	10,000	10,000	10,000	10,000
Profit before tax	0	0	0	0	0
Current tax expense (income)	(1,000)	(1,000)	(1,000)	(1,000)	4,000
Deferred tax expense (income)	1,000	1,000	1,000	1,000	(4,000)
Total tax expense (income)	0	0	0	0	0
Net profit for the year	0	0	0	0	0

4 Deductible temporary differences

Refer again to the definition given in Section 2 above.

The rule to remember here is that:

'All deductible temporary differences give rise to a deferred tax asset.'

There is a proviso, however. The deferred tax asset must also satisfy the **recognition criteria** given in IAS 12. This is that a deferred tax asset should be recognised for all deductible temporary differences to the extent that it is **probable that taxable profit will be available** against which it can be utilised. This is an application of prudence. Before we look at this issue in more detail, let us consider the examples of deductible temporary differences given in the standard.

4.1 Transactions that affect the statement of comprehensive income

- **Retirement benefit costs** (pension costs) are deducted from accounting profit as service is provided by the employee. They are not deducted in determining taxable profit until the entity pays either retirement benefits or contributions to a fund. (This may also apply to similar expenses.)
- **Accumulated depreciation** of an asset in the financial statements is greater than the accumulated depreciation allowed for tax purposes up to the year end.
- The **cost of inventories** sold before the year end is deducted from accounting profit when goods/services are delivered, but is deducted from taxable profit when the cash is received. (*Note.* There is also a taxable temporary difference associated with the related trade receivable, as noted in Section 3 above.)
- The **NRV** of inventory, or the **recoverable amount** of an item of property, plant and equipment falls and the carrying value is therefore **reduced**, but that reduction is ignored for tax purposes until the asset is sold.
- **Research costs** (or organisation/other start-up costs) are recognised as an expense for accounting purposes but are not deductible against taxable profits until a later period.
- Income is **deferred** in the statement of financial position, but has already been included in taxable profit in current/prior periods.
- A **government grant** is included in the statement of financial position as deferred income, but it will not be taxable in future periods. (*Note.* A deferred tax asset may *not* be recognised here according to the standard.)

4.2 Fair value adjustments and revaluations

Current investments or **financial instruments** may be carried at fair value which is less than cost, but no equivalent adjustment is made for tax purposes.

Other situations discussed by the standard relate to **business combinations** and consolidation (see Section 6).

4.3 Recognition of deductible temporary differences

We looked earlier at the important recognition criteria above. As with temporary taxable differences, there are also circumstances where the overall rule for recognition of deferred tax asset is *not* allowed. This applies where the deferred tax asset arises from **initial recognition** of an asset or liability in a transaction which is not a business combination, *and* at the time of the transaction, affects neither accounting nor taxable profit/ tax loss.

Let us lay out the reasoning behind the recognition of deferred tax assets arising from deductible temporary differences.

(a) When a **liability is recognised**, it is assumed that its carrying amount will be settled in the form of outflows of economic benefits from the entity in future periods.

(b) When these resources flow from the entity, part or all may be deductible in determining taxable profits of a **period later** than that in which the liability is recognised.

(c) A **temporary tax difference** then exists between the carrying amount of the liability and its tax base.

(d) A **deferred tax asset** therefore arises, representing the income taxes that will be recoverable in future periods when that part of the liability is allowed as a deduction from taxable profit.

(e) Similarly, when the carrying amount of an asset is **less than its tax base**, the difference gives rise to a deferred tax asset in respect of the income taxes that will be recoverable in future periods.

4.3.1 Example: Deductible temporary differences

Pargatha Co recognises a liability of $10,000 for accrued product warranty costs on 31 December 20X7. These product warranty costs will not be deductible for tax purposes until the entity pays claims. The tax rate is 25%.

Required

State the deferred tax implications of this situation.

Solution

What is the tax base of the liability? It is nil (carrying amount of $10,000 less the amount that will be deductible for tax purposes in respect of the liability in future periods).

When the liability is settled for its carrying amount, the entity's future taxable profit will be reduced by $10,000 and so its future tax payments by $10,000 × 25% = $2,500.

The difference of $10,000 between the carrying amount ($10,000) and the tax base (nil) is a deductible temporary difference. The entity should therefore recognise a deferred tax asset of $10,000 × 25% = $2,500 **provided that** it is probable that the entity will earn sufficient taxable profits in future periods to benefit from a reduction in tax payments.

4.4 Taxable profits in future periods

When can we be sure that sufficient taxable profit will be available against which a deductible temporary difference can be utilised? IAS 12 states that this will be assumed when sufficient **taxable temporary differences** exist which relate to the same taxation authority and the same taxable entity. These should be expected to reverse as follows.

(a)   In the same period as the expected reversal of the deductible temporary difference.

(b)   In periods into which a tax loss arising from the deferred tax asset can be carried back or forward.

Only in these circumstances is the deferred tax asset **recognised**, in the period in which the deductible temporary differences arise.

What happens when there are **insufficient taxable temporary differences** (relating to the same taxation authority and the same taxable entity)? It may still be possible to recognise the deferred tax asset, but only to the following extent.

(a)   **Taxable profits** are sufficient in the same period as the reversal of the deductible temporary difference (or in the periods into which a tax loss arising from the deferred tax asset can be carried forward or backward), ignoring taxable amounts arising from deductible temporary differences arising in future periods.

(b)   **Tax planning opportunities** exist that will allow the entity to create taxable profit in the appropriate periods.

With reference to (b), **tax planning opportunities** are actions that an entity would take in order to create or increase taxable income in a particular period before the expiry of a tax loss or tax credit carryforward. For example, in some countries it may be possible to increase or create taxable profit by electing to have interest income taxed on either a received or receivable basis, or deferring the claim for certain deductions from taxable profit.

In any case, where tax planning opportunities **advance taxable profit** from a later period to an earlier period, the utilisation of a tax loss or a tax credit carryforward will still depend on the existence of future taxable profit from sources other than future originating temporary differences.

If an entity has a **history of recent losses**, then this is evidence that future taxable profit may not be available (see below).

4.5 Initial recognition of an asset or liability

Consider Paragraph 3.6 on **initial recognition of an asset or liability**. The example given by the standard is of a non-taxable government grant related to an asset, deducted in arriving at the carrying amount of the asset. For tax purposes, however, it is *not* deducted from the asset's depreciable amount (ie its tax base). The carrying amount of the asset is less than its tax base and this gives rise to a deductible temporary difference. Paragraph 3.6 applies to this type of transaction.

4.6 Unused tax losses and unused tax credits

An entity may have unused tax losses or credits (ie which it can offset against taxable profits) at the end of a period. Should a deferred tax asset be recognised in relation to such amounts? IAS 12 states that a deferred tax asset may be recognised in such circumstances **to the extent that it is probable future taxable profit will be available against which the unused tax losses/credits can be utilised**.

The **criteria for recognition** of deferred tax assets here is the same as for recognising deferred tax assets arising from deductible differences. The existence of **unused tax losses** is strong evidence, however, that future taxable profit may not be available. So where an entity has a history of recent tax losses, a deferred tax asset arising from unused tax losses or credits should be recognised only to the extent that the entity has sufficient taxable temporary differences or there is other convincing evidence that sufficient taxable profit will be available against which the unused losses/credits can be utilised by the entity.

In these circumstances, the following criteria should be considered when assessing the probability that taxable profit will be available against which unused tax losses/credits can be utilised.

- Existence of **sufficient taxable temporary differences** (same tax authority/taxable entity) against which unused tax losses/credits can be utilised before they expire
- Probability that the entity will have **taxable profits** before the unused tax losses/credits expire
- Whether the unused tax losses result from **identifiable causes**, unlikely to recur
- Availability of **tax planning opportunities** (see above)

To the extent that it is **not probable** that taxable profit will be available, the deferred tax asset is *not* recognised.

4.7 Reassessment of unrecognised deferred tax assets

For *all* unrecognised deferred tax assets, at each year end an entity should **reassess the availability of future taxable profits** and whether part or all of any unrecognised deferred tax assets should now be recognised. This may be due to an improvement in trading conditions which is expected to continue.

4.8 Section summary

- Deductible temporary differences give rise to a **deferred tax asset**.
- **Prudence** dictates that deferred tax assets can only be recognised when **sufficient future taxable profits** exist against which they can be utilised.

5 Measurement and recognition of deferred tax

IAS 12 *Income taxes* covers both current and deferred tax. It has substantial presentation and disclosure requirements.

5.1 Basis of provision of deferred tax

IAS 12 adopts the full provision method of providing for deferred tax.

The **full provision method** has the **advantage** that it recognises that each timing difference at the year end has an effect on future tax payments. If a company claims an accelerated tax allowance on an item of plant, future tax assessments will be bigger than they would have been otherwise. Future transactions may well affect those assessments still further, but that is not relevant in assessing the position at the year end. The **disadvantage** of full provision is that, under certain types of tax system, it gives rise to large liabilities that may fall due only far in the future.

5.2 Example: Full provision

Suppose that Girdo Co begins trading on 1 January 20X7. In its first year it makes profits of $5m, the depreciation charge is $1m and the tax allowances on those assets is $1.5m. The rate of corporation tax is 30%.

Solution: Full provision

The tax liability is $1.35m again, but the debit to profit or loss is increased by the deferred tax liability of 30% × $0.5m = $150,000. The total charge to profit or loss is therefore $1.5m which is an effective tax rate of 30% on accounting profits (ie 30% × $5.0m). Again, no judgement is involved in using this method.

5.3 Deferral/liability methods: changes in tax rates

Where the corporate rate of income tax **fluctuates from one year to another**, a problem arises in respect of the amount of deferred tax to be credited (debited) to profit or loss in later years. The amount could be calculated using either of two methods.

(a)   The **deferral method** assumes that the deferred tax account is an item of 'deferred tax relief' which is credited to profits in the years in which the timing differences are reversed. Therefore the tax effects of timing differences are calculated using tax rates current when the differences **arise**.

(b)   The **liability method** assumes that the tax effects of timing differences should be regarded as amounts of tax ultimately due by or to the company. Therefore deferred tax provisions are calculated at the rate at which it is estimated that tax will be paid (or recovered) when the timing differences **reverse**.

The deferral method involves **extensive record keeping** because the timing differences on each individual capital asset must be held. In contrast, under the liability method, the total originating or reversing timing difference for the year is converted into a deferred tax amount at the current rate of tax (and if any change in the rate of tax has occurred in the year, only a single adjustment to the opening balance on the deferred tax account is required).

IAS 12 requires deferred tax assets and liabilities to be measured at the tax rates expected to apply in the period **when the asset is realised or liability settled**, based on tax rates and laws enacted (or substantively enacted) at the year end. In other words, IAS 12 requires the **liability method** to be used.

5.4 Different rates of tax

In addition, in some countries different tax rates apply to different levels of taxable income. In such cases, deferred tax assets and liabilities should be measured using the **average rates** that are expected to apply to the taxable profit (loss) of the periods in which the temporary differences are expected to reverse.

5.5 Manner of recovery or settlement

In some countries, the way in which an entity **recovers or settles** the carrying amount of an asset or liability may affect the following.

(a)   The tax rate applying when the entity recovers/settles the carrying amount of the asset/liability
(b)   The tax base of the asset/liability

In such cases, the entity must consider the expected manner of recovery or settlement. Deferred tax liabilities and assets must be measured accordingly, using an **appropriate tax rate and tax base**.

5.6 Example: Manner of recovery/settlement

Richcard Co has an asset with a carrying amount of $10,000 and a tax base of $6,000. If the asset were sold, a tax rate of 20% would apply. A tax rate of 30% would apply to other income.

Required

State the deferred tax consequences if the entity:

(a)   sells the asset without further use.
(b)   expects to return the asset and recover its carrying amount through use.

Solution

(a)   A deferred tax liability is recognised of $(10,000 – 6,000) × 20% = $800.
(b)   A deferred tax liability is recognised of $(10,000 – 6,000) × 30% = $1,200.

Question   Recovery 1

Emida Co has an asset which cost $100,000. In 20X9 the carrying value was $80,000 and the asset was revalued to $150,000. No equivalent adjustment was made for tax purposes. Cumulative depreciation for tax purposes is $30,000 and the tax rate is 30%. If the asset is sold for more than cost, the cumulative tax depreciation of $30,000 will be included in taxable income but sale proceeds in excess of cost will not be taxable.

Required

State the deferred tax consequences of the above. (*Hint.* Assume first that the entity expects to recover the carrying value through use, and secondly that it will not and therefore will sell the asset instead.)

Answer

The tax base of the asset is $70,000 ($150,000 – $80,000).

If the entity expects to recover the carrying amount by using the asset it must generate taxable income of $150,000, but will only be able to deduct depreciation of $70,000. On this basis there is a deferred tax liability of $24,000 ($80,000 × 30%).

If the entity expects to recover the carrying amount by selling the asset immediately for proceeds of $150,000, the deferred tax liability will be computed as follows.

	Taxable temporary difference	Tax rate	Deferred tax liability
	$		$
Cumulative tax depreciation	30,000	30%	9,000
Proceeds in excess of cost	50,000	Nil	–
Total	80,000		9,000

Note. The additional deferred tax that arises on the revaluation is charged directly to equity: see below.

Question   Recovery 2

The facts are as in Recovery 1 above, except that if the asset is sold for more than cost, the cumulative tax depreciation will be included in taxable income (taxed at 30%) and the sale proceeds will be taxed at 40% after deducting an inflation-adjusted cost of $110,000.

Required

State the deferred tax consequences of the above (use the same hint as in Recovery 1).

If the entity expects to recover the carrying amount by using the asset, the situation is as in Recovery 1 above in the same circumstances.

If the entity expects to recover the carrying amount by selling the asset immediately for proceeds of $150,000, the entity will be able to deduct the indexed costs of $110,000. The net profit of $40,000 will be taxed at 40%. In addition, the cumulative tax depreciation of $30,000 will be included in taxable income and taxed at 30%. On this basis, the tax base is $80,000 ($110,000 – $30,000), there is a taxable temporary difference of $70,000 and there is a deferred tax liability of $25,000 ($40,000 × 40% plus $30,000 × 30%).

Exam focus point

> If the tax base is not immediately apparent in Recovery 2 above, it may be helpful to consider the fundamental principle of IAS 12: that an entity should recognise a deferred tax liability (asset) whenever recovery or settlement of the carrying amount of an asset or liability would make future tax payments larger (smaller) than they would be if such recovery or settlement would have no consequences.

5.7 Discounting

IAS 12 states that deferred tax assets and liabilities **should not be discounted** because the complexities and difficulties involved will affect reliability. Discounting would require detailed scheduling of the timing of the reversal of each temporary difference, but this is often impracticable. If discounting were permitted, this would affect comparability, so it is barred completely. However, carrying amounts determine temporary differences even when such carrying amounts are discounted (eg retirement benefit obligations: see Chapter 6).

5.8 Carrying amount of deferred tax assets

The carrying amount of deferred tax assets should be **reviewed at each year end** and reduced where appropriate (insufficient future taxable profits). Such a reduction may be reversed in future years.

5.9 Recognition

As with current tax, deferred tax should normally be recognised as income or an expense and included in the net profit or loss for the period. The exceptions are where the tax arises from the events below.

(a)   A transaction or event which is recognised (in the same or a different period) **directly in equity**

(b)   A business combination that is an **acquisition** (see Part C)

The figures shown for deferred tax in profit or loss will consist of **two components**.

(a)   Deferred tax relating to **timing differences**.

(b)   Adjustments relating to **changes in the carrying amount of deferred tax assets/ liabilities** (where there is no change in timing differences), eg changes in tax rates/ laws, reassessment of the recoverability of deferred tax assets, or a change in the expected recovery of an asset.

Items in (b) will be recognised in the profit or loss, *unless* they relate to items previously charged/credited to equity.

Deferred tax (and current tax) should be **charged/credited directly to equity** if the tax relates to items also charged/credited directly to equity (in the same or a different period).

The following show examples of IASs which allow certain items to be credited/charged directly to equity.

(a)   **Revaluations** of property, plant and equipment (IAS 16)

(b)   The effect of a **change in accounting policy** (applied retrospectively) or correction of an **error** (IAS 8)

Where it is not possible to determine the amount of current/deferred tax that relates to items credited/charged to equity, such tax amounts should be based on a reasonable **prorata allocation** of the entity's current/deferred tax.

5.10 SIC 21 Income taxes – recovery of revalued non-depreciable assets

SIC 21 deals with cases where a non-depreciable asset (freehold land) is carried at revaluation under IAS 16. No part of the carrying amount of such an asset is considered to be recovered through its use. Therefore, SIC 21 concludes that the deferred tax liability or asset that arises from revaluation must be measured based on the tax consequences that would follow from the sale of the asset rather than through use.

In some jurisdictions, this will result in the use of a capital gains tax rate rather than the rate applicable to corporate earnings.

5.11 Section summary

- You should understand and be able to explain the different **bases for provision** of deferred tax.
    - **Flow-through method** (no tax provided)
    - **Full provision method** (tax provided in full, as per IAS 12)
    - **Partial provision method** (tax provided to the extent it is expected to be paid)
- There are two methods of calculating deferred tax when **tax rates change**.
    - **Deferral method** (use tax rates current when differences **arise**)
    - **Liability method** (use tax rate expected when differences **reverse**: per IAS 12)
- Where different rates of tax apply to different rates of income, the **manner of recovery/settlement** of assets/liabilities is important.

6 Deferred taxation and business combinations

FAST FORWARD

> You must appreciate the deferred tax aspects of **business combinations**: this is the aspect of deferred tax most likely to appear in the Paper P2 exam.

Much of the above will be familiar to you from your earlier studies. In Paper P2 you are likely to be asked about the **group aspects of deferred taxation**. Everything that IAS 12 states in relation to deferred tax and business combinations is brought together in this section.

6.1 Tax bases

Remember the definition of the tax base of an asset or liability given in Section 4 above? In relation to business combinations and consolidations, IAS 12 gives (in an appendix) examples of circumstances that give rise to taxable temporary differences and to deductible temporary differences.

6.1.1 Circumstances that give rise to taxable temporary differences

- The carrying amount of an asset is increased to **fair value** in a business combination that is an acquisition and no equivalent adjustment is made for tax purposes
- **Unrealised losses resulting from intragroup transactions** are eliminated by inclusion in the carrying amount of inventory or property, plant and equipment
- **Retained earnings** of subsidiaries, branches, associates and joint ventures are included in consolidated retained earnings, but income taxes will be payable if the profits are distributed to the reporting parent
- Investments in foreign subsidiaries, branches or associates or interests in foreign joint ventures are affected by **changes in foreign exchange rates**
- An entity accounts in its own currency for the cost of the non-monetary assets of a foreign operation that is **integral to the reporting entity's operations** but the taxable profit or tax loss of the foreign operation is determined in the foreign currency

What are the consequences of the above situations?

Note. You may want to read through to the end of this section before you attempt this question.

Answer

(a) *Fair value adjustment*

On initial recognition, the resulting deferred tax liability increases goodwill or decreases negative goodwill.

(b) *Unrealised losses*

The tax bases of the assets are unaltered.

(c) *Consolidated earnings*

IAS 12 does not allow recognition of the resulting deferred tax liability if the parent, investor or venturer is able to control the timing of the reversal of the temporary difference and it is probable that the temporary difference will not reverse in the foreseeable future.

(d) *Changes in exchange rates: investments*

There may be either a taxable temporary difference or a deductible temporary difference in this situation. IAS 12 does not allow recognition of the resulting deferred tax liability if the parent, investor or venturer is able to control the timing of the reversal of the temporary difference and it is probable that the temporary difference will not reverse in the foreseeable future.

(e) *Changes in exchange rates: use of own currency*

Again, there may be either a taxable temporary difference or a deductible temporary difference. Where there is a taxable temporary difference, the resulting deferred tax liability is recognised, because it relates to the foreign operation's own assets and liabilities, rather than to the reporting **entity**'s investment in that foreign operation. The deferred tax is charged to profit or loss.

6.1.2 Circumstances that give rise to deductible temporary differences

- A **liability is recognised at its fair value** in a business combination that is an acquisition, but none of the related expense is deducted in determining taxable profit until a later period
- **Unrealised profits resulting from intragroup transactions** are eliminated from the carrying amount of assets, such as inventory or property, plant or equipment, but no equivalent adjustment is made for tax purposes
- Investments in foreign subsidiaries, branches or associates or interests in foreign joint ventures are affected by **changes in foreign exchange rates**
- A foreign operation accounts for its non-monetary assets in its own (functional) currency. If its taxable profit or loss is determined in a different currency (under the presentation currency method) changes in the exchange rate result in temporary differences. The resulting deferred tax is charged or credited to profit or loss.

Question

Deferred tax and business combinations 2

What are the consequences of the above situations?

Note. Again, you should read to the end of this section before you answer this question.

Answer

(a) *Fair value of liabilities*

The resulting deferred tax asset decreases goodwill or increases negative goodwill.

(b) *Unrealised profits*

As in above

(c)   *Changes in exchange rates: investments*

As noted in Question 7, there may be a taxable temporary difference or a deductible temporary difference. IAS 12 requires recognition of the resulting deferred tax asset to the extent, and only to the extent, that it is probable that:

(i)   the temporary difference will reverse in the foreseeable future; and

(ii)   taxable profit will be available against which the temporary difference can be utilised.

(d)   *Changes in exchange rates: use of own currency*

As noted in the question before this, there may be either a taxable temporary difference or a deductible temporary difference. Where there is a deductible temporary difference, the resulting deferred tax asset is recognised to the extent that it is probable that sufficient taxable profit will be available, because the deferred tax asset relates to the foreign operation's own assets and liabilities, rather than to the reporting **entity**'s investment in that foreign operation. The deferred tax is charged to profit or loss.

6.2 Taxable temporary differences

In a business combination, the cost of the acquisition must be allocated to the fair values of the identifiable assets and liabilities acquired as at the date of the transaction. Temporary differences will arise when the tax bases of the identifiable assets and liabilities acquired are not affected by the business combination or are affected differently. For example, the carrying amount of an asset is increased to fair value but the tax base of the asset remains at cost to the previous owner; a taxable temporary difference arises which results in a deferred tax liability and this will also affect goodwill.

6.3 Deductible temporary differences

In a business combination that is an acquisition, as in Paragraph 6.2 above, when a **liability** is recognised on acquisition but the related costs are not deducted in determining taxable profits until a later period, a deductible temporary difference arises resulting in a deferred tax asset. A deferred tax asset will also arise when the fair value of an identifiable asset acquired is less than its tax base. In both these cases goodwill is affected (see below).

6.4 Investments in subsidiaries, branches and associates and interests in joint ventures

When such investments are held, **temporary differences** arise because the carrying amount of the investment (ie the parent's share of the net assets including goodwill) becomes different from the tax base (often the cost) of the investment. Why do these differences arise? These are some examples.

- There are **undistributable profits** held by subsidiaries, branches, associates and joint ventures
- There are **changes in foreign exchange rates** when a parent and its subsidiary are based in different countries
- There is a **reduction in the carrying amount** of an investment in an associate to its recoverable amount

The **temporary difference in the consolidated financial statements** may be different from the temporary difference associated with that investment in the parent's separate financial statements when the parent carries the investment in its separate financial statements at cost or revalued amount.

IAS 12 requires entities to **recognise a deferred tax liability** for all taxable temporary differences associated with investments in subsidiaries, branches and associates, and interests in joint ventures, *except* to the extent that both of these conditions are satisfied:

(a)   The parent/investor/venturer is able to **control the timing of the reversal** of the temporary difference

(b)   It is probable that the temporary difference **will not reverse** in the foreseeable future.

As well as the fact of parent control over reversal of temporary differences, it would often be **impracticable** to determine the amount of income taxes payable when the temporary differences reverses. So when the parent has determined that those profits will not be distributed in the foreseeable future, the parent does not recognise a deferred tax liability. The same applies to investments in branches.

Where a foreign operation's taxable profit or tax loss (and therefore the tax base of its non-monetary assets and liabilities) is determined in a **foreign currency**, changes in the exchange rate give rise to temporary differences. These relate to the foreign entity's own assets and liabilities, rather than to the reporting entity's investment in that foreign operation, and so the reporting entity should recognise the resulting deferred tax liability or asset. The resulting deferred tax is charged or credited to profit or loss.

An investor in an **associate** does not control that entity and so cannot determine its dividend policy. Without an agreement requiring that the profits of the associate should not be distributed in the foreseeable future, therefore, an investor should recognise a deferred tax liability arising from taxable temporary differences associated with its investment in the associate. Where an investor cannot determine the exact amount of tax, but only a minimum amount, then the deferred tax liability should be that amount.

In a **joint venture**, the agreement between the parties usually deals with profit sharing. When a venturer can control the sharing of profits and it is probable that the profits will not be distributed in the foreseeable future, a deferred liability is not recognised.

IAS 12 then states that a **deferred tax asset** should be recognised for all deductible temporary differences arising from investments in subsidiaries, branches and associates, and interests in joint ventures, to the extent that (and *only* to the extent that) both these are probable:

(a)   that the temporary difference will **reverse** in the foreseeable future, **and**

(b)   that **taxable profit** will be available against which the temporary difference can be utilised.

The **prudence principles** discussed above for the recognition of deferred tax assets should be considered.

6.5 Recognition of deferred tax arising from business combinations

As noted above, temporary differences may arise in a business combination. IFRS 3 *Business combinations* requires an entity to recognise any resulting deferred tax assets (to the extent that they meet the relevant recognition criteria) or deferred tax liabilities as identifiable assets and liabilities at the date of acquisition. These deferred tax assets and liabilities, consequently, will **affect goodwill or negative goodwill**. An entity will not, however, recognise deferred tax liabilities arising from the initial recognition of goodwill.

An acquirer may consider that, as a result of a business combination, it is probable that it will **recover its own deferred tax asset** that was not recognised prior to the business combination, eg by utilising unused tax losses against the future taxable profit of the acquiree. The acquirer should recognise a deferred tax asset but does not take it into account in calculating goodwill.

If deferred tax assets of an acquiree were not originally recognised as identifiable assets at the acquisition date but are realised and **recognised subsequently**, deferred tax income is recognised in profit or loss. The acquirer should also:

(a)   **Adjust (reduce) the carrying amount of goodwill** to the amount that would have been recognised if the deferred tax asset had been recognised at acquisition, and

(b)   **Recognise the reduction in the carrying amount** of goodwill as an expense.

The acquirer cannot, however, recognise negative goodwill. In other words, the acquirer cannot recognise a gain in the statement of comprehensive income.

Question

In 20X2 Jacko Co acquired a subsidiary, Jilly Co, which had deductible temporary differences of $3m. The tax rate at the date of acquisition was 30%. The resulting deferred tax asset of $0.9m was not recognised as an identifiable asset in determining the goodwill of $5m resulting from the business combination. Two years after the acquisition, Jacko Co decided that future taxable profit would probably be sufficient for the entity to recover the benefit of all the deductible temporary differences.

Required

(a)   Consider the accounting treatment of the subsequent recognition of the deferred tax asset in 20X4.

(b)   What would happen if the tax rate had risen to 40% by 20X4 or decreased to 20%?

Answer

(a)   The entity recognises a deferred tax asset of $0.9m ($3m × 30%) and, in profit or loss statement, deferred tax income of $0.9m. It also reduces the cost of the goodwill by $0.9m and recognises an expense of $0.9m in profit or loss. The cost of goodwill is reduced to $4.1m, ie the amount that would have been recorded if a deferred tax asset of $0.9m had been recognised as an identifiable asset at the date of the business combination.

(b)   If the tax rate rises to 40%, the entity should recognise a deferred tax asset of $1.2m ($3m × 40%) and, in profit or loss, deferred tax income of $0.12m.

        If the tax rate falls to 20%, the entity should recognise a deferred tax asset of $0.6m ($3m × 20%) and deferred tax income of $0.6m.

        In both cases, the entity will also reduce the cost of goodwill by $0.9m and recognise an expense for that amount in profit or loss.

6.6 Example: Deferred tax adjustments (1)

Red is a private limited company and has two 100% owned subsidiaries, Blue and Green, both themselves private limited companies. Red acquired Green on 1 January 20X2 for $5 million when the Fair value of the net assets was $4 million, and the tax base of the net assets was $3.5 million. The acquisition of Green and Blue was part of a business strategy whereby Red would build up the 'value' of the group over a three year period and then list its existing share capital on the stock exchange.

(a)   The following details relate to the acquisition of Green, which manufactures electronic goods.

        (i)   Part of the purchase price has been allocated to intangible assets because it relates to the acquisition of a database of key customers from Green. The recognition and measurement criteria for an intangible asset under IFRS 3 *Business combinations*/IAS 38 *Intangible assets* do not appear to have been met but the directors feel that the intangible asset of $0.5 million will be allowed for tax purposes and have computed the tax provision accordingly. However, the tax authorities could possibly challenge this opinion.

        (ii)   Green has sold goods worth $3 million to Red since acquisition and made a profit of $1 million on the transaction. The inventory of these goods recorded in Red's statement of financial position at the year end of 31 May 20X2 was $1.8 million.

        (iii)   The balance on the retained earnings of Green at acquisition was $2 million. The directors of Red have decided that, during the three years to the date that they intend to list the shares of the company, they will realise earnings through future dividend payments from the subsidiary amounting to $500,000 per year. Tax is payable on any remittance or dividends and no dividends have been declared for the current year.

(b)   Blue was acquired on 1 June 20X1 and is a company which undertakes various projects ranging from debt factoring to investing in property and commodities. The following details relate to Blue for the year ending 31 May 20X2.

        (i)   Blue has a portfolio of readily marketable government securities which are held as current assets. These investments are stated at market value in the statement of financial position with any gain or loss taken to the income statement. These gains and losses are taxed when the investments are sold. Currently the accumulated unrealised gains are $4 million.

        (ii)   Blue has calculated that it requires a specific allowance of $2 million against loans in its portfolio. Tax relief is available when the specific loan is written off.

        (iii)   When Red acquired Blue it had unused tax losses brought forward. At 1 June 20X1, it appeared that Blue would have sufficient taxable profit to realise the deferred tax asset created by these losses but subsequent events have proven that the future taxable profit will not be sufficient to realise all of the unused tax loss.

The current tax rate for Red is 30% and for public companies is 35%.

Required

Write a note suitable for presentation to the partner of an accounting firm setting out the deferred tax implications of the above information for the Red Group of companies.

Solution: Deferred tax adjustments (1)

Acquisition of the subsidiaries – general

Fair value adjustments have been made for consolidation purposes in both cases and these will **affect** the **deferred tax charge for the year**. This is because the deferred tax position is viewed **from the perspective of the group as a whole**. For example, it may be possible to recognise deferred tax assets which previously could not be recognised by individual companies, because there are now sufficient tax profits available within the group to utilise unused tax losses. Therefore a **provision** should be made for **temporary differences between fair values of the identifiable net assets acquired and their carrying values** ($4 million less $3.5 million in respect of Green). **No provision should be made for the temporary difference** of $1 million arising on goodwill recognised as a result of the combination with Green.

Future listing

Red plans to seek a listing in three years time. Therefore it will become a **public company** and will be subject to a **higher rate of tax**. IAS 12 states that deferred tax should be measured at the **average tax rates expected to apply in the periods in which the timing differences are expected to reverse**, based on current enacted tax rates and laws. This means that Red may be paying tax at the higher rate when some of its timing differences reverse and this should be taken into account in the calculation.

Acquisition of Green

(a) The directors have calculated the tax provision on the assumption that the intangible asset of $0.5 million will be allowed for tax purposes. However, this is not certain and the directors **may eventually have to pay the additional tax**. If the directors cannot be persuaded to adjust their calculations a **liability for the additional tax should be recognised**.

(b) The intra-group transaction has resulted in an **unrealised profit** of $0.6 million in the group accounts and this will be **eliminated on consolidation**. The tax charge in the group statement of comprehensive income includes the tax on this profit, for which **the group will not become liable to tax until the following period. From the perspective of the group, there is a temporary difference**. Because the temporary difference arises in the financial statements of Red, **deferred tax should be provided** on this difference (an asset) using the rate of tax payable by Red.

(c) **Deferred tax should be recognised on the unremitted earnings of subsidiaries** unless the parent is able to **control the timing of dividend payments** or it is **unlikely that dividends will be paid for the foreseeable future**. Red controls the dividend policy of Green and this means that there would normally be no need to make a provision in respect of unremitted profits. However, the profits of Green **will be distributed** to Red over the next few years and **tax will be payable** on the dividends received. Therefore a **deferred tax liability should be shown**.

Acquisition of Blue

(a) A **temporary difference arises** where non-monetary assets are **revalued upwards** and the **tax treatment of the surplus is different from the accounting treatment**. In this case, the revaluation surplus has been **recognised in profit or loss** for the current period, rather than in equity but no corresponding adjustment has been made to the tax base of the investments because the gains will be taxed in future periods. Therefore the company **should recognise a deferred tax liability on the temporary difference of $4 million**.

(b) A temporary difference arises when the provision for the loss on the loan portfolio is first recognised. The general allowance is expected to increase and therefore it is unlikely that the temporary difference will reverse in the near future. However, a **deferred tax liability should still be recognised**. The temporary difference gives rise to a **deferred tax asset**. IAS 12 states that **deferred tax assets should not be recognised unless it is probable that taxable profits will be available** against which the taxable profits can be utilised. **This is affected by the situation in point (c) below**.

(c)   In theory, unused tax losses give rise to a deferred tax asset. However, IAS 12 states that **deferred tax assets should only be recognised to the extent that they are regarded as recoverable**. They should be regarded as recoverable to the extent that on the basis of all the evidence available it is **probable that there will be suitable taxable profits against which the losses can be recovered**. The future taxable profit of Blue **will not be sufficient to realise all the unused tax loss. Therefore the deferred tax asset is reduced to the amount that is expected to be recovered**.

This reduction in the deferred tax asset implies that it was **overstated at 1 June 20X1**, when it was acquired by the group. As these are the first post-acquisition financial statements, **goodwill should also be adjusted**.

6.7 Example: Deferred tax adjustments 2

You are the accountant of Pay it. Your assistant is preparing the consolidated financial statements of the year ended 31 March 20X2. However, he is unsure how to account for the deferred tax effects of certain transactions as he has not studied IAS 12. These transactions are given below.

Transaction 1

During the year, Pay it sold goods to a subsidiary for $10 million, making a profit of 20% on selling price. 25% of these goods were still in the inventories of the subsidiary at 31 March 20X2. The subsidiary and Pay it are in the same tax jurisdiction and pay tax on profits at 30%.

Transaction 2

An overseas subsidiary made a loss adjusted for tax purposes of $8 million ($ equivalent). The only relief available for this tax loss is to carry it forward for offset against future taxable profits of the overseas subsidiary. Taxable profits of the oversees subsidiary suffer tax at a rate of 25%.

Required

Compute the effect of both the above transactions on the deferred tax amounts in the consolidated statement of financial position of Pay it at 31 March 20X2. You should provide a full explanation for your calculations and indicate any assumptions you make in formulating your answer.

Solution: Deferred tax adjustments 2

Transaction 1

This intra-group sale will give rise to a **provision for unrealised profit** on the unsold inventory of $10,000,000 \times 20\% \times 25\% = \$500,000$. This provision must be made in the consolidated accounts. However, this profit has already been taxed in the financial statements of Payit. In other words there is a **timing difference**. In the following year when the stock is sold outside the group, the provision will be released, but the profit will not be taxed. The timing difference therefore gives rise to a **deferred tax asset**. The asset is $30\% \times \$500,000 = \$150,000$.

Deferred tax assets are recognised to the extent that they are **recoverable**. This will be the case if **it is more likely than not** that **suitable tax profits** will exist from which the reversal of the timing difference giving rise to the asset can be deducted. The asset is carried forward on this assumption.

Transaction 2

An unrelieved tax loss gives rise to a **timing difference** because the loss is recognised in the financial statements but not yet allowed for tax purposes. When the overseas subsidiary generates sufficient taxable profits, the loss will be offset against these in arriving at taxable profits.

The amount of the deferred tax asset to be carried forward is $25\% \times \$8m = \$2m$.

As with Transaction 1, deferred tax assets are recognised to the extent that they are **recoverable.** This will be the case if **it is more likely than not** that **suitable tax profits** will exist from which the reversal of the timing difference giving rise to the asset can be deducted.

6.8 Section summary

In relation to deferred tax and business combinations you should be familiar with:

- Circumstances that give rise to **taxable temporary differences**
- Circumstances that give rise to **deductible temporary differences**
- Their **treatment** once an acquisition takes place
- Reasons **why deferred tax arises** when investments are held
- **Recognition** of deferred tax on business combinations

Chapter Roundup

- Taxation consists of **two components.**
  - Current tax
  - Deferred tax

- **Current tax** is the amount payable to the tax authorities in relation to the trading activities during the period. It is generally straightforward.

- **Deferred tax** is an accounting measure, used to match the tax effects of transactions with their accounting impact. It is quite complex.

- **Deferred tax assets and liabilities** arise from taxable and deductible temporary differences.

- **IAS 12** *Income taxes* covers both current and deferred tax. It has substantial presentation and disclosure requirements.

- You must appreciate the deferred tax aspects of **business combinations**: this is the aspect of deferred tax most likely to appear in the Paper P2 exam.

1   What is the difference between 'current tax' and 'deferred tax'?

2   How should current tax be measured?

    A   The total liability, including deferred tax
    B   The amount expected to be paid to (or recovered from) the tax authorities
    C   The amount calculated on profit at current tax rates
    D   The amount calculated on profit at future tax rates

3   A taxable temporary difference does *not* give rise to a deferred tax liability. *True or false*?

4   What is the basis of provision for deferred tax required by IAS 12?

5   What two methods can be used for calculating deferred tax when the tax rate changes?

6   Current tax assets and liabilities cannot be offset. *True or false*?

7   How do temporary differences arise when investments are held in subsidiaries, associates etc?

Answers to Quick Quiz

1   (a)   Current tax is the amount actually payable to the tax authorities.
    (b)   Deferred tax is used to match the tax effects of transactions with their accounting impact.

2   B   The amount expected to be paid to (or recovered from) the tax authorities.

3   True.

4   Full provision

5   • Deferral method
    • Liability method

6   False. They can be offset only if the entity has a legally enforceable right to offset *and* it intends to actually carry out the offset.

7   When the carrying amounts of the investment become different to the tax base of the investment.

Now try the question below from the Exam Question Bank

Number	Level	Marks	Time
Q8	Examination	25	45 mins

7

Financial instruments

Topic list	Syllabus reference
1 Financial instruments	C3
2 Presentation of financial instruments	C3
3 Recognition of financial instruments	C3
4 Measurement of financial instruments	C3
5 Embedded derivatives	C3
6 Hedging	C3
7 Reducing complexity	C3
8 Amended reclassification rules	C3
9 Disclosure of financial instruments	C3

Introduction

Financial instruments sounds like a daunting subject, and indeed this is a complex and controversial area. The numbers involved in financial instruments are often huge, but don't let this put you off. In this chapter we aim to simplify the topic as much as possible and to focus on the important issues.

The discussion paper on reducing complexity is topical.

Study guide

Exam guide

This is a highly controversial topic and therefore, likely to be examined, probably in Section B.

Exam focus point

> Although the very complexity of this topic makes it a highly likely subject for an exam question in Paper P2, there are limits as to how complicated and detailed a question the examiner can set with any realistic expectation of students being able to answer it. You should therefore concentrate on the essential points. To date, financial instruments have mainly been examined within a larger scenario based question. Candidates have been asked to advise on the broad financial reporting implications of an entity having financial instruments. However, a more detailed question with a main focus on this topic cannot be ruled out.

1 Financial instruments   6/08

FAST FORWARD

> Financial instruments can be very complex, particularly **derivative instruments**, although **primary instruments** are more straightforward.

1.1 Background

If you read the financial press you will probably be aware of **rapid international expansion** in the use of financial instruments. These vary from straightforward, traditional instruments, eg bonds, through to various forms of so-called 'derivative instruments'.

We can perhaps summarise the reasons why a project on the accounting for financial instruments was considered necessary as follows.

(a)   The **significant growth of financial instruments** over recent years has outstripped the development of guidance for their accounting.

(b)   The topic is of **international concern**, other national standard-setters are involved as well as the IASB.

(c)   There have been recent **high-profile disasters** involving derivatives (eg Barings) which, while not caused by accounting failures, have raised questions about accounting and disclosure practices.

These are three Standards on financial instruments:

(a)   IAS 32 Financial instruments: Presentation, which deals with:

(i)   The classification of financial instruments between liabilities and equity

(ii)   Presentation of certain compound instruments

(b)   IFRS 7 *Financial instruments: Disclosures*, which revised, simplified and incorporated disclosure requirements previously in IAS 32.

(c)   IAS 39 Financial instruments: Recognition and measurement, which deals with:

(i)   Recognition and derecognition
(ii)   The measurement of financial instruments
(iii)   Hedge accounting

1.2 Definitions

The most important definitions are common to both Standards.

The important definitions to learn are:

- **Financial asset**
- **Financial liability**
- **Equity instrument**

Key terms

Financial instrument. Any contract that gives rise to both a financial asset of one entity and a financial liability or equity instrument of another entity.

Financial asset. Any asset that is:

(a)   cash

(b)   an equity instrument of another entity

(c)   a contractual right to receive cash or another financial asset from another entity; or to exchange financial instruments with another entity under conditions that are potentially   favourable to the entity, or

(d)   a contract that will or may be settled in the entity's own equity instruments and is:

(i)   a non-derivative for which the entity is or may be obliged to receive a variable number of the entity's own equity instruments; or

(ii)   a derivative that will or may be settled other than by the exchange of a fixed amount of cash or another financial asset for a fixed number of the entity's own equity instruments.

Financial liability. Any liability that is:

(a)   a contractual obligation:

(i)   to deliver cash or another financial asset to another entity, or

(ii)   to exchange financial instruments with another entity under conditions that are potentially unfavourable; or

(b)   a contract that will or may be settled in the entity's own equity instruments and is:

(i)   a non-derivative for which the entity is or may be obliged to deliver a variable number of the entity's own equity instruments; or

(ii)   a derivative that will or may be settled other than by the exchange of a fixed amount of cash or another financial asset for a fixed number of the entity's own equity instruments.

Equity instrument. Any contract that evidences a residual interest in the assets of an entity after deducting all of its liabilities.

Fair value is the amount for which an asset could be exchanged, or a liability settled, between knowledgeable, willing parties in an arm's length transaction

Derivative. A financial instrument or other contract with all three of the following characteristics:

(a)   its value changes in response to the change in a specified interest rate, financial instrument price, commodity price, foreign exchange rate, index of prices or rates, credit rating or credit index, or other variable (sometimes called the 'underlying');

(b) it requires no initial net investment or an initial net investment that is smaller than would be required for other types of contracts that would be expected to have a similar response to changes in market factors; and

(c) it is settled at a future date.

(IAS 32 and IAS 39)

These definitions are very important – particularly the first three – so learn them.

We should clarify some points arising from these definitions. Firstly, one or two terms above should be themselves defined.

(a) A '**contract**' need not be in writing, but it must comprise an agreement that has 'clear economic consequences' and which the parties to it cannot avoid, usually because the agreement is enforceable in law.

(b) An '**entity**' here could be an individual, partnership, incorporated body or government agency.

The definitions of **financial assets and financial liabilities** may seem rather circular, referring as they do to the terms financial asset and financial instrument. The point is that there may be a chain of contractual rights and obligations, but it will lead ultimately to the receipt or payment of cash *or* the acquisition or issue of an equity instrument.

Examples of **financial assets** include:

(a) Trade receivables
(b) Options
(c) Shares (when used as an investment).

Examples of **financial liabilities** include:

(a) Trade payables
(b) Debenture loans payable
(c) Redeemable preference (non-equity) shares
(d) Forward contracts standing at a loss.

As we have already noted, financial instruments include both of the following.

(a) **Primary instruments**: eg receivables, payables and equity securities

(b) **Derivative instruments**: eg financial options, futures and forwards, interest rate swaps and currency swaps, **whether recognised or unrecognised**

IAS 32 makes it clear that the following items are *not* financial instruments.

- **Physical assets**, eg inventories, property, plant and equipment, leased assets and intangible assets (patents, trademarks etc)

- **Prepaid expenses**, deferred revenue and most warranty obligations

- Liabilities or assets that are **not contractual** in nature

- Contractual rights/obligations that **do not involve transfer of a financial asset**, eg commodity futures contracts, operating leases

Question

Why not?

Can you give the reasons why the first two items listed above do not qualify as financial instruments?

Answer

Refer to the definitions of financial assets and liabilities given above.

(a) **Physical assets**: control of these creates an opportunity to generate an inflow of cash or other assets, but it does not give rise to a present right to receive cash or other financial assets.

(b)   **Prepaid expenses, etc**: the future economic benefit is the receipt of goods/services rather than the right to receive cash or other financial assets.

(c)   **Deferred revenue, warranty obligations**: the probable outflow of economic benefits is the delivery of goods/services rather than cash or another financial asset.

Contingent rights and obligations meet the definition of financial assets and financial liabilities respectively, even though many do not qualify for recognition in financial statements. This is because the contractual rights or obligations exist because of a past transaction or event (eg assumption of a guarantee).

1.3 Derivatives

A **derivative** is a financial instrument that **derives** its value from the price or rate of an underlying item. Common **examples** of derivatives include:

(a)   **Forward contracts**: agreements to buy or sell an asset at a fixed price at a fixed future date

(b)   **Futures contracts**: similar to forward contracts except that contracts are standardised and traded on an exchange

(c)   **Options**: rights (but not obligations) for the option holder to exercise at a pre-determined price; the option writer loses out if the option is exercised

(d)   **Swaps**: agreements to swap one set of cash flows for another (normally interest rate or currency swaps).

The nature of derivatives often gives rise to **particular problems**. The **value** of a derivative (and the amount at which it is eventually settled) depends on **movements** in an underlying item (such as an exchange rate). This means that settlement of a derivative can lead to a very different result from the one originally envisaged. A company which has derivatives is exposed to **uncertainty and risk** (potential for gain or loss) and this can have a very material effect on its financial performance, financial position and cash flows.

Yet because a derivative contract normally has **little or no initial cost**, under traditional accounting it **may not be recognised** in the financial statements at all. Alternatively it may be recognised at an amount which bears no relation to its current value. This is clearly **misleading** and leaves users of the financial statements unaware of the **level of risk** that the company faces. IASs 32 and 39 were developed in order to correct this situation.

1.4 Section summary

-    Third accounting standards are relevant:
     -    **IAS 32**: Financial instruments: Presentation
     -    **IFRS 7**: Financial instruments: Disclosures
     -    **IAS 39**: Financial instruments: Recognition and measurement

-    The definitions of **financial asset, financial liability** and **equity instrument** are fundamental to the standards.

-    Financial instruments include:
     -    **Primary** instruments
     -    **Derivative** instruments

2 Presentation of financial instruments

2.1 Objective

The objective of IAS 32 is:

'to enhance financial statement users' understanding of the significance of on-balance-sheet and off-balance-sheet financial instruments to an entity's financial position, performance and cash flows.'

2.2 Scope

IAS 32 should be applied in the presentation of **all types of financial instruments**, whether recognised or unrecognised.

Certain items are **excluded**.

- Interests in subsidiaries (IAS 27: Chapter 12)
- Interests in associates (IAS 28: Chapter 12)
- Interests in joint ventures (IAS 31: Chapter 12)
- Pensions and other post-retirement benefits (IAS 19: Chapter 5)
- Insurance contracts
- Contracts for contingent consideration in a business combination
- Contracts that require a payment based on climatic, geological or other physical variables
- Financial instruments, contracts and obligations under share-based payment transactions (IFRS 2: Chapter 8)

2.3 Liabilities and equity

FAST FORWARD

> Financial instruments must be classified as **liabilities** or **equity** according to their **substance**.
>
> The critical feature of a financial liability is the **contractual obligation to deliver cash** or another financial asset.

The main thrust of IAS 32 here is that financial instruments should be presented according to their **substance, not merely their legal form**. In particular, entities which issue financial instruments should classify them (or their component parts) as **either financial liabilities, or equity**.

The classification of a financial instrument as a liability or as equity depends on the following.

- The substance of the contractual arrangement on initial recognition
- The definitions of a financial liability and an equity instrument

How should a **financial liability be distinguished from an equity instrument**? The critical feature of a **liability** is an **obligation** to transfer economic benefit. Therefore a financial instrument is a financial liability if there is a **contractual obligation** on the issuer either to deliver cash or another financial asset to the holder or to exchange another financial instrument with the holder under potentially unfavourable conditions to the issuer.

The financial liability exists **regardless of the way in which the contractual obligation will be settled**. The issuer's ability to satisfy an obligation may be restricted, eg by lack of access to foreign currency, but this is irrelevant as it does not remove the issuer's obligation or the holder's right under the instrument.

Where the above critical feature is *not* met, then the financial instrument is an **equity instrument**. IAS 32 explains that although the holder of an equity instrument may be entitled to a *pro rata* share of any distributions out of equity, the issuer does *not* have a contractual obligation to make such a distribution.

Although substance and legal form are often **consistent with each other**, this is not always the case. In particular, a financial instrument may have the legal form of equity, but in substance it is in fact a liability. Other instruments may combine features of both equity instruments and financial liabilities.

For example, many entities issue **preferred shares** which must be **redeemed** by the issuer for a fixed (or determinable) amount at a fixed (or determinable) future date. Alternatively, the holder may have the right to require the issuer to redeem the shares at or after a certain date for a fixed amount. In such cases, the issuer has an **obligation**. Therefore the instrument is a **financial liability** and should be classified as such.

The classification of the financial instrument is made when it is **first recognised** and this classification will continue until the financial instrument is removed from the entity's statement of financial position.

2.4 Contingent settlement provisions

An entity may issue a financial instrument where the way in which it is settled depends on:

(a)   The occurrence or non-occurrence of uncertain future events, or
(b)   The outcome of uncertain circumstances,

that are beyond the control of both the holder and the issuer of the instrument. For example, an entity might have to deliver cash instead of issuing equity shares. In this situation it is not immediately clear whether the entity has an equity instrument or a financial liability.

Such financial instruments should be classified as **financial liabilities** unless the possibility of settlement is remote.

2.5 Settlement options

When a derivative financial instrument gives one party a **choice** over how it is settled (eg, the issuer can choose whether to settle in cash or by issuing shares) the instrument is a **financial asset** or a **financial liability** unless **all the alternative choices** would result in it being an equity instrument.

2.6 Compound financial instruments

FAST FORWARD

Compound instruments are split into **equity** and **liability** components and presented accordingly in the statement of financial position.

Some financial instruments contain both a liability and an equity element. In such cases, IAS 32 requires the component parts of the instrument to be **classified separately**, according to the substance of the contractual arrangement and the definitions of a financial liability and an equity instrument.

One of the most common types of compound instrument is **convertible debt**. This creates a primary financial liability of the issuer and grants an option to the holder of the instrument to convert it into an equity instrument (usually ordinary shares) of the issuer. This is the economic equivalent of the issue of conventional debt plus a warrant to acquire shares in the future.

Although in theory there are several possible ways of calculating the split, the following method is recommended:

(a)   Calculate the value for the liability component.
(b)   Deduct this from the instrument as a whole to leave a residual value for the equity component.

The reasoning behind this approach is that an entity's equity is its residual interest in its assets amount after deducting all its liabilities.

The **sum of the carrying amounts** assigned to liability and equity will always be equal to the carrying amount that would be ascribed to the instrument **as a whole**.

2.7 Example: valuation of compound instruments

Rathbone Co issues 2,000 convertible bonds at the start of 20X2. The bonds have a three year term, and are issued at par with a face value of $1,000 per bond, giving total proceeds of $2,000,000. Interest is payable annually in arrears at a nominal annual interest rate of 6%. Each bond is convertible at any time up to maturity into 250 common shares.

When the bonds are issued, the prevailing market interest rate for similar debt without conversion options is 9%. At the issue date, the market price of one common share is $3. The dividends expected over the three year term of the bonds amount to 14c per share at the end of each year. The risk-free annual interest rate for a three year term is 5%.

Required

What is the value of the equity component in the bond?

Solution

The liability component is valued first, and the difference between the proceeds of the bond issue and the fair value of the liability is assigned to the equity component. The present value of the liability component is calculated using a discount rate of 9%, the market interest rate for similar bonds having no conversion rights, as shown.

	$
Present value of the principal: $2,000,000 payable at the end of three years ($2m × 0.772)*	1,544,000
Present value of the interest: $120,000 payable annually in arrears for three years ($120,000 × 2.531)*	303,725
Total liability component	1,847,720
Equity component (balancing figure)	152,280
Proceeds of the bond issue	2,000,000

* These figures can be obtained from discount and annuity tables.

The split between the liability and equity components remains the same throughout the term of the instrument, even if there are changes in the **likelihood of the option being exercised.** This is because it is not always possible to predict how a holder will behave. The issuer continues to have an obligation to make future payments until conversion, maturity of the instrument or some other relevant transaction takes place.

2.8 Treasury shares

If an entity **reacquires its own equity instruments**, those instruments ('treasury shares') shall be **deducted from equity**. No gain or loss shall be recognised in profit or loss on the purchase, sale, issue or cancellation of an entity's own equity instruments. Consideration paid or received shall be recognised directly in equity.

2.9 Interest, dividends, losses and gains

As well as looking at statement of financial position presentation, IAS 32 considers how financial instruments affect the profit or loss (and movements in equity). The treatment varies according to whether interest, dividends, losses or gains relate to a financial liability or an equity instrument.

(a)   Interest, dividends, losses and gains relating to a financial instrument (or component part) classified as a **financial liability** should be recognised as **income or expense** in profit or loss.

(b)   Distributions to holders of a financial instrument classified as an **equity instrument** should be **debited directly to equity** by the issuer.

(c)   **Transaction costs** of an equity transaction shall be accounted for as a **deduction from equity** (unless they are directly attributable to the acquisition of a business, in which case they are accounted for under IFRS 3).

You should look at the requirements of IAS 1 *Presentation of financial statements* for further details of disclosure, and IAS 12 *Income taxes* for disclosure of tax effects.

2.10 Offsetting a financial asset and a financial liability

A financial asset and financial liability should **only** be **offset**, with the net amount reported in the statement of financial position, when an entity:

(a)   has a legally enforceable right of set off, *and*

(b)   intends to settle on a net basis, or to realise the asset and settle the liability simultaneously, ie at the same moment.

This will reflect the expected **future cash flows** of the entity in these specific circumstances. In all other cases, financial assets and financial liabilities are presented separately.

2.11 Amendment to IAS 32: Puttable financial instruments and obligations arising on liquidation

This amendment was issued in February 2008. The changes deal with puttable financial instruments and the effect obligations that arise on liquidation have on determining whether an instrument is debt or equity.

IAS 32 requires that if the holder of a financial instrument can require the issuer to redeem it for cash it should be classified as a liability. Some ordinary shares and partnership interests allow the holder to 'put' the instrument (that is to require the issuer to redeem it in cash). Such shares might more usually be considered as equity, but application of IAS 32 results in their being classified as liabilities.

The amendment would requires entities to classify such instruments as equity, so long as they meet certain conditions. The amendment further requires that instruments imposing an obligation on an entity to deliver to another party a pro rata share of the net assets only on liquidation should be classified as equity.

2.12 Section summary

*   Financial instruments issued to raise capital must be classified as **liabilities** or **equity**
*   The **substance** of the financial instrument is more important than its **legal form**
*   The **critical feature of a financial liability** is the contractual obligation to deliver cash or another financial instrument
*   **Compound instruments** are split into equity and liability parts and presented accordingly
*   **Interest, dividends, losses and gains** are treated according to whether they relate to an equity instrument or a financial liability

3 Recognition of financial instruments

IAS 39 *Financial instruments: recognition and measurement* is a recent and most controversial standard.

The IAS states that all financial assets and liabilities should be recognised in the statement of financial position, including derivatives.

IAS 39 *Financial instruments: Recognition and measurement* establishes principles for recognising and measuring financial assets and financial liabilities.

3.1 Scope

IAS 39 applies to **all entities** and to **all types of financial instruments except** those specifically excluded, as listed below.

(a)   Investments in **subsidiaries, associates, and joint ventures** that are accounted for under IASs 27, 28 and 31

(b)   **Leases** covered in IAS 17

(c) **Employee benefit plans** covered in IAS 19

(d) **Insurance contracts**

(e) Equity instruments **issued by the entity** eg ordinary shares issued, or options and warrants

(f) **Financial guarantee** contracts

(g) **Contracts for contingent consideration** in a business combination, covered in IFRS 3

(h) Contracts requiring payment based on climatic, geological or other **physical variables**

(i) **Loan commitments** that cannot be settled net in cash or another financial instrument

(j) Financial instruments, contracts and obligations under **share based payment transactions,** covered in IFRS 2

3.2 Initial recognition

Financial instruments should be recognised in the statement of financial position when the entity becomes a party to the **contractual provisions of the instrument**.

<table>
<tr><td>Point to note</td><td>An important consequence of this is that all derivatives should be in the statement of financial position.</td></tr>
</table>

Notice that this is **different** from the recognition criteria in the *Framework* and in most other standards. Items are normally recognised when there is a probable inflow or outflow of resources and the item has a cost or value that can be measured reliably.

3.3 Example: initial recognition

An entity has entered into two separate contracts.

(a) A firm commitment (an order) to buy a specific quantity of iron.

(b) A forward contract to buy a specific quantity of iron at a specified price on a specified date, provided delivery of the iron is not taken.

Contract (a) is a **normal trading contract**. The entity does not recognise a liability for the iron until the goods have actually been delivered. (Note that this contract is not a financial instrument because it involves a physical asset, rather than a financial asset.)

Contract (b) is a **financial instrument**. Under IAS 39, the entity recognises a financial liability (an obligation to deliver cash) on the **commitment date**, rather than waiting for the closing date on which the exchange takes place.

Note that planned future transactions, no matter how likely, are not assets and liabilities of an entity – the entity has not yet become a party to the contract.

3.4 Derecognition

Derecognition is the removal of a previously recognised financial instrument from an entity's statement of financial position.

An entity should derecognise a **financial asset** when:

(a) The **contractual rights** to the cash flows from the financial asset **expire**, or

(b) The entity **transfers substantially all the risks and rewards of ownership** of the financial asset to another party.

Question

Risks and rewards

Can you think of an example of a situation in which:

(a) An entity has transferred substantially all the risks and rewards of ownership?

(b) An entity has retained substantially all the risks and rewards of ownership?

IAS 39 includes the following examples:

(a) (i) An unconditional sale of a financial asset
    (ii) A sale of a financial asset together with an option to repurchase the financial asset at its fair value at the time of repurchase

(b) (i) A sale and repurchase transaction where the repurchase price is a fixed price or the sale price plus a lender's return
    (ii) A sale of a financial asset together with a total return swap that transfers the market risk exposure back to the entity

Exam focus point

The principle here is that of **substance over form**.

An entity should derecognise a **financial liability** when it is **extinguished** – ie, when the obligation specified in the contract is discharged or cancelled or expires.

It is possible for only **part** of a financial asset or liability to be derecognised. This is allowed if the part comprises:

(a) only specifically identified cash flows; or
(b) only a fully proportionate (pro rata) share of the total cash flows.

For example, if an entity holds a bond it has the right to two separate sets of cash inflows: those relating to the principal and those relating to the interest. It could sell the right to receive the interest to another party while retaining the right to receive the principal.

On derecognition, the amount to be included in net profit or loss for the period is calculated as follows:

Formula to learn

	$	$
Carrying amount of asset/liability (or the portion of asset/liability) transferred		X
Less: Proceeds received/paid	X	
Any cumulative gain or loss reported in equity	X	
		(X)
Difference to net profit/loss		X

Where only part of a financial asset is derecognised, the carrying amount of the asset should be allocated between the part retained and the part transferred based on their relative fair values on the date of transfer. A gain or loss should be recognised based on the proceeds for the portion transferred.

3.5 Section summary

- **All financial assets** and **liabilities** should be **recognised in the statement of financial position**, including derivatives.
- Financial assets should be derecognised when the **rights to the cash flows** from the asset **expire** or where **substantially all the risks and rewards of ownership are transferred** to another party.
- Financial liabilities should be derecognised when they are **extinguished**.

4 Measurement of financial instruments

FAST FORWARD

Financial assets should initially be measured at cost = fair value.

Subsequently they should be re-measured to fair value except for

(a)   Loans and receivables not held for trading
(b)   Other held-to-maturity investments
(c)   Financial assets whose value cannot be reliably measured

4.1 Initial measurement

Financial instruments are initially measured at the **fair value** of the consideration given or received (ie, **cost**) **plus** (in most cases) **transaction costs** that are **directly attributable** to the acquisition or issue of the financial instrument.

The **exception** to this rule is where a financial instrument is designated as **at fair value through profit or loss** (this term is explained below). In this case, **transaction costs** are **not** added to fair value at initial recognition.

The fair value of the consideration is normally the transaction price or market prices. If market prices are not reliable, the fair value may be **estimated** using a valuation technique (for example, by discounting cash flows).

4.2 Subsequent measurement

For the purposes of measuring a financial asset held subsequent to initial recognition, IAS 39 classifies financial assets into four categories defined here. Note particularly the criteria for a financial asset or liability at fair value through profit and loss.

Key terms

> **A financial asset or liability at fair value through profit or loss** meets either of the following conditions:
>
> (a)   It is classified as held for trading. A financial instrument is classified as held for trading if it is:
>   (i)   Acquired or incurred principally for the purpose of selling or repurchasing it in the near term
>   (ii)   Part of a portfolio of identified financial instruments that are managed together and for which there is evidence of a recent actual pattern of short-term profit-taking, or
>   (iii) A derivative (unless it is a designated and effective hedging instrument).
>
> (b)   Upon initial recognition it is designated by the entity as at fair value through profit or loss. An entity may only use this designation in severely restricted circumstances:
>   (i)   It **eliminates** or significantly **reduces** a measurement or recognition **inconsistency** (mismatch) that would otherwise arise.
>   (ii)   A **group of** financial assets/liabilities is managed and its performance is evaluated **on a fair value basis**.
>
> **Held-to-maturity investments** are non-derivative financial assets with fixed or determinable payments and fixed maturity that an entity has the positive intent and ability to hold to maturity other than:
>
> (a)   Those that the entity upon initial recognition designates as at fair value through profit or loss
> (b)   Those that the entity designates as available for sale
> (c)   Those that meet the definition of loans and receivables
>
> **Loans and receivables** are non-derivative financial assets with fixed or determinable payments that are not quoted in an active market, other than:

(a) Those that the entity intends to sell immediately or in the near term, which should be classified as held for trading and those that the entity upon initial recognition designates as at fair value through profit or loss

(b) Those that the entity upon initial recognition designates as available-for-sale, or

(c) Those for which the holder may not recover substantially all of the initial investment, other than because of credit deterioration, which shall be classified as available for sale

An interest acquired in a pool of assets that are not loans or receivables (for example, an interest in a mutual fund or a similar fund) is not a loan or a receivable.

Available-for-sale financial assets are those financial assets that are not:

(a) Loans and receivables originated by the entity,

(b) Held-to-maturity investments, or

(c) Financial assets at fair value through profit or loss. *(IAS 39)*

After initial recognition, all financial assets should be **remeasured to fair value**, without any deduction for transaction costs that may be incurred on sale or other disposal, except for:

(a) Loans and receivables;

(b) Held to maturity investments;

(c) Investments in equity instruments that do not have a quoted market price in an active market and whose fair value cannot be reliably measured and derivatives that are linked to and must be settled by delivery of such unquoted equity instruments.

Loans and receivables and **held to maturity investments** should be measured at **amortised cost** using the **effective interest method**.

Amortised cost of a financial asset or financial liability is the amount at which the financial asset or liability is measured at initial recognition minus principal repayments, plus or minus the cumulative amortisation of any difference between that initial amount and the maturity amount, and minus any write-down (directly or through the use of an allowance account) for impairment or uncollectability.

The **effective interest method** is a method of calculating the amortised cost of a financial instrument and of allocating the interest income or interest expense over the relevant period.

The **effective interest rate** is the rate that exactly discounts estimated future cash payments or receipts through the expected life of the financial instrument to the net carrying amount of the financial asset or liability. *(IAS 39)*

4.3 Example: Amortised cost

On 1 January 20X1 Abacus Co purchases a debt instrument for its fair value of $1,000. The debt instrument is due to mature on 31 December 20X5. The instrument has a principal amount of $1,250 and the instrument carries fixed interest at 4.72% that is paid annually. (The effective interest rate is 10%.)

How should Abacus Co account for the debt instrument over its five year term?

Solution

Abacus Co will receive interest of $59 (1,250 × 4.72%) each year and $1,250 when the instrument matures.

Abacus must allocate the discount of $250 and the interest receivable over the five year term at a constant rate on the carrying amount of the debt. To do this, it must apply the effective interest rate of 10%.

The following table shows the allocation over the years:

Year	Amortised cost at beginning of year $	Profit or loss: Interest income for year (@10%) $	Interest received during year (cash inflow) $	Amortised cost at end of year $
20X1	1,000	100	(59)	1,041
20X2	1,041	104	(59)	1,086
20X3	1,086	109	(59)	1,136
20X4	1,136	113	(59)	1,190
20X5	1,190	119	(1,250+59)	–

Each year the carrying amount of the financial asset is increased by the interest income for the year and reduced by the interest actually received during the year.

Investments whose **fair value cannot be reliably measured** should be measured at **cost**.

4.4 Classification

There is a certain amount of flexibility in that **any** financial instrument can be designated as fair value through profit or loss. However, this is a **once and for all choice** and has to be made on initial recognition. Once a financial instrument has been classified in this way it **cannot be reclassified**, even if it would otherwise be possible to measure it at cost or amortised cost.

In contrast, it is quite difficult for an entity **not** to remeasure financial instruments to fair value.

Exam focus point

> Notice that derivatives **must** be remeasured to fair value. This is because it would be misleading to measure them at cost.

For a financial instrument to be held to maturity it must meet several extremely narrow criteria. The entity must have a **positive intent** and a **demonstrated ability** to hold the investment to maturity. These conditions are not met if:

(a) The entity intends to hold the financial asset for an undefined period

(b) The entity stands ready to sell the financial asset in response to changes in interest rates or risks, liquidity needs and similar factors (unless these situations could not possibly have been reasonably anticipated)

(c) The issuer has the right to settle the financial asset at an amount significantly below its amortised cost (because this right will almost certainly be exercised)

(d) It does not have the financial resources available to continue to finance the investment until maturity

(e) It is subject to an existing legal or other constraint that could frustrate its intention to hold the financial asset to maturity

In addition, an **equity** instrument is **unlikely** to meet the criteria for classification as held to maturity.

There is a **penalty** for selling or reclassifying a 'held-to-maturity' investment other than in certain very tightly defined circumstances. If this has occurred during the **current** financial year or during the **two preceding** financial years **no** financial asset can be classified as held-to-maturity.

If an entity can no longer hold an investment to maturity, it is no longer appropriate to use amortised cost and the asset must be re-measured to fair value. **All** remaining held-to-maturity investments must also be re-measured to fair value and classified as available-for-sale (see above).

4.5 Subsequent measurement of financial liabilities

After initial recognition, all financial liabilities should be measured at **amortised cost**, with the exception of financial liabilities at fair value through profit or loss (including most derivatives). These should be measured at **fair value**, but where the fair value **is not capable of reliable measurement**, they should be measured at **cost**.

Question

Galaxy Co issues a bond for $503,778 on 1 January 20X2. No interest is payable on the bond, but it will be held to maturity and redeemed on 31 December 20X4 for $600,000. The bond has **not** been designated as at fair value through profit or loss.

Required:

Calculate the charge to profit or loss of Galaxy Co for the year ended 31 December 20X2 and the balance outstanding at 31 December 20X2.

Answer

The bond is a 'deep discount' bond and is a financial liability of Galaxy Co. It is measured at amortised cost. Although there is no interest as such, the difference between the initial cost of the bond and the price at which it will be redeemed is a finance cost. This must be allocated over the term of the bond at a constant rate on the carrying amount.

To calculate amortised cost we need to calculate the effective interest rate of the bond:

$$\frac{600,000}{503,778} = 1.191 \text{ over three years}$$

To calculate an annual rate, we take the cube root, $(1.191)^{1/3} = 1.06$, so the annual interest rate is 6%.

The charge to the income statement is $30,226 (503,778 × 6%)

The balance outstanding at 31 December 20X2 is $534,004 (503,778 + 30,226)

4.6 Gains and losses

Instruments at **fair value through profit or loss**: gains and losses are recognised **in profit or loss**.

Available for sale financial assets: gains and losses are recognised **directly in equity** through the statement of changes in equity. When the asset is derecognised the cumulative gain or loss previously recognised in equity should be recognised in profit and loss.

Financial instruments carried at **amortised cost**: gains and losses are recognised **in profit and loss** as a result of the amortisation process and when the asset is derecognised.

Financial assets and financial liabilities that are **hedged items**: special rules apply (discussed later in this chapter).

Question

On 1 January 20X3 Deferred issued $600,000 loan notes. Issue costs were $200. The loan notes do not carry interest, but are redeemable at a premium of $152,389 on 31 December 20X4. The effective finance cost of the debentures is 12%.

What is the finance cost in respect of the loan notes for the year ended 31 December 20X4?

A $72,000
B $76,194
C $80,613
D $80,640

C   The premium on redemption of the preferred shares represents a finance cost. The effective rate of interest must be applied so that the debt is measured at amortised cost (IAS 39).

At the time of issue, the loan notes are recognised at their net proceeds of $599,800 (600,000 – 200).

The finance cost for the year ended 31 December 20X4 is calculated as follows:

	B/f	Interest @ 12%	C/f
	$	$	$
20X3	599,800	71,976	671,776
20X4	671,776	80,613	752,389

Question

On 1 January 20X5, an entity issued a debt instrument with a coupon rate of 3.5% at a par value of $6,000,000. The directly attributable costs of issue were $120,000. The debt instrument s repayable on 31 December 2011 at a premium of $1,100,000.

What is the total amount of the finance cost associated with the debt instrument?

A $1,470,000
B $1,590,000
C $2,570,000
D $2,690,000

Answer

D

	$
Issue costs	120,000
Interest $6,000,000 \times 3.5\% \times 7$	1,470,000
Premium on redemption	1,100,000
Total finance cost	2,690,000

Question

During the financial year ended 28 February 20X5, MN issued the two financial instruments described below. For *each* of the instruments, identify whether it should be classified as debt or equity, **explaining in not more than 40 words each** the reason for your choice. In each case you should refer to the relevant International Accounting Standard or International Financial Reporting Standard.

(i)   Redeemable preferred shares with a coupon rate 8%. The shares are redeemable on 28 February 20X9 at premium of 10%

(ii)   A grant of share options to senior executives. The options may be exercised from 28 February 20X8.

Answer

(i)   **Debt.** The preference shares require regular distributions to the holders but more importantly have the debt characteristic of being redeemable. Therefore according to IAS 32 *Financial instruments: presentation* they must be classified as debt.

(ii)   **Equity.** According to IFRS 2 *Share based payment* the grant of share options must be recorded as equity in the statement of financial position. It is an alternative method of payment to cash for the provision of the services of the directors.

Question

On 1 January 20X1, EFG issued 10,000 5% convertible bonds at their par value of $50 each. The bonds will be redeemed on 1 January 20X6. Each bond is convertible at the option of the holder at any time during the five year period. Interest on the bond will be paid annually in arrears.

The prevailing market interest rate for similar debt without conversion options at the date of issue was 6%.

At what value should the equity element of the hybrid financial instrument be recognised in the financial statements of EFG at the date of issue?

Answer

> **Top tip** The method to use here is to find the present value of the principal value of the bond, $500,000 (10,000 × $50) and the interest payments of $25,000 annually (5% × $500,000) at the market rate for non-convertible bonds of 6%, using the discount factor tables. The difference between this total and the principal amount of $500,000 is the equity element.

	$
Present value of principal $500,000 × 0.747	373,500
Present value of interest $25,000 × 4.212	105,300
Liability value	478,800
Principal amount	500,000
Equity element	21,200

Question

After initial recognition, all financial liabilities should be measured at amortised cost.

True ☐   False ☐

Answer

False. Some may be measured at fair value if certain criteria are net.

Question

Ellesmere Co entered into the following transactions during the year ended 31 December 20X3:

(1)   Entered into a speculative interest rate option costing $10,000 on 1 January 20X3 to borrow $6,000,000 from AB Bank commencing 31 March 20X5 for 6 months at 4%. The value of the option at 31 December 20X3 was $15,250.

(2)   Purchased 6% debentures in FG Co on 1 January 20X3 (their issue date) for $150,000 as an investment. Ellesmere Co intends to hold the debentures until their redemption at a premium in 5 year's time. The effective rate of interest of the bond is 8.0%.

(3)   Purchased 50,000 shares in ST Co on 1 July 20X3 for $3.50 each as an investment. The share price on 31 December 20X3 was $3.75.

Required

Show the accounting treatment and relevant extracts from the financial statements for the year ended 31 December 20X3. Ellesmere Co only designates financial assets as at fair value through profit or loss where this is unavoidable.

STATEMENT OF FINANCIAL POSITION EXTRACTS

	$
Financial assets:	
Interest rate option (W1)	15,250
6% debentures in FG Co (W2)	153,000
Shares in EG Co (W3)	187,500

STATEMENT OF COMPREHENSIVE INCOME EXTRACTS

	$
Finance income:	
Gain on interest rate option (W1)	5,250
Effective interest on 6% debentures (W2)	12,000

Workings

1   *Interest rate option*

This is a derivative and so it must be treated as at fair value through profit or loss.

Initial measurement (at cost):

DEBIT	Financial asset	$10,000	
CREDIT	Cash		$10,000

At 31.12.20X3 (re-measured to fair value)

DEBIT	Financial asset ($15,250 – $10,000)	$5,250	
CREDIT	Profit or loss		$5,250

2   *Debentures*

On the basis of the information provided, this can be treated as a held-to-maturity investment.

Initial measurement (at cost):

DEBIT	Financial asset	$150,000	
CREDIT	Cash		$150,000

At 31.12.20X3 (amortised cost):

DEBIT	Financial asset (150,000 × 8%)	$12,000	
CREDIT	Finance income		$12,000

DEBIT	Cash (150,000 × 6%)	$9,000	
CREDIT	Financial asset		$9,000

Amortised cost at 31.12.20X3:

(150,000 + 12,000 – 9,000) = $153,000

3   *Shares*

These are treated as an available for sale financial asset (shares cannot normally be held to maturity and they are clearly not loans or receivables).

Initial measurement (at cost):

DEBIT	Financial asset (50,000 × $3.50)	$175,000	
CREDIT	Cash		$175,000

At 31.12.20X3 (re-measured to fair value)

DEBIT	Financial asset ((50,000 × $3.75) – $175,000))	$12,500	
CREDIT	Equity		$12,500

4.7 Impairment and uncollectability of financial assets

At each year end, an entity should assess whether there is any objective evidence that a financial asset or group of assets is impaired.

Impairment

Give examples of indications that a financial asset or group of assets may be impaired.

Answer

IAS 39 lists the following:

(a)   Significant financial difficulty of the issuer

(b)   A breach of contract, such as a default in interest or principal payments

(c)   The lender granting a concession to the borrower that the lender would not otherwise consider, for reasons relating to the borrower's financial difficulty

(d)   It becomes probable that the borrower will enter bankruptcy

(e)   The disappearance of an active market for that financial asset because of financial difficulties

Where there is objective evidence of impairment, the entity should **determine the amount** of any impairment loss.

4.7.1 Financial assets carried at amortised cost

The impairment loss is the **difference** between the asset's **carrying amount** and its **recoverable amount**. The asset's recoverable amount is the present value of estimated future cash flows, discounted at the financial instrument's **original** effective interest rate.

The amount of the loss should be **recognised in profit or loss.**

If the impairment loss decreases at a later date (and the decrease relates to an event occurring **after** the impairment was recognised) the reversal is recognised in profit or loss. The carrying amount of the asset must not exceed the original amortised cost.

4.7.2 Financial assets carried at cost

Unquoted equity instruments are carried at cost if their fair value cannot be reliably measured. The impairment loss is the difference between the asset's **carrying amount** and the **present value of estimated future cash flows**, discounted at the current market rate of return for a similar financial instrument. Such impairment losses cannot be reversed.

4.7.3 Available for sale financial assets

Available for sale financial assets are carried at fair value and gains and losses are recognised directly in equity. Any impairment loss on an available for sale financial asset should be **removed from equity** and **recognised in net profit or loss for the period** even though the financial asset has not been derecognised.

The impairment loss is the difference between its **acquisition cost** (net of any principal repayment and amortisation) and **current fair value** (for equity instruments) or recoverable amount (for debt instruments), less any impairment loss on that asset previously recognised in profit or loss.

Impairment losses relating to equity instruments cannot be reversed. Impairment losses relating to debt instruments may be reversed if, in a later period, the fair value of the instrument increases and the increase can be objectively related to an event occurring after the loss was recognised.

4.8 Example: Impairment

Broadfield Co purchased 5% debentures in X Co on 1 January 20X3 (their issue date) for $100,000. The term of the debentures was 5 years and the maturity value is $130,525. The effective rate of interest on the debentures is 10% and the company has classified them as a held-to-maturity financial asset.

At the end of 20X4 X Co went into liquidation. All interest had been paid until that date. On 31 December 20X4 the liquidator of X Co announced that no further interest would be paid and only 80% of the maturity value would be repaid, on the original repayment date.

The market interest rate on similar bonds is 8% on that date.

Required

(a)   What value should the debentures have been stated at just before the impairment became apparent?

(b)   At what value should the debentures be stated at 31 December 20X4, after the impairment?

(c)   How will the impairment be reported in the financial statements for the year ended 31 December 20X4?

Solution

(a)   The debentures are classified as a held-to-maturity financial asset and so they would have been stated at amortised cost:

	$
Initial cost	100,000
Interest at 10%	10,000
Cash at 5%	(5,000)
At 31 December 20X3	105,000
Interest at 10%	10,500
Cash at 5%	(5,000)
At 31 December 20X4	110,500

(b)   After the impairment, the debentures are stated at their recoverable amount (using the **original** effective interest rate of 10%):

80% × $130,525 × 0.751 = $78,419

(c)   The impairment of $32,081 ($110,500 – $78,419) should be recorded:

DEBIT Statement of comprehensive income	$32,081
CREDIT Financial asset	$32,081

4.9 Section summary

- On initial recognition, financial instruments are measured at **cost**.
- Subsequent measurement depends on how a financial asset is **classified**.
- Financial assets at **fair value through profit or loss** are measured at **fair value**; gains and losses are recognised in **profit or loss**.
- **Available for sale** assets are measured at **fair value**; gains and losses are taken to **equity**.
- **Loans and receivables** and **held to maturity** investments are measured at **amortised cost**; gains and losses are recognised in **profit or loss**.
- Financial **liabilities** are normally measured at **amortised cost**, unless they have been classified as at fair value through profit or loss.

5 Embedded derivatives

Certain contracts that are not themselves derivatives (and may not be financial instruments) include derivative contracts that are 'embedded' within them. These non-derivatives are called **host contracts.**

> An **embedded derivative** is a derivative instrument that is combined with a non-derivative host contract to form a single hybrid instrument.

5.1 Examples of host contracts

Possible examples include:

(a) A lease
(b) A debt or equity instrument
(c) An insurance contract
(d) A sale or purchase contract
(e) A construction contract

5.2 Examples of embedded derivatives

Possible examples include:

(a) A term in a lease of retail premises that provides for contingent rentals based on sales:

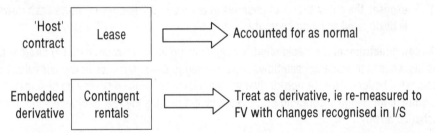

(b) A bond which is redeemable in five years' time with part of the redemption price being based on the increase in the FTSE 100 index.

(c) Construction contract priced in a foreign currency. The construction contract is a non-derivative contract, but the changes in foreign exchange rate is the embedded derivative.

5.3 Accounting treatment of embedded derivatives

IAS 39 requires that an embedded derivative be **separated from its host contract** and accounted for as a derivative when the following conditions are met.

(a) The economic characteristics and risks of the embedded derivative are not closely related to the economic characteristics and risks of the host contract.

(b) A separate instrument with the same terms as the embedded derivative would meet the definition of a derivative.

(c) The hybrid (combined) instrument is not measured at fair value with changes in fair value recognised in the profit or loss (a derivative embedded in a financial asset or financial liability need not be separated out if the entity holds the combined instrument at fair value through profit or loss).

5.4 IFRIC 9 Reassessment of embedded derivatives

IAS 39 describes an embedded derivative as a component of a financial instrument that has the features of a stand-alone derivative; that is, it causes cash flows under the instrument to vary with a specified interest rate, market price, foreign exchange rate or other financial variable. IAS 39 requires an embedded derivative to be separated from the non-derivative elements of the contract, and accounted for as a stand-alone derivative, unless the derivative features are 'closely related' to the non-derivative features of the compound instrument.

IFRIC 9 addresses the question of whether it is necessary to reassess the treatment of an embedded derivative throughout the life of a contract if certain events occur after an entity first becomes a party to the contract. **It concludes that reassessment is not permitted unless there is a significant change to the terms of the contract.**

6 Hedging

FAST FORWARD

Hedging is allowed in certain strictly defined circumstances.

6.1 Introduction

IAS 39 **requires hedge accounting** where there is a **designated hedging relationship** between a hedging instrument and a hedged item. It is **prohibited otherwise**.

Key terms

> **Hedging**, for accounting purposes, means designating one or more hedging instruments so that their change in fair value is an offset, in whole or in part, to the change in fair value or cash flows of a hedged item.
>
> A **hedged item** is an asset, liability, firm commitment, or forecasted future transaction that:
>
> (a)   exposes the entity to risk of changes in fair value or changes in future cash flows, and that
> (b)   is designated as being hedged.
>
> A **hedging instrument** is a designated derivative or (in limited circumstances) another financial asset or liability whose fair value or cash flows are expected to offset changes in the fair value or cash flows of a designated hedged item. (A non-derivative financial asset or liability may be designated as a hedging instrument for hedge accounting purposes only if it hedges the risk of changes in foreign currency exchange rates.)
>
> **Hedge effectiveness** is the degree to which changes in the fair value or cash flows of the hedged item attributable to a hedged risk are offset by changes in the fair value or cash flows of the hedging instrument.
>
> (*IAS 39*)

In simple terms, entities hedge to reduce their exposure to risk and uncertainty, such as changes in prices, interest rates or foreign exchange rates. Hedge accounting recognises hedging relationships by allowing (for example) losses on a hedged item to be offset against gains on a hedging instrument.

Generally only assets, liabilities etc that involve external parties can be designated as hedged items. The foreign currency risk of an intragroup monetary item (eg payable/receivable between two subsidiaries) may qualify as a hedged item in the group financial statements if it results in an exposure to foreign exchange rate gains or losses that are not fully eliminated on consolidation. This can happen (per IAS 21) when the transaction is between entities with different functional currencies.

In addition the foreign currency risk of a highly probable group transaction may qualify as a hedged item if it is in a currency other than the functional currency of the entity and the foreign currency risk will affect profit or loss.

6.2 Example: Hedging

A company owns inventories of 20,000 gallons of oil which cost $400,000 on 1 December 20X3.

In order to hedge the fluctuation in the market value of the oil the company signs a futures contract to deliver 20,000 gallons of oil on 31 March 20X4 at the futures price of $22 per gallon.

The market price of oil on 31 December 20X3 is $23 per gallon and the futures price for delivery on 31 March 20X4 is $24 per gallon.

Required

Explain the impact of the transactions on the financial statements of the company:

(a)   Without hedge accounting

(b)   With hedge accounting.

Solution

The futures contract was intended to protect the company from a fall in oil prices (which would have reduced the profit when the oil was eventually sold). However, oil prices have actually risen, so that the company has made a loss on the contract.

Without hedge accounting:

The futures contract is a derivative and therefore must be remeasured to fair value under IAS 39. The loss on the futures contract is recognised in profit or loss:

DEBIT	Profit or loss (20,000 × 24 – 22)	$40,000	
CREDIT	Financial liability		$40,000

With hedge accounting:

The loss on the futures contract is recognised in the profit or loss as before.

The inventories are revalued to fair value:

	$
Fair value at 31 December 20X4 (20,000 × 23)	460,000
Cost	(400,000)
Gain	60,000

The gain is also recognised in profit or loss:

DEBIT	Inventory	$60,000	
CREDIT	Profit or loss		$60,000

The net effect on the profit or loss is a gain of $20,000 compared with a loss of $40,000 without hedging.

The **standard** identifies three types of **hedging relationship**.

Key terms

Fair value hedge: a hedge of the exposure to changes in the fair value of a recognised asset or liability, or an identified portion of such an asset or liability, that is attributable to a particular risk and could affect profit or loss.

Cash flow hedge: a hedge of the exposure to variability in cash flows that

(a)   is attributable to a particular risk associated with a recognised asset or liability (such as all or some future interest payments on variable rate debt) or a highly probable forecast transaction (such as an anticipated purchase or sale), and that

(b)   could affect profit or loss.

Hedge of a net investment in a foreign operation: IAS 21 defines a net investment in a foreign operation as the amount of the reporting entity's interest in the net assets of that operation.   (*IAS 39*)

The hedge in the example above is a **fair value hedge** (it hedges exposure to changes in the fair value of a recognised asset: the oil).

6.3 Conditions for hedge accounting

Before a hedging relationship qualifies for hedge accounting, **all** of the following **conditions** must be met.

(a)   The hedging relationship must be **designated at its inception as a hedge** based on the entity's risk management objective and strategy. There must be formal documentation (including identification of the hedged item, the hedging instrument, the nature of the risk that is to be hedged and how the entity will assess the hedging instrument's effectiveness in offsetting the exposure to changes in the hedged item's fair value or cash flows attributable to the hedged risk).

(b) The hedge is expected to be **highly effective** in achieving offsetting changes in fair value or cash flows attributable to the hedged risk. (Note: the hedge need not necessarily be *fully* effective.)

(c) For **cash flow hedges**, a **forecast transaction** that is the subject of the hedge must be **highly probable** and must present an exposure to variations in cash flows that could ultimately affect profit or loss.

(d) The effectiveness of the hedge can be **measured reliably**.

(e) The hedge is **assessed** on an ongoing basis (annually) and has been **effective during the reporting period**.

6.4 Accounting treatment

6.4.1 Fair value hedges

The **gain or loss** resulting from **re-measuring** the hedging instrument at fair value is **recognised in profit or loss**.

The gain or loss on the hedged item attributable to the **hedged risk** should **adjust the carrying amount** of the hedged item and be **recognised in profit or loss**.

6.4.2 Example: fair value hedge

On 1 July 20X6 Joules acquired 10,000 ounces of a material which it held in its inventory. This cost $200 per ounce, so a total of $2 million. Joules was concerned that the price of this inventory would fall, so on 1 July 20X6 he sold 10,000 ounces in the futures market for $210 per ounce for delivery on 30 June 20X7. On 1 July 20X6 the conditions for hedge accounting were all met.

At 31 December 20X6, the end of Joules' reporting period, the fair value of the inventory was $220 per ounce while the futures price for 30 June 20X7 delivery was $227 per ounce. On 30 June 20X7 the trader sold the inventory and closed out the futures position at the then spot price of $230 per ounce.

Required

Set out the accounting entries in respect of the above transactions

Solution

At 31 December 20X6 the increase in the fair value of the inventory was $200,000 (10,000 × ($220 - $200)) and the increase in the forward contract liability was $170,000 (10,000 × ($227 - $210)). Hedge effectiveness was 85% (170,000 as a % of 200,000), so hedge accounting was still permitted.

31 December 20X6	Debit $	Credit $
Profit or loss	170,000	
Financial liability		170,000
(To record the loss on the forward contract)		
Inventories	200,000	
Profit or loss		200,000
(To record the increase in the fair value of the inventories)		

At 30 June 20X7 the increase in the fair value of the inventory was another $100,000 (10,000 × ($230 - $220)) and the increase in the forward contract liability was another $30,000 (10,000 × ($230 - $227)).

	Debit $	Credit $
30 June 20X7		
Profit or loss	30,000	
Financial liability		30,000
(To record the loss on the forward contract)		
Inventories	100,000	
Profit or loss		100,000
(To record the increase in the fair value of the inventories)		
Profit or loss	2,300,000	
Inventories		2,300,000
(To record the inventories now sold)		
Cash	2,300,000	
Profit or loss – revenue		2,300,000
(To record the revenue from the sale of inventories)		
Financial liability	200,000	
Cash		200,000
(To record the settlement of the net balance due on closing the financial liability)		

Note that because the fair value of the material rose, Joules made a profit of only £100,000 on the sale of inventories. Without the forward contract, the profit would have been £300,000 (2,300,000 – 2,000,000). In the light of the rising fair value the trader might in practice have closed out the futures position earlier, rather than waiting until the settlement date.

6.4.3 Cash flow hedges

The portion of the gain or loss on the hedging instrument that is determined to be an **effective** hedge shall be **recognised directly in equity** through the statement of changes in equity.

The **ineffective portion** of the gain or loss on the hedging instrument should be **recognised in profit or loss**.

When a hedging transaction results in the recognition of an asset or liability, changes in the value of the hedging instrument recognised in equity either:

(a)   Are adjusted against the carrying value of the asset or liability, or

(b)   Affect the profit or loss at the same time as the hedged item (for example, through depreciation or sale).

6.4.4 Example: Cash flow hedge

Bets Co signs a contract on 1 November 20X1 to purchase an asset on 1 November 20X2 for €60,000,000. Bets reports in US$ and hedges this transaction by entering into a forward contract to buy €60,000,000 on 1 November 20X2 at US$1: €1.5.

Spot and forward exchange rates at the following dates are:

	Spot	Forward (for delivery on 1.11.X2)
1.11.X1	US$1: €1.45	US$1: €1.5
31.12.X1	US$1: €1.20	US$1: €1.24
1.11.X2	US$1: €1.0	US$1: €1.0 (actual)

Required

Show the double entries relating to these transactions at 1 November 20X1, 31 December 20X1 and 1 November 20X2.

Solution

Entries at 1 November 20X1

The value of the forward contract at inception is zero so no entries recorded (other than any transaction costs), but risk disclosures will be made.

The contractual commitment to buy the asset would be disclosed if material (IAS 16).

Entries at 31 December 20X1

Gain on forward contract:

	$
Value of contract at 31.12.X1 (€60,000,000/1.24)	48,387,097
Value of contract at 1.11.X1 (€60,000,000/1.5)	40,000,000
Gain on contract	8,387,097

Compare to movement in value of asset (unrecognised):

Increase in $ cost of asset

(€60,000,000/1.20 – €60,000,000/1.45)	$8,620,690

As this is higher, the hedge is deemed fully effective at this point:

DEBIT Financial asset (Forward a/c)	$8,387,097	
CREDIT Equity		$8,387,097

Entries at 1 November 20X2

Additional gain on forward contract

	$
Value of contract at 1.11.X2 (€60,000,000/1.0)	60,000,000
Value of contract at 31.12.X1 (€60,000,000/1.24)	48,387,097
Gain on contract	11,612,903

Compare to movement in value of asset (unrecognised):

Increase in $ cost of asset

(€60,000,000/1.0 – €60,000,000/1.2)	$10,000,000

Therefore, the hedge is not fully effective during this period, but is still highly effective (and hence hedge accounting can be used):

$10,000,000/ $11,612,903 = 86% which is within the 80% – 125% bandings.

DEBIT Financial asset (Forward a/c)	$11,612,903	
CREDIT Equity		$10,000,000
CREDIT Profit or loss		$1,612,903

Purchase of asset at market price

DEBIT Asset (€60,000,000/1.0)	$60,000,000	
CREDIT Cash		$60,000,000

Settlement of forward contract

DEBIT Cash	$20,000,000	
CREDIT Financial asset (Forward a/c)		$20,000,000

Realisation of gain on hedging instrument

The cumulative gain of $18,387,097 recognised in equity:

- Is transferred to profit or loss as the asset is used, ie over the asset's useful life; or
- Adjusts the initial cost of the asset (reducing future depreciation).

6.5 ED Amendments to IAS 39: Exposures qualifying for hedge accounting

In September 2007, the ASB issued an Exposure Draft *Amendments to IAS 39 Financial instruments: recognition and measurement – Exposures qualifying for hedge accounting.* The proposed amendments are intended **to clarify the IASB's original intentions regarding what can be designated as a hedged risk and when an entity may designate a portion of the cash flows of a financial instrument as a hedged item**.

The **risks specified** are:

(a)   Interest rate risk
(b)   Foreign currency rate risk
(c)   Credit risk
(d)   Prepayment risk

The **portions of the cash flows** of a financial instrument that may be designated as a hedged item are one or more of the following.

(a)   The cash flows of a financial instrument for part of its time period to maturity.

(b)   A percentage of the cash flows of a financial instrument

(c)   The cash flows of a financial instrument associated with a one-sided risk of that instrument

(d)   Any contractually specified cash flows of a financial instrument that are independent from the other cash flows of that instrument.

(e)   The portion of the cash flows of an interest bearing financial instrument that is equivalent to a financial instrument with a risk-free rate

(f)   The portion of the cash flows of an interest bearing financial instrument that is equivalent to a financial instrument with a quoted or variable inter-bank rate.

6.6 Section summary

- **Hedge accounting** means designating one or more instruments so that their change in fair value is **offset** by the change in fair value or cash flows of another item.
- **Hedge accounting** is permitted in certain circumstances, provided the hedging relationship is **clearly defined**, **measurable** and actually **effective**.
- There are three types of hedge: **fair value** hedge; **cash flow** hedge; hedge of a **net investment in a foreign operation.**
- The accounting treatment of a hedge **depends on its type**.

7 Reducing complexity

FAST FORWARD

Many users and preparers of accounts have found financial instruments to be **complex.** The IASB has recently issued a Discussion Paper, which aims at reducing complexity.

7.1 Background

You may have found this chapter difficult. Question practice will help. It may be of some comfort to know that students are not alone in finding **financial instruments complex.** Preparers of financial statements, their users and auditors, have all found this to be the case.

In March 2008, the IASB issued a Discussion Paper *Reducing complexity in reporting financial instruments.* The Discussion Paper is also being considered for comment by the US Financial Accounting Standards Board (FASB). In fact this is a joint project between the IASB and FASB.

7.2 Objective

The objective of the joint project is to **develop less complex and principle-based standards** on accounting for financial instruments. The Discussion Paper aims to gather information in order to assist with this project.

7.3 Summary

The Discussion Paper covers the following matters.

(a)   The main **causes of complexity** in financial instrument accounting: multiple measurement methods

(b)   **A long-term solution** for reducing complexity and improving financial instrument accounting: measure all financial instruments at **fair value**

(c)   Three possible approaches for the medium term:

(i)   Amending the current measurement requirements
(ii)   Replacing the existing measurement requirements
(iii) Simplifying hedge accounting requirements

The determination of fair value and the classification of financial instruments as debt or equity are not discussed, as these matters are dealt with in separate projects.

7.4 Reasons for complexity in accounting for financial instruments

As the Discussion Paper acknowledges, the main reason for complexity in accounting for financial instruments is the **many different ways in which they can be measured**. A table lists twenty-four! The measurement method depends on:

(a)   The applicable financial reporting standard
(b)   The categorisation of the financial instrument under IAS 39 *Financial instruments: Recognition and measurement*
(c)   Whether hedge accounting has been applied

7.5 Long-term solution: fair value

The Discussion Paper maintains the view that **fair value is the only measure that is appropriate for all types of financial instruments**, and that a full fair value model would be much simpler to apply than the current mixed model. A single measurement method would, it is argued:

(a)   Significantly reduce complexity
(b)   Make reported information easier to understand
(c)   Improve the comparability of reported information between entities and between periods

7.5.1 IAS 39 requirements no longer needed

Fair value measurement for all financial instruments would mean that the following **requirements of IAS 39 could be dispensed with:**

(a)   **Classificatio**n of financial instruments into:

(i)   Fair value through profit or loss
(ii)   Available for sale
(iii)   Held-to-maturity
(iv)   Loans and receivables

(b)   **Accounting for transfers** between the above categories

(c)   Identification and quantification of **impairments**

7.5.2 Unresolved problems

The Discussion Paper acknowledges that a single measurement method would not resolve all of the current problems and notes that it would not be possible to achieve the long-term solution of measuring all financial instruments at fair value until the following issues have been resolved:

(a)   **Presentation.** How should the effects of changes in fair values be presented in earnings?

(b)   **Disclosure**. What information about financial instruments should be disclosed?

(c)   **Measurement**. What is the definition of fair value and how should it be measured?

(d)   **Scope.** What is the appropriate definition of a financial instrument and which financial instruments, if any, should be outside the scope of a standard?

7.6 Intermediate approaches

The long-term solution of measuring all financial instruments at **fair value** must be **postponed until certain other projects have been completed**. Accordingly, an intermediate solution must be found. The Discussion Paper proposes three intermediate approaches.

7.6.1 Amending the current measurement requirements

It is proposed to reduce the number of categories of financial instruments (see 7.5.1 above) and/or to simplify or eliminate some of the current requirements or restrictions.

7.6.2 Replacing the existing measurement requirements

This approach would involve replacing the existing measurement requirements with a fair value measurement principle, which would make fair value through profit or loss the default category. An exemption would be available, whereby some financial instruments could be measured at amortised cost. (This approach follows that proposed in the IASB Exposure Draft of an *IFRS for Small and Medium-sized Entities*.

7.6.3 Simplifying hedge accounting requirements

The hedge accounting requirements would be simplified in one of the following ways.

(a)   One or more of the existing hedge accounting models would be eliminated or replaced (eg with a less complex fair value hedging model).

(b)   The current hedge accounting models would be maintained and simplified (eg by changing the requirements for assessing effectiveness, hedging of portions and partial term hedges.

7.6.4 Benefits of intermediate approach

(a)   Reduced complexity
(b)   Greater relevance in information provided to users
(c)   Consistency with the long-term solution of measuring all financial instruments at fair value
(d)   Benefits outweighing costs

7.7 Section summary

- Financial instruments are found to be complex, mainly because there are so many different measurement methods.
- The IASB has addressed this in a Discussion Paper.
- In the long term all financial instruments will be measured at fair value.
- Solutions are proposed for the medium term.

8 Amended reclassification rules

Exam focus point

Only read this section if you are taking the exam in June 2010. The change came in October 2008, which is after the cut-off date for the December 2009 exam.

FAST FORWARD

Changes to IAS 39 introduced in October 2008 permit entities to **reclassify non-derivative financial assets out of the 'fair value through profit or loss' and 'available-for-sale' categories** in limited circumstances. Additional disclosures are required.

In October 2008, the IASB published amendments to IAS 39 *Financial instruments: recognition and measurement* and IFRS 7 *Financial instruments: disclosures.* The IASB had come under pressure, to bring the reclassification of financial assets into line with US GAAP, thus creating a 'level playing field'. The amendments are effective from 1 July 2008.

8.1 Scope

The amendment only applies to reclassification of some non-derivative financial assets recognised in accordance with IAS 39. Reclassification is not permitted for financial liabilities, derivatives and financial assets that are designated as at fair value through profit or loss (FVTPL) on initial recognition under the 'fair value option'.

The amendments therefore **only permit reclassification of debt and equity financial assets** subject to meeting specified criteria. They **do not permit reclassification into FVTPL**.

8.2 Criteria for reclassification out of fair value through profit or loss and available for sale

The criteria vary depending on whether the asset would have met the definition of 'loans and receivables' if it had not been classified as FVTPL or available for sale (AFS) on initial recognition.

(a)   If the debt instrument would have met the definition of loans and receivables, had it not been required to be classified as held for trading at initial recognition, it may be classified out of FVTPL **provided the entity has the intention and ability to hold the asset for the foreseeable future or until maturity**.

(b)   If a debt instrument was classified as AFS, but would have met the definition of loans and receivables if it had not been designated as AFS, it may be reclassified to the loans and receivables category **provided the entity has the intention and ability to hold the financial asset for the foreseeable future or until maturity**.

(c)   Other debt instruments or any equity instruments may be reclassified from FVTPL to AFS or, in the case of debt instruments only from FVTPL to held to maturity (HTM) **if the financial assets are no longer held for selling in the short term**. Such cases will be rare.

8.3 Measurement at the reclassification date

Reclassified assets must be measured at the **fair value of the financial asset at the date of reclassification**.

(a)   Previously recognised gains and losses cannot be reversed.

(b)   The fair value at the date of reclassification becomes the new cost, or amortised cost of the financial asset.

8.4 Measurement after the reclassification date

After the reclassification date, **the normal IAS 39 requirements apply**. For example, in the case of financial assets measured at amortised cost, a **new effective interest rate** will be determined. If a fixed rate debt is reclassified as loans and receivables and held to maturity, this effective interest rate will be used as the discount rate for future impairment calculations.

For assets reclassified out of AFS, amounts previously recognised in other comprehensive income must be reclassified to profit or loss.

8.4.1 Exception

Reclassified debt instruments are treated differently. If, after the instrument has been reclassified, an entity increases its estimate of recoverability of future cash flows, the carrying amount is not adjusted upwards (in accordance with existing IAS 39 rules). Instead, a **new effective interest rate must be applied from that date** on. This enables the increase in recoverability of cash flows to be recognised over the expected life of the financial asset.

8.5 Disclosures

Disclosures, covered by IFRS 7 (see the next section) are not important for your P2 syllabus. However, you should be aware **that IFRS 7 has been amended to require additional disclosures for reclassifications that fall within the scope of the above amendments**. They relate to the amounts reclassified in and out of each category, the fair values of reclassified assets, fair value gains or losses recognised in the period of reclassification and any new effective interest rate.

9 Disclosure of financial instruments

Skim through for background only – disclosures will not be tested in detail.

IFRS 7 specifies the **disclosures** required for financial instruments. The standard requires qualitative and quantitative disclosures about exposure to risks arising from financial instruments and specifies minimum disclosures about credit risk, liquidity risk and market risk.

The IASB maintains that users of financial instruments need information about an entity's exposures to risks and how those risks are managed, as this information can **influence a user's assessment of the financial position and financial performance of an entity** or of the amount, timing and uncertainty of its **future cash flows.**

There have been new techniques and approaches to measuring risk management, which highlighted the need for guidance.

Accordingly, IFRS 7 *Financial instruments: Disclosures* was issued in August 2005. The standard revises, enhances and replaces the disclosures in IAS 30 and IAS 32. The presentation aspects of IAS 32 are retained, and IAS 32 has been renamed *Financial instruments: Presentation.*

9.1 General requirements

The extent of disclosure required depends on the extent of the entity's use of financial instruments and of its exposure to risk. It **adds to the requirements previously in IAS 32** by requiring:

- Enhanced statement of financial position and statement of comprehensive income disclosures
- Disclosures about an allowance account when one is used to reduce the carrying amount of impaired financial instruments.

The standard requires **qualitative and quantitative disclosures about exposure to risks** arising from financial instruments, and specifies minimum disclosures about **credit risk**, **liquidity risk** and **market risk**.

9.2 Objective

The objective of the IFRS is to require entities to provide disclosures in their financial statements that enable users to evaluate:

(a) The significance of financial instruments for the entity's financial position and performance

(b) The nature and extent of risks arising from financial instruments to which the entity is exposed during the period and at the reporting date, and how the entity manages those risks.

The principles in IFRS 7 complement the principles for recognising, measuring and presenting financial assets and financial liabilities in IAS 32 *Financial instruments: Presentation* and IAS 39 *Financial instruments: Recognition and measurement.*

9.3 Classes of financial instruments and levels of disclosure

The entity must group financial instruments into classes **appropriate to the nature of the information disclosed**. An entity must decide in the light of its circumstances how much detail it provides. Sufficient information must be provided to permit reconciliation to the line items presented in the statement of financial position.

9.3.1 Statement of financial position

The following must be disclosed.

(a) **Carrying amount** of financial assets and liabilities by IAS 39 category

(b) **Reason for any reclassification** between fair value and amortised cost (and vice versa)

(c) **Details** of the assets and exposure to risk where the entity has made a **transfer** such that part or all of the financial assets do not qualify for derecognition.

(d) The **carrying amount** of financial assets the entity has **pledged as collateral** for liabilities or contingent liabilities and the associated terms and conditions.

(e) When financial assets are impaired by credit losses and the entity records the impairment in a separate account (eg an **allowance account** used to record individual impairments or a similar account used to record a collective impairment of assets) rather than directly reducing the carrying amount of the asset, it must disclose a **reconciliation** of changes in that account during the period for each class of financial assets.

(f) The **existence of multiple embedded derivatives**, where compound instruments contain these.

(g) Defaults and breaches

9.3.2 Statement of comprehensive income

The entity must disclose the following **items of income, expense, gains or losses**, either on the face of the financial statements or in the notes.

(a) Net gains/losses by IAS 39 category (broken down as appropriate: eg interest, fair value changes, dividend income)

(b) Interest income/expense

(c) Impairments losses by class of financial asset

9.3.3 Other disclosures

Entities must disclose in the summary of **significant accounting policies** the measurement basis used in preparing the financial statements and the other accounting policies that are relevant to an understanding of the financial statements.

Disclosures must be made relating to **hedge accounting**, as follows:

(a) Description of hedge

(b) Description of financial instruments designated as **hedging instruments** and their fair value at the reporting date

(c) The **nature of the risks** being hedged

(d) For **cash flow hedges**, periods **when the cash flows will occur** and when will affect profit or loss

(e) For fair value hedges, gains or losses on the hedging instrument and the hedged item.

(f) The **ineffectiveness recognised in profit or loss** arising from cash flow hedges and net investments in foreign operations.

Disclosures must be made relating to **fair value**:

(a) **By class** in a way that allows comparison to statement of financial position value in the statement of financial position. (Financial assets and liabilities may only be offset to the extent that their carrying amounts are offset in the statement of financial position.)

(b) The **methods and assumptions** used, for example by reference to an active market, and any change in these assumptions. If the market for a financial instrument is not active, a valuation technique, as per IAS 39, must be used. There could be a difference between the fair value at initial recognition and the amount that would be determined using the valuation technique. The accounting policy for recognising that difference in profit or loss, the aggregate difference yet to be recognised in profit or loss at the beginning and end of the period and a reconciliation of the changes in the balance of this difference, should be disclosed, as in the following example.

9.3.4 Example: Fair value disclosures

Background

On 1 January 20X1 an entity purchases for $15 million financial assets that are not traded in an active market. The entity has only one class of such financial assets.

The transaction price of $15 million is the fair value at initial recognition.

After initial recognition, the entity will apply a valuation technique to establish the financial assets fair value. This valuation technique includes variables other than data from observable markets.

At initial recognition, the same valuation technique would have resulted in an amount of $14 million, which differs from fair value by $1 million.

The entity has existing differences of $5 million at 1 January 20X1.

Application of requirements

The entity's 20X2 disclosure would include the following:

Accounting policies

The entity uses the following valuation technique to determine the fair value of financial instruments that are not traded in an active market: [description of technique, not included in this example]. Differences may arise between the fair value at initial recognition (which, in accordance with IAS 39, is generally the transaction price) and the amount determined at initial recognition using the valuation technique. Any such differences are [description of the entity's accounting policy].

In the notes to the financial statements

As discussed in note X, the entity uses [name of valuation technique]to measure the fair value of the following financial instruments that are not traded in an active market. However, in accordance with IAS 39, the fair value of an instrument at inception is generally the transaction price. If the transaction price differs from the amount determined at inception using the valuation technique, that difference is [description of the entity's accounting policy]. The differences yet to be recognised in profit or loss are as follows:

	31 Dec 20X2 $m	31 Dec 20X1 $m
Balance at beginning of year	5.3	5.0
New transactions		1.0
Amounts recognised in profit or loss during the year	(0.7)	(0.8)
Other increases		0.2
Other decreases	(0.1)	(0.1)
Balance at end of year	4.5	5.3

Disclosures of fair value are **not required** if carrying value is a reasonable approximation to fair value, or if fair value cannot be measured reliably.

9.4 Nature and extent of risks arising from financial instruments

In undertaking transactions in financial instruments, an entity may assume or transfer to another party one or more of **different types of financial risk** as defined below. The disclosures required by the standard show the extent to which an entity is exposed to these different types of risk, relating to both recognised and unrecognised financial instruments.

Credit risk	The risk that one party to a financial instrument will cause a financial loss for the other party by failing to discharge an obligation.
Currency risk	The risk that the fair value or future cash flows of a financial instrument will fluctuate because of changes in foreign exchange rates.
Interest rate risk	The risk that the fair value or future cash flows of a financial instrument will fluctuate because of changes in market interest rates.
Liquidity risk	The risk that an entity will encounter difficulty in meeting obligations associated with financial liabilities.
Loans payable	Loans payable are financial liabilities, other than short-term trade payables on normal credit terms.
Market risk	The risk that the fair value or future cash flows of a financial instrument will fluctuate because of changes in market prices. Market risk comprises three types of risk: **currency risk**, **interest rate risk** and **other price risk**.
Other price risk	The risk that the fair value or future cash flows of a financial instrument will fluctuate because of changes in market prices (other than those arising from **interest rate risk** or **currency risk**), whether those changes are caused by factors specific to the individual financial instrument or its issuer, or factors affecting all similar financial instruments traded in the market.
Past due	A financial asset is past due when a counterparty has failed to make a payment when contractually due.

9.4.1 Qualitative disclosures

For each type of risk arising from financial instruments, an entity must disclose:

(a)   The **exposures to risk** and how they arise

(b)   Its objectives, policies and processes for managing the risk and the methods used to measure the risk

(c)   Any **changes** in (a) or (b) from the previous period.

9.4.2 Quantitative disclosures

For each financial instrument risk, **summary quantitative data** about risk exposure must be disclosed. This should be based on the information provided internally to key management personnel. More information should be provided if this is unrepresentative.

Information about **credit risk** must be disclosed by class of financial instrument:

(a)   Maximum exposure at the year end

(b)   Any collateral pledged as security

(c)   In respect of the amount disclosed in (b), a description of collateral held as security and other credit enhancements

(d)   Information about the credit quality of financial assets that are neither **past due** nor impaired

(e)   Financial assets that are past due or impaired, giving an age analysis and a description of collateral held by the entity as security.

(f)   Collateral and other credit enhancements obtained, including the nature and carrying amount of the assets and policy for disposing of assets not readily convertible into cash.

For **liquidity risk** entities must disclose:

(a)   A maturity analysis of financial liabilities
(b)   A description of the way risk is managed

Disclosures required in connection with **market risk** are:

(a)   Sensitivity analysis, showing the effects on profit or loss of changes in each market risk
(b)   If the sensitivity analysis reflects interdependencies between risk variables, such as interest rates and exchange rates the method, **assumptions and limitations** must be disclosed.

9.5 Capital disclosures

Certain disclosures about **capital** are required. An entity's capital does not relate solely to financial instruments, but has more general relevance. Accordingly, those disclosures are included in IAS 1, rather than in IFRS 7.

Chapter Roundup

- Financial instruments can be very complex, particularly **derivative instruments**, although **primary instruments** are more straightforward.

- The important definitions to learn are:
  - **Financial asset**
  - **Financial liability**
  - **Equity instrument**

- Financial instruments must be classified as **liabilities** or **equity** according to their **substance**

- The critical feature of a financial liability is the **contractual obligation to deliver cash** or another financial asset.

- **Compound instruments** are split into **equity** and **liability** components and presented accordingly in the statement of financial position.

- **IAS 39** *Financial instruments: recognition and measurement* is a recent and most controversial standard.

- The IAS states that **all financial assets and liabilities** should be **recognised in the statement of financial position, including derivatives**.

- **Financial assets** should **initially** be measured at **cost = fair value**.

- Subsequently they should be **re-measured to fair value** except for

  (a)   Loans and receivables not held for trading
  (b)   Other **held-to-maturity investments**
  (c)   **Financial assets** whose value **cannot be reliably measured**

- An **embedded derivative** is a derivative instrument that is combined with a non-derivate host contract to form a single hybrid instrument.

- Changes to IAS 39 introduced in October 2008 permit entities to **reclassify non-derivative financial assets out of the 'fair value through profit or loss' and 'available-for-sale' categories** in limited circumstances. Additional disclosures are required.

- **Hedging** is allowed in certain strictly defined circumstances.

- **IFRS 7** specifies the **disclosures** required for financial instruments. The standard requires quantitative and qualitative disclosures about exposure to risks arising from financial instruments and specifies minimum disclosures about credit risk, liquidity risk and market risk.

- Many users and preparers of accounts have found financial instruments to be **complex.** The IASB has recently issued a Discussion Paper, which aims at reducing complexity.

Quick Quiz

1   Which four issues are dealt with by IAS 32?

2   What items are *not* financial instruments according to IAS 32?

3   What is the critical feature used to identify a financial liability?

4   How should compound instruments be presented in the statement of financial position?

5   Define interest rate risk and credit risk.

6   When should a financial asset be de-recognised?

7   How are financial instruments initially measured?

8   What is hedging?

9   Name the three types of hedging relationship identified by IAS 39.

Answers to Quick Quiz

1. Classification; presentation; offsetting and disclosure

2. Physical assets; prepaid expenses; non-contractual assets or liabilities; contractual rights not involving transfer of assets

3. The contractual obligation to deliver cash or another financial asset to the holder

4. By calculating the present value of the liability component and then deducting this from the instrument as a whole to leave a residual value for the equity component

5. See Key Terms, Section 3.4

6. Financial assets should be derecognised when the rights to the cash flows from the asset expire or where substantially all the risks and rewards of ownership are transferred to another party.

7. At cost

8. See Key Terms, Section 6.1

9. Fair value hedge; cash flow hedge; hedge of a net investment in a foreign operation

Now try the questions below from the Exam Question Bank

Number	Level	Marks	Time
Q9	Introductory	10	18 mins
Q10	Introductory	n/a	n/a

Share-based payment

Topic list	Syllabus reference
1 IFRS 2 *Share based payment*	C10
2 Deferred tax implications	C10
3 Recent developments	C10

Introduction

This chapter deals with IFRS 2 on share based payment, a controversial area.

Study guide

		Intellectual level
C10	**Share based payment**	
(a)	Apply and discuss the recognition and measurement criteria for share-based payment transactions.	3
(b)	Account for modifications, cancellations and settlements of share-based payment transactions.	2

Exam guide

This examiner is fond of testing share-based payment as part of a scenario question.

One of the competences you need to fulfil Objective 10 of the Practical Experience Requirement (PER) is to compile financial statements and accounts in line with appropriate standards and guidelines. You can apply the knowledge you obtain from this Chapter, on share-based payment, to demonstrate this competence.

1 IFRS 2 Share based payment   Pilot paper, 12/08

FAST FORWARD

Share-based payment transactions should be recognised in the financial statements. You need to understand and be able to advise on:

- Recognition
- Measurement
- Disclosure

of both equity settled and cash settled transactions.

1.1 Background

Transactions whereby entities purchase goods or services from other parties, such as suppliers and employees, by **issuing shares or share options** to those other parties are **increasingly common.** Share schemes are a common feature of director and executive remuneration and in some countries the authorities may offer tax incentives to encourage more companies to offer shares to employees. Companies whose shares or share options are regarded as a valuable 'currency' commonly use share-based payment to obtain employee and professional services.

The increasing use of share-based payment has raised questions about the accounting treatment of such transactions in company financial statements.

Share options are often granted to employees at an exercise price that is equal to or higher than the market price of the shares at the date the option is granted. Consequently the options have no intrinsic value and so **no transaction is recorded in the financial statements**.

This leads to an **anomaly:** if a company pays its employees in cash, an expense is recognised in profit or loss, but if the payment is in share options, no expense is recognised.

1.1.1 Arguments against recognition of share-based payment in the financial statements

There are a number of arguments against recognition. The IASB has considered and rejected the arguments below.

(a) **No cost therefore no charge**

There is no cost to the entity because the granting of shares or options does not require the entity to sacrifice cash or other assets. Therefore a charge should not be recognised.

This argument is unsound because it ignores the fact that a transaction has occurred. The employees have provided valuable services to the entity in return for valuable shares or options.

(b) **Earnings per share is hit twice**

It is argued that the charge to profit or loss for the employee services consumed reduces the entity's earnings, while at the same time there is an increase in the number of shares issued.

However, the dual impact on earnings per share simply reflects the two economic events that have occurred.

(i) The entity has issued shares or options, thus increasing the denominator of the earnings per share calculation.

(ii) It has also consumed the resources it received for those shares or options, thus reducing the numerator.

(c) **Adverse economic consequences**

It could be argued that entities might be discouraged from introducing or continuing employee share plans if they were required to recognise them on the financial statements. However, if this happened, it might be because the requirement for entities to account properly for employee share plans had revealed the economic consequences of such plans.

A situation where entities are able to obtain and consume resources by issuing valuable shares or options without having to account for such transactions could be perceived as a distortion.

1.2 Objective and scope

IFRS 2 requires an entity to **reflect the effects of share-based payment transactions** in its profit or loss and financial position.

IFRS 2 applies to all share-based payment transactions. There are three types.

(a) **Equity-settled share-based payment transactions**, in which the entity receives goods or services in exchange for equity instruments of the entity (including shares or share options)

(b) **Cash-settled share-based payment transactions**, in which the entity receives goods or services in exchange for amounts of cash that are based on the price (or value) of the entity's shares or other equity instruments of the entity

(c) Transactions in which the entity receives or acquires goods or services and either the entity or the supplier has a **choice** as to whether the entity settles the transaction in cash (or other assets) or by issuing equity instruments

Certain transactions are **outside the scope** of the IFRS:

(a) Transactions with employees and others in their capacity as a holder of equity instruments of the entity (for example, where an employee receives additional shares in a rights issue to all shareholders)

(b) The issue of equity instruments in exchange for control of another entity in a business combination

Key terms

> **Share-based payment transaction** A transaction in which the entity receives goods or services as consideration for equity instruments of the entity (including shares or share options), or acquires goods or services by incurring liabilities to the supplier of those goods or services for amounts that are based on the price of the entity's shares or other equity instruments of the entity.
>
> **Share-based payment arrangement** An agreement between the entity and another party (including an employee) to enter into a share-based payment transaction, which thereby entitles the other party to receive cash or other assets of the entity for amounts that are based on the price of the entity's shares or other equity instruments of the entity, or to receive equity instruments of the entity, provided the specified vesting conditions, if any, are met.
>
> **Equity instrument** A contract that evidences a residual interest in the assets of an entity after deducting all of its liabilities.
>
> **Equity instrument granted** The right (conditional or unconditional) to an equity instrument of the entity conferred by the entity on another party, under a share-based payment arrangement.

Share option A contract that gives the holder the right, but not the obligation, to subscribe to the entity's shares at a fixed or determinable price for a specified period of time.

Fair value The amount for which an asset could be exchanged, a liability settled, or an equity instrument granted could be exchanged, between knowledgeable, willing parties in an arm's length transaction.

Grant date The date at which the entity and another party (including an employee) agree to a share-based payment arrangement, being when the entity and the other party have a shared understanding of the terms and conditions of the arrangement. At grant date the entity confers on the other party (the counterparty) the right to cash, other assets, or equity instruments of the entity, provided the specified vesting conditions, if any, are met. If that agreement is subject to an approval process (for example, by shareholders), grant date is the date when that approval is obtained.

Intrinsic value The difference between the fair value of the shares to which the counterparty has the (conditional or unconditional) right to subscribe or which it has the right to receive, and the price (if any) the other party is (or will be) required to pay for those shares. For example, a share option with an exercise price of $15 on a share with a fair value of $20, has an intrinsic value of $5.

Measurement date The date at which the fair value of the equity instruments granted is measured. For transactions with employees and others providing similar services, the measurement date is grant date. For transactions with parties other than employees (and those providing similar services), the measurement date is the date the entity obtains the goods or the counterparty renders service.

Vest To become an entitlement. Under a share-based payment arrangement, a counterparty's right to receive cash, other assets, or equity instruments of the entity vests upon satisfaction of any specified vesting conditions.

Vesting conditions The conditions that must be satisfied for the counterparty to become entitled to receive cash, other assets or equity instruments of the entity, under a share-based payment arrangement. Vesting conditions include service conditions, which require the other party to complete a specified period of service, and performance conditions, which require specified performance targets to be met (such as a specified increase in the entity's profit over a specified period of time).

Vesting period The period during which all the specified vesting conditions of a share-based payment arrangement are to be satisfied.

1.3 Recognition: the basic principle

An entity should **recognise goods or services received or acquired in a share-based payment transaction when it obtains the goods or as the services are received.** Goods or services received or acquired in a share-based payment transaction **should be recognised as expenses unless they qualify for recognition as assets**. For example, services are normally recognised as expenses (because they are normally rendered immediately), while goods are recognised as assets.

If the goods or services were received or acquired in an **equity-settled** share-based payment transaction the entity should recognise **a corresponding increase in equity** (reserves).

If the goods or services were received or acquired in a **cash-settled** share-based payment transaction the entity should recognise a **liability**.

1.4 Equity-settled share-based payment transactions

1.4.1 Measurement

The issue here is how to measure the 'cost' of the goods and services received and the equity instruments (eg, the share options) granted in return.

The general principle in IFRS 2 is that when an entity recognises the goods or services received and the corresponding increase in equity, it should measure these at the **fair value of the goods or services received**. Where the transaction is with **parties other than employees**, there is a rebuttable presumption that the fair value of the goods or services received can be estimated reliably.

If the fair value of the goods or services received cannot be measured reliably, the entity should measure their value by reference to the **fair value of the equity instruments granted.**

Where the transaction is with a party other than an employee fair value should be measured at the date the entity obtains the goods or the counterparty renders service.

Where shares, share options or other equity instruments are granted to **employees** as part of their remuneration package, it is not normally possible to measure directly the services received. For this reason, the entity should measure the fair value of the employee services received by reference to the **fair value of the equity instruments granted**. The fair value of those equity instruments should be measured at **grant date**.

1.4.2 Determining the fair value of equity instruments granted

Where a transaction is measured by reference to the fair value of the equity instruments granted, fair value is based on **market prices** if available, taking into account the terms and conditions upon which those equity instruments were granted.

If market prices are not available, the entity should estimate the fair value of the equity instruments granted using a **valuation technique**. (These are beyond the scope of this exam.)

1.4.3 Transactions in which services are received

The issue here is **when** to recognise the transaction. When equity instruments are granted they may vest immediately, but often the counterparty has to meet specified conditions first. For example, an employee may have to complete a specified period of service. This means that the effect of the transaction normally has to be allocated over more than one accounting period.

If the equity instruments granted **vest immediately**, (ie, the counterparty is not required to complete a specified period of service before becoming unconditionally entitled to the equity instruments) it is presumed that the services have already been received (in the absence of evidence to the contrary). The entity should **recognise the services received in full**, with a corresponding increase in equity, **on the grant date**.

If the equity instruments granted do not vest until the counterparty completes a specified period of service, the entity should account for those services **as they are rendered** by the counterparty during the vesting period. For example if an employee is granted share options on condition that he or she completes three years' service, then the services to be rendered by the employee as consideration for the share options will be received in the future, over that three-year vesting period.

The entity should recognise an amount for the goods or services received during the vesting period based on the **best available estimate** of the **number of equity instruments expected to vest**. It should **revise** that estimate if subsequent information indicates that the number of equity instruments expected to vest differs from previous estimates. On **vesting date**, the entity should revise the estimate to **equal the number of equity instruments that actually vest**.

Once the goods and services received and the corresponding increase in equity have been recognised, the entity should make no subsequent adjustment to total equity after vesting date.

1.5 Example: Equity-settled share-based payment transaction

On 1 January 20X1 an entity grants 100 share options to each of its 400 employees. Each grant is conditional upon the employee working for the entity until 31 December 20X3. The fair value of each share option is $20.

During 20X1 20 employees leave and the entity estimates that 20% of the employees will leave during the three year period.

During 20X2 a further 25 employees leave and the entity now estimates that 25% of its employees will leave during the three year period.

During 20X3 a further 10 employees leave.

Required

Calculate the remuneration expense that will be recognised in respect of the share-based payment transaction for each of the three years ended 31 December 20X3.

Solution

IFRS 2 requires the entity to recognise the remuneration expense, based on the fair value of the share options granted, as the services are received during the three year vesting period.

In 20X1 and 20X2 the entity estimates the number of options expected to vest (by estimating the number of employees likely to leave) and bases the amount that it recognises for the year on this estimate.

In 20X3 it recognises an amount based on the number of options that actually vest. A total of 55 employees left during the three year period and therefore 34,500 options (400 – 55 × 100) vested.

The amount recognised as an expense for each of the three years is calculated as follows:

	Cumulative expense at year-end $	Expense for year $
20X1 40,000 × 80% × 20 × 1/3	213,333	213,333
20X2 40,000 × 75% × 20 × 2/3	400,000	186,667
20X3 34,500 × 20	690,000	290,000

 Question

During its financial year ended 31 January 20X6, TSQ issued share options to several of its senior employees. The options vest immediately upon issue.

Which *one* of the following describes the accounting entry that is required to recognise the options?

A	DEBIT the statement of changes in equity	CREDIT liabilities
B	DEBIT the statement of changes in equity	CREDIT equity
C	DEBIT profit or loss	CREDIT liabilities
D	DEBIT profit or loss	CREDIT equity

Answer

D   Under IFRS 2 a charge must be made to the profit or loss

 Question

On 1 January 20X3 an entity grants 250 share options to each of its 200 employees. The only condition attached to the grant is that the employees should continue to work for the entity until 31 December 20X6. Five employees leave during the year.

The market price of each option was $12 at 1 January 20X3 and $15 at 31 December 20X3.

Required

Show how this transaction will be reflected in the financial statements for the year ended 31 December 20X3.

The remuneration expense for the year is based on the fair value of the options granted at the grant date (1 January 20X3). As five of the 200 employees left during the year it is reasonable to assume that 20 employees will leave during the four year vesting period and that therefore 45,000 options (250 × 180) will actually vest.

Therefore the entity recognises a remuneration expense of $135,000 (45,000 × 12 × ¼) in the profit or loss and a corresponding increase in equity of the same amount.

1.6 Cash-settled share-based payment transactions

Examples of this type of transaction include:

(a)   **Share appreciation rights** granted to employees: the employees become entitled to a future cash payment (rather than an equity instrument), based on the increase in the entity's share price from a specified level over a specified period of time or

(b)   An entity might grant to its employees a right to receive a future cash payment by granting to them a **right to shares that are redeemable**

The basic principle is that the entity measures the goods or services acquired and the liability incurred at the **fair value of the liability**.

The entity should **remeasure** the fair value of the liability **at each reporting date** until the liability is settled **and at the date of settlement**. Any **changes** in fair value are recognised in **profit or loss** for the period.

The entity should recognise the services received, and a liability to pay for those services, **as the employees render service**. For example, if share appreciation rights do not vest until the employees have completed a specified period of service, the entity should recognise the services received and the related liability, over that period.

1.7 Example: cash-settled share-based payment transaction

On 1 January 20X1 an entity grants 100 cash share appreciation rights (SARS) to each of its 500 employees, on condition that the employees continue to work for the entity until 31 December 20X3.

During 20X1 35 employees leave. The entity estimates that a further 60 will leave during 20X2 and 20X3.

During 20X2 40 employees leave and the entity estimates that a further 25 will leave during 20X3.

During 20X3 22 employees leave.

At 31 December 20X3 150 employees exercise their SARs. Another 140 employees exercise their SARs at 31 December 20X4 and the remaining 113 employees exercise their SARs at the end of 20X5.

The fair values of the SARs for each year in which a liability exists are shown below, together with the intrinsic values at the dates of exercise.

	Fair value $	Intrinsic value $
20X1	14.40	
20X2	15.50	
20X3	18.20	15.00
20X4	21.40	20.00
20X5		25.00

Required

Calculate the amount to be recognised in the profit or loss for each of the five years ended 31 December 20X5 and the liability to be recognised in the statement of financial position at 31 December for each of the five years.

Solution

For the three years to the vesting date of 31 December 20X3 the expense is based on the entity's estimate of the number of SARs that will actually vest (as for an equity-settled transaction). However, the fair value of the liability is **re-measured** at each year-end.

The intrinsic value of the SARs at the date of exercise is the amount of cash actually paid.

	Liability at year-end $		Expense for year $
20X1 Expected to vest (500 – 95):			
405 × 100 × 14.40 × 1/3	<u>194,400</u>		194,400
20X2 Expected to vest (500 – 100):			
400 × 100 × 15.50 × 2/3	<u>413,333</u>		218,933
20X3 Exercised:			
150 ×100 × 15.00		225,000	
Not yet exercised (500 – 97 – 150):			
253 × 100 × 18.20	<u>460,460</u>	<u>47,127</u>	
			272,127
20X4 Exercised:			
140 × 100 × 20.00		280,000	
Not yet exercised (253 – 140):			
113 × 100 × 21.40	<u>241,820</u>	<u>(218,640)</u>	
			61,360
20X5 Exercised:			
113 × 100 × 25.00		282,500	
	Nil	<u>(241,820)</u>	
			<u>40,680</u>
			<u>787,500</u>

Transactions which either the entity or the other party has a choice of settling in cash or by issuing equity instruments

If the entity has incurred a liability to settle in cash or other assets it should account for the transaction as a cash-settled share-based payment transaction

If no such liability has been incurred the entity should account for the transaction as an equity-settled share-based payment transaction.

2 Deferred tax implications

2.1 Issue

An entity may receive a tax deduction that differs from related cumulative remuneration expense, and may arise in a later accounting period.

Eg: an entity recognises an expense for share options granted under IFRS 2, but does not receive a tax deduction until the options are exercised and receives the tax deduction at the share price on the exercise date.

2.2 Measurement

The deferred tax asset temporary difference is measured as:

		0
Carrying amount of share-based payment expense		0

Carrying amount of share-based payment expense   0
Less: tax base of share-based payment expense
     (estimated amount tax authorities will permit as a deduction
     in future periods, based on year end information)   (X)
Temporary difference   (X)
Deferred tax asset at X%   X

If the amount of the tax deduction (or estimated future tax deduction) exceeds the amount of the related cumulative remuneration expense, this indicates that the tax deduction relates also to an equity item.

The excess is therefore recognised directly in equity.

2.3 Example: Deferred tax implications of share-based payment

On 1 January 20X2, Bruce granted 5,000 share options to an employee vesting two years later on 31 December 20X3. The fair value of each option measured at the grant date was $3.

Tax law in the jurisdiction in which the entity operates allows a tax deduction of the intrinsic value of the options on exercise. The intrinsic value of the share options was $1.20 at 31 December 20X2 and $3.40 at 31 December 20X3 on which date the options were exercised.

Assume a tax rate of 30%.

Required

Show the deferred tax accounting treatment of the above transaction at 31 December 20X2, 31 December 20X3 (before exercise), and on exercise.

Solution

	31/12/20X2	31/12/20X3 before exercise
Carrying amount of share-based payment expense	0	0
Less: Tax base of share-based payment expense		
(5,000 × $1.2 × ½)/(5,000 × $3.40)		(17,000)
Temporary difference	(3,000)	(17,000)
Deferred tax asset @ 30%	900	5,100
Deferred tax (Cr I/S) (5,100 – 900 – (Working) 600)	900	3,600
Deferred tax (Cr Equity) (Working)	0	600

On exercise, the deferred tax asset is replaced by a current tax one. The double entry is:

Debit deferred tax (I/S)	4,500	
Debit deferred tax (equity)	600	} reversal
Credit deferred tax asset	5,100	
Debit current tax asset	5,100	
Credit current tax (I/S)	4,500	
Credit current tax (equity)	600	

Working

Accounting expense recognised (5,000 × $3 × ½)/(5,000 × $3)	7,500	15,000
Tax deduction	(3,000)	(17,000)
Excess temporary difference	0	(2,000)
Excess deferred tax asset to equity @ 30%	0	600

3 Recent developments

3.1 Amendment to IFRS 2

The ED *Amendment to IFRS 2 Share-based payment: vesting conditions and cancellations* was issued in January 2008.

3.1.1 Requirements

IFRS 2 was amended to define vesting conditions and clarify the accounting treatment of cancellations by parties other than the entity. The amendment restricts vesting conditions to service conditions and performance conditions.

The amendment additionally requires cancellations by the employee to be treated in the same way as cancellations by the employer, resulting in an **accelerated charge to profit or loss of the unamortised balance of the options granted.**

3.2 IFRIC 8 Scope of IFRS 2

IFRIC 2 has the effect of implementing the International Accounting Standards Board's (IASB's) International Financial Reporting Interpretations Committee (IFRIC) Interpretation 8 'Scope of IFRS 2' in the UK and the Republic of Ireland for entities preparing their financial statements in accordance with UK accounting standards and, in doing so, are applying IFRS 2 *Share-based payment.*

IFRS 2 requires an entity to recognise share-based payment transactions in its financial statements. Transactions in which an entity receives goods or services as consideration for equity instruments of the entity (including shares or share options) are share-based payment transactions. Such transactions give rise to expenses (or, if applicable, assets) that should be measured at fair value.

IFRIC 8 was developed to address situations in those parts of the world where, for public policy or other reasons, companies give their shares or rights to shares to individuals, organisations or groups that have not provided goods or services to the company. An example is the issue of shares to a charitable organisation for less than fair value, where the benefits are more intangible than usual goods or services. **IFRIC 2 confirms that such arrangements fall within the scope of IFRS 2**.

3.3 IFRIC 11 IFRS 2 Group and treasury share transactions

The IFRIC addresses how to apply IFRS 2 to arrangements involving an entity's own equity instruments or equity instruments of another entity in the same group. The IFRIC requires a share-based payment arrangement in which an entity receives goods or services as consideration for its own equity-instruments to be accounted for as an equity-settled share-based payment transaction, regardless of how the equity instruments needed are obtained. The IFRIC also provides guidance on whether share-based payment arrangements, in which suppliers of goods or services of an entity are provided with equity instruments of the entity's parent should be accounted for as cash-settled or equity-settled in the entity's financial statements.

3.4 Proposed amendment to IFRS 2

In December 2007, the IASB issued an ED of an amendment to IFRS 2 Share-based payment – Group cash-settled share-based payment transactions.

The proposed amendment gives guidance on how a group entity that receives goods or services from its suppliers (including employees) should account for the following arrangements:

(a) **Arrangement 1** – the entity's suppliers will receive cash payments that are linked to the price of the equity instruments of the entity

(b) **Arrangement 2** – the entity's suppliers will receive cash payments that are linked to the price of the equity instruments of the entity's parent.

Under either arrangement, the entity's parent has an obligation to make the required cash payments to the entity's suppliers. The entity itself does not have any obligation to make such payments.

The proposed amendment to IFRS 2 clarifies that **IFRS 2 applies to arrangements such as those described above** even if the entity that receives goods or services from its suppliers has no obligation to make the required share-based cash payments.

3.5 Section summary

IFRS 2 requires entities to **recognise** the goods or services received as a result of **share based payment transactions.**

- Equity settled transactions: DEBIT Asset/Expense, CREDIT Equity
- Cash settled transactions: DEBIT Asset/Expense, CREDIT Liability
- Transactions are **recognised when goods/services are obtained/received** (usually over the performance period)
- Transactions are measured at fair value

Chapter Roundup

- **Share-based payment** transactions should be recognised in the financial statements. You need to understand and be able to advise on:

  - Recognition
  - Measurement
  - Disclosure

  of both equity settled and cash settled transactions.

Quick Quiz

1   What is a cash-settled share based payment transaction?

2   What is grant date?

3   If an entity has entered into an equity settled share-based payment transaction, what should it recognise in its financial statements?

4   Where an entity has granted share options to its employees in return for services, how is the transaction measured?

Answers to Quick Quiz

1   A transaction in which the entity receives goods or services in exchange for amounts of cash that are based on the price (or value) of the entity's shares or other equity instruments of the entity.

2   The date at which the entity and another party (including an employee) agree to a share based payment arrangement, being when the entity and the other party have a shared understanding of the terms and conditions of the arrangement.

3   The goods or services received and a corresponding increase in equity.

4   By reference to the fair value of the equity instruments granted, measured at grant date.

Now try the question below from the Exam Question Bank

Number	Level	Marks	Time
Q11	Introductory	6	11 mins

9

Provisions, contingencies and events after the reporting period

Topic list	Syllabus reference
1 Revision of IAS 10 *Events after the reporting period*	C8
2 IAS 37 *Provisions, contingent liabilities and contingent assets*	C8

Introduction

You should be very familiar with IAS 10 from your earlier studies, but in the light of the Study Guide, you should concentrate on the issue of window dressing.

Provisions are a topical area in the light of IAS 37.

Discounting is of increasing importance.

Study guide

		Intellectual level
C8	**Provisions, contingencies, events after the reporting period**	
(a)	Apply and discuss the recognition, derecognition and measurement of provisions, contingent liabilities and contingent assets, including environmental provisions.	3
(b)	Apply and discuss the accrual of restructuring provisions.	3
(c)	Apply and discuss accounting for events after the reporting period.	3
(d)	Determine going concern issues arising after the reporting period.	3
F2	**Proposed changes to accounting standards**	
(a)	Identify the issues and deficiencies which have led to a proposed change to an accounting standard.	2
(b)	Apply and discuss the implications of a proposed change to an accounting standard on the performance and position of an entity	2

Exam guide

These standards are likely to be tested as part of a scenario question. You may also be asked to advise the directors on the implications for the financial statements of the changes proposed in the ED.

1 Revision of IAS 10 Events after the reporting period

FAST FORWARD

IAS 10 should be familiar from your earlier studies, but it still could come up in part of a question.

You have already studied IAS 10 *Events after the reporting period* extensively. Note, that the parts of IAS 10 that cover contingencies have been superseded by IAS 37, covered in the next section.

Knowledge brought forward from earlier studies

IAS 10: events after the reporting period

Definition

Events after the reporting period are those events, both favourable and unfavourable, that occur between the year end and the date on which the financial statements are authorised for issue. Two types of events can be identified:

* those that provide further evidence of conditions that existed at the year end, and
* those that are indicative of conditions that arose subsequent to the year end.

Accounting treatment

* **Adjust** assets and liabilities where events after the B/S date provide further evidence of conditions existing at the B/S date.
* **Do not adjust**, but instead disclose, important events after B/S date that do not affect condition of assets/liabilities at the B/S date.
* **Dividends** for period proposed/declared after the B/S date but before FS are approved should not be recognised as a liability at the B/S date. Dividends do not need the criteria of a present obligation in IAS 37 (see below). They should be disclosed as required by IAS 1.

Disclosure
- Nature of event
- Estimate of financial effect (or statement that estimate cannot be made)

Window dressing is the arranging of transactions, the substance of which is primarily to alter the appearance of the B/S: it is **not** falsification of accounts. IAS 10 does allow window dressing but **disclosure** should be made of such transactions.

2 IAS 37 Provisions, contingent liabilities and contingent assets   12/07

As we have seen with regard to events after the reporting period events, financial statements must include **all the information necessary for an understanding of the company's financial position**. Provisions, contingent liabilities and contingent assets are 'uncertainties' that must be accounted for consistently if are to achieve this understanding.

2.1 Objective

IAS 37 *Provisions, contingent liabilities and contingent assets* aims to ensure that appropriate **recognition criteria** and **measurement bases** are applied to provisions, contingent liabilities and contingent assets and that **sufficient information** is disclosed in the **notes** to the financial statements to enable users to understand their nature, timing and amount.

2.2 Provisions

FAST FORWARD

Under IAS 37, a **provision** should be recognised:

- When an entity has a **present obligation**, legal or constructive
- It is probable that a **transfer of economic benefits** will be required to settle it
- A reliable estimate can be made of its amount

You will be familiar with provisions for depreciation and doubtful debts from your earlier studies. The sorts of provisions addressed by IAS 37 are, however, rather different.

Before IAS 37, there was no accounting standard dealing with provisions. Companies wanting to show their results in the most favourable light used to make large 'one off' provisions in years where a high level of underlying profits was generated. These provisions, often known as 'big bath' provisions, were then available to shield expenditure in future years when perhaps the underlying profits were not as good.

In other words, provisions were used for profit smoothing. Profit smoothing is misleading.

Important

The key aim of IAS 37 is to ensure that provisions are made only where there are valid grounds for them.

IAS 37 views a provision as a liability.

Key terms

A **provision** is a **liability** of uncertain timing or amount.

A **liability** is an obligation of an entity to transfer economic benefits as a result of past transactions or events.   *(IAS 37)*

The IAS distinguishes provisions from other liabilities such as trade payables and accruals. This is on the basis that for a provision there is **uncertainty** about the timing or amount of the future expenditure. Whilst uncertainty is clearly present in the case of certain accruals the uncertainty is generally much less than for provisions.

2.3 Recognition

IAS 37 states that a provision should be **recognised** as a liability in the financial statements when:

- An entity has a **present obligation** (legal or constructive) as a result of a past event
- It is probable that a **transfer of economic benefits** will be required to settle the obligation
- A **reliable estimate** can be made of the obligation

2.4 Meaning of obligation

It is fairly clear what a legal obligation is. However, you may not know what a **constructive obligation** is.

Key term

> IAS 37 defines a constructive obligation as
>
> 'An obligation that derives from an entity's actions where:
>
> - by an established pattern of past practice, published policies or a sufficiently specific current statement the entity has indicated to other parties that it will accept certain responsibilities, and
> - as a result, the entity has created a valid expectation on the part of those other parties that it will discharge those responsibilities.

Question
Recognise a provision

In which of the following circumstances might a provision be recognised?

(a) On 13 December 20X9 the board of an entity decided to close down a division. The accounting date of the company is 31 December. Before 31 December 20X9 the decision was not communicated to any of those affected and no other steps were taken to implement the decision.

(b) The board agreed a detailed closure plan on 20 December 20X9 and details were given to customers and employees.

(c) A company is obliged to incur clean up costs for environmental damage (that has already been caused).

(d) A company intends to carry out future expenditure to operate in a particular way in the future.

Answer

(a) No provision would be recognised as the decision has not been communicated.

(b) A provision would be made in the 20X9 financial statements.

(c) A provision for such costs is appropriate.

(d) No present obligation exists and under IAS 37 no provision would be appropriate. This is because the entity could avoid the future expenditure by its future actions, maybe by changing its method of operation.

2.4.1 Probable transfer of economic benefits

For the purpose of the IAS, a transfer of economic benefits is regarded as **'probable'** if the event is **more likely than not** to occur. This appears to indicate a probability of more than 50%. However, the standard makes it clear that where there is a number of similar obligations the probability should be based on considering the population as a whole, rather than one single item.

2.5 Example: Transfer of economic benefits

If a company has entered into a warranty obligation then the probability of an outflow of resources embodying economic benefits (transfer of economic benefits) may well be extremely small in respect of one specific item. However, when considering the population as a whole the probability of some transfer of economic benefits is quite likely to be much higher. If there is a **greater than 50% probability** of some transfer of economic benefits then a **provision** should be made for the **expected amount**.

2.5.1 Measurement of provisions

> The amount recognised as a provision should be the best estimate of the expenditure required to settle the present obligation at the year end.

The estimates will be determined by the **judgement** of the entity's management supplemented by the experience of similar transactions.

Allowance is made for **uncertainty**. Where the provision being measured involves a large population of items, the obligation is estimated by weighting all possible outcomes by their discounted probabilities, ie **expected value**.

Question   Warranty

Parker Co sells goods with a warranty under which customers are covered for the cost of repairs of any manufacturing defect that becomes apparent within the first six months of purchase. The company's past experience and future expectations indicate the following pattern of likely repairs.

% of goods sold	Defects	Cost of repairs $m
75	None	–
20	Minor	1.0
5	Major	4.0

What is the expected cost of repairs?

Answer

The cost is found using 'expected values' (75% × $nil) + (20% × $1.0m) + (5% × $4.0m) = $400,000.

Where the effect of the **time value of money** is material, the amount of a provision should be the **present value** of the expenditure required to settle the obligation. An appropriate **discount** rate should be used.

The discount rate should be a **pre-tax rate** that reflects current market assessments of the time value of money. **The discount rate(s) should not reflect risks for which future cash flow estimates have been adjusted.**

2.5.2 Future events

Future events which are reasonably expected to occur (eg new legislation, changes in technology) may affect the amount required to settle the entity's obligation and should be taken into account.

2.5.3 Expected disposal of assets

Gains from the expected disposal of assets should not be taken into account in measuring a provision.

2.5.4 Reimbursements

Some or all of the expenditure needed to settle a provision may be expected to be recovered form a third party. If so, the **reimbursement should be recognised only when it is virtually certain that reimbursement will be received if the entity settles the obligation**.

- The reimbursement should be treated as a separate asset, and the amount recognised should not be greater than the provision itself.
- The provision and the amount recognised for reimbursement may be netted off in the profit and loss account.

2.5.5 Changes in provisions

Provisions should be renewed at each year end and adjusted to reflect the current best estimate. If it is no longer probable that a transfer of economic benefits will be required to settle the obligation, the provision should be reversed.

2.5.6 Use of provisions

A provision should be used only for expenditures for which the provision was originally recognised. Setting expenditures against a provision that was originally recognised for another purpose would conceal the impact of two different events.

2.5.7 Future operating losses

Provisions should not be recognised for future operating losses. They do not meet the definition of a liability and the general recognition criteria set out in the standard.

2.5.8 Onerous contacts

If an entity has a contract that is onerous, the present obligation under the contract **should be recognised and measured** as a provision. An example might be vacant leasehold property.

Key term

> An **onerous contract** is a contract entered into with another party under which the unavoidable costs of fulfilling the terms of the contract exceed any revenues expected to be received from the goods or services supplied or purchased directly or indirectly under the contract and where the entity would have to compensate the other party if it did not fulfil the terms of the contract.

2.6 Examples of possible provisions

It is easier to see what IAS 37 is driving at if you look at examples of those items which are possible provisions under this standard. Some of these we have already touched on.

(a) **Warranties**. These are argued to be genuine provisions as on past experience it is probable, ie more likely than not, that some claims will emerge. The provision must be estimated, however, on the basis of the class as a whole and not on individual claims. There is a clear legal obligation in this case.

(b) **Major repairs**. In the past it has been quite popular for companies to provide for expenditure on a major overhaul to be accrued gradually over the intervening years between overhauls. Under IAS 37 this will no longer be possible as IAS 37 would argue that this is a mere intention to carry out repairs, not an obligation. The entity can always sell the asset in the meantime. The only solution is to treat major assets such as aircraft, ships, furnaces etc as a series of smaller assets where each part is depreciated over shorter lives. Thus any major overhaul may be argued to be replacement and therefore capital rather than revenue expenditure.

(c) **Self insurance**. A number of companies have created a provision for self insurance based on the expected cost of making good fire damage etc instead of paying premiums to an insurance company. Under IAS 37 this provision would no longer be justifiable as the entity has no obligation until a fire or accident occurs. No obligation exists until that time.

(d) **Environmental contamination**. If the company has an environment policy such that other parties would expect the company to clean up any contamination or if the company has broken current environmental legislation then a provision for environmental damage must be made.

(e) **Decommissioning or abandonment costs**. When an oil company initially purchases an oilfield it is put under a legal obligation to decommission the site at the end of its life. Prior to IAS 37 most oil companies up the provision gradually over the field so that no one year would be unduly burdened with the cost.

IAS 37, however, insists that a legal obligation exists on the initial expenditure on the field and therefore a liability exists immediately. This would appear to result in a large charge to profit and loss in the first year of operation of the field. However, the IAS takes the view that the cost of purchasing the field in the first place is not only the cost of the field itself but also the costs of putting it right again. Thus all the costs of abandonment may be capitalised.

(f)   **Restructuring**. This is considered in detail below.

2.6.1 Provisions for restructuring

One of the main purposes of IAS 37 was to target abuses of provisions for restructuring. Accordingly, IAS 37 lays down **strict criteria** to determine when such a provision can be made.

> IAS 37 defines a **restructuring** as:
>
> A programme that is planned and is controlled by management and materially changes either:
>
> •   the scope of a business undertaken by an entity, or
> •   the manner in which that business is conducted.

(Key term — left margin)

The IAS gives the following **examples** of events that may fall under the definition of restructuring.

•   The **sale or termination** of a line of business
•   The **closure of business locations** in a country or region or the **relocation** of business activities from one country region to another
•   **Changes in management structure**, for example, the elimination of a layer of management
•   **Fundamental reorganisations** that have a material effect on the **nature and focus** of the entity's operations

The question is whether or not an entity has an obligation – legal or constructive – at the year end.

•   An entity must have a **detailed formal plan** for the restructuring.
•   It must have **raised a valid expectation** in those affected that it will carry out the restructuring by starting to implement that plan or announcing its main features to those affected by it.

> **A mere management decision is not normally sufficient**. Management decisions may sometimes trigger off recognition, but only if earlier events such as negotiations with employee representatives and other interested parties have been concluded subject only to management approval.

(Important — left margin)

Where the restructuring involves the **sale of an operation** then IAS 37 states that no obligation arises until the entity has entered into a **binding sale agreement**. This is because until this has occurred the entity will be able to change its mind and withdraw from the sale even if its intentions have been announced publicly.

2.6.2 Costs to be included within a restructuring provision

The IAS states that a restructuring provision should include only the **direct expenditures** arising from the restructuring.

•   **Necessarily entailed** by the restructuring
•   Not associated with the **ongoing activities** of the entity

The following costs should specifically **not** be included within a restructuring provision.

•   **Retraining** or relocating continuing staff
•   **Marketing**
•   **Investment in new systems** and distribution networks

2.6.3 Disclosure

Disclosures for provisions fall into two parts.

•   Disclosure of details of the **change in carrying value** of a provision from the beginning to the end of the year

- Disclosure of the **background** to the making of the provision and the uncertainties affecting its outcome

2.7 Contingent liabilities

FAST FORWARD

An entity should not recognise a contingent asset or liability, but they should be disclosed.

Now you understand provisions it will be easier to understand contingent assets and liabilities.

Key term

IAS 37 defines a **contingent liability** as:

- A possible obligation that arises from past events and whose existence will be confirmed only by the occurrence or non-occurrence of one or more uncertain future events not wholly within the entity's control, or
- A present obligation that arises from past events but is not recognised because:
  - It is not probable that a transfer of economic benefits will be required to settle the obligation, or
  - The amount of the obligation cannot be measured with sufficient reliability.

As a rule of thumb, probable means more than 50% likely. **If an obligation is probable, it is not a contingent liability** – instead, a **provision is needed**.

2.7.1 Treatment of contingent liabilities

Contingent liabilities **should not be recognised in financial statements** but they **should be disclosed**. The required disclosures are:

- A brief description of the nature of the contingent liability
- An estimate of its financial effect
- An indication of the uncertainties that exist
- The possibility of any reimbursement

2.8 Contingent assets

Key term

IAS 37 defines a **contingent asset** as:

A possible asset that arises from past events and whose existence will be confirmed by the occurrence of one or more uncertain future events not wholly within the entity's control.

A contingent asset must not be recognised. Only when the realisation of the related economic benefits is **virtually certain** should recognition take place. At that point, **the asset is no longer a contingent asset!**

2.8.1 Disclosure: contingent liabilities

A **brief description** must be provided of all material contingent liabilities unless they are likely to be remote. In addition, provide

- An estimate of their **financial effect**
- Details of **any uncertainties**

2.8.2 Disclosure: contingent assets

Contingent assets must only be disclosed in the notes if they are **probable**. In that case a brief description of the contingent asset should be provided along with an estimate of its likely financial effect.

2.8.3 'Let out'

IAS 37 permits reporting entities to avoid disclosure requirements relating to provisions, contingent liabilities and contingent assets if they would be expected to **seriously prejudice** the position of the entity in dispute with other parties. However, this should only be employed in **extremely rare** cases. Details of the general nature of the provision/contingencies must still be provided, together with an explanation of why it has not been disclosed.

You must practise the questions below to get the hang of IAS 37. But first, study the flow chart, taken from IAS 37, which is a good summary of its requirements.

Exam focus point

If you learn this flow chart you should be able to deal with most tasks you are likely to meet in a central assessment.

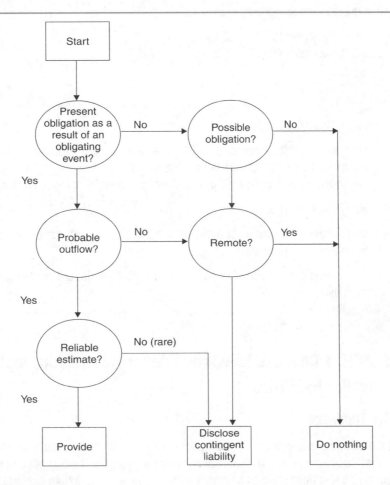

 ### Question

Recognise or not 1?

Warren Co gives warranties at the time of sale to purchasers of its products. Under the terms of the warranty the manufacturer undertakes to make good, by repair or replacement, manufacturing defects that become apparent within a period of three years from the year end. Should a provision be recognised?

Answer

Warren Co **cannot avoid** the cost of repairing or replacing all items of product that manifest manufacturing defects in respect of which warranties are given before the balance sheet date, and a provision for the cost of this should therefore be made.

Warren Co is obliged to repair or replace items that fail within the entire warranty period. Therefore, in respect of **this year's sales**, the obligation provided for at the year end should be the cost of making good items for which defects have been notified but not yet processed, **plus** an estimate of costs in respect of the other items sold for which there is sufficient evidence that manufacturing defects **will** manifest themselves during their remaining periods of warranty cover.

Question | Recognise or not 2?

After a wedding in 20X8 ten people died, possibly as a result of food poisoning from products sold by Callow Co. Legal proceedings are started seeking damages from Callow but it disputes liability. Up to the date of approval of the financial statements for the year to 31 December 20X8, Callow's lawyers advise that it is probable that it will not be found liable. However, when Callow prepares the financial statements for the year to 31 December 20X9 its lawyers advise that, owing to developments in the case, it is probable that it will be found liable.

What is the required accounting treatment:

(a) At 31 December 20X8?
(b) At 31 December 20X9?

Answer

(a) *At 31 December 20X8*

On the basis of the evidence available when the financial statements were approved, there is no obligation as a result of past events. No provision is recognised. The matter is disclosed as a contingent liability unless the probability of any transfer is regarded as remote.

(b) *At 31 December 20X9*

On the basis of the evidence available, there is a present obligation. A transfer of economic benefits in settlement is probable.

A provision is recognised for the best estimate of the amount needed to settle the present obligation.

2.9 IFRIC 1 Changes in existing decommissioning, restoration and similar liabilities

2.9.1 The issue

IFRIC 1 contains guidance on accounting for changes in decommissioning, restoration and similar liabilities that have previously been recognised both as part of the cost of an item of property, plant and equipment under IAS 16 and as a provision (liability) under IAS 37. An example would be a liability that was recognised by the operator of a nuclear power plant for costs that it expects to incur in the future when the plant is shut down (decommissioned). IFRIC 1 addresses subsequent changes to the amount of the liability that may arise from:

(a) A revision in the timing or amount of the estimated decommissioning or restoration costs, or
(b) A change in the current market-based discount rate

2.9.2 Required treatment

IAS 37 requires the amount recognised as a provision to be the best estimate of the expenditure required to settle the obligation at the balance sheet date. This is measured at its **present value,** which **IFRIC 1 confirms should be measured using a current market-based discount rate.** IFRIC 1 deals with three kinds of change in an existing liability for such costs.

The two main kinds of change dealt with in IFRIC 1 are those that arise from:

(a) The revision of estimated outflows of resources embodying economic benefits. For example, the estimated costs of decommissioning a nuclear power plant may vary significantly both in timing and amount

(b) Revisions to the current market-based discount rate

Most entities account for their property, plant and equipment using the cost model. Where this is so, these changes are required to be capitalised as part of the cost of the item and depreciated prospectively over the remaining life of the item to which they relate. This is consistent with the treatment under IAS 16 of other changes in estimate relating to property, plant and equipment.

Where entities account for their property, plant and equipment using the fair value model, a change in the liability does not affect the valuation of the item for accounting purposes. Instead, it alters the revaluation surplus or deficit on the item, which is the difference between its valuation and what would be its carrying amount under the cost model. The effect of the change is treated consistently with other revaluation surpluses or deficits. Any cumulative deficit is taken to profit or loss, but any cumulative surplus is credited to equity.

The third kind of change dealt with by IFRIC 1 is an increase in the liability that reflects the passage of time – also referred to as the **unwinding of the discount.** This is **recognised in profit or loss** as a finance cost as it occurs.

2.10 IFRIC 5 Rights to interests from decommissioning restoration and environmental rehabilitation funds

2.10.1 The issue

Some entities have **obligations to decommission assets** or to perform environmental restoration or rehabilitation. Some such entities **contribute to a fund** established to reimburse the decommissioning, restoration or rehabilitation costs when they are incurred. The fund may be set up to meet the decommissioning costs of a single contributor or for many contributors.

The issues addressed in IFRIC 5 are:

(a) How should a contributor account for its interest in a fund?

(b) When a contributor has an obligation to make additional contributions, how should that obligation be accounted for?

2.10.2 IFRIC 5 treatment

IFRIC 5 specifies the following treatment:

(a) If an entity recognises a decommissioning obligation under IFRSs and contributes to a fund to segregate assets to pay for the obligation, it should **apply IAS 27** *Consolidated and separate financial statements,* **SIC-12**, *Consolidation—Special Purpose Entities,* **IAS 28** *Investments in associates,* **and IAS 31** *Interests in joint ventures,* to determine whether decommissioning funds should be consolidated, proportionately consolidated or accounted for under the equity method.

(b) When **a fund is not consolidated, proportionately consolidated, or accounted for under the equity method**, and that fund does not relieve the contributor of its obligation to pay decommissioning costs, the contributor should **recognise**:

(i) Its obligation to pay decommissioning costs as a liability, and

(ii) Its **rights to receive reimbursement** from the fund as a reimbursement under IAS 37.

(c) A right to reimbursement should **be measured** at the lower of (i) the amount of the decommissioning obligation recognised and (ii) the contributor's share of the fair value of the net assets of the fund. Changes in the carrying amount of this right (other than contributions to and payments from the funds) should be recognised in profit or loss.

(d)   When a contributor has an obligation to make potential additional contributions to the fund, that obligation is a **contingent liability** within the scope of IAS 37. When it becomes probable that the additional contributions will be made, a provision should be recognised.

IFRIC 5 amends IAS 39 *Financial instruments: recognition and measurement* to exclude from its scope rights to reimbursement for expenditure required to settle a liability recognised as a provision. Such rights will be accounted for in accordance with IAS 37 Provisions, contingent liabilities and contingent assets.

2.11 Section summary

- The objective of IAS 37 is to ensure that appropriate recognition criteria and measurement bases are applied to provisions and contingencies and that sufficient information is disclosed.
- The IAS seeks to ensure that provisions are **only recognised** when a **measurable obligation** exists. It includes detailed rules that can be used to ascertain when an obligation exists and how to measure the obligation.
- The standard attempts to **eliminate** the **'profit smoothing'** which has gone on before it was issued.

Chapter Roundup

- **IAS 10** should be familiar from your earlier studies, but it still could come up in part of a question.
- Under IAS 37, a **provision** should be recognised:
  - When an entity has a **present obligation**, legal or constructive
  - It is probable that a **transfer of economic benefits** will be required to settle it
  - A reliable estimate can be made of its amount
- An entity **should not recognise a contingent asset or liability**, but they **should be disclosed**.
- An Exposure Draft issued in June 2005 proposes **amendments to IAS 37.**
  - The standard would be re-named 'non-financial' liabilities and be extended to include all liabilities not covered by other standards.
  - The terms contingent liability and contingent asset would be removed, and unconditional and conditional obligations introduced.
  - Expected values would be used.

1   According to IAS 37 when, and only when, can a provision be recognised?

2   A provision can be made for future operating losses. True or false?

3   When should a contingent liability be recognised?

Answers to Quick Quiz

1   • Present obligation
     • Probable transfer of economic benefits
     • Reliable estimate of value

2   False

3   Never. However they should be disclosed in a note to the accounts.

Now try the questions below from the Exam Question Bank

Number	Level	Marks	Time
Q12	Examination	25	45 mins

Related parties

Topic list	Syllabus reference
1 IAS 24 *Related party disclosures*	C9
2 Question	C9

Introduction

Section 1 deals with related party disclosures, and Section 2 deals with IFRS 2 on share based payment, a controversial area.

Study guide

		Intellectual level
C9	**Related parties**	
(a)	Determine the parties considered to be related to an entity.	3
(b)	Identify the implications of related party relationships and the need for disclosure	3

Exam guide

This examiner is fond of testing share-based payment as part of a scenario question.

1 IAS 24 Related party disclosures

FAST FORWARD

IAS 24 is primarily a disclosure standard. It is concerned to improve the quality of information provided by published accounts and also to strengthen their stewardship roles.

In the absence of information to the contrary, it is assumed that a reporting entity has **independent discretionary power** over its resources and transactions and pursues its activities independently of the interests of its individual owners, managers and others. Transactions are presumed to have been undertaken on an **arm's length basis**, ie on terms such as could have obtained in a transaction with an external party, in which each side bargained knowledgeably and freely, unaffected by any relationship between them.

These assumptions may not be justified when **related party relationships** exist, because the requisite conditions for competitive, free market dealings may not be present. Whilst the parties may endeavour to achieve arm's length bargaining the very nature of the relationship may preclude this occurring.

1.1 Objective

This is the related parties issue and IAS 24 tackles it by ensuring that financial statements contain the disclosures necessary to draw attention to the possibility that the reported financial position and results may have been affected by the existence of related parties and by material transactions with them. In other words, this is a standard which is primarily concerned with **disclosure**.

1.2 Scope

The standard requires disclosure of related party transactions and outstanding balances in the **separate financial statements** of a parent, venturer or investor presented in accordance with IAS 27 as well as in consolidated financial statements.

This is a **change** from the previous version of IAS 24, which did not require disclosure in the separate financial statements of a parent or wholly-owned subsidiary that are made available or published with consolidated financial statements for the group.

An entity's financial statements disclose related party transactions and outstanding balances with other entities in a group. **Intragroup** transactions and balances are **eliminated** in the preparation of consolidated financial statements.

1.3 Definitions

The following important definitions are given by the standard. Note that the definitions of **control** and **significant influence** are now the same as those given in IASs 27, 28 and 31.

Key terms

> **Related party**. A party is related to an entity if:
>
> (a) directly, or indirectly through one or more intermediaries, it:
>
>   (i) controls, is controlled by, or is under common control with, the entity (this includes parents, subsidiaries and fellow subsidiaries);
>
>   (ii) has an interest in the entity that gives it significant influence over the entity; or
>
>   (iii) has joint control over the entity;
>
> (b) it is an associate;
>
> (c) it is a joint venture in which the entity is a venturer;
>
> (d) it is a member of the key management personnel of the entity or its parent;
>
> (e) it is a close member of the family of any individual referred to in (a) or (d);
>
> (f) it is an entity that is controlled, jointly controlled or significantly influenced by; or for which significant voting power in such entity resides with, directly or indirectly, any individual referred to in (d) or (e); or
>
> (g) it is a post-employment benefit plan for the benefit of employees of the entity, or of any entity that is a related party of the entity.
>
> **Related party transaction**. A transfer of resources, services or obligations between related parties, regardless of whether a price is charged.
>
> **Control** is the power to govern the financial and operating policies of an entity so as to obtain benefits from its activities.
>
> **Significant influence** is the power to participate in the financial and operating policy decisions of an entity, but is not control over these policies. Significant ownership may be gained by share ownership, statute or agreement.
>
> **Joint control** is the contractually agreed sharing of control over an economic activity.
>
> **Key management personnel** are those persons having authority and responsibility for planning, directing and controlling the activities of the entity, directly or indirectly, including any director (whether executive or otherwise) of that entity.
>
> **Close members of the family of an individual** are those family members who may be expected to influence, or be influenced by, that individual in their dealings with the entity. They may include:
>
> (a) the individual's domestic partner and children;
>
> (b) children of the domestic partner; and
>
> (c) dependants of the individual or the domestic partner.   *(IAS 24)*

The most important point to remember here is that, when considering each possible related party relationship, attention must be paid to the **substance of the relationship, not merely the legal form**.

IAS 24 lists the following which are **not necessarily related parties**.

(a) **Two entities simply because they have a director or other key management in common** (notwithstanding the definition of related party above, although it is necessary to consider how that director would affect both entities)

(b) **Two venturers, simply because they share joint control over a joint venture**.

(c) Certain other bodies, simply as a result of their **role in normal business dealings** with the entity

    (i) Providers of finance

    (ii) Trade unions

    (iii) Public utilities

    (iv) Government departments and agencies

(d) **Any single customer, supplier, franchisor, distributor, or general agent** with whom the entity transacts a significant amount of business, simply by virtue of the resulting economic dependence.

1.4 Disclosure

As noted above, IAS 24 is almost entirely concerned with disclosure and its provisions are meant to **supplement** those disclosure requirements required by national company legislation and other IASs (particularly IASs 1, 22, 27 and 28).

The standard lists some **examples** of transactions that are disclosed if they are with a related party:

- Purchases or sales of goods (finished or unfinished)
- Purchases or sales of property and other assets
- Rendering or receiving of services
- Leases
- Transfer of research and development
- Transfers under licence agreements
- Provision of finance (including loans and equity contributions in cash or in kind)
- Provision of guarantees and collateral security
- Settlement of liabilities on behalf of the entity or by the entity on behalf of another party.

Relationships between **parents and subsidiaries** must be **disclosed irrespective** of **whether** any **transactions** have **taken place between** the related parties. An entity must disclose the **name** of its **parent** and, if different, the **ultimate controlling party**. This will enable a reader of the financial statements to be able to form a view about the effects of a related party relationship on the reporting entity.

If neither the parent nor the ultimate controlling party produces financial statements available for public use, the name of the next most senior parent that does so shall also be disclosed.

An entity should disclose key management personnel compensation in total for various categories:

Items of a similar nature may be **disclosed in aggregate** *unless* separate disclosure is necessary for an understanding of the effect on the financial statements.

Disclosures that related party transactions were made on terms equivalent to those that prevail in arm's length transactions are made only if such disclosures can be substantiated.

1.5 Section summary

IAS 24 is primarily concerned with **disclosure**. You should learn the following.

- **Definitions**: these are very important
- Relationships covered
- Relationships that **may not** necessarily be between related parties
- **Disclosures**: again, very important, representing the whole purpose of the standard

 Question   Related parties

Fancy Feet Co is a UK company which supplies handmade leather shoes to a chain of high street shoe shops. The company is also the sole importer of some famous high quality Greek stoneware which is supplied to an upmarket shop in London's West End.

Fancy Feet Co was set up 30 years ago by Georgios Kostades who left Greece when he fell out with the military government. The company is owned and run by Mr Kostades and his three children.

The shoes are purchased from a French company, the shares of which are owned by the Kostades Family Trust (Monaco).

Required

Identify the financial accounting issues arising out of the above scenario.

Issues

(a)   The basis on which Fancy Feet trades with the Greek supplier and the French company owned by the Kostades family trust.

(b)   Whether the overseas companies trade on commercial terms with the UK company or do the foreign entities control the UK company.

(c)   Who owns the Greek company: is this a related party under the provisions of IAS 24?

(d)   Should the nature of trade suggest a related party controls Fancy Feet Co? Detailed disclosures will be required in the accounts.

2 Question

Try this longer question on related parties.

Question   RP Group

Discuss whether the following events would require disclosure in the financial statements of the RP Group, a public limited company, under IAS 24 *Related party disclosures*.

The RP Group, merchant bankers, has a number of subsidiaries, associates and joint ventures in its group structure. During the financial year to 31 October 20X9 the following events occurred.

(a)   The company agreed to finance a management buyout of a group company, AB, a limited company. In addition to providing loan finance, the company has retained a 25% equity holding in the company and has a main board director on the board of AB. RP received management fees, interest payments and dividends from AB.

(b)   On 1 July 20X9, RP sold a wholly owned subsidiary, X, a limited company, to Z, a public limited company. During the year RP supplied X with second hand office equipment and X leased its factory from RP. The transactions were all contracted for at market rates.

(c)   The retirement benefit scheme of the group is managed by another merchant bank. An investment manager of the group retirement benefit scheme is also a non-executive director of the RP Group and received an annual fee for his services of $25,000 which is not material in the group context. The company pays $16m per annum into the scheme and occasionally transfers assets into the scheme. In 20X9, property, plant and equipment of $10m were transferred into the scheme and a recharge of administrative costs of $3m was made.

Answer

(a)   IAS 24 does not require disclosure of transactions between companies and providers of finance in the ordinary course of business. As RP is a merchant bank, no disclosure is needed between RP and AB. However, RP owns 25% of the equity of AB and it would seem significant influence exists (IAS 28, **greater than 20% existing holding means significant influence is presumed**) and therefore AB could be an associate of RP. IAS 24 regards associates as related parties.

The decision as to associate status depends upon the ability of RP to exercise significant influence especially as the other 75% of votes are owned by the management of AB.

Merchant banks tend to regard companies which would qualify for associate status as trade investments since the relationship is designed to provide finance.

IAS 28 presumes that a party owning or able to exercise control over 20% of voting rights is a related party. So an investor with a 25% holding and a director on the board would be expected to have significant influence over operating and financial policies in such a way as to inhibit the pursuit of separate interests. If it can be shown that this is not the case, there is no related party relationship.

If it is decided that there is a related party situation then **all material transactions** should be disclosed including **management fees, interest, dividends and the terms of the loan**.

(b) **IAS 24 does *not* require intragroup transactions and balances eliminated** on **consolidation to be disclosed.** IAS 24 does not deal with the situation where an undertaking becomes, or ceases to be, a subsidiary during the year.

Best practice indicates that related party transactions should be disclosed for the period when X was not part of the group. Transactions between RP and X should be disclosed between 1 July 20X9 an 31 October 20X9 but transactions prior to 1 July will have been eliminated on consolidation.

There is no related party relationship between RP and Z since it is a normal business transaction unless either parties interests have been influenced or controlled in some way by the other party.

(c) **Employee retirement benefit schemes** of the reporting entity are included in the IAS 24 definition of **related parties**.

The contributions paid, the non current asset transfer ($10m) and the charge of administrative costs ($3m) must be disclosed.

The **pension investment manager** would **not normally** be **considered** a **related party. However,** the manager is **key management personnel** by virtue of his **non-executive directorship.**

Directors are deemed to be related parties by IAS 24, and the manager receives a $25,000 fee. IAS 24 requires the disclosure of **compensation paid to key management personnel** and the fee falls within the definition of compensation. Therefore it must be disclosed.

Chapter Roundup

- **IAS 24** is primarily a disclosure standard. It is concerned to improve the quality of information provided by published accounts and also to strengthen their stewardship roles.

Quick Quiz

1   What is a related party transaction?

2   A managing director of a company is a related party.

   True   ☐   False   ☐

Answers to Quick Quiz

1   A transfer of resources, services or obligations between related parties, regardless of whether a price is charged.

2   True. A member of the key management personnel of an entity is a related party of that entity.

Now try the questions below from the Exam Question Bank

Number	Level	Marks	Time
Q13	Introductory	8	14 mins

11

Leases

Topic list	Syllabus reference
1 Forms of lease	C4
2 Lessee accounting	C4
3 Lessor accounting	C4
4 A criticism of IAS 17	C4

Introduction

Leasing transactions are extremely common in business and you will often
come across them in both your business and personal capacity. You should be
familiar with the more straightforward aspects of this topic from your earlier
studies, but we will go through these aspects in full as leasing can be very
complicated. The first section of this chapter goes over some of that basic
groundwork, before the chapter moves on to more complicated aspects.

Study guide

		Intellectual level
C4	**Leases**	
(a)	Apply and discuss the classification of leases and accounting by lessors and lessees.	3
(b)	Apply and discuss the accounting for sale and leaseback transactions.	3

Exam guide

The Study Guide and Pilot paper suggest that the emphasis may be on revenue recognition aspects or sale and leaseback ratter than the mechanics.

1 Forms of lease

> **FAST FORWARD**
>
> **IAS 17** covers the accounting under lease transactions for both lessees and lessors.
>
> There are **two forms of lease**:
>
> - Finance leases
> - Operating leases

A **lease** is a contract between a lessee for the hire of a specific asset. The lessor retains ownership of the asset but conveys the right of the use of the asset to the lessee for an agreed period of time in return for the payment of specified rentals. The term 'lease' also applies to other arrangements in which one party retains ownership of an asset but conveys the right to the use of the asset to another party for an agreed period of time in return for specified payments.

> **FAST FORWARD**
>
> The definition of a **finance lease** is very important: it is a lease that transfers all the risks and rewards of ownership of the asset, regardless of whether legal title passes.

Leasing can be considered, to be, like hire purchase, a form of instalment credit. Leases of this type are referred to as **finance leases.** Although there are many variations, in general a finance lease will have the following characteristics.

(a) The lease term will consist of a **primary period and a secondary period**. The primary period, which may be for three, four or five years, will be non-cancellable or cancellable only under certain conditions, for example on the payment of a heavy settlement figure. The secondary period is usually cancellable at any time at the lessee's option.

(b) The rentals payable during the primary period will be sufficient to **repay to the lessor** the cost of the equipment plus interest thereon.

(c) The rentals during the secondary period will be of a **nominal amount**.

(d) If the lessee wishes to **terminate the lease** during the secondary period, the equipment will be sold and substantially all of the sale proceeds will be paid to the lessee as a rebate of rentals.

(e) The lessee will be responsible for the **maintenance** and **insurance** of equipment throughout the lease.

It can be seen from the above that, from the point of view of the lessee, leasing an asset is very **similar to purchasing** it using a loan repayable over the primary period. The lessee has all of the benefits and responsibilities of ownership except for the capital allowances.

Other leases are of a very different nature. For example, a businessman may decide to hire (lease) a car whilst his own is being repaired. A lease of this nature is for a short period of time compared with the car's useful life and the lessor will expect to lease it to many different lessees during that life. Furthermore, the lessor rather than the lessee will be responsible for maintenance. Agreements of this type are usually called **operating leases**.

IAS 17 *Leases* requires that different accounting treatments should be adopted for finance and operating leases. In distinguishing between them, IAS 17 gives the following definitions.

> **Lease.** An agreement whereby the lessor conveys to the lessee in return for a payment or series of payments the right to use an asset for an agreed period of time.
>
> **Finance lease.** A lease that transfers substantially all the risks and rewards incidental to ownership of an asset. Title may or may not eventually be transferred.
>
> **Operating lease.** A lease other than a finance lease. *(IAS 17)*

When we talk of **risks** here, we specifically mean the risks of ownership, not other types of risk. Risks of **ownership** include the possibility of losses from idle capacity or technological obsolescence, or variations in return due to changing economic conditions. The **rewards** are represented by the expectation of profitable operation over the asset's economic life, and also any gain from appreciation in value or realisation of a residual value.

IAS 17 applies the same definitions and accounting principles to both lessees and lessors, but the **different circumstances** of each may lead each to classify the same lease differently.

Classification is made at the **inception of the lease**. Any revised agreement should be treated as a new agreement over its term. In contrast, changes in estimates (eg of economic life or residual value of the property) or changes in circumstances (eg default by the lessee) do not lead to a new classification of a lease for accounting purposes.

Land normally has an indefinite economic life. If the lessee does not receive legal title by the end of the lease, then the lessee does not receive substantially all the risks and rewards of ownership of the land, in which case the lease of land will be an operating lease. Any premium paid for such a leasehold is effectively a prepayment of lease payments. These are amortised over the lease term according to the pattern of benefits provided.

Where there is a lease of both land and buildings, the land and buildings elements are considered separately for the purpose of lease classification, unless title to both elements is expected to pass to the lessee by the end of the lease term (in which case both elements are classified as a financial lease). When the land has an indefinite economic life, the land element is classified as an operating lease unless title is expected to pass to the lessee by the end of the lease term; the buildings element is classified as a finance or operating lease.

Question   Finance lease

Given the above definition of a finance lease, can you think of examples of situations that would normally lead to a lease being classified as a finance lease?

Answer

Some of these (given by IAS 17) may seem fairly obvious, but others are quite complicated.

(a)   The lease transfers ownership of the asset to the lessee by the end of the lease term

(b)   The lessee has the option to purchase the asset at a price which is expected to be sufficiently lower than the fair value at the date the option becomes exercisable such that, at the inception of the lease, it is reasonably certain that the option will be exercised

(c)   The lease term is for the major part of the economic life of the asset even if title is not transferred

(d)   At the inception of the lease the present value of the minimum lease payments amounts to at least substantially all of the fair value of the leased asset

(e)   The leased assets are of a specialised nature such that only the lessee can use them without major modifications being made

There are also some indicators of situations which individually or in combination could also lead to a lease being classified as a finance lease.

(f)   If the lessee can cancel the lease, the lessor's losses associated with the cancellation are borne by the lessee

(g)   Gains or losses from the fluctuation in the fair value of the residual fall to the lessee (eg in the form of a rent rebate equalling most of the sales proceeds at the end of the lease)

(h)   The lessee has the ability to continue the lease for a secondary period at a rent which is substantially lower than market rent

1.1 Other definitions

FAST FORWARD

Make sure you learn these **important definitions** from IAS 17:

- Minimum lease payments
- Interest rate implicit in the lease
- Guaranteed/unguaranteed residual values
- Gross net investments in the lease

IAS 17 gives a substantial number of definitions.

Key terms

Minimum lease payments. The payments over the lease term that the lessee is or can be required to make, excluding contingent rent, costs for services and taxes to be paid by and be reimbursable to the lessor, together with:

(a)   For a lessee, any amounts guaranteed by the lessee or by a party related to the lessee

(b)   For a lessor, any residual value guaranteed to the lessor by one of the following.

　　(i)   The lessee
　　(ii)   A party related to the lessee
　　(iii)   An independent third party financially capable of meeting this guarantee

However, if the lessee has the option to purchase the asset at a price which is expected to be sufficiently lower than fair value at the date the option becomes exercisable for it to be reasonably certain, at the inception of the lease, that the option will be exercised, the minimum lease payments comprise the minimum payments payable over the lease term to the expected date of exercise of this purchase option and the payment required to exercise it

Interest rate implicit in the lease.

The discount rate that, at the inception of the lease, causes the aggregate present value of

(a)   the minimum lease payments, and
(b)   the unguaranteed residual value

to be equal to the sum of

(a)   the fair value of the leased asset, and
(b)   any initial direct costs.

Initial direct costs are **incremental costs** that are directly attributable to **negotiating** and **arranging** a lease, except for such costs incurred by manufacturer or dealer lessors. Examples of initial direct costs include amounts such as **commissions, legal fees** and relevant internal costs.

Lease term. The non-cancellable period for which the lessee has contracted to lease the asset together with any further terms for which the lessee has the option to continue to lease the asset, with or without further payment, when at the inception of the lease it is reasonably certain that the lessee will exercise the option.

A non-cancellable lease is a lease that is cancellable only in one of the following situations.

(a)   Upon the occurrence of some remote contingency
(b)   With the permission of the lessor
(c)   If the lessee enters into a new lease for the same or an equivalent asset with the same lessor

(d)   Upon payment by the lessee of an additional amount such that, at inception, continuation of the lease is reasonably certain

The **inception of the lease** is the earlier of the date of the lease agreement and the date of commitment by the parties to the principal provisions of the lease. As at this date:

(a)   a lease is classified as either an operating lease or a finance lease; and

(b)   in the case of a finance lease, the amounts to be recognised at the lease term are determined.

Economic life is either:

(a)   the period over which an asset is expected to be economically usable by one or more users, or

(b)   the number of production or similar units expected to be obtained from the asset by one or more users.

Useful life is the estimated remaining period, from the beginning of the lease term, without limitation by the lease term, over which the economic benefits embodied in the asset are expected to be consumed by the entity.

Guaranteed residual value is:

(a)   For a lessee, that part of the residual value which is guaranteed by the lessee or by a party related to the lessee (the amount of the guarantee being the maximum amount that could, in any event, become payable)

(b)   For a lessor, that part of the residual value which is guaranteed by the lessee or by a third party unrelated to the lessor who is financially capable of discharging the obligations under the guarantee.

Unguaranteed residual value is that portion of the residual value of the leased asset, the realisation of which by the lessor is not assured or is guaranteed solely by a party related to the lessor.

Gross investment in the lease is the aggregate of:

(a)   the minimum lease payments receivable by the lessor under a finance lease, and

(b)   any unguaranteed residual value accruing to the lessor.

Net investment in the lease is the gross investment in the lease discounted at the interest rate implicit in the lease.

Unearned finance income is the difference between:

(a)   the gross investment in the lease, and

(b)   the net investment in the lease.

The lessee's incremental borrowing rate of interest is the rate of interest the lessee would have to pay on a similar lease or, if that is not determinable, the rate that, at the inception of the lease, the lessee would incur to borrow over a similar term, and with a similar security, the funds necessary to purchase the asset.

Contingent rent is that portion of the lease payments that is not fixed in amount but is based on a factor other than just the passage of time (eg percentage of sales, amount of usage, price indices, market rates of interest).   *(IAS 17)*

Some of these definitions are only of relevance once we look at lessor accounting in Section 3.

You should also note here that IAS 17 **does not apply to** either (a) or (b) below.

(a)   Lease agreements to explore for or use of natural resources (eg oil, gas, timber).

(b)   Licensing agreements for items such as motion picture films, plays, etc.

1.1.1 SIC 15 Operating leases – incentives

In negotiating a new or renewed operating lease, the lessor may provide incentives for the lessee to enter into the agreement. Examples include an up-front cash payment to the lessee. The question arises as to how incentives in an operating lease should be recognised in the financial statements of both the lessee and the lessor.

SIC 15 provides that all incentives for the agreement of a new or renewed operating lease should be recognised as an integral part of the net consideration agreed for the use of the leased asset, irrespective of the incentive's nature or the form or the timing of payments.

The lessor should recognise the aggregate cost of incentives as a reduction of rental income over the lease term, generally on a straight-line basis.

The lessee should recognise the aggregate benefit of incentives as a reduction of rental expense over the lease term, generally on a straight line basis.

Costs incurred by the lessee, including costs in connection with a pre-existing lease should be accounted for in accordance with the relevant IAS.

1.2 Section summary

The following diagram should help you remember how to determine whether a lease is a **finance lease** or an **operating lease**.

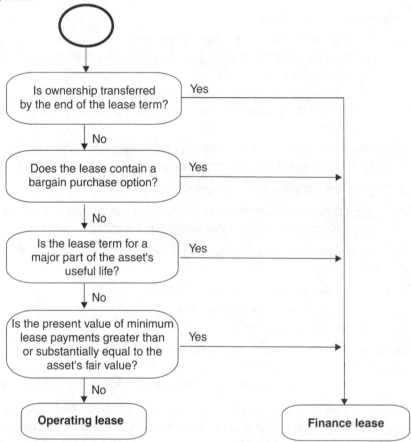

2 Lessee accounting

12/07

FAST FORWARD

Lessee accounting:

- **Finance leases:** record an asset in the statement of financial position and a liability to pay for it (fair value or PV of minimum lease payments), apportion the finance charge to give a constant periodic rate of return.

- **Operating leases:** write off rentals on a straight line basis.

Exam focus point

Your earlier studies concentrated on lessee accounting. This is therefore given fairly brief coverage before we go on to look at the more complex areas of lessor accounting.

2.1 Finance leases

From the lessee's point of view there are two main **accounting problems**.

(a)   Whether the asset should be **capitalised** as if it had been purchased.

(b)   How the **lease charges** should be allocated between different accounting periods.

2.1.1 Accounting treatment

IAS 17 requires that a finance lease should be recorded in the statement of financial position of a lessee as an asset and as an obligation to pay future lease payments. At the inception of the lease the sum to be recorded both as an asset and as a liability should be the **fair value of the leased property** or, if lower, at the **present value of the minimum lease payments**. The latter are derived by discounting them at the interest rate implicit in the lease.

If it is not practicable to determine the interest rate implied in the lease, then the lessee's **incremental borrowing rate** can be used.

Any **initial direct costs** of the lessee are added to the amount recognised as an asset. Such costs are often incurred in connection with securing or negotiating a lease. Only those costs which are directly attributable to activities performed by the lessee to obtain a finance lease should be added to the amount recognised as an asset.

IAS 17 states that it is not appropriate to show liabilities for leased assets as deductions from the leased assets. A distinction should be made between **current and non-current** lease liabilities, if the entity makes this distinction for other assets.

2.1.2 Lease payments

Minimum lease payments should be apportioned between the finance charge and a reduction of the outstanding obligation for future amounts payable. The total finance charge under a finance lease should be allocated to accounting periods during the lease term so as to produce a **constant periodic rate of interest** on the remaining balance of the obligation for each accounting period, or a reasonable approximation thereto.

Contingent rents should be charged in the periods in which they are incurred.

An asset leased under a finance lease should be **depreciated** over the shorter of the lease term or its useful life if there is no reasonable certainty that the lessee will obtain ownership by the end of the lease term. The policy of depreciation adopted should be **consistent** with similar non-leased assets and calculations should follow the bases set out in IAS 16 (see Chapter 4).

IAS 17 (revised) introduced guidance on **impairment** of leased assets by referring to IAS 36.

2.1.3 Lessees' disclosure for finance leases

IAS 17 (revised) introduced substantial disclosures (in addition to those required by IFRS 7: see Chapter 11).

- The **net carrying amount** at the year end for each class of asset
- A **reconciliation** between the total of minimum lease payments at the year end, and their present value. In addition, an entity should disclose the total of minimum lease payments at the year end, and their present value, for each of the following periods:
    - Not later than one year
    - Later than one year and not later than five years
    - Later than five years
- **Contingent rents** recognised as an expense for the period
- Total of **future minimum sublease payments** expected to be received under non-cancellable subleases at the year end

- A **general description** of the lessee's significant leasing arrangements including, but not limited to, the following:
  - The basis on which contingent rent payments are determined
  - The existence and terms of renewal or purchase options and escalation clauses
  - Restrictions imposed by lease arrangements, such as those concerning dividends, additional debt, and further leasing

2.1.4 Arguments against capitalisation

We have seen that the main argument in favour of capitalisation is substance over form. The main arguments **against** capitalisation are as follows.

(a) **Legal position.** The benefit of a lease to a lessee is an intangible asset, not the ownership of the equipment. It may be misleading to users of accounts to capitalise the equipment when a lease is legally quite different from a loan used to purchase the equipment. Capitalising leases also raises the question of whether other executory contracts should be treated similarly, for example contracts of employment.

(b) **Complexity**. Many small businesses will find that they do not have the expertise necessary for carrying out the calculations required for capitalisation.

(c) **Subjectivity**. To some extent, capitalisation is a somewhat arbitrary process and this may lead to a lack of consistency between companies.

(d) **Presentation**. The impact of leasing can be more usefully described in the notes to financial statements. These can be made readily comprehensible to users who may not understand the underlying calculations.

2.1.5 Allocating finance charge

There are two main ways of **allocating the finance charge** between accounting periods.

- Actuarial method (before tax)
- Sum of the digits method

Exam focus point

The sum of the digits method is not examinable.

The **actuarial method** is the best and most scientific method. It derives from the common-sense assumption that the interest charged by a lessor company will equal the rate of return desired by the company, multiplied by the amount of capital it has invested.

(a) At the beginning of the lease the capital invested is equal to the fair value of the asset (less any initial deposit paid by the lessee).

(b) This amount reduces as each instalment is paid. It follows that the interest accruing is greatest in the early part of the lease term, and gradually reduces as capital is repaid. In this section, we will look at a simple example of the actuarial method.

2.2 Example: actuarial method

On 1 January 20X0 Bacchus Co, wine merchants, buys a small bottling and labelling machine from Silenus Co under a finance lease. The cash price of the machine was $7,710 while the amount to be paid was $10,000. The agreement required the immediate payment of a $2,000 deposit with the balance being settled in four equal annual instalments commencing on 31 December 20X0. The charge of $2,290 represents interest of 15% per annum, calculated on the remaining balance of the liability during each accounting period. Depreciation on the plant is to be provided for at the rate of 20% per annum on a straight line basis assuming a residual value of nil.

You are required to show the breakdown of each instalment between interest and capital, using the actuarial method.

Solution

Interest is calculated as 15% of the outstanding *capital* balance at the beginning of each year. The outstanding capital balance reduces each year by the capital element comprised in each instalment. The outstanding capital balance at 1 January 20X0 is $5,710 ($7,710 fair value less $2,000 deposit).

	Total $	Capital $	Interest $
Capital balance at 1 Jan 20X0		5,710	
1st instalment			
(interest = $5,710 × 15%)	2,000	1,144	856
Capital balance at 1 Jan 20X1		4,566	
2nd instalment			
(interest = $4,566 × 15%)	2,000	1,315	685
Capital balance at 1 Jan 20X2		3,251	
3rd instalment			
(interest = $3,251 × 15%)	2,000	1,512	488
Capital balance at 1 Jan 20X3		1,739	
4th instalment			
(interest = $1,739 × 15%)	2,000	1,739	261
	8,000		2,290
Capital balance at 1 Jan 20X4		–	

2.3 Operating leases

IAS 17 requires that the **rentals** under operating leases should be written off as an expense on a **straight line basis** over the lease term even if the payments are not made on such a basis, unless another systematic and rational basis is justified by the circumstances.

2.3.1 Lessees' disclosures for operating leases

The following should be disclosed. (Remember that these are in addition to requirements under IAS 32: see Chapter 18.)

- The total of **future minimum lease payments** under non-cancellable operating leases for each of the following periods:
    - Not later than one year
    - Later than one year and not later than five years
    - Later than five years
- The total of **future minimum sublease payments** expected to be received under non-cancellable subleases at the year end
- Lease and sublease payments **recognised** as an expense for the period, with separate amounts for minimum lease payments, contingent rents, and sublease payments
- A **general description** of the lessee's significant leasing arrangements including, but not limited to, the following:
    - Basis on which contingent rent payments are determined
    - Existence and terms of renewal or purchase options and escalation clauses
    - Restrictions imposed by lease arrangements, such as those concerning dividends, additional debt, and further leasing

2.4 Section summary

The following diagram gives a useful summary of the **accounting treatment for a finance lease by a lessee**.

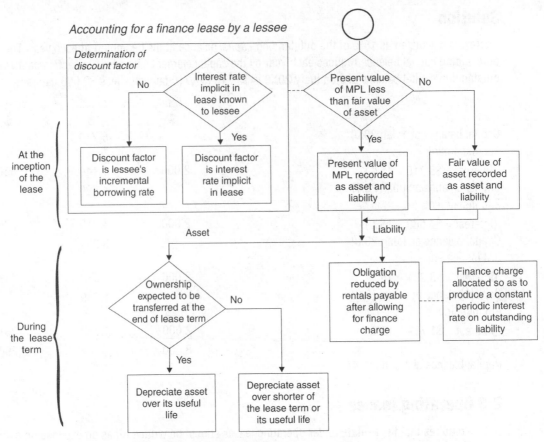

Accounting for a finance lease by a lessee

MPL = Minimum lease payments

3 Lessor accounting

Lessor accounting:

- Finance leases: record the amount due from the lessor in the statement of financial position at the net investment in the lease, recognise finance income to give a constant periodic rate of return.

- Operating leases: record as long-term asset and depreciate over useful life, record income on a straight-line basis over the lease term.

To a certain extent at least, the accounting treatment of leases adopted by lessors will be a **mirror image** of that used by lessees.

3.1 Finance leases

Several of the **definitions** given in Section 1 of this chapter are relevant to lessor accounting in particular and you should go back and look at them.

- Unguaranteed residual value
- Gross investment in the lease
- Unearned finance income
- Net investment in the lease

3.2 Accounting treatment

IAS 17 requires the **amount due from the lessee** under a finance lease to be recorded in the statement of financial position of a lessor as a receivable at the amount of the **net investment in the lease**.

The **recognition of finance income** under a finance lease should normally be based on a pattern to give a **constant periodic rate of return** on the lessor's net investment outstanding in respect of the finance lease in each period. In arriving at the constant periodic rate of return, a reasonable approximation may be made.

The lease payments (excluding costs for services) relating to the accounting period should be applied against the gross investment in the lease, so as to **reduce both the principal and the unearned finance income**.

The **estimated unguaranteed residual values** used to calculate the lessor's gross investment in a lease should be reviewed regularly. If there has been a reduction in the value, then the income allocation over the lease term must be revised. Any reduction in respect of amounts already accrued should be recognised immediately.

Initial direct costs incurred by lessors (eg commissions, legal fees and other costs that are directly attributable to negotiating and arranging a lease) are included in the initial measurement of the finance lease receivable.

FAST FORWARD

You should also know how to deal with:

* **Manufacturer/dealer lessors**
* **Sale and leaseback transactions**

3.3 Manufacturer/dealer lessors

IAS 17 (revised) looks at the situation where manufacturers or dealers offer customers the choice of either buying or leasing an asset. There will be two types of income under such a lease.

(a) Profit/loss equal to that from an **outright sale** (normal selling price less any discount)
(b) **Finance income** over the lease term

IAS 17 requires the following treatment.

(a) Recognise the **selling profit/loss** in income for the period as if it was an outright sale.
(b) If **interest rates are artificially low**, restrict the selling profit to that which would apply had a commercial rate been applied.
(c) Recognise **costs** incurred in connection with negotiating and arranging a lease as an **expense** when the **selling profit** is recognised (at the start of the lease term).

3.4 Lessors' disclosures for finance leases

The following should be disclosed (in addition to the requirements of IFRS 7).

* A **reconciliation** between the total gross investment in the lease at the year end, and the present value of minimum lease payments receivable at the year end. In addition, an entity should disclose the total gross investment in the lease and the present value of minimum lease payments receivable at the year end, for each of the following periods:
    – Not later than one year
    – Later than one year and not later than five years
    – Later than five years
* Unearned finance income
* The unguaranteed residual values accruing to the benefit of the lessor
* The accumulated allowance for uncollectible minimum lease payments receivable
* Contingent rents recognised in income
* A general description of the lessor's material leasing arrangements

3.5 Operating leases

3.5.1 Accounting treatment

An **asset** held for use in operating leases by a lessor should be recorded as a long-term asset and depreciated over its useful life. The basis for depreciation should be consistent with the lessor's policy on similar non-lease assets and follow the guidance in IAS 16.

Income from an operating lease, excluding charges for services such as insurance and maintenance, should be recognised on **a straight-line basis** over the period of the lease (even if the receipts are not on such a basis), unless another systematic and rational basis is more representative of the time pattern in which the benefit from the leased asset is receivable.

Initial direct costs incurred by lessors in negotiating and arranging an operating lease should be **added to the carrying amount** of the leased asset and recognised as an expense over the lease term on the same basis as lease income, ie capitalised and amortised over the lease term.

Lessors should refer to IAS 36 in order to determine whether a leased asset has become impaired.

A lessor who is a **manufacturer or dealer** should not recognise any selling profit on entering into an operating lease because it is not the equivalent of a sale.

3.5.2 Lessors' disclosures for operating leases

The following should be disclosed (on top of IAS 32 requirements).

- For each class of asset, the **gross carrying amount**, the accumulated depreciation and accumulated impairment losses at the year end:
  - Depreciation recognised in income for the period
  - Impairment losses recognised in income for the period
  - Impairment losses reversed in income for the period
- The **future minimum lease payments** under non-cancellable operating leases in the aggregate and for each of the following periods:
  - Not later than one year
  - Later than one year and not later than five years
  - Later than five years
- Total **contingent rents** recognised in income
- A **general description** of the lessor's leasing arrangements

3.6 Sale and leaseback transactions

In a sale and leaseback transaction, an asset is sold by a vendor and then the same asset is **leased back** to the same vendor. The lease payment and sale price are normally interdependent because they are negotiated as part of the same package. The accounting treatment for the lessee or seller should be as follows, depending on the type of lease involved.

(a)   In a sale and leaseback transaction which results in a **finance lease**, any apparent profit or loss (that is, the difference between the sale price and the previous carrying value) should be deferred and amortised in the financial statements of the seller/lessee over the lease term. It should not be recognised as income immediately.

(b)   If the leaseback is an **operating lease**:

(i)   Any profit or loss should be recognised immediately, provided it is clear that the transaction is established at a **fair value.**

(ii)   Where the **sale price is below fair value**, any profit or loss should be recognised immediately except that if the apparent loss is compensated by future lease payments at below market price it should to that extent be deferred and amortised over the period for which the asset is expected to be used.

(iii)   If the **sale price is above fair value**, the excess over fair value should be deferred and amortised over the period over which the asset is expected to be used.

In addition, for an operating lease where the fair value of the asset at the time of the sale is less than the **carrying amount**, the loss (carrying value less fair value) should be recognised immediately.

The buyer or lessor should account for a sale and leaseback in the **same way as other leases**.

The **disclosure requirements** for both lessees and lessors should force disclosure of sale and leaseback transactions. IAS 1 should be considered.

4 A criticism of IAS 17

IAS 17 (revised) closed many loopholes, but some still argue that it is **open to manipulation**.

IAS 17 has not been without its critics. The original standard **closed many loopholes** in the treatment of leases, but it has been open to abuse and manipulation. A great deal of this topic is tied up in the off balance sheet finance and creative accounting debate discussed in the last chapter.

4.1 The revised IAS 17

Some of the criticisms have been addressed by the revision of the standard in November 1997.

The changes in accounting for leases introduced by the revised standard were prompted by the unwillingness of **IOSCO** to recommend IAS 17 for the purpose of a core set of standards acceptable for the purpose of cross-border listings. In particular, IOSCO was dissatisfied with the following.

(a)   **Inadequate disclosures** by both lessors and lessees, for both finance and operating leases

(b)   The tendency of companies to prefer classifying leases as **operating leases** rather than finance leases

(c)   The free **choice of two methods for lessors** to account for finance income over the life of a lease

The main improvements in the new IAS 17 are substantially **increased disclosures** of all types of leasing transactions, particularly of the nature of leasing transactions undertaken.

IAS 17 (revised) allows only one method of recognising finance income in finance leases, the **net investment method**. This ignores external cash flow considerations such as taxation and the lessor's finance cost.

4.2 IASB projects

As mentioned earlier, leasing is the subject of a wider IASB project. This is at a very early stage but is expected to propose that the distinction between finance leases and operating leases should be abolished and that all leases should be treated as finance leases.

4.3 Unguaranteed residual value

This was defined in Section 1 above. As we have already seen, to qualify as a finance lease the risks and rewards of ownership must be transferred to the lessee. One reward of ownership is any **residual value** in the asset at the end of the primary period. If the asset is returned to the lessor then it is he who receives this reward of ownership, not the lessee. This might prevent the lease from being a finance lease if this reward is significant (IAS 17 allows insubstantial ownership risks and rewards not to pass).

IAS 17 does not state **at what point** it should normally be presumed that a transfer of substantially all the risks and rewards of ownership has occurred. To judge the issue it is necessary to compare the present value of the minimum lease payments against the fair value of the leased assets. This is an application of **discounting principles** to financial statements. The discounting equation is:

$$\text{Present value of minimum lease payment} + \text{Present value of unguaranteed residual amount accruing to lessor} = \text{Fair value of leased asset}$$

Note. Any **guaranteed residual amount** accruing to the lessor will be included in the minimum lease payments.

You should now be able to see the **scope for manipulation** involving lease classification. Whether or not a lease is classified as a finance lease can hinge on the size of the unguaranteed residual amount due to the lessor, and that figure will only be an estimate. A lessor might be persuaded to estimate a larger residual amount than he would otherwise have done and cause the lease to fail the test on present value of lease payments approximating to the asset's fair value, rather than lose the business.

4.4 Example: Unguaranteed residual value

A company enters into two leasing agreements. Let us assume that it has a 90% line to estimate whether the PV of the lease payments are 'substantially' equal to the fair value of the asset.

	Lease A $'000	Lease B $'000
Fair value of asset	210	120
Estimated residual value (due to lessor)	21	30
Minimum lease payments	238	108

How should each lease be classified?

Solution

You should note that it is unnecessary to perform any calculations for discounting in this example.

Lease A: it is obvious that the present value of the unguaranteed lease payments is less than $21,000, and therefore less than 10% of the fair value of the asset. This means that the present value of the minimum lease payments is over 90% of the fair value of the asset. Lease A is therefore a finance lease.

Lease B: the present value of the minimum lease payments is obviously less than $108,000 and therefore less than 90% of the fair value of the asset. Lease B is therefore an operating lease.

4.5 Implicit interest rate

It will often be the case that the lessee does not know the unguaranteed residual value placed on the asset by the lessor and he is therefore unaware of the interest rate implicit in the lease. In such a case, IAS 17 allows the lessee to provide his **own estimate**, to calculate the implicit interest rate and perform the test comparing the PV of the lease payments with fair value of the asset. It is obviously very easy to estimate a residual amount which fails the test. This situation would also lead to different results for the lessee and the lessor.

4.6 SIC 27 Evaluating the substance of transactions in the legal form of a lease

SIC 27 addresses issues that may arise when an arrangement between an entity and an investor involves the **legal form of a lease**. It contains the following provisions.

(a)   Accounting for arrangements between an entity and an investor should **reflect the substance of the arrangement.** All aspects of the arrangement should be evaluated to determine its substance, with weight given to those aspects and implications that have an **economic effect**. In this respect, SIC 27 includes a list of indicators that individually demonstrate that an arrangement may not, in substance, involve a lease under IAS 17 Leases.

(b)   If an arrangement **does not meet the definition of a lease**, SIC 27 considers:

(i)   Whether a separate investment **account** and lease payment obligation that might exist represent assets and liabilities of the entity

(ii)   How the entity should account for other obligations resulting from the arrangement

(iii)   How the entity should account for a fee it might receive from an Investor.

The SIC includes a list of **indicators** that collectively **demonstrate** that, in substance, a separate investment account and lease payment obligations **do not meet the definitions of an asset and a liability and should not be recognised** by the entity. Other obligations of an arrangement, including any guarantees provided and obligations incurred upon early termination, should be accounted for under IAS 37 or IAS 39, depending on the terms. Further, it agreed that the criteria in IAS 18.20 should be applied to the facts and circumstances of each arrangement in determining when to recognise a fee as income that an Entity might receive.

(c)   A series of transactions that involve the legal form of a lease is **linked**, and therefore should be accounted for as **one transaction**, when the overall economic effect cannot be understood without reference to the series of transactions as a whole.

4.7 IFRIC 4 Determining whether an arrangement contains a lease

4.7.1 The issue

In recent years arrangements have developed that do not take the legal form of a lease but which convey rights to use assets in return for a payment or series of payments. Examples of such arrangements include the following.

(a)   Outsourcing arrangements

(b)   Telecommunication contracts that provide rights to capacity

(c)   Take-or-pay and similar contracts, in which purchasers must make specified payments regardless of whether they take delivery of the contracted products or services

4.7.2 IFRIC 4 treatment

The Interpretation specifies that an arrangement that meets the following **criteria** is, or contains, a lease that should be **accounted for in accordance with IAS 17** *Leases:*

(a)   **Fulfilment of the arrangement depends upon a specific asset.** The asset need not be explicitly identified by the contractual provisions of the arrangement. Rather it may be implicitly specified because it is not economically feasible or practical for the supplier to fulfil the arrangement by providing use of alternative assets.

(b)   The arrangement conveys a **right to control the use of the underlying asset**. This is the case if any of the following conditions is met:

(i)   The purchaser in the arrangement has the **ability or right to operate the asset** or direct others to operate the asset (while obtaining more than an insignificant amount of the output of the asset).

(ii)   The purchaser has the **ability or right to control physical access to the asset** (while obtaining more than an insignificant amount of the output of the asset).

(iii)   There is **only a remote possibility that parties other than the purchaser will take more than an insignificant amount of the output of the asset** and the price that the purchaser will pay is neither fixed per unit of output nor equal to the current market price at the time of delivery.

Chapter Roundup

- **IAS 17** covers the accounting under lease transactions for both lessees and lessors.

- There are **two forms of lease**:
    - Finance leases
    - Operating leases

- The definition of a **finance lease** is very important: it is a lease that transfers all the risks and rewards of ownership of the asset, regardless of whether legal title passes.

- Make sure you learn these **important definitions** from IAS 17:
    - Minimum lease payments
    - Interest rate implicit in the lease
    - Guaranteed/unguaranteed residual values
    - Gross net investments in the lease

- **Lessee accounting**:

    - **Finance leases**: record an asset in the statement of financial position and a liability to pay for it (fair value or PV of minimum lease payments), apportion the finance charge to give a constant periodic rate of return.

    - **Operating leases**: write off rentals on a straight line basis.

- **Lessor accounting**:

    - **Finance leases**: record the amount due from the lessor in the statement of financial position at the net investment in the lease, recognise finance income to give a constant periodic rate of return.

    - **Operating leases**: record as long-term asset and depreciate over useful life, record income on a straight-line basis over the lease term.

- You should also know how to deal with:

    - **Manufacturer/dealer lessors**
    - **Sale and leaseback transactions**

- IAS 17 (revised) closed many loopholes, but some still argue that it is **open to manipulation**.

Quick quiz

1   Distinguish between a finance lease and an operating lease.

2   List the disclosure requirements for lessees under finance leases.

3   What are the arguments both for and against lessees capitalising leased assets?

4   How should manufacturer or dealer lessors account for finance leases?

5   What changes were introduced by the revision of IAS 17?

Answers to Quick Quiz

1   (a)   A finance lease transfers substantially all the risks and rewards incident to ownership of an asset. Title may or may not be transferred eventually.

       (b)   An operating lease is a lease other than a finance lease.

2   See Paragraph 2.3.1

3   *For*

       (a)   Substance over form.

    Against

       (a)   Legal position.
       (b)   Complexity.
       (c)   Subjectivity.
       (d)   Presentation.

4   (a)   Recognise the selling profit/loss in income for the period as if it were an outright sale.

       (b)   If interest rates are artificially low, restrict the selling price to that applying on a commercial rate of interest.

       (c)   Recognise indirect costs as an expense at the lease's start.

5   See Paragraph 4.1.

Now try the question below from the Exam Question Bank

Number	Level	Marks	Time
Q14	Examination	25	45 mins

Group financial statements

Revision of basic groups

12

Topic list	Syllabus reference
1 IFRS 3 (revised) and IAS 27 (revised): main points	D1
2 Other aspects of IFRS 3 (revised) and IAS 27 (revised)	D1
3 IFRS 3 (revised) and fair values	D1
4 IAS 28 Investments in associates	D1
5 IAS 31 Interest in joint ventures	D1

Introduction

Basic groups were covered in your earlier studies. In Paper P2, the emphasis is on the **more complex** aspects of consolidation. In this chapter, you will revise briefly the main principles of consolidation. If you have problems, then you should go back to your earlier study material and revise this topic more thoroughly. IFRS 3 and IAS 27 have recently been revised. The changes are significant.

Note. Throughout Part C, all undertakings are limited liability companies, unless otherwise stated. However, you should bear in mind that IAS 27 includes unincorporated entities such as partnerships within the definition of subsidiary.

IAS 28 requires that **consolidated accounts** should be extended so that they include the share of earnings or losses of companies which are associated companies. You have covered IAS 28 in your earlier studies, but it is an important standard and so is covered again here.

IAS 31 covers all types of **joint venture**. It looks at how joint ventures are accounted for in individual accounts and in consolidated accounts. Again, it is covered in full as an important standard.

> **Note.** The term 'income statement' is used for what is now generally the 'statement of comprehensive income'. This is because the ACCA have said they will use this term where the last line of the statement is 'profit for the year' and this has generally been the case in group questions.

Study guide

		Intellectual level
D1	**Group accounting including statement of cash flows**	
(a)	Apply the method of accounting for business combinations including complex group structures	3
(b)	Apply the principles relating to the cost of a business combination.	3
(c)	Apply the recognition and measurement criteria for identifiable acquired assets and liabilities and goodwill, including piecemeal acquisitions.	3
(f)	Account for and apply the equity method of accounting for associates.	3
(g)	Outline and apply the key definitions and accounting methods which relate to interests in joint ventures.	3

Exam guide

You are unlikely to be examined just on the basic principles. However, you will gain marks for knowing the basic principles in a more complex consolidation.

1 IFRS 3 (revised) and IAS 27 (revised): main points 12/08

One of the competences you need to fulfil Objective 10 of the Practical Experience Requirement (PER) is to record and understand financial transactions for single companies and combined entities. You can apply the knowledge you obtain from this Chapter, on combined entities, to demonstrate this competence.

In traditional accounting terminology, a **group of companies** consists of a **parent company** and one or more **subsidiary companies** which are controlled by the parent company. We will be looking at four accounting standards in this and the next few chapters.

- IFRS 3 (revised) Business combinations (goodwill aspects are covered in an earlier chapter).
- IAS 27 (revised) Consolidated and separate financial statements
- IAS 28 Investments in associates
- IAS 31 Interests in joint ventures

You should have studied IFRS 3 (revised) *Business combinations* for Paper F7. Here is a re-cap.

1.1 Objective of IFRS 3 (revised)

The objective of IFRS 3 (revised) is to improve the relevance, reliability and comparability of the information that a reporting entity provides in its financial statements about a business combination and its effects. To accomplish that, IFRS 3 (revised) establishes principles and requirements for how the acquirer:

(a)   Recognises and measures in its financial statements the identifiable assets acquired, the liabilities assumed and any non-controlling interest in the acquiree

(b)   Recognises and measures the goodwill acquired in the business combination or a gain from a bargain purchase

(c)   Determines what information to disclose to enable users of the financial statements to evaluate the nature and financial effects of the business combination

1.2 Definitions

All the definitions relating to group accounts are extremely important. You must **learn them** and **understand** their meaning and application.

Go back to your earlier study material and practice more questions if you are unsure of basic consolidation techniques.

Definitions are very important when looking at group accounts.

Some of these definitions are from IAS 27 (revised), 28 and 31 as well as IFRS 3 (revised) Some are new, and some you will have met before.

Control. The power to govern the financial and operating policies of an entity so as to obtain benefits from its activities. *(IFRS 3 (revised), 27, 28, 31)*

Subsidiary. An entity that is controlled by another entity (known as the parent). *(IFRS 3 (revised), IASs 27, 28)*

Parent. An entity that has one or more subsidiaries. *(IFRS 3 (revised), IAS 27 (revised))*

Group. A parent and all its subsidiaries. *(IAS 27 (revised))*

Associate. An entity, including an unincorporated entity such as a partnership, in which an investor has significant influence and which is neither a subsidiary nor a joint venture of the investor. *(IAS 28)*

Significant influence is the power to participate in the financial and operating policy decisions of an investee or an economic activity but is not control or joint control over those policies. *(IASs 28, 31)*

Joint venture. A contractual arrangement whereby two or more parties undertake an economic activity which is subject to joint control. *(IAS 31)*

Acquiree. The business or businesses that the **acquirer** obtains control of in a **business combination** *(IFRS 3 (revised))*

Acquirer. The entity that obtains control of the **acquiree** *(IFRS 3 (revised))*

Business combination. A transaction or other event in which an **acquirer** obtains control of one or more **businesses**. *(IFRS 3 (revised))*

Contingent consideration. Usually, an obligation of the **acquirer** to transfer additional assets or **equity** *(IFRS 3 (revised))* **interests** to the former owners of an **acquiree** as part of the exchange for **control** of the **acquiree** if specified future events occur or conditions are met. *(IFRS 3 (revised))*

Equity interests. Broadly used in IFRS 3 (revised) to mean ownership interests.

Fair value. The amount for which an asset could be exchanged, or a liability settled, between knowledgeable, willing parties in an arm's length transaction *(IFRS 3 (revised))*

Non-controlling interest. The equity in a subsidiary not attributable, directly or indirectly, to a parent. *(IFRS 3 (revised))*

Before discussing IFRS 3 (revised) in detail, we can summarise the different types of investment *and* the required accounting for them as follows.

Investment	Criteria	Required treatment in group accounts
Subsidiary	Control	Full consolidation
Associate	Significant influence	Equity accounting
Joint venture (jointly controlled entity)	Contractual arrangement	Proportional consolidation or equity accounting
Investment which is none of the above	Asset held for accretion of wealth	As for single company accounts per IAS 39

1.3 Identifying a business combination

IFRS 3 (revised) requires entities to determine whether a transaction or other event is a business combination by applying the definition in the IFRS.

1.4 The acquisition method

Entities must account for each business combination by applying the **acquisition method.** This requires:

(a)   **Identifying the acquirer.** This is generally the party that obtains control.

(b)   **Determining the acquisition date.** This is generally the date the consideration is legally transferred, but it may be another date if control is obtained on that date.

(c)   Recognising and measuring the **identifiable assets acquired, the liabilities assumed** and any non-controlling interest in the acquiree. (See below.)

(d)   Recognising and measuring goodwill or a gain from a bargain purchase (see Chapter 4)

The recognition and measurement of identifiable assets acquired and liabilities assumed other than non-controlling interest is dealt with in Section 3 Below we deal with the cost of the acquisition, the consideration transferred, the goodwill and the non-controlling interest, as these treatments have changed from your F7 studies.

1.5 Acquisition-related costs

The original IFRS 3 (revised) required fees (legal, accounting, valuation etc) paid in relation to a business acquisition to be included in the cost of the acquisition, which meant that they were measured as part of goodwill.

Under the revised IFRS 3 (revised) **costs relating to the acquisition must be recognised as an expense** at the time of the acquisition. They are not regarded as an asset. (Costs of issuing debt or equity are to be accounted for under the rules of IAS 39.)

1.6 Contingent consideration

FAST FORWARD

> The revised IFRS 3 (revised) **requires recognition of contingent consideration, measured at fair value, at the acquisition date**.

IFRS 3 (revised) defines contingent consideration as:

> Usually, an obligation of the acquirer to transfer additional assets or equity interests to the former owners of an acquiree as part of the exchange for control of the acquiree if specified future events occur or conditions are met. However, contingent consideration also may give the acquirer the right to the return of previously transferred consideration if specified conditions are met.

1.6.1 IFRS 3

The revised IFRS 3 (revised) recognises that, by entering into an acquisition, the acquirer becomes obliged to make additional payments. Not recognising that obligation means that the consideration recognised at the acquisition date is not fairly stated.

The revised IFRS 3 (revised) **requires recognition of contingent consideration, measured at fair value, at the acquisition date.** This is, arguably, consistent with how other forms of consideration are fair valued.

The acquirer may be required to pay contingent consideration in the form of equity or of a debt instrument or cash. Debt instruments are presented in accordance with IAS 32. Contingent consideration may occasionally be an asset, for example if the consideration has already been transferred and the acquirer has the right to the return of part of it, an asset may occasionally be recognised in respect of that right.

1.6.2 Post acquisition changes in the fair value of the contingent consideration

The treatment depends on the circumstances:

(a)   If the change in fair value is due to additional information obtained that affects the position at the acquisition date, goodwill should be re-measured.

(b)   If the change is due to events which took place after the acquisition date, for example, meeting earnings targets:

   (i)   Account for under IAS 39 if the consideration is in the form of a financial instrument, for example loan notes.

   (ii)   Account for under IAS 37 if the consideration is in the form of cash.

   (iii)   An equity instrument is not remeasured.

1.7 Goodwill and the non-controlling interest

1.7.1 IFRS 3 (revised) methods – an introduction

The revised IFRS 3 views the group as an economic entity. This means that it treats all providers of equity – including non-controlling interests – as shareholders in the group, even if they are not shareholders of the parent. Thus goodwill attributable to the non-controlling interest needs to be recognised.

We will come back to this point below, but first we need to consider how IFRS 3 (revised) sets out the calculation for goodwill.

1.7.2 IFRS 3 (revised) goodwill calculation

In words, IFRS 3 (revised) states:

Consideration paid by parent + fair value of non-controlling interest – fair value of the subsidiary's net identifiable assets = consolidated goodwill

1.7.3 BPP proforma goodwill calculation

The proforma goodwill calculation could be set out like this:

	$
Consideration transferred	X
Amount of any non-controlling interests	X
	X
Less net acquisition-date fair value of identifiable assets acquired and liabilities assumed	(X)
	X

While the above layout reflects the wording of the standard, for the purposes of your workings in the examination, the following layout is recommended:

		Group	NCI
	$	$	$
Consideration transferred/Fair value of non-controlling interests		X	X
Less: net fair value of identifiable assets acquired and liabilities assumed	X		
× Group/NCI %		(X)	(X)
		X	X
		X	

The NCI (non-controlling interest) column is only needed if the NCI interest is to be measured at fair value (see later). When the NCI is measured at fair value, goodwill arises that is attributable to the NCI.

1.7.4 Valuing non-controlling interest at acquisition

The non-controlling interest may be valued **either at fair value or at the non-controlling interest's proportionate share of the acquiree's identifiable net assets**.

The non-controlling interest now forms part of the calculation of goodwill. The question now arises as to how it should be valued.

The 'economic entity' principle (see 1.7.2) suggests that the non-controlling interest should be valued at fair value. In fact, IFRS 3 (revised) gives a **choice**:

> For each business combination, the acquirer shall measure any non-controlling interest in the acquiree **either at fair value or at the non-controlling interest's proportionate share of the acquiree's identifiable net assets.** (IFRS 3 (revised))

IFRS 3 (revised) revised suggests that the closest approximation to fair value will be the market price of the shares held by the non-controlling shareholders just before the acquisition by the parent.

Non-controlling interest at fair value will be different from non-controlling interest at proportionate share of the acquiree's net assets. The difference is goodwill attributable to non-controlling interest, which may be, but often is not, proportionate to goodwill attributable to the parent.

Exam focus point

The ACCA refer to valuation at the non-controlling interest's proportionate share of the acquiree's identifiable net assets as the 'old' method and to valuation at (full) fair value as the 'new' or 'full goodwill' method.

1.7.5 Goodwill calculation: simple examples

Now we will look at two simple goodwill calculations: the revised IFRS 3 (revised) 'old' method (proportion of net assets) and the revised IFRS 3 (revised) 'new' method (fair (or full) value).

(a)   **Revised IFRS 3 (revised) 'old' method**

On 31 December 20X8, Penn acquired 4 million of the 5 million $1 ordinary shares of Sylvania, paying $10m in cash. On that date, the fair value of Sylvania's net assets was $7.5m.

It is the group's policy to value the non-controlling interest at its proportionate share of the fair value of the subsidiary's identifiable net assets.

Calculate goodwill on the acquisition.

Answer

	$'000	$'000
Consideration transferred	10,000	
Non-controlling interest: 20% × $7.5m		1,500
Net assets acquired 80%/20%	(6,000)	(1,500)
Goodwill	4,000	–

BPP note. You will see that the NCI column is not needed because the figures cancel each other out.

(b)   **Revised IFRS 3 (revised) 'new' method**

On 31 December 20X8, Penn acquired 4 million of the 5 million $1 ordinary shares of Sylvania, paying $10m in cash. On that date, the fair value of Sylvania's net assets was $7.5m.

It is the group's policy to value the non-controlling interest at fair value. The market price of the shares held by the non-controlling shareholders just before the acquisition was $2.00

Calculate goodwill on the acquisition.

Answer

	$'000	$'000
Consideration transferred/FV NCI	10,000	2,000
Net assets acquired 80%/20%	(6,000)	(1,500)
Goodwill	4,000	500

Goodwill attributable to non-controlling interest is $500,000

Total goodwill on the acquisition (parent + NCI) is $4m + $0.5m = $4.5m.

BPP note. The goodwill attributable to the non-controlling interest is not in proportion to that attributable to the parent. If it were in proportion, the total goodwill would be $4m × 100%/80% = $5m, and so the goodwill attributable to the NCI would be $1m.

1.7.6 Why is the goodwill attributable to the NCI not always proportionate?

In Example (b) above, the goodwill attributable to the non-controlling interest is not in proportion to that attributable to the parent. Generally, this is because owners of the parent have paid a higher price in order to obtain control. You can calculate the share price the owners of the parent must have paid – it is $10m/4m, that is $2.50 per share. The premium to acquire control may reflect the value of synergies between the parent and subsidiary.

1.7.7 Non-controlling interest at the year end ('new' method)

It is important to realise that the new 'formula' only applies **at the date of acquisition**. Subsequent to acquisition both the non-controlling interest and the fair value of the subsidiary's net asset will have changed.

If you are using the revised IFRS 3 (revised) 'new method' (NCI at fair value), you **must include goodwill attributable to the non-controlling interest in your calculation of non-controlling interest at the year end.** Otherwise calculate NCI as normal.

Your calculation of non-controlling interest at the year end will look like this:

	$'000	$'000
Share capital	X	
Retained earnings	X	
Provision for unrealised profit	X	
NCI share of identifiable net assets (a × NCI %)		X
NCI share of goodwill		X
Non-controlling interest		X

Because the NCI share of goodwill appears in both the top half of the statement of financial position (as an asset, part of total goodwill), and the bottom half, the statement of financial position will balance.

1.7.8 Goodwill impairment under the 'new' method

The ACCA have given the following advice regarding allocation of impairment of goodwill. The advice relates to an example where the proportionate shareholding of the NCI is 25% (and so the parent controls 75%) and the amount of the impairment is $1 million:

> IAS 36 requires a subsidiary's goodwill impairment to be allocated between the parent and the non-controlling interest on the same basis as the subsidiary's profits and losses are allocated. Thus of the impairment of $1 million, $750,000 would be allocated to the parent (and debited to group retained earnings reducing them to $29.55 million (30,300 - 750)) and $250,000 would be allocated to the NCI writing it down to $3.65 million (3,900 - 250).
>
> It could be argued that this requirement represents an anomaly; of the recognised goodwill (before the impairment) of $5 million only $500,000 ie 10% relates to the NCI, but it suffers 25% (its proportionate shareholding in the subsidiary) of the goodwill impairment.

In other words, **the impairment of the goodwill is allocated proportionately, even if the goodwill on the non-controlling interest is not itself proportionate.**

1.7.9 Your P2 exam

The ACCA has stated that **both the 'old' and the 'new' methods are examinable.** Specifically, the advice is as follows:

ACCA will require students to know both methods. The wording is as follows

New method

'It is the group policy to value the non-controlling interest at full (or fair) value.'

Old method

'It is the group policy to value the non-controlling interest at its proportionate share of the (fair value of the) subsidiary's identifiable net assets.'

Questions will ask specifically for one or other method.

There are a number of ways of presenting the information to test the new method:

(i)   As above, the subsidiary's share price just before the acquisition could be given and then used to value the non-controlling interest. It would then be a matter of multiplying the share price by the number of shares held by the non-controlling interests. (Note: the parent is likely to have paid more than the subsidiary's pre acquisition share price in order to gain control).

(ii)   The question could simply state that the directors valued the non-controlling interest at the date of acquisition at $2 million

(iii)   An alternative approach would be to give (in the question) the value of the goodwill attributable to the non-controlling interest. In this case the NCI's goodwill would be added to the parent's goodwill (calculated by the traditional method) and to the carrying amount of the non-controlling interest itself. [In example (c) above this would be $500,000.

2 Other aspects of IFRS 3 (revised) and IAS 27 (revised)

Note. This will be revision from your earlier studies, amended where appropriate for the changes introduced by IFRS 3 (revised).

2.1 investment in subsidiaries

The important point here is **control**. In most cases, this will involve the holding company or parent owning a majority of the ordinary shares in the subsidiary (to which normal voting rights are attached). There are circumstances, however, when the parent may own only a minority of the voting power in the subsidiary, *but* the parent still has control.

IAS 27 (revised) states that control can usually be assumed to exist when the parent **owns more than half (ie over 50%) of the voting power** of an entity *unless* it can be clearly shown that **such ownership does not constitute control** (these situations will be very rare).

What about situations where this ownership criterion does not exist? IFRS 3 (revised) and IAS 27 list the following situations where control exists, even when the parent owns only 50% or less of the voting power of an entity.

(a)   The parent has power over more than 50% of the voting rights by virtue of agreement with other investors

(b)   The parent has power to govern the financial and operating policies of the entity by statute or under an agreement

(c)   The parent has the power to appoint or remove a majority of members of the board of directors (or equivalent governing body)

(d)   The parent has power to cast a majority of votes at meetings of the board of directors

IAS 27 (revised) also states that a parent loses control when it loses the power to govern the financial and operating policies of an investee. Loss of control can occur without a change in ownership levels. This may happen if a subsidiary becomes subject to the control of a government, court administrator or regulator (for example, in bankruptcy).

Exam focus point

You should learn the contents of the above paragraph as you may be asked to apply them in the exam.

2.1.1 Accounting treatment in group accounts

IAS 27 (revised) requires a parent to present consolidated financial statements, in which the accounts of the parent and subsidiary (or subsidiaries) are combined and presented **as a single entity**.

2.2 Investments in associates

This type of investment is something less than a subsidiary, but more than a simple investment (nor is it a joint venture). The key criterion here is **significant influence**. This is defined as the 'power to participate', but *not* to 'control' (which would make the investment a subsidiary).

Significant influence can be determined by the holding of voting rights (usually attached to shares) in the entity. IAS 28 states that if an investor holds **20% or more** of the voting power of the investee, it can be presumed that the investor has significant influence over the investee, *unless* it can be clearly shown that this is not the case.

Significant influence can be presumed *not* to exist if the investor holds **less than 20%** of the voting power of the investee, unless it can be demonstrated otherwise.

The **existence of significant influence** is evidenced in one or more of the following ways.

(a) Representation on the **board of directors** (or equivalent) of the investee
(b) Participation in the **policy making process**
(c) **Material transactions** between investor and investee
(d) Interchange of **management personnel**
(e) Provision of **essential technical information**

2.2.1 Accounting treatment in group accounts

IAS 28 requires the use of the **equity method** of accounting for investments in associates. This method will be explained in detail in Section 4.

2.3 Accounting for investments in joint ventures

There are situations where venturers control jointly either operations or assets of the joint venture. The case of a **jointly controlled entity** will be considered in detail in Section 5.

2.3.1 Accounting treatment in group accounts

IAS 31 allows two treatments for investments in joint entities.

(a) Proportionate consolidation
(b) Equity method

2.4 Other investments

Investments which do not meet the definitions of any of the above should be accounted for according to IAS 39 *Financial instruments: recognition and measurement*.

The section summary after this question will give a reminder of the table above. Before you look at it, see if you can write out the table yourself.

2.5 Revision: IAS 27 (revised) Consolidated and separate financial statements

FAST FORWARD

> **IAS 27 (revised)** covers the basic definitions and consolidation requirements. In particular you should learn the rules on **exemptions** from preparing group accounts

IAS 27 (revised) requires a parent to present consolidated financial statements.

Key term

> **Consolidated financial statements**. The financial statements of a group presented as those of a single economic entity.
> *(IAS 27 (revised))*

When a parent issues consolidated financial statements, it should consolidate **all subsidiaries**, both foreign and domestic.

2.5.1 Exemption from preparing group accounts

A parent **need not present** consolidated financial statements if and only if:

(a)   It is a **wholly-owned subsidiary** or it is a **partially owned subsidiary** of another entity and its other owners, including those not otherwise entitled to vote, have been informed about, and do not object to, the parent not presenting consolidated financial statements

(b)   Its securities are **not publicly traded**

(c)   It is **not in the process of issuing securities** in public securities markets

(d)   The **ultimate or intermediate parent** publishes consolidated financial statements that comply with International Financial Reporting Standards

A parent that does not present consolidated financial statements must comply with the IAS 27 (revised) rules on separate financial statements (discussed later in this section).

2.5.2 Potential voting rights

An entity may own share warrants, share call options, or other similar instruments that are **convertible into ordinary shares** in another entity. If these are exercised or converted they may give the entity voting power or reduce another party's voting power over the financial and operating policies of the other entity (potential voting rights). The **existence and effect** of potential voting rights, including potential voting rights held by another entity, should be considered when assessing whether an entity has control over another entity (and therefore has a subsidiary).

In assessing whether potential voting rights give rise to control, the entity examines all facts and circumstances that affect the rights (for example, terms and conditions), except the intention of management and the financial ability to exercise the rights or convert them into equity shares.

2.5.3 Exclusion of a subsidiary from consolidation

The rules on exclusion of subsidiaries from consolidation are necessarily strict, because this is a common method used by entities to manipulate their results. If a subsidiary which carries a large amount of debt can be excluded, then the gearing of the group as a whole will be improved. In other words, this is a way of taking debt **off the statement of financial position**.

The previous version of IAS 27 (revised) required a subsidiary to be excluded from consolidation where **control is intended to be temporary**: the subsidiary was acquired and is held *exclusively* with a view to its subsequent disposal within twelve months from acquisition *and* management is actively seeking a buyer. This exclusion has now been **removed**; subsidiaries held for sale must be consolidated.

Subsidiaries held for sale are accounted for in accordance with IFRS 5 *Non-current assets held for sale and discontinued operations* (see Chapter 15).

It has been argued that subsidiaries should be excluded from consolidation on the grounds of **dissimilar activities**, ie the activities of the subsidiary are so different to the activities of the other companies within the group that to include its results in the consolidation would be misleading. IAS 27 (revised) rejects this argument: exclusion on these grounds is not justified because better (relevant) information can be provided about such subsidiaries by consolidating their results and then giving additional information about the different business activities of the subsidiary, eg under IFRS 8 *Operating segments.*

The previous version of IAS 27 (revised) permitted exclusion where the subsidiary operates under **severe long-term restrictions** and these significantly impair its ability to transfer funds to the parent. This exclusion has now been **removed**. Control must actually be lost for exclusion to occur.

2.5.4 Different reporting dates

In most cases, all group companies will prepare accounts to the same reporting date. One or more subsidiaries may, however, prepare accounts to a different reporting date from the parent and the bulk of other subsidiaries in the group.

In such cases the subsidiary may prepare additional statements to the reporting date of the rest of the group, for consolidation purposes. If this is not possible, the subsidiary's accounts may still be used for the consolidation, *provided that* the gap between the reporting dates is **three months or less**.

Where a subsidiary's accounts are drawn up to a different accounting date, **adjustments should be made** for the effects of significant transactions or other events that occur between that date and the parent's reporting date.

2.5.5 Uniform accounting policies

Consolidated financial statements should be prepared using **the same accounting policies** for like transactions and other events in similar circumstances.

Adjustments must be made where members of a group use different accounting policies, so that their financial statements are suitable for consolidation.

2.5.6 Date of inclusion/exclusion

The results of subsidiary undertakings are included in the consolidated financial statements from:

(a)   The date of 'acquisition', ie the **date control passes to the parent**, to
(b)   The date of 'disposal', ie the **date control passes from the parent**

Once an investment is no longer a subsidiary, it should be treated as an associate under IAS 28 (if applicable) or as an investment under IAS 39.

2.5.7 Accounting for subsidiaries, jointly controlled entities and associates in the parent's separate financial statements

A parent company will usually produce its own, single company financial statements. In these statements, investments in subsidiaries, jointly controlled entities and associates included in the consolidated financial statements should be *either*:

(a)   Accounted for at **cost**, *or*
(b)   In accordance with **IAS 39**.

Where subsidiaries are **classified as held for sale** in accordance with IFRS 5 they should be accounted for in accordance with IFRS 5 (see Chapter 15).

2.6 Attribution of losses

Under the previous version of IAS 27 (revised), non-controlling interest could not be negative. Losses exceeding the non-controlling interest were attributed to the parent. Under the revised standard, non-controlling interests can be negative. This is consistent with the idea that non-controlling interests are part of the equity of the group.

2.7 Revision: summary of techniques

FAST FORWARD

Consider the nature of the **current definitions and accounting requirements**. You should be able to discuss why they are so complex and detailed.

The summary given below is very brief but it encompasses all the major, but basic, rules of consolidation for, firstly, the consolidated statement of financial position.

Knowledge brought forward from earlier studies

Summary of technique: consolidated statement of financial position

- **Net assets**: 100% P plus 100% S.
- **Share capital**: P only.
- **Reserves**: 100% P plus group share of post-acquisition retained reserves of S less consolidation adjustments.
- **Non-controlling interest**: NCI share of S's consolidated net assets (**'old' method**).
  NCI share of S's consolidated net assets plus NCI share of goodwill (**'new method'**)

The method of consolidation is as follows.

- Determine the **group structure**. Draw chart showing the percentages holdings and dates of acquisition.
- Consider **adjustments** for:
  - Dividends
  - Provisions for unrealised profits (PUP)
  - Revaluations to fair value
  - Intragroup inventory and cash in transit
- Combine **net assets**, cancelling any **intra-group balances**.
  - Current accounts
  - Debentures
- **Share capital** of P only

- Calculate the **non-controlling interest** in net assets

NCI % of share capital	X
NCI % of reserves	X
NCI % of revaluations to fair value	X
NCI % of unrealised profit	(X)
	X

If using new method, include NCI share of goodwill.

- Calculate the **goodwill (positive or negative)**

Consideration transferred	X
NCI	X
Assets acquired	
Share capital	(X)
Pre-acquisition reserves	(X)
Revaluation to fair value	(X)
Goodwill	X

- If cost is **greater than** the share of net assets acquired then the difference is **positive** goodwill, which should be capitalised and retained in the statement of financial position, subject to annual impairment reviews (see Chapter 4).

- If cost is **less than** the share of net assets acquired then the difference is **negative** goodwill. The treatment of this is discussed in Chapter 4.

- **Calculate retained earnings reserve**

	P	S	A
Per question	X	X	X
Adjustments	X(X)	X(X)	X(X)
Fair value adjustment (% x adj)		X/X)	X/(X)
Accumulated profits at acquisition	-	(X)	(X)
	X	X	X
Share of post acquisition profits of subsidiary (% x X)	X		
Share of post acquisition profits reserves of associate/JCE (% x Y)	X		
	X		

The technique for the preparation of a **consolidated statement of comprehensive income** is given below, with two additional (and very important) points.

Summary of technique: consolidated statement of comprehensive income

Adjustments required for consolidation of a subsidiary are as follows.

- Eliminate **intra-group sales and purchases**.
- Eliminate any **unrealised profits** on intra-group purchases still in inventory at the year end.
- Eliminate any **intra-group** dividends received and paid, ie show only P's dividends.
- Analyse profit for the year between owners of the parent and N.C.I.

For the inclusion of a subsidiary carry out the following.

- **Combine all P and S results** from turnover to profit after tax (where the acquisition is mid-year, use a time-apportioned basis).
- Exclude any **investment income** that is intra-group.

- **Calculate NCI**:
  - Where there are no preference shares: NCI = % × profit after tax
  - Where there are preference shares an additional working is required

Pre-acquisition dividends

There are two ways to calculate the pre-acquisition element of a dividend.

- To the extent that post-acquisition profits are **insufficient** to cover the dividend, the distribution must be out of pre-acquisition profits. This method is more commonly used in practice.

- **Apportion** the dividend on a time basis between the pre– and post-acquisition periods, so that only post-acquisition dividends are taken to P's reserves. This method is recommended in ACCA exams.
  - For **pre-acquisition dividends**: *Debit* Dividend receivable/cash, *Credit* Cost of investment.
  - For **post-acquisition dividends**: *Debit* Dividend receivable/cash, *Credit* Reserves.

Unrealised profits/losses

Only where **S sells to P**, allocate the unrealised profit between NCI and P: *Debit* Group reserves, *Debit* non-controlling interest, *Credit* Inventory.

Now try the following question to refresh your memory on the topics listed above.

Exam focus point

The consolidation questions in the Paper P2 exam are much more difficult than those in your earlier studies. The examiner will not bother to test basic consolidation techniques directly, although they may come up in a question: rather he will ask about one of the more complex areas which we will look at in the next few chapters.

Question   Revision of basic groups

Boo Co has owned 80% of Goose Co's equity since its incorporation. On 31 December 20X8 it despatched goods which cost $80,000 to Goose, at an invoiced cost of $100,000. Goose received the goods on 2 January 20X9 and recorded the transaction then. The two companies' draft accounts as at 31 December 20X8 are shown below.

INCOME STATEMENTS

	Boo	Goose
	$'000	$'000
Revenue	5,000	1,000
Cost of sales	2,900	600
Gross profit	2,100	400
Other expenses	1,700	320
Net profit	400	80
Income tax	130	25
Profit for the year	270	55

STATEMENT OF CHANGES IN EQUITY

	$'000	$'000
Opening balance	2,260	285
Total comprehensive income (profit) for the year	270	55
Dividends	(130)	(40)
Closing balance	2,400	300

STATEMENTS OF FINANCIAL POSITION

	Boo		Goose	
	$'000	$'000	$'000	$'000
Assets				
Non-current assets				
Property, plant and equipment		1,920		200
Investment in Goose		80		–
		2,000		200
Current assets				
Inventory	500		120	
Trade debtors	650		40	
Bank and cash	390		35	
		1,540		195
		3,540		395
Equity and liabilities				
Equity				
Share capital		2,000		100
Retained earnings		400		200
		2,400		300
Current liabilities				
Trade payables	910		30	
Dividend payable	100		40	
Tax	130		25	
		1,140		95
		3,540		395

Required

Prepare draft consolidated financial statements.

Answer

BOO GROUP
CONSOLIDATED INCOME STATEMENT
FOR THE YEAR ENDED 31 DECEMBER 20X8

	$'000
Revenue (5,000 + 1,000 – 100)	5,900
Cost of sales (2,900 + 600 – 80)	3,420
Gross profit	2,480
Other expenses (1,700 + 320)	2,020
Net profit	460
Income tax (130 + 25)	155
Profit for the year	305
Profit attributable to:	
Owners of the parent	294
Non-controlling interest	11
	305

CONSOLIDATED STATEMENT OF CHANGES IN EQUITY
FOR THE YEAR ENDED 31 DECEMBER 20X8

	$'000
Opening balance	2,408
Group profit for the year	294
Dividends	(130)
Closing balance	2,572

CONSOLIDATED STATEMENT OF FINANCIAL POSITION AS AT 31 DECEMBER 20X8

	$'000	$'000
Assets		
Non-current assets (1,920 + 200)		2,120
Current assets		
Inventory (500 + 120 + 80)	700	
Trade receivables (650 – 100 + 40)	590	
Bank and cash (390 + 35)	425	
		1,715
		3,835
Equity and liabilities		
Equity		
Share capital (Boo only)		2,000
Retained earnings (W)		572
Shareholders' funds		2,572
Non-controlling interest (20% × 300)		60
		2,632
Current liabilities		
Trade payables (910 + 30)	940	
Dividend payable: Boo Ltd	100	
to non-controlling interest in Goose Ltd	8	
Income tax (130 + 25)	155	
		1,203
		3,835

Working: group retained earnings

	Boo	Goose
	$'000	$'000
Per question	400	200
Closing inventory in transit (at cost)	80	
Inter company sale	(100)	
Dividend receivable ($40 × 80%)	32	
Share of Goose ($200 × 80%)	160	
Group net owned profits	572	

This working is, of course, only necessary when you are not required to prepare the consolidated income statement. Here, it serves as a proof of the consolidated income statement as well as of the reserves figure in the statement of financial position.

Question   NCI at its proportionate share of fair value of subsidiary's identifiable net assets

The draft statements of financial position of Oak and its subsidiary Chestnut at 30 September 20X8 are as follows.

	Oak		Chestnut	
	$	$	$	$
Non-current assets				
Tangible assets, net book value				
Land and buildings		225,000		270,000
Plant		202,500		157,500
		427,500		427,500
Investment				
Shares in Chestnut at cost		562,500		
Current assets				
Inventory	255,000		180,000	
Receivables	375,000		90,000	
Bank	112,500		22,500	
		742,500		292,500
		1,732,500		720,000

	Oak $	Chestnut $
Equity		
Called up share capital – issued and fully paid		
$1 ordinary shares	1,125,000	450,000
Retained earnings	450,000	202,500
	1,575,000	652,500
Current liabilities	157,500	67,500
	1,732,500	720,000

The following information is also available.

(a) Oak purchased 360,000 shares in Chestnut some years ago when that company had a credit balance of $105,000 in retained earnings. The goodwill had been impaired and was fully written off through the income statement by 30 September 20X7.

(b) For the purpose of the takeover, the land of Chestnut was revalued at $120,000 in excess of its book value. This was not reflected in the accounts of Chestnut. Land is not depreciated.

(c) At 30 September 20X8 Chestnut owed Oak $15,000 for goods purchased.

(d) The inventory of Chestnut includes goods purchased from Oak at a price which includes a profit to Oak of $10,500.

(e) It is the group's policy to value the non-controlling interest at its proportionate share of the fair value of the subsidiary's identifiable net assets.

Required

Prepare the consolidated statement of financial position (balance sheet) for Oak as at 30 September 20X8.

BPP hint. You don't need a separate column for non-controlling interest in the goodwill working.

Answer

OAK
CONSOLIDATED STATEMENT OF FINANCIAL POSITION AS AT 30 SEPTEMBER 20X8

	$	$
Non-current assets		
Land and buildings (W5)		615,000
Plant		360,000
		975,000
Current assets		
Inventory (W6)	424,500	
Receivables (W7)	450,000	
Bank	135,000	
		1,009,500
		1,984,500
Equity		
Ordinary $1 shares		1,125,000
Retained earnings (W3)		495,000
		1,620,000
Non-controlling interest (W4)		154,500
Current liabilities one year (W8)		210,000
		1,984,500

Workings

1 Group structure: $\dfrac{360,000}{450,000} = 80\%$

2 *Goodwill*

	$	$
Consideration transferred		562,500
Net assets acquired		
Share capital	450,000	
Reserves	105,000	
Revaluation reserve	120,000	
	675,000	
Group share: 80%		540,000
Goodwill		22,500

3 *Retained earnings*

	$
Oak	450,000
Chestnut (202,500 – 105,000) × 80%	78,000
Goodwill written off as impaired	(22,500)
Unrealised profit	(10,500)
	495,000

4 *Non-controlling interests*

	$
Share capital	450,000
Retained earnings	202,500
Revaluation	120,000
	772,500
20% × $772,500 =	$154,500

5 *Land and buildings*

	$	$
Oak		225,000
Chestnut:		
Net book value	270,000	
Revaluation	120,000	
		390,000
		615,000

6 *Inventory*

	$
Oak	225,000
Chestnut	180,000
Less unrealised profit	10,500
	424,500

7 *Receivables*

	$
Oak	375,000
Chestnut	90,000
Less intragroup	(15,000)
	450,000

8   *Current liabilities*

	$
Oak	157,500
Chestnut	67,500
Less intragroup	(15,000)
	210,000

Question	Non-controlling interest at fair value

You are provided with the following statements of financial position (balance sheets) for Shark and Minnow.

STATEMENTS OF FINANCIAL POSITION AS AT 31 OCTOBER 20X0

	Shark		Minnow	
	$'000	$'000	$'000	$'000
Non-current assets, at net book value				
Plant		325		70
Fixtures		200		50
		525		120
Investment				
Shares in Minnow at cost		200		
Current assets				
Inventory at cost	220		70	
Receivables	145		105	
Bank	100		0	
		465		175
		1,190		295
Equity				
$1 Ordinary shares		700		170
Retained earnings		215		50
		915		220
Current liabilities				
Payables	275		55	
Bank overdraft	0		20	
		275		75
		1,190		295

The following information is also available.

(a)   Shark purchased 70% of the issued ordinary share capital of Minnow four years ago, when the retained earnings of Minnow were $20,000. There has been no impairment of goodwill.

(b)   For the purposes of the acquisition, plant in Minnow with a book value of $50,000 was revalued to its fair value of $60,000. The revaluation was not recorded in the accounts of Minnow. Depreciation is charged at 20% using the straight-line method.

(c)   Shark sells goods to Minnow at a mark up of 25%. At 31 October 20X0, the inventories of Minnow included $45,000 of goods purchased from Shark.

(d)   Minnow owes Shark $35,000 for goods purchased and Shark owes Minnow $15,000.

(e)   It is the group's policy to value the non-controlling interest at fair value.

(f)   The market price of the shares of the non-controlling shareholders just before the acquisition was $1.50.

Required

Prepare the consolidated statement of financial position of Shark as at 31 October 20X0.

SHARK
CONSOLIDATED STATEMENT OF FINANCIAL POSITION (BALANCE SHEET) AS AT 31 OCTOBER 20X0

	$'000	$'000
Non-current assets		
Plant (W2)	397	
Fixtures (200 + 50)	250	
		647
Intangible asset: goodwill (W1)		77
		724
Current assets		
Inventory (W5)	281	
Receivables (W6)	200	
Bank	100	
		581
		1,305
Capital and reserves		
Share capital		700
Retained earnings (W2)		221
		921
Non-controlling interests (W3)		84
		1,005
Current liabilities		
Payables (W7)	280	
Bank overdraft	20	
		300
		1,305

Workings

1   *Goodwill*

		Group	NCI
	$'000	$'000	$'000
Consideration transferred/FV NCI		200	76.5
(30% × 170,000 × $1.50)			
Net assets acquired			
Share capital	170		
Retained earnings	20		
Revaluation surplus (60 – 50)	10		
	200		
Group/NCI share: 70%/30%		140	60.0
Goodwill in parent		60	16.5
			$76.5m

2   *Retained earnings*

	$'000	$'000
Shark		215
PUP (W3)	9.0	
Excess depn on plant (8 (W2) × 70%)	5.6	
		14.6
		200.4
Minnow: 70% × (50 – 20)		21.0
		221.4

3   Non-controlling interests

	$'000	$'000
Share capital		170
Revaluation	10	
Less excess depreciation	(8)	
		2
Retained earnings		50
		222

NCI in sub's identifiable net assets: 30% × $222,000		67
Goodwill attributable to NCI (W1)		17
Non-controlling interest		84

4   Plant

	$'000	$'000
Shark		325
Minnow		
Per question	70	
Revalued (60 – 50)	10	
Depreciation on revalued plant (10 × 20% × 4)	(8)	
		72
		397

5   Inventory

	$'000	$'000
Shark		220
Minnow	70	
Less PUP (45 × $^{20}/_{100}$)	(9)	
		61
		281

6   Receivables

	$'000	$'000
Shark		145
Less intragroup		35
		110
Minnow	105	
Less intragroup	15	
		90
		200

7   Payables

	$'000	$'000
Shark		275
Less intragroup		15
		260
Minnow	55	
Less intragroup	35	
		20
		280

3 IFRS 3 (revised) and fair values

To understand the importance of fair values in the acquisition of a subsidiary consider again the definition of goodwill.

> **Goodwill**. Any excess of the cost of the acquisition over the acquirer's interest in the fair value of the identifiable assets and liabilities acquired as at the date of the exchange transaction.

The **statement of financial position of a subsidiary company** at the date it is acquired may not be a guide to the fair value of its net assets. For example, the market value of a freehold building may have risen greatly since it was acquired, but it may appear in the statement of financial position at historical cost less accumulated depreciation.

3.1 What is fair value?

Fair value is defined as follows by IFRS 3 (revised) and various other standards – it is an important definition.

> **Fair value**. The amount for which an asset could be exchanged, or a liability settled, between knowledgeable, willing parties in an arm's length transaction.

We will look at the requirements of IFRS 3 (revised) regarding fair value in more detail below. First let us look at some practical matters.

3.2 Fair value adjustment calculations

Until now we have calculated goodwill as the difference between the cost of the investment and the **book value** of net assets acquired by the group. If this calculation is to comply with the definition above we must ensure that the book value of the subsidiary's net assets is the same as their **fair value**.

There are two possible ways of achieving this.

(a) The **subsidiary company** might **incorporate any necessary revaluations** in its own books of account. In this case, we can proceed directly to the consolidation, taking asset values and reserves figures straight from the subsidiary company's statement of financial position.

(b) The **revaluations** may be made as a **consolidation adjustment without being incorporated** in the subsidiary company's books. In this case, we must make the necessary adjustments to the subsidiary's statement of financial position as a working. Only then can we proceed to the consolidation.

Note. Remember that when depreciating assets are revalued there may be a corresponding alteration in the amount of depreciation charged and accumulated.

3.3 Example: Fair value adjustments

P Co acquired 75% of the ordinary shares of S Co on 1 September 20X5. At that date the fair value of S Co's non-current assets was $23,000 greater than their net book value, and the balance of retained earnings was $21,000. The statements of financial position of both companies at 31 August 20X6 are given below. S Co has not incorporated any revaluation in its books of account.

P CO
STATEMENT OF FINANCIAL POSITION AS AT 31 AUGUST 20X6

	$	$
Assets		
Non-current assets		
Tangible assets	63,000	
Investment in S Co at cost	51,000	
		114,000
Current assets		82,000
Total assets		196,000

	$	$
Equity and liabilities		
Equity		
Ordinary shares of $1 each	80,000	
Retained earnings	96,000	
		176,000
Current liabilities		20,000
Total equity and liabilities		196,000

S CO

STATEMENT OF FINANCIAL POSITION AS AT 31 AUGUST 20X6

	$	$
Assets		
Tangible non-current assets		28,000
Current assets		43,000
Total assets		71,000
Equity and liabilities		
Equity		
Ordinary shares of $1 each	20,000	
Retained earnings	41,000	
		61,000
Current liabilities		10,000
Total equity and liabilities		71,000

If S Co had revalued its non-current assets at 1 September 20X5, an addition of $3,000 would have been made to the depreciation charged to profit or loss for 20X5/X6. It is the group's policy to value the non-controlling interest at acquisition at its proportionate share or the fair value the subsidiary's net asset.

Required

Prepare P Co's consolidated statement of financial position as at 31 August 20X6.

Solution

S Co has not incorporated the revaluation in its draft statement of financial position. Before beginning the consolidation workings we must therefore adjust the company's balance of profits at the date of acquisition and at the year end.

S Co adjusted balance of retained earnings

	$	$
Balance per accounts at 1 September 20X5		21,000
Consolidation adjustment: revaluation surplus		23,000
∴ Pre-acquisition profits for consolidation purposes		44,000
Profit for year ended 31 August 20X6		
Per draft accounts $(41,000 – 21,000)	20,000	
Consolidation adjustment: increase in depreciation		
Charge	(3,000)	
		17,000
Adjusted balance of retained profits at 31 August 20X6		61,000

In the consolidated statement of financial position, S Co's non-current assets will appear at their revalued amount: $(28,000 + 23,000 – 3,000) = $48,000. The consolidation workings can now be drawn up.

1 Goodwill

	$	$
Consideration transferred		51,000
Non-controlling interest (64,000 × 25%)		16,000
		77,000
Share of net assets acquired as represented by		
Ordinary share capital	20,000	
Retained earnings		
$(21,000 + 23,000)	44,000	
		(64,000)
Goodwill		3,000

2 Retained earnings

	P Co	S Co
	$	$
Per question	96,000	41,000
Pre acquisition profits		(21,000)
Depreciation adjustment		(3,000)
Post acquisition S Co		17,000
Group share in S Co		
($17,000 × 75%)	12,750	
Group retained earnings	108,750	

3 Non-controlling interest

	$
Share capital (25% × $20,000)	5,000
Retained earnings (25% × $61,000)	15,250
	20,250

P CO CONSOLIDATED STATEMENT OF FINANCIAL POSITION AS AT 31 AUGUST 20X6

	$	$
Assets		
Tangible non-current assets $(63,000 + 48,000)	111,000	
Goodwill	3,000	
		114,000
Current assets		125,000
		239,000
Equity and liabilities		
Equity		
Ordinary shares of $1 each	80,000	
Retained earnings	108,750	
		188,750
Non-controlling interest		20,250
		204,000
Current liabilities		30,000
		239,000

 Question

Fair value

An asset is recorded in S Co's books at its historical cost of $4,000. On 1 January 20X5 P Co bought 80% of S Co's equity. Its directors attributed a fair value of $3,000 to the asset as at that date. It had been depreciated for two years out of an expected life of four years on the straight line basis. There was no expected residual value. On 30 June 20X5 the asset was sold for $2,600. What is the profit or loss on disposal of this asset to be recorded in S Co's accounts and in P Co's consolidated accounts for the year ended 31 December 20X5?

S Co: NBV at disposal (at historical cost) = $4,000 × 1½/4 = $1,500

∴ Profit on disposal = $1,100 (depreciation charge for the year = $500)

P Co: NBV at disposal (at fair value) = $3,000 × 1½/2 = $2,250

∴ Profit on disposal for consolidation = $350 (depreciation for the year = $750).

The non-controlling interest would be credited with 20% of both items as part of the one line entry in the income statement.

3.4 IFRS 3 (revised): Fair values

FAST FORWARD

The accounting requirements and disclosures of the **fair value exercise** are covered by **IFRS 3 (revised).**

IFRS 3 does not allow combinations to be accounted for as a **uniting of interests; all combinations must be treated as acquisitions.**

The general rule under the revised IFRS 3 (revised) is that the subsidiary's assets and liabilities **must be measured at fair value** except in **limited, stated cases**. The assets and liabilities must:

(a) Meet the destinations of assets and liabilities in the *Framework*.

(b) Be part of what the acquiree (or its former owners) exchanged in the business combination rather than the result of separate transactions

3.4.1 Restructuring and future losses

An acquirer **should not recognise liabilities for future losses** or other costs expected to be incurred as a result of the business combination.

IFRS 3 (revised) explains that a plan to restructure a subsidiary following an acquisition is not a present obligation of the acquiree at the acquisition date. Neither does it meet the definition of a contingent liability. Therefore an acquirer **should not recognise a liability for** such **a restructuring plan** as part of allocating the cost of the combination unless the subsidiary was already committed to the plan before the acquisition.

This **prevents creative accounting**. An acquirer cannot set up a provision for restructuring or future losses of a subsidiary and then release this to profit or loss in subsequent periods in order to reduce losses or smooth profits.

3.4.2 Intangible assets

The acquiree may have **intangible assets**, such as development expenditure. These can be recognised separately from goodwill only if they are **identifiable**. An intangible asset is identifiable only if it:

(a) Is **separable**, ie capable of being separated or divided from the entity and sold, transferred, or exchanged, either individually or together with a related contract, asset or liability, or

(b) Arises from **contractual or other legal rights**

3.4.3 Contingent liabilities

Contingent liabilities of the acquirer are **recognised** if their **fair value can be measured reliably**. A **contingent liability** must be recognised even if the outflow is not probable, provided there is a present obligation.

This is a departure from the normal rules in IAS 37; contingent liabilities are not normally recognised, but only disclosed.

After their initial recognition, the acquirer should measure contingent liabilities that are recognised separately at the higher of:

(a)   The amount that would be recognised in accordance with IAS 37

(b)   The amount initially recognised

3.4.4 Other exceptions to the recognition or measurement principles

(a)   **Deferred tax:** use IAS 12 values.

(b)   **Employee benefits:** use IAS 19 values.

(c)   **Indemnification assets:** measurement should be consistent with the measurement of the indemnified item, for example an employee benefit or a contingent liability.

(d)   **Reacquired rights**: value on the basis of the remaining contractual term of the related contract regardless of whether market participants would consider potential contractual renewals in determining its fair value.

(e)   **Share-based payment**: use IFRS 2 values.

(f)   **Assets held for sale**: use IFRS 5 values.

IFRS 3 (revised) goes on to list some **general guidelines** for arriving at the fair values of assets and liabilities.

Asset	Fair valuation
Marketable securities	Current market value
Non-marketable securities	Estimated values that take into consideration features such as: (a) Price earnings ratios (b) Dividend yield (c) Expected growth rates of comparable securities of entity with similar characteristics
Receivables, beneficial contracts and other identifiable assets	Present values of the amounts to be received, determined at appropriate current interest rates, less allowances for uncollectability and collection costs if necessary. Discounting is not required for short term receivables when the difference when the difference between the nominal and the discounted amount is not material.
Inventories: finished goods and merchandise	Selling price less the sum of: (a) the costs of disposal, and (b) a reasonable profit allowance for the selling effort of the acquirer based on profit for similar finished goods and merchandise.
Inventories: work in progress	Selling price of finished goods less the sum of: (a) Costs to complete, (b) Costs of disposal, and (c) A reasonable profit for the completing and selling effort based on profit for similar finished goods.
Inventories: raw materials	Current replacement costs
Land and buildings	Market value
Plant and equipment (to be **used** in the business)	Market value normally determined by appraisal. When there is no evidence of market value because of the specialised nature of the plant and equipment or because the items are rarely sold, except as part of a continuing business, they should be valued at their depreciated replacement cost.

Asset	Fair valuation
Intangible assets, as defined in IAS 38 *Intangible assets*	At a value determined: (a) By reference to an active market as defined in IAS 38, and (b) If no active market exists on a basis that reflects the amount that the acquirer would have paid for the asset in an arm's length transaction between knowledgeable, willing parties based on the best information available.
Tax assets and liabilities	Amount of the tax benefit arising from tax losses or the taxes payable in respect of the net profit or loss, assessed from the perspective of the combined entity. The tax asset or liability is determined after allowing for the tax effect of restating identifiable assets and liabilities to their fair values.
Accounts and notes payable, long-term debt, liabilities, accruals and other claims payable	Present values of amounts to be disbursed in meeting the liability determined at appropriate current interest rates. However, discounting is not required for short-term liabilities when the difference between the nominal amount of the liability and the discounted amount is not material.
Onerous contracts, and other identifiable liabilities of the acquirer.	Present values of amounts to be disbursed in settling the obligations determined at the appropriate current interest rates.

Some of the above guidelines assume that fair values will be determined by the use of **discounting**. When the guidelines do *not* refer to the use of discounting, discounting may or may not be used in determining the fair values of identifiable assets and liabilities.

Question

More fair values

Tyzo Co prepares accounts to 31 December. On 1 September 20X7 Tyzo Co acquired 6 million $1 shares in Kono Co at $2.00 per share. At that date Kono Co produced the following interim financial statements.

	$m		$m
Property, plant and equipment		Trade payables	3.2
(note 1)	16.0	Taxation	0.6
Inventories (note 2)	4.0	Bank overdraft	3.9
Receivables	2.9	Long-term loans	4.0
Cash in hand	1.2	Share capital ($1 shares)	8.0
		Reserves	4.4
	24.1		24.1

Notes

1   The following information relates to the property, plant and equipment of Kono Co at 1 September 20X7.

	$m
Gross replacement cost	28.4
Net replacement cost	16.6
Economic value	18.0
Net realisable value	8.0

The property, plant and equipment of Kono Co at 1 September 20X7 had a total purchase cost to Kono Co of $27.0 million. They were all being depreciated at 25% per annum pro rata on that cost. This policy is also appropriate for the consolidated financial statements of Tyzo Co. No non-current assets of Kono Co which were included in the interim financial statements drawn up as at 1 September 20X7 were disposed of by Kono Co prior to 31 December 20X7. No non-current asset was fully depreciated by 31 December 20X7.

2   The inventories of Kono Co which were shown in the interim financial statements are raw materials at cost to Kono Co of $4 million. They would have cost $4.2 million to replace at 1 September

20X7. Of the inventory of Kono Co in hand at 1 September 20X7, goods costing Kono Co $3.0 million were sold for $3.6 million between 1 September 20X7 and 31 December 20X7.

3   On 1 September 20X7 Tyzo Co took a decision to rationalise the group so as to integrate Kono Co. The costs of the rationalisation were estimated to total $3.0 million and the process was due to start on 1 March 20X8. No provision for these costs has been made in any of the financial statements given above.

Required

Compute the goodwill on consolidation of Kono Co that will be included in the consolidated financial statements of the Tyzo Co group for the year ended 31 December 20X7, explaining your treatment of the items mentioned above. You should refer to the provisions of relevant accounting standards.

Answer

Goodwill on consolidation of Kono Co

	$m	$m
Consideration ($2.00 × 6m)		12.0
Non-controlling interest (13.2% × 25%)		3.3
		15.3
Group share of fair value of net assets acquired		
Share capital	8.0	
Pre-acquisition reserves	4.4	
Fair value adjustments		
Property, plant and equipment (16.6 – 16.0)	0.6	
Inventories (4.2 – 4.0)	0.2	
		(13.2)
Goodwill		2.1

Notes on treatment

(a)   Share capital and pre-acquisition profits represent the book value of the net assets of Kono Co at the date of acquisition. Adjustments are then required to this book value in order to give the fair value of the net assets at the date of acquisition. For short-term monetary items, fair value is their carrying value on acquisition.

(b)   IFRS 3 (revised) states that the fair value of property, plant and equipment should be determined by market value or, if information on a market price is not available (as is the case here), then by reference to depreciated replacement cost, reflecting normal business practice. The net replacement cost (ie $16.6m) represents the gross replacement cost less depreciation based on that amount, and so further adjustment for extra depreciation is unnecessary.

(c)   IFRS 3 (revised) also states that raw materials should be valued at replacement cost. In this case that amount is $4.2m.

(d)   The rationalisation costs cannot be reported in pre-acquisition results under IFRS 3 (revised) as they are not a liability of Kono Co at the acquisition date.

3.5 Goodwill arising on acquisition

Goodwill should be carried in the statement of financial position at **cost less any accumulated impairment losses**. The treatment of goodwill is covered in detail in Chapter 4.

3.6 Adjustments after the initial accounting is complete

Sometimes the fair values of the acquiree's identifiable assets, liabilities or contingent liabilities or the cost of the combination can only be determined **provisionally** by the **end of the period in which the combination takes place**. In this situation, the acquirer **should account for the combination using those provisional values**. The acquirer should **recognise any adjustments** to those provisional values as a result of completing the initial accounting:

(a)   **Within twelve months** of the acquisition date, and

(b)   **From** the acquisition date (ie, retrospectively)

This means that:

(a)   The **carrying amount** of an item that is recognised or adjusted as a result of completing the initial accounting shall be calculated **as if its fair value** at the acquisition date **had been recognised from that date.**

(b)   **Goodwill should be adjusted** from the acquisition date by an amount equal to the adjustment to the fair value of the item being recognised or adjusted.

Any further adjustments after the initial accounting is complete should be **recognised only to correct an error** in accordance with IAS 8 *Accounting policies, changes in accounting estimates and errors*. Any subsequent changes in estimates are dealt with in accordance with IAS 8 (ie, the effect is recognised in the current and future periods). IAS 8 requires an entity to account for an error correction retrospectively, and to present financial statements as if the error had never occurred by restating the comparative information for the prior period(s) in which the error occurred.

3.7 Reverse acquisitions

IFRS 3 (revised) also addresses a certain type of acquisition, known as a **reverse acquisition or takeover**. This is where Company A acquires ownership of Company B through a share exchange. (For example, a private entity may arrange to have itself 'acquired' by a smaller public entity as a means of obtaining a stock exchange listing.) The number of shares issued by Company A as consideration to the shareholders of Company B is so great that control of the combined entity after the transaction is with the shareholders of Company B.

In legal terms Company A may be regarded as the parent or continuing entity, but IFRS 3 (revised) states that, as it is the Company B shareholders who control the combined entity, **Company B should be treated as the acquirer**. Company B should apply the acquisition (or purchase) method to the assets and liabilities of Company A.

Exam focus point

> Look out for a reverse takeover in the exam – it may look like a normal acquisition. You must analyse the takeover deal given in a question carefully to determine the correct treatment.

4 IAS 28 Investments in associates

FAST FORWARD

> **IAS 28** deals with accounting for associates. The definitions are important as they govern the accounting treatment, particularly **'significant influence'**.

We looked at investments in associates briefly in Section 1. IAS 28 *Investments in associates* covers this type of investment. IAS 28 does not apply to investments in associates or joint ventures held by venture capital organisations, mutual funds, unit trusts, and similar entities that are measured at fair value in accordance with IAS 39.

Some of the important definitions in Section 1 are repeated here, with some additional important terms.

Key terms

> **Associate.** An entity, including an unincorporated entity such as a partnership, over which an investor has significant influence and which is neither a subsidiary nor a joint venture of the investor.
>
> **Significant influence** is the power to participate in the financial and operating policy decisions of an economic activity but is not control or joint control over those policies.
>
> **Joint control** is the contractually agreed sharing of control over an economic activity.
>
> **Equity method.** A method of accounting whereby the investment is initially recorded at cost and adjusted thereafter for the post acquisition change in the investor's share of net assets of the investee. The profit or loss of the investor includes the investor's share of the profit or loss of the investee.

We have already looked at how the **status** of an investment in an associate should be determined. Go back to Section 2 to revise it. (Note that, as for an investment in a subsidiary, any **potential voting rights** should be taken into account in assessing whether the investor has **significant influence** over the investee.)

IAS 28 requires all investments in associates to be accounted for using the equity method, *unless* the investment is classified as 'held for sale' in accordance with IFRS 5 in which case it should be accounted for under IFRS 5 (see Chapter 15).

An investor is exempt from applying the equity method if:

(a)   It is a parent exempt from preparing consolidated financial statements under IAS 27 (revised) or

(b)   All of the following apply:

    (i)   The investor is a **wholly-owned subsidiary** or it is a **partially owned subsidiary** of another entity and its other owners, including those not otherwise entitled to vote, have been informed about, and do not object to, the investor not applying the equity method;

    (ii)   Its securities are **not publicly traded**;

    (iii)   It is **not in the process of issuing securities** in public securities markets; and

    (iv)   The **ultimate or intermediate parent** publishes consolidated financial statements that comply with International Financial Reporting Standards.

The revised version of IAS 28 **no longer allows** an investment in an associate to be excluded from equity accounting when an investee operates under severe long-term restrictions that significantly impair its ability to transfer funds to the investor. Significant influence must be lost before the equity method ceases to be applicable.

The use of the equity method should be **discontinued** from the date that the investor **ceases to have significant influence.**

From that date, the investor shall account for the investment in accordance with IAS 39 *Financial instruments: recognition and measurement.* The carrying amount of the investment at the date that it ceases to be an associate shall be regarded as its cost on initial measurement as a financial asset under IAS 39.

4.1 Separate financial statements of the investor

If an investor that **issues consolidated financial statements** (because it has subsidiaries), an investment in an associate should be *either.*

(a)   Accounted for at **cost**, *or*

(b)   In accordance with **IAS 39**

in its separate financial statements.

If an investor that does ***not*** **issue consolidated financial statements** (ie it has no subsidiaries) has an investment in an associate this should be included in the financial statements of the investor using the **equity method**.

4.2 Application of the equity method: consolidated accounts

The **equity method** should be applied in the consolidated accounts:

- **Statement of financial position**: investment in associate at cost plus (or minus) the group's share of the associate's post-acquisition profits (or losses)
- **Income statement (statement of comprehensive income)**: group share of associate's profit after tax.

Many of the procedures required to apply the equity method are the same as are required for full consolidation. In particular, **intra-group unrealised profits** must be excluded.

Goodwill is calculated as the difference (positive or negative) between the cost of acquisition and the investor's share of the fair values of the net identifiable assets of the associate. This should be treated as required by IFRS 3 (revised) (see Chapter 3). Appropriate adjustments should be made to the investor's share of the profits or losses after acquisition, to account for depreciation.

4.2.1 Consolidated income statement/statement of comprehensive income

The basic principle is that the investing company (X Co) should take account of its **share of the earnings** of the associate, Y Co, whether or not Y Co distributes the earnings as dividends. X Co achieves this by adding to consolidated profit the group's share of Y Co's profit after tax.

Notice the difference between this treatment and the **consolidation** of a subsidiary company's results. If Y Co were a subsidiary X Co would take credit for the whole of its sales revenue, cost of sales etc and would then make a one-line adjustment to remove any by the non-controlling interest share owner.

Under equity accounting, the associate's sales revenue, cost of sales and so on are *not* amalgamated with those of the group. Instead the group share only of the associate's profit before tax and tax charge for the year is added to the corresponding lines of the parent company and its subsidiaries. In effect, this is the corresponding treatment to the associate's parent company's treatment: the investing company is the non-controlling interest here.

4.2.2 Consolidated statement of financial position

A figure for **investment in associates** is shown which at the time of the acquisition must be stated at cost. This amount will increase (decrease) each year by the amount of the group's share of the associated associate's profit (loss) for the year.

4.3 Example: Associate

P Co, a company with subsidiaries, acquires 25,000 of the 100,000 $1 ordinary shares in A Co for $60,000 on 1 January 20X8. In the year to 31 December 20X8, A Co earns profits after tax of $24,000, from which it declares a dividend of $6,000.

How will A Co's results be accounted for in the individual and consolidated accounts of P Co for the year ended 31 December 20X8?

Solution

In the **individual accounts** of P Co, the investment will be recorded on 1 January 20X8 at cost. Unless there is an impairment in the value of the investment (see below), this amount will remain in the individual statement of financial position of P Co permanently. The only entry in P Co's individual income statement (statement of comprehensive income) will be to record dividends received. For the year ended 31 December 20X8, P Co will:

DEBIT	Cash	$1,500
CREDIT	Income from shares in associated companies	$1,500

In the **consolidated accounts** of P Co equity accounting principles will be used to account for the investment in A Co. Consolidated profit after tax will include the group's share of A Co's profit after tax

(25% × $24,000 = $6,000). To the extent that this has been distributed as dividend, it is already included in P Co's individual accounts and will automatically be brought into the consolidated results. That part of the group's profit share which has not been distributed as dividend ($4,500) will be brought into consolidation by the following adjustment.

DEBIT   Investment in associates $4,500
CREDIT   Income from shares in associates $4,500

The asset 'Investment in associates' is then stated at $64,500, being cost plus the group share of post-acquisition retained profits.

4.4 Consolidated income statement (statement of comprehensive income)

The treatment of associates' profits in the following proforma should be studied carefully.

4.4.1 Pro-forma consolidated income statement

The following is a **suggested layout** (using the figures given in the illustration above) for an income statement for a company having subsidiaries as well as associates.

	$'000
Sales revenue	1,400
Cost of sales	770
Gross profit	630
Distribution costs and administrative expenses	290
	340
Interest and similar income receivable	30
	370
Finance costs	(20)
	350
Share of profit (after tax) of associate	17
Profit before taxation	367
Income tax expense	
Parent company and subsidiaries	145
Profit for the year	222
Profit attributable to:	
Owners of the parent	200
Non-controlling interest	22
	222

4.4.2 Income statement: parent with no subsidiaries

The treatment required by the standard is given above. The following layout is suggested.

	$
Sales revenue	X
Cost of sales	(X)
Gross profit	X
Distribution costs/administrative expenses	(X)
	X
Interest payable and similar charges	X
Share of profit after tax of associate	X
Profit before taxation	(X)
	X
Taxation	X
Profit for the year	X

4.5 Consolidated statement of financial position

As explained earlier, the consolidated statement of financial position will contain an **asset 'Investment in associated companies'**. The amount at which this asset is stated will be its original cost plus the group's share of any **profits earned since acquisition** which have not been distributed as dividends.

4.6 Example: Consolidated statement of financial position

On 1 January 20X6 the net tangible assets of A Co amount to $220,000, financed by 100,000 $1 ordinary shares and retained earnings of $120,000. P Co, a company with subsidiaries, acquires 30,000 of the shares in A Co for $75,000. During the year ended 31 December 20X6 A Co's profit after tax is $30,000, from which dividends of $12,000 are paid.

Show how P Co's investment in A Co would appear in the consolidated statement of financial position at 31 December 20X6.

Solution

CONSOLIDATED STATEMENT OF FINANCIAL POSITION
AS AT 31 DECEMBER 20X6 (extract)

	$
Non-current assets	
Investment in associate	
Cost	75,000
Group share of post-acquisition retained earnings	
(30% × $18,000)	5,400
	80,400

Set out below are the draft accounts of Parent Co and its subsidiaries and of Associate Co. Parent Co acquired 40% of the equity capital of Associate Co three years ago when the latter's retained earnings stood at $40,000.

SUMMARISED STATEMENT OF FINANCIAL POSITION

	Parent Co & subsidiaries $'000	Associate Co $'000
Property, plant and equipment	220	170
Investment in Associate at cost	60	–
Loan to Associate Co	20	–
Current assets	100	50
Loan from Parent Co	–	(20)
	400	200
Share capital ($1 shares)	250	100
Retained earnings	150	100
	400	200

SUMMARISED INCOME STATEMENTS

	Parent Co & subsidiaries $'000	Associate Co $'000
Net profit	95	80
Taxation	35	30
	60	50

You are required to prepare the summarised consolidated accounts of Parent Co.

Notes

(1) Assume that the associate's assets/liabilities are stated at fair value.
(2) Assume that there are no non-controlling interest in the subsidiary companies.

Answer

PARENT CO

CONSOLIDATED INCOME STATEMENT	$'000
Net profit	95
Share of profits of associate (50 × 40%)	20
Profit before tax	115
Income tax expense	35
Profit attributable to the owners of Parent Co	80

PARENT CO
CONSOLIDATED STATEMENT OF FINANCIAL POSITION

	$'000
Assets	
Property, plant and equipment	220
Interest in associate (see note)	104
Current assets	100
Total assets	424
Equity and liabilities	
Share capital	250
Retained earnings (W)	174
Total equity and liabilities	424

Note	$'000
Interest in associate	
Cost	60
Share of post-acquisition retained earnings 40% × (100 – 40)	24
	84
Loan to associate	20
	104

Workings: retained earnings

	Parent & subsidiaries $'000	Associate $'000
Per question	150	100
Pre-acquisition		40
Post-acquisition		60
Group share in associate ($60 × 40%)	24	
Group retained earnings	174	

Question

Associate 2

Alfred Co bought 25,000 ordinary shares on 31 December 20X8 in Grimbald Co at a cost of $38,000 when the statement of financial position of Grimbald was as follows.

GRIMBALD CO
DRAFT STATEMENT OF FINANCIAL POSITION AT DATE OF SHARE PURCHASE

	$
Assets	
Non-current assets	
Goodwill	30,000
Tangible assets	120,000
	150,000
Current assets	40,000
Total assets	190,000
Equity and liabilities	
Equity	
Called up share capital in ordinary shares of $1	100,000
Retained earnings	40,000
Non-current liabilities	
12% debentures	50,000
Total equity and liabilities	190,000

During the year to 31 December 20X9 Grimbald Co made a profit before tax of $82,000 and the taxation charge on the year's profits was $32,000. A dividend of $20,000 was paid on 31 December out of these profits.

The statement of financial position of Grimbald Co on 31 December 20X9 was as follows.

	$
Assets	
Non-current assets	
Goodwill	30,000
Tangible assets	140,000
	170,000
Current assets	50,000
Total assets	220,000
Equity and liabilities	
Equity	
Called up share capital in ordinary shares of $1	100,000
Retained earnings	70,000
Non-current liabilities	
12% loan notes	50,000
Total equity and liabilities	220,000

Calculate the entries for the associate which would appear in the consolidated accounts of the Alfred group, in accordance with the requirements of IAS 28. (Assume no impairment of goodwill.)

Answer

Net tangible assets of Grimbald Co at date of acquisition.

	$
Total assets	190,000
Less goodwill	(30,000)
Less non-current liabilities	(50,000)
Net tangible assets	110,000

At the date of the share acquisition
Alfred Co share of Grimbald's net tangible assets owned

by equity (25% of $110,000)	27,500
Alfred Co share of Grimbald Co goodwill (25% of $30,000)	7,500
	35,000
Cost of the shares	38,000
Premium arising on acquisition	3,000

At 31 December 20X8, the investment by Alfred Co in shares of Grimbald would have appeared in the consolidated statement of financial position as follows.

	$
Group share of net assets other than goodwill	27,500
Goodwill and premium arising on acquisition $(7,500 + 3,000)	10,500
Total investment in associate	38,000

Grimbald Co	Total $	Group share $
Profits before taxation for the year to 31.12.X9	82,000	20,500
Taxation	32,000	8,000
Profits after taxation	50,000	12,500
Dividend	20,000	5,000
Retained earnings carried forward	30,000	7,500

CONSOLIDATED INCOME STATEMENT

	$
Group share of associate's profit after tax (20,500 – 8,000)	12,500

CONSOLIDATED STATEMENT OF FINANCIAL POSITION

	$
Interest in associate	45,500
The asset 'interest in associate' comprises:	
Cost	
($27,500 + retained profits of $7,500)	38,000
Share of post-acquisition retained earnings 25% × (70 – 40)	7,500
	45,500

The following points are also relevant and are similar to a parent-subsidiary consolidation situation.

(a) Use financial statements drawn up to the **same reporting date.**

(b) If this is impracticable, adjust the financial statements for **significant transactions/ events** in the intervening period. The difference between the reporting date of the associate and that of the investor must be no more than three months.

(c) Use **uniform accounting policies** for like transactions and events in similar circumstances, adjusting the associate's statements to reflect group policies if necessary.

(d) If an associate has **cumulative preferred shares** held by outside interests, calculate the share of the investor's profits/losses after adjusting for the preferred dividends (whether or not declared).

4.7 'Upstream' and 'downstream' transactions

'Upstream' transactions are, for example, sales of assets from an associate to the investor. 'Downstream' transactions are, for example, sales of assets from the investor to an associate.

Profits and losses resulting from 'upstream' and 'downstream' transactions between an investor (including its consolidated subsidiaries) and an associate are eliminated to the extent of the investor's interest in the associate. This is very similar to the procedure for eliminating intra-group transactions between a parent and a subsidiary. The important thing to remember is that **only the group's share is eliminated**.

The double entry is as follows, where A% is the parent's holding in the associate, and PUP is the provision for unrealised profit.

DEBIT	Retained earnings of parent	PUP × A%
CREDIT	Group inventories		PUP × A%

For upstream transactions (associate sells to parent/subsidiary) where the parent holds the inventories.

OR

DEBIT	Retained earnings of parent /subsidiary	PUP × A%
CREDIT	Investment in associate	PUP × A%

For downstream transactions, (parent/subsidiary sells to associate) where the associate holds the inventory.

4.8 Example: downstream transaction

A Co, a parent with subsidiaries, holds 25% of the equity shares in B Co. During the year, A Co makes sales of $1,000,000 to B Co at cost plus a 25% mark-up. At the year-end, B Co has all these goods still in inventories.

Solution

A Co has made an unrealised profit of $200,000 (1,000,000 × 25/125) on its sales to the associate. The group's share of this is 25%, ie $50,000. This must be eliminated.

The double entry is:

DEBIT	A: Retained earnings	$50,000	
CREDIT	Investment in associate (B)		$50,000

Because the sale was made to the associate, the group's share of the unsold inventories forms part of the investment in associate at the year end. If the sale had been from the associate B to A, ie an upstream transaction, the double entry would have been.

DEBIT	A: Retained earnings	$50,000	
CREDIT	A: Inventories		$50,000

If preparing the consolidated income statement, you would deduct the $50,000 from the group share of the associate's profit.

4.9 Associate's losses

When the equity method is being used and the investor's share of losses of the associate equals or exceeds its interest in the associate, the investor should **discontinue** including its share of further losses. The investment is reported at nil value. The interest in the associate is normally the carrying amount of the investment in the associate, but it also includes any other long-term interests, for example, preference shares or long term receivables or loans.

After the investor's interest is reduced to nil, **additional losses** should only be recognised where the investor has incurred obligations or made payments on behalf of the associate (for example, if it has guaranteed amounts owed to third parties by the associate).

4.10 Impairment losses

IAS 39 sets out a list of indications that a financial asset (including an associate) may have become impaired. Any impairment loss is recognised in accordance with IAS 36 *Impairment of assets* for each associate individually. An impairment loss is not allocated to any asset, including goodwill, that forms part of the carrying amount of the investment in associate. Accordingly any reversal of that impairment loss is recognised in accordance with IAS 36 to the extent that the recoverable amount of the investment subsequently increases.

4.11 Non-controlling interest/associate held by a subsidiary

Where the investment in an associate is held by a subsidiary in which there are non-controlling interest, the non-controlling interest shown in the consolidated financial statements of the group should include the

non-controlling interest of the subsidiary's interest in the results and net assets of the associated company.

This means that the group accounts must include the 'gross' share of net assets, pre-tax profits and tax, in accounting for the **non-controlling interest separately**. For example, we will suppose that P Co owns 60% of S Co which owns 25% of A Co, an associate of P Co. The relevant amounts for inclusion in the consolidated financial statements would be as follows.

CONSOLIDATED INCOME STATEMENT
Operating profit (P 100% + S 100%)
Share of profit after tax of associate (A 25%)
Tax (P 100% + S 100%)
Non-controlling interest (S 40% + A 10%*)
Retained profits (P 100% + S 60% + A 15%)

CONSOLIDATED STATEMENT OF FINANCIAL POSITION
Investment in associated company (figures based on 25% holding)
Non-controlling interest ((40% × shareholders' funds of S) + (10%* × post-acquisition retained earnings of A))
Unrealised reserves (15% × post-acquisition reserves of A)
Group retrained earnings ((100% × P) + (60% × post-acquisition of S))
* 40% × 25% = 10%

4.12 Section summary

Income statement (statement of comprehensive income)	Profit before tax) Parent and subsidiary + associate's profit after tax
	Tax) Parent and subsidiary only

Statement of financial position	Interests in associated companies should be stated at:	$
	Cost	X
	Share of post acquisition retained earnings	X
		X

Also disclose group's share of post-acquisition reserves of associated companies and movements therein.

5 IAS 31 Interests in joint ventures

FAST FORWARD

IAS 31 *Financial reporting of interests in joint ventures* is concerned with how venturers **report their interests** in joint ventures in their accounts.

Two or more persons may decide to enter into a business venture together without wishing to form a formal long-term partnership. Usually the venturers agree to place limitations on their activities, for example, a joint venture to manufacture and sell 'total eclipse of the sun' souvenirs could be limited by time, while a joint venture to buy and sell a bankrupt's inventory (a fairly common occurrence in practice) comes to an end when all the inventory has been sold.

Joint ventures are often found when each party can **contribute in different ways** to the venture. For example, one venturer may provide finance, another purchases or manufactures goods, while a third offers his marketing skills.

Joint ventures generally have the following characteristics.

- They are **limited by time and/or activity**
- The venturers usually **carry on their principal businesses** at the same time
- **Separate books** for the venture are **not** normally maintained
- The venturers usually agree to a **profit/ loss sharing ratio** for the purpose of the venture

IAS 31 *Interests in joint ventures* covers all types of joint ventures. It is not concerned with the accounts of the joint venture itself (if separate accounts are maintained), but rather **how the interest in a joint venture is accounted for by each joint venturer** (ie each 'partner' in the joint venture).

The assets and liabilities, income and expenses of the joint venture must be reported in the financial statements of the venturers and investors, whatever the form of the joint venture.

IAS 31 looks at the various forms of joint venture which may be undertaken and then looks at how joint ventures are dealt with in the **individual financial statements** of the venturer *and* the **group financial statements**.

5.1 Definitions

The IAS begins by listing some important definitions.

Joint venture. A contractual arrangement whereby two or more parties undertake an economic activity which is subject to joint control.

Control. The power to govern the financial and operating policies of an economic activity so as to obtain benefits from its activities.

Joint control. The contractually agreed sharing of control over an economic activity.

Significant influence. The power to participate in the financial and operating policy decisions of an economic activity but is not control or joint control over those policies.

Venturer. A party to a joint venture that has joint control over that joint venture.

Proportionate consolidation. A method of accounting whereby a venturer's share of each of the assets, liabilities, income and expenses of a jointly controlled entity is combined line-by-line with similar items in the venturer's financial statements or reported as separate line items in the venturer's financial statements.

Equity method. A method of accounting whereby an interest in a jointly controlled entity is initially recorded at cost and adjusted thereafter for the post acquisition change in the venturer's share of net assets of the jointly controlled entity. The income statement reflects the venturer's share of the profit or loss of the jointly controlled entity.

(IAS 31)

5.2 Forms of joint venture

The **form and structure** of joint ventures can vary enormously. There are, however, three main types identified by the standard.

- **Jointly controlled operations**
- **Jointly controlled assets**
- **Jointly controlled entities**

We will look at each of these below. They are all usually described as joint ventures and fulfil the definition of a joint venture given above.

Whatever the form and structure, every joint venture will have **two characteristics.**

- Two (or more) venturers are bound by a **contractual arrangement**.
- The contractual relationship establishes **joint control**.

5.2.1 Contractual arrangement

The existence of a contractual agreement distinguishes a joint venture from an investment in an associate. **If there is no contractual arrangement, then a joint venture does not exist**.

Evidence of a contractual arrangement could be in one of several forms.

- **Contract** between the venturers
- **Minutes** of discussion between the venturers
- Incorporation in the **articles or by-laws** of the joint venture

The contractual arrangement is usually **in writing**, whatever its form, and it will deal with the following issues surrounding the joint venture.

- **Its activity, duration and reporting obligations**
- The appointment of its **board of directors** (or equivalent) and the **voting rights** of the venturers
- **Capital contributions** to it by the venturers
- How its output, income, expenses or results are **shared** between the venturers

It is the contractual arrangement which establishes **joint control** over the joint venture, so that no single venturer can control the activity of the joint venture on its own.

One venturer, identified by the contractual agreement, may be the **operator of the joint venture**. This does *not* mean that the operator controls the joint venture, the operator must act within the policies (financial and operation) agreed by all the venturers as laid out in the contractual arrangement. If this is not the case, if the operator effectively controls the joint venture rather than only acting within the arrangements delegated to it, then the activity is *not* a joint venture.

5.2.2 SIC 13 – Jointly controlled entities – non-monetary contributions by venturers

The SIC states that, in applying IAS 31 to non-monetary contributions to a jointly controlled entity (JCE), **a venturer should recognise in profit or loss for the period the portion of a gain or loss attributed to the equity interests of the other venturers except** in certain circumstances.

(a) The significant risks and rewards of ownership of the contributed non-monetary asset(s) have not been transferred to the JCE.

(b) The gain or loss on the non-monetary contributions cannot be measured reliably.

(c) The non-monetary assets contributed are similar to those contributed by the other venturers.

5.3 Section summary

- There are three **common types of joint venture**: jointly controlled operations, assets or entities
- A **contractual arrangement** must exist which establishes joint control
- **Joint control** is important: an **operator** must not be able to govern the financial and operating policies of the joint venture

5.4 Forms of joint venture

FAST FORWARD

There are three usual forms of joint venture.
- Jointly controlled operations
- Jointly controlled assets
- Jointly controlled entities

5.4.1 Jointly controlled operations

In this type of joint venture, there is no separate entity set up to deal with the joint venture, whether in the form of a corporation, partnership or other entity. Instead, the venturers **use their own assets and**

resources for the joint venture, ie their own property, plant and equipment is used and they carry their own inventories.

The venturers also incur their own expenses and liabilities, and raise their own finance which then represent their own obligations. In these situations, the activities of the joint venture will often be performed by the venturers' staff alongside the venturers' **other similar activities**. The way that income and expenses are shared between the venturers is usually laid out in the joint venture agreement.

Question
Joint venture

Can you think of an example of a situation where such a joint venture might occur?

Answer

IAS 31 uses the example of building an aircraft. Say that Boeing is to build the body of the aircraft and the engines are to be built by Rolls Royce as specified by the airline customer for the aircraft. You can see that different parts of the manufacturing process are carried out by each of the venturers. In the Rolls Royce factory, workers will work on the engines for the Boeing plane alongside others working on engines for different aircraft.

Each venturer, Boeing and Rolls Royce, bears its own costs and takes a share of revenue from the aircraft sale. That share is decided in the contractual arrangement between the venturers.

Can you think of other examples?

Accounting treatment

> **FAST FORWARD**
>
> Joint ventures are characterised by **joint control** evidenced by a **contractual arrangement.**

When a joint venture in the nature of jointly controlled operations exists, IAS 31 requires a venturer to recognise the following in its financial statements.

(a)   The **assets** it controls and the **liabilities** it incurs

(b)   The **expenses** it incurs and the **income** it earns from the sale of goods or services by the joint venture

Separate accounts for the joint venture are not required, although the venturers may prepare management accounts for the joint venture, in order to assess its performance.

5.4.2 Jointly controlled assets

In this type of joint venture, the venturers have **joint control**, and often **joint ownership** of some or all of the assets in the joint venture. These assets may have been contributed to the joint venture or purchased for the purpose of the joint venture, but in any case they are **dedicated to the activities of the joint venture**. These assets are used to produce benefits for the venturers; each venturer takes a share of the output and bears a share of the incurred expenses.

As with jointly controlled operations, this type of joint venture does *not* involve setting up a corporation, partnership or any other kind of entity. The venturers **control their share of future economic benefits** through their share in the jointly controlled asset.

Question
Jointly controlled asset

Can you think of examples of situations where this type of joint venture might take place?

IAS 31 gives examples in the oil, gas and mineral extraction industries. In such industries companies may, say, jointly control and operate on oil or gas pipeline. Each company transports its own products down the pipeline and pays an agreed proportion of the expenses of operating the pipeline (perhaps based on volume).

A further example is a property which is jointly controlled, each venturer taking a share of the rental income and bearing a portion of the expense.

Accounting treatment

IAS 31 requires each venturer to recognise (ie include in their financial statements) the following in respect of its interest in jointly controlled assets.

(a)   Its **share of the jointly controlled assets**, classified by their nature, eg a share of a jointly controlled oil pipeline should be classified as property, plant and equipment

(b)   Any **liabilities** it has incurred, eg in financing its share of the assets

(c)   Its share of any **liabilities incurred jointly** with the other venturers which relate to the joint venture

(d)   Any **income** from the sale or use of its share of the joint venture's output, together with its share of any **expenses** incurred by the joint venture

(e)   Any **expenses** which it has incurred in respect of its interest in the joint venture, eg those relating to financing the venturer's interest in the assets and selling its share of the output

This treatment of jointly controlled assets reflects the **substance and economic reality,** and (usually) the legal form of the joint venture. Separate accounting records need not be kept for the joint venture and financial statements for the joint venture need not be prepared. Management accounts may be produced, however, in order to monitor the performance of the joint venture.

5.4.3 Jointly controlled entities

FAST FORWARD

Jointly controlled entities may be accounted for in different ways:

*   **Proportionate consolidation**: combine items on a line by line basis
*   **Equity method**: see above

This type of joint venture involves the setting up of a corporation, partnership or other entity. This **operates in the same way as any other entity**, except that the venturers have a contractual arrangement establishing their joint control over the economic activity of the entity.

A jointly controlled entity effectively operates as a **separate entity**: it controls the joint venture's assets, incurs liabilities and expenses and earns income. It can, as a separate entity, enter into contracts in its own name and raise finance to fund the activities of the joint venture. The venturers share the results of the jointly controlled entity, and in some cases they may also share the output of the joint venture.

Question

Jointly controlled entities

Can you think of some examples of situations where jointly controlled entities might be set up?

Answer

A common situation is where two or more entities transfer the relevant assets and liabilities to a jointly controlled entity in order to combine their activities in a particular line of business.

In other situations, an entity wishing to start operations in a foreign country will set up a jointly controlled entity with the government of the foreign country (or an agency of it).

The **substance** of jointly controlled entities are often similar in substance to the joint ventures discussed above (jointly controlled assets/operations). In the case of the oil/gas pipeline mentioned in Question 4, the asset might be transferred to a jointly controlled entity for tax or similar reasons. In other circumstances, a jointly controlled entity may be set up to deal with only certain aspects of the jointly controlled operations, eg marketing or after-sales service, design or distribution.

As a separate entity, the jointly controlled entity must maintain its **own accounting records** and will **prepare financial statements** according to national requirements and IASs. The accounting treatment for jointly controlled entities is discussed in the next section.

5.4.4 Transactions between a venturer and a joint venture

A venturer may **sell or contribute assets** to a joint venture. The value attributed to such assets may create a gain or loss. However, any such gain or loss should only be recognised to the extent that it reflects the substance of the transaction.

What this means is that only the **gain** attributable to the interest of the other venturers should be recognised. However, the full amount of any **loss** should be recognised when the transaction shows evidence that the net realisable value of current assets is less than cost, or that there is an impairment loss (determined by applying IAS 36).

Inventories

Kirstan Co contributes inventories to a 50:50 joint venture it has undertaken with Pirstan Co. The recorded historical cost of the inventories is $2m.

What gain or loss should Kirstan Co recognise in its financial statements when the fair value (net realisable value) of the inventories is estimated at the date of transfer and recorded by the joint venture as:

(a) $2.2m?
(b) $1.8m?

Answer

(a)   Kirstan Co has made a profit of $0.2m, but only 50% of this can be considered as realised, ie that part attributable to the other venturer. Kirstan Co should therefore recognise a gain of $0.1m.

(b)   A loss of $0.2m has been made on the inventories, the entire amount of which should be recognised by Kirstan Co. It is known that the loss will be made, even though the inventories have not yet been sold, and so prudence requires that the full loss should be recognised.

A venturer may **purchase assets** from a joint venture. When it does so, the venturer should not recognise its share of the profit made by the joint venture on the transaction in question until it resells the assets to an independent third party, ie until the profit is realised. Losses should be treated in the same way, *except* losses should be recognised immediately if they represent a reduction in the net realisable value of current assets, or a permanent decline in the carrying amount of non-current assets.

5.4.5 Investors in joint ventures

There may be investors in joint ventures who **do *not* have joint control**. Such interests should be reported in accordance with IAS 39 (see Chapter 7) or IAS 28 *Investments in associates* (see Section 1), depending on the circumstances.

5.4.6 Operators of joint ventures

Operators of joint ventures will often **receive fees** for their work in directly managing the joint venture. Such fees should be accounted for according to IAS 18 *Revenue*. Such management fees will be treated by the joint venture as an expense.

5.4.7 Special purpose entities

These are dealt with here because they do not fit in readily anywhere else! An entity may be created to accomplish a specific, defined objective. Examples include research and development, or securitisation of financial assets. Such special purpose entities (SPE) may be incorporated or unincorporated. Often there are strict and permanent limits on the decision-making powers of their governing board or other management. They operate on 'autopilot', ie the policy guiding their activities cannot be modified other than perhaps by their sponsor. The sponsor frequently transfers assets to the SPE or performs services for it.

SPEs are dealt with in SIC 12 *Consolidation – special purpose entities*. The SIC states that **an SPE should be consolidated** when the **substance of the relationship between an entity and the SPE indicates that the SPE is controlled by that entity**. There are several circumstances which might indicate **control**.

5.5 Accounting treatment of jointly controlled entities

5.5.1 Separate financial statements of a venturer

IAS 31 states that where a venturer prepares separate financial statements (as a single company), investments in jointly controlled entities should be *either*:

(a)   accounted for at **cost**, *or*

(b)   in accordance with **IAS 39**.

The same accounting treatment must be applied consistently to all jointly controlled entities.

Exam focus point

This type of joint venture is most likely to appear in the Paper 2 exam.

5.5.2 Consolidated financial statements of a venturer

IAS 31 requires all interests in jointly controlled entities to be accounted for using *either* proportionate consolidation *or* the equity method.

However, several exemptions are available and neither of these methods need be applied where:

(a)   The interest is classified as held for sale in accordance with IFRS 5, or

(b)   The venturer is a parent exempt from preparing consolidated financial statements under IAS 27 (revised), or

(c)   All of the following apply:

(i)   The venturer is a **wholly-owned subsidiary** or it is a **partially owned subsidiary** of another entity and its other owners, including those not otherwise entitled to vote, have been informed about, and do not object to, the investor not applying proportionate consolidation or the equity method.

(ii)   Its securities are **not publicly traded**.

(iii)   It is **not in the process of issuing securities** in public securities markets; and

(iv)   The **ultimate or intermediate parent** publishes consolidated financial statements that comply with International Financial Reporting Standards.

Where an interest is classified as held for sale it should be accounted for in accordance with IFRS 5 (see Chapter 15).

5.5.3 Proportionate consolidation

A venturer should report its interest in a jointly controlled entity in its consolidated financial statements using one of the two reporting formats for **proportionate consolidation**.

IAS 31 maintains that this treatment reflects the **substance and economic reality** of the arrangement, ie the control the venturer has over its share of future economic benefits through its share of the assets and liabilities of the venture.

The proportionate consolidation method differs from normal consolidation in that only the group share of assets and liabilities, income and expenses are brought into account. There is therefore **no non-controlling interest**.

There are **two different formats** with which the proportionate consolidation method can be used.

(a)   **Combine on a line-by-line basis** the venturer's share of each of the assets, liabilities, income and expenses of the jointly controlled entity with the similar items in the venturer's consolidated financial statements.

(b)   Include in the venturer's consolidated financial statements **separate line items** for the venturer's share of the assets and liabilities, income and expenses of the jointly controlled entity.

5.5.4 Example: Proportionate consolidation

Both of the above methods produce exactly the same results and they are demonstrated in this example. We will use similar information as in the question above.

Set out below are the draft accounts of Parent Co and its subsidiaries and of Joint Venture Co. Parent Co acquired 50% of the equity capital of Joint Venture Co three years ago when the latter's retained earnings stood at $40,000.

SUMMARISED STATEMENTS OF FINANCIAL POSITION

	Parent Co & subsidiaries $'000	Joint Venture Co $'000
Tangible non-current assets	220	170
Investment in joint venture	75	–
Current assets	100	50
Loan to Joint Venture	20	–
	415	220
Share capital ($1 shares)	250	100
Retained earnings	165	100
Loan from Parent Co	–	20
	415	220

SUMMARISED INCOME STATEMENTS

	Parent Co & subsidiaries $'000	Joint Venture Co $'000
Profit before tax	95	80
Income tax expense	35	30
	60	50
Dividends paid	50	10
Profit for the year	10	40

Parent Co has taken credit for the dividend paid by Joint Venture Co.

You are required to prepare the summarised consolidated statement of financial position of Parent Co, under both the formats of proportionate consolidation recommended by IAS 31.

Solution: Line-by-line format

PARENT CO
CONSOLIDATED STATEMENT OF FINANCIAL POSITION

	$'000
Goodwill (W1)	5
Tangible non-current assets (220 + (50% × 170))	305
Current assets (100 + (50% × 50))	125
Loan to joint venturer (note)	10
	445
Share capital	250
Retained earnings (W2)	195
	445

Note. The loan is the proportion of the $20,000 lent to the other venturer.

Workings

1   *Goodwill*

	$'000
Consideration transferred	75
Share of net assets acquired (50% × 140)	70
Premium on acquisition	5

2   *Retained earnings*

	Parent Co & subsidiaries	Joint Venture Co
	$'000	$'000
Per question	165	100
Pre-acquisition		(40)
Post-acquisition		60
Group share in joint venture ($60 × 50%)	30	
Group retained earnings	195	

Solution: Separate line method

PARENT CO
CONSOLIDATED STATEMENT O FINANCIAL POSITION

	$'000	$'000
Goodwill (as above)		5
Tangible non-current assets		
Group	220	
Joint venture (170 × 50%)	85	
		305
Current assets		
Group	100	
Joint venture (50% × 50)	25	
		125
Loan to joint venturer		10
		445
Share capital		250
Retained earnings (as above)		195
		445

In both these cases the **consolidated income statements** would be shown in the same way.

The use of the proportionate consolidation method should be **discontinued** from the date the venturer ceases to have joint control over the entity.

5.5.5 Equity method

A venturer can report its interest in a joint venture in its consolidated financial statements under the **equity method**, as discussed in Section 1. The argument for this method is that it is misleading to combine controlled items with jointly controlled items. It is also felt by some that venturers have significant influence over the entity, not merely joint control.

IAS 31 does not agree with this approach, preferring the proportionate consolidation method for the reasons given above, but it allows the equity method, **as laid out in IAS 28**, to be used.

The use of the equity method should be **discontinued** from the date on which the venturer ceases to have joint control over, or have significant influence on, a jointly controlled entity.

5.5.6 Section summary

In **consolidated accounts**, two treatments are allowed for the consolidation of an investment in a jointly controlled entity.

- **Proportionate consolidation**, using either of two formats

    - **Line-by-line combined results**
    - **Separate line item method**

- **Equity method** as under IAS 28

Question

What are the advantages and disadvantages of accounting for joint ventures using the proportionate consolidation method?

Answer

Advantages

(a)   This method clearly shows the size of an investor's interest in a joint venture and any related liabilities. The financing and structure of the venture is also shown, in relating to the rest of the group. All this information helps users to judge past performance and assess future prospects.

(b)   This method treats the investment as if the investor had direct control of its share of the assets and results of the joint venture, which is very close to the reality of the situation, even though in fact it shares control of the entire venture.

(c)   Proportional consolidation is used for joint ventures which consist of a sharing of facilities and so other joint ventures should use this method for consistency.

Disadvantages

(a)   It may not be made clear (and it may not be possible to make clear) which assets and liabilities are controlled (directly or indirectly) by the group and those which are not. This will muddy the waters around the group results and confuse users of accounts. In particular, group figures which include consolidated *and* proportionately consolidated figures might be seen as meaningless.

(b)   The assets and liabilities included in the group accounts from the joint venture do not meet the definitions of assets and liabilities in the IASB's *Framework*. 'Assets' include the ability to control rights or other access to benefits, but in a joint venture this control is not present; the investor only controls the net investment.

(c)   What does 50% of a piece of machinery mean? Taking fractions of items and adding them into the group accounts may only confuse users.

Chapter Roundup

- Go back to your earlier study material and practice more questions if you are unsure of basic consolidation techniques.

- **Definitions** are very important when looking at group accounts. Learn the definitions of:

– Control	– Associate
– Subsidiary	– Significant influence
– Parent	– Joint venture
– Group	– Non-controlling interest

- **IAS 27 (revised)** covers the basic definitions and consolidation requirements. In particular you should learn the rules on **exemptions** from preparing group accounts

- Consider the nature of the **current definitions and accounting requirements**. You should be able to discuss why they are so complex and detailed.

- The revised IFRS 3 **requires recognition of contingent consideration, measured at fair value, at the acquisition date**.

- The revised IFRS 3 (revised) views the group as an economic entity. This means that it treats all providers of equity – including non-controlling interests – as shareholders in the group, even if they are not shareholders of the parent. Thus **goodwill attributable to the non-controlling interest needs to be recognised**.

- The non-controlling interest may be valued **either at fair value or at the non-controlling interest's proportionate share of the acquiree's identifiable net assets**.

- **Goodwill arising on consolidation** is the difference between the purchase consideration and the fair value of the identifiable assets and liabilities acquired.

- **Goodwill** should be calculated **after revaluing** the subsidiary company's assets.

- If the subsidiary does not incorporate the revaluation in its own accounts, it should be done as a **consolidation adjustment**.

- The accounting requirements and disclosures of the **fair value exercise** are covered by **IFRS 3 (revised)**.

- IFRS 3 (revised) does not allow combinations to be accounted for as a **uniting of interests; all combinations must be treated as acquisitions.**

- You should learn the three main indications of **when an acquirer exists**.

- **IAS 28** deals with accounting for associates. The definitions are important as they govern the accounting treatment, particularly **'significant influence'**.

- The **equity method** should be applied in the consolidated accounts:

  - **Statement of financial position**: investment in associate at cost plus (or minus) the group's share of the associate's post-acquisition profits (or losses)
  - **Income statement (statement of comprehensive income)**: group share of associate's profit after tax.

- IAS 31 *Financial reporting of interests in joint ventures* is concerned with how venturers **report their interests** in joint ventures in their accounts.

- There are three usual **forms of joint venture**.

  - Jointly controlled operations
  - Jointly controlled assets
  - Jointly controlled entities

- Joint ventures are characterised by **joint control** evidenced by a **contractual arrangement**.

- **Jointly controlled entities** may be accounted for in different ways:
    - **Proportionate consolidation**: combine items on a line by line basis
    - **Equity method**: see above

Quick Quiz

1   **Fill in the blanks** in the statements below, using the words in the box.

Per IAS 27 (revised), A is a parent of B if:

(a)   A holds (1) ……………….. in B

(b)   A can appoint or remove (2) ………………..

(c)   A has the right to exercise (3) ……………….. over B

(d)   B is a (4) ……………….. of A

• Sub-subsidiary	• Control
• Directors holding a majority of the voting rights	• A majority of the voting rights

2   If a company holds 20% or more of the shares of another company, it has significant influence. True or false?

3   What is significant influence?

4   What is a non-controlling interest?

5   How is the non-controlling interest on acquisition to be valued?

6   How should an investment in a subsidiary be accounted for in the separate financial statements of the parent?

7   Describe the requirement of IFRS 3 (revised) in relation to the revaluation of a subsidiary company's assets.

8   What guidelines are given by IFRS 3 in relation to valuing land and buildings fairly?

9   Which party to a business combination is the acquirer?

10   An associate is a _____ in which a investor has a _____ , but which is not a subsidiary or a joint venture of the investor. *Complete the blanks.*

11   What is the effect of the equity method on the income statement and the statement of financial position?

12   The equity method has no effect on ratios. True or false?

13   A joint venture is a _____ whereby two or more parties undertake an economic activity which is subject to _____ . *Complete the blanks.*

14   What forms of evidence of a contractual agreement might exist?

15   How should a venturer account for its share of jointly controlled operations?

16   Which standard should an operator of a joint venture follow when dealing with management fees received?

17   What is the procedure for proportionate consolidation?

Answers to Quick Quiz

1   (a)   A majority of the voting rights
    (b)   Directors holding a majority of the voting rights
    (c)   Control
    (d)   Sub-subsidiary

2   True.

3   The power to participate but not to control.

4   The part of the net profit or loss and the net assets attributable to interests not owned by the parent.

5   Either at fair value or at the non-controlling interest's proportionate share of the acquiree's identifiable net assets.

6   (a)   At cost using the equity method
    (b)   At cost or revaluation as a long-term investment

7   Fair value is not affected by the acquirer's intentions. Therefore only intentions after acquisition are reflected in the statement of comprehensive income after acquisition.

8   Market value

9   The acquirer is the entity that obtains control of the other combining entities or businesses.

10 An associates is an **entity** in which an investor has a **significant influence**, but which is not a subsidiary or a joint venture of the investor.

11 (a)   *Income statement.* Investing entity includes its share of the earnings of the associate, by adding its share of profit after tax.

    (b)   *Statement of financial position.* Investment in associates is included in assets at cost. This will increase or decrease each year according to whether the associate makes a profit or loss.

12 False. See Paragraph 4.13

13 A joint venture is a **contractual arrangement** whereby two or more parties undertake an economic activity which is subject to **joint control**.

14 •   Contractual arrangement
    •   Joint control

14 (a)   The assets it controls and the liabilities it incurs
    (b)   The expenses it incurs and the income it earns

16 IAS 18 *Revenue*

17 (a)   Line-by-line basis with venturer's own assets, liabilities, income and expenses.
    (b)   Show as separate line items within the venturer's accounts.

    Note. Remember only the venturer's share is included, so there is **no** non-controlling interest.

Now try the question below from the Exam Question Bank

Number	Level	Marks	Time
Q15	Introductory	18	32 mins

13

Complex groups

Topic list	Syllabus reference
1 Complex groups	D1
2 Consolidating sub-subsidiaries	D1
3 Direct holdings in sub-subsidiaries	D1

Introduction

This chapter introduces the first of several more complicated consolidation topics. The best way to tackle these questions is to be logical and to carry out the consolidation on a **step by step** basis.

In questions of this nature, it is very helpful to sketch a **diagram of the group structure**, as we have done. This clarifies the situation and it should point you in the right direction: always sketch the group structure as your first working and double check it against the information in the question.

fs

Study guide

		Intellectual level
D1	**Group accounting: statement of cash flows**	
(a)	Apply the method of accounting for business combinations including complex group structures	3

Exam guide

If the groups questions does not involve an acquisition or disposal or a statement of cash flows, then it is likely to involve a complex group.

1 Complex groups

When a holding company has **several subsidiaries**, the consolidated statement of financial position shows a single figure for non-controlling interests and for goodwill arising on consolidation. In cases where there are several subsidiary companies the technique is to open up a single non-controlling interest working and a columnar goodwill working.

1.1 Introduction

In this section we shall consider how the principles of statement of financial position consolidation may be applied to more complex structures of companies within a group.

(a) **Several subsidiary companies**

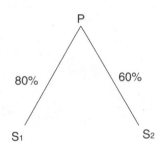

You have already seen this type of structure in your previous studies.

(b) **Sub-subsidiaries**

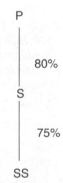

P holds a controlling interest in S which in turn holds a controlling interest in SS. SS is therefore a subsidiary of a subsidiary of P, in other words, a *sub-subsidiary* of P.

(c) **Direct holdings in sub-subsidiaries: 'D' shaped groups**

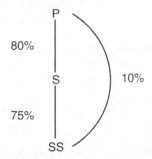

In this example, SS is a sub-subsidiary of P with additional shares held directly by P.

In practice, groups are usually larger, and therefore more complex, but the procedures for consolidation of large groups will not differ from those we shall now describe for smaller ones.

1.2 A parent company which has several subsidiaries

Where a company P has several subsidiaries S_1, S_2, S_3 and so on, the technique for consolidation is exactly as previously described. **Cancellation** is from the holding company, which has assets of investments in subsidiaries S_1, S_2, S_3, to each of the several subsidiaries.

The consolidated statement of financial position will show:

(a)   A single figure for **non-controlling interest**, and
(b)   A single figure for **goodwill** arising.

A single working should be used for each of the constituents of the consolidated statement of financial position: one working for goodwill, one for non-controlling interest, one for retained earnings (reserves), and so on.

1.3 Sub-subsidiaries

A slightly different problem arises when there are sub-subsidiaries in the group, which is how should we **identify the non-controlling interest** in the retained earnings of the group? Suppose P owns 80% of the equity of S, and that S in turn owns 60% of the equity of SS.

It would appear that in this situation:

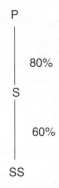

(a)   P owns 80% of 60% = 48% of SS
(b)   The non-controlling interest in S owns 20% of 60% = 12% of SS
(c)   The non-controlling interest in SS itself owns the remaining 40% of the SS equity

SS is nevertheless a **sub-subsidiary** of P, because it is a subsidiary of S which in turn is a subsidiary of P. The chain of control thus makes SS a sub-subsidiary of P which owns only 48% of its equity.

The total non-controlling interest in SS may be checked by considering a **dividend** of $100 paid by SS where S then distributes its share of this dividend in full to its own shareholders.

		$
S will receive	$60	
P will receive	80% × $60 =	48
Leaving for the total minority in SS		52
		100

Top owns 60% of the equity of Middle Co, which owns 75% of the equity of Bottom Co. What is Top Co's effective holding in Bottom Co?

Answer

Top owns 60% of 75% of Bottom Co = 45%.

1.4 Date of effective control

The date the sub-subsidiary comes under the **control of the holding company** is either:

(a) The date P acquired S if S already holds shares in SS, or

(b) If S acquires shares in SS later, then that later date.

Exam focus point

The examiner has strongly indicated that fair value NCI will generally be tested with more difficult group topics in December 2009 and June 2010. However, this chapter uses examples where the NCI is valued at its proportionate share of the subsidiary's identifiable net assets. Fair value NCI is shown as an alternative. This is to enable you to learn the new techniques. Fair value NCI is used in the questions in the exam question bank. You should keep an eye on *Student Accountant* magazine for articles by the examiner giving further advice on this point.

2 Consolidating sub-subsidiaries

FAST FORWARD

When dealing with **sub-subsidiaries,** you will need to calculate effective interest owned by the group and by the non-controlling interest. The date of acquisition is important when dealing with sub-subsidiaries. Remember that it is the post-acquisition reserves from a group perspective which are important.

Exam focus point

Don't panic when a question seems very complicated – sketch the group structure and analyse the information in the question methodically.

The basic consolidation method is as follows.

(a) **Net assets**: show what the group controls.

(b) **Equity (capital and reserves)**: show who owns the net assets included elsewhere in the statement of financial position. Reserves (retained earnings), therefore, are based on **effective holdings**.

As indicated earlier, the major problem on consolidation is to identify the non-controlling interest share of the retained earnings of S and (especially) SS.

2.1 Example: subsidiary acquired first

The draft statements of financial position of P Co, S Co and SS Co on 30 June 20X7 were as follows.

	P Co $	S Co $	SS Co $
Assets			
Non-current assets			
Tangible assets	105,000	125,000	180,000
Investments, at cost			
80,000 shares in S Co	120,000	–	–
60,000 shares in SS Co	–	110,000	–
Current assets	80,000	70,000	60,000
	305,000	305,000	240,000
Equity and liabilities			
Equity			
Ordinary shares of $1 each	80,000	100,000	100,000
Retained earnings	195,000	170,000	115,000
	275,000	270,000	215,000
Payables	30,000	35,000	25,000
	305,000	305,000	240,000

P Co acquired its shares in S Co on 1 July 20X4 when the reserves of S Co stood at $40,000; and

S Co acquired its shares in SS Co on 1 July 20X5 when the reserves of SS Co stood at $50,000.

It is the group's policy to measure the non-controlling interest at acquisition at its proportionate share of the fair value of the subsidiary's net assets.

Required

Prepare the draft consolidated statement of financial position of P Group at 30 June 20X7.

Note. Assume no impairment of goodwill.

Solution

In 20X4, the group buys 80% of S. Then in 20X5 S (which is now part of the P group) buys 60% of SS.

P buys 80% of S, then S (80% of S from the group's point of view) buys 60% of SS.

Having calculated the non-controlling interest and the P group interest (see working 1 below), the workings can be constructed. You should, however, note the following.

(a) Group structure working (see working 1)

(b) **Goodwill working**: compare the costs of investments with the effective group interests acquired (80% of S Co and 48% of SS Co).

(c) **Retained earnings working**: bring in the share of S Co's and SS Co's post-acquisition retained earnings in the normal way.

(d) **Non-controlling interest working**: bring in the total non-controlling interests in S Co's net assets (20%), and the total non-controlling interests in SS Co's net assets (52%).

1 Group structure

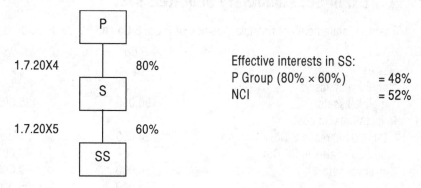

1.7.20X4   80%

S

1.7.20X5   60%

SS

Effective interests in SS:
P Group (80% × 60%) = 48%
NCI = 52%

2 Goodwill

	P in S		S in SS	
	$	$	$	$
Consideration transferred		120,000	(80 × 110,000)	88,000
Fair value of identifiable NA acquired:				
Share capital	100,000		100,000	
Retained earnings	40,000		50,000	
	140,000		150,000	
Group share	80%		48%	
		(112,000)		(72,000)
		8,000		16,000
			24,000	

3 Retained earnings

	P Co $	S Co $	SS Co $
Per question	195,000	170,000	115,000
Pre-acquisition		(40,000)	(50,000)
Post-acquisition		130,000	65,000
Group share:			
In S Co ($130,000 × 80%)	104,000		
In SS Co ($65,000 × 48%)	31,200		
Group retained earnings	330,200		

4 Non-controlling interests

	S $	SS $
Net assets per Q	270,000	215,000
Less investment in SS	(110,000)	-
	160,000	215,000
	× 20%	× 52%
	32,000	111,800
	$ 143,800	

Note. The cost of the investment in SS Co must be split between the non-controlling interest and the goodwill workings to ensure that we have only P Co's share of the goodwill arising in the S Co subgroup appearing in the consolidated statement of financial position. This is done by taking the group share of the subsidiary's 'cost' in the goodwill working and by deducting the cost from the net assets allocated to the non-controlling interests.

P CO
CONSOLIDATED STATEMENT OF FINANCIAL POSITION AT 30 JUNE 20X7

	$
Assets	
Non-current assets	
Tangible assets	410,000
Goodwill	24,000
Current assets	210,000
	644,000
Equity	
Ordinary shares of $1 each fully paid	80,000
Retained earnings	330,200
	410,200
Non-controlling interest	143,800
	554,000
Payables	90,000
	644,000

2.2 Date of acquisition

Care must be taken when consolidating sub-subsidiaries, because (usually) either:

(a)   The parent company acquired the subsidiary **before** the subsidiary bought the sub-subsidiary (as in the example in 2.1 above); *OR*

(b)   The parent holding company acquired the subsidiary **after** the subsidiary bought the sub-subsidiary

Depending on whether (a) or (b) is the case, the retained earnings of the subsidiary at acquisition wil be different.

The rule to remember here, when considering pre- and post-acquisition profits, is that we are only interested in the consolidated results of the **parent company**. We will use the example above to demonstrate the required approach.

2.3 Example: Sub-subsidiary acquired first

In this version, SS only becomes part of the group when P acquires S.

The calculation is the same as in Section 2.1, but we use the retained earnings of SS of 1 July 20X5, when it became part of the P group, that is $60,000.

Again using the figures in Section 2.1, assume that:

(a)   S Co purchased its holding in SS Co on 1 July 20X4
(b)   P Co purchased its holding in S Co on 1 July 20X5

It is the group's policy to measure the non-controlling interest at its proportionate share of the fair value of the subsidiary's net assets.

Solution

The point here is that SS Co only became part of the P group on 1 July 20X5, *not* on 1 July 20X4. This means that only the retained earnings of SS Co arising *after* 1 July 20X5 can be included in the post-acquisition reserves of P Co group. Goodwill arising on the acquisition will be calculated by comparing P's share of S's cost of the investment by S in SS to the effective group interests acquired represented by the share capital of SS and its retained earnings **at the date P acquired S** (here $60,000).

P CO
CONSOLIDATED STATEMENT OF FINANCIAL POSITION AS AT 30 JUNE 20X7

	$
Non-current assets	
Tangible	410,000
Goodwill (W2)	19,200
	429,200
Current assets	210,000
	639,200
Equity and liabilities	
Ordinary shares $1 each, fully paid	80,000
Retained earnings (W3)	325,400
	405,400
Non-controlling interest (W4)	143,800
	549,200
Payables	90,000
	639,200

Workings

1   *Group structure*

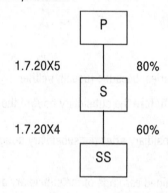

1.7.20X5   80%

S

1.7.20X4   60%

SS

P owns an effective interest of 48% in SS. NCI in SS is 52%.

2   *Goodwill*

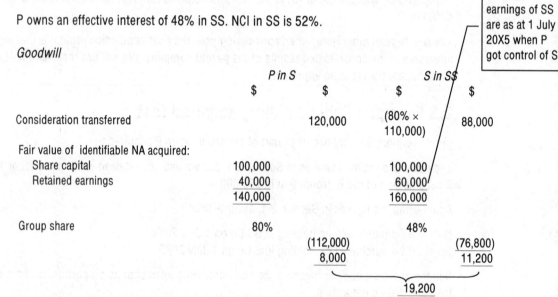

	P in S		S in SS	
	$	$	$	$
Consideration transferred		120,000	(80% × 110,000)	88,000
Fair value of identifiable NA acquired:				
Share capital	100,000		100,000	
Retained earnings	40,000		60,000	
	140,000		160,000	
Group share	80%		48%	
		(112,000)		(76,800)
		8,000		11,200
			19,200	

> Retained earnings of SS are as at 1 July 20X5 when P got control of S

3   *Retained earnings*

		$
P Co (as above)		195,000
S Co (as above)		104,000
SS Co (115 – 60) × 48%		26,400
		325,400

4   *Non-controlling interests*

The cost of investment in SS is again deducted as the NCI is being calculated on the net assets that have been consolidated (see note above).

	S	SS
	$	$
Net assets per Q	270,000	215,000
Less investment in SS	(110,000)	-
	160,000	215,000
	× 20%	× 52%
	32,000	111,800

$ 143,800

2.4 Example: subsidiary acquired first: non-controlling interest at fair value

Exam focus point

The examiner has indicated that fair value NCI will be tested with more difficult group topics from December 2009. Keep an eye on *Student Accountant* for further guidance from the examiner.

The draft statements of financial position of P Co, S Co and SS Co on 30 June 20X7 were as follows.

	P Co	S Co	SS Co
	$	$	$
Assets			
Non-current assets			
Tangible assets	105,000	125,000	180,000
Investments, at cost			
80,000 shares in S Co	120,000	–	–
60,000 shares in SS Co	–	110,000	–
Current assets	80,000	70,000	60,000
	305,000	305,000	240,000
Equity and liabilities			
Equity			
Ordinary shares of $1 each	80,000	100,000	100,000
Retained earnings	195,000	170,000	115,000
	275,000	270,000	215,000
Payables	30,000	35,000	25,000
	305,000	305,000	240,000

P Co acquired its shares in S Co on 1 July 20X4 when the reserves of S Co stood at $40,000; and

S Co acquired its shares in SS Co on 1 July 20X5 when the reserves of SS Co stood at $50,000.

It is the group's policy to measure the non-controlling interest at fair value at the date of acquisition. The fair value of the non-controlling interests in S on 1 July 20X4 was $29,000. The fair value of the 52% non-controlling interest on 1 July 20X5 was $80,000.

Required

Prepare the draft consolidated statement of financial position of P Group at 30 June 20X7.

Note. Assume no impairment of goodwill.

Solution

The main difference from the example in 2.1 above is that extra columns are needed in the goodwill calculation for the goodwill attributable to the non-controlling interest. As explained in Chapter 12, the goodwill attributable to the non-controlling interest is also added to the NCI figure at the year end.

P CO
CONSOLIDATED STATEMENT OF FINANCIAL POSITION AT 30 JUNE 20X7

	$
Assets	
Non-current assets	
Tangible assets	410,000
Goodwill (W2)	27,000
Current assets	210,000
	647,000
Equity	
Ordinary shares of $1 each fully paid	80,000
Retained earnings (W3)	330,200
	410,200
Non-controlling interest (W4)	146,800
	557,000
Payables	90,000
	647,000

1   *Group structure*

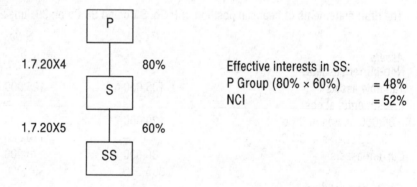

1.7.20X4		80%
1.7.20X5		60%

Effective interests in SS:
P Group (80% × 60%) = 48%
NCI   = 52%

2 Goodwill

		P in S			S in SS	
		Group	NCI		Group	NCI
	$	$	$	$	$	$
Consideration transferred/ FV NCI		120,000	29,000	(80% × 110,000)	88,000	80,000
Fair value of identifiable net assets acquired						
Share capital	100,000				100,000	
Retained earnings	40,000				50,000	
	140,000				150,000	
Group/NCI Share	80%		(20%)	48%		(52%)
		(112,000)	(28,000)		(72,000)	(78,000)
		8,000	1,000		16,000	2,000

$27,000

3 Retained earnings

	P Co $	S Co $	SS Co $
Per question	195,000	170,000	115,000
Pre-acquisition		(40,000)	(50,000)
Post-acquisition		130,000	65,000
Group share:			
In S Co ($130,000 × 80%)	104,000		
In SS Co ($65,000 × 48%)	31,200		
Group retained earnings	330,200		

4 Non-controlling interests

The non-controlling interest working in this example has one extra step: adding on the non-controlling interest in goodwill as calculated in working 2. The cost of investment in SS is again deducted as the NCI is being calculated on the net assets that have been consolidated (see note above).

	S $	SS $
Net assets per Q	270,000	215,000
Less investment in SS	(110,000)	-
	160,000	215,000
	× 20%	× 52%
	32,000	111,800
Non-controlling interests in goodwill (W2)	1,000	2,000
	33,000	113,800

146,800

Question

Sub-subsidiary

Learning outcome: A (ii)

The statements of financial position of Antelope Co, Yak Co and Zebra Co at 31 March 20X4 are summarised as follows.

	Antelope Co		Yak Co		Zebra Co	
Assets	$	$	$	$	$	$
Non-current assets						
Freehold property		100,000		100,000		–
Plant and machinery		210,000		80,000		3,000
		310,000		180,000		3,000
Investments in subsidiaries						
Shares, at cost	110,000		6,200			–
Loan account	–		3,800			–
Current accounts	10,000		12,200			–
		120,000		22,200		3,000
Current assets						
Inventories	170,000		20,500		15,000	
Receivables	140,000		50,000		1,000	
Cash at bank	60,000		16,500		4,000	
		370,000		87,000		20,000
		800,000		289,200		23,000
Equity and liabilities						
Equity						
Ordinary share capital	200,000		100,000		10,000	
Retained earnings	379,600		129,200		(1,000)	
		579,600		229,200		9,000
Current liabilities						
Trade payables	160,400		40,200		800	
Due to Antelope Co	–		12,800		600	
Due to Yak Co	–				12,600	
Taxation	60,000		7,000		–	
				–		–
		220,400		60,000		14,000
		800,000		289,200		23,000

Antelope Co acquired 75% of the shares of Yak Co in 20X1 when the credit balance on the retained earnings of that company was $40,000. No dividends have been paid since that date. Yak Co acquired 80% of the shares in Zebra Co in 20X3 when there was a debit balance on the retained earnings of that company of $3,000. Subsequently $500 was received by Zebra Co and credited to its retained earnings, representing the recovery of a bad debt written off before the acquisition of Zebra's shares by Yak Co. During the year to 31 March 20X4 Yak Co purchased inventory from Antelope Co for $20,000 which included a profit mark-up of $4,000 for Antelope Co. At 31 March 20X4 one half of this amount was still held in the inventories of Yak Co. Group accounting policies are to make a full allowance for unrealised intra-group profits.

It is the group's policy to measure the non-controlling interest at its proportionate share of the fair value of the subsidiary's net assets.

Prepare the draft consolidated statement of financial position of Antelope Co at 31 March 20X4. (Assume no impairment of goodwill.)

A

20X1		75%

Y

20X3		80%

Z

Effective interests in Z:
A Group (75% × 80%) = 60%
NCI = 40%

Workings

1 *Goodwill*

	A in Y		Y in Z	
	$	$	$	$
			(75% ×	
Consideration transferred		110,000	6,200)	4,650
Fair value of identifiable NA acquired:				
Share capital	100,000		10,000	
Retained earnings: ($3,000) + $500	40,000		(2,500)	
	140,000		7,500	
Group share	75%		60%	
		(105,000)		(4,500)
		5,000		150

$ 5,150

2 *Retained earnings*

	Antelope	Yak	Zebra
	$	$	$
Per question	379,600	129,200	(1,000)
Adjustment bad debt recovery			(500)
Pre-acquisition profit/losses		(40,000)	3,000
Post-acquisition profits		89,200	1,500
Group share			
In Yak ($89,200 × 75%)	66,900		
In Zebra ($1,500 × 60%)	900		
Unrealised profit in inventories sitting in parent ($4,000) × ½)	(2,000)		
Group retained earnings	445,400		

3   *Non-controlling interests*

	Yak	Zebra
	$	$
Net assets per Q	229,200	9,000
Less investment in Zebra	(6,200)	-
	223,000	9,000
	× 25%	× 40%
	55,750	3,600

59,350

ANTELOPE CO
CONSOLIDATED STATEMENT OF FINANCIAL POSITION AS AT 31 MARCH 20X4

	$	$
Assets		
Non-current assets		
Freehold property		200,000
Plant and machinery		293,000
		493,000
Goodwill (W1)		5,150
Current assets		498,150
Inventories $(205,500 – 2,000)$	203,500	
Receivables	191,000	
Cash at bank	80,500	
		475,000
		973,150
Equity and liabilities		
Equity		
Ordinary share capital		200,000
Retained earnings (W2)		445,400
Shareholders' funds		645,400
Non-controlling interests (W3)		59,350
		704,750
Current liabilities		
Trade payables	201,400	
Taxation	67,000	
		268,400
		973,150

2.5 Section summary

You should follow this **step by step approach** in all questions using the single-stage method. This applies to Section 3 below as well.

Step 1   Set up **proforma**

Step 2   Sketch the **group structure** and check it to the question

Step 3   **Add details** to the sketch of dates of acquisition, holdings acquired (percentage and nominal values) and cost

Step 4   **Goodwill working**: compare costs of investment with the **effective** group interests acquired.

Step 5   **Non-controlling interest working**: total NCI in subsidiary plus total NCI in sub-subsidiary

Step 6   **Reserves working**: include the group share of subsidiary and sub-subsidiary post-acquisition retained earnings (effective holdings again)

Step 7   Complete the **consolidated statement of financial position** (and statement of comprehensive income if required).

3 Direct holdings in sub-subsidiaries

Consider the following structure, sometimes called a **'D-shaped' group**.

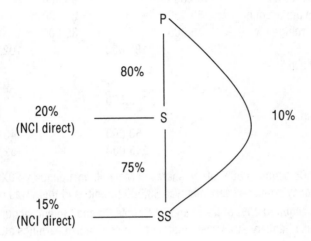

In the structure above, there is:

(a)	A **direct** non-controlling share in S of	20%
(b)	A **direct** non-controlling share in SS of	15%
(c)	An **indirect** non-controlling share in SS of 20% × 75% =	15%
		30%

The effective interest in SS is:

Group 80% × 75%	=	60% interest
		10%
		70%
∴ NCI		30%
		100%

Having ascertained the structure and non-controlling interests, proceed as for a typical sub-subsidiary situation.

Question   'D' shaped group

Learning outcome: A (ii)

The draft statements of financial position of Hulk Co, Molehill Co and Pimple Co as at 31 May 20X5 are as follows.

	Hulk Co		Molehill Co		Pimple Co	
	$	$	$	$	$	$
Assets						
Non-current assets						
Tangible assets		90,000		60,000		60,000
Investments in subsidiaries(cost)						
Shares in Molehill Co	90,000		–		–	
Shares in Pimple Co	25,000		42,000		–	
		115,000		42,000		–
		205,000		102,000		60,000
Current assets		40,000		50,000		40,000
		245,000		152,000		100,000

	Hulk Co		Molehill Co		Pimple Co	
	$	$	$	$	$	$
Equity and liabilities						
Equity						
Ordinary shares $1	100,000		50,000		50,000	
Share premium account	50,000		20,000			
Retained earnings	45,000		32,000		25,000	
		195,000		102,000		75,000
Non-current liabilities						
12% loan		–	10,000			–
		195,000		112,000		75,000
Current liabilities						
Payables		50,000		40,000		25,000
		245,000		152,000		100,000

(a)   Hulk Co acquired 60% of the shares in Molehill on 1 January 20X3 when the balance on that company's retained earnings was $8,000 (credit) and there was no share premium account.

(b)   Hulk acquired 20% of the shares of Pimple Co and Molehill acquired 60% of the shares of Pimple Co on 1 January 20X4 when that company's retained earnings stood at $15,000.

(c)   There has been no payment of dividends by either Molehill or Pimple since they became subsidiaries.

(d)   There was no impairment of goodwill.

(e)   It is the group's policy to measure the non-controlling interest at acquisition at its proportionate share of the fair value of the subsidiary's net assets.

Required

Prepare the consolidated statement of financial position of Hulk Co as at 31 May 20X5.

Answer

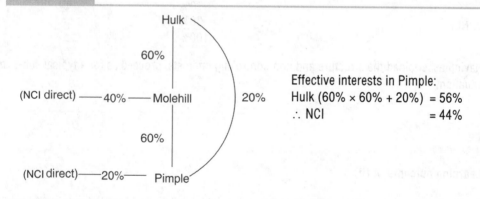

The direct non-controlling interest in Molehill Co is   40%

The direct non-controlling interest in Pimple Co is   20%

The indirect non-controlling interest in Pimple Co is (40% of 60%)   24%

The total non-controlling interest in Pimple Co is   44%

The group share of Molehill Co is 60% and of Pimple Co is (100 – 44)% = 56%

Workings

1   *Goodwill*

	Hulk in Molehill		*Molehill in Pimple*		*Hulk in Pimple*	
	$	$	$	$	$	$
Consideration transferred		90,000	(60% × 42,000)	25,200		25,000
Fair value at NA acquired						
Share capital	50,000		50,000		50,000	
Retained earnings	8,000		15,000		15,000	
	58,000		65,000		65,000	
Group share	60%		36%		20%	13,000
		(34,800)		(23,400)		
		55,200		1,800		12,000

$69,000

2   *Retained earnings*

	Hulk	*Molehill*	*Pimple*
	$	$	$
Per question	45,000	32,000	25,000
Pre-acquisition profits		(8,000)	(15,000)
Post-acquisition retained earnings		24,000	10,000
Group share:			
In Molehill ($24,000 × 60%)	14,400		
In Pimple ($10,000 × 56%)	5,600		
Group retained earnings	65,000		

3   *Non-controlling interests*

	Molehill	*Pimple*
	$	$
Net assets per question	102,000	75,000
Investment in Pimple	(42,000)	–
	60,000	75,000
	× 40%	× 44%
	$24,000	$33,000

Type here $57,000

4   *Share premium account*

	$
Hulk Co	50,000
Molehill Co: all post-acquisition ($20,000 × 60%)	12,000
	62,000

HULK CO
CONSOLIDATED STATEMENT OF FINANCIAL POSITION AS AT 31 MAY 20X8

	$	$
Assets		
Non-current assets		
Tangible assets	210,000	
Goodwill (W1)	69,000	
		279,000
Current assets		130,000
		409,000
Equity and liabilities		
Equity		
Ordinary shares $1	100,000	
Share premium (W4)	62,000	
Retained earnings (W2)	65,000	
Shareholders' funds	227,000	
Non-controlling interests (W3)	57,000	
		284,000
Non-current liabilities		
12% loan		10,000
		294,000
Current liabilities		
Payables		115,000
		409,000

Chapter Roundup

- When a holding company has **several subsidiaries**, the consolidated statement of financial position shows a single figure for non-controlling interests and for goodwill arising on consolidation. In cases where there are several subsidiary companies the technique is to open up a single non-controlling interest working and a single goodwill working.

- When dealing with **sub-subsidiaries,** you will need to calculate effective interest. The date of acquisition is important when dealing with sub-subsidiaries. Remember that it is the post-acquisition reserves from a group perspective which are important.

Quick Quiz

1 B Co owns 60% of the equity of C Co which owns 75% of the equity of D Co. What is the total non-controlling interest percentage ownership in D Co?

2 What is the basic consolidation method for sub-subsidiaries?

3 P Co owns 25% of R Co's equity and 75% of Q Co's equity. Q Co owns 40% of R Co's equity. What is the total non-controlling interest percentage ownership in R Co?

1   B
      | 60%
    C
      | 75%
    D

Non-controlling interest = 25% + (40% of 75%) = 55%

2   ●   Net assets: show what the group controls
     ●   Equity (capital and reserves): show who owns the net assets

3

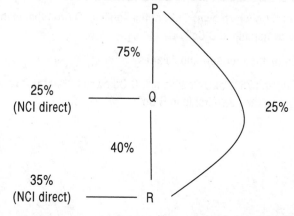

Total non-controlling interest in R is 35% + (25% × 40%) = 35%

Now try the question below from the Exam Question Bank

Number	Level	Marks	Time
Q16	Examination	10	18 mins

14

Changes in group structures

Topic list	Syllabus reference
1 Disposals	D3
2 Business combinations achieved in stages	D3

Introduction

Complex consolidation issues are very likely to come up in this, the final stage of your studies on financial accounting. Your approach should be the same as for more simple consolidation questions: **methodical and logical**. If you understand the basic principles of consolidation, you should be able to tackle these complicated questions.

Study guide

		Intellectual level
D3	**Changes in group structure**	
(a)	Discuss the reasons behind a group reorganisation	3
(b)	Evaluate and assess the principal terms of a proposed group reorganisation	3

Exam guide

IFRS 3 has changed the way piecemeal acquisitions and disposals are accounted for.

One of the competences you need to fulfil Objective 10 of the Practical Experience Requirement (PER) is to prepare financial statements for single companies and combined entities. You can apply the knowledge you obtain from this Chapter, on combined entities, to demonstrate this competence.

1 Disposals

FAST FORWARD

Disposals can drop a subsidiary holding to associate status, long-term investment status and to zero, or a the parent might still retain a subsidiary with a reduced holding. Once again, you should be able to deal with all these situations. Remember particularly how to deal with **goodwill**.

1.1 Types of disposal

1.1.1 Disposals where control is lost

There are three main kinds of disposals in which control is lost:

(a) Full disposal: all the holding is sold (say, 80% to nil)
(b) Subsidiary to associate (say, 80% to 30%)
(c) Subsidiary to trade investment (say, 80% to 10%)

In your exam, you are most likely to meet a partial disposal, either subsidiary to associate or subsidiary to trade investment.

1.1.2 Disposals where control is retained

There is only one kind of disposal where control is retained: **subsidiary to subsidiary**, for example an 80% holding to a 60% holding.

Disposals where control is lost are treated differently from disposals where control is retained. There is a reason for this.

1.2 General principle: 'crossing an accounting boundary'

Under the revised IFRS 3 disposal occurs only when one entity loses control over another, which is generally when its holding is decreased to less than 50%. The Deloitte guide: *Business Combinations and Changes in Ownership Interests* calls this 'crossing an accounting boundary'.

On disposal of a controlling interest, any retained interest (an associate or trade investment) is measured at fair value on the date that control is lost. This fair value is used in the calculation of the gain or loss on disposal, and also becomes the carrying amount for subsequent accounting for the retained interest.

If the **50%** boundary is **not crossed**, as when the interest in a subsidiary is reduced, the event is treated as a **transaction between owners**.

> Whenever you cross the 50% boundary, you revalue, and a gain or loss is reported in profit or loss for the year. If you do not cross the 50% boundary, no gain or loss is reported; instead there is an adjustment to the parent's equity.

The following diagram, from the *Deloittes* guide may help you visualise the boundary:

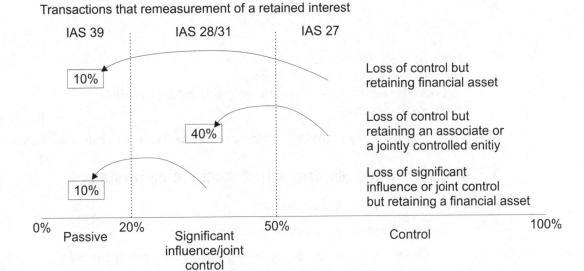

Transactions that remeasurement of a retained interest

As you will see from the diagram, the situation in paragraph 1.1.2, where an interest in a subsidiary is reduced from say 80% to 60%, does not involve crossing that all-important 50% threshold.

1.3 Effective date of disposal

The effective date of disposal is **when control passes**: the date for accounting for an undertaking ceasing to be a subsidiary undertaking is the date on which its former parent undertaking relinquishes its control over that undertaking. The consolidated income statement (statement of comprehensive income) should include the results of a subsidiary undertaking up to the date of its disposal. IAS 37 on provisions (Chapter 9) and IFRS 5 on disclosure of discontinued operations will have an impact here (see Chapter 15).

1.4 Control lost: calculation of group gain on disposal

A proforma calculation is shown below. This needs to be adapted for the circumstances in the question, in particular whether it is a full or partial disposal:

		$
Fair value of consideration received		X
Fair value of investment retained		X
Less:	net assets × share (%) held at date control lost	(X)
	goodwill less any NCI in goodwill at date control lost	(X)
Add/less:	gains/(losses) previously recognised in OCI	X/(X)
Group profit/(loss)		X/(X)

Following IAS 1, this gain may need to be disclosed separately if it is material.

1.4.1 Analogy: trading in a large car for a smaller one

It may seem counter-intuitive that the investment retained is now part of the 'proceeds' for the purposes of calculating the gain. One way of looking at it is to imagine that you are selling a larger car and putting part of the proceeds towards a smaller one. If the larger car you are selling cost you less than the smaller car and cash combined, you have made a profit. Likewise, the company making the disposal sold a larger stake to gain, at fair value, a smaller stake and some cash on top, which is the 'consideration received'.

This analogy is not exact, but may help.

1.5 Control lost: calculation of gain in parent's separate financial statements

This calculation is more straightforward: the proceeds are compared with the carrying value of the investment sold. The investment will be held at cost or at fair value if held as an available-for-sale financial asset:

	$
Fair value of consideration received	X
Less carrying value of investment disposed	(X)
Add/(less) fair value changes previously recognised in OCI (if an AFSFA)	X/(X)
Profit/(loss) on disposal	X/(X)

The profit on disposal is generally taxable, and the **tax based on the parent's gain** rather than the group's.

1.6 Disposals where control is lost: accounting treatment

For a **full disposal**, apply the following treatment.

(a) **Statement of comprehensive income (income statement)**

    (i)   Consolidate results and non-controlling interest to the date of disposal.

    (ii)   Show the group profit or loss on disposal.

(b) **Statement of financial position**

    There will be no non-controlling interest and no consolidation as there is no subsidiary at the date the statement of financial position is being prepared.

For **partial disposals**, use the following treatments.

(a) **Subsidiary to associate**

    (i)   **Statement of comprehensive income (income statement)**

        (1)   Treat the undertaking as a subsidiary up to the date of disposal, ie consolidate for the correct number of months and show the non-controlling interest in that amount.

        (2)   Show the profit or loss on disposal.

        (3)   Treat as an associate thereafter.

    (ii)   **Statement of financial position**

        (1)   The investment remaining is at its fair value at the date of disposal (to calculate the gain)

        (2)   Equity account (as an associate) thereafter, using the fair value as the new 'cost'. (Post 'acquisition' retained earnings are added to this cost in future years to arrive at the carrying value of the investment in the associate in the statement of financial position.)

(b) **Subsidiary to trade investment**

    (i)   **Income statement (statement of comprehensive income)**

        (1)   Treat the undertaking as a subsidiary up to the date of disposal, ie consolidate.

        (2)   Show profit or loss on disposal.

        (3)   Show dividend income only thereafter.

    (ii)   **Statement of financial position**

        (i)   The investment remaining is at its fair value at the date of disposal (to calculate the gain).

        (2)   Thereafter, treat as an available-for-sale financial asset under IAS 39.

1.7 Disposals where control is retained

Control is retained where the disposal is from **subsidiary to subsidiary.** The accounting treatment is treatment is as follows:

1.7.1 Statement of comprehensive income (income statement)

(a)   The subsidiary is **consolidated in full** for the whole period.

(b)   The **non-controlling interest in the income statement** will be based on percentage before and after disposal, ie time apportion.

(c)   There is no profit or loss on disposal.

1.7.2 Statement of financial position

(a)   The non-controlling interest in the statement of financial position is based on the year end percentage.

(b)   The change (increase) in non-controlling interests is shown as an adjustment to the parent's equity.

(c)   Goodwill on acquisition is unchanged in the consolidated statement of financial position.

1.7.3 Adjustment to the parent's equity

This reflects the fact that the non-controlling share has increased (as the parent's share has reduced). A subsidiary to subsidiary disposal is, in effect, **a transaction between owners.** Specifically, it is a reallocation of ownership between parent and non-controlling equity holders. **The goodwill is unchanged,** because it is a historical figure, unaffected by the reallocation. The adjustment to the parent's equity is calculated as follows:

	$
Fair value of consideration received	X
Increase in NCI in net assets at disposal	(X)
Increase in NCI in goodwill at disposal *	(X)
Adjustment to parent's equity	X

* **Note.** This line is only required where non-controlling interests are measured at fair value at the date of acquisition (ie where there is an increase in the non-controlling interest share of goodwill already recognised). It is included for completeness only, as the examiner has strongly indicated that he will not test fair value NCI in this context in December 2008 or June 2009.

If you are wondering why the decrease in shareholding is treated as a transaction between owners, look back to Chapter 12, where we explained that the revised IFRS 3 views **the group as an economic entity,** and views **all providers of equity,** including non-controlling interests, as **owners of the group.** Non-controlling shareholders are not outsiders, they are owners of the group just like the parent.

You can practise the adjustment to parent's equity in the example and question below.

1.7.4 Gain in the parent's separate financial statements

This is calculated as for disposals where control is lost: see Paragraph 1.5 above.

1.8 Example: Partial disposals

Chalk Co bought 100% of the voting share capital of Cheese Co on its incorporation on 1 January 20X2 for $160,000. Cheese Co earned and retained $240,000 from that date until 31 December 20X7. At that date the statements of financial position of the company and the group were as follows.

	Chalk Co $'000	Cheese Co $'000	Consolidated $'000
Investment in Cheese	160	–	–
Other net assets	1,000	500	1,400
	1,160	500	1,400
Share capital	400	160	400
Retained earnings	560	240	800
Current liabilities	200	100	200
	1,160	500	1,400

It is the group's policy to value the non-controlling interest at its proportionate share of the fair value of the subsidiary's identifiable net assets.

On 1 January 20X8 Chalk Co sold 40% of its shareholding in Cheese Co for $280,000. The profit on disposal (ignoring tax) in the financial statements of the parent company is calculated as follows.

	Chalk $'000
Fair value of consideration received	280
Carrying value of investment (40% × 160)	64
Profit on sale	216

We now move on to calculate the adjustment to equity for the group financial statements.

Because only 40% of the 100% subsidiary has been sold, leaving a 60% subsidiary, **control is retained**. This means that there is **no group profit on disposal in profit or loss for the year**. Instead, there is an **adjustment to the parent's equity**, which affects group retained earnings.

Point to note

> Remember that, when control is retained, the disposal is just a transaction between owners. The non-controlling shareholders are owners of the group, just like the parent.

The adjustment to parent's equity is calculated as follows:

	$'000
Fair value of consideration received	280
Increase in non-controlling interest in net assets at the date of disposal (40% × 400)	160
Adjustment to parent's equity	120

This increases group retained earnings and does not go through group profit or loss for the year. (Note that there is no goodwill in this example, or non-controlling interest in goodwill, as the subsidiary was acquired on incorporation.)

Solution: subsidiary status

The statements of financial position immediately after the sale will appear as follows.

	Chalk Co $'000	Cheese Co $'000	Consolidated $'000
Investment in Cheese (160-64)	96		
Other assets	1,280	500	1,780
	1,376	500	1,780
Share capital	400	160	400
Retained earnings*	776	240	920
Current liabilities	200	100	300
	1,376	500	1,620
Non-controlling interest			160
			1,780

*Chalk's retained earnings are $560,000 + $216,000 profit on disposal. Group retained earnings are increased by the adjustment above: $800,000 + $120,000 = $920,000.

Solution: associate status

Using the above example, assume that Chalk Co sold 60% of its holding in Cheese Co for $440,000. The fair value of the 40% holding retained was $200,000. The gain or loss on disposal in the books of the parent company would be calculated as follows.

	Parent company $'000
Fair value of consideration received	440
Carrying value of investment (60% × 160)	96
Profit on sale	344

This time control is lost, so there will be a gain in group profit or loss, calculated as follows:

	$'000
Fair value of consideration received	440
Fair value of investment retained	
Less Chalk's share of consolidated carrying	200
value at date control lost 100% × 400	(400)
Group profit on sale	240

Note that there was no goodwill arising on the acquisition of Cheese, otherwise this too would be deducted in the calculation.

The statements of financial position would now appear as follows.

	Chalk Co $'000	Cheese Co $'000	Consolidated $'000
Investment in Cheese (Note 1)	64		200
Other assets	1,440	500	1,440
	1,504	500	1,640
Share capital	400	160	400
Retained earnings (Note 2)	904	240	1,040
Current liabilities	200	100	200
	1,504	500	1,640

Notes

1   The investment in Cheese is at fair value in the group SOFP. In fact it is equity accounted at fair value at date control lost plus share of post-'acquisition' retained earnings. But there are no retained earnings yet because control has only just been lost.

2   Group retained earnings are $800,000 (per question) plus group profit on the sale of $240,000, ie $1,040,000.

The following comprehensive question should help you get to grips with disposal problems. Try to complete the whole question without looking at the solution, and then check your answer very carefully. **Give yourself at least two hours**. This is a very difficult question.

Exam focus point

Questions may involve part-disposals leaving investments with both subsidiary and associate status. Disposals could well come up at P2, since you have not covered them before.

Question

Disposal

Smith Co bought 80% of the share capital of Jones Co for $324,000 on 1 October 20X5. At that date Jones Co's retained earnings balance stood at $180,000. The statements of financial position at 30 September 20X8 and the summarised statements of comprehensive income (income statements) to that date are given below.

	Smith Co	Jones Co
	$'000	$'000
Non-current assets	360	270
Investment in Jones Co	324	–
Current assets	370	370
	1,054	640
Equity		
$1 ordinary shares	540	180
Retained earnings	414	360
Current liabilities	100	100
	1,054	640
Profit before tax	153	126
Tax	(45)	(36)
Profit for the year	108	90

No entries have been made in the accounts for any of the following transactions.

Assume that profits accrue evenly throughout the year.

It is the group's policy to value the non-controlling interest at its proportionate share of the fair value of the subsidiary's identifiable net assets.

Ignore taxation.

Required

Prepare the consolidated statement of financial position and income statement at 30 September 20X8 in each of the following circumstances. (Assume no impairment of goodwill.)

(a)   Smith Co sells its entire holding in Jones Co for $650,000 on 30 September 20X8.

(b)   Smith Co sells one quarter of its holding in Jones Co for $160,000 on 30 June 20X8.

(c)   Smith Co sells one half of its holding in Jones Co for $340,000 on 30 June 20X8, and the remaining holding (fair value $250,000) is to be dealt with as an associate.

(d)   Smith Co sells one half of its holding in Jones Co for $340,000 on 30 June 20X8, and the remaining holding (fair value $250,000) is to be dealt with as an available-for-sale financial asset.

Answer

(a)   *Complete disposal at year end (80% to 0%)*

CONSOLIDATED STATEMENT OF FINANCIAL POSITION
AS AT 30 SEPTEMBER 20X8

	$'000
Non-current assets	360
Current assets (370 + 650)	1,020
	1,380
Equity	
$1 ordinary shares	540
Retained earnings (W2)	740
Current liabilities	100
	1,380

CONSOLIDATED INCOME STATEMENT
FOR THE YEAR ENDED 30 SEPTEMBER 20X8

	$'000
Profit before tax (153 + 126)	279
Profit on disposal (W1)	182
Tax (45 + 36)	(81)
	380

Profit attributable to:
Owners of the parent   362
Non-controlling interest (20% × 90)   18
                                                        380

Workings

1   *Profit on disposal of Jones Co*

	$'000	$'000
Fair value of consideration received		650
Less share of consolidated carrying value when control lost:		
net assets (540 × 80%)	432	
goodwill	36	
		(468)
		182

Note: goodwill

	$'000
Consideration transferred	324
Acquired: 80% × (180 + 180)	(288)
	36

2   *Retained earnings carried forward*

	$'000
Smith per question	414
Jones: 80% × (360 − 180)	144
Profit on disposal (W1)	182
	740

(b)   *Partial disposal: subsidiary to subsidiary (80% to 60%)*

CONSOLIDATED STATEMENT OF FINANCIAL POSITION AS AT 30 SEPTEMBER 20X8

	$'000
Non-current assets (360 + 270)	630
Goodwill (part (a))	36
Current assets (370 + 160 + 370)	900
	1,566

Equity

	$'000
$1 ordinary shares	540
Retained earnings (W2)	610
	1,150
Non-controlling interest (40% × 540)	216
Current liabilities (100 + 100)	200
	1,566

CONSOLIDATED INCOME STATEMENT
FOR THE YEAR ENDED 30 SEPTEMBER 20X8

	$'000	$'000
Profit before tax (153 + 126)		279
Tax (45 + 36)		(81)
Profit for the period		198
Profit attributable to:		
Owners of the parent		175.5
Non-controlling interest		
20% × 90 × 9/12	13.5	
40% × 90 × 3/12	9.0	
		22.5
		198.0

Workings

1   *Adjustment to parent's equity on disposal of 20% of Jones*

	$'000	$'000
Fair value of consideration received		160.0
Less increase in NCI in net assets at disposal		
20% × (540 − (3/12 × 90))		(103.5)
		56.5

2   *Group retained earnings*

	Smith	Jones 80%	Jones 60% retained
	$'000	$'000	$'000
At date of disposal (360 − (90 × 3/12))/per question	414.0	337.5	360.0
Adjustment to parent's equity on disposal (W1)	56.5		
Retained earnings at acquisition/on disposal		(180.0)	(337.5)
		157.5	22.5
Jones: share of post acqn. earnings (157.5 × 80%)	126.0		
Jones: share of post acqn. earnings (22.5 × 60%)	13.5		
	610.0		

(c)   (i)   *Partial disposal: subsidiary to associate (80% to 40%)*

CONSOLIDATED STATEMENT OF FINANCIAL POSITION AS AT 30 SEPTEMBER 20X8

	$'000
Non-current assets	360
Investment in associate (W3)	259
Current assets (370 + 340)	710
	1,329
Equity	
$1 ordinary shares	540
Retained earnings (W2)	689
Current liabilities	100
	1,329

CONSOLIDATED INCOME STATEMENT
FOR THE YEAR ENDED 30 SEPTEMBER 20X8

	$'000
Profit before tax (153 + 9/12 × 126)	247.5
Profit on disposal (W1)	140.0
Share of profit of associate (90 × 3/12 × 40%)	9.0
Tax 45 + (9/12 × 36)	(72.0)
Profit for the period	324.5
Profit attributable to:	
Owners of the parent	311.0
Non-controlling interest (20% × 90 × 9/12)	13.5
	324.5

Workings

1   Profit on disposal in Smith Co

	$'000	$'000
Fair value of consideration received		340
Fair value of 40% investment retained		250
Less share of consolidated carrying value when control lost		
80% × ((540 – (90 × 3/12))	414	
Goodwill (part (a))	36	
		(450)
		140

2   Group retained earnings

	Smith $'000	Jones $'000	Jones 40% retained $'000
At date of disposal (360 – (90 × 3/12))/per question	414	337.5	360.0
Group profit on disposal (W1)	140		
Retained earnings at acquisition/ on disposal		(180.0)	(337.5)
		157.5	22.5
Jones: share of post acqn. earnings (157 × 80%)	126		
Jones: share of post acqn. earnings (22.5 × 40%)	9		
	689		

3   Investment in associate

	$'000
Fair value at date control lost (new 'cost')	250
Share of post 'acq'n' retained reserves (90 × 3/12 × 40%)	9
	259

(d)   *Partial disposal: subsidiary to available-for-sale financial asset (80% to 40%)*

CONSOLIDATED STATEMENT OF FINANCIAL POSITION
AS AT 30 SEPTEMBER 20X8

	$'000
Non-current assets	360
Investment	250
Current assets (370 + 340)	710
	1,320
Equity	
$1 ordinary shares	540
Retained earnings (W)	680
Current liabilities	100
	1,320

CONSOLIDATED INCOME STATEMENT
FOR THE YEAR ENDED 30 SEPTEMBER 20X8

	$'000
Profit before tax (153 + (9/12 × 126))	247.5
Profit on disposal (See (c) above)	140.0
Tax (45 + (9/12 × 36))	(72.0)
Profit for the period	315.5
Profit attributable to:	
Owners of the parent	302.0
Non-controlling interest	13.5
	315.5

Working: retained earnings

	Smith $'000	Jones $'000
Per question/at date of disposal (360 − (90 × 3/12))	414	337.5
Group profit on disposal (W1)	140	
Retained earnings at acquisition		(180.0)
		157.5
Jones: share of post acqn. earnings (157.5 × 80%)	126	
	680	

1.9 Section summary

Disposals occur frequently in Paper 2 consolidation questions.

- The effective date of disposal is when **control passes**.
- Treatment of **goodwill** is according to IFRS 3.
- Disposals may be **full** or **partial**, to subsidiary, associate or investment status.

  – **if control is lost,** the interest retained is **fair valued** and becomes part of the calculation of the gain on disposal.

  – **if control is retained**, the change in non-controlling interests is shown as **an adjustment to parent's equity.**

- **Gain or loss** on disposal is calculated for the parent company and the group.

2 Business combinations achieved in stages

FAST FORWARD

Transactions of the type described in this chapter can be very complicated and certainly look rather daunting. Remember and apply the **basic techniques** and you should find such questions easier than you expected.

Business combinations achieved in stages (piecemeal acquisitions) can lead to a company becoming a non-current asset investment, an associate and then a subsidiary over time. Make sure you can deal with each of these situations.

A parent company may acquire a controlling interest in the shares of a subsidiary as a result of **several successive share purchases**, rather than by purchasing the shares all on the same day. Business combinations achieved in stages may also be known as 'piecemeal acquisitions'.

Point to note

Business combinations achieved in stages are in many ways a mirror image of disposals. The same principles underly both.

2.1 Types of business combination achieved in stages

There are three possible types of business combinations achieved in stages:

(a) A previously held **interest**, say 10%, with **no significant influence** (accounted for under IAS 39) is **increased to a controlling interest** of 50% or more.

(b) A **previously held equity interest**, say 35%, accounted for as an **associate** under IAS 28, is increased to a controlling interest of 50% or more.

(c) A **controlling interest** in a subsidiary is **increased**, say from 60% to 80%.

The first two transactions are treated in the same way, but the third is not. There is a reason for this.

2.2 General principle: 'crossing an accounting boundary'

Under the revised IFRS 3 a business combination occurs only when one entity **obtains control over another**, which is generally when 50% or more has been acquired. The Deloitte guide: *Business Combinations and Changes in Ownership interests* calls this '**crossing an accounting boundary**'.

When this happens, the original investment – whether an investment under IAS 39 with no significant influence, or an associate – is treated as if it were **disposed of at fair value and re-acquired at fair value**. This **previously held interest** at fair value, together with any consideration transferred, is the **'cost' of the combination** used in calculating the goodwill.

If the 50% **boundary is not crossed**, as when the interest in a subsidiary is increased, the event is treated as a **transaction between owners**.

Whenever you cross the 50% boundary, you revalue, and a gain or loss is reported in profit or loss for the year. If you do not cross the 50% boundary, no gain or loss is reported; instead there is an adjustment to the parent's equity.

The following diagram, from the *Deloitte* guide may help you visualise the boundary:

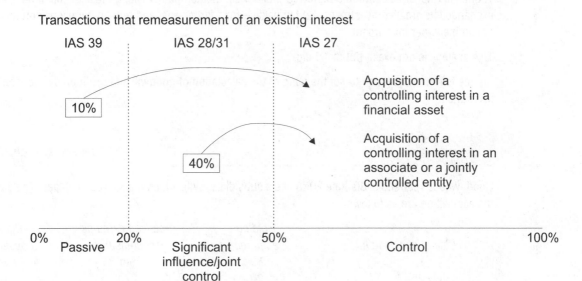

Transactions that remeasurement of an existing interest

As you will see from the diagram, the third situation in paragraph 2.1, where an interest in a subsidiary is increased from, say, 60% to 80%, does not involve crossing that all-important 50% threshold. Likewise, purchases of stakes of up to 50% do not involve crossing the boundary, and therefore do not trigger a calculation of goodwill.

Exam focus point

In an exam, if you get a question with a business combination achieved in stages, ignore all purchases made before control is achieved, that is purchases bringing the total holding to less than 50%.

2.3 Investment or associate becomes a subsidiary: calculation of goodwill

The previously held investment is re-measured to fair value, with any gain being reported in profit and loss, and the goodwill calculated as follows:

	Group	NCI
Consideration transferred/Fair value of NCI	X	X
Fair value of acquirer's previously held equity interest	X	
Less: Net fair value of identifiable assets acquired and liabilities assumed	X	
× Group/NCI %	(X)	(X)
	X	X

Note. You only need the NCI if NCI at acquisition are measured at fair value. The examiner has strongly indicated that he will not examine fair value NCI in the same question as the more difficult group topics.

2.3.1 Analogy: trading in a small car for a larger one

It may seem counter-intuitive that the previous investment is now part of the 'cost' for the purposes of calculating the goodwill. One way of looking at it is to imagine that you are part-exchanging a small car for a larger one. The value of the car you trade in is put towards the cost of the new vehicle, together with your cash (the 'consideration transferred'). Likewise, the company making the acquisition has part-exchanged its smaller investment – at fair value – for a larger one, and must naturally pay on top of that to obtain the larger investment.

This analogy is not exact, but may help.

Try the following question to get the hang of the calculation of goodwill and profit on de-recognition of the investment.

Question	Piecemeal acquisition 2

Good, whose year end is 30 June 20X9 has a subsidiary, Will, which it acquired in stages. The details of the acquisition are as follows:

Date of acquisition	Holding acquired %	Retained earnings at acquisition $m	Purchase consideration $m
1 July 20X7	20	270	120
1 July 20X8	60	450	480

The share capital of Will has remained unchanged since its incorporation at $300m. The fair values of the net assets of Will were the same as their carrying amounts at the date of the acquisition. Good did not have significant influence over Will at any time before gaining control of Will. The group policy is to measure non-controlling interest at its proportionate share of the fair value of the subsidiary's identifiable net assets.

Required

(a) Calculate the goodwill on the acquisition of Will that will appear in the consolidated statement of financial position at 30 June 20X9.

(b) Calculate the profit on the derecognition of any previously held investment in Will to be reported in group profit or loss for the year ended 30 June 20X9.

(a)   *Goodwill (at date control obtained)*

	$m	$m
Consideration transferred		480
Fair value of previously held equity interest ($480m × 20/60)		160
Fair value of identifiable assets acquired and liabilities assumed		
Share capital	300	
Retained earnings	450	
	750	
× 80%		(600)
		40

(b)   *Profit on derecognition of investment*

	$m
Fair value at date control obtained	160
Cost	(120)
	40

In this short example, the figures for goodwill and profit on derecognition are the same. In the more complicated examples, such as the one in Paragraph 2.5 below, they may different because the investment (an available for sale financial asset) may be revalued before or after control was obtained.

2.4 Increase in previously held controlling interest: adjustment to parent's equity

An example of this would be where an investment goes from a 60% subsidiary to an 80% subsidiary. The 50% threshold has not been crossed, so there is no re-measurement to fair value and no gain or loss to profit or loss for the year. The increase is treated as a **transaction between owners**. As with disposals, ownership has been **reallocated** between parent and non-controlling shareholders.

Accordingly the parent's equity is adjusted. The required adjustment is calculated by comparing the consideration paid with the decrease in non-controlling interest. (As the parent's share has increased, the NCI share has decreased.) The **calculation is as follows**:

	$
Fair value of consideration paid	(X)
Decrease in NCI in net assets at date of transaction	X
Decrease in NCI in goodwill at date of transaction *	X
Adjustment to parent's equity	(X)

*Note. This line is only required where non-controlling interests are measured at fair value at the date of acquisition (ie where there is an decrease in the non-controlling interest share of goodwill already recognised). It is included for completeness only, as the examiner has strongly indicated that he will not test fair value NCI in this context in December 2008 or June 2009.

If you are wondering why the increase in shareholding is treated as a transaction between owners, look back to Chapter 12, where we explained that the revised IFRS 3 views **the group as an economic entity,** and **views all providers of equity**, including non-controlling interests, as **owners of the group.**

You can practise this adjustment in the example below.

2.5 Comprehensive example: piecemeal acquisition of a subsidiary

Peace acquired 25% of Miel on 1 January 20X1 for $2,020,000 when Miel's reserves were standing at $5,800,000. The fair value of Miel's identifiable assets and liabilities at that date was $7,200,000. Both Peace and Miel are stock market listed entities.

At 31 December 20X1, the fair value of Peace's 25% stake in Miel was $2,440,000.

A further 35% stake in Miel was acquired on 30 September 20X2 for $4,025,000 (equivalent to the fair value of $14.375 per share acquired on that date) giving Peace control over Miel. The fair value of Miel's identifiable assets and liabilities at that date was $9,400,000, and Miel's reserves stood at $7,800,000.

For consistency with the measurement of other shares, Peace holds all investments in subsidiaries and associates as available-for-sale financial assets in its separate financial statements as permitted by IAS 27.

At 31 December 20X2, the fair value of Peace's 60% holding in Miel was $7,020,000 (and total cumulative gains recognised in other comprehensive income in Peace's separate financial statements amounted to $975,000).

Summarised statements of financial position of the two companies at that date show:

	Peace $'000	Miel $'000
Non-current assets		
Property, plant and equipment	38,650	7,600
Investment in Miel	7,020	–
	45,670	7,600
Current assets	12,700	2,200
	58,370	9,800
Equity		
Share capital	10,200	800
Reserves	40,720	7,900
	50,920	8,700
Liabilities	7,450	1,100
	58,370	9,800

The difference between the fair value of the identifiable assets and liabilities of Miel and their book value relates to the value of a plot of land. The land had not been sold by 31 December 20X2.

Income and expenses are assumed to accrue evenly over the year. Neither company paid dividends during the year.

Group policy is to measure non-controlling interests at the date of acquisition at their proportionate share of the net fair value of the identifiable assets acquired and liabilities assumed.

No impairment losses on recognised goodwill have been necessary to date.

Required

(a)   Prepare the consolidated statement of financial position of Peace Group as at 31 December 20X2 in the following circumstances:

(i)   The 25% interest in Miel allowed Peace significant influence over the financial and operating policy decisions of Miel.

(ii)   The other 75% of shares were held by a single shareholder and Peace was allowed no influence in the running of Miel until acquiring control.

(b)   Show the consolidated current assets, non-controlling interests and reserves figures if Peace acquired an *additional* 10% interest in Miel on 1 January 20X3 for $1,200,000.

Solution

Parts (a)(i) and (a)(ii) to the example would generate the same overall answer.

(a)   PEACE GROUP
      CONSOLIDATED STATEMENT OF FINANCIAL POSITION AS AT 31 DECEMBER 20X2

	$'000
Non-current assets	
Property, plant and equipment (38,650 + 7,600 + (W2) 800)	47,050
Goodwill (W2)	1,260
	48,310
Current assets (12,700 + 2,200)	14,900
	63,210
Equity attributable to owners of the parent	
Share capital	10,200
Reserves (W3)/(W4)	40,660
	50,860
Non-controlling interests (W5)	3,800
	54,660
Liabilities (7,450 + 1,100)	8,550
	63,210

Workings

1   Group structure

Part (i)

1.1.X2		30.9.X2	31.12.X2

SOCI ← Associate – Equity account × 9/12 → ← Consolidate × 3/12 →

Had 25% associate	Acquired 35% 25% + 35% = 60% Subsidiary	Consol in SOFP with 40% NCI

Part (ii)

1.1.X2		30.9.X2	31.12.X2

SOCI

← Consolidate × 3/12 →

Had 25% financial asset	Acquired 35% 25% + 35% = 60% Subsidiary	Consol in SOFP with 40% NCI

2 Goodwill

	$'000	$'000
Consideration transferred		4,025
FV of P's previously held equity interest (800,000 × 25% × $14.375)		2,875
Fair value of identifiable assets acq'd & liabilities assumed:		
Share capital	800	
Reserves	7,800	
Fair value adjustments (W6)	800	
	9,400	
× Group share 60%		(5,640)
		1,260

3 Consolidated reserves (if previously held as an associate) (i)

	Peace $'000	Miel $'000 25%	Miel $'000 60%
Per question	40,720	7,800	7,900
Profit on derecognition of investment *	355		
Fair value movement (W6)		(0)	(0)
Reserves at acquisition		(5,800)	(7,800)
		2,000	100
Share of post acquisition reserves			
Miel – 25% (2,000 × 25%)	500		
Miel – 60% (100 × 60%)	60		
Less: Fair value gain recognised in Peace's separate FS	(975)		
	40,660		

* *Profit on derecognition of 25% associate*

	$'000
Fair value at date control obtained (200,000 shares × $14.375)	2,875
P's share of carrying value [2,020 + ((7,800 – 5,800) × 25%]	(2,520)
	355

4 Consolidated reserves (if previously held as an AFSFA) (ii)

	Peace $'000	Miel $'000
Per question	40,720	7,900
Profit on derecognition of investment*	855	
Fair value movement (W6)	(0)	(0)
Reserves at acquisition		(7,800)
		100
Miel – Share of post acquisition reserves		
(100 × 60%)	60	
Less: Fair value gain recognised in Peace's separate FS	(975)	
	40,660	

* *Profit on derecognition of 25% investment*

	$'000
Fair value at date control obtained (200,000 shares × $14.375)	2,875
Cost	(2,020)
	855

Note. The profit would be the same whether the available-for-sale financial asset had been revalued or not, as any revaluation above original cost previously recognised in other comprehensive income is transferred to profit or loss.

5	Non-controlling interests	$'000	$'000
	Net assets at year end per question	8,700	
	Fair value adjustment (W6)	800	
		9,500	
	× NCI share 40%		3,800

6   Fair value adjustments

Measured at date control achieved (only)

	At acquisition 30.9.X2 $'000	Movement $'000	At year end 31.12.X2 $'000
Land (9,400 − (800 + 7,800))	800	–	800

(b)   Current assets (14,900 − 1,200)   13,700

Non-controlling interests

	$'000	$'000
Net assets at year end per question	8,700	
Fair value adjustment (W2)	800	
	9,500	
× 30%		2,850

Consolidated reserves

	$'000
Per part (a)	40,660
Adjustment to parent's equity on acq'n of 10% (W)	(250)
	40,410

Note: no other figures in the statement of financial position are affected.

Working: Adjustment to parent's equity on acquisition of additional 10% of Miel

	$'000
Fair value of consideration paid	(1,200)
Decrease in NCI in net assets at acq'n (9,500 × 10%)	950
	(250)

2.6 Comprehensive example: piecemeal acquisition of a subsidiary with non-controlling interest at fair value

So far, the examples in this chapter have been with non-controlling interest at acquisition valued at its proportionate share of the fair value of the subsidiary's net assets. This is simpler than fair value NCI, and therefore more suited to learning these complex topics initially. However, the examiner has strongly indicated that he is more likely to test fair value NCI in the exam. Accordingly, a version of the above example with fair value NCI is included below. Additionally, the questions in the question bank at the end of this Study Text have fair value NCI.

The facts are the same as in Example 2.5 above, except that group policy is to measure non-controlling interests at the date of acquisition at fair value. The fair value of the non-controlling interest at acquisition was $4,600,000.

Solution

Parts (a)(i) and (a)(ii) to the example would generate the same overall answer.

(a) PEACE GROUP
CONSOLIDATED STATEMENT OF FINANCIAL POSITION AS AT 31 DECEMBER 20X2

	$'000
Non-current assets	
Property, plant and equipment (38,650 + 7,600 + (W2) 800)	47,050
Goodwill (W2)	2,100
	49,150
Current assets (12,700 + 2,200)	14,900
	64,050
Equity attributable to owners of the parent	
Share capital	10,200
Reserves (W3)/(W4)	40,660
	50,860
Non-controlling interests (W5)	4,640
	55,500
Liabilities (7,450 + 1,100)	8,550
	64,050

Workings

1 *Group structure*

Part (i)

1.1.X2	30.9.X2	31.12.X2
SOCI		

Associate – Equity account × 9/12

Consolidate × 3/12

Had 25% associate	Acquired 35%	Consol in SOFP with 40% NCI
	25% + 35% = 60% Subsidiary	

Part (ii)

1.1.X2	30.9.X2	31.12.X2
SOCI		

Consolidate × 3/12

Had 25% financial asset	Acquired 35%	Consol in SOFP with 40% NCI
	25% + 35% = 60% Subsidiary	

2 Goodwill

	Group $'000	Group $'000	NCI $'000
Consideration transferred		4,025	
FV NCI			4,600
FV P's previously held equity interest		2,875	
Fair value of identifiable assets acq'd & liabilities assumed:			
Share capital	800		
Reserves	7,800		
Fair value adjustments (W6)	800		
	9,400		
× 60%/40%		(5,640)	(3,760)
		1,260	840

2,100

3 Consolidated reserves (if previously held as an associate) (i)

	Peace $'000	Miel $'000 25%	Miel $'000 60%
Per question	40,720	7,800	7,900
Profit on derecognition of investment *	355		
Fair value movement (W6)		(0)	(0)
Reserves at acquisition		(5,800)	(7,800)
		2,000	100
Share of post acquisition reserves			
Miel – 25% (2,000 × 25%)	500		
Miel – 60% (100 × 60%)	60		
Less: Fair value gain recognised in Peace's separate FS	(975)		
	40,660		

* Profit on derecognition of 25% associate

Fair value at date control obtained (200,000 shares × $14.375)		2,875
P's share of carrying value [2,020 + ((7,800 – 5,800) × 25%]		(2,520)
		355

4 Consolidated reserves (if previously held as an AFSFA) (ii)

	Peace $'000	Miel $'000
Per question	40,720	7,900
Profit on derecognition of investment*	855	
Fair value movement (W6)	(0)	(0)
Reserves at acquisition		(7,800)
		100
Miel - Share of post acquisition reserves		
(100 × 60%)	60	
Less: Fair value gain recognised in Peace's separate FS	(975)	
	40,660	

* Profit on derecognition of 25% investment

	$'000
Fair value at date control obtained (200,000 shares × $14.375)	2,875
Cost	(2,020)
	855

Note. The profit would be the same whether the available-for-sale financial asset had been revalued or not, as any revaluation above original cost previously recognised in other comprehensive income is transferred to profit or loss.

5 *Non-controlling interests*

	$'000	$'000
Net assets at year end per question	8,700	
Fair value adjustment (W2)	800	
	9,500	
× 40%		3,800
NCI in goodwill (W3)		840
		4,640

6 *Fair value adjustments*

Measured at date control achieved (only)

	At acquisition 30.9.X2	*Movement*	*At year end 31.12.X2*
	$'000	$'000	$'000
Land (9,400 − (800 + 7,800))	800	–	800

2.7 Section summary

Where control is **achieved in stages:**

- **Remeasure** any previously held equity interest to **fair value at the date control is achieved.**

- Report any **gain in profit or loss**

- Where a **controlling interest is increased** treat as a transaction between owners and **adjust parent's equity**

Chapter Roundup

- Transactions of the type described in this chapter can be very complicated and certainly look rather daunting. Remember and apply the basic techniques and you should find such questions easier than you expected.

- Disposals can drop a subsidiary holding to associate status, long-term investment status and to zero, or a the parent might still retain a subsidiary with a reduced holding. Once again, you should be able to deal with all these situations. Remember particularly how to deal with goodwill.

- Business combinations achieved in stages (piecemeal acquisitions) can lead to a company becoming a non-current asset investment, an associate and then a subsidiary over time. Make sure you can deal with each of these situations.

Quick Quiz

1   Control is always lost when there is a disposal? True or false?

2   Why is the fair value of the interest retained used in the calculation of a gain on disposal where control is lost?

3   When is the effective date of disposal of shares in an investment?

4   Subside owns 60% of Diary at 31 December 20X8. On 1 July 20X9, it buys a further 20% of Diary. How should this transaction be treated in the group financial statements at 31 December 20X9.

5   Ditch had a 75% subsidiary, Dodge, at 30 June 20X8. On 1 January 20X9, it sold two-thirds of this investment, leaving it with a 25% holding, over which it retained significant influence. How will the remaining investment in Dodge appear in the group financial statements for the year ended 30 June 20X9?

Answers to Quick Quiz

1   False. Control may be retained if the disposal is from subsidiary to subsidiary, even though the parent owns less and the non-controlling interest owns more.

2   It may be viewed as part of the consideration received.

3   When control passes

4   As a transaction between owners, with an adjustment to the parent's equity to reflect the difference between the consideration paid and the decrease in non-controlling interest.

5   At its fair value at the date of disposal plus a 25% share of the profits accrued between the date of disposal and the year end, less any impairment at the year end.

Now try the questions below from the Exam Question Bank

Number	Level	Marks	Time
Q17	Examination	10	18 mins
Q18	Examination	22	40 mins

Continuing and discontinued interests

Introduction

Separate analysis of discontinued operations and of non-current assets held for sale allows the user of the accounts to make more accurate assessments of a company's prospects in the future, because it excludes these items.

Study guide

		Intellectual level
C2	**Non-current assets**	
(b)	Apply and discuss the treatment of non-current assets held for sale	3
D2	**Continuing and discontinued interests**	
(a)	Prepare group financial statements where activities have been classified as discontinued or have been acquired or disposed in the period.	3
(b)	Apply and discuss the treatment of a subsidiary which has been acquired exclusively with a view to subsequent disposal.	3

Exam guide

IFRS 5 was test in December 2007.

1 IFRS 5 Non-current assets held for sale and discontinued operations
12/07

Background

FAST FORWARD

> **IFRS 5** requires assets 'held for sale' to be presented separately in the statement of financial position.
>
> The results of discontinued operations should be presented separately in the statement of comprehensive income.

IFRS 5 was the result of a short-term convergence project with the US Financial Accounting Standards Board (FASB). It replaced IAS 35 Discontinuing operations.

IFRS 5 requires assets and groups of assets that are 'held for sale' to be presented separately in the statement of financial position and the results of discontinued operations to be presented separately in the statement of comprehensive income. This is required so that users of financial statements will be better able to make projections about the financial position, profits and cash flows of the entity.

Key term

> **Disposal group**: a group of assets to be disposed of, by sale or otherwise, together as a group in a single transaction, and liabilities directly associated with those assets that will be transferred in the transaction. (In practice a disposal group could be a subsidiary, a cash-generating unit or a single operation within an entity.) (*IFRS 5*)

IFRS 5 does not apply to certain assets covered by other accounting standards:

(a) Deferred tax assets (IAS 12)

(b) Assets arising from employee benefits (IAS 19)

(c) Financial assets (IAS 39)

(d) Investment properties accounted for in accordance with the fair value model (IAS 40)

(e) Agricultural and biological assets that are measured at fair value less estimated point of sale costs (IAS 41)

(f) Insurance contracts (IFRS 4)

2 Classification of assets held for sale

A non-current asset (or disposal group) should be classified as **held for sale** if its carrying amount will be recovered **principally through a sale transaction** rather than **through continuing use**. A number of detailed criteria must be met:

(a) The asset must be **available for immediate sale** in its present condition.

(b) Its sale must be **highly probable** (ie, significantly more likely than not).

For the sale to be highly probable, the following must apply.

(a) Management must be **committed** to a plan to sell the asset.

(b) There must be an active programme to **locate a buyer.**

(c) The asset must be marketed for sale at a **price that is reasonable** in relation to its current fair value.

(d) The sale should be expected to take place **within one year** from the date of classification.

(e) It is unlikely that significant changes to the plan will be made or that the plan will be withdrawn.

An asset (or disposal group) can still be classified as held for sale, even if the sale has not actually taken place within one year. However, the delay must have been **caused by events or circumstances beyond the entity's control** and there must be sufficient evidence that the entity is still committed to sell the asset or disposal group. Otherwise the entity must cease to classify the asset as held for sale.

If an entity acquires a disposal group (eg, a subsidiary) exclusively with a view to its subsequent disposal it can classify the asset as held for sale only if the sale is expected to take place within one year and it is highly probable that all the other criteria will be met within a short time (normally three months).

An asset that is to be **abandoned** should not be classified as held for sale. This is because its carrying amount will be recovered principally through continuing use. However, a disposal group to be abandoned may meet the definition of a discontinued operation and therefore separate disclosure may be required (see below).

Question

On 1 December 20X3, a company became committed to a plan to sell a manufacturing facility and has already found a potential buyer. The company does not intend to discontinue the operations currently carried out in the facility. At 31 December 20X3 there is a backlog of uncompleted customer orders. The subsidiary will not be able to transfer the facility to the buyer until after it ceases to operate the facility and has eliminated the backlog of uncompleted customer orders. This is not expected to occur until spring 20X4.

Required

Can the manufacturing facility be classified as 'held for sale' at 31 December 20X3?

Answer

The facility will not be transferred until the backlog of orders is completed; this demonstrates that the facility is not available for immediate sale in its present condition. The facility cannot be classified as 'held for sale' at 31 December 20X3. It must be treated in the same way as other items of property, plant and equipment: it should continue to be depreciated and should not be separately disclosed.

3 Measurement of assets held for sale

Key terms

Fair value: the amount for which an asset could be exchanged, or a liability settled, between knowledgeable, willing parties in an arm's length transaction.

Costs to sell: the incremental costs directly attributable to the disposal of an asset (or disposal group), excluding finance costs and income tax expense.

Recoverable amount: the higher of an asset's fair value less costs to sell and its value in use.

Value in use: the present value of estimated future cash flows expected to arise from the continuing use of an asset and from its disposal at the end of its useful life.

A non-current asset (or disposal group) that is held for sale should be measured at the **lower of** its **carrying amount** and **fair value less costs to sell**. Fair value less costs to sell is equivalent to net realisable value.

An impairment loss should be recognised where fair value less costs to sell is lower than carrying amount. Note that this is an exception to the normal rule. IAS 36 *Impairment of assets* requires an entity to recognise an impairment loss only where an asset's recoverable amount is lower than its carrying value. Recoverable amount is defined as the higher of net realisable value and value in use. IAS 36 does not apply to assets held for sale.

Non-current assets held for sale **should not be depreciated**, even if they are still being used by the entity.

A non-current asset (or disposal group) that is **no longer classified as held for sale** (for example, because the sale has not taken place within one year) is measured at the **lower of**:

(a) Its **carrying amount** before it was classified as held for sale, adjusted for any depreciation that would have been charged had the asset not been held for sale

(b) Its **recoverable amount** at the date of the decision not to sell

4 Presenting discontinued operations

Discontinued operation: a component of an entity that has either been disposed of, or is classified as held for sale, and:

(a) Represents a separate major line of business or geographical area of operations

(b) Is part of a single co-ordinated plan to dispose of a separate major line of business or geographical area of operations, or

(c) Is a subsidiary acquired exclusively with a view to resale.

Component of an entity: operations and cash flows that can be clearly distinguished, operationally and for financial reporting purposes, from the rest of the entity.

An entity should **present and disclose information** that enables users of the financial statements to evaluate the financial effects of **discontinued operations** and disposals of non-current assets or disposal groups.

An entity should disclose a **single amount** in the **statement of comprehensive income** comprising the total of:

(a) The **post-tax profit or loss** of discontinued operations and

(b) The post-tax gain or loss recognised on the **measurement to fair value less costs to sell** or on the disposal of the assets or disposal group(s) constituting the discontinued operation.

An entity should also disclose an **analysis** of the above single amount into:

(a) The revenue, expenses and pre-tax profit or loss of discontinued operations

(b) The related income tax expense

(c) The gain or loss recognised on the measurement to fair value less costs to sell or on the disposal of the assets or the discontinued operation

(d) The related income tax expense

This may be presented either in the statement of comprehensive income or in the notes. If it is presented in the statement of comprehensive income it should be presented in a section identified as relating to discontinued operations, ie separately from continuing operations. This analysis is not required where the discontinued operation is a newly acquired subsidiary that has been classified as held for sale.

An entity should disclose the **net cash flows** attributable to the operating, investing and financing activities of discontinued operations. These disclosures may be presented either on the face of the statement of cash flows or in the notes.

Gains and losses on the remeasurement of a disposal group that is not a discontinued operation but is held for sale should be included in profit or loss from continuing operations.

4.1 Illustration

The following illustration is taken from the implementation guidance to IFRS 5. Profit for the year from discontinued operations would be analysed in the notes.

XYZ GROUP
INCOME STATEMENT
FOR THE YEAR ENDED 31 DECEMBER 20X2

	20X2	20X1
Continuing operations	$'000	$'000
Revenue	X	X
Cost of sales	(X)	(X)
Gross profit	X	X
Other income	X	X
Distribution costs	(X)	(X)
Administrative expenses	(X)	(X)
Other expenses	(X)	(X)
Finance costs	(X)	(X)
Share of profit of associates	X	X
Profit before tax	X	X
Income tax expense	(X)	(X)
Profit for the year from continuing operations	X	X
Discontinued operations		
Profit for the year from discontinued operations	X	X
Profit for the year	X	X
Period attributable to:		
Owners of the parent	X	X
Non-controlling interest	X	X
	X	X

An alternative to this presentation would be to analyse the profit from discontinued operations in a separate column in the statement of comprehensive income.

Question	Treatment of closure

On 20 October 20X3 the directors of a parent company made a public announcement of plans to close a steel works. The closure means that the group will no longer carry out this type of operation, which until recently has represented about 10% of its total turnover. The works will be gradually shut down over a period of several months, with complete closure expected in July 20X4. At 31 December output had been significantly reduced and some redundancies had already taken place. The cash flows, revenues and expenses relating to the steel works can be clearly distinguished from those of the subsidiary's other operations.

Required

How should the closure be treated in the financial statements for the year ended 31 December 20X3?

Answer

Because the steel works is being closed, rather than sold, it cannot be classified as 'held for sale'. In addition, the steel works is not a discontinued operation. Although at 31 December 20X3 the group was firmly committed to the closure, this has not yet taken place and therefore the steel works must be included in continuing operations. Information about the planned closure could be disclosed in the notes to the financial statements.

4.2 Presentation of a non-current asset or disposal group classified as held for sale

Non-current assets and disposal groups classified as held for sale should be **presented separately** from other assets in the statement of financial position. The liabilities of a disposal group should be presented separately from other liabilities in the balance sheet.

(a) Assets and liabilities held for sale **should not be offset**.

(b) The **major classes** of assets and liabilities held for sale should be **separately disclosed** either in the statement of financial position or in the notes.

4.3 Additional disclosures

In the period in which a non-current asset (or disposal group) has been either classified as held for sale or sold the following should be disclosed.

(a) A **description** of the non-current asset (or disposal group)

(b) A description of the **facts and circumstances** of the disposal

(c) Any **gain or loss** recognised when the item was classified as held for sale

(d) If applicable, the **segment** in which the non-current asset (or disposal group) is presented in accordance with IFRS 8 *Operating segments*

Where an asset previously classified as held for sale is **no longer held for sale**, the entity should disclose a description of the facts and circumstances leading to the decision and its effect on results.

Chapter Roundup

- **IFRS 5** requires assets 'held for sale' to be presented separately in the statement of financial position.

- The results of discontinued operations should be presented separately in the statement of comprehensive income.

Quick Quiz

1   For a non-current asset to be held for sale, a buyer must already have been found. True or false?

2   An asset held for sale should be measured at the lower of… and …*(Fill in the blanks.)*

Answers to Quick Quiz

1   False. There must be an **active programme** to locate a buyer.

2   The lower of **its carrying amount** and **fair value less costs to sell.**

Foreign currency transactions and entities

16

Topic list	Syllabus reference
1 Foreign currency translation	D4
2 IAS 21: Individual company stage	D4
3 IAS 21: Consolidated financial statements stage	D4
4 Hyperinflation	D4

Introduction

Many of the largest companies in any country, while based there, have subsidiaries and other interests all over the world: they are truly **global companies** and so foreign currency consolidations take place frequently in practice.

Study guide

		Intellectual level
D4	**Foreign transactions and entities**	
(a)	Outline and apply the translation of foreign currency amounts and transactions into the functional currency and the presentation currency.	3
(b)	Account for the consolidation of foreign operations and their disposal.	3
(c)	Describe the principal objectives of establishing a standard for enterprises reporting in the currency of a hyperinflationary economy.	1

Exam guide

Foreign currency consolidation questions are likely to appear frequently in Paper P2. Students have always found such questions difficult but, as with most financial accounting topics, you only need to adopt a **logical approach** and to **practice plenty of questions**.

1 Foreign currency translation

FAST FORWARD

Questions on foreign currency translation have always been popular with examiners. In general you are required to prepare **consolidated accounts** for a group which includes a foreign subsidiary.

If a company trades overseas, it will buy or sell assets in foreign currencies. For example, an Indian company might buy materials from Canada, and pay for them in US dollars, and then sell its finished goods in Germany, receiving payment in €uros, or perhaps in some other currency. If the company owes money in a foreign currency at the end of the accounting year, or holds assets which were bought in a foreign currency, those liabilities or assets must be translated into the local currency (in this text $), in order to be shown in the books of account.

A company might have a subsidiary abroad (ie a foreign entity that it owns), and the subsidiary will trade in its own local currency. The subsidiary will keep books of account and prepare its annual accounts in its own currency. However, at the year end, the holding company must 'consolidate' the results of the overseas subsidiary into its group accounts, so that somehow, the assets and liabilities and the annual profits of the subsidiary must be translated from the foreign currency into $.

If foreign currency exchange rates remained constant, there would be no accounting problem. As you will be aware, however, foreign exchange rates are continually changing, and it is not inconceivable for example, that the rate of exchange between the Polish zlotych and sterling might be Z6.2 to £1 at the start of the accounting year, and Z5.6 to £1 at the end of the year (in this example, a 10% increase in the relative strength of the zlotych).

There are two distinct types of foreign currency transaction, conversion and translation.

1.1 Conversion gains and losses

Conversion is the process of exchanging amounts of one foreign currency for another. For example, suppose a local company buys a large consignment of goods from a supplier in Germany. The order is placed on 1 May and the agreed price is €124,250. At the time of delivery the rate of foreign exchange was €3.50 to $1. The local company would record the amount owed in its books as follows.

DEBIT	Inventory account (124,250 ÷ 3.5)	$35,500	
CREDIT	Payables account		$35,500

When the local company comes to pay the supplier, it needs to obtain some foreign currency. By this time, however, if the rate of exchange has altered to €3.55 to $1, the cost of raising €124,250 would be (÷ 3.55) $35,000. The company would need to spend only $35,000 to settle a debt for inventories 'costing'

$35,500. Since it would be administratively difficult to alter the value of the inventories in the company's books of account, it is more appropriate to record a profit on conversion of $500.

DEBIT	Payables account	$35,500	
CREDIT	Cash		$35,000
CREDIT	Profit on conversion		$500

Profits (or losses) on conversion would be included in profit of loss for the year in which conversion (whether payment or receipt) takes place.

Suppose that another home company sells goods to a Chinese company, and it is agreed that payment should be made in Chinese Yuan at a price of Y116,000. We will further assume that the exchange rate at the time of sale is Y10.75 to $1, but when the debt is eventually paid, the rate has altered to Y10.8 to $1. The company would record the sale as follows.

DEBIT	Receivables account (116,000 ÷ 10.75)	$10,800	
CREDIT	Sales account		$10,800

When the Y116,000 are paid, the local company will convert them into $, to obtain (÷ 10.8) $10,750. In this example, there has been a loss on conversion of $50 which will be written off to profit of loss for the year:

DEBIT	Cash	$10,750	
DEBIT	Loss on conversion	$50	
CREDIT	Payables account		$10,800

There are **no accounting difficulties** concerned with foreign currency conversion gains or losses, and the procedures described above are uncontroversial.

1.2 Translation

Foreign currency translation, as distinct from conversion, does not involve the act of exchanging one currency for another. **Translation is required at the end of an accounting period when a company still holds assets or liabilities in its statement of financial position which were obtained or incurred in a foreign currency.**

These assets or liabilities might consist of any of the following.

(a) An individual home company holding individual **assets** or **liabilities** originating in a foreign currency 'deal'.

(b) An individual home company with a separate **branch** of the business operating abroad which keeps its own books of account in the local currency.

(c) A home company which wishes to consolidate the **results of a foreign subsidiary**.

There has been great **uncertainty** about the method which should be used to translate the following.

- Value of assets and liabilities from a foreign currency into $ for the year end statement of financial position

- Profits of an independent foreign branch or subsidiary into $ for the annual statement of comprehensive income

Suppose, for example, that a Belgian subsidiary purchases a piece of property for €2,100,000 on 31 December 20X7. The rate of exchange at this time was €70 to $1. During 20X8, the subsidiary charged depreciation on the building of €16,800, so that at 31 December 20X8, the subsidiary recorded the asset as follows.

	€
Property at cost	2,100,000
Less accumulated depreciation	16,800
Net book value	2,083,200

At this date, the rate of exchange has changed to €60 to $1.

The local holding company must translate the asset's value into $, but there is a **choice of exchange rates**.

(a) Should the rate of exchange for translation be the rate which existed at the date of purchase, which would give a net book value of 2,083,200 ÷ 70 = $29,760?

(b) Should the rate of exchange for translation be the rate existing at the end of 20X8 (the closing rate of €60 to $1)? This would give a net book value of $34,720.

Similarly, should depreciation be charged to group profit or loss at the rate of €70 to $1 (the historical rate), €60 to $1 (the closing rate), or at an average rate for the year (say, €64 to $1)?

1.3 Consolidated accounts

If a parent has a subsidiary whose accounts are presented in a foreign currency, those accounts must be translated into the local currency before they can be included in the consolidated financial statements.

- Should the subsidiary's accounts be translated as if the subsidiary is an extension of the parent?
- Or should they be translated as if the subsidiary is a separate business?

Where the affairs of a foreign operation are very closely interlinked with those of the investing company, it should be included in the consolidated financial statements as if the transactions had been entered into by the investing company in its own currency. Non-monetary assets and depreciation are translated at **historical rate** and sales, purchase and expenses at **average rate**. **Exchange differences** arising on retranslation are reported as part of **profit or loss** on ordinary activities.

Where a foreign operation is effectively a separate business, the **closing rate** is used for most items in the financial statements. **Exchange differences** are taken **directly** to **equity**.

We will look at the consolidation of foreign subsidiaries in much more detail in Section 3 of this chapter.

2 IAS 21: Individual company stage

The questions discussed above are addressed by IAS 21 *The effects of changes in foreign exchange rates.* We will examine those matters which affect single company accounts here.

2.1 Definitions

These are some of the definitions given by IAS 21.

Key terms

> **Foreign currency**. A currency other than the functional currency of the entity.
>
> **Functional currency**. The currency of the primary economic environment in which the entity operates.
>
> **Presentation currency**. The currency in which the financial statements are presented.
>
> **Exchange rate**. The ratio of exchange for two currencies.
>
> **Exchange difference**. The difference resulting from translating a given number of units of one currency into another currency at different exchange rates.
>
> **Closing rate**. The spot exchange rate at the year end date.
>
> **Spot exchange rate**. The exchange rate for immediate delivery.
>
> **Monetary items**. Units of currency held and assets and liabilities to be received or paid in a fixed or determinable number of units of currency.
>
> *(IAS 21)*

Each entity – whether an individual company, a parent of a group, or an operation within a group (such as a subsidiary, associate or branch) – should determine its **functional currency** and **measure its results and financial position in that currency**.

For most individual companies the functional currency will be the currency of the country in which they are located and in which they carry out most of their transactions. Determining the functional currency is much more likely to be an issue where an entity operates as part of a group. IAS 21 contains detailed guidance on how to determine an entity's functional currency and we will look at this in more detail in Section 3.

An entity can present its financial statements in any currency (or currencies) it chooses. IAS 21 deals with the situation in which financial statements are presented in a currency other than the functional currency.

Again, this is unlikely to be an issue for most individual companies. Their presentation currency will normally be the same as their functional currency (the currency of the country in which they operate). A company's presentation currency may be different from its functional currency if it operates within a group and we will look at this in Section 3.

2.2 Foreign currency transactions: initial recognition

IAS 21 states that a foreign currency transaction should be recorded, on initial recognition in the functional currency, by applying the exchange rate between the reporting currency and the foreign currency **at the date of the transaction** to the foreign currency amount.

An **average rate** for a period may be used if exchange rates do not fluctuate significantly.

2.3 Reporting at subsequent year ends

The following rules apply at each subsequent year end.

(a) Report foreign currency **monetary items** using the **closing rate**

(b) Report **non-monetary items** (eg non-current assets, inventories) which are carried at **historical cost** in a foreign currency using the **exchange rate at the date of the transaction** (historical rate)

(c) Report **non-monetary items** which are carried at **fair value** in a foreign currency using the exchange rates that existed **when the values were determined.**

2.4 Recognition of exchange differences

Exchange differences occur when there is a **change in the exchange rate** between the transaction date and the date of settlement of monetary items arising from a foreign currency transaction.

Exchange differences arising on the settlement of monetary items (receivables, payables, loans, cash in a foreign currency) or on translating an entity's monetary items at rates different from those at which they were translated initially, or reported in previous financial statements, should be **recognised in profit or loss** in the period in which they arise.

There are two situations to consider.

(a) The transaction is **settled in the same period** as that in which it occurred: all the exchange difference is recognised in that period.

(b) The transaction is **settled in a subsequent accounting period**: the exchange difference recognised in each intervening period up to the period of settlement is determined by the change in exchange rates during that period.

In other words, where a monetary item has not been settled at the end of a period, it should be **restated using the closing exchange rate** and any gain or loss taken to the income statement.

Question	Entries

White Cliffs Co, whose year end is 31 December, buys some goods from Rinka SA of France on 30 September. The invoice value is €40,000 and is due for settlement in equal instalments on 30 November and 31 January. The exchange rate moved as follows.

	€= $1
30 September	1.60
30 November	1.80
31 December	1.90
31 January	1.85

Required

State the accounting entries in the books of White Cliffs Co.

Answer

The purchase will be recorded in the books of White Cliffs Co using the rate of exchange ruling on 30 September.

DEBIT	Purchases	$25,000	
CREDIT	Trade payables		$25,000

Being the $ cost of goods purchased for €40,000 (€40,000 ÷ €1.60/$1)

On 30 November, White Cliffs must pay €20,000. This will cost €20,000 ÷ €1.80/$1 = $11,111 and the company has therefore made an exchange gain of $12,500 – $11,111 = $1,389.

DEBIT	Trade payables	$12,500	
CREDIT	Exchange gains: I & E account		$1,389
CREDIT	Cash		$11,111

On 31 December, the year end, the outstanding liability will be recalculated using the rate applicable to that date: €20,000 ÷ €1.90/$1 = $10,526. A further exchange gain of $1,974 has been made and will be recorded as follows.

DEBIT	Trade payables	$1,974	
CREDIT	Exchange gains: I & E account		$1,974

The total exchange gain of $3,363 will be included in the operating profit for the year ending 31 December.

On 31 January, White Cliffs must pay the second instalment of €20,000. This will cost them $10,811 (€20,000 ÷ €1.85/$1).

DEBIT	Trade payables	$10,526	
	Exchange losses: I & E account	$285	
CREDIT	Cash		$10,811

When a gain or loss on a non-monetary item is recognised **directly in equity** (for example, where property is revalued), any **related exchange differences** should also be **recognised directly in equity.**

3 IAS 21: Consolidated financial statements stage   6/08

3.1 Definitions

The following definitions are relevant here.

Key terms

Foreign operation. A subsidiary, associate, joint venture or branch of a reporting entity, the   activities of which are based or conducted in a country or currency other than those of the reporting entity.

Net investment in a foreign operation. The amount of the reporting entity's interest in the net assets of that operation.
(IAS 21)

3.2 Determining functional currency

FAST FORWARD

You may have to make the decision yourself as to whether the subsidiary has the same functional currency as the parent or a different functional currency from the parent. This determines whether the subsidiary is treated as an **extension of the parent** or as a **net investment.**

A holding or parent company with foreign operations must **translate the financial statements** of those operations into its own reporting currency before they can be consolidated into the group accounts. There are two methods: **the method used depends** upon **whether** the foreign operation has the **same functional currency as the parent**.

IAS 21 states that an entity should consider the following factors in determining its functional currency:

(a)   The currency that mainly **influences sales prices** for goods and services (often the currency in which prices are denominated and settled)

(b)   The currency of the **country whose competitive forces and regulations** mainly determine the sales prices of its goods and services

(c)   The currency that mainly **influences labour, material and other costs** of providing goods or services (often the currency in which prices are denominated and settled)

Sometimes the functional currency of an entity is not immediately obvious. Management must then exercise judgement and may also need to consider:

(a)   The currency in which **funds from financing activities** (raising loans and issuing equity) are generated

(b)   The currency in which **receipts from operating activities** are usually retained

Where a parent has a foreign operation a number of factors are considered:

(a)   Whether the activities of the foreign operation are carried out as an **extension of the parent**, rather than being carried out with a **significant degree of autonomy**.

(b)   Whether **transactions with the parent** are a high or a low proportion of the foreign operation's activities.

(c)   Whether **cash flows** from the activities of the foreign operation **directly affect the cash flows of the parent** and are readily available for remittance to it.

(d)   Whether the activities of the foreign operation are **financed from its own cash flows** or by **borrowing from the parent**.

Exam focus point

> A question involving foreign currency is almost certain, in P2, to consist of a foreign operation consolidation.

To sum up: in order to determine the functional currency of a foreign operation it is necessary to consider the **relationship** between the foreign operation and its parent:

- If the foreign operation carries out its business as though it were an **extension of the parent's operations**, it almost certainly has the **same functional currency** as the parent.

- If the foreign operation is **semi-autonomous** it almost certainly has **a different functional currency** from the parent.

The translation method used has to reflect the economic reality of the relationship between the reporting entity (the parent) and the foreign operation.

3.2.1 Same functional currency as the reporting entity

In this situation, the foreign operation normally carries on its business as though it were an **extension of the reporting entity's operations.** For example, it may only sell goods imported from, and remit the proceeds directly to, the reporting entity.

Any **movement in the exchange rate** between the reporting currency and the foreign operation's currency will have an **immediate impact** on the reporting entity's cash flows from the foreign operations. In other words, changes in the exchange rate affect the **individual monetary items** held by the foreign operation, *not* the reporting entity's net investment in that operation.

3.2.2 Different functional currency from the reporting entity

In this situation, although the reporting entity may be able to exercise control, the foreign operation normally operates in a **semi-autonomous** way. It accumulates cash and other monetary items, generates income and incurs expenses, and may also arrange borrowings, all **in its own local currency**.

A change in the exchange rate will produce **little or no direct effect on the present and future cash flows** from operations of either the foreign operation or the reporting entity. Rather, the change in exchange rate affects the reporting entity's **net investment** in the foreign operation, not the individual monetary and non-monetary items held by the foreign operation.

Exam focus point

> Where the foreign operation's functional currency is different from the parent's, the financial statements need to be translated before consolidation.

3.3 Accounting treatment: different functional currency from the reporting entity

The financial statements of the foreign operation must be translated to the functional currency of the parent. Different procedures must be followed here, because the functional currency of the parent is the **presentation currency** of the foreign operation.

(a)   The **assets and liabilities** shown in the foreign operation's statement of financial position are translated at the **closing rate** at the year end, regardless of the date on which those items originated. The balancing figure in the translated statement of financial position represents the reporting entity's net investment in the foreign operation.

(b)   Amounts in the **statement of comprehensive income** should be translated at the rate ruling at the date of the transaction (an **average rate** will usually be used for practical purposes).

(c)   **Exchange differences** arising from the re-translation at the end of each year of the parent's net investment should be **taken to equity**, not through the profit or loss for the year, until the disposal of the net investment.

3.4 Example: different functional currency from the reporting entity

A dollar-based company, Stone Co, set up a foreign subsidiary on 30 June 20X7. Stone subscribed €24,000 for share capital when the exchange rate was €2 = $1. The subsidiary, Brick Inc, borrowed €72,000 and bought a non-monetary asset for €96,000. Stone Co prepared its accounts on 31 December 20X7 and by that time the exchange rate had moved to €3 = $1. As a result of highly unusual circumstances, Brick Inc sold its asset early in 20X8 for €96,000. It repaid its loan and was liquidated. Stone's capital of €24,000 was repaid in February 20X8 when the exchange rate was €3 = $1.

Required

Account for the above transactions as if the entity has a different functional currency from the parent.

Solution

From the above it can be seen that Stone Co will record its initial investment at $12,000 which is the starting cost of its shares. The statement of financial position of Brick Inc at 31 December 20X7 is summarised below.

	€'000
Non-monetary asset	96
Share capital	24
Loan	72
	96

This may be translated as follows.

	$'000
Non-monetary asset (€3 = $1)	32
Share capital and reserves (retained earnings) (balancing figure)	8
Loan (€3 = $1)	24
	32

Exchange gain/(loss) for 20X7	(4)

The exchange gain and loss are the differences between the value of the original investment ($12,000) and the total of share capital and reserves (retained earnings) as disclosed by the above statements of financial position.

On liquidation, Stone Co will receive $8,000 (€24,000 converted at €3 = $1). No gain or loss will arise in 20X8.

3.5 Some practical points

The following points apply.

(a)   For consolidation purposes calculations are simpler if a subsidiary's share capital is translated at the **historical rate** (the rate when the investing company acquired its interest) and reserves are found as a balancing figure.

(b)   **Dividends declared** by a subsidiary should always be translated at the **closing rate** in the income statement and at the actual rate on the date of payment. This is because the investing company will record the items at these rates in its own books.

FAST FORWARD

You must be able to calculate **exchange differences**.

Practising examination questions is the best way of learning this topic.

3.6 Summary of method

A summary of the translation method is given below, which shows the main steps to follow in the consolidation process.

Exam focus point

You should learn this summary.

	Translation
Step 1	
Translate the **closing statement of financial position** (net assets/ shareholders' funds) and use this for preparing the consolidated statement of financial position in the normal way.	Use the **closing rate** at the year end for all items (see note).
Step 2	
Translate the **income statement**. (In all cases, dividends should be translated at the rate ruling when the dividend was paid or, in the case of proposed dividends, the closing rate at the year end.)	Use the **average rate** for the year for all items (but see comment on dividends). The figures obtained can then be used in preparing the consolidated income statement.
Step 3	
Translate the **shareholders' funds** (net assets) at the beginning of the year.	Use the **closing rate** at the beginning of the year (the opening rate for the current year).

	Translation
Step 4	
Calculate the **total exchange difference** for the year as follows.	This stage will be **unnecessary** unless you are asked to state the total exchange differences or are asked to prepare a statement of the movement on reserves, where the exchange difference will be shown.

	$
Closing net assets at closing rate (Step 1)	X
Less opening net Assets at opening rate (Step 3)	X
	X
Less retained profit per translated income statement (Step 2)	X
Exchange differences	X
Group share (%)	X

For **exam purposes** you can translate the closing shareholders' funds as follows.

It may be necessary to adjust for any profits or losses taken direct to reserves during the year.

(a) Share capital + pre-acquisition reserves at historical rate.

(b) Post-acquisition reserves as a balancing figure.

As mentioned above, the share capital may be translated at the historical rate. The reserves will then be the balancing figure. The advantage of this method is that it simplifies the 'cancellation' of the share capital on consolidation.

Question — Consolidated financial statements

The abridged statements of financial position and income statements of Darius Co and its foreign subsidiary, Xerxes Inc, appear below.

DRAFT STATEMENT OF FINANCIAL POSITION AS AT 31 DECEMBER 20X9

	Darius Co		Xerxes Inc	
	$	$	€	€
Assets				
Non-current assets				
Plant at cost	600		500	
Less depreciation	(250)		(200)	
		350		300
Investment in Xerxes				
100 €1 shares		25		–
		375		300
Current assets				
Inventories	225		200	
Receivables	150		100	
		375		300
		750		600
Equity and liabilities				
Equity				
Ordinary $1/€1 shares	300		100	
Retained earnings	300		280	
		600		380
Long-term loans		50		110
Current liabilities		100		110
		750		600

INCOME STATEMENTS
FOR THE YEAR ENDED 31 DECEMBER 20X9

	Darius Co	Xerxes Inc
	$	€
Profit before tax	200	160
Tax	100	80
Profit after tax, retained	100	80

The following further information is given.

(a) Darius Co has had its interest in Xerxes Inc since the incorporation of the company.

(b) Depreciation is 8% per annum on cost.

(c) There have been no loan repayments or movements in non-current assets during the year. The opening inventory of Xerxes Inc was €120. Assume that inventory turnover times are very short.

(d) Exchange rates: €4 to $1 when Xerxes Inc was incorporated
€2.5 to $1 when Xerxes Inc acquired its non-current assets
€2 to $1 on 31 December 20X8
€1.6 to $1 average rate of exchange year ending 31 December 20X9
€1 to $1 on 31 December 20X9.

Required

Prepare the summarised consolidated financial statements of Darius Co.

Answer

Step 1 The statement of financial position of Xerxes Inc at 31 December 20X9, other than share capital and retained earnings, should be translated at €1 = $1.

SUMMARISED STATEMENT OF FINANCIAL POSITION AT 31 DECEMBER 20X9

	$	$
Non-current assets (NBV)		300
Current assets		
Inventories	200	
Receivables	100	
		300
		600
Non-current liabilities		110
Current liabilities		110

∴ Equity = 600 − 110 − 110 = $380

Since Darius Co acquired the whole of the issued share capital on incorporation, the post-acquisition retained earnings including exchange differences will be the value of shareholders' funds arrived at above, less the original cost to Darius Co of $25. Post-acquisition retained earnings = $380 − $25 = $355.

SUMMARISED CONSOLIDATED STATEMENT OF FINANCIAL POSITION AS AT 31 DECEMBER 20X9

		$	$
Assets			
Non-current assets (NBV)	$(350 + 300)		650
Current assets			
Inventories	$(225 + 200)	425	
Receivables	$(150 + 100)	250	
			675
			1,325

	$	$
Equity and liabilities		
Equity		
Ordinary $1 shares (Darius only)		300
Retained earnings	$(300 + 355)	655
		955
Non-current liabilities: loans	$(50 + 110)	160
Current liabilities	$(100 + 110)	210
		1,325

Note. It is quite unnecessary to know the amount of the exchange differences when preparing the consolidated statement of financial position.

Step 2 The income statement should be translated at average rate (€1.6 = $1).

SUMMARISED INCOME STATEMENT OF XERXES INC
FOR THE YEAR ENDED 31 DECEMBER 20X9

	$
Profit before tax	100
Tax	50
Profit after tax, retained	50

SUMMARISED CONSOLIDATED INCOME STATEMENT
FOR THE YEAR ENDED 31 DECEMBER 20X9

		$
Profit before tax	$(200 + 100)	300
Tax	$(100 + 50)	150
Profit after tax, retained	$(100 + 50)	150

Step 3 The equity interest at the beginning of the year can be found as follows.

	€
Equity value at 31 December 20X9	380
Retained profit for year	80
Equity value at 31 December 20X8	300
Translated at €2 = $1, this gives	$150

Step 4 The exchange difference can now be calculated.

	$
Equity interest at 31 December 20X9 (stage 1)	380
Equity interest at 1 January 20X9 (stage 3)	150
	230
Less retained profit (stage 2)	50
Exchange gain	180

CONSOLIDATED STATEMENT OF MOVEMENTS ON RESERVES
FOR THE YEAR ENDED 31 DECEMBER 20X9

	$
Consolidated reserves at 31 December 20X8	325
Exchange gains arising on consolidation	180
Retained profit for the year	150
Consolidated reserves at 31 December 20X9	655

(*Note.* The post-acquisition reserves of Xerxes Inc at the beginning of the year must have been $150 – $25 = $125 and the reserves of Darius Co must have been $300 – $100 = $200. The consolidated reserves must therefore have been $325.)

3.7 Analysis of exchange differences

The exchange differences in the above exercise could be reconciled by splitting them into their component parts.

Exam focus point

> Such a split is not required by IAS 21, nor is it required in your exam, but it may help your understanding of the subject.

The exchange difference consists of those exchange gains/losses arising from:

- Translating **income/expense items** at the exchange rates at the date of transactions, whereas **assets/liabilities** are translated at the closing rate.
- Translating the **opening net investment** (opening net assets) in the foreign entity at a closing rate different from the closing rate at which it was previously reported.

This can be demonstrated using the above question.

Using the opening statement of financial position and translating at €2 = $1 and €1 = $1 gives the following.

	€2 = $1 $	€1 = $1 $	Difference $
Non-current assets at NBV	170	340	170
Inventories	60	120	60
Net current monetary liabilities	(25)	(50)	(25)
	205	410	205
Equity	150	300	150
Loans	55	110	55
	205	410	205

Translating the income statement using €1.60 = $1 and €1 = $1 gives the following results.

	€1.60 = $1 $	€1 = $1 $	Difference $
Profit before tax, depreciation and increase in inventory values	75	120	45
Increase in inventory values	50	80	30
	125	200	75
Depreciation	(25)	(40)	(15)
	100	160	60
Tax	(50)	(80)	(30)
Profit after tax, retained	50	80	30

The overall position is then:

	$	$
Gain on non-current assets ($170 – $15)		155
Loss on loan		(55)
Gain on inventories ($60 + $30)	90	
Loss on net monetary current assets/ Liabilities (all other differences) ($45 – $30 – $25)	(10)	
		80
Net exchange gain: as above		180

3.8 Further matters relating to foreign operations

3.8.1 Goodwill and fair value adjustments

Goodwill and fair value adjustments arising on the acquisition of a foreign operation should be treated as assets and liabilities of the acquired entity. This means that they should be expressed in the functional currency of the foreign operation and translated at the **closing rate**.

Here is a layout for calculating goodwill and the exchange gain or loss. The parent holds 90% of the shares. NCI is valued as the proportionate share of the fair value of the subsidiary's as identifiable net assets.

Goodwill

	F'000	F'000	*Rate*	$'000
Consideration transferred (12,000 × 6)		72,000		
Non-controlling interest		6,600		
66,000 × 10%		78,600		
Less:				
Less share capital	40,000			
Pre acquisition retained earnings	26,000			
		(66,000)		
At 1.4.X1		12,600	6**	2,100
Foreign exchange gain		–	Balance	420
At 31.3.X7		12,600	5***	2,520

*   Percentage controlled by parent
**   Historic rate
*** Closing rate

3.8.2 Consolidation procedures

Follow normal consolidation procedures, except that where an exchange difference arises on **long– or short-term intra-group monetary items**, these cannot be offset against other intra-group balances. This is because these are commitments to convert one currency into another, thus exposing the reporting entity to a gain or loss through currency fluctuations.

If the foreign operation's **reporting date** is different from that of the parent, it is acceptable to use the accounts made up to that date for consolidation, as long as adjustments are made for any significant changes in rates in the interim.

3.8.3 Hyperinflationary economies

We will look at IAS 29 *Financial reporting in hyperinflationary economies* in Section 4. The financial statements of a foreign operation operating in a hyperinflationary economy must be adjusted under IAS 29 before they are translated into the parent's reporting currency and then consolidated. When the economy **ceases to be hyperinflationary**, and the foreign operation ceases to apply IAS 29, the amounts restated to the price level at the date the entity ceased to restate its financial statements should be used as the historical costs for translation purposes.

3.8.4 Disposal of foreign entity

When a parent disposes of a foreign entity, the cumulative amount of deemed exchange differences relating to that foreign entity should be **recognised as an income or expense** in the same period in which the gain or loss on disposal is recognised. Effectively, this means that these exchange differences are recognised once by taking them to reserves and then are recognised for a second time ('recycled') by transferring them to the income statement on disposal of the foreign operation.

3.8.5 In the parent's accounts

In the parent company's own accounts, exchange differences arising on a **monetary item** that is effectively part of the parent's net investment in the foreign entity should be recognised **in profit or loss** in the separate financial statements of the reporting entity or the individual financial statements of the foreign operation, as appropriate.

3.9 Change in functional currency

The functional currency of an entity can be changed only if there is a change to the underlying transactions, events and conditions that are relevant to the entity. For example, an entity's functional currency may change if there is a change in the currency that mainly influences the sales price of goods and services.

Where there is a change in an entity's functional currency, the entity translates all items into the new functional currency **prospectively** (ie, from the date of the change) using the exchange rate at the date of the change.

3.10 Tax effects of exchange differences

IAS 12 *Income taxes* should be applied when there are tax effects arising from gains or losses on foreign currency transactions and exchange differences arising on the translation of the financial statements of foreign operations.

3.11 Foreign associated undertakings

Foreign associates will be companies with substantial autonomy from the group and so their **functional currency will be different** from that of the parent.

3.12 Section summary

- Where the functional currency of a foreign operation is **different** from that of the parent/reporting entity, they need to be translated before consolidation

  - Operation is semi-autonomous
  - Translate assets and liabilities at **closing rate**
  - Translate income statement at **average rate**
  - Exchange differences through **reserves/equity**

4 Hyperinflation

IAS 29 requires financial statements of entities operating within a hyperinflationary economy to be restated in terms of measuring units current at the year end.

In a hyperinflationary economy, **money loses its purchasing power very quickly**. Comparisons of transactions at different points in time, even within the same accounting period, are misleading. It is therefore considered inappropriate for entities to prepare financial statements without making adjustments for the **fall in the purchasing power of money over time**.

IAS 29 *Financial reporting in hyperinflationary economies* applies to the **primary financial statements** of entities (including consolidated accounts and statements of cash flows) whose functional currency is the currency of a hyperinflationary economy. In this section, we will identify the hyperinflationary currency as $H.

The standard does not define a **hyperinflationary economy** in exact terms, although it indicates the characteristics of such an economy, for example, where the cumulative inflation rate over three years approaches or exceeds 100%.

Question

What other factors might indicate a hyperinflationary economy?

Answer

These are examples, but the list is not exhaustive.

(a)   The population prefers to retain its wealth in non-monetary assets or in a relatively stable foreign currency. Amounts of local currency held are immediately invested to maintain purchasing power.

(b)   The population regards monetary amounts not in terms of the local currency but in terms of a relatively stable foreign currency. Prices may be quoted in that currency.

(c)   Sales/purchases on credit take place at prices that compensate for the expected loss of purchasing power during the credit period, if that period is short.

(d)   Interest rates, wages and prices are linked to a price index.

The reported value of **non-monetary assets**, in terms of current measuring units, increases over time. For example, if a fixed asset is purchased for $H1,000 when the price index is 100, and the price index subsequently rises to 200, the value of the asset in terms of current measuring units (ignoring accumulated depreciation) will rise to $H2,000.

In contrast, the value of **monetary assets and liabilities**, such as a debt for 300 units, is unaffected by changes in the prices index, because it is an actual money amount payable or receivable. If a debtor owes $H300 when the price index is 100, and the debt is still unpaid when the price index has risen to 150, the debtor still owes just $H300. The purchasing power of monetary assets, however, will decline over time as the general level of prices goes up.

4.1 Requirement to restate financial statements in terms of measuring units current at the year end

In most countries, financial statements are produced on the basis of either:

(a)   **historical cost**, except to the extent that some assets (eg property and investments) may be revalued, or

(b)   **current cost**, which reflects the changes in the values of specific assets held by the entity.

In a hyperinflationary economy, neither of these methods of financial reporting are meaningful unless adjustments are made for the fall in the purchasing power of money. IAS 29 therefore requires that the **primary financial statements** of entities in a hyperinflationary economy should be produced by restating the figures prepared on either a historical cost basis or a current cost basis in terms of **measuring units current at the year end**.

Key term

> **Measuring unit current at the year end date**. This is a unit of local currency with a purchasing power as at the date of the statement of financial position, in terms of a general prices index.

Financial statements that are not restated (ie that are prepared on a historical cost basis or current cost basis without adjustments) may be presented as **additional statements** by the entity, but this is discouraged. The primary financial statements are those that have been restated.

After the assets, liabilities, equity and statement of comprehensive income of the entity have been restated, there will be a **net gain or loss on monetary assets and liabilities (the 'net monetary position')** and this should be recognised separately in profit or loss for the period.

4.2 Making the adjustments

IAS 29 recognises that the resulting financial statements, after restating all items in terms of measuring units current at the year end, will **lack precise accuracy**. However, it is more important that certain procedures and judgements should be applied consistently from year to year. The implementation guidelines to the Standard suggest what these procedures should be.

4.3 Statement of financial position: historical cost

Where the entity produces its accounts on a historical cost basis, the following procedures should be applied.

(a)   Items that are not already expressed in terms of measuring units current at the year end should be restated, using a **general prices index**, so that they are valued in measuring units current at the year end.

(b)   **Monetary assets and liabilities** are not restated, because they are already expressed in terms of measuring units current at the year end.

(c)   Assets that are **already stated at market value or net realisable value** need not be restated, because they too are already valued in measuring units current at the year end.

(d)   Any assets or liabilities **linked by agreement to changes in the general level of prices**, such as indexed-linked loans or bonds, should be adjusted in accordance with the terms of the agreement to establish the amount outstanding as at the year end.

(e)   All **other non-monetary assets**, ie tangible long-term assets, intangible long-term assets (including accumulated depreciation/amortisation) investments and inventories, should be restated in terms of measuring units as at the year end, by applying a general prices index.

The **method of restating** these assets should normally be to multiply the original cost of the assets by a factor: [prices index at year end /prices index at date of acquisition of the asset]. For example, if an item of machinery was purchased for $H2,000 units when the prices index was 400 and the prices index at the year end is 1,000, the restated value of the long-term asset (before accumulated depreciation) would be:

$$\$H2,000 \times [1,000/400] = \$H5,000$$

If, in the above example, the non current asset has been held for half its useful life and has no residual value, the **accumulated depreciation** would be restated as $H2,500. (The depreciation charge for the year should be the amount of depreciation based on historical cost, multiplied by the same factor as above: 1,000/400.)

If an asset has been **revalued** since it was originally purchased (eg a property), it should be restated in measuring units at the year end date by applying a factor: (prices index at year end/prices index at revaluation date) to the revalued amount of the asset.

If the restated amount of a non-monetary asset **exceeds its recoverable value** (ie its net realisable value or market value), its value should be reduced accordingly.

The **owners' equity** (all components) as at the start of the accounting period should be restated using a general prices index from the beginning of the period.

4.4 Statement of comprehensive income: historical cost

In the statement of comprehensive income, all amounts of income and expense should be **restated in terms of measuring units current at the year end**. All amounts therefore need to be restated by a factor that allows for the change in the prices index since the item of income or expense was first recorded.

4.5 Gain or loss on net monetary position

In a period of inflation, an entity that holds monetary assets (cash, receivables) will suffer a fall in the purchasing power of these assets. By the same token, in a period of inflation, the value of monetary liabilities, such as a bank overdraft or bank loan, declines in terms of current purchasing power.

(a)   If an entity has an **excess of monetary assets over monetary liabilities**, it will suffer a loss over time on its net monetary position, in a period of inflation, in terms of measuring units as at 'today's date'.

(b)   If an entity has an **excess of monetary liabilities over monetary assets**, it will make a gain on its net monetary position, in a period of inflation.

4.6 Example: Hyperinflationary accounts

An entity maintains an unchanged position over time. At 1 January, when the general prices index was 100, its statement of financial position was as follows.

	$H
Assets	
Non-monetary assets	2,000
Monetary assets	2,000
	4,000
Liabilities and equity	
Monetary liabilities	1,000
Equity	3,000
	4,000

Suppose that the general prices index rises to 150 at 31 December.

Required

Show the adjustments required in the statement of financial position.

Solution

Restating this statement of financial position in terms of measuring units when the prices index is 50% higher gives the following.

	$H
Assets	
Non-monetary assets ($\times$ 150/100)	3,000
Monetary assets	2,000
	5,000
Liabilities and equity	
Monetary liabilities	1,000
Equity ($\times$ 150/100)	4,500
	5,500

The entity has suffered a loss on its net monetary position of $H500, in terms of measuring units at the current date $H(5,500 – 5,000). This is because it has held net monetary assets of $H1,000 during the period.

In the financial statements of an entity reporting in the currency of a hyperinflationary economy, the gain or loss on the net monetary position:

(a)   may be derived as the **difference between total assets and total equity and liabilities**, after restating the non-monetary assets, owners' equity, statement of comprehensive income items and index-linked items, *or*

(b)   may be estimated by **applying the change in the general prices index** for the period to the weighted average of the net monetary position of the entity in the period.

The gain or loss on the net monetary position should be **included in net income** and disclosed separately. (Any adjustment that was made to index-linked items can be set off against this net monetary gain or loss.)

4.7 Current cost accounts: restating the accounts

A similar procedure is required to restate the accounts of an entity that prepares its accounts using a current cost basis.

(a) Items stated in the statement of financial position at current cost do not need to be restated. Other items should be restated in the same way as for adjusting accounts prepared on a historical cost basis.

(b) In the **statement of comprehensive income**, cost of sales and depreciation are generally reported at current costs at the time of consumption and sales and other expenses at money amounts at the time they occurred. These items will need to be restated in terms of measuring units as at the year end by making a prices index adjustment.

(c) There will be a **gain or loss on the net monetary position**, which will be established in the same way as for accounts based on historical cost.

4.8 Economies ceasing to be hyperinflation economies

When an economy ceases to be a hyperinflation economy, entities reporting in the currency of the economy are no longer required to produce financial statements in compliance with IAS 29.

Suppose for example that in 20X4 an entity reports in compliance with IAS 29, but in 20X5 it reverts to historical cost accounting because the economy is no longer a hyperinflation economy. As a starting point for reverting to historical cost accounts reporting, the entity should use the amounts expressed in terms of measuring units as at the end of 20X4 as the basis for its carrying amounts in 20X5 and subsequent years.

4.9 Disclosures

IAS 29 calls for the following disclosures.

*   The fact that the **financial statements have been restated** for the changes in general purchasing power.
*   Whether the financial statements as shown are based on **historical cost or current cost**.
*   The **identity of the prices index** used to make the restatements, its level at the year end the movement in the index during the current and the previous reporting periods.

In financial statements prepared under IAS 29, corresponding figures for the previous year should be **restated using the general prices index**.

4.10 Hyper-inflation and changes in foreign exchange rates

IAS 21 *The effects of changes in foreign exchange rates* was covered in an earlier chapter. A parent may have a foreign operation whose functional currency is the currency of a hyperinflationary economy. When the parent prepares consolidated financial statements it should:

(a) **restate the financial statements** of the foreign operation in accordance with IAS 29; **before**

(b) **translating all amounts** from the foreign operation's functional currency to the presentation currency **at the closing rate**.

The following example is a simple illustration of the problems that can arise where a foreign subsidiary operates in a hyper-inflationary economy.

4.11 Example: 'Disappearing assets'

A company has a subsidiary in a country which suffers from hyper-inflation. On 31 December 20X2 the subsidiary acquired freehold land for $H1,000,000. At that date the exchange rate was $H4 = $1 and the relevant price index was 100.

At 31 December 20X3 the exchange rate was $H10 = $1 and the price index was 300.

Required:

Show the value at which the freehold land is included in the consolidated financial statements of the parent at 31 December 20X3 if the subsidiary's financial statements:

(a)   are not restated to reflect current price levels;
(b)   are restated to reflect current price levels.

Solution

(a)   Without restatement

Assuming that the subsidiary has a different functional currency ($H) from that of its parent ($) the statement of financial position is translated at the closing rate.

At 31 December 20X3 the land is included at $100,000 ($H1,000,000 @ 10).

At 31 December 20X2 (the date of purchase) its was stated at $250,000 ($H1,000,000 @ 4). Therefore there has been an exchange loss of $150,000 (which may significantly reduce equity) and the land appears to have fallen to only 40% of its original value.

(b)   With restatement

At 31 December 20X3 the land is included at $300,000 ($H1,000,000 × 300/100 @ 10).

The value of the land is now adjusted so that it reflects the effect of inflation over the year and the 'disappearing assets' problem is overcome.

Where the financial statements of an entity whose functional currency is that of a hyperinflationary economy are translated into a different presentation currency, **comparative amounts** should be those that were presented as current year amounts in the relevant prior year financial statements (ie, **not adjusted** for subsequent changes in the price level or subsequent changes in exchange rates).

4.12 IFRIC 7 Applying the restatement approach under IAS 29 Financial reporting in hyperinflationary economies

4.12.1 The issue

IAS 29 *Financial reporting in hyperinflationary economies* requires that the financial statements of an entity that reports in the currency of a hyperinflationary economy should be **stated in terms of the measuring unit current at the year end.** Comparative figures for prior period(s) should be restated into the same current measuring unit. **IFRIC 7 contains guidance** on how an entity would restate its financial statements in the first year it identifies the existence of hyperinflation in the economy of its functional currency.

The restatement approach on which IAS 29 is based distinguishes between monetary and non-monetary items. However, in practice there has been uncertainty about how an entity goes about restating its financial statements for the first time, especially deferred tax balances and comparatives.

4.12.2 IFRIC 7 requirements

The main requirements of the IFRIC 7 are:

(a)   In the period in which the economy of an entity's functional currency becomes hyperinflationary, the entity must **apply** the requirements of **IAS 29 as though the economy had always been hyperinflationary.** The effect of this requirement is that restatements of non-monetary items carried at historical cost are made from the dates at which those items were first recognised; for other non-monetary items the restatements are made from the dates at which revised current values for those items were established.

(b) **Deferred tax amounts** in the opening balance sheet are determined in two stages:

(i) Deferred tax items are **remeasured** in accordance with IAS 12 after restating the nominal carrying amounts of the non-monetary items in the opening balance sheet by applying the measuring unit at that date.

(ii) The deferred tax items remeasured in this way are restated for the change in the measuring unit from the date of the opening balance sheet to the date of the closing balance sheet.

4.13 Section summary

- IAS 29 does not define **hyperinflationary economies**, but they have various characteristics

- Financial statements should be **restated based on a measuring unit current** at the year end

  - **Monetary assets/liabilities** do not need to be restated
  - **Non-monetary assets/liabilities** must be restated by applying a general prices index
  - **Items of income/expense** must be restated
  - **Gain/loss on net monetary items** must be reported in profit or loss for the year

Chapter Roundup

- Questions on foreign currency translation have always been popular with examiners. In general you are required to prepare **consolidated accounts** for a group which includes a foreign subsidiary.

- You may have to make the decision yourself as to whether the subsidiary has the same functional currency as the parent or a different functional currency from the parent. This determines whether the subsidiary is treated as an **extension of the parent** or as a **net investment**.

- **Practising** examination questions is the best way of learning this topic.

- **IAS 29** requires financial statements of entities operating within a hyperinflationary economy to be restated in terms of measuring units current at the year end.

Quick Quiz

1 What is the difference between conversion and translation?

2 Define 'monetary' items according to IAS 21.

3 How should foreign currency transactions be recognised initially in an individual enterprise's accounts?

4 What factors must management take into account when determining the functional currency of a foreign operation?

5 How should goodwill and fair value adjustments be treated on consolidation of a foreign operation?

6 When can an entity's functional currency be changed?

Answers to Quick Quiz

1   (a)   Conversion is the process of exchanging one currency for another.
    (b)   Translation is the restatement of the value of one currency in another currency.

2   Money held and assets and liabilities to be received or paid in fixed or determinable amounts of money.

3   Use the exchange rate at the date of the transaction. An average rate for a period can be used if the exchange rates did not fluctuate significantly.

4   See Section 3.2

5   Treat as assets/liabilities of the foreign operation and translate at the closing rate.

6   Only if there is a change to the underlying transactions relevant to the entity.

Now try the question below from the Exam Question Bank

Number	Level	Marks	Time
Q19	Examination	18	36 mins

17

Group statements of cash flows

Topic list	Syllabus reference
1 Cash flows and funds flows	D1
2 IAS 7 Statement of cash flows: single company	D1
3 Consolidated statements of cash flows	D1

Introduction

A statement of cash flows is an additional primary statement of **great value** to users of financial statements for the extra information it provides.

You should be familiar with the basic principles, techniques and definitions relating to statements of cash flows from your earlier studies. This chapter develops the principles and preparation techniques to include **consolidated financial statements**.

Study guide

		Intellectual level
D1	**Group accounting including statements of cash flows**	
(h)	Prepare and discuss group statements of cash flows.	3

Exam guide

A group statement of cash flows could well appear in the case study question in compulsory Section A of the paper as it did in the Pilot Paper.

1 Cash flows and funds flows

Statements of cash flows are a useful addition to the financial statements of companies because it is recognised that accounting profit is not the only indicator of a company's performance.

Statements of cash flows concentrate on the sources and uses of cash and are a useful indicator of a company's **liquidity and solvency**.

1.1 Funds flows

'Funds statements' have been used in the past and are still used in some countries. They are generally deficient in that they often do not specify the 'focus' of the statement, ie the **definition of funds** to be adopted by the reporting entity. Some companies will report movements in net liquid funds, some in working capital, some in net borrowings and some in total external financing. This means that a whole range of different funds flow statements might be given in company accounts.

In spite of this problem, some standards on funds flow require that the 'all financial resources' approach should be adopted in presentation. This means that the definition of funds adopted by the company is effectively ignored as **all movements in financial resources** have to be shown, whether they affect the 'funds' or not. For example, if a company adopted a working capital definition of funds, it would still have to show a conversion of shares into debt (say) in the statement, even though this has no impact on working capital 'funds'.

The overall effect of such an approach is a **lack of uniformity and definition**, the result of which is often a simple mathematical exercise comparing opening and closing statement of financial position. It is also perceived as relatively meaningless to most users.

1.2 Cash flows: advantages

Cash flows are much easier to understand as a concept. The main advantages of using cash flow accounting (including both historical and forecast cash flows) are as follows.

(a)   **Survival** of a company depends on its ability to generate cash. Cash flow accounting directs attention towards this critical issue.

(b)   Cash flow is more **comprehensive** than 'profit' which is dependent on accounting conventions and concepts.

(c)   Creditors (long– and short-term) are more interested in an entity's **ability to repay** them than in its profitability. Whereas 'profits' might indicate that cash is likely to be available, cash flow accounting is more direct with its message.

(d)   Cash flow reporting provides a better means of **comparing** the results of different companies than traditional profit reporting.

(e)   Cash flow reporting satisfies the **needs of all users** better.

(i) For **management**. It provides the sort of information on which decisions should be taken (in management accounting, 'relevant costs' to a decision are future cash flows). Traditional profit accounting does not help with decision-making.

(ii) For **shareholders and auditors**. Cash flow accounting can provide a satisfactory basis for stewardship accounting.

(iii) For **creditors and employees**. Their information needs will be better served by cash flow accounting.

(f) **Cash flow forecasts** are easier to prepare, as well as more useful, than profit forecasts.

(g) Cash flow accounts can be **audited more easily** than accounts based on the accruals concept.

(h) The accruals concept is confusing, and cash flows are more **easily understood**.

(i) Cash flow accounting can be both **retrospective**, and also include a **forecast** for the future. This is of great information value to all users of accounting information.

(j) Forecasts can subsequently be monitored by the use of **variance statements** which compare actual cash flows against the forecast.

Looking at the same question from a different angle, readers of accounts can be **misled** by the profit figure.

(a) Shareholders might believe that if a company makes a profit after tax of, say $100,000 then this is the amount which it could afford to pay as a **dividend**. Unless the company has sufficient cash available to stay in business and also to pay a dividend, the shareholders' expectations would be wrong.

(b) Employees might believe that if a company makes profits, it can afford to pay **higher wages** next year. This opinion may not be correct: the ability to pay wages depends on the availability of cash.

(c) Creditors might consider that a profitable company is a **going concern**.

(i) If a company builds up large amounts of **unsold inventories** of goods, their cost would not be chargeable against profits, but cash would have been used up in making them, thus weakening the company's liquid resources.

(ii) A company might capitalise large **development costs**, having spent considerable amounts of money on R & D, but only charge small amounts against current profits. As a result, the company might show reasonable profits, but get into severe difficulties with its liquidity position.

(d) Management might suppose that if their company makes a historical cost profit, and reinvests some of those profits, then the company must be **expanding**. This is not the case: in a period of inflation, a company might have a historical cost profit but a current cost accounting loss, which means that the operating capability of the firm will be declining.

(e) **Survival** of a business entity depends not so much on profits as on its ability to pay its debts when they fall due. Such payments might include 'P&L' items such as material purchases, wages, interest and taxation etc, but also capital payments for new fixed assets and the repayment of loan capital when this falls due (eg on the redemption of debentures).

2 IAS 7 Statement of cash flows: single company

FAST FORWARD

You need to be aware of the **format** of the statement as laid out in **IAS 7**. Setting out the format is an essential first stage in preparing the statement, so this format must be learnt.

The aim of IAS 7 is to provide information to users of financial statements about the cash flows of an entity's **ability to generate cash and cash equivalents**, as well as indicating the cash needs of the entity. The statement of cash flows provides *historical* information about cash and cash equivalents, classifying cash flows between operating, investing and financing activities.

2.1 Scope

A statement of cash flows should be presented as an **integral part** of an entity's financial statements. All types of entity can provide useful information about cash flows as the need for cash is universal, whatever the nature of their revenue-producing activities. Therefore **all entities are required by the standard to produce a statement of cash flows.**

2.2 Benefits of cash flow information

The use of statements of cash flows is very much **in conjunction** with the rest of the financial statements. Users can gain further appreciation of the change in net assets, of the entity's financial position (liquidity and solvency) and the entity's ability to adapt to changing circumstances by affecting the amount and timing of cash flows. Statements of cash flows **enhance comparability** as they are not affected by differing accounting policies used for the same type of transactions or events.

Cash flow information of a historical nature can be used as an indicator of the amount, timing and certainty of future cash flows. Past forecast cash flow information can be **checked for accuracy** as actual figures emerge. The relationship between profit and cash flows can be analysed as can changes in prices over time.

2.3 Definitions

The standard gives the following definitions, the most important of which are **cash** and **cash equivalents**.

Key terms

> **Cash** comprises cash on hand and demand deposits.
>
> **Cash equivalents** are short-term, highly liquid investments that are readily convertible to known amounts of cash and which are subject to an insignificant risk of changes in value.
>
> **Cash flows** are inflows and outflows of cash and cash equivalents.
>
> **Operating activities** are the principal revenue-producing activities of the entity and other activities that are not investing or financing activities.
>
> **Investing activities** are the acquisition and disposal of long-term assets and other investments not included in cash equivalents.
>
> **Financing activities** are activities that result in changes in the size and composition of the equity capital and borrowings of the entity.
>
> *(IAS 7)*

2.4 Cash and cash equivalents

The standard expands on the definition of cash equivalents: they are not held for investment or other long-term purposes, but rather to meet short-term cash commitments. To fulfil the above definition, an investment's **maturity date should normally be three months from its acquisition date**. It would usually be the case then that equity investments (ie shares in other companies) are *not* cash equivalents. An exception would be where preferred shares were acquired with a very close maturity date.

Loans and other borrowings from banks are classified as investing activities. In some countries, however, **bank overdrafts** are repayable on demand and are treated as part of an entity's total cash management system. In these circumstances an overdrawn balance will be included in cash and cash equivalents. Such banking arrangements are characterised by a balance which fluctuates between overdrawn and credit.

Movements between different types of cash and cash equivalent are not included in cash flows. The investment of surplus cash in cash equivalents is part of cash management, not part of operating, investing or financing activities.

2.5 Presentation of a statement of cash flows

IAS 7 requires statements of cash flows to report cash flows during the period classified by **operating, investing and financing activities.**

The manner of presentation of cash flows from operating, investing and financing activities **depends on the nature of the entity**. By classifying cash flows between different activities in this way users can see the impact on cash and cash equivalents of each one, and their relationships with each other. We can look at each in more detail.

2.5.1 Operating activities

This is perhaps the key part of the statement of cash flows because it shows whether, and to what extent, companies can **generate cash from their operations**. It is these operating cash flows which must, in the end pay for all cash outflows relating to other activities, ie paying loan interest, dividends and so on.

Most of the components of cash flows from operating activities will be those items which **determine the net profit or loss of the entity**, ie they relate to the main revenue-producing activities of the entity. The standard gives the following as examples of cash flows from operating activities.

- Cash receipts from the sale of goods and the rendering of services
- Cash receipts from royalties, fees, commissions and other revenue
- Cash payments to suppliers for goods and services
- Cash payments to and on behalf of employees
- Cash payments/refunds of income taxes unless they can be specifically identified with financing or investing activities
- Cash receipts and payments from contracts held for dealing or trading purposes

Certain items may be included in the net profit or loss for the period which do *not* relate to operational cash flows, for example the profit or loss on the sale of a piece of plant will be included in net profit or loss, but the cash flows will be classed as **financing**.

2.5.2 Investing activities

The cash flows classified under this heading show the extent of new investment in **assets which will generate future profit and cash flows**. The standard gives the following examples of cash flows arising from investing activities.

- Cash payments to acquire property, plant and equipment, intangibles and other long-term assets, including those relating to capitalised development costs and self-constructed property, plant and equipment
- Cash receipts from sales of property, plant and equipment, intangibles and other long-term assets
- Cash payments to acquire shares or debentures of other entities
- Cash receipts from sales of shares or debentures of other entities
- Cash advances and loans made to other parties
- Cash receipts from the repayment of advances and loans made to other parties
- Cash payments for or receipts from futures/forward/option/swap contracts except where the contracts are held for dealing purposes, or the payments/receipts are classified as financing activities

2.5.3 Financing activities

This section of the statement of cash flows shows the share of cash which the entity's capital providers have claimed during the period. This is an indicator of **likely future interest and dividend payments**. The standard gives the following examples of cash flows which might arise under these headings.

- Cash proceeds from issuing shares
- Cash payments to owners to acquire or redeem the entity's shares

- Cash proceeds from issuing debentures, loans, notes, bonds, mortgages and other short or long-term borrowings
- Cash repayments of amounts borrowed
- Cash payments by a lessee for the reduction of the outstanding liability relating to a finance lease

2.6 Reporting cash flows from operating activities

The standard offers a choice of method for this part of the statement of cash flows.

(a) **Direct method:** disclose major classes of gross cash receipts and gross cash payments

(b) **Indirect method:** net profit or loss is adjusted for the effects of transactions of a non-cash nature, any deferrals or accruals of past or future operating cash receipts or payments, and items of income or expense associated with investing or financing cash flows

The **direct method is the preferred method** because it discloses information, not available elsewhere in the financial statements, which could be of use in estimating future cash flows. The example below shows both methods.

2.6.1 Using the direct method

There are different ways in which the **information about gross cash receipts and payments** can be obtained. The most obvious way is simply to extract the information from the accounting records. This may be a laborious task, however, and the indirect method below may be easier.

2.6.2 Using the indirect method

This method is undoubtedly **easier** from the point of view of the preparer of the statement of cash flows. The net profit or loss for the period is adjusted for the following.

(a) Changes during the period in inventories, operating receivables and payables

(b) Non-cash items, eg depreciation, provisions, profits/losses on the sales of assets

(c) Other items, the cash flows from which should be classified under investing or financing activities.

A **proforma** of such a calculation is as follows and this method may be more common in the exam.

	$
Profit before taxation (statement of comprehensive income)	X
Add depreciation	X
Loss (profit) on sale of non-current assets	X
(Increase)/decrease in inventories	(X)/X
(Increase)/decrease in receivables	(X)/X
Increase/(decrease) in payables	X/(X)
Cash generated from operations	X
Interest (paid)/received	(X)
Income taxes paid	(X)
Net cash flows from operating activities	X

It is important to understand why **certain items are added and others subtracted**. Note the following points.

(a) Depreciation is not a cash expense, but is deducted in arriving at the profit figure in the statement of comprehensive income. It makes sense, therefore, to eliminate it by adding it back.

(b) By the same logic, a loss on a disposal of a non-current asset (arising through underprovision of depreciation) needs to be added back and a profit deducted.

(c) An increase in inventories means less cash – you have spent cash on buying inventory.

(d) An increase in receivables means the company's debtors have not paid as much, and therefore there is less cash.

(e) If we pay off payables, causing the figure to decrease, again we have less cash.

2.6.3 Indirect versus direct

The direct method is encouraged where the necessary information is not too costly to obtain, but IAS 7 does not require it, and **favours the indirect method**. In practice, therefore, the direct method is rarely used. It is not obvious that IAS 7 is right in favouring the indirect method. It could be argued that companies ought to monitor their cash flows carefully enough on an ongoing basis to be able to use the direct method at minimal extra cost.

2.7 Interest and dividends

Cash flows from interest and dividends received and paid should each be **disclosed separately**. Each should be classified in a consistent manner from period to period as either operating, investing or financing activities.

Dividends paid by the entity can be classified in **one of two ways**.

(a)   As a **financing cash flow**, showing the cost of obtaining financial resources.

(b)   As a component of **cash flows from operating activities** so that users can assess the entity's ability to pay dividends out of operating cash flows.

2.8 Taxes on income

Cash flows arising from taxes on income should be **separately disclosed** and should be classified as cash flows from operating activities *unless* they can be specifically identified with financing and investing activities.

Taxation cash flows are often **difficult to match** to the originating underlying transaction, so most of the time all tax cash flows are classified as arising from operating activities.

2.9 Components of cash and cash equivalents

The components of cash and cash equivalents should be disclosed and a **reconciliation** should be presented, showing the amounts in the statement of cash flows reconciled with the equivalent items reported in the statement of financial position.

It is also necessary to disclose the **accounting policy** used in deciding the items included in cash and cash equivalents, in accordance with IAS 1, but also because of the wide range of cash management practices worldwide.

2.10 Other disclosures

All entities should disclose, together with a **commentary by management**, any other information likely to be of importance.

(a)   Restrictions on the use of or access to any part of cash equivalents.

(b)   The amount of undrawn borrowing facilities which are available.

(c)   Cash flows which increased operating capacity compared to cash flows which merely maintained operating capacity.

2.11 Example of a statement of cash flows

In the next section we will look at the procedures for preparing a statement of cash flows. First, look at this **example**, adapted from the example given in the standard.

2.11.1 Direct method

STATEMENT OF CASH FLOWS (DIRECT METHOD)
YEAR ENDED 20X7

	$m	$m
Cash flows from operating activities		
Cash receipts from customers	30,150	
Cash paid to suppliers and employees	(27,600)	
Cash generated from operations	2,550	
Interest paid	(270)	
Income taxes paid	(900)	
Net cash from operating activities		1,380
Cash flows from investing activities		
Purchase of property, plant and equipment	(900)	
Proceeds from sale of equipment	20	
Interest received	200	
Dividends received	200	
Net cash used in investing activities		(480)
Cash flows from financing activities		
Proceeds from issuance of share capital	250	
Proceeds from long-term borrowings	250	
Payment of finance lease liabilities	(90)	
Dividends paid*	(1,200)	
Net cash used in financing activities		(790)
Net increase in cash and cash equivalents		110
Cash and cash equivalents at beginning of period (Note)		120
Cash and cash equivalents at end of period (Note)		230

* This could also be shown as an operating cash flow

2.11.2 Indirect method

STATEMENT OF CASH FLOWS (INDIRECT METHOD)
YEAR ENDED 20X7

	$m	$m
Cash flows from operating activities		
Profit before taxation	3,390	
Adjustments for:		
Depreciation	450	
Investment income	(500)	
Interest expense	400	
	3,740	
Increase in trade and other receivables	(500)	
Decrease in inventories	1,050	
Decrease in trade payables	(1,740)	
Cash generated from operations	2,550	
Interest paid	(270)	
Income taxes paid	(900)	
Net cash from operating activities		1,380
Cash flows from investing activities		
Purchase of property, plant and equipment	(900)	
Proceeds from sale of equipment	20	
Interest received	200	
Dividends received	200	
Net cash used in investing activities		(480)
Cash flows from financing activities		
Proceeds from issue of share capital	250	
Proceeds from long-term borrowings	250	
Payment of finance lease liabilities	(90)	
Dividends paid*	(1,200)	
Net cash used in financing activities		(790)
Net increase in cash and cash equivalents		110
Cash and cash equivalents at beginning of period (Note)		120
Cash and cash equivalents at end of period (Note)		230

* This could also be shown as an operating cash flow

	20X7	20X6
	$m	$m
Cash on hand and balances with banks	40	25
Short-term investments	190	95
Cash and cash equivalents	230	120

2.12 Section summary

FAST FORWARD

> Remember the **step-by-step preparation procedure** and use it for all the questions you practise.

Remember the steps involved in preparation of a statement of cash flows.

Step 1 Set out the proforma leaving plenty of space.

Step 2 Complete the reconciliation of operating profit to net cash from operating activities, as far as possible.

Step 3   Calculate the following where appropriate.

- Tax paid
- Dividends paid
- Purchase and sale of non-current assets
- Issues of shares
- Repayment of loans

Step 4   Work out the profit if not already given using: opening and closing balances, tax charge and dividends.

Step 5   Complete the note of gross cash flows. Alternatively the information may go straight into the statement.

Step 6   Slot the figures into the statement and any notes required.

Question	Single company

Kane Co's income statement for the year ended 31 December 20X8 and statements of financial position at 31 December 20X7 and 31 December 20X8 were as follows.

KANE CO
INCOME STATEMENT FOR THE YEAR ENDED 31 DECEMBER 20X8

	$'000	$'000
Sales		720
Raw materials consumed	70	
Staff costs	94	
Depreciation	118	
Loss on disposal of long-term asset	18	
		300
		420
Interest payable		28
Profit before tax		392
Income tax expense		124
Profit for the year		268

KANE CO
STATEMENT OF FINANCIAL POSITION AS AT 31 DECEMBER

	20X8		20X7	
	$'000	$'000	$'000	$'000
Assets				
Non-current assets				
Cost	1,596		1,560	
Depreciation	318		224	
		1,278		1,336
Current assets				
Inventory	24		20	
Trade receivables	76		58	
Bank	48		56	
		148		134
Total assets		1,426		1,470

	20X8		20X7	
	$'000	$'000	$'000	$'000
Equity and liabilities				
Equity				
Share capital	360		340	
Share premium	36		24	
Retained earnings	686		490	
		1,082		854
Non-current liabilities				
Long-term loans		200		500
Current liabilities				
Trade payables	42		30	
Taxation	102		86	
		144		116
		1,426		1,470

During the year, the company paid $90,000 for a new piece of machinery.

Required

Prepare a statement of cash flows for Kane Co for the year ended 31 December 20X8 in accordance with the requirements of IAS 7, using the indirect method.

Answer

KANE CO
STATEMENT OF CASH FLOWS FOR THE YEAR ENDED 31 DECEMBER 20X8

	$'000	$'000
Net cash flow from operating activities		
Operating profit	420	
Depreciation charges	118	
Loss on sale of tangible non-current assets	18	
Increase in inventories	(4)	
Increase in receivables	(18)	
Increase in payables	12	
Cash generated from operations	546	
Interest paid	(28)	
Dividends paid (268 + 490 – 686)	(72)	
Tax paid (86 + 124 – 102)	(108)	
Net cash flow from operating activities		338
Cash flows from investing activities		
Payments to acquire tangible non-current assets	(90)	
Receipts from sales of tangible non-current assets (W)	12	
Net cash outflow from investing activities		(78)
Cash flows from financing activities		
Issues of share capital (360 + 36 – 340 – 24)	32	
Long-term loans repaid (500 – 200)	(300)	
Net cash flows from financing		(268)
Decrease in cash and cash equivalents		(8)
Cash and cash equivalents at 1.1.X8		56
Cash and cash equivalents at 31.12.X8		48

Working: non-current asset disposals

COST

	$'000		$'000
At 1.1.X8	1,560	At 31.12.X8	1,596
Purchases	90	Disposals (balance)	54
	1,650		1,650

ACCUMULATED DEPRECIATION

	$'000		$'000
At 31.1.X8	318	At 1.1.X8	224
Depreciation on disposals		Charge for year	118
(balance)	24		
	342		342
NBV of disposals			30
Net loss reported			(18)
Proceeds of disposals			12

3 Consolidated statements of cash flows   Pilot paper, 12/08

Consolidated cash flows should not present a great problem if you understand how to deal with acquisitions and disposals of subsidiaries, non-controlling interest and dividends.

Consolidated statements of cash flows follow the same principles as for single company statements, with some additional complications.

Cash flows that are **internal to the group** should be eliminated in the preparation of a consolidated statement of cash flows. Where a subsidiary undertaking **joins or leaves** a group during a financial year the cash flows of the group should include the cash flows of the subsidiary undertaking concerned for the same period as that for which the group's income statement includes the results of the subsidiary undertaking.

3.1 Acquisitions and disposals of subsidiaries and other business units

An entity should present separately the aggregate cash flows arising from acquisitions and from disposals of subsidiaries or other business units and classify them as **investing activities**.

Disclosure is required of the following, in aggregate, in respect of both acquisitions and disposals of subsidiaries or other business units during the period.

- Total purchase/disposal consideration
- Portion of purchase/disposal consideration discharged by means of cash/cash equivalents
- Amount of cash/cash equivalents in the subsidiary or business unit disposed of
- Amount of assets and liabilities other than cash/cash equivalents in the subsidiary or business unit acquired or disposed of, summarised by major category

The amounts shown in the statements of cash flows for purchase or disposal of subsidiaries or business units will be the amounts paid or received **net** of cash/cash equivalents acquired or disposed of.

3.2 Consolidation adjustments and non-controlling interest

The group statement of cash flows should only deal with flows of cash and cash equivalents external to the group, so all intra-group cash flows should be eliminated. **Dividends paid to non-controlling interest** should be included under the heading 'cash flow from financing' and disclosed separately.

3.3 Example: Non-controlling interest

The following are extracts of the consolidated results for Jarvis Co for the year ended 31 December 20X8.

CONSOLIDATED INCOME STATEMENT (EXTRACT)

	$'000
Group profit before tax	90
Income tax expense	(30)
Profit for the year	60
Profit attributable to:	
Owners of the parent	45
Non-controlling interest	15
	60

CONSOLIDATED STATEMENT OF FINANCIAL POSITION (EXTRACT)

	20X1	20X2
	$'000	$'000
Non-controlling interest	300	306

Calculate the dividends paid to the non-controlling interest during the year

Solution

The non-controlling interest share of profit after tax represents retained profit plus dividends paid.

NON-CONTROLLING INTEREST

	£'000		£'000
Dividend paid	9	Balance b/fwd	300
Balance c/fwd	306	Profit for period (I/S)	15
	315		315

3.4 Associates and joint ventures

Where an interest in a **jointly controlled entity** (see IAS 31) is accounted for using **proportionate consolidation**, the reporting entity's proportionate share of the jointly controlled entity's cash flows in the consolidated statement of cash flows.

When the equity method is used, only the actual cash flows from sales or purchases between the group and the associate/joint venture, and investments in and dividends from the entity should be included. Dividends should be included in **operating cash flows**, where they are shown within operating profit in the statement of comprehensive income.

3.5 Example: Associate

The following are extracts of the consolidated results of Pripon Co for the year ended 31 December 20X8.

CONSOLIDATED INCOME STATEMENT (EXTRACT)

	$'000
Group profit before tax	150
Share of associate's profit after tax (60 – 30)	30
	180
Tax (group)	75
	105
Profit after tax	

CONSOLIDATED STATEMENT OF FINANCIAL POSITION (EXTRACTS)

	20X1	20X2
	$'000	$'000
Investment in associate	264	276

Calculate the dividend received from the associate.

Solution

The associate profit before tax represents retained profit plus dividend plus tax.

ASSOCIATE

	£'000		£'000
Balance b/fwd	264	Dividend from associate	18
Profit after tax (60 – 30)	30	Balance c/fwd	276
	294		294

3.6 Finance lease transactions

When rentals under a finance lease are paid the **capital and interest elements are split out** and included under the 'financing' and 'servicing of finance' headings respectively.

Exam focus point

Various complications may arise in a consolidated statement of cash flows in the exam, the most important of which are covered above. Question 3, given below, is comprehensive. The Pilot Paper asked for the preparation of a consolidated statement of cash flows and a report on the usefulness of group statements of cash flows, generally and specifically to the entity in the question.

3.7 Section summary

The preparation of consolidated statements of cash flows will, in many respects, be the same as those for single companies, with the following **additional complications.**

- Acquisitions and disposals of subsidiary undertaking
- Cancellation of intra-group transactions
- Non-controlling interest
- Associates and joint ventures
- Finance leases

Question

Consolidated cash flow 1

Topiary Co is a 40 year old company producing garden statues carved from marble. Twenty two years ago it acquired a 100% interest in a marble importing company, Hardstuff Co. In 20W9 it acquired a 40% interest in a competitor, Landscapes Co and on 1 January 20X7 it acquired a 75% interest in Garden Furniture Designs. The draft consolidated accounts for the Topiary Group are as follows.

DRAFT CONSOLIDATED INCOME STATEMENT
FOR THE YEAR ENDED 31 DECEMBER 20X7

	$'000	$'000
Operating profit		4,455
Share of profit after tax of associate		1,050
Income from long-term investment		600
Interest payable		(450)
Profit before taxation		5,655
Tax on profit		
Income tax	1,173	
Deferred taxation	312	
Tax attributable to investment income	135	
		(1,620)
Profit for the year		4,035
Non-controlling interest		
Attribute to: owners of the parent		3,735
non-controlling interest		300
		4,035

DRAFT CONSOLIDATED STATEMENT OF FINANCIAL POSITION
AS AT 31 DECEMBER

	20X6 $'000	20X6 $'000	20X7 $'000	20X7 $'000
Assets				
Non-current assets				
Tangible assets				
Buildings at net book value		6,600		6,225
Machinery: cost	4,200		9,000	
aggregate depreciation	(3,300)		(3,600)	
net book value		900		5,400
		7,500		11,625
Goodwill				300
Investments in associates		3,000		3,300
Long-term investments		1,230		1,230
		11,730		16,455
Current assets				
Inventories	3,000		5,925	
Receivables	3,825		5,550	
Cash	5,460		13,545	
		12,285		25,020
		24,015		41,475
Equity and liabilities				
Equity				
Share capital: 25c shares	6,000		11,820	
Share premium account	6,285		8,649	
Retained earnings	7,500		10,335	
Total equity	19,785		30,804	
Non-controlling interest	–		345	
		19,785		31,149
Non-current liabilities				
Obligations under finance leases	510		2,130	
Loans	1,500		4,380	
Deferred tax	39		90	
		2,049		6,600
Current liabilities				
Trade payables	840		1,500	
Obligations under finance leases	600		720	
Income tax	651		1,386	
Accrued interest and finance charges	90		120	
		2,181		3,726
		24,015		41,475

Note

1   There had been no acquisitions or disposals of buildings during the year.

Machinery costing $1.5m was sold for $1.5m resulting in a profit of $300,000. New machinery was acquired in 20X7 including additions of $2.55m acquired under finance leases.

2   *Information relating to the acquisition of Garden Furniture Designs*

	$'000
Machinery	495
Inventories	96
Trade receivables	84
Cash	336
Trade payables	(204)
Income tax	(51)
	756
Non-controlling interest	(189)
	567
Goodwill	300
	867
2,640,000 shares issued as part consideration	825
Balance of consideration paid in cash	42
	867

3   Loans were issued at a discount in 20X7 and the carrying amount of the loans at 31 December 20X7 included $120,000 representing the finance cost attributable to the discount and allocated in respect of the current reporting period.

Required

Prepare a consolidated statement of cash flows for the Topiary Group for the year ended 31 December 20X7 as required by IAS 7, using the indirect method. There is no need to provide notes to the statement of cash flows.

TOPIARY CO
CONSOLIDATED STATEMENT OF CASH FLOWS
FOR THE YEAR ENDED 31 DECEMBER 20X7

	$'000	$'000
Cash flows from operating activities		
Net profit before tax	5,655	
Adjustments for:		
Depreciation (W1)	975	
Profit on sale of plant	(300)	
Share of associate's profit after tax	(1,050)	
Investment income	(600)	
Interest payable	450	
Operating profit before working capital changes	5,130	
Increase in trade and other receivables (5,500 – 3,825 – 84)	(1,641)	
Increase in inventories (5,925 – 3,000 – 96)	(2,829)	
Increase in trade payables (1,500 – 840 – 204)	456	
Cash generated from operations	1,116	
Interest paid (W2)	(300)	
Income taxes paid (W3)	(750)	
Net cash from operating activities		66
Cash flows from investing activities		
Purchase of subsidiary undertaking (W4)	294	
Purchase of property, plant and equipment (W5)	(3,255)	
Proceeds from sale of plant	1,500	
Dividends from investment (600 – 135)	465	
Dividends from associate (W6)	750	
Dividends paid to non-controlling interest (W7)	(144)	
Net cash used in investing activities		(390)
Cash flows from financing activities		
Issue of ordinary share capital (W8)	7,359	
Issue of loan notes (W9)	2,760	
Capital payments under finance leases (W10)	(810)	
Dividends paid (3,735 + 7,500 – 10,335)	(900)	
Net cash flows from financing activities		8,409
Net increase in cash and cash equivalents		8,085
Cash and cash equivalents at 1.1.X7		5,460
Cash and cash equivalents at 31.12.X7		13,545

Workings

1   *Depreciation charges*

	$'000	$'000
Freehold buildings (6,600 – 6,225)		375
Plant		
Closing balance	3,600	
Opening balance	3,300	
	300	
Depreciation on disposal	300	
		600
		975

2   Interest

	$'000
Accrued interest b/f	90
Expense	450
Discount	(120)
Less accrued interest c/f	(120)
	300

3   Taxation

	$'000	$'000
Opening balance		
Income tax	651	
Deferred tax	39	
		690
Income statement transfer (1,173 + 312)		1,485
Closing balances		
Income tax	1,386	
Deferred tax	90	
		(1,476)
		699
On acquisition		51
Cash outflow		750

4   Purchase of subsidiary

	$'000
Cash received on acquisition	336
Less cash consideration	(42)
Cash inflow	294

5   Purchase of tangible non-current assets: machinery

	$'000	$'000
Cost at 31 December 20X7		9,000
Cost at 1 January 20X7		4,200
		4,800
Disposal		1,500
		6,300
On acquisition	495	
Leased	2,550	
		(3,045)
Cash outflow		3,255

6   Dividends from associate

	$'000
Opening balance	3,000
Share of profit after tax	1,050
	4,050
Closing balance	3,300
	750

7   Non-controlling interest

	$'000
Opening balance	
Profit for year	300
On acquisition	189
	489
Closing balance	(345)
Cash outflow	144

8   Issue of ordinary share capital

	$'000	$'000
Closing balance		
Shares	11,820	
Premium	8,649	
		20,469
Non-cash consideration		
Shares	660	
Premium	165	
		(825)
Opening balance		
Shares	6,000	
Premium	6,285	
		(12,285)
Cash inflow		7,359

9   Issue of loan notes

	$'000
Closing balance	4,380
Opening balance	1,500
	2,880
Finance cost	120
Cash inflow	2,760

10   Capital payments under leases

	$'000	$'000
Opening balances		
Current		600
Long-term		510
		1,110
New lease commitment		2,550
Closing balances		
Current	720	
Long-term	2,130	
		(2,850)
Cash outflow		810

The following are extracts from the financial statements of Tastydesserts and one of its wholly owned subsidiaries, Custardpowders, the shares in which were acquired on 31 October 20X2.

Statements of financial position

| | Tastydesserts and subsidiaries | | Custardpowders |
	31 December 20X2 $'000	31 December 20X1 $'000	31 October 20X2 $'000
Non-current assets			
Property, plant & equipment	4,764	3,685	694
Goodwill	42		
Investment in associates	2,195	2,175	–
	7,001	5,860	694
Current assets			
Inventories	1,735	1,388	306
Receivables	2,658	2,436	185
Bank balances and cash	43	77	7
	4,436	3,901	498
	11,437	9,761	1,192
Equity			
Share capital	4,896	4,776	400
Share premium	216		
Retained earnings	2,540	2,063	644
	7,652	6,839	1,044
Non-current liabilities			
Loans	1,348	653	–
Deferred tax	111	180	–
	1,459	833	–
Current liabilities			
Payables	1,915	1,546	148
Bank overdrafts	176	343	
Current tax payable	235	200	–
	2,326	2,089	148
	11,437	9,761	1,192

CONSOLIDATED STATEMENT OF COMPREHENSIVE INCOME
FOR THE YEAR ENDED 31 DECEMBER 20X2

	$'000
Profit before interest and tax	546
Finance costs	
Share of profit of associates	120
Profit before tax	666
Income tax expense	126
PROFIT/TOTAL COMPREHENSIVE INCOME FOR THE YEAR	540
Attributable to:	
Owners of the parent	540
Non-controlling interests	0
	540

The following information is also given:

(a) The consolidated figures at 31 December 20X2 include Custardpowders.

(b) The amount of depreciation on property, plant and equipment during the year was $78,000. There were no disposals.

(c) The cost on 31 October 20X2 of the shares in Custardpowders was $1,086,000 comprising the issue of $695,000 unsecured loan stock at par, 120,000 ordinary shares of $1 each at a value of 280c and $55,000 in cash.

(d) No write down of goodwill was required during the period.

(e) Total dividends paid by Tastydesserts (parent) during the period amounted to $63,000.

Required

Prepare a statement of cash flows for Tastydesserts and subsidiaries for the year ended 31 December 20X2 using the indirect method.

Notes to the statement of cash flows are not required.   **(15 marks)**

Answer

STATEMENT OF CASH FLOWS FOR THE YEAR ENDED 31 DECEMBER 20X2

	$'000	$'000
Cash flows from operating activities		
Profit before taxation	666	
Adjustments for:		
Depreciation	78	
Share of profit of associates	(120)	
Interest expense	–	
	624	
Increase in receivables (2,658 – 2,436 – 185)	(37)	
Increase in inventories (1,735 – 1,388 – 306)	(41)	
Increase in payables (1,915 – 1,546 – 148)	221	
Cash generated from operations	767	
Interest paid	–	
Income taxes paid (W5)	(160)	
Net cash from operating activities		607
Cash flows from investing activities		
Acquisition of subsidiary Custardpowders net of cash acquired (55 – 7)	(48)	
Purchase of property, plant and equipment (W1)	(463)	
Dividends received from associates (W3)	100	
Net cash used in investing activities		(411)
Cash flows from financing activities		
Dividends paid	(63)	
Net cash used in financing activities		(63)
Net increase in cash and cash equivalents		133
Cash and cash equivalents at beginning of year		(266)
Cash and cash equivalents at end of year		(133)

Workings

1   *Purchase of property, plant and equipment*

PROPERTY, PLANT AND EQUIPMENT

	$'000		$'000
b/d	3,685		
Acquisition of Custardpowders	694	Depreciation	78
∴ Cash additions	463	c/d	4,764
	4,842		4,842

2   *Goodwill*

GOODWILL

	$'000		$'000
b/d	-		
Acquisition of Custardpowders	42	∴ Impairment losses	0
(1,086 – (1,044 × 100%))		c/d	42
	42		42

3   *Dividends received from associates*

INVESTMENT IN ASSOCIATE

	$'000		$'000
b/d	2,175		
Share of profit	120	∴ Dividends received	100
		c/d	2,195
	2,295		2,295

4   *Reconciliation of share capital*

	$'000
Share capital plus premium b/d	4,776
Issued to acquire sub (120,000 × $2.80)	336
Share capital plus premium c/d (4,896 + 216)	5,112

∴ no shares have been issued for cash during the year.

5   *Income taxes paid*

INCOME TAX PAYABLE

	$'000			$'000
		b/d	– current tax	200
			– deferred tax	180
∴ Cash paid	160	P/L		126
c/d – current tax	235			
– deferred tax	111			
	506			506

Chapter Roundup

- **Statements of cash flows** are a useful addition to the financial statements of companies because it is recognised that accounting profit is not the only indicator of a company's performance.

- Statements of cash flows concentrate on the sources and uses of cash and are a useful indicator of a company's **liquidity and solvency**.

- You need to be aware of the **format** of the statement as laid out in **IAS 7**. Setting out the format is an essential first stage in preparing the statement, so this format must be learnt.

- Remember the **step-by-step preparation procedure** and use it for all the questions you practise.

- **Consolidated cash flows** should not present a great problem if you understand how to deal with acquisitions and disposals of subsidiaries, non-controlling interest and dividends.

Quick Quiz

1   What is the objective of IAS 7?

2   What are the benefits of cash flow information according to IAS 7?

3   What are the standard headings required by IAS 7 to be included in a statement of cash flows?

4   What is the 'indirect method' of preparing a statement of cash flows?

5   How should an acquisition or disposal of a subsidiary be shown in the statement of cash flows?

Answers to Quick Quiz

1   To provide users of financial statements with information about the entity's ability to generate cash and cash equivalents, and the entity's cash needs

2   See Paragraphs 2.3 – 2.4

3   Operating, investing and financing activities.

4   The net profit or loss for the period is adjusted for non-cash items; changes in inventories, receivables and payables from operations; and other items resulting from investing or financing activities.

5   Cash flows from acquisitions and disposal are disclosed separately under investing activities.

Now try the question below from the Exam Question Bank

Number	Level	Marks	Time
Q20	Examination	25	45 mins

Performance reporting

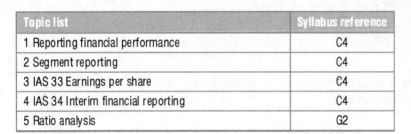

Performance reporting

Topic list	Syllabus reference
1 Reporting financial performance	C4
2 Segment reporting	C4
3 IAS 33 Earnings per share	C4
4 IAS 34 Interim financial reporting	C4
5 Ratio analysis	G2

Introduction

This chapter covers a great many standards, but you are very familiar with some of them. **IAS 1** has been revised fairly recently. The changes are covered in detail in this Chapter.

Note that **IFRS 8** *Operating segments* is also a recent standard.

Earnings per share is important: it is used internationally as a comparative performance figure.

Ratio analysis at P2 is likely to come up in the category of changing accounting policies.

Study guide

		Intellectual level
C1	**Performance reporting**	
(a)	Prepare reports relating to corporate performance for external stakeholders	3
C5	**Segment reporting**	
(a)	Determine business and geographical segments and reportable segments	3
(b)	Specify and discuss the nature of information to be disclosed.	
G2	**Analysis and interpretation of financial information and measurement of performance**	
(a)	Select and calculate relevant indicators of financial and non-financial performance.	3
(b)	Identify and evaluate significant features and issues in financial statements	3
(c)	Highlight inconsistencies in financial information through analysis and application of knowledge	3
(d)	Make inferences from the analysis of the information, taking into account the limitation of the information, the analytical methods used and the business environment in which the entity operates.	3

Exam guide

EPS is covered at an earlier level, so the details are not covered here. However, you may need to know how the earnings figure can be manipulated.

1 Reporting financial performance

FAST FORWARD

Go back to your earlier studies and revise **IAS 1** and **IAS 8**. **IAS 1 has been revised**. The changes and new formats are given in this section.

1.1 Revision of IAS 1 Presentation of Financial Statements

Exam focus point

You have studied IAS 1 at F7. However, the standard was revised in September 2007. In this section we focus on the changes from the old standard. The new formats are given. Elsewhere in this study text, the new terminology and formats are used where appropriate.

1.1.1 Introduction

A revised IAS 1 *Presentation of financial statements* was issued in September 2007. The **main changes** to the previous version are as follows:

(a) Changes in **terminology**, notably 'balance sheet' to statement of financial position.

(b) Single **statement of comprehensive income**. This **can be split into two** (income statement to profit for the year and 'other comprehensive income').

(c) Entities must **disclose reclassification adjustments** relating to each component of other recognised income and expense. These are amounts reclassified in the current period from other recognised income and expense to profit or loss.

(d) **Tax effects** of each item of comprehensive income must be shown. Entities should **disclose income tax relating to each component of other recognised income and expense**. This information will be useful, because often different tax rates are applied to these items than are applied to profit or loss.

(d) **Dividends cannot be shown in profit or loss** (income statement). . **Dividends must be presented on the face of the statement of changes in equity or in the notes**. This change reflects the fact that a dividend distribution is an owner change in equity, which must be presented separately from non-owner changes in equity.

(e) Statement of changes in equity for **owner changes in equity**. Non-owner changes must be shown in the statement of comprehensive income. The purpose of the changes is to provide better information to users by requiring **aggregation of items with shared characteristics**.

    (i) All owner changes in equity, that is changes in equity arising from transactions with owners in their capacity as owners, should be presented separately from non-owner changes. **Entities would no longer be permitted to present components of income and expense (non-owner changes in equity) in the statement of changes in equity**.

    (ii) Income and expenses must be presented in one or two statements, separately from owner changes in equity.

    (iii) Profit or loss and total recognised income and expense should be presented in the financial statements.

The most common application of this change is in **revaluation gains**, which could formerly be shown in the statement of changes in equity, but must now be shown the 'other comprehensive income' part of the statement of comprehensive income.

1.1.2 Most important terminology changes

Old standard	New standard
Balance sheet	Statement of financial position
Income statement	Statement of comprehensive income (one statement) *or*
	Income statement (separate) and statement of comprehensive income (two statements)
Statement of recognised income and expense	'Other comprehensive income' section of new comprehensive income statement. 'Other comprehensive income' for short.
Cash flow statement	Statement of cash flows
Recognised in the income statement	Recognised in profit or loss (Note **or** not **and.**)

You should be aware that, in practice, the new terminology is not mandatory. It is unlikely that you would lose marks in an exam if you accidentally said 'balance sheet', but it is better – and easier in the long run – to get into the habit of referring to the statements by their new names.

1.1.3 Other terminology/wording changes

Old standard	New standard
'On the face of'	'in'
'Reporting date'	'end of the reporting period'
'Each balance sheet date'	'the end of each reporting period'

Old standard	New standard
'Equity holders'	'owners'
'Removed from equity and recognised in profit or loss' (recycling)	'reclassified from equity to profit or loss as a reclassification adjustment'
'Standard or interpretation'	'IFRS'

1.1.4 Changes to titles of IFRS

Old title	New title
IAS 7 *Cash flow statements*	IAS 7 *Statement of cash flows*
IAS 10 *Events after the balance sheet date*	IAS 10 *Events after the reporting period*

1.1.5 New formats

Below are the new IAS 1 formats, with principal changes indicated by 'speech bubbles'.

New title

XYZ GROUP – STATEMENT OF FINANCIAL POSITION AT 31 DECEMBER

	20X7	20X6
Assets	$'000	$'000
Non-current assets		
Property, plant and equipment	350,700	360,020
Goodwill	80,800	91,200
Other intangible assets	227,470	227,470
Investments in associates	100,150	110,770
Available-for-sale financial assets	142,500	156,000
	901,620	945,460
Current assets		
Inventories	135,230	132,500
Trade receivables	91,600	110,800
Other current assets	25,650	12,540
Cash and cash equivalents	312,400	322,900
	564,880	578,740
Total assets	1,466,500	1,524,200

Instead of 'equity holders' (This affects all group balance sheets.)

Was 'other reserves' (also order changed)

	20X7	20X6
Equity and liabilities		
Equity attributable to owners of the parent		
Share capital	650,000	600,000
Retained earnings	243,500	161,700
Other components of equity	10,200	21,200
	903,700	782,900
Non-controlling interest*	70,050	48,600
Total equity	973,750	831,500
Non-current liabilities		
Long-term borrowings	120,000	160,000
Deferred tax	28,800	26,040
Long-term provisions	28,850	52,240
Total non-current liabilities	117,650	238,280

Current liabilities	20X7	20X8
Trade and other payables	115,100	187,620
Short-term borrowings	150,000	200,000
Current portion of long-term borrowings	10,000	20,000
Current tax payable	35,000	42,000
Short-term provisions	5,000	4,800
Total current liabilities	315,100	454,420
Total liabilities	492,750	692,700
Total equity and liabilities	1,466,500	1,524,200

*Non-controlling interest is the new name for minority interest. The name was changed in IFRS 3, which was issued after IAS 1 revised.

New title

XYZ GROUP – STATEMENT OF COMPREHENSIVE INCOME FOR THE YEAR ENDED 31 DECEMBER 20X7

	20X7	20X8
	$'000	$'000
Revenue	39,000	355,000
Cost of sales	(245,000)	(230,000)
Gross profit	145,000	125,000
Other income	20,667	11,300
Distribution costs	(9,000)	(8,700)
Administrative expenses	(20,000)	(21,000)
Other expenses	(2,100)	(1,200)
Finance costs	(8,000)	(7,500)
Share of profit of associates	35,100	30,100
Profit before tax	161,667	128,000
Income tax expense	(40,417)	(32,000)
Profit for the year from continuing operations	121,250	96,000
Loss for the year from discontinued operations	–	(30,500)
Profit for the year	121,250	65,500

Was 'profit for the period'. Affects all income statements.

Other comprehensive income:	20X7	20X8
Exchange differences on translating foreign operations	5,334	10,667
Available-for-sale financial assets	(24,000)	26,667
Cash flow hedges	(667)	(4,000)
Gains on property revaluation	933	3,367
Actuarial gains (losses) on defined benefit pension plans	(667)	1,333
Share of other comprehensive income of associates	400	(700)
Income tax relating to component of other comprehensive income	4,667	(9,334)
Other comprehensive income for the year, net of tax	(14,000)	28,000
Total comprehensive income for the year	107,250	93,500

Note. 'Profit' added. This affects all group income statements (needed to add to distinguish from comprehensive income)

Profit attributable to:	20X7	20X8
Owners of the parent	97,000	52,400
Minority interest	24,250	13,100
	121,250	65,500
Total comprehensive income attributable to		
Owners of the parent	85,800	74,800
Minority interest	21,450	18,700
	107,250	93,500

Earnings per share (in currency units)
   Basic and diluted   0.46   0.30

XYZ GROUP – STATEMENT OF CHANGES IN EQUITY FOR THE YEAR ENDED 31 DECEMBER 20X7

> New title – was 'translation

> Note. Was 31 December 20X5

> Cannot be split now

	Share capital	Retained earnings	Translation of foreign operations	Available for-sale financial assets	Cash flow Hedges	Revaluation surplus	Total	Minority interest	Total equity
	$'000	$'000	$'000	$'000	$'000	$'000	$'000	$'000	$'000
Balance at 1 January 20X6	600,000	118,100	(4,000)	1,600	2,000	–	717,700	29,800	747,500
Changes in accounting policy	–	400	–	–	–	–	400	100	500
Restated balance	600,000	118,500	(4,000)	1,600	2,000	–	718,100	29,900	748,000
Changes in equity for 20X6									
Dividends	–	(10,000)	–	–	–	–	(10,000)	–	(10,000)
Total comprehensive income for the year	–	53,200	6,400	16,000	(2,400)	1,600	74,800	18,700	93,500
Balance at 31 December 20X6	600,000	161,700	2,400	17,600	(400)	1,600	782,900	48,600	831,500
Changes in equity for 20X7									
Issue of share capital	50,000	–	–	–	–	–	50,000	–	50,000
Dividends	–	(15,000)	–	–	–	–	(15,000)	–	(15,000)
Total comprehensive income for the year	–	96,600	3,200	(14,400)	(400)	800	85,800	21,450	107,250
Transfer to retained earnings	–	200	–	–	–	200	–	–	–
Balance at 31 December 20X7	650,000	243,500	5,600	3,200	(800)	2,200	903,700	70,050	973,750

One of the competences you need to fulfil Objective 11 of the Practical Experience Requirement (PER) is to draw valid conclusions from the information contained within financial statements or financial data You can apply the knowledge you obtain from this Chapter, on performance reporting, to demonstrate this competence.

1.1.6 ACCA and examinability of Revised IAS 1

Reproduced below are extracts from the ACCA's article *When is a Balance Sheet not a Balance Sheet?*, amended where appropriate. In the shaded box below, BPP has added emphasis on the part referring to the statement of comprehensive income.

1.1.7 When is a Balance Sheet not a Balance Sheet?

The IASB reissued IAS 1 *Presentation of financial statements* in September 2007. Amendments to the old IAS 1 are mainly to presentation and terminology. The revised IAS 1 has been examined since the June 2008 examinations.

1.1.8 How will this affect your P2 examination?

The IAS 1 update impacts on all ACCA's examination papers which may refer to 'Balance Sheets' or 'Cash Flow Statements'. IAS 1 has changed the name of these financial statements to 'Statement of Financial Position' and 'Statement of Cash Flows' respectively.

The following applies to all companies, partnerships and sole traders for examination purposes.

'Balance Sheet' has been 'Statement of Financial Position' since the June 2008 examination sitting.

'Cash Flow Statement' has been 'Statement of Cash Flows' since the June 2008 examination sitting.

Another amendment made by the standard is to require the presentation of 'other comprehensive income' items, such as revaluation gains and losses, and actuarial gains and losses, as well as the usual income statement items on the face of the primary financial statements. IAS 1 allows this information to be presented in one 'Statement of Comprehensive Income' (see Table A) or in two separate statements; an 'Income Statement' and a 'Statement of Comprehensive Income'.

In the examinations, if a 'Statement of Comprehensive Income' is referred to, this will always relate to the single statement format (see Table A). (Please refer to Examination study guides for examinability of line items).

If 'Income Statements' are referred to, this relates to the statement from 'Revenue' to 'Profit for the year'.

Examinations may also refer to 'Other Comprehensive Income' which relates to the Other Comprehensive Income section of the Statement of Comprehensive Income.

1.1.9 Example of Statement of Comprehensive Income (in one statement) given in IAS 1

	20X7	20X8
Revenue	390,000	355,000
Cost of sales	(245,000)	(230,000)
Gross profit	145,000	125,000
Other income	20,667	11,300
Distribution costs	(9,000)	(8,700)
Administrative expenses	(20,000)	(21,000)
Other expenses	(2,100)	(1,200)
Finance costs	(8,000)	(7,500)
Share of profit of associates	35,100	30,100
Profit before tax	161,667	128,000
Income tax expense	(40,417)	(32,000)
Profit for the year from continuing operations	121,250	96,000
Loss for the year from discontinued operations	-	(30,500)
Profit for the year	121,250	65,500
Other comprehensive income:		
Exchange differences on translating foreign operations	5,334	10,667
Available-for-sale financial assets	(24,000)	26,667
Cash flow hedges	(667)	(4,000)
Gains on property revaluation	933	3,367
Actuarial gains (losses) on defined benefit pension plans	(667)	1,333
Share of other comprehensive income of associates	400	(700)
Income tax relating to components of other comprehensive Income	4,667	(9,334)
Other comprehensive income for the year, net of tax	(14,000)	28,000
Total comprehensive income for the year	107,250	93,500
Profit attributable to:		
Owners of the parent	97,000	52,400
Minority interest	24,250	13,100
	121,250	65,500
Total comprehensive income attributable to:		
Owners of the parent	85,800	74,800
Minority interest	21,450	18,700
	107,250	93,500

> **Exam focus point**
>
> IAS 1 is very straightforward, but it is important. If necessary, go back to your previous study material. In particular you need to be aware of the **current/non-current distinction**, which is not discussed above. You should also be aware of the recent revisions to IAS 1.

1.2 Other aspects of IAS 1

You should note the following further aspects of IAS 1.

(a)　The standard includes various definitions.

> **Key term**
>
> • **Material** Omissions or misstatements of items are material if they could, individually or collectively, influence the economic decisions of users taken on the basis of the financial statements. Materiality depends on the size and nature of the omission or misstatement judged in the surrounding circumstances. The size or nature of the item, or a combination of both, could be the determining factor.

- **Impracticable** Applying a requirement is impracticable when the entity cannot apply it after making every reasonable effort to do so.

(b) Guidance is provided on the meaning of **present fairly**, ie represent **faithfully** the effects of transactions and other events in accordance with the **definitions** and recognition criteria for assets, liabilities, income and expenses as set out in the **Framework** for the Preparation and Presentation of Financial Statements.

(c) The application of **IFRSs** with **additional disclosure** where necessary, is presumed to result in financial statements that achieve a **fair presentation**.

(d) In extremely rare circumstances, **compliance** with a requirement of an IFRS or IFRIC may be so **misleading** that it would conflict with the objective of financial statements set out in the Framework, the entity shall **depart from that specific requirement**.

   (i) Where the relevant regulatory framework requires or does not prohibit such a departure, the entity must disclose:

      (1) That management has concluded that the financial statements present fairly the entity's financial position, financial performance and cash flows

      (2) That it has complied with applicable IFRSs except that it has departed from a particular requirement to achieve a fair presentation

      (3) Full details of the departure

      (4) The impact on the financial statements for each item affected and for each period presented

   (ii) where the relevant regulatory framework prohibits departure from the requirement, the entity shall, to the **maximum extent possible**, **reduce** the perceived **misleading aspects** of compliance by **disclosing**:

      (1) The relevant IFRS, the nature of the requirement and the reason why complying with the requirement is misleading

      (2) For each period presented, the adjustments to each item in the financial statements that would be necessary to achieve a fair presentation

(e) An entity must present **current** and **non-current assets**, and **current** and **non-current liabilities**, as **separate classifications** in the statement of financial position. A presentation based on liquidity should only be used where it provides more relevant and reliable information, in which cases, all assets and liabilities shall be presented broadly in order of liquidity.

(f) A **long-term financial liability** due to be **settled within twelve months** of the year end date should be classified as a **current liability**, even if an agreement to refinance, or to reschedule payments, on a long-term basis is completed after the reporting period and before the financial statements are authorised for issue.

Year end	Agreement to refinance on long-term basis	Date financial statements authorised for issue	Settlement date <12 months after year end

(g) A **long-term financial liability** that is payable on **demand** because the entity **breached** a **condition** of its loan agreement should be classified as **current** at the year end even if the **lender** has agreed **after the year end**, and **before** the financial statements are **authorised for issue**, **not** to **demand payment** as a consequence of the breach.

Condition of loan agreement breached. Long-term liability becomes payable on demand	Year end	Lender agrees not to enforce payment resulting from breach	Date financial statements approved for issue

However, if the **lender** has **agreed** by the **year end** to provide a **period of grace** ending **at least twelve months after the year end** within which the entity can rectify the breach and during that time the lender cannot demand immediate repayment, the liability is classified as **non-current.**

(h) All requirements previously set out in other Standards for the presentation of particular line items in the statement of financial position and income statement are now dealt with in IAS 1. These line items are: biological assets; liabilities and assets for current tax and deferred tax; and pre-tax gain or loss recognised on the disposal of assets or settlement of liabilities attributable to discontinuing operations.

(i) The section that set out the **presentation requirements** for the **net profit or loss** for the period in **IAS 8** has now been **transferred** to **IAS 1** instead.

(j) The following **disclosures** are **no longer required:**

 (i) The results of operating activities, as a line item on the face of the income statement. **'Operating activities'** are **not defined in IAS 1**

 (ii) **Extraordinary items**, as a line item on the face of the income statement (note that the disclosure of 'extraordinary items' is now **prohibited**)

 (iii) The **number** of an **entity's employees**

(k) An entity must disclose, in the summary of significant accounting policies and/or other notes, the **judgements** made by management in **applying** the **accounting policies** that have the **most significant effect** on the amounts of items recognised in the financial statements.

(l) An entity must disclose in the notes information regarding **key assumptions** about the **future**, and other sources of **measurement uncertainty**, that have a significant **risk of** causing a **material adjustment** to the carrying amounts of assets and liabilities within the **next financial year**.

(m) The following items must be disclosed on the **face of the income statement**.

 (i) Profit or loss attributable to **non-controlling interest**

 (ii) Profit or loss attributable to **equity** holders of the parent

 The allocated amounts must not be presented as items of income or expense. There is a similar requirement for the statement of changes in equity or statement of recognised income and expense. (See the example formats above.)

1.3 Revision of IAS 8

You have studied this standard already but it is long and important. If you do not understand any of this or if you have problems with the revision question, go back and revise your earlier study material.

There have been extensive revisions to the standard, which is now called IAS 8 *Accounting policies, changes in accounting estimates and errors*. The new title reflects the fact that the material on determining net profit and loss for the period has been transferred to IAS 1.

Knowledge brought forward from earlier studies

IAS 8 *Accounting policies, changes in accounting estimates and errors*

Definitions

- **Accounting policies** are the specific principles, bases, conventions, rules and practices adopted by an entity in preparing and presenting financial statements.

The remaining definitions are either new or heavily amended.

- A **change in accounting estimate** is an adjustment of the carrying amount of an asset or a liability or the amount of the periodic consumption of an asset, that results from the assessment of the present status of, and expected future benefits and obligations associated with, assets and liabilities. Changes in accounting estimates result from new information or new developments and, accordingly, are not corrections of errors.

- **Material**: as defined in IAS 1 (see above)
- **Prior period errors** are omissions from, and misstatements in, the entity's financial statements for one or more prior periods arising from a failure to use, or misuse of, reliable information that:
    - (a)   Was available when financial statements for those periods were authorised for issue, and
    - (b)   Could reasonably be expected to have been obtained and taken into account in the preparation and presentation of those financial statements.

    Such errors include the effects of mathematical mistakes, mistakes in applying accounting policies, oversights or misinterpretations of facts, and fraud.

- **Retrospective application** is applying a new accounting policy to transactions, other events and conditions as if that policy had always been applied.
- **Retrospective restatement** is correcting the recognition, measurement and disclosure of amounts of elements of financial statements as if a prior period error had never occurred.
- **Prospective application** of a change in accounting policy and of recognising the effect of a change in an accounting estimate, respectively, are:
    - (a)   Applying the new accounting policy to transactions, other events and conditions occurring after the date as at which the policy is changes; and
    - (b)   Recognising the effect of the change in the accounting estimate in the current and future periods affected by the change.

- **Impracticable** Applying a requirement is impracticable when the entity cannot apply it after making every reasonable effort to do so. It is impracticable to apply a change in an accounting policy retrospectively or to make a retrospective restatement to correct an error if one of the following apply.
    - (a)   The effects or the retrospective application or retrospective restatement are not determinable.
    - (b)   The retrospective application or retrospective restatement requires assumptions about what management's intent would have been in that period.
    - (c)   The retrospective application or retrospective restatement requires significant estimates of amounts and it is impossible to distinguish objectively information about those estimates that: provides evidence of circumstances that existed on the date(s) at which those amounts are to be recognised, measured or disclosed; and would have been available when the financial statements for that prior period were authorised for issue from other information.

Accounting policies

This material has been transferred into IAS 8 from IAS 1.

- Accounting policies are determined by **applying the relevant IFRS or IFRIC** and considering any relevant Implementation Guidance issued by the IASB for that IFRS/IFRIC.
- Where there is no applicable IFRS or IFRIC management should use its **judgement** in developing and applying an accounting policy that results in information that is **relevant** and **reliable**. Management should refer to:
    - (a)   The requirements and guidance in IFRSs and IFRICs dealing with **similar** and **related issues.**
    - (b)   The definitions, recognition criteria and measurement concepts for assets, liabilities and expenses in the *Framework*.

    Management may also consider the most recent pronouncements of other standard setting bodies that use a similar conceptual framework to develop standards, other accounting literature and accepted industry practices if these do not conflict with the sources above.

- An entity shall select and apply its accounting policies for a period **consistently** for similar transactions, other events and conditions, unless an IFRS or an IFRIC specifically requires or permits categorisation of items for which different policies may be appropriate. If an IFRS or an IFRIC requires or permits categorisation of items, an appropriate accounting policy shall be selected and applied consistently to each category.

Changes in accounting policies

- These are **rare**: only required by statute/standard-setting body/results in reliable and more relevant information.
- **Adoption of new IAS**: follow transitional provisions of IAS. If no transitional provisions: **retrospective** application.
- **Other changes in policy**: **retrospective** application. Adjust opening balance of each affected component of equity, ie as if new policy has always been applied.
- **Prospective** application is **no longer allowed** unless it is **impracticable** to determine the cumulative effect of the change. (See definition of impracticable above).
- An entity should **disclose** information relevant to assessing the **impact of new IFRSs/IFRICs** on the financial statements where these have been **issued but have not yet come into force**.

Changes in accounting estimates

- Estimates arise because of **uncertainties inherent within them**, judgement is required but this does not undermine reliability.
- Effect of a change in accounting estimate should be included in net profit/loss in:
    - Period of change, if change affects only current period, or
    - Period of change and future periods, if change affects both.

Errors

(See definition of prior period error above; this **replaces** definition of **fundamental error** in previous version of IAS 8.)

- **Prior period errors**: correct **retrospectively**. There is **no** longer any **allowed alternative** treatment.
- This involves:
    (a) Either restating the comparative amounts for the prior period(s) in which the error occurred,
    (b) Or when the error occurred before the earliest prior period presented, restating the opening balances of assets, liabilities and equity for that period so that the financial statements are presented as if the error had never occurred.
- Only where it is **impracticable** to determine the cumulative effect of an error on prior periods can an entity correct an error **prospectively**.

The following question will allow you to revise IAS 8.

Question

Prior period error

During 20X7 Lubi Co discovered that certain items had been included in inventory at 31 December 20X6, valued at $4.2m, which had in fact been sold before the year end. The following figures for 20X6 (as reported) and 20X7 (draft) are available.

	20X6	20X7 (draft)
	$'000	$'000
Sales	47,400	67,200
Cost of goods sold	(34,570)	(55,800)
Profit before taxation	12,830	11,400
Income taxes	(3,880)	(3,400)
Net profit	8,950	8,000

Reserves at 1 January 20X6 were $13m. The cost of goods sold for 20X7 includes the $4.2m error in opening inventory. The income tax rate was 30% for 20X6 and 20X7.

Required

Show the income statement for 20X7, with the 20X6 comparative, and retained earnings.

Answer

INCOME STATEMENT

	20X6	*20X7*
	$'000	$'000
Sales	47,400	67,200
Cost of goods sold (W1)	(38,770)	(51,600)
Profit before tax	8,630	15,600
Income tax (W2)	(2,620)	(4,660)
Net profit	6,010	10,940

RETAINED EARNINGS

	20X6	*20X7*
Opening retained earnings		
As previously reported	13,000	21,950
Correction of prior period		
error (4,200 – 1,260)	–	(2,940)
As restated	13,000	19,010
Net profit for year	6,010	10,940
Closing retained earnings	19,010	29,950

Workings

1	Cost of goods sold	*20X6*	*20X7*
		$'000	$'000
	As stated in question	34,570	55,800
	inventory adjustment	4,200	(4,200)
		38,770	51,600

2	Income tax	*20X6*	*20X7*
		$'000	$'000
	As stated in question	3,880	3,400
	Inventory adjustment (4,200 × 30%)	1,260	1,260
		2,620	4,660

1.3.1 A complete set of financial statements

IAS 1 currently uses the terms ' statement of financial position' and 'statement of cash flows' to describe two of the statements that constitute a complete set of financial statements. It was felt necessary to reflect more closely the function of these statements as referred to in the IASB *Framework*. Accordingly, the **ED proposes to use the terms 'statement of financial position' and 'statement of cash flows**'.

It is also proposed that a **statement of financial position as at the beginning of the period** should be included in a complete set of financial statements. This will provide information that is useful to users.

1.3.2 Reporting owner changes in equity and recognised income and expenses

IAS 1 requires the presentation of an income statement that includes income and expenses recognised in profit or loss. Other components of income and expense not recognised in profit or loss may currently be presented in the statement of changes in equity, together with owner changes in equity.

This will change under the proposals in the ED. The purpose of the changes is to provide better information to users by requiring **aggregation of items with shared characteristics**.

(a) All owner changes in equity, that is changes in equity arising from transactions with owners in their capacity as owners, should be presented separately from non-owner changes. **Entities would no longer be permitted to present components of income and expense (non-owner changes in equity) in the statement of changes in equity**.

(b) Income and expenses must be presented in one or two statements, separately from owner changes in equity.

(c) Profit or loss and total recognised income and expense should be presented in the financial statements.

1.3.3 Reclassification adjustments and related tax effects

Entities must **disclose reclassification adjustments** relating to each component of other recognised income and expense. These are amounts reclassified in the current period from other recognised income and expense to profit and loss.

Entities should **disclose income tax relating to each component of other recognised income and expense**. This information will be useful, because often different tax rates are applied to these items than are applied to profit or loss.

1.3.4 Presentation of dividends

Entities will no longer have the choice currently allowed in IAS 1 of presenting dividends on the face of the income statement, the statement of changes in equity or the notes. **Dividends must be presented on the face of the statement of changes in equity or in the notes**.

This change reflects the fact that a dividend distribution is an owner change in equity, which must be presented separately from non-owner changes in equity.

2 Segment reporting

6/08

FAST FORWARD

An important aspect of reporting financial performance is **segment reporting**. This is covered by IFRS 8 *Operating segments,* which replaced IAS 14 *Segment reporting* in 2006.

2.1 Introduction

Large entities produce a wide range of products and services, often in several different countries. Further information on how the overall results of entities are made up from each of these product or geographical areas will help the users of the financial statements. This is the reason for **segment reporting**.

* The entity's **past performance** will be better understood
* The entity's **risks and returns** may be better assessed
* More **informed judgements** may be made about the entity as a whole

Risks and returns of a **diversified, multi-national company** can only be assessed by looking at the individual risks and rewards attached to groups of products or services or in different groups of products or services or in different geographical areas. These are subject to differing rates of profitability, opportunities for growth, future prospects and risks.

Segment reporting is covered by IFRS 8 *Operating segments*, which replaced IAS 14 *Segment reporting* in November 2006.

2.2 Objective

An entity must disclose information to enable users of its financial statements to evaluate the nature and financial effects of the business activities in which it engages and the economic environments in which it operates.

2.3 Scope

Only entities whose **equity or debt securities are publicly traded** (ie on a stock exchange) need disclose segment information. In group accounts, only **consolidated** segmental information needs to be shown. (The statement also applies to entities filing or in the process of filing financial statements for the purpose of issuing instruments.)

2.4 Definition of operating segment

Reportable segments are **operating segments** or aggregation of operating segments that meet specified criteria.

You need to learn this definition, as it is crucial to the standard.

Key term

Operating segment: This is a component of an entity:

(a) That engages in business activities from which it may earn revenues and incur expenses (including revenues and expenses relating to transactions with other components of the same entity)

(b) Whose operating results are regularly reviewed by the entity's chief operating decision maker to make decisions about resources to be allocated to the segment and assess its performance, and

(c) For which discrete financial information is available.

IFRS 8

The term 'chief operating decision maker' identifies a function, not necessarily a manager with a specific title. That function is to allocate resources and to assess the performance of the entity's operating segments

2.5 Aggregation

Two or more operating segments may be **aggregated** if the segments have **similar economic characteristics**, and the segments are similar in *each* of the following respects:

- The **nature of the products or services**
- The **nature of the production process**
- The **type or class of customer for their products or services**
- The **methods used to distribute their products or provide their services**, and
- If applicable, the **nature of the regulatory environment**

2.6 Determining reportable segments

An entity must report separate information about **each operating segment** that:

(a) Has been identified as meeting the **definition of an operating segment**; and

(b) Segment total is **10% or more of total**:

    (i) **Revenue** (internal and external), or

    (ii) All **segments not reporting a loss** (or all segments in loss if greater), or

    (iii) **Assets**

At least **75% of total external revenue** must be reported by operating segments. Where this is not the case, additional segments must be identified (even if they do not meet the 10% thresholds).

Two or more operating segments **below** the thresholds may be aggregated to produce a reportable segment if the segments have similar economic characteristics, and the segments are similar in a **majority** of the aggregation criteria above.

Operating segments that do not meet **any of the quantitative thresholds** may be reported separately if management believes that information about the segment would be useful to users of the financial statements.

2.6.1 Decision tree to assist in identifying reportable segments

The following decision tree will assist in identifying reportable segments.

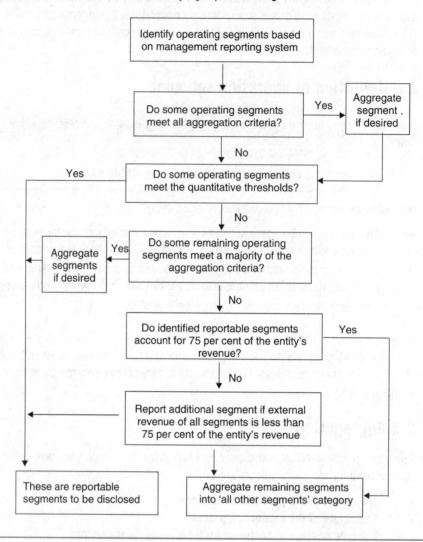

2.7 Disclosures

FAST FORWARD

- IFRS 8 disclosures are of:
    - Operating segment profit or loss
    - Segment assets
    - Segment liabilities
    - Certain income and expense items
- Disclosures are also required about the revenues derived from products or services and about the countries in which revenues are earned or assets held, even if that information is not used by management in making decisions.

Disclosures required by the IFRS are extensive, and best learned by looking at the example and proforma, which follow the list.

(a) Factors used to identify the entity's reportable segments

(b) **Types of products and services** from which each reportable segment derives its revenues

(c) Reportable segment revenues, profit or loss, assets, liabilities and other material items:

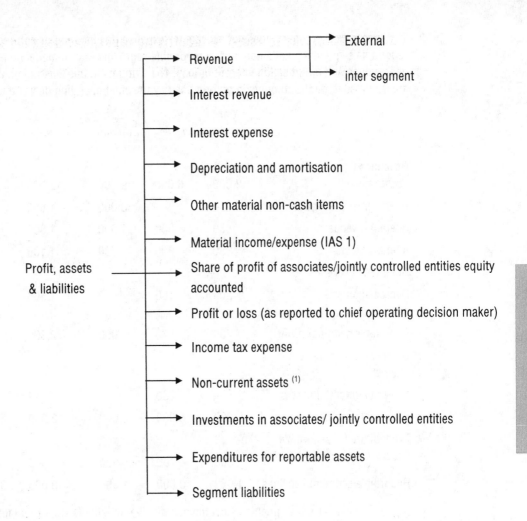

A **reconciliation** of the each of the above material items to the entity's reported figures is required.

Reporting of a measure of **profit or loss** and **total assets** by segment is compulsory. Other items are disclosed if included in the figures reviewed by or regularly provided to the chief operating decision maker.

(d) **External revenue** by each product and service (if reported basis is not products and services)

(e) **Geographical information**:

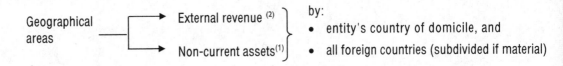

Notes

(1) External revenue is allocated based on the customer's location.

(2) Non-current assets excludes financial instruments, deferred tax assets, post-employment benefit assets, and rights under insurance contracts.

(f) Information about **reliance on major customers** (ie those who represent more than 10% of external revenue)

2.7.1 Disclosure example from IFRS 8

The following example is adapted from the IFRS 8 *Implementation Guidance*, which emphasises that this is for illustrative purposes only and that the information must be presented in the most understandable manner in the specific circumstances.

The hypothetical company does not allocate tax expense (tax income) or non-recurring gains and losses to reportable segments. In addition, not all reportable segments have material non-cash items other than depreciation and amortisation in profit or loss. The amounts in this illustration, denominated as dollars, are assumed to be the amounts in reports used by the chief operating decision maker.

	Car parts $	Motor vessel $	Software $	Electronics $	Finance $	All other $	Totals $
Revenues from external customers	3,000	5,000	9,500	12,000	5,000	1,000[a]	35,500
Intersegment revenues	–	–	3,000	1,500	–	–	4,500
Interest revenue	450	800	1,000	1,500	–	–	3,750
Interest expense	350	600	700	1,100	–	–	2,750
Net interest revenue [b]	–	–	–	–	1,000	–	1,000
Depreciation and amortisation	200	100	50	1,500	1,100	–	2,950
Reportable segment profit	200	70	900	2,300	500	100	4,070
Other material non-cash items:							
Impairment of assets	–	200	–	–	–	–	200
Reportable segment assets	2,000	5,000	3,000	12,000	57,000	2,000	81,000
Expenditure for reportable segment non-current assets	300	700	500	800	600	–	2,900
Reportable segment liabilities	1,050	3,000	1,800	8,000	30,000	–	43,850

(a) Revenues from segments below the quantitative thresholds are attributable to four operating segments of the company. Those segments include a small property business, an electronics equipment rental business, a software consulting practice and a warehouse leasing operation. None of those segments has ever met any of the quantitative thresholds for determining reportable segments.

(b) The finance segment derives a majority of its revenue from interest. Management primarily relies on net interest revenue, not the gross revenue and expense amounts, in managing that segment. Therefore, as permitted by IFRS 8, only the net amount is disclosed.

2.7.2 Suggested proforma

Information about profit or loss, assets and liabilities

	Segment A	Segment B	Segment C	All other segments	Inter segment	Entity total
Revenue – external customers	X	X	X	X	–	X
Revenue – inter segment	X̲	X̲	X̲	X̲	X̲	–̳
	X	X	X	X	(X)	X
Interest revenue	X	X	X	X	(X)	X
Interest expense	(X)	(X)	(X)	(X)	X	(X)
Depreciation and amortisation	(X)	(X)	(X)	(X)	–	(X)
Other material non-cash items	X/(X)	X/(X)	X/(X)	X/(X)	X/(X)	X/(X)
Material income/expense (IAS 1)	X/(X)	X/(X)	X/(X)	X/(X)	X/(X)	X/(X)
Share of profit of associate/JVs	X	X	X	X	–	X
Segment profit before tax	X	X	X	X	(X)	X
Income tax expense	(X)	(X)	(X)	(X)	–	(X)
Unallocated items						X/(X)
Profit for the year						X̲
Segment assets	X	X	X	X	(X)	X
Investments in associate/JVs	X	X	X	X	–	X
Unallocated assets						X
Entity's assets						X̲
Expenditures for reportable assets	X	X	X	X	(X)	X
Segment liabilities	X	X	X	X	(X)	X
Unallocated liabilities						X
Entity's liabilities						X̲

Information about geographical areas

	Country of domicile	Foreign countries	Total
Revenue – external customers	X	X	X
Non-current assets	X	X	X

2.8 Advantages and disadvantages of the old and new segment definition approaches

	Advantages	Disadvantages
'Risks and Returns' approach (IAS 14)	• The information can be reconciled to the financial statements • It is a consistent method • The method helps to highlight the profitability, risks and returns of an identifiable segment	• The information may be commercially sensitive. • The segments may include operations with different risks and returns
'Managerial approach (IFRS 8)	• It is cost effective because the marginal cost of reporting segmental data will be low. • Users can be sure that the segment data reflects the operational strategy of the business	• Segment determination is the responsibility of directors and is subjective • Management may report segments which are not consistent for internal reporting and control purposes making its usefulness questionable

2.9 Criticisms of IFRS 8

(a) Some commentators have criticized the 'management approach' as leaving segment identification **too much to the discretion of the entity.**

(b) The management approach may mean that financial statements of different entities are **not comparable.**

(c) Segment determination is the responsibility of directors and is **subjective.**

(d) Management may report segments which are **not consistent** for internal reporting and control purposes, making its usefulness questionable.

(e) For accounting periods beginning on or after 1 January 2005 listed entities within the EU are required to use adopted international standards in their consolidated financial statements. The **EU has not yet adopted IFRS 8** and until it does IAS 14 will continue to apply here. Some stakeholders believe the standard to be flawed due to the amount of discretion it gives to management.

(f) **Geographical information** has been **downgraded.** It could be argued that this **breaks the link between a company and its stakeholders.**

(g) There is **no defined measure** of segment profit or loss.

2.10 Recent summary

IFRS 8 is a **disclosure standard D**:

• **Segment reporting** is necessary for a better understanding and assessment of:
    – Past performance
    – Risks and returns
    – Informed judgements
• IFRS 8 adopts the **managerial approach** to identifying segments
• The standard gives guidance on how segments should be **identified** and **what information should be disclosed** for each

It also sets out **requirements for related disclosures** about products and services, geographical areas and major customers.

3 IAS 33 Earnings per share

Earnings per share is a measure of the amount of profits earned by a company for each ordinary share. Earnings are profits after tax and preferred dividends.

You studied the bulk of IAS 33 for earlier papers, The examiner has stated that it is not going to form the basis of a full question. However, you may have to talk about the potential for manipulation.

Remember that the objective of IAS 33 is to improve the **comparison** of the performance of different entities in the same period and of the same entity in different accounting periods.

3.1 Definitions

The following definitions are given in IAS 33.

Ordinary share: an equity instrument that is subordinate to all other classes of equity instruments.

Potential ordinary share: a financial instrument or other contract that may entitle its holder to ordinary shares.

Options, warrants and their equivalents: financial instruments that give the holder the right to purchase ordinary shares.

Contingently issuable ordinary shares are ordinary shares issuable for little or no cash or other consideration upon the satisfaction of certain conditions in a contingent share agreement.

Contingent share agreement: an agreement to issue shares that is dependent on the satisfaction of specified conditions.

Dilution is a reduction in earnings per share or an increase in loss per share resulting from the assumption that convertible instruments are converted, that options or warrants are exercised, or that ordinary shares are issued upon the satisfaction of certain conditions.

Antidilution is an increase in earnings per share or a reduction in loss per share resulting from the assumption that convertible instruments are converted, that options or warrants are exercised, or that ordinary shares are issued upon the satisfaction of certain conditions.   *(IAS 33)*

3.1.1 Ordinary shares

There may be more than one class of ordinary shares, but ordinary shares of the same class will have the same rights to receive dividends. Ordinary shares participate in the net profit for the period **only after other types of shares**, eg preference shares.

3.1.2 Potential ordinary shares

IAS 33 identifies the following examples of financial instrument and other contracts generating potential ordinary shares.

(a)   **Debts** (financial liabilities) **or equity instruments**, including preference shares, that are convertible into ordinary shares

(b)   **Share warrants and options**

(c)   Shares that would be issued upon the satisfaction of **certain conditions** resulting from contractual arrangements, such as the purchase of a business or other assets

3.2 Scope

IAS 33 has the following **scope restrictions**.

(a)   Only companies with (potential) ordinary shares which are **publicly traded** need to present EPS (including companies in the process of being listed).

(b)   EPS need only be presented on the basis of **consolidated results** where the parent's results are shown as well.

(c)   Where companies **choose** to present EPS, even when they have no (potential) ordinary shares which are traded, they must do so according to IAS 33.

3.3 Basic EPS

Basic EPS is calculated by dividing the net profit or loss for the period attributable to ordinary shareholders by the weighted average number of ordinary shares outstanding during the period.

You should know how to calculate **basic EPS** and how to deal with related complications (issue of shares for cash, bonus issue, share splits/reverse share splits, rights issues).

Basic EPS should be calculated for **profit or loss attributable to ordinary equity holders** of the parent entity and **profit or loss from continuing operations** attributable to those equity holders (if this is presented).

Basic EPS should be calculated by dividing the **net profit** or loss for the period attributable to ordinary equity holders by the **weighted average number of ordinary shares** outstanding during the period.

$$\frac{\text{Net profit/(loss) attribtable to ordinary shareholders}}{\text{Weighted average number of ordinary shares outstanding during the period}}$$

3.3.1 Earnings

Earnings includes **all items of income and expense** (including tax and non-controlling interest) *less* net profit attributable to **preference shareholders**, including preference dividends.

Preference dividends deducted from net profit consist of the following:

(a)   Preference dividends on non-cumulative preference shares declared in respect of the period.

(b)   Preference dividends for cumulative preference shares required for the period, *whether or not* they have been declared (*excluding* those paid/declared during the period in respect of previous periods).

If an entity purchases its own preference shares for more than their carrying amount the excess should be treated as a return to the preference shareholders and deducted from profit or loss attributable to ordinary equity holders.

3.3.2 Per share

The number of ordinary shares used should be the weighted average number of ordinary shares during the period. This figure (for all periods presented) should be **adjusted for events**, other than the conversion of potential ordinary shares, that have changed the number of shares outstanding without a corresponding change in resources.

The **time-weighting factor** is the number of days the shares were outstanding compared with the total number of days in the period. A reasonable approximation is usually adequate.

Shares are usually included in the weighted average number of shares from the **date consideration is receivable** which is usually the date of issue. In other cases consider the specific terms attached to their issue (consider the substance of any contract). The treatment for the issue of ordinary shares in different circumstances is as follows.

Consideration	Start date for inclusion
In exchange for cash	When cash is receivable
On the voluntary reinvestment of dividends on ordinary or preferred shares	The dividend payment date
As a result of the conversion of a debt instrument to ordinary shares	Date interest ceases accruing
In place of interest or principal on other financial instruments	Date interest ceases accruing
In exchange for the settlement of a liability of the entity	The settlement date
As consideration for the acquisition of an asset other than cash	The date on which the acquisition is recognised
For the rendering of services to the entity	As services are rendered

Ordinary shares issued as **purchase consideration** in an acquisition should be included as of the date of acquisition because the acquired entity's results will also be included from that date.

Where a **uniting of interests** takes place the number of ordinary shares used for the calculation is the aggregate of the weighted average number of shares of the combined entities, adjusted to equivalent shares of the entity whose shares are outstanding after the combination.

Ordinary shares that will be issued on the **conversion** of a mandatorily convertible instrument are included in the calculation from the **date the contract is entered into**.

If ordinary shares are **partly paid**, they are treated as a fraction of an ordinary share to the extent they are entitled to dividends relative to fully paid ordinary shares.

Contingently issuable shares (including those subject to recall) are included in the computation when all necessary conditions for issue have been satisfied.

3.4 Effect on basic EPS of changes in capital structure

3.4.1 New issues/buy backs

When there has been an issue of new shares or a buy-back of shares, the corresponding figures for EPS for the previous year will be comparable with the current year because, as the weighted average of shares has risen or fallen, there has been a **corresponding increase or decrease in resources**. Money has been received when shares were issued, and money has been paid out to repurchase shares. It is assumed that the sale or purchase has been made at full market price.

There are other events, however, which change the number of shares outstanding, **without a corresponding change in resources**. In these circumstances (four of which are considered by IAS 33) it is necessary to make adjustments so that the current and prior period EPS figures are comparable.

3.4.2 Capitalisation/bonus issue and share split/reverse share split

These two types of event can be considered together as they have a similar effect. In both cases, ordinary shares are issued to existing shareholders for **no additional consideration**. The number of ordinary shares has increased without an increase in resources.

This problem is solved by **adjusting the number of ordinary shares outstanding before the event** for the proportionate change in the number of shares outstanding as if the event had occurred at the beginning of the earliest period reported.

3.4.3 Rights issue

A rights issue of shares is an issue of new shares to existing shareholders **at a price below the current market value**. The offer of new shares is made on the basis of x new shares for every y shares currently held, eg a 1 for 3 rights issue is an offer of 1 new share at the offer price for every 3 shares currently held. This means that there is a bonus element included.

To arrive at figures for EPS when a rights issue is made, we first calculate the **theoretical ex-rights price**. This is a weighted average value per share.

The procedures for calculating the EPS for the current year and a corresponding figure for the previous year are as follows.

(a)   The **EPS for the corresponding previous period** should be multiplied by the following fraction. (*Note.* The market price on the last day of quotation is taken as the fair value immediately prior to exercise of the rights, as required by the standard.)

$$\frac{\text{Theoretical ex-rights price}}{\text{Market price on last day of quotation (with rights)}}$$

(b)   To obtain the **EPS for the current year** you should:

(i)   multiply the number of shares before the rights issue by the fraction of the year before the date of issue and by the following fraction.

$$\frac{\text{Market price on last day of quotation with rights}}{\text{Theoretical ex-rights price}}$$

(ii)   multiply the number of shares after the rights issue by the fraction of the year after the date of issue and add to the figure arrived at in (i).

The total earnings should then be divided by the total number of shares so calculated.

Question
Basic EPS

Macarone Co has produced the following net profit figures.

	$m
20X6	1.1
20X7	1.5
20X8	1.8

On 1 January 20X7 the number of shares outstanding was 500,000. During 20X7 the company announced a rights issue with the following details.

Rights: 1 new share for each 5 outstanding (100,000 new shares in total)

Exercise price: $5.00

Last date to exercise rights: 1 March 20X7

The market (fair) value of one share in Marcoli immediately prior to exercise on 1 March 20X7 = $11.00.

Required

Calculate the EPS for 20X6, 20X7 and 20X8.

Answer

Computation of theoretical ex-rights price

This computation uses the total fair value and number of shares.

$$\frac{\text{Fair value of all outstanding shares} + \text{total received from exercise of rights}}{\text{No shares outstanding prior to exercise} + \text{no shares issued in exercise}}$$

$$= \frac{(\$11.00 \times 500,000) + (\$5.00 \times 100,000)}{500,000 + 100,000} = \$10.00$$

Computation of EPS

		20X6 $	20X7 $	20X8 $

20X6   EPS as originally reported

$$\frac{\$1,100,000}{500,000}$$ 2.20

20X6   EPS restated for rights issue =

$$\frac{\$1,100,000}{500,000} \times \frac{10}{11}$$ 2.00

20X7   EPS including effects of rights issue

$$\frac{\$1,500,000}{(500,000 \times 2/12 \times 11/10) + (600,000 \times 10/12)}$$ 2.54

20X8 $EPS = \dfrac{\$1,800,000}{600,000}$ 3.00

3.5 Diluted EPS

Diluted EPS is calculated by adjusting the net profit attributable to ordinary shareholders and the weighted average number of shares outstanding for the effects of all dilutive potential ordinary shares.

At the end of an accounting period, a company may have in issue some **securities** which do not (at present) have any 'claim' to a share of equity earnings, but **may give rise to such a claim in the future**.

(a)   A **separate class of equity shares** which at present is not entitled to any dividend, but will be entitled after some future date.

(b)   **Convertible loan stock** or **convertible preferred shares** which give their holders the right at some future date to exchange their securities for ordinary shares of the company, at a pre-determined conversion rate.

(c)   **Options** or **warrants**.

In such circumstances, the future number of shares ranking for dividend might increase, which in turn results in a fall in the EPS. In other words, a **future increase** in the **number of equity shares will cause a dilution or 'watering down' of equity**, and it is possible to calculate a **diluted earnings per share** (ie the EPS that would have been obtained during the financial period if the dilution had already taken place). This will indicate to investors the possible effects of a future dilution.

3.5.1 Earnings

The earnings calculated for basic EPS should be adjusted by the **post-tax** (including deferred tax) effect of the following.

(a)   Any **dividends** on dilutive potential ordinary shares that were deducted to arrive at earnings for basic EPS.

(b)   **Interest recognised** in the period for the dilutive potential ordinary shares.

(c)   Any **other changes in income or expenses** (fees and discount, premium accounted for as yield adjustments) that would result from the conversion of the dilutive potential ordinary shares.

The conversion of some potential ordinary shares may lead to changes in **other income or expenses**. For example, the reduction of interest expense related to potential ordinary shares and the resulting increase in net profit for the period may lead to an increase in the expense relating to a non-discretionary employee profit-sharing plan. When calculating diluted EPS, the net profit or loss for the period is adjusted for any such consequential changes in income or expense.

3.5.2 Per share

The number of ordinary shares is the weighted average number of ordinary shares calculated for basic EPS plus the weighted average number of ordinary shares that would be issued on the conversion of all the **dilutive potential ordinary shares** into ordinary shares.

It should be assumed that dilutive ordinary shares were converted into ordinary shares at the **beginning of the period** or, if later, at the actual date of issue. There are two other points.

(a) The computation assumes the most **advantageous conversion rate** or exercise rate from the standpoint of the holder of the potential ordinary shares.

(b) A **subsidiary, joint venture or associate** may issue potential ordinary shares that are convertible into either ordinary shares of the subsidiary, joint venture or associate, or ordinary shares of the reporting entity. If these potential ordinary shares have a dilutive effect on the consolidated basic EPS of the reporting entity, they are included in the calculation of diluted EPS.

<table>
<tr><td>Exam focus
point</td><td>Read through the example for background only – you won't need to calculate a dilutive EPS in the exam.</td></tr>
</table>

3.6 Example: Diluted EPS

In 20X7 Farrah Co had a basic EPS of 105c based on earnings of $105,000 and 100,000 ordinary $1 shares. It also had in issue $40,000 15% Convertible Loan Stock which is convertible in two years' time at the rate of 4 ordinary shares for every $5 of stock. The rate of tax is 30%. In 20X7 gross profit of $135,000 was recorded.

Required

Calculate the diluted EPS.

Solution

Diluted EPS is calculated as follows.

Step 1 **Number of shares**: the additional equity on conversion of the loan stock will be 40,000 × 4/5 = 32,000 shares

Step 2 **Earnings**: Farrah Co will save interest payments of $6,000 but this increase in profits will be taxed. Hence the earnings figure may be recalculated:

	$
Gross profit $(150,000 + 6,000)	156,000
Tax (30%)	46,800
Profit after taxation	109,200

Step 3 **Calculation**: Diluted EPS = $\dfrac{\$109{,}200}{132{,}000}$ = 82.7c

Step 4 **Dilution**: the dilution in earnings would be 105c – 82.7c = 22.3c per share.

Ardent Co has 5,000,000 ordinary shares of 25 cents each in issue, and also had in issue in 20X4:

(a) $1,000,000 of 14% convertible loan stock, convertible in three years' time at the rate of 2 shares per $10 of stock.

(b) $2,000,000 of 10% convertible loan stock, convertible in one year's time at the rate of 3 shares per $5 of stock.

The total earnings in 20X4 were $1,750,000.

The rate of income tax is 35%.

Required

Calculate the EPS and diluted EPS.

(a)   EPS = $\dfrac{\$1{,}750{,}000}{5 \text{ million}}$ = 35 cents

(b)   On dilution, the (maximum) number of shares in issue would be:

	Shares
Current	5,000,000
On conversion of 14% stock	200,000
On conversion of 10% stock	1,200,000
	6,400,000

	$	$
Current earnings		1,750,000
Add interest saved (140,000 + 200,000)	340,000	
Less tax thereon at 35%	119,000	
		221,000
Revised earnings		1,971,000

Fully diluted EPS = $\dfrac{\$1{,}971{,}000}{6.4 \text{ million}}$ = 30.8 cents

3.7 Presentation

A entity should present in the **statement of comprehensive income** basic and diluted EPS for:

(a)   profit or loss from continuing operations; and
(b)   profit or loss for the period

for each class of ordinary share that has a different right to share in the net profit for the period.

The basic and diluted EPS should be presented with **equal prominence** for all periods presented.

Basic and diluted EPS for any **discontinuing operations** must also be presented.

Disclosure must still be made where the EPS figures (basic and/or diluted) are **negative** (ie a loss per share).

3.8 Alternative EPS figures

An entity may present **alternative EPS figures if it wishes**. However, IAS 33 lays out certain rules where this takes place.

(a)   The weighted average number of shares as calculated under IAS 33 **must** be used.
(b)   A **reconciliation** must be given between the component of profit used in the alternative EPS (if it is not a line item in the statement of comprehensive income) and the line item for profit reported in profit or loss
(c)   The entity must indicate the basis on which the **numerator** is determined.
(d)   Basic and diluted EPS must be shown with **equal prominence**.

3.9 Significance of earnings per share

Earnings per share (EPS) is one of the most frequently quoted statistics in financial analysis. Because of the widespread use of the price earnings **(P/E) ratio** as a yardstick for investment decisions, it became increasingly important.

It seems that reported and forecast EPS can, through the P/E ratio, have a **significant effect on a company's share price**. Thus, a share price might fall if it looks as if EPS is going to be low. This is not very rational, as EPS can depend on many, often subjective, assumptions used in preparing a historical statement, namely the statement of comprehensive income. It does not necessarily bear any relation to the value of a company, and of its shares. Nevertheless, the market is sensitive to EPS.

3.10 Exposure draft: Simplifying earnings per share

The objective of the EPS project is to simplify and converge the calculation of EPS between IAS 33 *Earnings per share* and its US equivalent, SFAS No. 128 *Earnings per share*. To this end, the IASB issued, in August 2008, an Exposure Draft: *Simplifying earnings per share*. This focuses on:

- Simplifying the earnings per share (EPS) calculation

- Establishing a common denominator for the EPS calculation

- Reducing differences between IAS 33 and U.S. Statement of Financial Accounting Standard (SFAS) No. 28 Earnings per Share.

Exam focus point

> Because IAS 33 will not be tested in detail for P2, you do not need to know the Exposure Draft in detail either. The most important aspect is the proposed simplification of the calculation of diluted EPS with share options. **End-of-period market price would be used, rather than average market price** during the period when calculating the dilutive effect of share options.

Other changes include the following:

(a) The ED proposes a **principle to determine which instruments would be included in the basic EPS calculation.** Under the proposed principle the weighted average number of ordinary shares would include only those instruments that give their holder the right to share in the profit or loss for the current period.

(b) The ED proposes **that if a contract requires an entity to repurchase its own ordinary shares for cash or other financial assets** (eg, a gross physically settled contract), then **such shares to be repurchased are treated as if the entity had already repurchased them**. As a result, these shares would be excluded from the denominator of the EPS calculation.

(c) For the **diluted EPS calculation**, the ED proposes that **no adjustment be made to reflect the assumed exercise or conversion of instruments measured at fair value through profit or loss.**

(d) The ED proposes to extend the scope of the application guidance of IAS 33 to **include participating instruments classified as liabilities.**

3.11 The P2 exam

Beware EPS was covered at an earlier level, it is assumed knowledge. You are unlikely to have to deal with the complications, except as they relate to **manipulation by the directors**, particularly of the earnings figure. Have a go at the Case Study question Wingit, at the end of the text.

EPS has also served as a means of assessing the **stewardship and management** role performed by company directors and managers. Remuneration packages might be linked to EPS growth, thereby increasing the pressure on management to improve EPS. The danger of this, however, is that management effort may go into distorting results to produce a favourable EPS.

3.12 Section summary

EPS is an important measure for investors.

- **Basic EPS** is straightforward, although it may require adjustments for **changes in capital structure**
- **Diluted EPS** is more complex
- **In an exam**, you may have to deal with ways in which EPS can be **manipulated**.

4 IAS 34 Interim financial reporting

IAS 34 recommends that **entities should produce interim financial reports**, and for entities that do publish such reports, it lays down principles and guidelines for their production.

The following definitions are used in IAS 34.

> - **Interim period** is a financial reporting period shorter than a full financial year.
> - **Interim financial report** means a financial report containing either a complete set of financial statements (as described in IAS 1) or a set of condensed financial statements (as described in this standard) for an interim period.
>   *(IAS 34)*

4.1 Scope

The standard does not make the preparation of interim financial reports **mandatory**, taking the view that this is a matter for governments, securities regulators, stock exchanges or professional accountancy bodies to decide within each country. The IASB does, however, strongly recommend to governments, etc, that interim financial reporting should be a requirement for companies whose equity or debt securities are **publicly traded**.

(a)   An interim financial report should be produced by such companies for **at least the first six months of their financial year** (ie a half year financial report).

(b)   The report should be **available no later than 60 days** after the end of the interim period.

Thus, a company with a year ending 31 December would be required as a minimum to prepare an interim report for the half year to 30 June and this report should be available before the end of August.

4.2 Minimum components

The proposed standard specifies the **minimum component elements** of an interim financial report.

- Condensed statement of financial position
- Condensed statement of comprehensive income
- Condensed statement of changes in equity
- Condensed statement of cash flows
- Selected note disclosures

The rationale for requiring only condensed statements and selected note disclosures is that entities need not duplicate information in their interim report that is contained in their report for the previous financial year. Interim statements should **focus more on new events, activities and circumstances**.

4.3 Form and content

Where **full financial statements** are given as interim financial statements, IAS 1 should be used as a guide, otherwise IAS 34 specifies minimum contents.

The **condensed statement of financial position** should include, as a minimum, each of the major components of assets, liabilities and equity as were in the statement of financial position at the end of the previous financial year, thus providing a summary of the economic resources of the entity and its financial structure.

The **condensed statement of comprehensive income** should include, as a minimum, each of the component items of income and expense as are shown in profit or loss for the previous financial year, together with the earnings per share and diluted earnings per share.

The **condensed statement of cash flows** should show, as a minimum, the three major sub-totals of cash flow as required in cash flow statements by IAS 7, namely: cash flows from operating activities, cash flows from investing activities and cash flow from financing activities.

The **condensed statement of changes in equity** should include, as a minimum, each of the major components of equity as were contained in the statement of changes in equity for the previous financial year of the entity.

4.3.1 Selected explanatory notes

IAS 34 states that **relatively minor changes** from the most recent annual financial statements need not be included in an interim report. However, the notes to interim report should include the following (unless the information is contained elsewhere in the report).

- A statement that the **same accounting policies and methods of computation** have been used for the interim statements as were used for the most recent annual financial statements. If not, the nature of the differences and their effect should be described. (The accounting policies for preparing the interim report should only differ from those used for the previous annual accounts in a situation where there has been a change in accounting policy since the end of the previous financial year, and the new policy will be applied for the annual accounts of the current financial period.)
- Explanatory comments on the **seasonality or 'cyclicality'** of operations in the interim period. For example, if a company earns most of its annual profits in the first half of the year, because sales are much higher in the first six months, the interim report for the first half of the year should explain this fact
- The **nature and amount** of items during the interim period affecting assets, liabilities, capital, net income or cash flows, that are unusual, due to their nature, incidence or size
- The **issue or repurchase** of equity or debt securities
- Nature and amount of any **changes in estimates** of amounts reported in an earlier interim report during the financial year, or in prior financial years if these affect the current interim period
- **Dividends paid** on ordinary shares and the dividends paid on other shares
- **Segmental results** for the business segments or geographical segments of the entity (see IFRS 8)
- Any **significant events since the end of the interim period**
- Effect of the acquisition or disposal of subsidiaries during the interim period
- Any significant change in a **contingent liability or a contingent asset** since the date of the last annual statement of financial position

The entity should also disclose the fact that the interim report has been produced **in compliance with** IAS 34 on interim financial reporting.

Question   Disclosures

Give some examples of the type of disclosures required according to the above list of explanatory notes.

Answer

The following are examples.

(a) Write-down of inventories to net realisable value and the reversal of such a write-down
(b) Recognition of a loss from the impairment of property, plant and equipment, intangible assets, or other assets, and the reversal of such an impairment loss
(c) Reversal of any provisions for the costs of restructuring
(d) Acquisitions and disposals of items of property, plant and equipment
(e) Commitments for the purchase of property, plant and equipment
(f) Litigation settlements
(g) Corrections of fundamental errors in previously reported financial data
(h) Any debt default or any breach of a debt covenant that has not been corrected subsequently
(i) Related party transactions

4.4 Periods covered

The standard requires that interim financial reports should provide financial information for the following periods or as at the following dates.

- **Statement of financial position data** as at the end of the current interim period, and comparative data as at the end of the most recent financial year
- **Statement of comprehensive income data** for the current interim period and cumulative data for the current year to date, together with comparative data for the corresponding interim period and cumulative figures for the previous financial year
- **Statement of cash flows data** should be *cumulative* for the current year to date, with comparative cumulative data for the corresponding interim period in the previous financial year
- **Data for the statement of changes in equity** should be for both the current interim period and for the year to date, together with comparative data for the corresponding interim period, and cumulative figures, for the previous financial year

4.5 Materiality

Materiality should be assessed in relation to the interim period financial data. It should be recognised that interim measurements **rely to a greater extent on estimates** than annual financial data.

4.6 Recognition and measurement principles

A large part of IAS 34 deals with recognition and measurement principles, and guidelines as to their practical application. The **guiding principle** is that an entity should use the **same recognition and measurement principles in its interim statements as it does in its annual financial statements**.

This means, for example, that a cost that would not be regarded as an asset in the year-end statement of financial position should not be regarded as an asset in the statement of financial position for an interim period. Similarly, an accrual for an item of income or expense for a transaction that has not yet occurred (or a deferral of an item of income or expense for a transaction that has already occurred) is inappropriate for interim reporting, just as it is for year-end reporting.

Applying this principle of recognition and measurement may result, in a subsequent interim period or at the year-end, in a **remeasurement** of amounts that were reported in a financial statement for a previous interim period. **The nature and amount of any significant remeasurements should be disclosed**.

4.6.1 Revenues received occasionally, seasonally or cyclically

Revenue that is received as an occasional item, or within a seasonal or cyclical pattern, should not be anticipated or deferred in interim financial statements, if it would be inappropriate to anticipate or defer the revenue for the annual financial statements. In other words, the principles of revenue recognition should be applied consistently to the interim reports and year-end reports.

4.6.2 Costs incurred unevenly during the financial year

These should only be anticipated or deferred (ie treated as accruals or prepayments) if it would be appropriate to anticipate or defer the expense in the annual financial statements. For example, it would be appropriate to anticipate a cost for property rental where the rental is paid in arrears, but it would be inappropriate to anticipate part of the cost of a major advertising campaign later in the year, for which no expenses have yet been incurred.

The standard goes on, in an appendix, to deal with **specific applications** of the recognition and measurement principle. Some of these examples are explained below, by way of explanation and illustration.

4.6.3 Payroll taxes or insurance contributions paid by employers

In some countries these are assessed on an annual basis, but paid at an uneven rate during the course of the year, with a large proportion of the taxes being paid in the early part of the year, and a much smaller proportion paid later on in the year. In this situation, it would be appropriate to use an estimated average annual tax rate for the year in an interim statement, not the actual tax paid. This treatment is appropriate because it reflects the fact that the taxes are assessed on an annual basis, even though the payment pattern is uneven.

4.6.4 Cost of a planned major periodic maintenance or overhaul

The cost of such an event later in the year must not be anticipated in an interim financial statement *unless* there is a legal or constructive obligation to carry out this work. The fact that a maintenance or overhaul is planned and is carried out annually is not of itself sufficient to justify anticipating the cost in an interim financial report.

4.6.5 Other planned but irregularly-occurring costs

Similarly, these costs such as charitable donations or employee training costs, should not be accrued in an interim report. These costs, even if they occur regularly and are planned, are nevertheless discretionary.

4.6.6 Year-end bonus

A year-end bonus should not be provided for in an interim financial statement *unless* there is a constructive obligation to pay a year-end bonus (eg a contractual obligation, or a regular past practice) and the size of the bonus can be reliably measured.

4.6.7 Holiday pay

The same principle applies here. If holiday pay is an enforceable obligation on the employer, then any unpaid accumulated holiday pay may be accrued in the interim financial report.

4.6.8 Non-mandatory intangible assets

The entity might incur expenses during an interim period on items that might or will generate non-monetary intangible assets. IAS 38 *Intangible assets* requires that costs to generate non-monetary intangible assets (eg development expenses) should be recognised as an expense when incurred *unless* the costs form part of an identifiable intangible asset. Costs that were initially recognised as an expense cannot subsequently be treated instead as part of the cost of an intangible asset. IAS 34 states that interim financial statements should adopt the same approach. This means that it would be inappropriate in an interim financial statement to 'defer' a cost in the expectation that it will eventually be part of a non-monetary intangible asset that has not yet been recognised: such costs should be treated as an expense in the interim statement.

4.6.9 Depreciation

Depreciation should only be charged in an interim statement on non-current assets that have been acquired, not on non-current assets that will be acquired later in the financial year.

4.7 Foreign currency translation gains and losses

These should be calculated by the same principles as at the financial year end, in accordance with IAS 21.

4.7.1 Tax on income

An entity will include an expense for income tax (tax on profits) in its interim statements. The **tax rate** to use should be the estimated average annual tax rate for the year. For example, suppose that in a particular jurisdiction, the rate of tax on company profits is 30% on the first $200,000 of profit and 40% on profits above $200,000. Now suppose that a company makes a profit of $200,000 in its first half year, and expects to make $200,000 in the second half year. The rate of tax to be applied in the interim financial report should be 35%, not 30%, ie the expected average rate of tax for the year as a whole. This approach is appropriate because income tax on company profits is charged on an annual basis, and an effective annual rate should therefore be applied to each interim period.

As another illustration, suppose a company earns pre-tax income in the first quarter of the year of $30,000, but expects to make a loss of $10,000 in each of the next three quarters, so that net income before tax for the year is zero. Suppose also that the rate of tax is 30%. In this case, it would be inappropriate to anticipate the losses, and the tax charge should be $9,000 for the first quarter of the year (30% of $30,000) and a negative tax charge of $3,000 for each of the next three quarters, if actual losses are the same as anticipated.

Where the tax year for a company does not coincide with its financial year, a separate estimated weighted average tax rate should be applied for each tax year, to the interim periods that fall within that tax year.

Some countries give entities tax credits against the tax payable, based on amounts of capital expenditure or research and development, etc. Under most tax regimes, these credits are calculated and granted on an annual basis; therefore it is appropriate to include anticipated tax credits within the calculation of the estimated average tax rate for the year, and apply this rate to calculate the tax on income for interim periods. However, if a tax benefit relates to a specific one-time event, it should be recognised within the tax expense for the interim period in which the event occurs.

4.7.2 Inventory valuations

Within interim reports, inventories should be valued in the same way as for year-end accounts. It is recognised, however, that it will be necessary to rely more heavily on estimates for interim reporting than for year-end reporting.

In addition, it will normally be the case that the net realisable value of inventories should be estimated from selling prices and related costs to complete and dispose at interim dates.

4.8 Use of estimates

Although accounting information must be reliable and free from material error, it may be necessary to sacrifice some accuracy and reliability for the sake of timeliness and cost-benefits. This is particularly the case with interim financial reporting, where there will be much less time to produce reports than at the financial year end. The proposed standard therefore recognises that estimates will have to be used to a greater extent in interim reporting, to assess values or even some costs, than in year-end reporting.

An appendix to IAS 34 gives some examples of the use of estimates.

(a)   **Inventories**. An entity might not need to carry out a full inventory count at the end of each interim period. Instead, it may be sufficient to estimate inventory values using sales margins.

(b)   **Provisions**. An entity might employ outside experts or consultants to advise on the appropriate amount of a provision, as at the year end. It will probably be inappropriate to employ an expert to make a similar assessment at each interim date. Similarly, an entity might employ a professional valuer to revalue fixed assets at the year end, whereas at the interim date(s) the entity will not rely on such experts.

(c)   **Income taxes**. The rate of income tax (tax on profits) will be calculated at the year end by applying the tax rate in each country/jurisdiction to the profits earned there. At the interim stage, it may be sufficient to estimate the rate of income tax by applying the same 'blended' estimated weighted average tax rate to the income earned in all countries/jurisdictions.

The principle of **materiality** applies to interim financial reporting, as it does to year-end reporting. In assessing materiality, it needs to be recognised that interim financial reports will rely more heavily on estimates than year-end reports. Materiality should be assessed in relation to the interim financial statements themselves, and should be independent of 'annual materiality' considerations.

4.9 IFRIC 10 Interim financial reporting and impairment

The Interpretation addresses an apparent conflict between the requirements of IAS 34 *Interim financial reporting* and those in other standards on the recognition and reversal in financial statements of impairment losses on goodwill and certain financial assets. IFRIC 10 concludes that:

(a)   An entity **must not reverse an impairment loss** recognised in a previous interim period in respect of goodwill or an investment in either an equity instrument or a financial asset carried at cost.

(b)   An entity **must not extend this consensus** by analogy to other areas of potential conflict between IAS 34 and other standards.

4.10 Section summary

- IAS 34 in concept makes **straightforward proposals** for the production of interim financial reports by entities.

- It is essential to apply **principles of recognition and measurement** that will prevent entities from 'massaging' the interim figures.

- The **detail** in the guidelines is therefore very important, and the application of the recognition and measurement principles to particular valuations and measurements needs to be understood.

5 Ratio analysis

FAST FORWARD

Keep the various **sources of financial information** in mind and the effects of insider dealing, the efficient market hypothesis and Stock Exchange regulations.

The accounts of a business are designed to provide users with information about its performance and financial position. The bare figures, however, are not particularly useful and it is only through **comparisons** (usually of ratios) that their significance can be established. Comparisons may be made with previous financial periods, with other similar businesses or with averages for the particular industry. The choice will depend on the purpose for which the comparison is being made and the information that is available.

Various groups are interested in the performance and financial position of a company.

(a)   **Management** will use comparisons to ensure that the business is performing efficiently and according to plan

(b)   **Employees**, trade unions and so on

(c)   **Government**

(d)   Present and potential **investors** will assess the company with a view to judging whether it is a sound investment

(e)   **Lenders** and **suppliers** will want to judge its creditworthiness

This text is concerned with financial rather than management accounting and the ratios discussed here are therefore likely to be calculated by external users. The following sources of information are readily available to external users.

- Published accounts and interim statements
- Documents filed as required by company legislation
- Statistics published by the government
- Other published sources eg *Investors Chronicle*, *The Economist*, *Wall Street Journal*

5.1 Financial analysis

The **lack of detailed information** available to the outsider is a considerable disadvantage in undertaking ratio analysis. The first difficulty is that there may simply be insufficient data to calculate all of the required ratios. A second concerns the availability of a suitable 'yardstick' with which the calculated ratios may be compared.

5.1.1 Inter-temporal analysis

Looking first at inter-temporal or trend analysis (comparisons for the same business over time), some of the **problems** include the following.

- Changes in the nature of the business
- Unrealistic depreciation rates under historical cost accounting
- The changing value of the pound
- Changes in accounting policies

Other factors will include changes in government incentive packages, changes from purchasing equipment to leasing and so on.

5.1.2 Cross-sectional analysis

When undertaking 'cross-sectional' analysis (making comparisons with other companies) the position is even more difficult because of the problem of identifying companies that are comparable. **Comparability** between companies may be impaired due to the following reasons.

(a) Different degrees of diversification

(b) Different production and purchasing policies (if an investor was analysing the smaller car manufacturers, he would find that some of them buy in engines from one of the 'majors' whilst others develop and manufacture their own)

(c) Different financing policies (eg leasing as opposed to buying)

(d) Different accounting policies (one of the most serious problems particularly in relation to non-current assets and inventory valuation)

(e) Different effects of government incentives

The major **intragroup comparison organisations** (whose results are intended for the use of participating companies and are not generally available) go to considerable length to adjust accounts to comparable bases. The external user will rarely be in a position to make such adjustments. Although the position is improved by increases in disclosure requirements direct comparisons between companies will inevitably, on occasion, continue to give rise to misleading results.

5.2 Social and political considerations

Social considerations tend to be **short-lived** or 'fashionable' and therefore each set of statements can be affected by a different movement or fad. In recent years, the social aspect much in evidence has been that of environmental issues. Companies have gone for a 'green' image, although this has been more in evidence in glossy pictures than in the accounts themselves.

Political considerations may be more far reaching. The regulatory regime may be instituted by statutes, but often self-regulation is encouraged through bodies such as the stock exchange.

5.3 Multinational companies

Multinational companies have great difficulties sometimes because of the need to comply with **legislation** in a large number of countries. As well as different reporting requirements, different rules of incorporation exist, as well as different directors' rules, tax legislation and so on. Sometimes the local rules can be so harsh that companies will avoid them altogether. In California, for example, multinational companies with operations there are taxed on their *world wide* profits, not just their US profits. Local tax regimes may also require information about the group as a whole because of the impact of internal transfer pricing on tax.

Different local reporting requirements will also make **consolidation** more difficult. The results of subsidiaries must be translated, not only to the company's base currency, but also using the accounting rules used by head office. This is a requirement of IASs as 'uniform accounting policies' are called for.

5.4 The efficient market hypothesis and stock exchanges

It has been argued that stock markets in the most sophisticated economies, eg the USA, are **efficient capital markets**.

(a)   The prices of securities bought and sold reflect all the relevant information which is available to the buyers and sellers. In other words, share prices change quickly to reflect all new information about future prospects.

(b)   No individual dominates the market.

(c)   Transaction costs are not so high as to discourage trading significantly.

If the stock market is efficient, share prices should vary in a **rational way**, ie reflecting the known profits or losses of a company and the state of return required based on interest states.

Research in both Britain and the USA has suggested that market prices anticipate mergers several months before they are formally announced, and the conclusion drawn is that the stock market in these countries *do* exhibit **semi-strong efficiency**. It has also been argued that the market displays sufficient efficiency for investors to see through 'window dressing' of accounts by companies which use accounting conventions to overstate profits (ie creative accounting).

Evidence suggests that stock markets show efficiency that is **at least weak form**, but tending more towards a semi-strong form. In other words, current share prices reflect all or most publicly available information about companies and their securities. However, it is very difficult to assess the market's efficiency in relation to shares which are not usually actively traded.

Fundamental analysis and **technical analysis** carried out by analysts and investment managers play an important role in creating an efficient stock market. This is because an efficient market depends on the widespread availability of cheap information about companies, their shares and market conditions, and this is what the firms of market makers and other financial institutions *do* provide for their clients and for the general investing public. In a market which demonstrates strong-form efficiency, such analysis would not identify profitable opportunities, ie where shares are undervalued, because such information would already be known and reflected in the share price.

On the other hand stock market crashes raise serious questions about the validity of the **fundamental theory of share values** and the efficient market hypothesis. If these theories are correct, how can shares that were valued at one level on one day suddenly be worth 40% less the next day, without any change in expectations of corporate profits and dividends? On the other hand, a widely feared crash may fail to happen, suggesting that stock markets may not be altogether out of touch with the underlying values of companies.

5.5 Insider dealing

In theory, the rules of various countries on **insider dealing** should limit the efficiency of the capital markets to semi-strong form.

Key term

> **Insider dealing** is dealing in securities while in possession of insider information as an insider, the securities being price-affected by the information. Off-market transactions between or involving 'professional intermediaries' may be included, not just transactions on a designated exchange.

There are various possible anti-avoidance measures, including disclosure of information to other parties.

Examples of securities

(a)   Shares or stock in the share capital of a company

(b)   Debt securities (eg gilts)

(c)   All forms of warrants, depository receipts, options, futures, contracts for differences based on individual securities or an index

Insider information is 'price-sensitive information' relating to a particular issue of securities that are price-affected and not to securities generally; it must be specific or precise and, if made public, be likely to have a significant effect on price.

General defences may be available where the individual concerned can show that:

(a)   he did not expect there to be a profit or avoidance of loss,

(b)   he had reasonable grounds to believe that the information had been disclosed widely, or

(c)   he would have done what he did even if he had not had the information, for example where securities are sold to pay a pressing debt.

In order to avoid false markets in shares and to keep investors and their advisors properly informed, listed companies should notify the relevant stock exchange of any **necessary information**. This is then public knowledge. More specific requirements may include the following.

- Preliminary announcements of profits and losses
- Major acquisitions
- Redemption of debt capital
- Changes in nature of business
- Proposals to purchase own shares
- Declaration of dividends

To publish information quickly is an effective way of reducing the opportunity for insider dealing.

The evil of insider dealing is obvious enough. On the other hand some **reasonable limits** have to be set on the prohibition on insider dealing. There are practical problems in applying rules on insider dealing. In particular it is doubtful whether a director of a public company, who receives confidential information (say management accounts) at each board meeting, is ever in a position to deal in securities of his company without technical infringement of insider dealing rules.

5.6 The broad categories of ratios

FAST FORWARD

Much of the material here on **basic ratios** should have been revision for you. The next few chapters will cover much more complicated aspects of financial analysis.

Make sure that you can **define** all the ratios. Look out for variations in definitions of ratios which might appear in questions.

Ratio analysis involves **comparing one figure against another** to produce a ratio, and assessing whether the ratio indicates a weakness or strength in the company's affairs.

Exam focus point

You are unlikely to be asked to calculate many ratios in the P2 exam, or not directly at any rate. If, say, you were asked to comment on a company's past or potential future performance, you would be expected to select your own ratios in order to do so. The skill here is picking the key ratios in the context of the question and not calculating a lot of useless ratios.

Broadly speaking, basic ratios can be grouped into five categories.

- Profitability and return
- Long-term solvency and stability
- Short-term solvency and liquidity
- Efficiency (turnover ratios)
- Shareholders' investment ratios

Ratio analysis on its own is **not sufficient** for interpreting company accounts, and that there are other items of information which should be looked at.

(a)   The content of any **accompanying commentary** on the accounts and other statements

(b)   The age and nature of the **company's assets**

(c)   Current and future **developments** in the company's markets, at home and overseas, recent acquisitions or disposals of a subsidiary by the company

(d)   Any other **noticeable features** of the report and accounts, such as events after the reporting period, contingent liabilities, a qualified auditors' report, the company's taxation position

The following sections summarise what you already know about ratio analysis from your earlier studies. You should then perform the comprehensive questions given in this chapter. The following chapters look at more complex areas of analysis and interpretation, which build on the knowledge in this chapter.

5.7 Profitability and return on capital

One profit figure that should be calculated and compared over time is **PBIT, profit before interest and tax**, the amount of profit which the company earned before having to pay interest to the providers of loan capital. By providers of loan capital, we usually mean longer-term loan capital, such as debentures and medium-term bank loans, which will be shown in the statement of financial position as 'non-current liabilities'. Also, tax is affected by unusual variations which have a distorting effect.

Profit before interest and tax is therefore:

(a)   The profit on operating activities before taxation, plus
(b)   Interest charges on long-term loan capital.

Published accounts do not always give sufficient detail on interest payable to determine how much is interest on long-term finance.

5.7.1 A warning about comments on profit margin and asset turnover

It might be tempting to think that a high profit margin is good, and a low asset turnover means sluggish trading. In broad terms, this is so. But there is **a trade-off** between profit margin and asset turnover, and you cannot look at one without allowing for the other.

(a)   A high profit margin means a high profit per $1 of sales, but if this also means that sales prices are high, there is a strong possibility that sales revenue will be depressed, and so asset turnover lower.

(b)   A high asset turnover means that the company is generating a lot of sales, but to do this it might have to keep its prices down and so accept a low profit margin per $1 of sales.

Knowledge brought forward from earlier studies

Profitability

Return on capital employed

$$ROCE = \frac{PBIT}{Capital\ employed} = \frac{PBIT}{Total\ assets\ less\ current\ liabilities}$$

When **interpreting** ROCE look for the following.

- How risky is the business?
- How capital intensive is it?
- What ROCE do similar businesses have?

Problems: which items to consider to achieve comparability:

- Revaluation reserves
- Policies, eg, R & D
- Bank overdraft: short/long-term liability
- Investments and related income: exclude

The following **considerations** are important.

- Change year to year
- Comparison to similar companies
- Comparison with current market borrowing rates

Return on equity

$$ROE = \frac{Profit\ after\ tax\ and\ pref\ div}{Ordinary\ share\ capital + reserves}\%$$

This gives a more **restricted view** of capital than ROCE, but the same principles apply.

Secondary ratios

Profit margin × Asset turnover = ROCE

Profit margin

$$\text{Profit margin} = \frac{\text{PBIT}}{\text{Revenue}}\% \quad \text{Gross profit margin} = \frac{\text{Gross profit}}{\text{Revenue}}\%$$

It is useful to compare profit margin to gross profit % to investigate movements which do not match. Take into account:

- Gross profit margin
    - Sales prices, sales volume and sales mix
    - Purchase prices and related costs (discount, carriage etc)
    - Production costs, both direct (materials, labour) and indirect (overheads both fixed and variable)
    - Inventory levels and inventory valuation, including errors, cut-off and stock-out costs

- Net profit margin
    - Sales expenses in relation to sales levels
    - Administrative expenses, including salary levels
    - Distribution expenses in relation to sales levels

    Depreciation should be considered as a separate item for each expense category.

Asset turnover

$$\text{Asset turnover} = \frac{\text{Revenue}}{\text{Total assets less current liabilities}}$$

This measures the **efficiency** of the use of assets. Amend to just non-current assets for capital intensive businesses.

5.8 Liquidity and working capital

Profitability is of course an important aspect of a company's performance and debt or gearing is another. Neither, however, addresses directly the key issue of liquidity in the **short term**.

Liquidity is the amount of cash a company can put its hands on quickly to settle its debts (and possibly to meet other unforeseen demands for cash payments too). Liquid funds consist of the following.

- Cash
- Short-term investments for which there is a ready market (as distinct from shares held in subsidiaries or associated companies)
- Fixed-term deposits with a bank (eg a six month high-interest deposit)
- Trade receivables (because they will pay what they owe within a short period of time)
- Bills of exchange receivable (because these represent cash due to be received within a relatively short period of time)

A company can obtain liquid assets from sources other than sales, such as the issue of shares for cash, a new loan or the sale of long-term assets. But a company cannot rely on these at all times, and in general obtaining liquid funds depends on making sales and profits. Even so, **profits do not always lead to increases in liquidity**. This is mainly because funds generated from trading may be immediately invested in long-term assets or paid out as dividends.

Efficiency ratios indicate how well a business is controlling aspects of its working capital.

Liquidity and working capital

This was very topical in the late 1980s as interest rates were high, and there was a recession Can a company meet its short-term debts?

Current ratio

$$\text{Current ratio} = \frac{\text{Current assets}}{\text{Current liabilities}}$$

Assume assets realised at book value ∴ theoretical. 2:1 acceptable? 1.5:1? It depends on the industry.

Quick ratio

$$\text{Quick ratio (acid test)} = \frac{\text{Current assets - Inventory}}{\text{Current liabilities}}$$

Eliminates illiquid and subjectively valued inventory. Care is needed: it could be high if **overtrading** with receivables, but no cash. Is 1:1 OK? Many supermarkets operate on 0.3.

Collection period

$$\text{Average collection period} = \frac{\text{Trade receivables}}{\text{Credit turnover}} \times 365$$

Is it **consistent** with quick/current ratio? If not, investigate.

Inventory turnover period

$$\text{Inventory turnover} = \frac{\text{Cost of sales}}{\text{Inventory}} \qquad \text{Inventory turnover period} = \frac{\text{Inventory}}{\text{Cost of sales}} \times 365$$

Higher the better? But remember:

- Lead times
- Seasonal fluctuations in orders
- Alternative uses of warehouse space
- Bulk buying discounts
- Likelihood of inventory perishing or becoming obsolete

Accounts payable payment period

$$\text{Accounts payable payment period} = \frac{\text{Trade payables}}{\text{Purchases}} \times 365$$

Use **cost of sales** if purchases are not disclosed.

Cash cycle

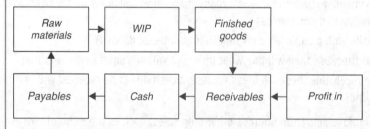

- Cash flow timing does not match sales/cost of sales timing as credit is taken
- Holding stock delays the time between payments for goods and sales receipts

Reasons for changes in liquidity

- **Credit control** efficiency altered
- Altering **payment period** of creditors as a source of funding
- Reduce **stock holdings** to maintain liquidity

5.9 Long-term solvency: debt and gearing/leverage

Debt and gearing ratios are concerned with a company's long-**term stability**: how much the company owes in relation to its size, whether it is getting into heavier debt or improving its situation, and whether its debt burden seems heavy or light.

(a) When a company is heavily in debt, banks and other potential lenders may be unwilling to advance further funds.

(b) When a company is earning only a modest profit before interest and tax, and has a heavy debt burden, there will be very little profit left (if any) over for shareholders after the interest charges have been paid. And so if interest rates were to go up (on bank overdrafts and so on) or the company were to borrow even more, it might soon be incurring interest charges in excess of PBIT. This might eventually lead to the liquidation of the company.

Debt and gearing/leverage

Debt/equity

$$\text{Debt/equity ratio} = \frac{\text{Interest bearing net debt}}{\text{Shareholders' funds}} \% \, (>100\% = \text{high})$$

Or

$$\frac{\text{Interest bearing net debt}}{\text{Shareholders' funds} + \text{interest bearing net debt}} \% \, (>50\% = \text{high})$$

There is **no definitive answer**; elements included are subjective. The following could have an impact.

- Convertible loan stock
- Preferred shares
- Deferred tax
- Goodwill and development expenditure capitalisation
- Revaluation reserve

Gearing/leverage

$$\text{Gearing ratio} = \frac{\text{Prior charge capital}}{\text{Total capital}} \qquad \text{Leverage} = \frac{\text{Total capital}}{\text{Prior charge capital}}$$

Interest cover

$$\text{Interest cover} = \frac{\text{PBIT (incl int receivable)}}{\text{Interest payable}}$$

Is this a better way to **measure gearing** or **leverage**? Company must generate enough profit to cover interest. Is a figure of 3+ safe?

5.9.1 The implications of high or low gearing

Gearing or leverage is, amongst other things, an attempt to quantify the **degree of risk** involved in holding equity shares in a company, both in terms of the company's ability to remain in business and in terms of expected ordinary dividends from the company. The problem with a highly geared company is that, by definition, there is a lot of debt. Debt generally carries a fixed rate of interest (or fixed rate of dividend if in the form of preferred shares), hence there is a given (and large) amount to be paid out from profits to holders of debt before arriving at a residue available for distribution to the holders of equity.

The more highly geared the company, the greater the risk that little (if anything) will be available to distribute by way of dividend to the ordinary shareholders. The more highly geared the company, the greater the percentage change in profit available for ordinary shareholders for any given percentage change in profit before interest and tax. The relationship similarly holds when profits increase. This means that there will be greater **volatility** of amounts available for ordinary shareholders, and presumably therefore greater volatility in dividends paid to those shareholders, where a company is highly geared. That is the risk. You may do extremely well or extremely badly without a particularly large movement in the PBIT of the company.

The risk of a company's ability to remain in business was referred to earlier. Gearing is relevant to this. A highly geared company has a large amount of interest to pay annually. If those borrowings are 'secured' in any way (and debentures in particular are secured), then the holders of the debt are perfectly entitled to force the company to realise assets to pay their interest if funds are not available from other sources. Clearly, the more highly geared a company, the more likely this is to occur when and if profits fall. Note that problems related to **off balance sheet finance** hiding the level of gearing have gradually become rarer, due to standards such as IAS 17 (on leasing).

Companies will only be able to increase their gearing if they have **suitable assets** to offer for security. Companies with assets which are depreciated rapidly or which are at high risk of obsolescence will be unable to offer sufficient security, eg computer software companies. On the other hand, a property company will have plenty of assets to offer as security whose value is fairly stable (but note the effect of a property slump).

Ideally, the following **gearing profiles** would apply, so that only certain types of company could have higher gearing.

Type of company	Assets	Profits
Highly geared companies	Holding value, long-term	Stable, steady trends
Low geared companies	Rapid depreciation/change	Erratic, volatile

5.9.2 The effect of GAAP on gearing/leverage

Variations in accounting policy can have a significant impact on gearing and it will be necessary to consider the individual policies of companies. The main areas which are likely to require consideration area as follows.

(a)   Revaluation of non-current assets will have an impact on equity and it will be necessary to consider the frequency of such revaluations.

(b)   Assets held under leases may be excluded from a company's statement of financial position if the leases are classified as operating leases.

(c)   The structure of group accounts and methods of consolidation will also have a substantial impact on gearing.

5.10 Shareholders' investment ratios

These are the ratios which help equity shareholders and other investors to assess the value and quality of an investment in the **ordinary shares** of a company.

The value of an investment in ordinary shares in a **listed company** is its market value, and so investment ratios must have regard not only to information in the company's published accounts, but also to the current price.

Earnings per share is a valuable indicator of an ordinary share's performance and you should refer to Chapter 15 to revise its calculation.

> **Knowledge brought forward from earlier studies**

Investors' ratios

Dividend yield

$$\text{Dividend yield} = \frac{\text{Div per share}}{\text{Mid - market price}}\%$$

- **Low yield**: the company retains a large proportion of profits to reinvest
- **High yield**: this is a risky company or slow-growing

Dividend cover

$$\text{Dividend cover} = \frac{\text{EPS}}{\text{Net div per share}}$$

Or

$$\frac{\text{Profit after tax and pref div}}{\text{Div on ordinary shares}}$$

This shows **how safe the dividend is**, or the extent of profit retention. Variations are due to maintaining dividend when profits are declining.

P/E ratio

$$\text{P/E ratio} = \frac{\text{Mid - market price}}{\text{EPS}}$$

The **higher the better** here: it reflects the confidence of the market. A rise in EPS will cause an increase in P/E ratio, but maybe not to same extent: Look at the context of the market and industry norms.

Earnings yield

$$\text{Earnings yield} = \frac{\text{EPS}}{\text{Mid - market price}}$$

This shows the dividend yield if there is no retention of profit. It allows you to compare companies with **different dividend policies**, showing growth rather than earnings.

Net assets per share

$$\text{Net assets per share} = \frac{\text{Net assets}}{\text{No of shares}}$$

This is a **crude measure** of value of a company, liable to distortion.

See also **EPS** and **dividend per share**

> **FAST FORWARD**
>
> Always remember that 'profit' and 'net assets' are fairly **arbitrary figures**, affected by different accounting policies and manipulation.
>
> Financial analysis is a vital tool for **auditors**.

Exam focus point

It cannot be overemphasised that question practice is *vital* in this area. By answering as many questions as possible you will become more and more adept at spotting the major issues in these types of question – which means you will gain most of the marks!

BPP LEARNING MEDIA

 **Question**

Ratio analysis report

RST Co is considering purchasing an interest in its competitor XYZ Co. The managing director of RST Co has obtained the three most recent statements of comprehensive income and statements of financial position of XYZ Co as shown below.

XYZ CO
STATEMENTS OF COMPREHENSIVE INCOME FOR YEARS ENDED 31 DECEMBER

	20X6	20X7	20X8
	$'000	$'000	$'000
Revenue	18,000	18,900	19,845
Cost of sales	10,440	10,340	11,890
Gross profit	7,560	8,560	7,955
Distribution costs	1,565	1,670	1,405
Administrative expenses	1,409	1,503	1,591
Operating profit	4,586	5,387	4,959
Interest payable on bank overdraft	104	215	450
Interest payable on 12% debentures	600	600	600
Profit before taxation	3,882	4,572	3,909
Income tax	1,380	2,000	1,838
Profit after taxation	2,502	2,572	2,071

XYZ CO
STATEMENTS OF FINANCIAL POSITION AS AT 31 DECEMBER

	20X6		20X7		20X8	
	$'000	$'000	$'000	$'000	$'000	$'000
Assets						
Non-current assets						
Land and buildings	11,460		12,121		11,081	
Plant and machinery	8,896		9,020		9,130	
		20,356		21,141		20,211
Current assets						
Inventory	1,775		2,663		3,995	
Trade receivables	1,440		2,260		3,164	
Cash	50		53		55	
		3,265		4,976		7,214
		23,621		26,117		27,425
Equity and liabilities						
Equity						
Share capital	8,000		8,000		8,000	
Retained earnings	6,434		7,313		7,584	
		14,434		15,313		15,584
Non-current liabilities						
12% debentures 20Y1 – 20Y4		5,000		5,000		5,000
Current liabilities						
Trade payables	390		388		446	
Bank	1,300		2,300		3,400	
Taxation	897		1,420		1,195	
Dividend payable	1,600		1,696		1,800	
		4,187		5,804		6,841
		23,621		26,117		27,425

Required

Prepare a report for the managing director of RST Co commenting on the financial position of XYZ Co and highlighting any areas that require further investigation.

(Marks will be awarded for ratios and other financial statistics where appropriate.)

To: MD of RST Co
From: An Accountant
Date: XX.XX.XX
Subject: *The financial position of XYZ Co*

Introduction

This report has been prepared on the basis of the three most recent statements of comprehensive income and statement of financial position of XYZ Co covering the years 20X6 to 20X8 inclusive. Ratio analysis used in this report is based on the calculations shown in the appendix attached.

Performance

Sales have increased at a steady 5% per annum over the three year period.

In contrast, the gross profit percentage has increased from 42% in 20X6 to 45% in 20X7 before dropping back to 40% in 20X8. Similarly, operating profit as a percentage of sales was 26% in 20X6, 28.5% in 20X7 and 25% in 20X8. This may indicate some misallocation of costs between 20X7 and 20X8 and should be investigated or it may be indicative of a longer downward trend in profitability.

Return on capital employed, as one would expect, has shown a similar pattern with an increase in 20X7 with a subsequent fall in 20X8 to a level below that of 20X6.

Debt and liquidity

The debt ratio measures the ratio of a company's total debt to its total assets. Although we have no information as to the norm for the industry as a whole, the debt ratios appear reasonable. However, it should be noted that it has risen steadily over the three year period.

When reviewing XYZ Co's liquidity the situation has improved over the period. The current ratio measures a company's ability to meet its current liabilities out of current assets. A ratio of at least 1 should therefore be expected. XYZ Co did not meet this expectation in 20X6 and 20X7.

This ratio can be misleading as inventory is included in current assets. Because inventory can take some time to convert into liquid assets a second ratio, the quick ratio, is calculated which excludes inventory. As can be seen, the quick ratio, although improving, is low and this shows that current liabilities cannot be met from current assets if inventory is excluded. As a major part of current liabilities is the bank overdraft, the company is obviously relying on the bank's continuing support with short-term funding. It would be useful to find out the terms of the bank funding and the projected cash flow requirements for future funding.

Efficiency ratios

The efficiency ratios, receivables ratio and inventory turnover, give a useful indication of how the company is managing its current assets.

As can be seen from the appendix the debtors collection period has increased over the three years from 29 days to 58 days. This may indicate that the company is failing to follow up its debts efficiently or that it has given increased credit terms to some or all of its customers.

Looking at inventory turnover, this has also risen from 62 days to 122 days. This may be an indication of over-stocking, stocking up on the expectation of a substantial sales increase or the holding of obsolete or slow-moving inventory items which should be written down. More investigation needs to be done on both receivables and inventory.

The financing of additional receivables and inventory has been achieved in the main through the bank overdraft as the trade payables figure has not increased significantly.

Conclusion

The review of the three year financial statements for XYZ Co has given rise to a number of queries which need to be resolved before a useful conclusion can be reached on the financial position of XYZ Co. It may also be useful to compare XYZ Co's ratios to those of other companies in the same industry in order to obtain some idea of the industry norms.

APPENDIX TO MEMORANDUM

	20X6	20X7	20X8
% sales increase		5%	5%
Gross profit %	42%	45%	40%
Operating profit %	25.5%	28.5%	25%

Return on capital employed

$$= \frac{\text{Profit before interest and tax}}{\text{Capital employed}} \times 100\%$$

	20X6	20X7	20X8
	$\frac{4,586-104}{14,434+5,000}$	$\frac{5,387-215}{15,313+5,000}$	$\frac{4,959-450}{15,584+5,000}$
	= 23%	= 25.5%	= 21.9%

Debt ratio

$$= \frac{\text{Total debt}}{\text{Total assets}} \times 100\%$$

	20X6	20X7	20X8
	$\frac{4,187+5,000}{20,356+3,265}$	$\frac{5,804+5,000}{21,114+4,976}$	$\frac{6,841+5,000}{20,211+7,214}$
	= 38.9%	= 41.4%	= 43.2%

Current ratio

$$= \frac{\text{Current assets}}{\text{Current liabilities}}$$

	20X6	20X7	20X8
	$\frac{3,265}{4,187}$	$\frac{4,976}{5,804}$	$\frac{7,214}{6,814}$
	= 0.78	= 0.86	= 1.06

Quick ratio

$$= \frac{\text{Current assets} - \text{inventory}}{\text{Current liabilities}}$$

	20X6	20X7	20X8
	$\frac{3,265-1,775}{4,187}$	$\frac{4,976-2,663}{5,804}$	$\frac{7,214-3,995}{6,814}$
	= 0.36	= 0.40	= 0.47

Receivables ratio

$$= \frac{\text{Trade receivables}}{\text{Sales}} \times 365 \text{ days}$$

	20X6	20X7	20X8
	$\frac{1,440}{18,000}$	$\frac{2,260}{18,900}$	$\frac{3,164}{19,845}$
	= 29.2 days	= 43.6 days	= 58.2 days

Inventory turnover

$$= \frac{\text{Inventory}}{\text{Cost of sales}} \times 365 \text{ days}$$

	20X6	20X7	20X8
	$\frac{1,775}{10,440}$	$\frac{2,663}{10,340}$	$\frac{3,995}{11,890}$
	= 62 days	= 94 days	= 122.6 days

Question

Ratio analysis report 2

You are the management accountant of Fry Co. Laurie Co is a competitor in the same industry and it has been operating for 20 years. Summaries of Laurie Co's statements of comprehensive income and financial position for the previous three years are given below.

SUMMARISED STATEMENTS OF COMPREHENSIVE INCOME
FOR THE YEAR ENDED 31 DECEMBER

	20X6 $m	20X7 $m	20X8 $m
Revenue	840	981	913
Cost of sales	554	645	590
Gross profit	286	336	323
Selling, distribution and administration expenses	186	214	219
Profit before interest	100	122	104
Interest	6	15	19
Profit before taxation	94	107	85
Taxation	45	52	45
Profit after taxation	49	55	40
Dividends	24	24	24

SUMMARISED STATEMENTS OF FINANCIAL POSITION AS AT 31 DECEMBER

	20X6 $m	20X7 $m	20X8 $m
Assets			
Non-current assets			
Intangible assets	36	40	48
Tangible assets at net book value	176	206	216
	212	246	264
Current assets			
Inventories	237	303	294
Receivables	105	141	160
Bank	52	58	52
	606	748	770
Equity and liabilities			
Equity			
Ordinary share capital	100	100	100
Retained earnings	299	330	346
	399	430	446
Non-current liabilities			
Long-term loans	74	138	138
Current liabilities			
Trade payables	53	75	75
Other payables	80	105	111
	606	748	770

You may assume that the index of retail prices has remained constant between 20X0 and 20X2.

Required

Write a report to the finance director of Fry Co:

(a)   Analysing the performance of Laurie Co and showing any calculations in an appendix to this report.

(b)   Summarising five areas which require further investigation, including reference to other pieces of information which would complement your analysis of the performance of Laurie Co.

Answer

(a)   To: Finance Director
       From: Management accountant
       Subject: *Performance of Laurie Co 20X6 to 20X8*

An appendix is attached to this report which shows the ratios calculated as part of the performance review.

Profitability

The gross profit margin has remained relatively static over the three year period, although it has risen by approximately 1% in 20X8. ROCE, while improving very slightly in 20X7 to 21.5% has dropped dramatically in 20X8 to 17.8%. The net profit margin has also fallen in 20X8, in spite of the improvement in the gross profit margin. This marks a rise in expenses which suggests that they are not being well controlled. The utilisation of assets compared to the turnover generated has also declined reflecting the drop in trading activity between 20X7 and 20X8.

Trading levels

It is apparent that there was a dramatic increase in trading activity between 20X7 and 20X8, but then a significant fall in 20X8. Revenue rose by 17% in 20X7 but fell by 7% in 20X8. The reasons for this fluctuation are unclear. It may be the effect of some kind of one-off event, or it may be the effect of a change in product mix. Whatever the reason, it appears that improved credit terms granted to customers (receivables payment period up from 46 to 64 days) has not stopped the drop in sales.

Working capital

Both the current ratio and quick ratio demonstrate an adequate working capital situation, although the quick ratio has shown a slight decline. There has been an increased investment over the period in inventories and receivables which has been only partly financed by longer payment periods to trade payables and a rise in other payables (mainly between 20X6 and 20X7).

Capital structure

The level of gearing of the company increased when a further $64m was raised in long-term loans in 20X7 to add to the $74m already in the statement of financial position. Although this does not seem to be a particularly high level of gearing, the debt/equity ratio did rise from 18.5% to 32.0% in 20X7. The interest charge has risen to $19m from $6m in 20X6. The 20X7 charge was $15m, suggesting that either the interest rate on the loan is flexible, or that the full interest charge was not incurred in 20X7. The new long-term loan appears to have funded the expansion in both fixed and current assets in 20X7.

APPENDIX

Ratio	Working	20X6	20X7	20X8
Gross profit margin	(1)	34.0%	34.3%	35.4%
ROCE	(2)	21.1%	21.5%	17.8%
Profit margin	(3)	11.9%	12.4%	11.4%
Assets turnover	(4)	1.78	1.73	1.56
Gearing ratio	(5)	15.6%	24.3%	23.6%
Debt/equity ratio	(6)	18.5%	32.0%	30.9%
Interest cover	(7)	16.7	8.1	5.5
Current ratio	(8)	3.0	2.8	2.7
Quick ratio	(9)	1.2	1.1	1.1
Receivables payment period (days)	(10)	46	52	64
Inventory turnover period (days)	(11)	156	171	182
Payables turnover period	(12)	35	42	46

Workings (all in $m)

		20X6	20X7	20X8
1	Gross profit margin	$\dfrac{286}{840}$	$\dfrac{336}{981}$	$\dfrac{323}{913}$
2	ROCE *	$\dfrac{100}{473}$	$\dfrac{122}{568}$	$\dfrac{104}{584}$
3	Profit margin	$\dfrac{100}{840}$	$\dfrac{122}{981}$	$\dfrac{104}{913}$
4	Assets turnover	$\dfrac{840}{473}$	$\dfrac{981}{568}$	$\dfrac{913}{584}$
5	Gearing ratio	$\dfrac{74}{74 + 399}$	$\dfrac{138}{138 + 430}$	$\dfrac{138}{138 + 446}$
6	Debt/equity ratio	$\dfrac{74}{399}$	$\dfrac{138}{430}$	$\dfrac{138}{446}$
7	Interest cover	$\dfrac{100}{6}$	$\dfrac{122}{15}$	$\dfrac{104}{19}$
8	Current ratio	$\dfrac{394}{133}$	$\dfrac{502}{180}$	$\dfrac{506}{186}$
9	Quick ratio	$\dfrac{157}{133}$	$\dfrac{199}{180}$	$\dfrac{212}{186}$
10	Receivables payment period	$\dfrac{105}{840} \times 365$	$\dfrac{141}{981} \times 365$	$\dfrac{160}{913} \times 365$
11	Inventory turnover period	$\dfrac{237}{554} \times 365$	$\dfrac{303}{645} \times 365$	$\dfrac{294}{590} \times 365$
12	Payables payment period	$\dfrac{53}{554} \times 365$	$\dfrac{75}{645} \times 365$	$\dfrac{75}{590} \times 365$

* ROCE has been calculated here as:

$$\frac{\text{Profit on ordinary activities before interest and taxation (PBIT)}}{\text{Capital employed}}$$

where capital employed = shareholders' funds plus creditors falling due after one year and any long-term provision for liabilities and charges. It is possible to calculate ROCE using net profit after taxation and interest, but this admits variations and distortions into the ratio which are not affected by *trading* activity.

(b) Areas for further investigation include the following.

(i) *Long-term loan*

There is no indication as to why this loan was raised and how it was used to finance the business. Further details are needed of interest rate(s), security given and repayment dates.

(ii) *Trading activity*

The level of sales has fluctuated in quite a strange way and this requires further investigation and explanation. Factors to consider would include pricing policies, product mix, market share and any unique occurrence which would affect sales.

(iii) *Further breakdown*

It would be useful to break down some of the information in the financial statements, perhaps into a management accounting format. Examples would include the following.

(1) Sales by segment, market or geographical area
(2) Cost of sales split, into raw materials, labour and overheads
(3) Inventory broken down into raw materials, work in progress and finished goods
(4) Expenses analysed between administrative expenses, sales and distribution costs

(iv)   *Accounting policies*

Accounting policies may have a significant effect on certain items. In particular, it would be useful to know what the accounting policies are in relation to intangible assets (and what these assets consist of), and whether there has been any change in accounting policies.

(v)   *Dividend policy*

The company has maintained the level of dividend paid to shareholders (although it has not been raised during the three year period). Presumably the company would have been able to reduce the amount of long-term debt taken on if it had retained part or all of the dividend during this period. It would be interesting to examine the share price movement during the period and calculate the dividend cover.

Tutorial note. Other matters raised could have included:

(1)   Working capital problems, particularly inventory turnover and control over receivables

(2)   EPS (which cannot be calculated here as the number of shares is not given) and other related investor statistics, such as the P/E ratio.

Chapter Roundup

- Go back to your earlier studies and revise **IAS 1** and **IAS 8**. IAS 1 has been revised. The changes and new formats are given in this section.

- An important aspect of reporting financial performance is **segment reporting.** This is covered by IFRS 8 *Operating segments*, which replaced IAS 14 *Segment reporting* in November 2006.

- IFRS 8 adopts a **managerial approach** to identifying reportable segments.

- **Reportable segments** are operating segments or aggregation of operating segments that meet specified criteria.

- IFRS 8 **disclosures** are of:

    –   Operating segment profit or loss
    –   Segment assets
    –   Segment liabilities
    –   Certain income and expense items

- Disclosures are also required about the **revenues derived from products or services** and about the **countries** in which revenues are earned or assets held, even if that information is not used by management in making decisions.

- **Earnings per share** is a measure of the amount of profits earned by a company for each ordinary share. Earnings are profits after tax and preferred dividends.

- **Basic EPS** is calculated by dividing the net profit or loss for the period attributable to ordinary shareholders by the weighted average number of ordinary shares outstanding during the period.

- You should know how to calculate **basic EPS** and how to deal with related complications (issue of shares for cash, bonus issue, share splits/reverse share splits, rights issues).

- **Diluted EPS** is calculated by adjusting the net profit attributable to ordinary shareholders and the weighted average number of shares outstanding for the effects of all dilutive potential ordinary shares.

- Keep the various **sources of financial information** in mind and the effects of insider dealing, the efficient market hypothesis and Stock Exchange regulations.

- Much of the material here on **basic ratios** should have been revision for you. The next few chapters will cover much more complicated aspects of financial analysis.

- Make sure that you can **define** all the ratios. Look out for variations in definitions of ratios which might appear in questions.

- Always remember that 'profit' and 'net assets' are fairly **arbitrary figures**, affected by different accounting policies and manipulation.

- Financial analysis is a vital tool for **auditors**.

Quick Quiz

1   The new statement introduced by the revised IAS 1 is:

    A   Statement of total recognised gains and losses
    B   Statement of comprehensive income
    C   Statement of recognised income and expenses
    D   Statement of recognised gains and losses

2   What new terms are defined in the revised IAS 1?

3   What is the full name for the revised IAS 8? (*Fill in the blanks.*)

        Accounting................., changes in accounting......................... and ....

4   All entities must disclose segment information. True or false?

5   Geographical and segment information is no longer required. True or false?

6   Which numerator is used to rank dilutive shares?

7   Why is the numerator adjusted for convertible bonds when calculating diluted EPS?

8   What are the main sources of financial information available to the external users?

9   What is the efficient market hypothesis?

10   Apart from ratio analysis, what other information might be helpful in interpreting a company's accounts?

11   In a period when profits are fluctuating, what effect does a company's level of gearing have on the profits available for ordinary shareholders?

Answers to Quick Quiz

1   The correct answer is B.

2   'Materiality'; 'impracticable'

3   Accounting **policies**, changes in accounting **estimates** and **errors**

4   False. Only entities whose equity or debt securities are publicly traded need disclose segment information.

5   False. Information about revenues from different countries must be disclosed unless it is not available and the cost to develop it would be excessive. It should always be disclosed if it is used by management in making operating decisions.

6   Net profit from continuing operations only

7   Because the issue of shares will affect earnings by the interest saving.

8   Published accounts and interim statement, filed documents, government statistics.

9   See Section 5.4

10   •   Other comments in the accounts eg Directors' Report
     •   Age and nature of the assets
     •   Current and future market developments
     •   Recent acquisition or disposal of subsidiaries
     •   Notes to the accounts, auditors' report, after the reporting period events, etc.

11   Profits available for the shareholders will be highly volatile and some years there may not be an ordinary dividend paid.

When you have done Chapter 15, try the question below from the Exam Question Bank

Number	Level	Marks	Time
Q21	Introductory	n/a	n/a

19

Current developments

Topic list	Syllabus reference
1 Current issues in corporate reporting	F2, H4
2 Fair value measurements	F2
3 Financial instruments	F2
4 Management Commentary – a global Operating and Financial Review?	F2
5 Managing the change to IFRS	F2
6 International harmonisation and move towards US GAAP	F2
7 IASB Work Plan	F2

Introduction

This chapter deals with a number of current issues and developments. Section 2 highlights the latest developments. These are dealt with within the relevant chapters in this text.

You should be familiar with the accounting standards covered in Part B. If you are in a hurry or revising, go straight to the sections highlighted in this chapter as current issues.

Study guide

		Intellectual level
F1	**The effect of changes in accounting standards on accounting systems.**	
(a)	Apply and discuss the accounting implications of the first time adoption of a body of new accounting standards	3
(b)	Outline the issues in implementing a change to new accounting standards, including organisational, behavioural and procedural changes within the entity.	3
F2	**Proposed changes to accounting standards**	
(a)	Identify the issues and deficiencies which have led to a proposed change to an accounting standard.	2
(b)	Apply and discuss the implications of a proposed change to an accounting standard on the performance and position of an entity	2
H2	**Convergence between national and international reporting standards**	
(a)	Evaluate the implications, nationally and globally, of convergence with International Financial Reporting Standards	3
(b)	Discuss the implementation issues arising from convergence process	3
H3	**Comparison of national reporting requirements**	
(a)	Identify the reasons for major differences in accounting practices, including culture	2
(b)	Discuss the influence of national regulators on international financial reporting	2
H4	**Current reporting issues**	
(a)	Discuss current issues in corporate reporting.	3

Exam guide

Current issues may come up in the context of a question requiring advice. For example, in the scenario question involving groups, perhaps you might have to explain the difference that the proposed changes will make.

Current issues are summarised here, but discussed in detail in the context of the topic to which they relate.

International harmonisation is very topical.

1 Current issues in corporate reporting   6/08, 12/08

FAST FORWARD

> You should know which are the **current issues** and concentrate your studying on these.

Exam focus point

The P2 examiner has given the following guidance on current issues:

'The IASB's work programme will be the basis for many of the current issue discursive questions asked in the paper. However the work programme will not be the exclusive source of questions.'

The Pilot Paper had part of a question on the business combination proposals.

1.1 Hot topics

The IASB workplan, as at April 2009 is reproduced in section F. Below are the examinable current issues, with an indication of where to find them. Most are dealt with in the chapters on the individual topic.

Hot topic	Where to find it
Discussion Paper on Management Commentary	Section 3 of this chapter
Discussion Paper on fair value measurement	Section 2 of this Chapter
Exposure draft on Revenue Recognition	Chapter 1
Exposure draft on EPS	Chapter 18
Exposure draft on Conceptual Framework	Chapter 1
Discussion Paper on Pensions	Chapter 5
Discussion Paper on Conceptual Framework (Joint IASB FASB project)	Chapter 1
Discussion Paper on complexity in financial instruments	Chapter 7
Amendment to rules on reclassification of financial instruments	Chapter 7
Non-active markets	Section 3 of this chapter

2 Fair value measurements

In November 2006, the IASB published a Discussion Paper, *Fair value measurements*. The Discussion Paper arose as a result of the Memorandum of Understanding between the IASB and FASB (February 2006) reaffirming their commitment to the convergence of IFRSs and US GAAP.

2.1 Objective

The objective of the project is to codify, clarify and simplify existing guidance that is dispersed widely in IFRSs. The intention is not therefore to expand the use of fair value in financial reporting.
The Discussion Paper focuses on the recent US Statement of Financial Accounting Standards No. 157 *Fair Value Measurements* (SFAS 157) as a starting point, on which work was well advanced before the Memorandum of Understanding was published.

2.2 Definitions

SFAS 157 defines fair value as 'the price that would be received to sell an asset or paid to transfer a liability in an orderly transaction between market participants at the measurement date.'
The IFRS definition is generally 'the amount for which an asset could be exchanged, or a liability settled, between knowledgeable, willing parties in an arm's length transaction'.

2.3 Differences between definitions

There are three key differences between the SFAS 157 and IFRS definitions:

(a)   The SFAS definition is explicitly an exit (selling) price, whereas the IFRS definition is neither explicitly an exit price nor an entry (buying) price.

(b)   The SFAS definition refers explicitly to market participants, whereas the IFRS definition refers to knowledgeable, willing parties in an arm's length transaction.

(c)   For liabilities, the SFAS definition rests on the notion that the liability is transferred (the liability to the counterparty continues; it is not settled with the counterparty). The IFRS definition refers to the amount at which a liability could be settled between knowledgeable, willing parties in an arm's length transaction.

2.4 Valuation techniques

SFAS 157 establishes a three-level hierarchy for the inputs that valuation techniques use to measure fair value:

Level 1   Quoted prices (unadjusted) in active markets for identical assets or liabilities that the reporting entity has the ability to access at the measurement date

Level 2   Inputs other than quoted prices included within Level 1 that are observable for the asset or liability, either directly or indirectly, eg quoted prices for similar assets in active markets or for identical or similar assets in non active markets or use of quoted interest rates for valuation purposes

Level 3   Unobservable inputs for the asset or liability, ie using the entity's own assumptions about market exit value.

The Discussion Paper analyses each of these principles in detail and provides a copy of the SFAS in order to seek a public opinion on this as a starting point for an IFRS ED to be published in early 2009.

2.5 Is the project necessary?

The IASB is already considering the matter of the measurement basis for assets and liabilities in financial reporting as part of its conceptual framework project. It could therefore be argued that it is not necessary to have a separate project on fair value. The conceptual framework might be the more appropriate forum for discussing **when** fair value should be used **as well as how to define and measure it.**

However, it has been argued that a concise definition and clear measurement framework is needed because there is so much inconsistency in this area, and this may form the basis for discussions in the conceptual framework project.

3 Financial instruments

3.1 Amended reclassification rules

In October 2008 the ASB issued amendments to IAS 39 *Financial instruments: recognition and measurement* permitting entities to **reclassify derivative financial assets** out of the 'fair value through profit or loss' and 'available for sale' categories in limited circumstances. IFRS 7 was also amended to include the required disclosures. The issue is covered in Chapter 7 of this Study Text.

Exam focus point

> EFP The amendments are not examinable until June 2010, so ignore that section if you are taking the exam in December 2009.

3.2 Fair value and derivatives

IAS 39 requires that derivatives be measured initially at **fair value** in the statement of financial position with changes through profit or loss for the year. This was seen to be **more appropriate than historical cost** because:

(a)   Historical cost can be zero, which does not reflect the underlying reality.

(b)   Fair values should have more predictive value.

(c)   Comparability is improved because derivatives valued at different historical costs are not being compared.

(d)   Derivatives are usually (but not always – see below) traded on an active market.

(e)   Fair value reflects the way risks are managed.

However, **fair value is not without problems**.

(a) Some of the changes in fair value will never be realised, which makes the figure reported in profit or loss misleading.

(b) Fair value may not be reliable, and in a non-active market, it may be irrelevant.

(c) Fair valuing derivatives result in volatile profits.

3.3 Non-active markets

An as yet unresolved issue concerns the relation between the market value of equity and the fair value of financial derivatives determined according to IAS 39 in non-active markets. This issue was explored in a Working Paper by Beate Juettner-Nauroth of the University of Applied Sciences of the Deutsche Bundesbank.

This paper has shown:

(a) The fair value of a financial derivative determined by a valuation model is **not relevant in a non-active market**.

(b) In the setting of a non-active market, determining the fair value under the fiction of an active market **does not take all available information into account**.

The paper also notes two consequences of the IAS 39 definition of fair value:

(a) The market value of equity at the end of the reporting period reflects the entity's value in a fictive (made-up) market situation.

(b) The fair value calculated by one valuation model is not unique.

3.3.1 IASB's Expert Advisory Panel (EAB)

In September 2008 the IASB issued a draft report summarising the EAP's discussions on fair value measurement and the related disclosures.

(a) **Measurement**

The draft report notes that, in inactive markets – a **thorough understanding of the instrument subject to valuation** is important so that all relevant available market information is considered. Other main points and guidance include:

(i) Fair value should not, as was suggested, be determined using a 'fundamental value' approach based primarily on **management's estimate of future cash flows**. The basis provided for this view is that fundamental value is **not consistent with the objective of a fair value measurement**.

(ii) Even where markets are inactive, where a current transaction **price for the same or a similar instrument can be found it provides evidence of fair value**. It notes that forced transactions, involuntary liquidations and distress sales are rare and evidence is needed before it is determined that a transaction has not taken place at fair value.

(iii) When valuing instruments for which there is not an active market, an entity uses a valuation technique **involving models and assumptions calibrated on a regular basis**.

(iv) The **need for judgement** is emphasised and the draft report acknowledges that, in exercising such judgement, different entities might arrive at different estimates of fair value for the same instrument and both entities might still meet the objective of fair value measurement.

(b) **Disclosure**

The draft report highlights the requirements of IFRS 7 and notes that the requirement for entities to use **judgement** in deciding how they disclose information about fair value measurement allows the most relevant information in the most understandable format to be provided on how entities measure fair value and the assumptions used. The section highlights areas which would be helpful for entities to consider when providing the disclosures and a number of recent examples of such disclosures.

This is very much a grey area.

4 Management commentary – a global operating and financial review?

FAST FORWARD Recent proposals have been put forward for a **management commentary** to supplement and complement the financial statements.

4.1 Need for management commentary

In the UK, companies have been encouraged to produce an Operating and Financial Review, explaining the main factors underlying a company's financial position and performance, and analysing the main trends affecting this. A Reporting Statement on the OFR was issued in January 2006.

Financial statements alone are not considered sufficient without an **accompanying explanation of the performance**, eg highlighting a restructuring that has reduced profits or the cost of developing a new business channel in the current period which will generate profits in the future.

Perhaps more importantly a good management commentary not only talks about the past position and performance, but how this will translate **into future financial position** and performance.

The *Framework for the Preparation and Presentation of Financial Statements* acknowledges, 'financial statements do not provide all the information that users may need to make economic decisions since they largely portray the financial effects of past events and do not necessarily provide non-financial information.' (para 13)

Typically, larger companies are already making disclosures similar to those debated in the management commentary discussion paper, eg as a 'Director's Report', but the aim of the proposed standard would be **to define internationally what a management commentary** should contain. For example, a good commentary should be balanced and not just highlight the company's successes.

A management commentary would also address **risks and issues** facing the entity that may not be apparent from a review of the financial statements, and how they will be addressed

4.2 Discussion paper

In 2005, the IASB issued a Discussion Paper *Management Commentary*, which is the international equivalent of the Operating and Financial Review.

The main conclusion in the paper is that the IASB can **improve the quality of financial reports** by developing a standard on management commentary. In reaching this conclusion, the team has reviewed existing requirements around the world, such as the OFR, Management's Discussion and Analysis (MD&A) in the USA and Canada, and the German accounting standard on Management Reporting.

4.2.1 Definition of management commentary

The following preliminary definition is given in the Discussion Paper:

Key term

> **Management commentary.** Information that accompanies financial statements as part of an entity's financial reporting. It explains the main trends and factors underlying the development, performance and position of the entity's business during the period covered by the financial statements. It also explains the main trends and factors that are likely to affect the entity's future development, performance and position.

4.2.2 Purpose of management commentary

The purpose of management commentary is to help investors to:

(a) Interpret and assess the related financial statements in the **context of the environment** in which the entity operates

(b) Assess what management views as the **most important issues** facing the entity and how it intends to manage those issues

(c) Assess the **strategies adopted by the entity** and the potential for those strategies to succeed

4.2.3 Proposed contents

The Paper's proposals for what a standard on management commentary should contain are largely similar to those in the ASB's Reporting Statement *Operating and Financial Review*. They specify a number **of principles and qualitative characteristics** that should underlie the preparation and presentation of management commentary.

In particular the principles state that MC should:

- **Supplement and complement** financial statement information
- Provide an analysis of the entity through the eyes of **management**
- Have an orientation to the **future**
- Be understandable, relevant, supportable, balanced and comparable over time

The proposals also adopt the same approach as the UK Reporting Statement in setting out a **disclosure framework** identifying the areas that management must consider, **rather than any more specific disclosure requirements.**

4.3 Section summary

- You should be able to discuss the need for corporate governance and the measures which should typically be in place in a large company.
- Make sure you are aware of the Discussion Paper on the proposed Management Commentary.

5 Managing the change to IFRS

6/08

FAST FORWARD

The **change to IFRS** must be carefully managed.

5.1 Practical issues

The implementation of the change to IFRS is likely to entail careful management in most companies. Here are some of the **change management considerations** that should be addressed.

(a) **Accurate assessment of the task involved**. Underestimation or wishful thinking may hamper the effectiveness of the conversion and may ultimately prove inefficient.

(b) **Proper planning**. This should take place at the overall project level, but a **detailed** task **analysis** could be drawn up to **control work performed**.

(c) **Human resource management**. The project must be properly structured and staffed.

(d) **Training**. Where there are **skills gaps**, remedial training should be provided.

(e) **Monitoring and accountability**. A relaxed 'it will be alright on the night' attitude could spell danger. Implementation **progress** should be **monitored** and **regular meetings** set up so that participants can **personally account for what they are doing** as well as **flag up any problems** as early as possible. **Project drift should be avoided**.

(f) **Achieving milestones**. Successful completion of key steps and tasks should be appropriately acknowledged, ie what managers call 'celebrating success', so as to **sustain motivation and performance**.

(g) **Physical resourcing.** The need for IT **equipment** and **office space** should be properly assessed.

(h) **Process review**. Care should be taken not to perceive the change as a one-off quick fix. Any charge in **future systems** and processes should be assessed and properly implemented.

(i) **Follow-up procedures**. As with general good management practice, the **follow up procedures** should be planned in to **make sure that the changes stick** and that any further changes are identified and addressed.

5.1.1 Financial reporting infrastructure

As well as sound management judgement, implementation of IFRS requires a sound financial reporting infrastructure. Key aspects of this include the following.

(a) A **robust regulatory framework**. For IFRS to be successful, they must be rigorously enforced.

(b) **Trained and qualified staff**. Many preparers of financial statements will have been trained in local GAAP and not be familiar with the principles underlying IFRS, let alone the detail. Some professional bodies provide conversion qualifications – for example, the ACCA's Diploma in International Financial Reporting – but the availability of such qualifications and courses may vary from country to country.

(c) **Availability and transparency of market information**. This is particularly important in the determination of fair values, which are such a key component of many IFRSs.

(d) **High standards of corporate governance and audit**. This is all the more important in the transition period, especially where there is resistance to change.

Overall, there are significant advantages to the widespread adoption of IFRS, but if the transition is to go well, there must be a realistic assessment of potential challenges.

5.2 Other implementation challenges

5.2.1 More detailed rules

Implementation of International Financial Reporting Standards entails **a great deal of work** for many companies, particularly those in countries where local GAAP has not been so onerous. For example, many jurisdictions will not have had such detailed rules about recognition, measurement and presentation of financial instruments, and many will have had no rules at all about share-based payment.

A challenge for preparers of financial statements is also **a challenge for users**. When financial statements become far more complex under IFRS than they were under local GAAP, users may find them hard to understand, and consequently of little relevance.

5.2.2 Presentation

Many developed countries have legislation requiring set formats and layouts for financial statements. For example, in the UK there is the Companies Act 2006. IFRS demands that presentation is in accordance with IAS 1 *Presentation of financial statements,* but this standard allows alternative forms of presentation. In choosing between alternatives, **countries tend to adopt the format that is closest to local GAAP**, even if this is not necessarily the best format. For example, UK companies are likely to adopt the two-statement format for the statement of comprehensive income, because this is closest to the old profit and loss account and statement of total recognised gains and losses.

5.2.3 Concepts and interpretation

Although later IAS and IFRS are based to an extent on the IASB *Framework,* there is **no consistent set of principles** underlying them. The *Framework* itself is being revised, and there is controversy over the direction the revision should take. Consequently, preparers of accounts are likely to think in terms of the conceptual frameworks – if any – that they have used in developing local GAAP, and these may be different from that of the IASB. German accounts, for example, have traditionally been aimed at the tax authorities.

Where IFRS themselves give clear guidance, this may not matter, but where there is uncertainty, preparers of accounts will fall back on their traditional conceptual thinking.

5.2.4 Choice of accounting treatment

Although many so-called 'allowed alternatives' have been eliminated from IFRS in recent years, choice of treatment remains. For example, IAS 16 *Property, plant and equipment* gives a choice of either the cost model or the revaluation model for a class of property, plant or equipment. IAS 31 *Interests in joint ventures* also gives a choice of treatment, allowing interests in jointly controlled entities to be accounted for using either proportionate consolidation or the equity method.

It could be argued that choice is a good thing, as companies should be able to select the treatment that most fairly reflects the underlying reality. However, in the context of change to IFRS, there is a danger that companies **will choose the alternative that closely matches the approach followed under local GAAP, or the one that is easier to implement**, regardless of whether this is the best choice.

5.2.5 Inconsistency in recognition or measurement methods

As well as the broader choice of which accounting model to adopt (cost or revaluation, and so on), IFRS allows further choice on recognition and measurement within a particular reporting standard. For example, IAS 39 *Financial instruments: recognition and measurement* allows certain instruments to be designated as being at fair value through profit or loss, with 'available for sale' sometimes being the default category if this choice is not made. In countries where local GAAP is not very developed on this matter, preparers of accounts might well **choose the least complex option**, or the option that does not involve making a decision, rather than the correct one.

5.2.6 Timing and exemptions taken

IFRSs have provision for early adoption, and this can affect comparability, although impact of a new standard must be disclosed under IAS 8 *Accounting policies, changes in accounting estimates and errors*. Further, IFRS 1 *First time adoption of International Financial Reporting Standards* permits a number of exemptions during the periods of transition to IFRS. This gives scope for manipulation, if **exemptions are 'cherry-picked'** to produce a favourable picture.

5.3 Subjectivity

The extent of the impact will vary, depending on how developed local GAAP was before the transition. However, in general it is likely that **management judgement will have a greater impact** on financial statements prepared under IFRS than under local GAAP. The main reasons for this are as follows.

(a)   The **volume** of rules and number of areas addressed by IFRS is likely to be greater than that under local GAAP.

(b)   Many issues are perhaps **addressed for the first time**, for example share-based payment.

(c)   IFRSs are likely to be **more complex** than local standards.

(d)   IFRSs allow **choice** in many cases, which leads to subjectivity.

(e)   Selection of **valuation method** (see above)

6 International harmonisation and move towards US GAAP

Harmonisation in accounting is likely to come from international accounting standards, but not in the near future. There are enormous difficulties to overcome, both technical and political.

You should be able to discuss the **barriers to harmonisation** and the advantages of and **progress towards harmonisation**.

Before we look at any other countries in particular, we must consider what barriers there are to international harmonisation and why harmonisation is considered so desirable, before looking at comparative accounting systems.

6.1 Barriers to harmonisation

There are undoubtedly many barriers to international harmonisation: if there were not then greater progress would probably have been made by now. The main problems are as follows.

(a) **Different purposes of financial reporting**. In some countries the purpose is solely for tax assessment, while in others it is for investor decision-making.

(b) **Different legal systems**. These prevent the development of certain accounting practices and restrict the options available.

(c) **Different user groups**. Countries have different ideas about who the relevant user groups are and their respective importance. In the USA investor and creditor groups are given prominence, while in Europe employees enjoy a higher profile.

(d) **Needs of developing countries**. Developing countries are obviously behind in the standard setting process and they need to develop the basic standards and principles already in place in most developed countries.

(e) **Nationalism** is demonstrated in an unwillingness to accept another country's standard.

(f) **Cultural differences** result in objectives for accounting systems differing from country to country.

(g) **Unique circumstances**. Some countries may be experiencing unusual circumstances which affect all aspects of everyday life and impinge on the ability of companies to produce proper reports, for example hyperinflation, civil war, currency restriction and so on.

(h) **The lack of strong accountancy bodies**. Many countries do not have strong independent accountancy or business bodies which would press for better standards and greater harmonisation.

These are difficult problems to overcome, and yet attempts are being made continually to do so. We must therefore consider what the perceived advantages of harmonisation are, which justify so much effort.

6.2 Advantages of global harmonisation

The advantages of harmonisation will be based on the benefits to users and preparers of accounts, as follows.

(a) **Investors**, both individual and corporate, would like to be able to compare the financial results of different companies internationally as well as nationally in making investment decisions. Differences in accounting practice and reporting can prove to be a barrier to such cross-border analysis. There is a growing amount of investment across borders and there are few financial analysts able to follow shares in international markets. For example, it is not easy for an analyst familiar with UK accounting principles to analyse the financial statements of a Dutch or German company. Harmonisation would therefore be of benefit to such analysts.

(b) **Multinational companies** would benefit from harmonisation for many reasons including the following.

(i) Better access would be gained to foreign investor funds.

(ii) Management control would be improved, because harmonisation would aid internal communication of financial information.

(iii) Appraisal of foreign entities for take-overs and mergers would be more straightforward.

(iv) It would be easier to comply with the reporting requirements of overseas stock exchanges.

(v) Consolidation of foreign subsidiaries and associated companies would be easier.

(vi) A reduction in audit costs might be achieved.

(vii) Transfer of accounting staff across national borders would be easier.

(c) **Governments of developing countries** would save time and money if they could adopt international standards and, if these were used internally, governments of developing countries could attempt to control the activities of foreign multinational companies in their own country. These companies could not 'hide' behind foreign accounting practices which are difficult to understand.

(d) **Tax authorities**. It will be easier to calculate the tax liability of investors, including multinationals who receive income from overseas sources.

(e) **Regional economic groups** usually promote trade within a specific geographical region. This would be aided by common accounting practices within the region.

(f) **Large international accounting firms** would benefit as accounting and auditing would be much easier if similar accounting practices existed throughout the world.

6.3 Progress with harmonisation to date

The barriers to harmonisation may be daunting but some progress has been made. There are various bodies which are working on different aspects of harmonisation and these are discussed below. The most important of these bodies, in the light of recent developments, are the IASB and the UK ASB.

6.3.1 ASB and international standards

The UK ASB considers the development of international standards of **fundamental importance**. In addition, the UK ASB meets on a formal, and regular basis with standard-setters around the world.

Exam focus point

> The UK's FRS 12 *Provisions, contingent liabilities and contingent assets* is almost identical to IAS 37 of the same name.

6.4 The EC regulation

FAST FORWARD

> The EC has required that **since 2005** consolidated accounts of all listed companies should **comply with IAS.**

As we have already seen, the EC regulations form one part of a broader programme for the harmonisation of company law in member states. The commission is uniquely the only organisation to produce **international** standards of accounting practice which are legally enforceable, in the form of directives which must be included in the national legislation of member states. The directives have been criticised as they might become constraints on the application of world-wide standards and bring accounting standardisation and harmonisation into the political arena.

The EC has adopted a regulation stating that **from 2005 consolidated accounts of listed companies have been required to comply with international accounting standards.** The implications of this proposal are far reaching.

Many commentators believe that, in the light of the above, it is only a matter of time before national standard setting bodies like the ASB are, in effect, replaced by the IASB and national standards fall into disuse. However, national standards were designed for the national environment, which includes small companies. Moreover, the IASB will need input and expertise from valued national standard setters like the ASB.

6.5 Convergence with US GAAP

Convergence with EC countries has been more or less put on hold while **IFRS moves closer to US GAAP**.

6.5.1 Norwalk agreement

In October 2002, the IASB reached an agreement with the US's FASB (Financial Accounting Standards Board) (the **'Norwalk' agreement**) to undertake a short-term convergence project aimed at removing a variety of individual differences between US GAAP and International standards. The first standard resulting from this project was IFRS 5 *Non-current assets held for sale and discontinued operations* (published March 2004).

6.5.2 Principles-based approach

In March 2003, an 'identical style and wording' approach was agreed for standards issued by FASB and the IASB on joint projects. Revised business combinations standards were issued as a result of this approach in January 2008.

FASB also recognised the need to follow a **'principles-based' approach** to standard-setting (as the IASB has always done) in the light of recent corporate failures and scandals which have led to criticism of the 'rules-based' approach.

6.5.3 Common conceptual framework

In October 2004 the IASB and FASB agreed to develop a **common conceptual framework** which would be a significant step towards harmonisation of future standards. The project has been divided into two phases:

(a)   The initial focus is on particular aspects of the frameworks dealing with objectives, qualitative characteristics, elements, recognition, and measurement, giving priority to issues affecting projects for new/ revised Standards.

(b)   Later, they will consider the applicability of those concepts to other sectors, beginning with not-for-profit entities in the private sector.

6.5.4 Memorandum of understanding

In February 2006, the two Boards signed a **'Memorandum of Understanding'**. This laid down a 'roadmap of convergence' between IFRSs and US GAAP in the period 2006-2008.

The aim was to remove by 2009 the requirement for foreign companies reporting under IFRSs listed on a US stock exchange to have to prepare a reconciliation to US GAAP.

Events moved faster than expected, and in November 2007 the US Securities and Exchange Commission (SEC) decided to allow non-US filers to report under IFRSs for years ended after 15 November 2007 with no reconciliation to US GAAP.

Consultation is also underway on the possibility of the use of IFRSs by US filers. In November 2008, the SEC published a proposal, titled *Roadmap for the Potential Use of Financial Statements Prepared in accordance with International Financial Reporting Standards by U.S. Issuers*. The proposed roadmap sets out milestones that, if achieved, could lead to the adoption of IFRSs in the US in 2014. It also proposes to permit the early adoption of IFRSs from 2010 for some US entities.

6.6 Dialogue with other key standard setters

The IASB maintains a policy of dialogue with other key standard setters around the world, in the interest of harmonising standards across the globe.

Partner standard setters are often involved in the development of Discussion Papers and Exposure Drafts on new areas.

6.6.1 China and Japan

In February 2006, China officially released a new set of Chinese Accounting Standards (CASs) which are substantially converged with IFRSs, and reaffirmed its commitment to international convergence.

In January 2005, the IASB and the Accounting Standards Board of Japan (ASBJ) announced a joint project to reduce differences between IFRSs and Japanese accounting standards, which is currently in progress.

6.7 The situation today and in the future

Many organisations committed to global harmonisation have done a great deal of work towards this goal. It is the case at present, however, that fundamental disagreements exist between countries and organisations about the way forward. One of the major gulfs is between the reporting requirements in developed countries and those in non-developed countries. It will be some time before these difficulties can be overcome. The IASB is likely to be the lead body in attempting to do so, as discussed above.

7 IASB Work Plan

Below is the latest (April 2009) version of the IASB Workplan. Not all the topics are examinable (see next chapter) but all examinable aspects are covered in this text.

IASB Work Plan – projected timetable as at 30 April 2009

The timetable shows the current best estimate of document publication dates. The effective date of amendments and new standards is usually 6-18 months after publication date, although in setting an effective date the Board considers all relevant factors. In appropriate circumstances, early adoption of new standards will be allowed.

The work plan anticipates the completion of several projects in 2010 and 2011. The Board will consider staggering effective dates of standards to help entities that apply IFRSs undertake an orderly transition to any new requirements.

The Board undertakes this work using its established due process, including consultation with interested parties. The timetable for completion is subject to change depending on input received throughout a project's development.

Financial Crisis related projects

| | Estimated publication date | | | | | | | IASB-FASB Collaboration | |
	2009 Q2	2009 Q3	2009 Q4	2010 H1	2010 H2	2011	2011+	MoU[1]	Joint[2]
Proposals out for public comment									
Derecognition [ED, comments due by 31 July 2009]	RT			IFRS				✓	✓
Documents currently being developed									
Consolidation	RT		IFRS					✓	✓
Fair value measurement guidance	ED		RT	IFRS				✓	
Financial instruments (IAS 39 replacement)			ED	IFRS				✓	✓

Recently completed projects

Embedded derivatives (IAS 39/IFRIC 9). Amendments issued in February 2009, for annual periods ending on or after 30 June 2009.

Financial instruments: enhanced disclosures. Amendments issued in February 2009, for annual periods beginning on or after 1 January 2009.

Investments in debt instruments. In the light of comments received, the Board decided not to proceed with the amendments. The Board will assess the impairment requirements as part of a wider examination of IAS 39.

Fair value measurement and impairment of financial instruments [FASB FSPs – *Request for Views*]. In the light of comments received, the Board decided to consider impairment as part of its wider, and urgent, examination of IAS 39.

New standards

| | Estimated publication date | | | | | | | IASB-FASB Collaboration | |
	2009 Q2	2009 Q3	2009 Q4	2010 H1	2010 H2	2011	2011+	MoU[1]	Joint[2]
Proposals out for public comment									
Revenue recognition [DP, comments due 19 June 2009]				ED		IFRS		✓	✓
Leases [DP, comments due 17 July 2009]				ED		IFRS		✓	✓
Income taxes [ED, comments due by 31 July 2009]					IFRS			✓	✓

Documents currently being developed	Estimated publication date							IASB-FASB Collaboration	
	2009 Q2	2009 Q3	2009 Q4	2010 H1	2010 H2	2011	2011+	MoU[1]	Joint[2]
Emissions trading schemes			ED		IFRS			✓	✓
Financial statement presentation				ED		IFRS		✓	✓
FI with characteristics of equity			ED			IFRS		✓	✓
IFRS for SMEs	IFRS								
Insurance contracts			ED			IFRS			✓
Joint ventures		IFRS						✓	
Management commentary	ED				CG				
Post-employment benefits (incl. pensions)		ED				IFRS		✓	
Rate-regulated activities		ED		IFRS					

Amendments

Proposals out for public comment

Nil

Documents currently being developed	Estimated publication date							IASB-FASB Collaboration	
	2009 Q2	2009 Q3	2009 Q4	2010 H1	2010 H2	2011	2011+	MoU[1]	Joint[2]
Annual improvements 2008-2010		ED		IFRS					
Annual improvements 2009-2011					ED	IFRS			
Discontinued operations (IFRS 5)			IFRS						✓
Earnings per share (IAS 33)					IFRS				✓
First-time adoption of IFRSs (IFRS 1): additional exemptions		IFRS							
Amendments to IFRIC 14	IFRS								
Liabilities (IAS 37 amendments)			IFRS						
Related party disclosures (IAS 24)		IFRS							
Share-based payment: group cash-settled transactions (IFRS 2 and IFRIC 11)	IFRS								

Recently completed projects

Annual improvements 2007-2009. IFRS published in April 2009.

Conceptual Framework

Proposals out for public comment

Nil

Documents currently being developed	Estimated publication date							IASB-FASB Collaboration	
	2009 Q2	2009 Q3	2009 Q4	2010 H1	2010 H2	2011	2011 +	MoU[1]	Joint[2]
Phase A: Objectives and qualitative characteristics		Final chapter							✓
Phase B: Elements and recognition					DP				✓
Phase C: Measurement			DP		ED				✓
Phase D: Reporting entity		ED		Final chapter					✓

The IASB and the FASB will amend sections of their conceptual frameworks as they complete individual phases of the project. Phases E to H *Presentation and disclosure, Purpose and Status, Application to not-for-profit entities* and *Remaining issues* have not yet started.

Research and other projects

Documents currently being developed	2009 Q2	2009 Q3	2009 Q4	2010 H1	2010 H2	2011	2011 +	IASB-FASB Collaboration	
								MoU[1]	Joint[2]
Extractive activities (prepared for the IASB by representatives from the national standard-setters of Australia, Canada, Norway and South Africa).	DP				AD				

Common control transactions was added to the agenda in December 2007. Work will begin when staff working on projects related to the financial crisis become available.

Work on the **government grants** project has been deferred pending progress in the revenue recognition, related parties and emissions trading schemes projects.

In December 2007 the IASB decided not to add a project on **intangible assets** to its active agenda. National standard-setters are carrying out research for a possible future project. The Australian Accounting Standards Board has published a discussion paper *Initial Accounting for Internally Generated Intangible Assets*.

Abbreviations			
AD	Agenda Decision (to add the topic to the active agenda)	AG	Advisory Group
CG	Completed Guidance	DP	Discussion Paper
ED	Exposure Draft	IFRS	International Financial Reporting Standard
RT	Roundtables	TBD	To be determined

Endnotes

1. These projects are part of the Memorandum of Understanding that sets out the milestones that the FASB and the IASB have agreed to achieve in order to demonstrate standard-setting convergence.

2. These projects are being undertaken with the FASB. Even though *joint ventures* and *post-employment benefits* are not being undertaken with the FASB, in each case the IASB has committed to improve the related IFRSs.

Chapter Roundup

- **Harmonisation** in accounting is likely to come from international accounting standards, but not in the near future. There are enormous difficulties to overcome, both technical and political.

- Recent proposals have been put forward for a **management commentary** to supplement and complement the financial statements.

- You should be able to discuss the **barriers to harmonisation** and the advantages of and **progress towards harmonisation**.

- The EC has required that **since 2005** consolidated accounts of all listed companies should **comply with IAS.**

- Convergence with EC countries has been more or less put on hold while **IFRS moves closer to US GAAP**.

- The **change to IFRS** must be carefully managed.

Quick Quiz

1   Which preparers and users of accounts can be expected to benefit from global harmonisation of accounting?

2   How many IFRSs are in existence at the moment?

3   The proposed Management Commentary provides detailed disclosures.

   True   ☐
   False ☐

4   What is the Norwalk agreement?

5   Which standards have recently undergone major revisions?

Answers to Quick Quiz

1   Investors, multinational companies, governments of developing countries, the authorities (overseas income), regional economic groups, large international accounting firms.

2   8

3   False. It provides a disclosure framework only.

4   An agreement between the IASB and FASB to undertake a short-term convergence project aimed at removing differences between US GAAP and IFRS.

5   IAS 1 and IFRS 3.

| Now try the question below from the Exam Question Bank | | | |

Number	Level	Marks	Time
Q22	Examination	25	45 mins

Reporting for specialised entities

20

Topic list	Syllabus reference
1 Specialised entities and the exam	E1
2 The not-for-profit sector: primary aims	E1
3 The not-for-profit sector: regulatory framework	E1
4 The not-for-profit sector: performance measurement	E1
5 Smaller entities	E2
6 IAS 41 Agriculture	E1

Introduction

Concentrate on Section 1 – this is the most important for your exam.

You should be aware that not-for-profit entities and smaller entities may have different accounting needs from the larger profit-making entities that you are used to. This chapter gives you the background you need to set you thinking about whether a one-size-fits-all set of standards is adequate.

We also include a couple of standards relating to specialist businesses.

Section 5 is important because smaller companies are a current issue but the res should be read for background only.

473

Study guide

		Intellectual level
E1	**Financial reporting in specialised, not-for-profit and public sector entities**	
(a)	Apply knowledge from the syllabus to straightforward transactions and events arising in specialised, not-for-profit and public sector entities	3
E2	**Reporting requirements of small and medium entities (SMEs)**	
(a)	Outline the principal considerations in developing a set of accounting standards for SMEs.	3
(b)	Discuss solutions to the problem of differential financial reporting.	3

Exam guide

The examiner has stated specifically that specialised entities will be tested in terms of **current IFRS**.

This could be tested in essay form, or you could be given a scenario of a not-for-profit entity and have to apply your knowledge from the rest of the syllabus to it. The examiner has said that he will give you the information you need for a question on specialised entities.

1 Specialist entities and the exam

FAST FORWARD

Questions on specialist entities will be set in terms of **current IFRS**.

1.1 Examiner's approach

The P2 examiner has stated explicitly that questions on specialist entities will be sent in terms of current accounting standards. So do not be alarmed if the setting for a question is a club, or a local council rather than a company. The principles will be the same.

1.2 Typical specialist entity questions

Below are some typical questions. The examiner is simply testing whether you are flexible enough to apply your knowledge and understanding of accounting standards in a fresh context.

1.2.1 An agricultural college

An agricultural college is not the kind of setting you are used to encountering in your accountancy studies. It doesn't manufacture or trade in goods. But there are issues that it will have in common with companies that do.

> ## Question   Agricultural college

Swindale Agricultural College derives its income from a variety of sources. It receives a grant from Central Government, further subsidies from the European Union and money from the local Council Tax. In addition, students pay fees.

The Diploma in Agriculture course lasts nine months – from October till the end of June. The College's accounting year end is 31 December 20X8. Students pay $3,000 subsidised tuition fees. As at 1 October 20X8, twenty students have enrolled, each paying a non-refundable deposit of $1,200. The balance of $1,800 per student is to be paid in nine monthly instalments of $200.

The College Bursar argues that because the deposit is non-refundable, the fee income should be recognised on a cash receipt basis.

Required

Advise the College Bursar on the correct accounting treatment for the fee income. Show the journal entries for this treatment.

Answer

This question deals with revenue recognition, specifically in the context of the provision of a service.

Total fee income from students for this course (deposits and instalments) will be:

(20 × $1,200) + (20 × $200 × 9) = $60,000

Currently it is proposed to recognised revenue on the basis of cash received, which, as at 31 December 20X8, is the deposit plus three monthly instalments:

(20 × $1,200) + (20 × $200 × 3) = $36,000

This is wrong, as it does not take account of the matching process. As at 31 December 20X8, only one third of the course (three out of nine months) has been delivered, so only one third of the total fee income should be recognised. Income recognised should be $20,000.

There is an element of deferred consideration. As this is over months, rather than years, it will not be necessary to discount to arrive at the fair value of the consideration. But it must be matched. The deposits received of $24,000 (20 × $1,200) but not yet recognised as revenue at the year end are to be regarded as deferred income. These deposits are non-refundable, but they create an obligation to complete the contract. Accordingly they should be a liability in the balance sheet.

The journal entries are as follows:

DEBIT	Cash	$36,000	
CREDIT	Fee income (recognised)		$20,000
CREDIT	Deferred income (received in advance of delivery of services)		$16,000

Note that one third of the deposit ($24,000 ÷ $8,000) has been recognised in the period, which is correct, because one third of the course has been delivered.

1.2.2 A football club

This question, from a past exam paper was specifically mentioned by the examiner as being the sort of setting that could be tested. Note the advice given at the end of the question: you do not need any specialist knowledge of the football club finance sector to answer this question.

Question

Football club

Seejoy is a famous football club but has significant cash flow problems. The directors and shareholders wish to take steps to improve the club's financial position. The following proposals had been drafted in an attempt to improve the cash flow of the club. However, the directors need advice upon their implications.

(a) **Sale and leaseback of football stadium (excluding the land element)**

The football stadium is currently accounted for using the cost model in IAS 16 *Property, plant and equipment*. The carrying value of the stadium will be $12 million at 31 December 20X6. The stadium will have a remaining life of 20 years at 31 December 20X6, and the club uses straight line depreciation. It is proposed to sell the stadium to a third party institution on 1 January 20X7 and lease it back under a 20 year finance lease. The sale price and fair value are $15 million which is the present value of the minimum lease payments. The agreement transfers the title of the stadium back to the football club at the end of the lease at nil cost. The rental is $1.2 million per annum in advance commencing on 1 January 20X7. The directors do not wish to treat this transaction as the raising of a secured loan. The implicit interest rate on the finance in the lease is 5.6%.   **(9 marks)**

(b)   **Player registrations**

The club capitalises the unconditional amounts (transfer fees) paid to acquire players.

The club proposes to amortise the cost of the transfer fees over ten years instead of the current practice which is to amortise the cost over the duration of the player's contract. The club has sold most of its valuable players during the current financial year but still has two valuable players under contract.

Player	Transfer fee capitalised $m	Amortisation to 31 December 20X6 $m	Contract commenced	Contract expires
A Steel	20	4	1 January 20X6	31 December 20Y0
R Aldo	15	10	1 January 20X5	31 December 20X7

If Seejoy win the national football league, then a further $5 million will be payable to the two players' former clubs. Seejoy are currently performing very poorly in the league.   **(5 marks)**

(c)   **Issue of bond**

The club proposes to issue a 7% bond with a face value of $50 million on 1 January 20X7 at a discount of 5% that will be secured on income from future ticket sales and corporate hospitality receipts, which are approximately $20 million per annum. Under the agreement the club cannot use the first $6 million received from corporate hospitality sales and reserved tickets (season tickets) as this will be used to repay the bond. The money from the bond will be used to pay for ground improvements and to pay wages to players.

The bond will be repayable, both capital and interest, over 15 years with the first payment of $6 million due on 31 December 20X7. it has an effective interest rate of 7.7%. There will be no active market for the bond and the company does not wish to use valuation models to value the bond.

     (6 marks)

(d)   **Player trading**

Another proposal is for the club to sell its two valuable players, Aldo and Steel. It is thought that it will receive a total of $16 million for both players. The players are to be offered for sale at the end of the current football season on 1 May 20X7.   **(5 marks)**

Required

Discuss how the above proposals would be dealt with in the financial statement of Seejoy for the year ending 31 December 20X7, setting out their accounting treatment and appropriateness in helping the football club's cash flow problems.

(Candidates do not need knowledge of the football finance sector to answer this question.)

     (Total = 25 marks)

Answer

(a)   **Sale and leaseback of football stadium**

The proposal is for a sale and leaseback which be treated as a **finance lease**. The accounting treatment for such a transaction is dealt with by IAS 17 *Leases*. As the **substance of the transaction is a financing transaction** this would not be dealt with as a sale so the **stadium would remain on the balance sheet as an item of property, plant and equipment** and be depreciated but it will now be valued at the sales value of $15 million. The **excess of the sales value over the carrying value** will be recognised as **deferred income** and credited to the income statement over the period of the finance lease.

When the sale takes place on 1 January 20X7 the double entry will be:

	$m	$m
DEBIT Cash	15	
CREDIT Properties, plant and equipment		12
CREDIT Deferred income		3

On this same date the finance lease will also be recognised:

	$m	$m
DEBIT Properties, plant and equipment	15	
CREDIT Finance lease payables		15

In the financial statements for the year ending 31 December 20X7 the effects will be as follows:

INCOME STATEMENT

	$'000
Depreciation of stadium ($15m/20 years)	(750)
Finance charge (($15m – $1.2m) × 5.6%)	(773)
Deferred income ($3m/20 years)	150

BALANCE SHEET

Properties, plant and equipment	
Stadium ($15m – $0.75m)	14,250
Current liabilities	
Rental payment	1,200
Non-current liabilities	
Finance lease payables ($15m – ($1.2m × 2) + $0.773m)	13,373
Deferred income ($3m – $0.15m)	2,850

There is little doubt that this form of sale and leaseback will improve the cash flow of the club as $15 million will be received on 1 January 20X7. However, the required accounting treatment by IAS 17 will mean that the sale and leaseback has **significant and detrimental affects** on the financial statements. The **profit** shown in the income statement is likely to **decrease** as the finance charge on the lease significantly outweighs the deferred income credit to the income statement. If the $15 million receipt is not used to pay off existing long term loans then the overall **gearing** of the club will **increase** as the finance lease payables are included on the balance sheet.

It might be worth investigating the possibility of a **sale and leaseback** agreement which **results in an operating lease rather** than a finance lease. In such a leaseback, as the sale is at fair value, the **profit can be recognised immediately** in the income statement and the stadium will be deemed to have been sold and removed from the balance sheet. There will also be no finance leases payables as liabilities on the balance sheet. The downside however is that any increase in the residual value of the stadium would be lost.

(b) **Player registrations**

The player registrations are **capitalised** by the club as intangible non-current assets under IAS 38 *Intangible assets*. This is an **acceptable** accounting treatment; the transfer fees classify as assets as it is probable that expected future benefits will flow to the club as a result of the contracts and the cost can be measured reliably at the amount of the transfer fees actually paid.

According to IAS 38, intangible non-current assets which are capitalised should be **amortised over their useful life**. Therefore on the face of it claiming a useful life of 10 years might be acceptable. However IAS 38 recommends that amortisation reflects the useful life of the assets and the pattern of economic benefits. Therefore the proposal to amortise the transfer fees over a period of **10 years is not acceptable as the contracts are only for 5 years and 3 years**.

In terms of **cash flow** this proposal regarding the amortisation would have **no effect** at all. It would simply be a bookkeeping entry which would reduce the amortisation charge to the income statement.

The potential payment to the two players' former clubs of $5 million would **not** appear to be **probable** due to the current form of the club. Therefore under IAS 37 *Provisions, contingent*

liabilities and contingent assets no provision would be recognised for this amount. However, the possible payment does fall within the IAS 37 definition of a contingent liability which is a possible obligation arising out of past events whose existence will be confirmed only by the occurrence or non-occurrence of one or more uncertain future events not wholly within the control of the entity. Therefore as a contingent liability the amount and details would be **disclosed** in the notes to the financial statements.

(c) **Issue of bond**

What the club is proposing here is known as **securitisation**. This particular type of securitisation is often called 'future flow' securitisation. In some forms of securitisation a special purpose vehicle is set up to administer the income stream or assets involved in which case there is potentially an off balance sheet effect. However, in this case there is **no special purpose vehicle** and therefore the only accounting issue is how the bond is to be treated under IAS 39 *Financial instruments: recognition and measurement*.

The bond will be recorded as a **financial liability** and will either be classified as a financial liability at fair value through profit or loss or as a financial liability measured at amortised cost. To be a financial liability at fair value through profit or loss the bond must either be held for trading or be part of a group of financial assets, financial liabilities, or both, that are managed on a fair value basis. It is unlikely that this is the case, therefore the bond will be **classified as measured at amortised cost**.

The bond will be **initially recognised at its fair value** which is the amount for which the liability can be settled between knowledgeable and willing parties in an arm's length transaction. Fair value at inception will normally be the amount of the consideration received for the instrument. Subsequent to initial recognition the instrument will be measured using amortised cost or fair value. In this case the club does not wish to use the valuation model therefore the bond will be measured at amortised cost.

When the bond is issued on 1 January 20X7 it will be measured at the value of the consideration received of $47.5 million ($50m × 95%).

At 31 December 20X7 the valuation will be:

	$m
Initial value	47.5
Interest at 7.7%	3.7
Cash paid	(6.0)
Balance sheet value	45.2

In terms of cash flow the issue of the bond will **bring $47.5 million into the club**. The bond is effectively secured on the income stream of the future corporate hospitality sales and season tickets receipts and due to this security the coupon rate of interest is lower than the market rates. The money is to be used to improve the grounds which is an appropriate use of long-term funds. However, the proposal to pay the **short term costs of the players' wages** out of these long term funds is a **misuse of long-term capital** which is likely to lead to future liquidity problems.

(d) **Player trading**

In accounting terms there is no issue to deal with at 31 December 20X6 as the potential sale of the players will not fall to be classified as 'held for sale' non-current assets under IFRS 5 *Non-current assets held for sale and discontinued operations*. In order for these players to classify as held for sale they would need to be available for immediate sale which they are not.

However, the club must consider carrying out an **impairment review** of these assets at 31 December 20X6. If the players are sold for the anticipated figure of $16 million then the following loss will be incurred:

	$m
Carrying value at 1 May 20X7	
A Steel ($20m – ($4m + 4/12 × $4m)	14.7
R Aldo ($15m – ($10 + 4/12 × $5)	3.3
	18.0
Potential sales value	16.0
Potential loss	2.0

This potential loss of $2 million on the sale of these players may be evidence of impairment and a review should be carried out at 31 December 20X6 and the **players' value written down to recoverable amount** if necessary.

In terms of cash flow, the sale of the players would **provide much needed cash**. However, as the club is performing poorly currently the sale of the two best players **may lead to even worse performance** which is likely to have a detrimental affect on ticket sales and the liquidity of the club in future.

1.3 Other possibilities

Another recent exam question was set in the entertainment industry. The possibilities are wide ranging, and you need to apply common sense. Suppose, for example, you got a property dealer, who was trying to classify his properties as investment properties? This would not be permitted, because the properties are for sale and not for investment potential.

1.4 Section summary

Questions on specialised entities will be set in terms of **current IFRS.**

- You will not need specialist knowledge, beyond a common sense awareness that different organisations do things in different ways.
- Any required specialist information (unlikely) will be given to you.
- Any setting, type of company or organisation could come up.

2 The not-for-profit sector: primary aims

FAST FORWARD

The not-for-profit sector includes **public sector entities** and **private** not-for-profit entities such as charities.

Not-for-profit entities have **different goals** from profit making entities, but they still need to be **properly managed** and their accounts need to present the information fairly

What organisations do we have in mind when we refer to **Not-for-profit and public sector entities**? These are the most obvious examples:

(a) Central government departments and agencies
(b) Local or federal government departments
(c) Publicly-funded bodies providing healthcare (in the UK this would be the NHS) and social housing
(d) Further and higher education institutions
(e) Charitable bodies

The first four are **public sector entities**. Charities are **private** not-for-profit entities.

Not-for-profit entities have different goals and purposes to profit-making entities and are responsible to different stakeholders. However, they are dealing in very large sums of money and it is important that they are properly managed and that their accounts present fairly the results of their operations.

Until recently, **public sector** accounts were prepared on a **cash basis**. A transition is still in progress which will get them operating on an **accruals basis**, in line with normal practice in the private sector.

2.1 Conceptual framework for not-for profit entities

The IASB and the FASB are currently in a project to produce a new, improved conceptual framework for financial reporting, entitled: *The Objective of Financial Reporting and Qualitative Characteristics of Decision-Useful Financial Reporting Information*. This project is being undertaken in phases. Phase G is entitled *Application to not-for-profit entities in the private and public sector*. A monitoring group, including ASB members, set up to advise on this has made the following points:

(a)   Not-for profit entities have different objectives, different operating environments and other different characteristics to private sector businesses.

(b)   The following issues exist regarding application of the proposals to not-for-profit entities:

- Insufficient emphasis on accountability/stewardship
- A need to broaden the definition of users and user groups
- The emphasis on future cash flows is inappropriate to not-for-profit entities
- Insufficient emphasis on budgeting

2.2 Accountability/stewardship

Not-for-profit entities are not reporting to shareholders, but it is very important that they can account for funds received and show how they have been spent. In some cases, resources may be contributed for specific purposes and management is required to show that they have been utilised for that purpose. Perhaps most importantly, taxpayers are entitled to see how the government is spending their money.

2.3 Users and user groups

The primary user group for not-for-profit entities is providers of funds. In the case of public bodies, such as government departments, this primary group will consist of taxpayers. In the case of private bodies such as charities it will be financial supporters, and also potential future financial supporters. There is also a case for saying that a second primary user group should be recognised, being the recipients of the goods and services provided by the not-for-profit entity.

2.4 Cash flow focus

The new framework, like the existing framework, emphasises the need to provide information which will enable users to assess an entity's ability to generate net cash inflows. Not-for-profit entities also need to generate cash flows, but other aspects are generally more significant – for instance, the resources the entity has available to deliver future goods and services, the cost and effectiveness of those it has delivered in the past and the degree to which it is meeting its objectives.

2.5 Budgeting

The IASB has decided to leave consideration of whether financial reporting should include forecast information until later in the project. However, for not-for-profit entities, budgets and variance analyses are more important. In some cases, funding is supplied on the basis of a formal, published budget.

3 The not-for-profit sector: regulatory framework

The **IASB** and the **FASB** are working on a **framework** for reporting, which includes not-for-profit entities.

The International Public Sector Accounting Standards Board (IPSAB) is developing a set of **International Public Sector Accounting Standard** based on IFRS.

Regulation of public not-for-profit entities, principally local and national governments and governmental agencies, is by the International Public Sector Accounting Standards Board (IPSAB), which comes under the International Federation of Accountants (IFAC).

3.1 International public sector accounting standards

The IPSASB is developing a set of International Public Sector Accounting Standards (IPSASs), based on IFRSs. To date 21 IPSASs have been issued.

Exam focus point

You don't need to know these – skim over for background only.

1	Presentation of financial statements
2	Statements of cash flows
3	Net surplus or deficit for the period, fundamental errors and changes in accounting policies
4	The effect of changes in foreign exchange rates
5	Borrowing costs
6	Consolidated financial statements and accounting for controlled entities
7	Accounting for investments in associates
8	Financial reporting of Interests in joint ventures
9	Revenue from exchange transactions
10	Financial reporting in hyperinflationary economies
11	Construction contracts
12	Inventories
13	Leases
14	Events after the reporting date
15	Financial instruments: disclosure and presentation
16	Investment property
17	Property, plant and equipment
18	Segment reporting
19	Provisions, contingent liabilities and contingent assets
10	Related party disclosures
21	Impairment of non-cash-generating assets

You are not required to remember this list of IPSAs, or know any of their detailed provisions, but you can see that they closely mirror the IAS/IFRSs and each one is based on the relevant International Accounting Standard.

The IPSAs are all based on the accrual method of accounting and one of the aims of the IPSAB is to move public sector organisations from the cash to the accruals basis of accounting.

3.2 Characteristics of not-for-profit entities

As part of its preliminary report on the new *Framework*, the IASB sets out some of the characteristics of not-for-profit entities as follows:

3.2.1 Private Sector

Not-for-profit entities in the private sector have the following characteristics:

- Their objective is to provide goods and services to various recipients and not to make a profit
- They are generally characterised by the absence of defined ownership interests (shares) that can be sold, transferred or redeemed
- They may have a wide group of stakeholders to consider (including the public at large in some cases)
- Their revenues generally arise from contributions (donations or membership dues) rather than sales
- Their capital assets are typically acquired and held to deliver services without the intention of earning a return on them

3.2.2 Public Sector

Nor-for-profit entities in the public sector have similar key characteristics to those in the private sector. They are typically established by legislation and:

- Their objective is to provide goods and services to various recipients or to develop or implement policy on behalf of governments and not to make a profit
- They are characterised by the absence of defined ownership interests that can be sold, transferred or redeemed
- They typically have a wide group of stakeholders to consider (including the public at large)
- Their revenues are generally derived from taxes or other similar contributions obtained through the exercise of coercive powers
- Their capital assets are typically acquired and held to deliver services without the intention of earning a return on them

3.3 Not-for-profit entities – specific issues

While the general trend is to get not-for-profit entities producing accounts which are based as far as possible on the provisions of IFRS and which are generally comparable to those produced for profit-making entities, there are two issues which have yet to be resolved.

3.3.1 Cost of transition

While there has been a general assumption that for public sector entities the move to the accruals basis will result in more relevant and better quality financial reporting, no actual cost-benefit analysis has been undertaken on this.

One of the arguments in favour of the adoption of the accruals basis is that it will be possible to compare the cost of providing a service against the same cost in the private sector. It will then be possible to see how goods and services can be most cheaply sourced.

However, it is questionable whether governments get a good deal anyway when they involve themselves with the private sector and the move to accruals accounting has not gained universal acceptance. The governments of Germany, Italy and Holland have so far made no plans for the transition and the governments of China, Japan, Malaysia and Singapore have decided against it. The main issue is the huge cost involved in terms of the number of qualified accountants required. For developing countries this cost is considered to be prohibitive.

3.3.2 Definition of a liability

The *Framework* defines a liability as 'a present obligation of the entity arising from past events, the settlement of which is expected to result in an outflow from the entity of resources embodying economic benefits'. A liability is recognised when the amount of the outflow can be reliably measured.

Public benefit entities are subject to a commitment to provide public benefits, but there is an issue to be resolved over whether this commitment meets the definition of a liability. In this situation there has been no 'exchange'. The entity has not received any goods or services for which it is required to make 'settlement'. A distinction can be drawn between 'general commitments to provide public benefits' and 'specific commitments to provide public benefits'. The specific commitment can be regarded as a 'present obligation', but it can be argued that the obligation only arises when the entity formally undertakes to provide something such as a non-performance-related grant. (If the grant were performance-related, the entity would be able to withdraw from the agreement if the performance targets were not reached.)

There is also the issue of 'reliable measurement'. Governments in particular often find themselves funding projects which go a long way over budget, suggesting that reliable measurement was not obtained at the outset.

This issue is still being debated by the IPSAB. It is of major importance in the financial reporting of the social policies of governments.

3.4 Charities

Charities are regulated by accounting standards, charity law, relevant company law and best practice. This will vary from country to country. Here we are taking the UK as a typical example.

3.4.1 Statement of financial activities

In addition to a statement of financial position, charities also produce a Statement of Financial Activities (SOFA), an Annual Report to the Charity Commission and sometimes an income and expenditure account. The Statement of Financial Activities is the primary statement showing the results of the charity's activities for the period.

The SoFA shows Incoming resources, Resources expended, and the resultant Net movement in funds. Under incoming resources, income from all sources of funds are listed. These can include:

Subscription or membership fees

- Public donations
- Donations from patrons
- Government grants
- Income from sale of goods
- Investment income
- Publication sales
- Royalties

The resources expended will show the amount spent directly in furtherance of the Charity's objects. It will also show items which form part of any income statement, such as salaries, depreciation, travelling and entertaining, audit and other professional fees. These items can be very substantial.

Charities, especially the larger charities, now operate very much in the way that profit-making entities do. They run high-profile campaigns which cost money and they employ professional people who have to be paid. At the same time, their stakeholders will want to see that most of their donation is not going on running the business, rather than achieving the aims for which funds were donated.

One of the problems charities experience is that, even although the accruals basis is being applied, they will still have income and expenditure recognised in different periods, due to the difficulty of correlating them. The extreme example is a campaign to persuade people to leave money to the charity in their will. The costs will have to be recognised, but there is no way to predict when the income will arise.

4 The not-for-profit sector: performance measurement

Not-for-profit and public sector entities produce financial statements in the same way as profit-making entities do but, while they are expected to remain solvent, their performance cannot be measured simply by the bottom line.

A public sector entity is not expected to show a profit or to underspend its budget. In practice, central government and local government departments know that if they underspend the budget, next year's allocation will be correspondingly reduced. This leads to a rash of digging up the roads and other expenditure just before the end of the financial year as councils strive to spend any remaining funds.

Private and public sector entities are judged principally on the basis of what they have achieved, not how much or how little they have spent in achieving it. So how is performance measured?

4.1 Public sector entities

These will have performance measures laid down by government. The emphasis is on economy, efficiency and effectiveness. Departments and local councils have to show how they have spent public money and what level of service they have achieved. Performance measurement will be based on Key Performance Indicators (KPIs). Examples of these for a local council could be:

- Number of homeless people rehoused

- % of rubbish collections made on time
- Number of children in care adopted

Public sector entities use the services of outside contractors for a variety of functions. They then have to be able to show that they have obtained the best possible value for what they have spent on outside services. This principle is usually referred to as Value For Money (VFM). In the UK, local authorities are required to report under a system known as Best Value. They have to show that they applied 'fair competition' in awarding contracts.

Best Value is based on the principle of the 'four Cs':

1   **Challenging** why, how and by whom a service is provided
2   **Comparing** performance against other local authorities
3   **Consulting** service users, the local community etc
4   Using fair **Competition** to secure efficient and effective services

4.2 Charities

While charities must demonstrate that they have made proper use of whatever funds they have received, their stakeholders will be more interested in what they have achieved in terms of their stated mission. People who donate money to a relief fund for earthquake victims will want to know what help has been given to survivors, before enquiring how well the organisation has managed its funds. Although it must be said that any mismanagement of funds by a charity is taken very seriously by the donating public.

Some charities produce 'impact reports' which highlight what the charity set out to achieve, what it has achieved and what it has yet to do. Stakeholders should know what the organisation is aiming to achieve and how it is succeeding. Each charity will have its own performance indicators which enable it to measure this.

Question	Definite variables

Choose a charity with which you are familiar and produce a possible set of performance indicators for it.

5 Smaller entities

FAST FORWARD

> The IASB has begun to address the **Big GAAP/Little GAAP** debate. An **exposure draft** has been published

5.1 Background

5.1.1 Scope Of IFRS

Any limitation of the applicability of a specific IFRS is made clear within that standard. IASs are **not intended to be applied to immaterial items, nor are they retrospective**. Each individual IAS lays out its scope at the beginning of the standard.

5.1.2 Application

Within each individual country **local regulations** govern, to a greater or lesser degree, the issue of financial statements. These local regulations include accounting standards issued by the national regulatory bodies and/or professional accountancy bodies in the country concerned.

The IASs **concentrate on essentials** and are designed not to be too complex, otherwise they would be impossible to apply on a worldwide basis.

IASs do not override local regulations on financial statements. Members of the IASB should simply disclose the fact where IASs are complied with in all material respects. Members of the IASB in individual counties will attempt to persuade local authorities, where current regulations deviate from IASs, that the benefits of harmonisation make local change worthwhile.

5.2 Application of IFRS to smaller entities

In most countries the majority of companies or other types of entity are **very small**. They are generally owned and managed by one person or a family. The owners have invested their own money in the business and there are no outside shareholders to protect.

Large entities, by contrast, particularly companies listed on a stock exchange, may have shareholders who have invested their money, possibly through a pension fund, with no knowledge whatever of the company. These shareholders need protection and the regulations for such companies need to be more stringent.

It could therefore be argued that company accounts should be of two types.

(a)   'Simple' ones for small companies with fewer regulations and disclosure requirements

(b)   'Complicated' ones for larger companies with extensive and detailed requirements

This is sometimes called the **big GAAP/little GAAP divide**.

It is certainly the case that there are several IASs which very rarely have any bearing on small company accounts, whereas others almost always have an impact. In particular, almost all small companies will be affected by the IASs on:

- Property, plant and equipment
- Depreciation
- Inventories
- Presentation of financial statements
- Events after the reporting period
- Taxes on income
- Revenue
- Provisions and contingencies

Does this mean that companies below a certain size should be exempt from other IASs? An alternative approach would be to reduce the exposure of small companies to IASs on a **standard by standard basis**. For those 'core' standards listed above, small companies would be required to follow all or most of their provisions. For more complicated standards, small companies would face nothing but very brief general obligations.

It is difficult to see how the IASB could impose any kind of specific size limits to define small companies if such an approach were adopted. Instead, it might specify that size limits which are already given in national legislation or standards could be adopted for the purpose.

IASs have been developed to deal with the problems arising in limited liability companies' financial statements.

However, this can cause small entities problems of the cost of compliance. For example, impairment reviews can be time consuming and a smaller entity may not have sufficient staff to spare to carry out these reviews.

Other standards may simply not apply to a smaller entity. For example, a company with equity not quoted on a stock exchange has no need to comply with IAS 33 *Earnings per share*. Also an entity with a small local market, may find IFRS 8 *Operating segments* to be superfluous.

The general rule to be followed by a smaller entity is to comply with all IASs that apply in its own particular case.

If the cost of compliance exceeds the benefits to users, an entity may decide not to follow an IAS. This applies to all reporting entities, not just smaller ones. However, smaller entities are more likely to make use of this exception.

Another point to note is that IASs apply to **material** items. In the case of smaller entities, the amount that is material may be very small in monetary terms. However, the affect of not reporting that item may be material in that it would mislead users of the financial statements. A case in point is IAS 24 *Related party disclosures*. Smaller entities may well rely on trade with relatives of the directors/shareholders and this needs to be disclosed.

The IASB has now begun a project to examine ways in which existing IASs and IFRSs could be adapted for smaller entities. This project is still at a very early stage.

5.3 Recent developments

5.3.1 Discussion paper

In June 2004, the **IASB** published a Discussion Paper *Preliminary Views on Accounting Standards for Small and Medium-sized Entities (SMEs)*. The purpose of the Discussion Paper is to invite comments on the IASB's preliminary views on its basic **approach to the project on accounting standards for SMEs.**

In the IASB's view, the set of accounting standards for SMEs should be a **modified version of full IFRS**, published in a separate printed volume and following the numbering system of International Financial Reporting Standards. It proposes a rebuttable presumption that **no modifications** would be made to the **recognition and measurement principles in IFRS**.

The IASB's proposals, if implemented, would result in standards for SMEs which differ from the UK equivalent standard (Financial Reporting Standard for Smaller Entities or FRSSE) in a number of ways.

(a)   The IASB project focuses on **non-public accountability** as the key test for determining who might be eligible to use the standards for SMEs. The focus, unlike that of the FRSSE, is **not on smaller entities**. If smaller entities are to enjoy a substantially reduced burden, this could imply the need for a 'three tier' system of accounting standards.

(b)   **Each IFRS** and interpretation would have its **SME equivalent**. Companies would therefore be using a series of separate standards rather than the one special standard for smaller entities. Furthermore, those SME standards would **change in line with IFRS** rather than be changed at most only once a year.

(c)   The IASB proposes **mandatory fallback to IFRS** for any particular accounting or measurement issue that is not addressed in the SME standards. The FRSSE, in contrast, encourages such reference only as a possible means of establishing generally accepted practice.

(d)   The IASB proposes a **'pick and mix' approach** from IFRS and IFRS for SMEs. Eligible entities could choose to follow IFRS in some areas and IFRS for SMEs in others. The FRSSE is not mandatory but once an entity has chosen to follow the FRSSE it must consider all its requirements.

5.3.2 Exposure draft: IFRS for small and medium sized entities

In February 2007, the IASB published an **exposure draft** of a proposed *IFRS for small and medium-sized entities*. This invites comments on eleven questions:

(a)   The proposed *IFRS for SMEs* is intended to be a **stand-alone document**. Is additional information needed to make it more self-contained?

(b)   Are there other **recognition or measurement simplifications** that the Board should consider?

(c)   Are there recognition and measurement simplifications that the Board should re-consider?

(d)   Should *all* **accounting policy options** in full IFRS be available to SMEs?

(e)   Should SMEs be allowed to **choose** either the **expense model or the capitalisation model** for borrowing costs, and why?

(f)   Should any **additional topics** be omitted from the IFRS for SMEs and replaced by a cross reference?

(g)   The proposed *IFRS for SMEs* is intended as a stand-alone document, but it contains **cross references** to full IFRS in specific circumstances. Is this appropriate?

(h)   Are there specific areas for which SMEs are likely to need **additional guidance**?

(i)   Should there be **disclosure requirements** in addition to those specified in the draft implementation guidance *Illustrative Financial Statements and Disclosure Checklist*?

(j)   Is the **transition guidance** adequate?

(k)   The IASB expects to amend the *IFRS for SMEs* **every other year**. Is this adequate?

5.3.3 Pluses and minuses of the ED

Pluses

(a)   It is virtually a '**one stop shop**'.

(b)   It is **structured according to topics**, which should make it practical to use.

(c)   It is written in an **accessible style**.

(d)   There is **considerable reduction in disclosure requirements**.

(e)   Guidance **not relevant** to SMEs is **excluded**.

Minuses

(a)   It **does not focus on the smallest companies**.

(b)   The scope extends to 'non-publicly accountable' entities. Potentially, the **scope is too wide**.

(c)   The standard will be **onerous** for small companies.

(d)   **Further simplifications could be made**. These might include:

    (i)   Amortisation for goodwill and intangibles

    (ii)   No requirement to value intangibles separately from goodwill on a business combination.

    (iii)   No recognition of deferred tax.

    (iv)   No measurement rules for equity-settled share-based payment.

    (v)   No requirement for consolidated accounts (as for EU SMEs currently)

    (vi)   All leases accounted for as operating leases with enhanced disclosures

    (vii)   Fair value measurement when readily determinable without undue cost or effort.

6 IAS 41 Agriculture

The importance of the agricultural sector in a country's economy will vary. It is reasonable to assume, however, that although agriculture is important in first world countries, it is likely to be of greater significance to **developing countries** in terms of the proportion of Gross Domestic Product it represents.

The IASC is prepared to develop standards that are specific to certain industries or businesses where the issues are considered to be of sufficient substance and significance. As a start in the case of agriculture, the IASC issued IAS 41 *Agriculture* in February 2001.

Exam focus point

This not a core topic for Paper P2, but may be tested in outline.

The main reason for developing a standard on agriculture is the same reason that any standard is developed, ie because there is great **diversity in practice in accounting** for agriculture at both a transnational and national level. Accounting guidelines have been piecemeal, developed as required to tackle specific issues in specific countries.

Question   **Agriculture**

If you work in agriculture, or if agriculture is important in your country, you may like to investigate the accounting treatment of items such as forestry activity or livestock activity in your country. Are there differences within your own country? How do these practices compare with other countries?

Perhaps more interestingly, it is quite difficult to apply **traditional accounting methods** to agricultural activities, which explains why agriculture is excluded from many IASs.

(a)   When and how do you account for the **critical events** associated with biological transformation (growth, procreation, production and degeneration), which alter the substance of biological assets?

(b)   **Statement of financial position classification** is made difficult by the variety and characteristics of the living assets of agriculture.

(c)   The nature of the management of agricultural activities also causes problems, particularly determination of the **unit of measurement**, ie whether biological assets are a perpetual group of assets or a number of limited life assets.

A standard would improve and harmonise practice in accounting for agriculture, which demonstrates fundamental **differences in its nature and characteristics** to other business activities.

6.1 Definitions

FAST FORWARD

IAS 41 *Agriculture* is examinable in outline only.

The following definitions are used in IAS 41 (you should be familiar with the definitions of fair value and carrying amount by now).

Key terms

> **Agricultural activity** is the management by an entity of the biological transformation of biological assets for sale, into agricultural produce or into additional biological assets.
>
> **Agricultural produce** is the harvested product of an entity's biological assets.
>
> A **biological asset** is a living animal or plant.
>
> **Biological transformation** comprises the processes of growth, degeneration, production and procreation that cause qualitative and quantitative changes in a biological asset.
>
> A **group of biological assets** is an aggregation of similar living animals or plants.
>
> **Harvest** is the detachment of produce from a biological asset or the cessation of a biological asset's life processes
>
> **Fair value** is the amount for which an asset could be exchanged, or a liability settled, between knowledgeable, willing parties in an arm's length transaction.
>
> **Carrying amount** is the amount at which an asset is recognised in the statement of financial position.
>
> *(IAS 41)*

Note the key parts of the definition of **agriculture**.

(a)   **Biological**: agriculture relates to 'life phenomena', living animals and plants with an innate capacity of biological transformation which are dependent upon a combination of natural resources (sunlight, water, etc).

(b)   **Transformation**: agriculture involves physical transformation, whereby animals and plants undergo a change in biological quantity (fat cover, density, etc) and/or quantity (progeny, live weight etc) over time, which is measured and monitored (increasingly objectively) as part of management control.

(c)   **Management**: biological transformation is managed.

(i)   Conditions are stabilised or enhanced

(ii)   The transparency of the relationship between inputs and outputs is determined by the degree of control (intensive versus extensive)

(iii) It is different from exploitation through extraction, where no attempt is made to facilitate the transformation

(iv)   Biological assets are managed in groups of plant or animal classes, using individual assets to ensure the sustainability of the group

(v)   Sustainability of an agricultural activity is a function of quality and quantity

(d)   **Produce**: agricultural produce is diverse and may require further processing before ultimate consumption.

Before we look at the way the standard tackles accounting for agriculture, can you think of some of the main accounting issues, given some of the things we have looked at so far?

Answer

The standard lists the following.

(a)   Biological assets meet the definition and recognition criteria of tangible assets (see IAS 16).

(b)   Biological transformation is the source of sector uniqueness and significant events within agricultural activities.

(c)   Biological transformations are critical events separable from the transactions entered into to facilitate them.

(d)   In agricultural activities there is a general lack of clarity in the relationship between inputs and outputs which increases the complexity of the allocation process, ie between joint costs and joint products.

(e)   A consistent basis of management must be applied to all outcomes to produce meaningful representations of current period performance, because of the range of outcomes and lack of traceability. This means that both biological assets and agricultural produce should be measured using the same basis.

(f)   Active and efficient markets for both biological assets and agricultural produce increases the reliability of measures of net market value and existing use value respectively.

(g)   Using the class or collective of biological assets as a unit of measurement has implications for: measurement (the class is more reliable than the individual, future benefits not confined to immediately available uses, values are normally expressed in the collective); for classification (a collective is a regenerative perpetual asset, even though individual members have a limited life); and for going concern (sustainability is an important indicator of going concern).

(h)   Different agricultural activities have different risk and reward characteristics and will therefore be reported under different segments (see IAS 14).

6.2 Scope

The standard applies to the three elements that form part of, or result from, agricultural activity.

- Biological assets
- Agricultural produce at the point of harvest
- Government grants

The standard does not apply to agricultural land (IASs 16 and 40) or intangible assets related to agricultural activity (IAS 38). After harvest, IAS 2 is applied.

6.3 Biological assets

We have seen the definition given above. Biological assets are the core income-producing assets of agricultural activities, held for their transformative capabilities. Biological transformation leads to various different outcomes.

- **Asset changes:**
    - Growth: increase in quantity and or quality
    - Degeneration: decrease in quantity and/or quality

- **Creation of new assets:**
    - Production: producing separable non-living products
    - Procreation: producing separable living animals

We can distinguish between the importance of these by saying that asset changes are **critical to the flow of future economic benefits** both in and beyond the current period, but the relative importance of new asset creation will depend on the purpose of the agricultural activity.

The IAS distinguishes therefore between two broad categories of agricultural production system.

(a)   **Consumable**: animals/plants themselves are harvested
(b)   **Bearer**: animals/plants bear produce for harvest

A few further points are made.

(a)   Biological assets are usually managed in groups of animal or plant classes, with characteristics (eg male/female ratio) which allow **sustainability in perpetuity**.
(b)   **Land often forms an integral part** of the activity itself in pastoral and other land-based agricultural activities.

The Standard then goes on to look at the principal issues in accounting for biological assets.

6.3.1 Recognition of biological assets

The recognition criteria are very **similar to those for other assets**, in that animals or plants should be recognised as assets in the following circumstances.

(a)   The entity **controls** the asset as a result of past events.
(b)   It is probable that the **future economic benefits** associated with the asset will flow to the entity
(c)   The fair value or cost of the asset to the entity can be **measured reliably**

The significant physical attributes of biological assets can be measured using various methods (which are used by markets to measure value) and generally indicate the source of future economic benefits. The **certainty** of the flow of rewards can be determined by formal ownership records, eg land title, branding. The availability of both cost and value for biological assets indicates the reliability aspect of the measurement criteria is fulfilled.

6.3.2 Measurement of biological assets

The IAS requires that at each year end **all biological assets should be measured at fair value** less estimated point-of-sale costs.

The IAS allows an alternative method of valuation, if a fair value cannot be determined because market-determined prices or values are not available. Then the biological asset can be measured at cost less accumulated depreciation and impairment losses.

This alternative basis is only allowed on **initial recognition.**

The **measurement basis** used to depict the fair value of a biological asset will differ depending on the existence of an active market, market efficiency and the use made of the asset.

In summary, it is felt that **fair value**, when compared to historical cost, has greater relevance, reliability, comparability and understandability as a measure of future economic benefits.

6.3.3 Determining fair value

The standard states that the primary indicator of fair value should be **net market value**. This is reasonable as efficient markets exist for most biological assets in most locations and net market value is usually considered as providing the best evidence of fair value where an active market exists. Markets will generally differentiate between differing **qualities and quantities**. Market value is not generally predicted on management's intended use, however, but recognises alternative uses.

An active and efficient market may not be available for a class of biological assets in a specific location, or there may be imperfections in the market. The standard goes into some detail about **how fair value should be estimated** in such circumstances, but in summary the valuation techniques should be consistent with the objectives of measuring fair value and should attain an appropriate balance between relevance and reliability.

6.3.4 Recognition

This is an important principle, whereby the change in the carrying amount for a group of biological assets should be allocated between:

(a)   the change attributable to **differences in fair value,** and

(b)   the **physical change** in biological assets held.

The total change in carrying value between the beginning and end of the period thus consists of two components. Although the separation of these two components might appear impractical, the Standard states that separate disclosure of each is **fundamental to appraising current period performance and future prospects**. This is because they will not be reported in the same way in the financial statements.

(a)   The change in carrying amount attributable to the **physical change in biological assets** must be recognised as income or expense and described as the change in biological assets. This allows management's performance to be evaluated in relation to the production from, and maintenance and renewal of, biological assets. This is the 'operating' part of the change in carrying amount.

(b)   The change in carrying amount attributable to **differences in fair value** should be recognised in the statement of non-owner movements in equity and presented in equity under the heading of surplus/(deficit) on fair valuation of biological assets. This is the 'holding' part of the change in carrying amount.

In the **statement of financial position** the biological assets must be shown at fair value, incorporating the consequences of all biological transformations. These assets, with their differing risk and return characteristics, should be identified clearly.

The recommended **method of separating the above components** is to calculate the change attributable to the differences in fair value by restating biological assets on hand at the opening reporting date using end of period fair values and comparing this with the closing carrying amount. The biological assets on hand at the beginning and end of the period will then be expressed in a common measurement unit, ie period-end fair value. This allows the relative significance of sales, disposals, purchases, additions and biological transformations to be evaluated in relation to the overall change in substance of the biological assets held during the period.

There are **exceptions to this approach** in certain situations. For example, in some agricultural systems the predominant activity has a production cycle of less than a year (eg broiler chickens, mushroom growing, cereal crops). In such cases the total change in carrying amount is reported in the statement of comprehensive income as a single item of income or expense.

Any other events giving rise to a change in biological assets of such a **size, nature or incidence** that their disclosure is relevant to explain the entity's performance (as defined in IAS 8) should be included in the change in biological assets recognised as income or expense. They should, however, be shown as a in the statement of financial position item in the reconciliation required to determine the change attributable to biological transformation.

6.3.5 Presentation and disclosure

In the statement of financial position biological assets should be classified as a separate class of assets falling under neither current nor non-current classifications. This reflects the view of such assets as having an unlimited life on a collective basis; it is the total exposure of the entity to this type of asset that is important.

Biological assets should also be **sub-classified** (either in the statement of financial position or as a note to the accounts).

(a)   Class of animal or plant

(b)   Nature of activities (consumable or bearer)

(c)   Maturity or immaturity for intended purpose

Where activities are **consumable**, the maturity criterion will be attainment of harvestable specifications, whereas in **bearer** activities, it will be attainment of sufficient maturity to sustain economic harvests.

In the **statement of comprehensive income**, entities with significant agricultural activity are encouraged to provide, in the statement of comprehensive income, an analysis of the income and expenses used in determining profit from operating activities based on the nature of income and expenses (ie rather than the cost of sales method).

The IAS also lists some detailed disclosure requirements including the measurement base used for fair value, the details of the reconciliation of the change in carrying value for the year and so on.

6.4 Agricultural produce

This was defined in the key terms above. It is **recognised at the point of harvest** (eg detachment from the biological asset). Agricultural produce is either incapable of biological process or such processes remain dormant (eg stored grain). **Recognition ends** once the produce enters trading activities or production processes within integrated agribusinesses, although processing activities that are incidental to agricultural activities and that do not materially alter the form of the produce (eg drying or cleaning) are not counted as processing. Following harvest, the provisions of IAS 2 apply.

6.4.1 Measurement and presentation

Following the treatment of biological assets above, the IAS states that agricultural produce should be **measured at each year end at fair value** less estimated point-of-sale costs, to the extent that it is sourced from an entity's biological assets, which are also valued at fair value. This is logical when you consider that, until harvest, the agricultural produce was valued at fair value anyway as part of the biological asset.

The **change in the carrying amount** of the agricultural produce held at year end should be recognised as **income or expense** in profit or loss. This will be rare as such produce is usually sold or processed within a short time, so that produce held over two balance sheet dates is being held for a specific management purpose and the consequences of that should be reflected in the current period.

Agricultural produce that is harvested for **trading or processing activities** within integrated agricultural/agribusiness operations should be measured at **fair value** at the date of harvest and this amount is deemed cost for application of IAS 2 to consequential inventories.

Presentation in the statement of financial position

Agricultural produce should be classified as inventory in the statement of financial position and disclosed separately either in the statement of financial position or in the notes.

6.5 Government grants

An unconditional government grant related to a biological asset measured at its fair value less estimated point-of-sale costs should be recognised as income when, and only when, the grant becomes receivable.

If a government grant requires an entity not to engage in specified agricultural activity (eg the EU's set aside grant), an entity should only recognise the grant as income when, and only when, the conditions are met.

IAS 20 does not apply to a government grant on biological assets measured at fair value less estimated point-of-sale costs. However if a biological asset is measured at cost less accumulated depreciation and accumulated impairment losses then IAS 20 does apply.

6.6 Section summary

In relation to agriculture you should be able to discuss:

- Accounting for **biological assets**
- **Transformation** and changes in substance
- **Unit of measurement** and changes in the carrying amount

Chapter Roundup

- Questions on specialist entities will be set in terms of **current IFRS**.

- The not-for-profit sector includes **public sector entities** and **private** not-for-profit entities such as charities.

- Not-for-profit entities have **different goals** from profit making entities, but they still need to be **properly managed** and their accounts need to present the information fairly

- The **IASB** and the **FASB** are working on a **framework** for reporting, which includes not-for-profit entities.

- The International Public Sector Accounting Standards Board (IPSAB) is developing a set of **International Public Sector Accounting Standard** based on IFRS.

- The IASB has begun to address the **Big GAAP/Little GAAP** debate. An **exposure draft** has been published

- IAS 41 *Agriculture* is examinable in outline only.

Quick Quiz

1   Charities are public sector entities. True or false?

2   Why do not-for-profit entities need to keep accounts if they are not reporting to shareholders?

3   Are there any special IFRSs for the public sector?

4   Are there any special IFRSs for small companies?

5   IAS 41 has abolished the concept of cost for measurement purposes.

    True ☐

    False ☐

Answers to Quick Quiz

1   False. charities are private not-for-profit profit entities.

2   They often deal in large sums of money.

3   Yes, the IPSASB is developing a set of International Public Sector Accounting Standards

4   Not yet. However, an exposure draft of a proposed *IFRS for small– and medium-sized entities* has been published

5   False. Cost is still allowed if fair value is not available at initial recognition.

Now try the question below from the Exam Question Bank

Number	Level	Marks	Time
Q23	Introductory	n/a	n/a
Q24	Examination	25	45 mins

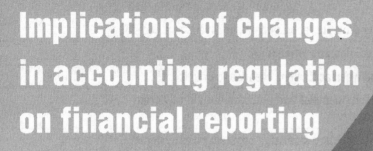

Implications of changes in accounting regulation on financial reporting

Topic list	Syllabus reference
1 Impact of changes in accounting standards and policies	B1
2 Performance measurement	B1
3 Benefits and problems of performance measures	B1
4 Accounting theory and practice	B3

Introduction

This is a 'mixed bag' chapter, drawing together some general issues you have touched on earlier and introducing the topic of performance measurement. You should be aware that there are non-financial performance measures.

Study guide

		Intellectual level
B1	**The contribution and limitations of financial statements in meeting user's and capital markets' needs.**	
(a)	Evaluate the consistency and clarity of corporate reports.	3
(b)	Assess the insight into financial and operational risks provided by corporate reports.	3
(c)	Discuss the usefulness of corporate reports in making investment decisions.	3
B3	**Critical evaluation of principles and practices**	
(a)	Identify the relationship between accounting theory and practice.	2
(b)	Critically evaluate accounting principles and practices used in corporate reporting	3
F1	**The effect of changes in accounting standards on accounting systems.**	
(a)	Apply and discuss the accounting implications of the first time adoption of a body of new accounting standards	3
(b)	Outline the issues in implementing a change to new accounting standards, including organisational, behavioural and procedural changes within the entity.	3
F2	**Proposed changes to accounting standards**	
(a)	Identify the issues and deficiencies which have led to a proposed change to an accounting standard.	2
(b)	Apply and discuss the implications of a proposed change to an accounting standard on the performance and position of an entity	2

Exam guide

Weaknesses in current financial reporting may come up as part of a discussion on the impact of change. Perhaps alternative types of reporting will be presented, and you will need to point out strengths and weaknesses.

1 Impact of changes in accounting standards and policies   12/08

> **FAST FORWARD**
>
> Accounting policies may be adopted for the purpose of **manipulation**.
>
> **Changes in accounting standards** can have a significant impact on the financial statements.

We discussed the disclosure of accounting policies in your earlier studies. The choice of accounting policy and the effect of its implementation are almost as important as its disclosure in that the results of a company can be altered significantly by the choice of accounting policy.

1.1 The effect of choice of accounting policies

Where accounting standards allow alternative treatment of items in the accounts, then the accounting policy note should declare which policy has been chosen. It should then be applied consistently.

Consider, though, the **radically different effects produced by the different treatment of some items**. An example is the treatment of joint ventures, which may be proportionally consolidated or equity accounted.

You should be able to think of other examples of how the choice of accounting policy can affect the financial statements.

1.2 Changes in accounting policy

The effect of a change of accounting policy is treated as a retrospective adjustment to the opening balance of each affected component of equity, as if the accounting policy had always applied.

IAS 8 (revised) states that changes in accounting policies are rare, and only allowed if **required by statute** or if the change results in **more reliable and relevant information.**

There is still some scope for directors to **manipulate the results** through change(s) of accounting policies. This would be done to avoid the effect of an old accounting policy or gain the effect of a new one. It is likely to be done in a sensitive period, perhaps when the company's profits are low or the company is about to announce a rights issue. The management would have to convince the auditors that the new policy was much better, but it is not difficult to produce reasons in such cases.

The effect of such a change is **very short-term**. Most analysts and sophisticated users will discount its effect immediately, except to the extent that it will affect any dividend (because of the effect on distributable profits). It may help to avoid breaches of banking covenants because of the effect on certain ratios.

Obviously, the accounting policy for any item in the accounts could only be changed once in quite a long period of time. No auditors would allow another change, even back to the old policy, unless there was a wholly exceptional reason.

The managers of a company can choose accounting policies **initially** to suit the company or the type of results they want to get. Any changes in accounting policy must be justified, but some managers might try to change accounting policies just to manipulate the results.

1.3 Changes in accounting standards

FAST FORWARD

> You will probably be asked to **advise the directors** on the implication of a change in accounting standards, or on the effect of using the correct accounting treatment.

The effect of a change of accounting standard can be far reaching. For example when IFRS 3 *Business combinations* was brought in, goodwill arising on consolidation could no longer be amortised, but had to be reviewed annually for impairment. Impairment tests are more subjective than amortisation, although both methods have their drawbacks. Further significant amendments in the area of business combinations are proposed.

1.4 The impact of change and the P2 examination

Judging from the Pilot Paper and from the approach taken by the P2 examiner in the past, this topic is likely to be examined regularly. Usually you will be in the position of advising the directors. The directors may have adopted an accounting treatment that is incorrect. You will need to advise them of the correct accounting treatment and show, usually with supporting calculations, the effect on the financial statements of adopting the correct treatment.

Ethics are an important aspect of the ACCA's qualification. If the directors, in adopting certain accounting treatments, are acting unethically, you may need to discuss this. This happened in Question 1 of the Pilot paper.

Alternatively the treatment may not be wrong, but a matter of accounting policy which the directors wish to change. As before, you will be asked to explain, with supporting calculations, the effect of the change.

You are very likely to be asked to explain the significance of a proposed change in accounting standards. For example, the Pilot Paper required you to discuss the effect of the changes proposed in to IFRS 3 and IAS 27.

1.5 Practise case study questions

The impact of change in standards, policies or treatment is unlikely to comprise a whole question. It is more likely to come up as part of a longer question. For example, it may come up as part of the compulsory 50 mark case study question, the first part of which will always be on groups. You should therefore practise this type of question. Have a go at Question 1 of the Pilot Paper at the end of this Study Text, and the question Wingit in the Exam Question Bank. Further questions of this type can be found in BPP's Practice & Revision Kit for this Paper.

Exam focus point

Case study questions to try: Planet, Wingit and the case study questions in the Practice and Revision Kit. The December 2008 paper had a question on accounting standards and disclosures, which required student to think broadly.

2 Performance measurement

FAST FORWARD

Key areas for performance measurement are **profitability**, **activity** and **productivity**. Profitability is often a key objective but other **'success factors'** are also critical. **Benchmarking** is increasingly common.

Both quantitative and qualitative performance measures are equally valuable.

Performance measurement aims to establish **how well** something or somebody is doing in relation to the **planned activity** and **desired results**. The 'thing' may be a machine, a factory, a subsidiary company or an organisation as a whole. The 'body' may be an individual employee, a manager, or a group of people.

A typical business requires performance measurement in the following areas.

(a)   In relation to **external parties** (customers, market, suppliers, competitors)
(b)   **Across the organisation** as a whole (divisional performance measurement)
(c)   **Within** each of the main sub-divisions of the business
(d)   At the level of **individual activities**

Measurement can be in terms of **profitability**, **activity** and **productivity**.

Point of reference	Comment
Profitability	Profit has two components: cost and income. All parts of an organisation and all activities within it incur costs, and so their success needs to be judged in relation to cost. Only some parts of an organisation receive income, and their success should be judged in terms of both cost and income.
Activity	All parts of an organisation are also engaged in activities (activities cause costs). Activity measures could include the following. • Number of orders received from customers, a measure of the effectiveness of marketing • Number of deliveries made, a measure of the effectiveness of distribution • Number of production runs achieved by a particular factory Each of these items could be measured in terms of physical numbers, monetary value, or time spent.
Productivity	This is the quantity of the product or service produced in relation to the resources put in, for example so many units produced per hour, or per employee, or per tonne of material. It defines how *efficiently* resources are being used.

Question   Types of performance measure

An invoicing assistant works in a department with three colleagues. She is paid $8,000 per annum. The department typically handles 10,000 invoices per week. One morning she spends half an hour on the phone to her grandfather, who lives in Australia, at the company's expense. The cost of the call proves to be £32.

Required

From this scenario identify as many different performance measures as possible, explaining what each is intended to measure. Make any further assumptions you wish.

Answer

Invoices per employee per week: 2,500 (activity)
Staff cost per invoice: $0.06 (cost/profitability)
Invoices per hour: 2,500/(7 × 5) = 71.4 (productivity)
Cost of idle time: $32 + $2.14 = $34.14 (cost/profitability)

You may have thought of other measures and probably have slight rounding differences.

2.1 Profit and other objectives

A traditional view has been that a desire to achieve greater profitability often entails a **sacrifice** in some other aspect of performance. One obvious example is quality: if cheaper materials are used to make a product or less highly trained workers deliver a service, money will be saved (increasing profits), but quality will fall.

In other cases there may not be a clear link between an objective and the profitability objective. A company may aim to improve **working conditions** for its staff, and measure its success in terms of the cost of improved facilities, falls in staff turnover, or absenteeism and so on. Some of the successes are directly contrary to profitability, while others can only with difficulty be linked to extra productivity.

A third example is where a company aims to fulfil its **social and moral responsibilities**, for example by incurring costs to make a manufacturing process more environmentally friendly.

2.2 Control and performance measurement

FAST FORWARD

> Financial measures generally derive from the accounting system (or other businesses' accounting systems).

Performance measurement is a vital part of **control**: it is the part of the control process where **feedback** is compared with the plan, and it is also a means of **feedforward control** in the sense that it sets targets to be aimed at in the future.

Exam focus point

> An exam question might refer to the need to exercise control over the process of performance measurement and asked how measurement itself acted as a control mechanism.

2.3 Measuring productivity

Earlier we identified **productivity** as a key area for measurement of a business, so let us see how that might be 'controlled', in other words how we can make sure that the 'right' productivity gets measured.

Key term

> **Productivity** expresses a relationship between outputs from a system and the inputs which go into their creation, as output ÷ input.

The lower the input and the higher the output, the higher will be the resulting productivity. However it needs to be understood by those measuring and those being measured that **high productivity is not a virtue** in itself. It might be possible to produce a larger number of items by spreading the inputs available more thinly, but **if the final output does not then serve its intended purpose** high productivity is worthless.

Inputs should be measured accurately and fairly.

(a)   In some cases it is very **easy** to measure inputs: the material inputs for a mass-produced product can be **weighed** or **counted** and a standard established. The more finished items that can be got out of standard inputs the more productive the process is.

(b)   Sometimes it can be more **difficult**, however, perhaps because **people** do not keep accurate records of the time they put into a task (or falsify records), or because satisfactory outputs depend upon **quality** of input rather than quantity.

(c)   Arguably, a fair measure should be **neutral**, that is, not manipulated by the measurer to encourage certain behaviour. An example might be the exclusion from time measurements of an arbitrary allowance for time that management considers to be 'wasted' chatting to colleagues.

Outputs must also be measured fairly and accurately.

(a)   In a manufacturing context outputs are likely to consist of finished products, but a fair measurement should also take account of goods subsequently **returned** for repair or replacement.

(b)   In a service context (for example, the delivery of products or after-sales care), outputs can be difficult to define: *how* satisfied is a satisfied customer, for example?

The measure needs to exhibit all the qualities of **good information**. For example it needs to be understood by those using it to make decisions, it needs to be available to them on time so that they can act if necessary, it should not cost more to obtain and calculate the measurement than the benefit derived from it, and so on.

The measurement should be **interpreted in context**. Low productivity in a particular month may be an isolated occurrence or part of a worsening trend. High productivity in one part of the factory may be overburdening workers in the next part of the process, causing them to cut corners and produce less satisfactory finished output.

As a **means of control**, productivity measures can be used in the following ways.

(a)   They can be linked to, and so help to achieve, the organisation's overall **strategy** and **objectives**. (A certain level of productivity may, in fact, be an objective itself.)

(b)   Once established they can be used to **predict** future performance.

(c)   They can indicate when and **where action is needed** to correct a process that is out of control.

(d)   They can be used as a **motivation** device if appropriate incentives are offered for achieving productivity targets (or disincentives for failing to achieve them).

2.4 Critical success factors

The use of critical success factors (CSFs) can help to determine the information requirements of senior management.

> **Critical success factors** are the few key areas of the job where things must go right for the organisation to flourish. They are all critical to the furtherance of the organisation's aims and the organisation cannot afford to fall behind in any of these areas.

There are usually **fewer than ten** of these factors that any one executive should monitor. They are very **time dependent**, so they should be **re-examined** as often as necessary to keep abreast of the current business climate.

Critical success factors are derived from the concerns of senior management and cover such areas as industry trends, market positioning and the wider business environment. Here are four sources of CSFs.

(a)   The **industry** that the business is in

(b)   The **company** itself and its situation within the industry

(c)   The **environment**, for example consumer trends and the economy

(d)   **Temporal organisational factors** (areas of corporate activity which are currently **unacceptable** and represent a cause of concern, such as high inventory levels)

A famous study of GEC examined a management reporting system that produced reports on the following factors.

(a)	Profitability	(e)	Personnel development
(b)	Market share	(f)	Employee attitudes
(c)	Productivity	(g)	Public responsibility
(d)	Product leadership	(h)	Balance between short-range and long-range goals

One approach to asking users to define the factors which are critical to success in performing their functions or making decisions is as follows.

Step 1 List the organisation's corporate objectives and goals.

Step 2 Determine which factors are critical for accomplishing the objectives.

Step 3 Determine a small number of prime measures for each factor.

Two separate types of critical success factor can be identified. A **monitoring** CSF is used to keep abreast of existing activities and operations. A **building** CSF helps to measure the progress of new initiatives and is more likely to be relevant at senior executive level.

2.5 Behavioural implications of performance measurement

If people **know** that their performance is being measured then this will affect the standard of their performance, particularly if they know that they will be **rewarded** for achieving a certain level of performance.

Ideally, performance measures will be devised that reward behaviour that maximises the **corporate good**. In practice, however, it is not quite so simple.

(a) There is a danger that managers and staff will concentrate **only** upon what they know is being measured. This is not a problem if every important issue has a measure attached to it, but such a system is difficult to devise and implement.

(b) Individuals have their own **personal goals**, but performance that satisfies their own sense of what is important will not necessarily work towards the corporate good.

Point (b) is the problem of **goal congruence**.

2.5.1 Attitudes

There are a number of factors which may affect the **attitude** of staff to their work.

(a) The feeling of **belonging** to a group with similar aims can be a great motivating force.

(b) The feeling of having **fulfilled one's personal potential** by introducing a new method or receiving praise from a customer can motivate staff.

(c) The amount of **resources** available will affect how staff work. If resources provided are inadequate they will feel as if their task is almost impossible.

(d) **Pay**, **promotion** prospects and bonuses will also be influencing factors.

Staff attitude can be measured in a number of ways.

(a) By the level of **quality** of their work and their **productivity** relative to other staff.

(b) By responses to **customer questionnaires** about the attitude of staff

(c) By reviews written by **colleagues** and **bosses**.

2.6 Financial performance measures

Financial measures (or *monetary* measures) are very familiar to you. Here are some examples, accompanied by comments from a single page of the *Financial Times*.

Part D Performance reporting | **21: Implications of changes in accounting regulation on financial reporting** 501

Measure	Example
Profit	*Profit* is the commonest measure of all. Profit maximisation is usually cited as the main objective of most business organisations: 'ICI increased pre-tax profits to $233m'; 'General Motors... yesterday reported better-than-expected first-quarter net income of $513.
Revenue	'the US businesses contributed $113.9m of total group turnover of $409m'.
Costs	'Sterling's fall benefited pre-tax profits by about $50m while savings from the cost-cutting programme instituted in 1991 were running at around $100m a quarter'; 'The group interest charge rose from $48m to $61m'.
Share price	'The group's shares rose 31c to 1,278c despite the market's fall'.
Cash flow	'Cash flow was also continuing to improve, with cash and marketable securities totalling $8.4bn on March 31, up from $8bn at December 31'.

Note here that monetary amounts stated are only given meaning in **relation to something else**. Here is a list of yard-sticks against which financial results are usually placed so as to become measures, perhaps in the form of **variances.**

- Budgeted **sales**, **costs** and **profits**
- **Standards** in a standard costing system
- The **trend** over time (last year/this year, say)
- The results of **other parts** of the business
- The results of **other businesses**
- The **economy** in general
- **Future potential**

2.6.1 Modern trends: customer profitability analysis

In certain circumstances a useful approach to performance evaluation may be the analysis of **profitability by customer** or customer group. Profitability can vary widely between different customers because various overhead costs are, to some extent, variable and **'customer-driven'**. These overheads include things like discounts and distribution costs.

Customer profitability analysis relates these variabilities in cost to individual customers or customer groups. Managers can use this information to check whether or not individual customers are actually profitable to sell to, and to assess whether profitability can be improved for any customer by switching effort from one type of overhead activity to another, or by reducing spending on some overhead activities.

2.6.2 Modern trends: activity based costing

The implications of ABC for performance measurement are highly significant. For example if a large part of production overheads used to be known as 'warehousing', but are now recognised as 'materials handling costs' that are incurred in relation to the number of production runs, then a materials handling rate per production run can be established. Many such insights will become possible using ABC and they are useful not only for costing products, but also as a **measurement** that will help in the **management** of costs.

2.6.3 Modern trends: benchmarking

Benchmarking has been described as 'the formalisation of the basic notion of comparing practices. It is a **systematic analysis of one's own performance against that of another organisation** ... the overall objective of benchmarking is to improve performance by learning from the experience of others' (Smith). Benchmarking, which is becoming increasingly popular, therefore aims to **achieve competitive advantage** by **learning from others' experiences and mistakes**, finding **best practice** and translating this best practice into **use in the organisation**.

Types of benchmarking

External benchmarking involves comparing the performance of an organisation with that of a **direct competitor** – ideally one that is acknowledged to be the 'best in class' (**competitive benchmarking**) or comparing the performance of an internal function with those of the best **external practitioners of those functions**, regardless of the industry within which they operate (**functional benchmarking**). Given that the benchmark is the 'best' in a particular field, it provides a meaningful target towards which the organisation should aim.

Internal benchmarking, on the other hand, involves comparing the performance of **one part of a business with that of a different part of the same business** with the aim of establishing best practice throughout an organisation. Some external benchmarking is still required, however, in order to establish best practice.

A 1994 survey of *The Times* Top 1000 companies (half of which were in manufacturing) revealed that the business functions most subjected to benchmarking in the companies using the technique were **customer services, manufacturing, human resources** and **information services.**

Why benchmark?

'Perhaps performance measures, when done correctly, help everyone in the company focus on the right things in the right place at the right time. However ... there are many stories of dysfunctional behaviour – the telephone company which pledged to have at least 90% of payphones working, then achieving this figure by simply removing all public payphones from those areas most often vandalised. Or the bus operator which, plagued by delays, decided to pay bonuses to drivers who arrived at the terminus on time. As a result, most buses arrived at the terminus on time – however, drivers no longer tended to stop for passengers along the way!

Measuring performance by itself has no meaning. Meaning can only be achieved through comparison, either against poor performance, which usually provides no true indication of future or competitive position, or through benchmarking.' (*Management Accounting*, November 1996)

2.6.4 Limitations

Both approaches to benchmarking suffer from a number of **limitations**.

(a) Limitations of external benchmarking
- Deciding which activities to benchmark
- Identifying which organisation is the 'best in class' at an activity
- **Persuading that organisation to share information**
- Successful practices in one organisation may not transfer successfully to another

(b) The principal limitation of **internal benchmarking** centres on the **relevance of the other part of the business**.
- The amount of resources devoted to the units may differ.
- There may be local differences (use of different computer hardware).
- Inputs and outputs may be difficult to define.

Benchmarking **works**, it is claimed, **for the following reasons**.

(a) The comparisons are carried out by the **managers who have to live with any changes implemented** as a result of the exercise.

(b) Benchmarking focuses on improvement in key areas and sets **targets** which are **challenging but 'achievable'**. What is *really* achievable can be discovered by examining what others have achieved: managers are thus able to accept that they are not being asked to perform miracles.

Benchmarking can also provide **early warning of competitive disadvantage** and should lead to a greater incidence of **teamworking** and **cross-functional learning**.

2.7 Non-financial performance measures

2.7.1 Quantitative and qualitative performance measures

As you know it is possible to distinguish between **quantitative** information, which is capable of being expressed in numbers, and **qualitative** information, which can only be expressed in numerical terms with difficulty.

An example of a **quantitative** performance measure is 'You have been late for work *twice* this week and it's only Tuesday!'. An example of a **qualitative** performance measure is 'My bed is *very* comfortable'.

The first measure is likely to find its way into a staff appraisal report. The second would feature in a bed manufacturer's customer satisfaction survey. Both are indicators of whether their subjects are doing as good a job as they are required to do.

Qualitative measures are by nature **subjective** and **judgmental** but this does not mean that they are not valuable. They are especially valuable when they are derived from several different sources because then they can be expressed in a mixture of quantitative and qualitative terms which is more meaningful overall.

Consider the following statement.

> 'Seven out of ten customers think our beds are very comfortable.'

This is a **quantitative** measure of customer satisfaction as well as a **qualitative** measure of the perceived performance of the beds. (But it does not mean that only 70% of the total beds produced are comfortable, nor that each bed is 70% comfortable and 30% uncomfortable: 'very' is the measure of comfort.)

2.7.2 Non-financial indicators (NFIs)

FAST FORWARD

> An imaginative approach to performance measurement is becoming a necessity in the modern business environment, and many businesses now recognise the need to supplement traditional financial measures with other, **non-financial indicators.**
>
> Non-monetary measures also include **ratios**, **percentages** and **indices**.

Financial measures do not convey the full picture of a company's performance, especially in a **modern business environment**.

> 'In today's worldwide competitive environment companies are competing in terms of product quality, delivery, reliability, after-sales service and customer satisfaction. None of these variables is directly measured by the traditional responsibility accounting system, despite the fact that they represent the major goals of world-class manufacturing companies.'

Many companies are discovering the usefulness of quantitative and qualitative **non-financial indicators (NFIs)** such as the following.

- Quality
- Lead times
- Rework
- Number of customer complaints and warranty claims
- Delivery to time
- Non-productive hours
- System (machine) down time, and so on

Unlike traditional variance reports, measures such as these can be provided quickly for managers, per shift, **daily** or even **hourly** as required. They are likely to be easy to calculate, and easier for non-financial managers to understand and therefore to use effectively.

The beauty of non-financial indicators is that **anything can be compared** if it is **meaningful** to do so. The measures should be **tailored** to the circumstances so that, for example, number of coffee breaks per 20 pages of Study Text might indicate to you how hard you are studying!

Many suitable measures combine elements from the chart shown below. The chart is not intended to be prescriptive or exhaustive.

Errors/failure	Time	Quantity	People
Defects	Second	Range of products	Employees
Equipment failures	Minute	Parts/components	Employee skills
Warranty claims	Hour	Units produced	Customers
Complaints	Shift	Units sold	Competitors
Returns	Cycle	Services performed	Suppliers
Stockouts	Day	kg/litres/metres	
Lateness/waiting	Month	m²/m³	
Misinformation	Year	Documents	
Miscalculation		Deliveries	
Absenteeism		Enquiries	

Traditional measures derived from these lists like 'kg (of material) per unit produced' or 'units produced per hour' are fairly obvious, but what may at first seem a fairly **unlikely combination** may also be very revealing. 'Absenteeism per customer', for example, may be of no significance at all or it may reveal that a particularly difficult customer is being avoided, and hence that some action is needed.

There is clearly a need for the information provider to work more closely with the managers who will be using the information to make sure that their needs are properly understood. The measures used are likely to be **developed and refined over time**. It may be that some will serve the purpose of drawing attention to areas in need of improvement but will be of no further relevance once remedial action has been taken. A flexible, responsive approach is essential.

Question

Non-financial indicators

Using the above chart make up five non-financial indicators and explain how each might be useful.

Answer

Here are five indicators, showing you how to use the chart, but there are many other possibilities.

(a)   Services performed late v total services performed
(b)   Total units sold v total units sold by competitors (indicating market share)
(c)   Warranty claims per month
(d)   Documents processed per employee
(e)   Equipment failures per 1,000 units produced

Don't forget to explain how the ones that you chose might be useful.

2.7.3 NFIs and financial measures

Arguably, NFIs are less likely to be **manipulated** than traditional profit-related measures and they should, therefore, offer a means of counteracting short-termism, since short-term profit at any (non-monetary) expense is rarely an advisable goal. The ultimate goal of commercial organisations in the long run is likely to remain the maximisation of **profit**, however, and so the financial aspect cannot be ignored.

There is a danger that too many such measures could be reported, leading to **information overload** for managers, providing information that is not truly useful, or that sends conflicting signals. A further danger of NFIs is that they might lead managers to pursue detailed **operational goals** and become blind to the **overall strategy** in which those goals are set.

A **combination** of financial and non-financial indicators is therefore likely to be most successful.

Question

What do the following indicate about an organisation's operational performance?

(a) Actual late deliveries as a percentage of total orders are greater than the budgeted figure.
(b) Actual process losses as a percentage of input are greater than the budgeted figure.
(c) Actual sales volumes are lower than budgeted sales volumes.

Answer

(a) This could indicate problems with either production planning or distribution.
(b) This could indicate faulty material, poor quality work or machine faults.
(c) This could indicate a fall in demand or too great a proportion of replacements or too many losses in process so that production cannot meet demand.

2.7.4 Ratios

Ratios (covered in Chapter 18) are a useful way of measuring performance for a number of reasons.

(a) It is easier to look at **changes over time** by comparing ratios in one time period with the corresponding ratios for periods in the past.

(b) Ratios are often **easier to understand than absolute measures** of physical quantities or money values. For example, it is easier to understand that 'productivity in March was 94%' than 'there was an adverse labour efficiency variance in March of $3,600'.

(c) Ratios **relate one item to another**, and so help to put performance into context. For example the profit/sales ratio sets profit in the context of how much has been earned per $1 of sales, and so shows how wide or narrow profit margins are.

(d) Ratios can be used as **targets**. In particular, targets can be set for ROI, profit/sales, asset turnover, capacity fill and productivity. Managers will then take decisions which will enable them to achieve their targets.

(e) Ratios provide a way of **summarising** an organisation's results, and **comparing** them with similar organisations. For example, the results of one investment centre/profit centre/company can be compared directly with the results of another.

2.7.5 Percentages

A **percentage** expresses one number as a proportion of another and gives meaning to absolute numbers. Examples are as follows.

(a) **Market share**. A company may aim to achieve a 25% share of the total market for its product, and measure both its marketing department and the quality of the product against this.

(b) **Capacity levels** are usually measured in this way. 'Factory A is working at 20% below full capacity' is an example which indicates relative inefficiency.

(c) **Wastage** is sometimes expressed in percentage terms. 'Normal loss' may be 10%, a measure of *in*efficiency.

(d) **Staff turnover** is often measured in this way. In the catering industry for example, staff turnover is typically greater than 100%, and so a hotel with a lower percentage could take this as an indicator both of the experience of its staff and of how well it is treating them.

2.7.6 Indices

FAST FORWARD

Indices can be used in a variety of ways in performance measurement, for example in **forecasting** and for **intragroup comparisons**.

Indices show how a particular variable has changed **relative to a base value**. The base value is usually the level of the variable at an earlier date. The 'variable' may be just one particular item, such as material X, or several items, such as 'raw materials' generally.

In its simplest form an index is calculated as (current value/base value) × 100. Thus if materials cost $15 per kg in 20X0 and now (20X3) cost $27 per kg, the 20X0 value would be expressed in index form as 100 (15/15 × 100) and the 20X3 value as 180 (27/15 × 100). If you find it easier to think of this as a percentage, then do so.

3 Benefits and problems of performance measures

Berry, Broadbent and Otley's list of **benefits of performance measures** is as follows.

1   'Clarifying the objectives of the organisation
2   Developing agreed measures of activity
3   Greater understanding of the processes
4   Facilitating comparison of performance in different organisations
5   Facilitating the setting of targets for the organisation and its managers
6   Promoting accountability of the organisation to its stakeholders'

Their list of **problems of performance measures** is also included in the article.

Problem	Comment
Tunnel vision	Undue focus on performance measures to the detriment of other areas
Sub-optimisation	Focus on some objectives so that others are not achieved
Myopia	Short-sightedness leading to the neglect of longer-term objectives
Measure fixation	Measures and behaviour in order to achieve specific performance indicators which may not be effective
Misrepresentation	'Creative' reporting to suggest that a result is acceptable
Misinterpretation	Failure to recognise the complexity of the environment in which the organisation operates
Gaming	Deliberate distortion of a measure to secure some strategic advantage
Ossification	An unwillingness to change the performance measure scheme once it has been set up

The article suggests ways in which the **problems may be reduced**, and they are summarised here.

(a)   **Involvement of staff** at all levels in the development and implementation of the scheme should help to reduce gaming and tunnel vision.

(b)   A **flexible use** of performance measures should help to reduce measure fixation and misrepresentation.

(c)   Keeping the performance measurement system under **constant review** should help to overcome the problems of ossification and gaming.

(d)   Give careful consideration to the **dimensions of performance**. Quantifying all objectives should help to overcome sub-optimisation, while a focus on measuring customer satisfaction should reduce tunnel vision and sub-optimisation.

(e)   Consideration should be given to the **audit of the system**. Expert interpretation of the performance measurement scheme should help to provide an idea of the incidence of the problems, while a careful audit of the data used should help to reduce the incidence and impact of measure fixation, misinterpretation and gaming.

(f)   **Recognition of the key feature** necessary in any scheme (a long-term view/perspective amongst staff, a sensible number of measures, benchmarks which are independent of past activity) should help to overcome the range of problems listed above.

4 Accounting theory and practice

4.1 The nature of profit

We have seen throughout this text that accounting 'profit' is an arbitrary figure, subject to the whims and biases of accountants and the variety of treatments in accounting standards. Go back to the contents page and pick out all the topics which demonstrate or indicate how company results are manipulated. Isn't it nearly all of them? Let us briefly mention some of them again.

4.1.1 IAS 2 Inventories

Companies are allowed to use different methods of valuing inventory under IAS 2, which means that the final inventory figure in the statement of financial position will be different under each method. Profit will be affected by the closing inventory valuation, particularly where the level of inventory fluctuates to a great extent.

4.1.2 IAS 16 Property, plant and equipment

As with IAS 2, IAS 16 allows different accounting bases for depreciation. Choosing to use the reducing balance method rather than the straight line method can front-load the depreciation charge for assets. It is also the case that the subjectivity surrounding the estimated economic lives of assets can lead to manipulation of profits. (Note. Remember that some companies refuse to depreciate some assets at all – mainly freehold property.)

4.2 Other problems with financial analysis

Two frequent problems affecting financial analysis are discussed here.

- Seasonal fluctuations
- Window dressing

4.2.1 Seasonal fluctuations

Many companies are located in industries where trade is seasonal. For example:

- Firework manufacturers
- Swimwear manufacturers
- Ice cream makers
- Umbrella manufacturers
- Gas companies
- Travel agents
- Flower suppliers and deliverers
- Football clubs

Year on year the seasonal fluctuations affecting such companies does not matter; a year end has to be chosen and as long as the fluctuations are at roughly the same time every year, then there should be no problem. Occasionally a perverse sense of humour will cause a company to choose an accounting period ending in the middle of the busy season: this may affect the cut off because the busy season might be slightly early or late.

A major difficulty can arise if companies affected by seasonal fluctuations change their accounting date. A shorter period (normally) may encompass part, all or none of the busy season. Whatever happens, the figures will be distorted and the comparatives will be meaningless. Analysts would not know how to extrapolate the figures from the shorter period to produce a comparison for the previous year. Weightings could be used, but these are likely to be inaccurate.

Case Study

An example of the problems this can cause occurred when the UK company British Gas plc changed its accounting period to 31 December from 31 March. The company published two reports and accounts.

- For the year to 31 March 1991
- For the year to 31 December 1991

thus including the first three months of the calendar year in both reports. As a note to the later accounts, the company produced a profit and loss account for the last nine months of the calendar year.

Although the British Gas auditors did not qualify the audit report, the Review Panel was not very happy about this double counting of results. The nine month profit and loss account did not meet the provisions of CA 1985 'either as to its location or its contents, nor did it contain the relevant earnings per share figure'. British Gas had to promise that, in their 1992 results, the 1991 comparative would be for the nine months period only.

The effect here is obvious. The first three months of the calendar year are when British Gas earns a high proportion of its profits (winter!). If the 1991 results had covered the period from 1 April only, then the profits would have been reduced by more than an average loss of three months' profit. By using a 12 month period, British Gas avoided the risk of the period's results looking too bad.

4.2.2 Window dressing

Window dressing transactions were made largely redundant by IAS 10 *Events after the reporting period*. Note that window dressing transactions were not outlawed, but full disclosure would render such transactions useless.

One example of window dressing is a situation where a large cheque is written against one group company's positive bank balance in favour of another group company with a large overdraft. The cheque is put through at the year end and then cancelled at the beginning of the next year, thus concealing the overdraft in the consolidated statement of financial position (where positive and negative bank balances cannot be netted off).

You may be able to think of other examples of window dressing and you should look for any potential examples which come up in examination questions.

Summary of limitations of financial analysis

(a) Information problems
   (i)   The base information is often out of date, so timeliness of information leads to problems of interpretation.
   (ii) Historic cost information may not be the most appropriate information for the decision for which the analysis is being undertaken.
   (iii) Information in published accounts is generally summarised information and detailed information may be needed.
   (iv) Analysis of accounting information only identifies symptoms not causes and thus is of limited use.
(b) Comparison problems: inter-temporal
   (i)   Effects of price changes make comparisons difficult unless adjustments are made.
   (ii) Impacts of changes in technology on the price of assets, the likely return and the future markets.
   (iii) Impacts of a changing environment on the results reflected in the accounting information.
   (iv) Potential effects of changes in accounting policies on the reported results.
   (v)   Problems associated with establishing a normal base year to compare other years with.

(c)   Comparison problems: inter-firm

  (i)   Selection of industry norms and the usefulness of norms based on averages.

  (ii)   Different firms having different financial and business risk profiles and the impact on analysis.

  (iii)   Different firms using different accounting policies.

  (iv)   Impacts of the size of the business and its comparators on risk, structure and returns.

  (v)   Impacts of different environments on results, for example different countries or home-based versus multinational firms.

You should use this summary as a type of checklist.

Chapter Roundup

- **Changes in accounting standards** can have a significant impact on the financial statements.

- You will probably be asked to **advise the directors** on the implication of a change in accounting standards, or on the effect of using the correct accounting treatment.

- Key areas for performance measurement are **profitability, activity** and **productivity**. Profitability is often a key objective but other **'success factors'** are also critical. **Benchmarking** is increasingly common.

- Both quantitative and qualitative performance measures are equally valuable.

- Financial measures generally derive from the accounting system (or other businesses' accounting systems).

- An imaginative approach to performance measurement is becoming a necessity in the modern business environment, and many businesses now recognise the need to supplement traditional financial measures with other, **non-financial indicators.**

- Non-monetary measures also include **ratios**, **percentages** and **indices**.

- **Indices** can be used in a variety of ways in performance measurement, for example in **forecasting** and for **intragroup comparisons**.

Quick Quiz

1   Give an example of a proposed changes to IFRS which will have a significant impact on the financial statements.

2   What is the latest IFRS?

3   What is the aim of performance management?

4   What is a critical success factor?

5   Which of the following are examples of non-financial indicators? Circle all that apply.

- Number of customer complaints
- Lead times
- Cash flow
- Delivery to time
- Revenue

6   Financial indicators are superior to non-financial indicators.

True ☐

False ☐

Answers to Quick Quiz

1   The EDs proposing amendments to IFRS 3 Business combinations and IAS 27 Consolidated and separate financial statements.

2   IFRS 8 Operating segments

3   To establish how well something or somebody is doing in relation to the planned activity and desired results.

4   An area of the job where things must go right for the organisation to flourish.

5   Number of customer complaints

     Lead times

     Delivery to time

6   False. A combination of financial and non-financial indicators is desirable.

Now try the question below from the Exam Question Bank

Number	Level	Marks	Time
Q25	Introductory	n/a	n/a
Q26	Examination	25	45 mins
Q27	Examination	50	90 mins

Mathematical tables

Present value table

Present value of £1 = $(1+r)^{-n}$ where r = interest rate, n = number of periods until payment or receipt.

Periods					Discount rates (r)					
(n)	1%	2%	3%	4%	5%	6%	7%	8%	9%	10%
1	0.990	0.980	0.971	0.962	0.952	0.943	0.935	0.926	0.917	0.909
2	0.980	0.961	0.943	0.925	0.907	0.890	0.873	0.857	0.842	0.826
3	0.971	0.942	0.915	0.889	0.864	0.840	0.816	0.794	0.772	0.751
4	0.961	0.924	0.888	0.855	0.823	0.792	0.763	0.735	0.708	0.683
5	0.951	0.906	0.863	0.822	0.784	0.747	0.713	0.681	0.650	0.621
6	0.942	0.888	0.837	0.790	0.746	0.705	0.666	0.630	0.596	0.564
7	0.933	0.871	0.813	0.760	0.711	0.665	0.623	0.583	0.547	0.513
8	0.923	0.853	0.789	0.731	0.677	0.627	0.582	0.540	0.502	0.467
9	0.914	0.837	0.766	0.703	0.645	0.592	0.544	0.500	0.460	0.424
10	0.905	0.820	0.744	0.676	0.614	0.558	0.508	0.463	0.422	0.386
11	0.896	0.804	0.722	0.650	0.585	0.527	0.475	0.429	0.388	0.350
12	0.887	0.788	0.701	0.625	0.557	0.497	0.444	0.397	0.356	0.319
13	0.879	0.773	0.681	0.601	0.530	0.469	0.415	0.368	0.326	0.290
14	0.870	0.758	0.661	0.577	0.505	0.442	0.388	0.340	0.299	0.263
15	0.861	0.743	0.642	0.555	0.481	0.417	0.362	0.315	0.275	0.239
16	0.853	0.728	0.623	0.534	0.458	0.394	0.339	0.292	0.252	0.218
17	0.844	0.714	0.605	0.513	0.436	0.371	0.317	0.270	0.231	0.198
18	0.836	0.700	0.587	0.494	0.416	0.350	0.296	0.250	0.212	0.180
19	0.828	0.686	0.570	0.475	0.396	0.331	0.277	0.232	0.194	0.164
20	0.820	0.673	0.554	0.456	0.377	0.312	0.258	0.215	0.178	0.149

Periods					Discount rates (r)					
(n)	11%	12%	13%	14%	15%	16%	17%	18%	19%	20%
1	0.901	0.893	0.885	0.877	0.870	0.862	0.855	0.847	0.840	0.833
2	0.812	0.797	0.783	0.769	0.756	0.743	0.731	0.718	0.706	0.694
3	0.731	0.712	0.693	0.675	0.658	0.641	0.624	0.609	0.593	0.579
4	0.659	0.636	0.613	0.592	0.572	0.552	0.534	0.516	0.499	0.482
5	0.593	0.567	0.543	0.519	0.497	0.476	0.456	0.437	0.419	0.402
6	0.535	0.507	0.480	0.456	0.432	0.410	0.390	0.370	0.352	0.335
7	0.482	0.452	0.425	0.400	0.376	0.354	0.333	0.314	0.296	0.279
8	0.434	0.404	0.376	0.351	0.327	0.305	0.285	0.266	0.249	0.233
9	0.391	0.361	0.333	0.308	0.284	0.263	0.243	0.225	0.209	0.194
10	0.352	0.322	0.295	0.270	0.247	0.227	0.208	0.191	0.176	0.162
11	0.317	0.287	0.261	0.237	0.215	0.195	0.178	0.162	0.148	0.135
12	0.286	0.257	0.231	0.208	0.187	0.168	0.152	0.137	0.124	0.112
13	0.258	0.229	0.204	0.182	0.163	0.145	0.130	0.116	0.104	0.093
14	0.232	0.205	0.181	0.160	0.141	0.125	0.111	0.099	0.088	0.078
15	0.209	0.183	0.160	0.140	0.123	0.108	0.095	0.084	0.074	0.065
16	0.188	0.163	0.141	0.123	0.107	0.093	0.081	0.071	0.062	0.054
17	0.170	0.146	0.125	0.108	0.093	0.080	0.069	0.060	0.052	0.045
18	0.153	0.130	0.111	0.095	0.081	0.069	0.059	0.051	0.044	0.038
19	0.138	0.116	0.098	0.083	0.070	0.060	0.051	0.043	0.037	0.031
20	0.124	0.104	0.087	0.073	0.061	0.051	0.043	0.037	0.031	0.026

Cumulative present value table

This table shows the present value of £1 per annum, receivable or payable at the end of each year for n years.

Periods					Discount rates (r)					
(n)	**1%**	**2%**	**3%**	**4%**	**5%**	**6%**	**7%**	**8%**	**9%**	**10%**
1	0.990	0.980	0.971	0.962	0.952	0.943	0.935	0.926	0.917	0.909
2	1.970	1.942	1.913	1.886	1.859	1.833	1.808	1.783	1.759	1.736
3	2.941	2.884	2.829	2.775	2.723	2.673	2.624	2.577	2.531	2.487
4	3.902	3.808	3.717	3.630	3.546	3.465	3.387	3.312	3.240	3.170
5	4.853	4.713	4.580	4.452	4.329	4.212	4.100	3.993	3.890	3.791
6	5.795	5.601	5.417	5.242	5.076	4.917	4.767	4.623	4.486	4.355
7	6.728	6.472	6.230	6.002	5.786	5.582	5.389	5.206	5.033	4.868
8	7.652	7.325	7.020	6.733	6.463	6.210	5.971	5.747	5.535	5.335
9	8.566	8.162	7.786	7.435	7.108	6.802	6.515	6.247	5.995	5.759
10	9.471	8.983	8.530	8.111	7.722	7.360	7.024	6.710	6.418	6.145
11	10.37	9.787	9.253	8.760	8.306	7.887	7.499	7.139	6.805	6.495
12	11.26	10.58	9.954	9.385	8.863	8.384	7.943	7.536	7.161	6.814
13	12.13	11.35	10.63	9.986	9.394	8.853	8.358	7.904	7.487	7.103
14	13.00	12.11	11.30	10.56	9.899	9.295	8.745	8.244	7.786	7.367
15	13.87	12.85	11.94	11.12	10.38	9.712	9.108	8.559	8.061	7.606
16	14.718	13.578	12.561	11.652	10.838	10.106	9.447	8.851	8.313	7.824
17	15.562	14.292	13.166	12.166	11.274	10.477	9.763	9.122	8.544	8.022
18	16.398	14.992	13.754	12.659	11.690	10.828	10.059	9.372	8.756	8.201
19	17.226	15.678	14.324	13.134	12.085	11.158	10.336	9.604	8.950	8.365
20	18.046	16.351	14.877	13.590	12.462	11.470	10.594	9.818	9.129	8.514

Periods					Discount rates (r)					
(n)	**11%**	**12%**	**13%**	**14%**	**15%**	**16%**	**17%**	**18%**	**19%**	**20%**
1	0.901	0.893	0.885	0.877	0.870	0.862	0.855	0.847	0.840	0.833
2	1.713	1.690	1.668	1.647	1.626	1.605	1.585	1.566	1.547	1.528
3	2.444	2.402	2.361	2.322	2.283	2.246	2.210	2.174	2.140	2.106
4	3.102	3.037	2.974	2.914	2.855	2.798	2.743	2.690	2.639	2.589
5	3.696	3.605	3.517	3.433	3.352	3.274	3.199	3.127	3.058	2.991
6	4.231	4.111	3.998	3.889	3.784	3.685	3.589	3.498	3.410	3.326
7	4.712	4.564	4.423	4.288	4.160	4.039	3.922	3.812	3.706	3.605
8	5.146	4.968	4.799	4.639	4.487	4.344	4.207	4.078	3.954	3.837
9	5.537	5.328	5.132	4.946	4.772	4.607	4.451	4.303	4.163	4.031
10	5.889	5.650	5.426	5.216	5.019	4.833	4.659	4.494	4.339	4.192
11	6.207	5.938	5.687	5.453	5.234	5.029	4.836	4.656	4.486	4.327
12	6.492	6.194	5.918	5.660	5.421	5.197	4.988	4.793	4.611	4.439
13	6.750	6.424	6.122	5.842	5.583	5.342	5.118	4.910	4.715	4.533
14	6.982	6.628	6.302	6.002	5.724	5.468	5.229	5.008	4.802	4.611
15	7.191	6.811	6.462	6.142	5.847	5.575	5.324	5.092	4.876	4.675
16	7.379	6.974	6.604	6.265	5.954	5.668	5.405	5.162	4.938	4.730
17	7.549	7.120	6.729	6.373	6.047	5.749	5.475	5.222	4.990	4.775
18	7.702	7.250	6.840	6.467	6.128	5.818	5.534	5.273	5.033	4.812
19	7.839	7.366	6.938	6.550	6.198	5.877	5.584	5.316	5.070	4.843
20	7.963	7.469	7.025	6.623	6.259	5.929	5.628	5.353	5.101	4.870

Exam question and answer bank

Exam question bank

1 Framework

(a) Explain the main purposes of the International Accounting Standards Board's Framework for the Preparation and Presentation of Financial Statements.

(b) Identify any four user groups of financial statements and explain what information they are likely to want from them.

2 Fundamental principles

Fundamental Principles require that a member of a professional accountancy body should behave with integrity in all professional, business and financial relationships and should strive for objectivity in all professional and business judgements. Objectivity can only be assured if the member is and is seen to be independent. Conflicts of interest have an important bearing on independence and hence also on the public's perception of the integrity, objectivity and independence of the accounting profession.

The following scenario is an example of press reports in recent years which deal with issues of objectivity and independence within a multinational firm of accountants:

'A partner in the firm was told by the regulatory body that he must resign because he was in breach of the regulatory body's independence rules, as his brother-in-law was financial controller of an audit client. He was told that the alternative was that he could move his home and place of work at least 400 miles from the offices of the client, even though he was not the reporting partner. This made his job untenable. The regulatory body was seen as 'taking its rules to absurd lengths' by the accounting firm. Shortly after this comment, the multinational firm announced proposals to split the firm into three areas between audit, tax and business advisory services; management consultancy; and investment advisory services.'

Required

Discuss the impact that the above events may have on the public perception of the integrity, objectivity and independence of the multinational firm of accountants.

3 Tree

You are the accountant of Tree, a listed limited liability company that prepares consolidated financial statements. Your Managing Director, who is not an accountant, has recently attended a seminar at which key financial reporting issues were discussed. She remembers being told the following.

- Financial statements of an entity should reflect the substance of its transactions;
- Revenue from the 'sale' of goods should only be recognised when certain conditions have been satisfied. Transfer of legal title to the goods is not necessarily sufficient for an entity to recognise revenue from their 'sale'.

The year end of Tree is 31 August. In the year to 31 August 20X1, the company entered into the following transactions.

Transaction 1

On 1 March 20X1, Tree sold a property to a bank for $5 million. The market value of the property at the date of the sale was $10 million. Tree continues to occupy the property rent-free. Tree has the option to buy the property back from the bank at the end of every month from 31 March 20X1 until 28 February 20X6. Tree has not yet exercised this option. The repurchase price will be $5 million plus $50,000 for every complete month that has elapsed from the date of sale to the date of repurchase. The bank cannot require Tree to repurchase the property and the facility lapses after 28 February 20X6. The directors of Tree expect property prices to rise at around 5% each year for the foreseeable future.

Transaction 2

On 1 September 20X0, Tree sold one of its branches to Vehicle for $8 million. The net assets of the branch in the financial statements of Tree immediately before the sale were $7 million. Vehicle is a subsidiary of a bank and was specifically incorporated to carry out the purchase – it has no other business operations. Vehicle received the $8 million to finance this project from its parent in the form of a loan.

Tree continues to control the operations of the branch and receives an annual operating fee from Vehicle. The annual fee is the operating profit of the branch for the 12 months to the previous 31 August less the interest payable on the loan taken out by Vehicle for the 12 months to the previous 31 August. If this amount is negative, then Tree must pay the negative amount to Vehicle.

Any payments to or by Tree must be made by 30 September following the end of the relevant period. In the year to 31 August 20X1, the branch made an operating profit of $2,000,000. Interest payable by Vehicle on the loan for this period was $800,000.

Required

(a)   Explain the conditions that need to be satisfied before revenue can be recognised from the sale of goods. You should support your answer with reference to International Accounting Standards as appropriate.

(b)   Explain how the transactions described above will be dealt with in the consolidated financial statements (statement of financial position and statement of comprehensive income) of Tree for the year ended 31 August 20X1.

4 Greensmith (20 marks)   36 mins

(a)   You have recently had a meeting with the finance director of a large company, Greensmith Co. He is concerned about a recent broker's circular which ranked his company as a 'sell'. The reasons for this were:

(i)   low earnings per share;
(ii)   a poor return on capital employed; and
(iii)   a weak net assets per share figure.

He had identified various items of property, plant and equipment that he thinks could be revalued. He is reluctant to involve his auditor in preliminary discussions so has turned to you as an independent adviser. He wishes you to advise him on the following matters:

(i)   Does he have to revalue the assets?
(ii)   Can any of the revaluations be pooled or will they all be dealt with separately?
(iii)   What are the accounting effects of any revaluations or devaluations?
(iv)   What will be the effect on profit or loss in the future when he sells revalued assets? and
(v)   What will be the effect of the revaluations on earnings per share, return on capital employed and net assets per share?

The assets in question are:

(i)   The company's head office in Conway Square, London. It has a book value (cost) of $4 million but is now estimated to be worth $3.3 million. They do not intend to sell the building and are sure property prices will recover in the longer term. The building is not depreciated as they argue that residual value is at least equal to book value.

(ii)   The company has a residential training centre in Berkshire which it leases on a 20-year lease from the freeholder. It is at present in the books at a cost of $5 million less two years' amortisation. It is now felt to be worth $8 million.

(b) The finance director is also unsure how to account for the following items:

(i) Last year Greensmith purchased a 15-year franchise for a tanning shop within the Berkshire training centre. The cost was $500,000.

(ii) The training centre has been generating considerable income over the past few years and the finance director has been approached by a potential purchaser offering a price of $1,000,000 in excess of the fair value of the individual net assets. The company wishes to include this as a brand value in the statement of financial position.

Required

Prepare a memorandum for the finance director summarising your response to the questions he has raised, and indicate your recommended course of action.

5 Acquirer (25 marks)   45 mins

Acquirer is an entity that regularly purchases new subsidiaries. On 30 June 20X0, the entity acquired all the equity shares of Prospects for a cash payment of $260 million. The net assets of Prospects on 30 June 20X0 were $180 million and no fair value adjustments were necessary upon consolidation of Prospects for the first time.

On 31 December 20X0, Acquirer carried out a review of the goodwill on consolidation of Prospects for evidence of impairment. The review was carried out despite the fact that there were no obvious indications of adverse trading conditions for Prospects. The review involved allocating the net asset of Prospects into three cash-generating units and computing the value in use of each unit. The carrying values of the individual units before any impairment adjustments are given below.

	Unit A $ million	Unit B $ million	Unit C $ million
Patents	5		
Property, plant and equipment	60	30	40
Net current assets	20	25	20
	85	55	60
Value in use of unit	72	60	65

It was not possible to meaningfully allocate the goodwill on consolidation to the individual cash-generating units, but all other net assets of Prospects are allocated in the table shown above. The patents of Prospects have no ascertainable market value but all the current assets have a market value that is above carrying value. The value in use of Prospects as a single cash-generating unit at 31 December 20X1 is £205 million.

Required

(a) Explain what is meant by a cash generating unit.   **(5 marks)**

(b) Explain why it was necessary to review the goodwill on consolidation of Prospects for impairment at 31 December 20X0.   **(3 marks)**

(c) Explain briefly the purpose of an impairment review and why the net assets of Prospects were allocated into cash-generating units as part of the review of goodwill for impairment.   **(5 marks)**

(d) Demonstrate how the impairment loss in unit A will affect the carrying value of the net assets of unit A in the consolidated financial statements of Acquirer.   **(5 marks)**

(e) Explain and calculate the effect of the impairment review on the carrying value of the goodwill on consolidation of Prospects at 31 December 20X0.   **(7 marks)**

6 Investor (25 marks)   45 mins

Investor is a listed company with a number of subsidiaries located throughout the United Kingdom.
Investor currently appraises investment opportunities using a cost of capital of 10 per cent.

On 1 April 20X9 Investor purchased 80 per cent of the equity share capital of Cornwall for a total cash
price of $60m. Half the price was payable on 1 April 20X9; the balance was payable on 1 April 20Y1. The
net identifiable assets that were actually included in the statement of financial position of Cornwall had a
carrying value totalling $55m at 1 April 20X9. With the exception of the pension provision (see below), you
discover that the fair values of the net identifiable assets of Cornwall at 1 April 20X9 are the same as their
carrying values. When performing the fair-value exercise at 1 April 20X9, you discover that Cornwall has a
defined-benefit pension scheme that was actuarially valued three years ago and found to be in deficit. As a
result of that valuation, a provision of $6m has been built up in the statement of financial position. The
fair-value exercise indicates that on 1 April 20X9, the pension scheme was in deficit by $11m. This
information became available on 31 July 20X9.

Assume that today's date is 31 October 20X9. You are in the process of preparing the consolidated
financial statements of the group for the year ended 30 September 20X9. Intangible assets are normally
written off on a pro-rata basis over twenty years. Your financial director is concerned that profits for the
year will be lower than originally anticipated. She is therefore wondering about changing the accounting
policy used by the group, so that all intangible assets are treated as having an indefinite useful life.

Required

(a)   Calculate the value of goodwill on acquisition of Cornwall in the consolidated accounts of Investor
      for the year ended 30 September 20X9. You should fully explain and justify all parts of the
      calculation.   **(10 marks)**

(b)   Write a memorandum to your financial director.

      (i)   Evaluate the policy of writing off all intangible assets over twenty years

      (ii)   Explain whether it is ever permissible to select a longer write-off period for intangible
             assets, and describe the future implications of selecting such a period   **(10 marks)**

(c)   Cornwall has purchased some valuable brands, which are included in the statement of financial
      position. Explain the justification for including purchased brands in the statement of financial
      position and how non-purchased brands should be treated.   **(5 marks)**

7 Radost (17 marks)   31 mins

Radost Co has a defined benefit pension scheme for its staff. Staff are eligible for an annual pension
between the date of their retirement and the date of their death equal to:

$$\text{Annual pension} = \frac{\text{Final salary per year}}{50} \times \text{Years' service.}$$

You are given the following data relating to the year ended 31 December 20X3:

(a)   Unrecognised actuarial gains at 1 January 20X3: $6 million

(b)   Yield on high quality corporate bonds: 10% pa.

(c)   Expected return on pension fund investments: 11% pa.

(d)   Contributions paid by Radost Co to pension plan: $12 million

(e)   Pensions paid to former employees: $8 million

(f)   Current service cost was $3.75 million

(g)   NPV of the pension obligation at:
      1.1.X3 – $45 million
      31.12.X3 – $44 million (as given by the actuary)

(h)   Fair value of the plan assets, as valued by the actuary:
       1.1.X3 – $52 million
       31.12.X3 – $64.17 million

(i)   The average remaining working life of employees who are members of the pension scheme is
       20 years

Required

(a)   Produce the notes to the statement of financial position and statement of comprehensive income in
       accordance with IAS 19.   **(12 marks)**

(b)   Explain why the pension plan assets are recognised in the financial statements of Radost, even
       though they are held in a separate legal trust for Radost's employees.   **(5 marks)**

Notes:

1   Work to the nearest $1,000 throughout.
2   You should assume contributions and benefits were paid on the last day of the year.

8 DT Group (25 marks)   45 mins

(a)   IAS 12 *Income taxes* focuses on the statement of financial position in accounting for deferred
       taxation, which is calculated on the basis of temporary differences. The methods used in IAS12 can
       lead to accumulation of large tax assets or liabilities over a prolonged period and this could be
       remedied by discounting these assets or liabilities. There is currently international disagreement
       over the discounting of deferred tax balances.

       Required:

       (i)   Explain what the terms 'focus on the statement of financial position' and 'temporary
              differences' mean in relation to deferred taxation.   **(6 marks)**

       (ii)   Discuss the arguments for and against discounting long-term deferred tax balances.
                                                                                               (6 marks)

(b)   DT, a public limited company, has decided to adopt the provisions of IFRSs for the first time in its
       financial statements for the year ending 30 November 20X1. The amounts of deferred tax provided
       as set out in the notes of the group financial statements for the year ending 30 November 20X0
       were as follows:

                                                                                                    $m
       Tax depreciation in excess of accounting depreciation   38
       Other temporary differences   11
       Liabilities for health care benefits   (12)
       Losses available for offset against future taxable profits   (34)
                                                                                                     3

       The following notes are relevant to the calculation of the deferred tax liability as at 30 November
       20X1:

       (i)   DT acquired a 100% holding in a foreign company on 30 November 20X1. The subsidiary
              does not plan to pay any dividends for the financial year to 30 November 20X1 or in the
              foreseeable future. The carrying amount in DT's consolidated financial statements of its
              investment in the subsidiary at 30 November 20X1 is made up as follows:

                                                                                                    $m
              Carrying value of net assets acquired excluding deferred tax   76
              Goodwill (before deferred tax and impairment losses)   14
              Carrying amount/cost of investment   90

              The tax base of the net assets of the subsidiary at acquisition was $60m. No deduction is
              available in the subsidiary's tax jurisdiction for the cost of the goodwill.

              Immediately after acquisition on 30 November 20X1, DT had supplied the subsidiary with
              inventories amounting to $30m at a profit of 20% on selling price. The inventories had not

been sold by the year end and the tax rate applied to the subsidiary's profit is 25%. There was no significant difference between the fair values and carrying values on the acquisition of the subsidiary.

(ii)   The carrying amount of the property, plant and equipment (excluding that of the subsidiary) is $2,600m and their tax base is $1,920m. Tax arising on the revaluation of properties of $140m, if disposed of at their revalued amounts, is the same at 30 November 20X1 as at the beginning of the year. The revaluation of the properties is included in the carrying amount above.

Other taxable temporary differences (excluding the subsidiary) amount to $90m as at 30 November 20X1.

(iii)   The liability for health care benefits in the statement of financial position had risen to $100m as at 30 November 20X1 and the tax base is zero. Health care benefits are deductible for tax purposes when payments are made to retirees. No payments were made during the year to 30 November 20X1.

(iv)   DT Group incurred $300m of tax losses in 20X0. Under the tax law of the country, tax losses can be carried forward for three years only. The taxable profits for the years ending 30 November were anticipated to be as follows:

20X1	20X2	20X3
$m	$m	$m
110	100	130

The auditors are unsure about the availability of taxable profits in 20X3 as the amount is based upon the projected acquisition of a profitable company. It is anticipated that there will be no future reversals of existing taxable temporary differences until after 30 November 20X3.

(v)   Income tax of $165m on a property disposed of in 20X0 becomes payable on 30 November 20X4 under the deferral relief provisions of the tax laws of the country. There had been no sales or revaluations of property during the year to 30 November 20X1.

(vi)   Income tax is assumed to be 30% for the foreseeable future in DT's jurisdiction and the company wishes to discount any deferred tax liabilities at a rate of 4% if allowed by IAS 12.

(vii)   There are no other temporary differences other than those set out above. The directors of DT have calculated the opening balance of deferred tax using IAS 12 to be $280m.

Required

Calculate the liability for deferred tax required by the DT Group at 30 November 20X1 and the deferred tax expense in profit or loss for the year ending 30 November 20X1 using IAS 12, commenting on the effect that the application of IAS 12 will have on the financial statements of the DT Group.   **(13 marks)**

9 PQR (10 marks)   18 mins

PQR has the following financial instruments in its financial statements for the year ended 31 December 20X5:

(a)   An investment in the debentures of STU, nominal value $40,000, purchased on their issue on 1 January 20X5 at a discount of $6,000 and carrying a 4% coupon. PQR plans to hold these until their redemption on 31 December 20X8. The internal rate of return of the debentures is 8.6%.

(b)   A foreign currency forward contract purchased to hedge the commitment to purchase a machine in foreign currency six months after the year end.

(c)   100,000 redeemable preference shares issued in 20X0 at $1 per share with an annual dividend payment of 6 cents per share, redeemable in 20X8 at their nominal value.

Required

Advise the directors (insofar as the information permits) about the accounting for the financial instruments stating the effect of each on the gearing of the company. Your answer should be accompanied by calculations where appropriate.

10 Hedging

A company owns 100,000 barrels of crude oil which were purchased on 1 July 20X2 at a cost of $26.00 per barrel.

In order to hedge the fluctuation in the market value of the oil the company signs a futures contract on the same date to deliver 100,000 barrels of oil on 31 March 20X3 at a futures price of $27.50 per barrel.

Due to unexpected increased production by OPEC, the market price of oil on 31 December 20X2 slumped to $22.50 per barrel and the futures price for delivery on 31 March 20X3 was $23.25 per barrel at that date

Required

Explain the impact of the transactions on the financial statements of the company for the year ended 31 December 20X2.

11 Share-based payment (6 marks)   11 mins

J&B granted 200 options on its $1 ordinary shares to each of its 800 employees on 1 January 20X1. Each grant is conditional upon the employee being employed by J&B until 31 December 20X3.

J&B estimated at 1 January 20X1 that:

(i)   The fair value of each option was $4 (before adjustment for the possibility of forfeiture).

(ii)   Approximately 50 employees would leave during 20X1, 40 during 20X2 and 30 during 20X3 thereby forfeiting their rights to receive the options. The departures were expected to be evenly spread within each year.

The exercise price of the options was $1.50 and the market value of a J&B share on 1 January 20X1 was $3.

In the event, only 40 employees left during 20X1 (and the estimate of total departures was revised down to 95 at 31 December 20X1), 20 during 20X2 (and the estimate of total departures was revised to 70 at 31 December 20X2) and none during 20X3, spread evenly during each year.

Required

The directors of J&B have asked you to illustrate how the scheme is accounted for under IFRS 2 *Share-based Payment*.

(a)   Show the double entries for the charge to profit or loss for employee services over the three years and for the share issue, assuming all employees entitled to benefit from the scheme exercised their rights and the shares were issued on 31 December 20X3.

(b)   Explain how your solution would differ had J&B offered its employees cash based on the share value rather than share options.

12 Clean (25 marks)   45 mins

Clean prepares its financial statements in accordance with International Accounting Standards. On 25 June 20X0, Clean made a public announcement of a decision to reduce the level of emissions of harmful chemicals from its factories. The average useful lives of the factories on 30 June 20X0 (the accounting reference date) was 20 years. The depreciation of the factories is computed on a straight-line basis and charged to cost of sales. The directors formulated the proposals for emission reduction following agreement in principle earlier in the year.

The directors prepared detailed estimates of the costs of their proposals and these showed that the following expenditure would be required.

- $30 million on 30 June 20X1
- $30 million on 30 June 20X2
- $40 million on 30 June 20X3

All estimates were for the actual anticipated cash payments. No contracts were entered into until after 1 July 20X0. The estimate proved accurate as far as the expenditure due on 30 June 20X1 was concerned. When the directors decided to proceed with this project, they used discounted cash flow techniques to appraise the proposed investment. The annual discount rate they used was 8%. The entity has a reputation of fulfilling its financial commitments after it has publicly announced them. Clean included a provision for the expected costs of its proposal in its financial statements for the year ended 30 June 20X0.

Required

(a) Explain why there was a need for an accounting standard dealing with provisions, and summarise the criteria that need to be satisfied before a provision is recognised. **(10 marks)**

(b) Explain the decision of the directors of Clean to recognise the provision in the statement of financial position at 30 June 20X0. **(5 marks)**

(c) Compute the appropriate provision in the statements of financial position in respect of the proposed expenditure at 30 June 20X0 AND 30 June 20X1. **(4 marks)**

(d) Compute the two components of the charge to profit or loss in respect of the proposal for the year ended 30 June 20X1. You should explain how each component arises and identify where in the statement of comprehensive income each component is reported. **(6 marks)**

13 Ace (8 marks)   14 mins

On 1 April 20X1, Ace Co owned 75% of the equity share capital of Deuce Co and 80% of the equity share capital of Trey Co. On 1 April 20X2, Ace Co purchased the remaining 25% of the equity shares of Deuce Co. In the two years ended 31 March 20X3, the following transactions occurred between the three companies:

(a) On 30 June 20X1 Ace Co manufactured a machine for use by Deuce Co. The cost of manufacture was $20,000. The machine was delivered to Deuce Co for an invoiced price of $25,000. Deuce Co paid the invoice on 31 August 20X1. Deuce Co depreciated the machine over its anticipated useful life of five years, charging a full year's depreciation in the year of purchase.

(b) On 30 September 20X2, Deuce Co sold some goods to Trey Co at an invoiced price of $15,000. Trey Co paid the invoice on 30 November 20X2. The goods had cost Deuce Co $12,000 to manufacture. By 31 March 20X3, Trey Co had sold all the goods outside the group.

(c) For each of the two years ended 31 March 20X3, Ace Co provided management services to Deuce Co and Trey Co. Ace Co did not charge for these services in the year ended 31 March 20X2 but in the year ended 31 March 20X3 decided to impose a charge of $10,000 per annum to Trey Co. The amount of $10,000 is due to be paid by Trey Co on 31 May 20X3.

Required

Summarise the related party disclosures which will be required in respect of transactions (a) to (c) above for both of the years ended 31 March 20X2 and 31 March 20X3 in the financial statements of Ace Co, Deuce Co and Trey Co.

Note. You may assume that Ace Co presents consolidated financial statements for both of the years dealt with in the question.

14 Able (25 marks)   45 mins

(a) The development of conceptual frameworks for financial reporting by accounting standard setters could fundamentally change the way in which financial contracts such as leases are accounted for. These frameworks identify the basic elements of financial statements as assets, liabilities, equity, income and expenses and set down their recognition rules. In analysing the definitions of assets and liabilities one could conclude that most leases, including non-cancellable operating leases, qualify for recognition as assets and liabilities because the lessee is likely to enjoy the future economic benefits embodied in the leased asset and will have an unavoidable obligation that will result in an outflow of resources embodying economic benefits to the lessor. Because of the problems of accounting for leases, there have been calls for the capitalisation of all non-cancellable operating leases so that the only problem would be the definition of the term 'non-cancellable'.

Required

(i)   Explain how leases are accounted for in the books of the lessee under IAS 17 *Leases*.

(7 marks)

(ii) Discuss the current problems relating to the recognition and classification of leases in corporate financial statements. (Candidates should give examples where necessary).

(8 marks)

(b)   (i)   During the financial year to 31 May 20X8, Able a public limited liability company disposed of electrical distribution systems from its electrical power plants to Cain a public limited liability company for a consideration of $198m. At the same time Able entered into a long-term distribution agreement with Cain whereby the assets were leased back under a 10-year operating lease. The fair value of the assets sold was $98m and the carrying value based on depreciated historic cost of the assets was $33m. The lease rentals were $24m per annum which represented twice the normal payment for leasing this type of asset.   **(5 marks)**

(ii) Additionally on 1 June 20X7, Able sold plant with a book value of $100m to Esau a public limited liability company when there was a balance on the revaluation reserve of $30m which related to the plant. The fair value and selling price of the plant at that date was $152m. The plant was immediately leased back over a lease term of four years which is the asset's remaining useful life. The residual value at the end of the lease period is estimated to be a negligible amount. Able can purchase the plant at the end of the lease for a nominal sum of $1. The lease is non-cancellable and requires equal rental payments of $43.5m at the commencement of each financial year. Able has to pay all of the costs of maintaining and insuring the plant.

The implicit interest rate in the lease is 10% per annum. The plant is depreciated on a straight-line basis. (The present value of an ordinary annuity of $1 per period for 3 years at 10% interest is $2.49.)   **(5 marks)**

Required

Show and explain how the above transactions should be dealt with in the financial statements of Able for the year ending 31 May 20X8 in accordance with IAS 17 *Leases* and the *Framework for the Preparation and Presentation of Financial Statements*.

15 Highland (18 marks)   32 mins

Highland owns two subsidiaries acquired as follows:

1 July 20X1   80% of Aviemore for $5 million when the book value of the net assets of Aviemore was $4 million.

30 November 20X7   65% of Buchan for $2.6 million when the book value of the net assets of Buchan was $3.35 million.

The companies' statements of comprehensive income for the year ended 31 March 20X8 were:

	Highland	Aviemore	Buchan
	$'000	$'000	$'000
Revenue	5,000	3,000	2,910
Cost of sales	(3,000)	(2,300)	(2,820)
Gross profit	2,000	700	90
Administrative expenses	(1,000)	(500)	(150)
Other income	230	–	–
Finance costs		(50)	(210)
Profit/(loss) before tax	1,230	150	(270)
Income tax expense	(300)	(50)	–
PROFIT/(LOSS) FOR THE YEAR	930	100	(270)
Other comprehensive income, net of tax	130	40	120
TOTAL COMPREHENSIVE INCOME FOR THE YEAR	1,060	140	(150)
Dividends paid during the year	200	50	–

Additional information

(a) On 1 April 20X7, Buchan issued $2.1 million 10% loan stock to Highland. Interest is payable twice yearly on 1 October and 1 April. Highland has accounted for the interest received on 1 October 20X7 only.

(b) On 1 July 20X7, Aviemore sold a freehold property to Highland for $800,000 (land element – $300,000). The property originally cost $900,000 (land element – $100,000) on 1 July 20W7. The property's total useful life was 50 years on 1 July 20W7 and there has been no change in the useful life since. Aviemore has credited the profit on disposal to 'Administrative expenses'.

(c) The property, plant and equipment of Buchan on 30 November 20X7 was valued at $500,000 (book value $350,000) and was acquired in April 20X7. The property, plant and equipment has a total useful life of ten years. Buchan has not adjusted its accounting records to reflect fair values. The group accounting policy to measure non-controlling interests at the proportionate share of the fair value of net identifiable assets at acquisition.

(d) All companies use the straight-line method of depreciation and charge a full year's depreciation in the year of acquisition and none in the year of disposal. Depreciation on fair value adjustments is time apportioned from the date of acquisition.

(e) Highland charges Aviemore an annual fee of $85,000 for management services and this has been included in 'Other income'.

(f) Highland has accounted for its dividend received from Aviemore in 'Other income'.

(g) Impairment tests conducted at the year end revealed recoverable amounts of $7,040,000 for Aviemore and $3,700,000 for Buchan versus book values of net assets of $4,450,000 and $3,300,000 in the separate financial statements of Aviemore and Buchan respectively (adjusted for the effects of group fair value adjustments). No impairment losses had previously been recognised.

Required

Prepare the consolidated statement of comprehensive income for Highland for the year ended 31 March 20X8. **(18 marks)**

16 Armoury (10 marks)   18 mins

Bayonet, a public limited company, purchased 6m shares in Rifle, a public limited company, on 1 January 20X5 for $10m. Rifle had purchased 4m shares in Pistol, a public limited company for $9m on 31 December 20X2 when its retained earnings stood at $5m. The balances on retained earnings of the acquired companies were $8m and $6.5m respectively at 1 January 20X5. The book value of the identifiable assets and liabilities of Rifle and Pistol was equivalent to their book values at the acquisition dates.

The statements of financial position of the three companies as at 31 December 20X9 are as follows:

	Bayonet $'000	Rifle $'000	Pistol $'000
Non-current assets			
Property, plant and equipment	14,500	12,140	17,500
Investment in Rifle	10,000		
Investment in Pistol	–	9,000	–
	24,500	21,140	17,500
Current assets			
Inventories	6,300	2,100	450
Trade receivables	4,900	2,000	2,320
Cash	500	1,440	515
	11,700	5,540	3,285
	36,200	26,680	20,785
Equity			
50c ordinary shares	5,000	4,000	2,500
Retained earnings	25,500	20,400	16,300
	30,500	24,400	18,800
Current liabilities	5,700	2,280	1,985
	36,200	26,680	20,785

Group policy is to value non-controlling interests at fair value at acquisition. The fair value of the non-controlling interests in Rifle was calculated as $980,000 on 1 January 20X5. The fair value of the 40% non-controlling interests in Pistol on 1 January 20X5 was $4.6m.

Impairment tests in previous years did not reveal any impairment losses.

Required

Prepare the consolidated statement of financial position of Bayonet Co as at 31 December 20X9.

(10 marks)

17 Murder, Mystery and Suspense (18 marks)   32 mins

On 1 January 20X3 Murder acquired 60% of Mystery.

On 30 July 20X1 Murder acquired 10% of Suspense and on the same day Mystery acquired 80% of Suspense.

The statements of financial position of the three companies as at 31 December 20X7 are as follows:

	Murder $m	Mystery $m	Suspense $m
Non-current assets			
Property, plant and equipment	2,458	1,410	870
Investment in Mystery	900		
Investment in Suspense	27	240	–
	3,385	1,650	870
Current assets			
Inventories	450	200	260
Trade receivables	610	365	139
Cash	240	95	116
	1,300	660	515
	4,685	2,310	1,385

	$m	$m	$m
Equity			
Ordinary share capital	500	200	100
Share premium	250	120	50
Retained earnings	2,805	1,572	850
	3,555	1,892	1,000
Current liabilities			
Trade payables	1,130	418	385
	4,685	2,310	1,385

During the year, Mystery sold goods to Suspense of $260,000 including a mark-up of 25%. All of these goods remain in inventories at the year end.

The retained earnings of the three companies at the acquisition dates was:

	30.7.X1	1.1.X3
	$m	$m
Murder	1,610	1,860
Mystery	700	950
Suspense	40	100

The book values of the identifiable net assets at the acquisition date are equivalent to their fair values. The fair value of Murder's 10% holding in Suspense on 1 January 20X3 was $50m.

Murder and Mystery hold their investments in subsidiaries at cost in their separate financial statements. It is group policy to value the non-controlling interests at fair value on acquisition. The directors valued the non-controlling interests in Mystery at $536m and in Suspense at $210m at the 1 January 20X3.

No impairment losses have been necessary in the consolidated financial statements to date.

Required

Prepare the consolidated statement of financial position of Murder group as at 31 December 20X7.

(18 marks)

18 Holmes & Deakin (22 marks) 40 mins

Holmes, a public limited company, has owned 85% of the ordinary share capital of Deakin, a pubic limited company, for some years. The shares were bought for $255m and Deakin's reserves at the time of purchase were $20m.

On 28 February 20X3 Holmes sold 40m of the Deakin shares for $160m. The only entry made in respect of this transaction has been the receipt of the cash, which was credited to the 'investment in subsidiary' account. No dividends were paid by either entity in the period.

The following draft summarised financial statements are available:

STATEMENTS OF COMPREHENSIVE INCOME FOR THE YEAR TO 31 MAY 20X3

	Holmes	*Deakin*
	$m	$m
Profit before tax	130	60
Income tax expense	(40)	(20)
Profit for the year	90	40
Other comprehensive income, net of tax	20	10
Total comprehensive income for the year	110	50

STATEMENTS OF FINANCIAL POSITION AS AT 31 MAY 20X3

	$m	$m
Non-current assets		
Property, plant and equipment	535	178
Investment in Deakin	95	–
	630	178
Current assets		
Inventories	320	190
Trade receivables	250	175
Cash	80	89
	650	454
	1,280	632
Equity		
Share capital $1 ordinary shares	500	200
Reserves	310	170
	810	370
Current liabilities		
Trade payables	295	171
Income tax payable	80	60
Provisions	95	31
	470	262
	1,280	632

No impairment losses have been necessary in the group financial statements to date.

Assume that the gain as calculated in the parent's separate financial statements will be subject to corporate income tax at a rate of 30% and that profit and other comprehensive income accrue evenly throughout the year.

Holmes group policy is to measure non-controlling interests at fair value at the date of acquisition. The fair value of the non-controlling interests in Deakin was $45m at the date of acquisition. No control premium was paid on acquisition.

Required

Prepare:

(a) The statement of comprehensive income and a statement of changes in equity (total) of Holmes Co for the year ended 31 May 20X3 **(5 marks)**

(b) The consolidated statement of comprehensive income of Holmes for the same period **(6 marks)**

(c) A consolidated statement of financial position as at 31 May 20X3 **(9 marks)**

(d) A consolidated statement of changes in equity (total) for the year ended 31 May 20X3 **(2 marks)**

(Total = 22 marks)

19 Harvard (18 marks)

The draft financial statements of Harvard and its subsidiary, Krakow sp. z o.o. are set out below.

STATEMENTS OF FINANCIAL POSITION AT 31 DECEMBER 20X5

	Harvard $'000	Krakow PLN'000
Non-current assets		
Property, plant and equipment	2,870	4,860
Investment in Krakow	840	–
	3,710	4,860
Current assets		
Inventories	1,990	8,316
Trade receivables	1,630	4,572
Cash	240	2,016
	3,860	14,904
	7,570	19,764
Equity		
Share capital ($1/PLN1)	118	1,348
Retained reserves	502	14,060
	620	15,408
Non-current liabilities		
Loans	1,920	–
Current liabilities		
Trade payables	5,030	4,356
	7,570	19,764

STATEMENTS OF COMPREHENSIVE INCOME FOR THE YEAR ENDED 31 DECEMBER 20X5

Revenue	40,425	97,125
Cost of sales	(35,500)	77,550
Gross profit	4,925	19,575
Distribution and administrative expenses	(4,400)	(5,850)
Investment income	718	–
Profit before tax	1,243	13,725
Income tax expense	(300)	(4,725)
Profit/total comprehensive income for the year	943	9,000
Dividends paid during the period	700	3,752

The following additional information is given:

(i) Exchange rates

	Zloty (PLN) to $
31 December 20X2	4.40
31 December 20X3	4.16
31 December 20X4	4.00
15 May 20X5	3.92
31 December 20X5	3.60
Average for 20X5	3.75

(ii) Harvard acquired 1,011,000 shares in Krakow for $840,000 on 31 December 20X2 when Krakow's retained reserves stood at PLN 2,876,000. Krakow operates as an autonomous subsidiary. Its functional currency is the Polish zloty.

The fair value of the identifiable net assets of Krakow were equivalent to their book values at the acquisition date. Group policy is to measure non-controlling interests at fair value at the acquisition date. The fair value of the non-controlling interests in Krakow was measured at $270,000 on 31 December 20X2.

(iii)   Krakow paid an interim dividend of PLN 3,752,000 on 15 May 20X5. No other dividends were paid or declared in the period.

(iv)   No impairment losses were necessary in the consolidated financial statements by 31 December 20X5.

Required

(a)   Prepare the consolidated statement of financial position at 31 December 20X5.   **(6 marks)**

(b)   Prepare the consolidated statement of comprehensive income and an extract from the statement of changes in equity for retained reserves for the year ended 31 December 20X5.   **(12 marks)**

Ignore deferred tax on translation differences.   **(Total = 18 marks)**

20 Porter (25 marks)   45 mins

The following consolidated financial statements relate to Porter, a public limited company:

PORTER GROUP: STATEMENT OF FINANCIAL POSITION AS AT 31 MAY 20X6

	20X6 $'m	20X5 $'m
Non-current assets		
Property, plant and equipment	958	812
Goodwill	15	10
Investment in associate	48	39
	1,021	861
Current assets		
Inventories	154	168
Trade receivables	132	112
Financial assets at fair value through profit or loss	16	0
Cash and cash equivalents	158	48
	460	328
	1,481	1,189
Equity attributable to owners of the parent		
Share capital ($1 ordinary shares)	332	300
Share premium account	212	172
Retained earnings	188	165
Revaluation surplus	101	54
	833	691
Non-controlling interests	84	28
	917	719
Non-current liabilities		
Long-term borrowings	380	320
Deferred tax liability	38	26
	418	346
Current liabilities		
Trade and other payables	110	98
Interest payable	8	4
Current tax payable	28	22
	146	124
	1,481	1,189

PORTER GROUP: STATEMENT OF COMPREHENSIVE INCOME
FOR THE YEAR ENDED 31 MAY 20X6

	$'m
Revenue	956
Cost of sales	(634)
Gross profit	322
Other income	6
Distribution costs	(97)
Administrative expenses	(115)
Finance costs	(16)
Share of profit of associate	12
Profit before tax	112
Income tax expense	(34)
PROFIT FOR THE YEAR	78
Other comprehensive income:	
Gains on property revaluation	58
Share of other comprehensive income of associate	8
Income tax relating to components of other comprehensive income	(17)
Other comprehensive income for the year, net of tax	49
TOTAL COMPREHENSIVE INCOME FOR THE YEAR	127

Profit attributable to:	
Owners of the parent	68
Non-controlling interests	10
	78

Total comprehensive income attributable to:	
Owners of the parent	115
Non-controlling interests	12
	127

The following information relates to the consolidated financial statements of Porter:

(a) During the period, Porter acquired 60% of a subsidiary. The purchase was effected by issuing shares of Porter on a 1 for 2 basis, at their market value on that date of $2.25 per share, plus $26m in cash.

A statement of financial position of the subsidiary, prepared at the acquisition date for consolidation purposes showed the following position:

	$'m
Property, plant and equipment	92
Inventories	20
Trade receivables	16
Cash and cash equivalents	8
	136
Share capital ($1 shares)	80
Reserves	40
	120
Trade payables	12
Income taxes payable	4
	136

An impairment test conducted at the year end, resulted in a write-down of goodwill relating to another wholly owned subsidiary. This was charged to cost of sales.

Group policy is to value non-controlling interests at the date of acquisition at the proportionate share of the fair value of the acquiree's identifiable assets acquired and liabilities assumed.

(b)　Depreciation charged to the consolidated profit or loss amounted to $44m. There were no disposals of property, plant and equipment during the year.

(c)　Other income represents gains on financial assets at fair value through profit or loss. The financial assets represent investments in quoted shares were purchased shortly before the year end with surplus cash, and were designated at fair through profit loss as they are expected to be sold after the year end. No dividends have yet been received.

(d)　Included in 'trade and other payables' is the $ equivalent of an invoice for 102m shillings for some equipment purchased from a foreign supplier. The asset was invoiced on 5 March 20X6, but had not been paid for at the year end, 31 May 20X6.

Exchange gains or losses on the transaction have been included in administrative expenses. Relevant exchange rates were as follows:

	Shillings to $1
5 March 20X6	6.8
31 May 20X6	6.0

(e)　Movement on retained earnings was as follows:

	$'m
At 31 May 20X5	165
Total comprehensive income	68
Dividends paid	(45)
At 31 May 20X6	188

Required

Prepare a consolidated statement of cash flows for Porter for the year ended 31 May 20X6 in accordance with IAS 7 *Statements of Cash Flows*, using the indirect method.

Notes to the statement of cash flows are not required.

(Total = 25 marks)

21 Grow by acquisition

Expand is a large group that seeks to grow by acquisition. The directors of Expand have identified two potential target entities (A and B) and obtained copies of their financial statements. Extracts from these financial statements, together with notes providing additional information, are given below.

INCOME STATEMENTS
YEAR ENDED 31 DECEMBER 20X1

	A	B
	$'000	$'000
Revenue	68,000	66,000
Cost of sales	(42,000)	(45,950)
Gross profit	26,000	20,050
Other operating expenses	(18,000)	(14,000)
Profit from operations	8,000	6,050
Finance cost	(3,000)	(4,000)
Profit before tax	5,000	2,050
Income tax expense	(1,500)	(1,000)
Profit for the year	3,500	1,050
Other comprehensive income surplus on revaluation of properties	NIL	6,000
Total comprehensive income	3,500	7,050

STATEMENTS OF CHANGES IN EQUITY
YEAR ENDED 31 DECEMBER 20X1

	A	B
	$'000	$'000
Balance at 1 January 20X1	22,000	16,000
Total comprehensive income for the year	3,500	7,050
Dividends paid	(2,000)	(1,000)
Balance at 31 December 20X1	23,500	22,050

STATEMENTS OF FINANCIAL POSITION AT 31 DECEMBER 20X1

	A		B	
	$'000	$'000	$'000	$'000
Non-current assets				
Property, plant and equipment	32,000		35,050	
		32,000		35,050
Current assets				
Inventories	6,000		7,000	
Trade receivables	12,000		10,000	
		18,000		17,000
		50,000		52,050
Equity				
Issued capital ($1 shares)		16,000		12,000
Revaluation reserve		Nil		5,000
Retained earnings		7,500		5,050
		23,500		22,050
Non-current liabilities				
Interest bearing borrowings		16,000		18,000
Current liabilities				
Trade payables	5,000		5,000	
Income tax	1,500		1,000	
Short-term borrowings	4,000		6,000	
		10,500		12,000
		50,000		52,050

Notes

1   *Sale by A to X*

On 31 December 20X1, A supplied goods, at the normal selling price of $2.4 million, to another entity, X. A's normal selling price is at a mark up of 60% on cost. X paid for the goods in cash on the same day. The terms of the selling agreement were that A repurchase these goods on 30 June 20X2 for $2.5 million. A has accounted for the transaction as a sale.

2   *Revaluation of non-current assets by B*

B revalued its non-current assets for the first time on 1 January 20X1. The non-current assets of A are very similar in age and type to the non-current assets of B. However, A has a policy of maintaining all its non-current assets at depreciated historical cost. Both entities charge depreciation of non-current assets to cost of sales. B has transferred the excess depreciation on the revalued assets from the revaluation reserve to retained earnings as permitted in IAS 16 – *Property, plant and equipment.*

Expand uses ratio analysis to appraise potential investment opportunities. It is normal practice to base the appraisal on four key ratios.

- Return on capital employed
- Gross profit margin
- Turnover of capital employed
- Leverage

For the purposes of the ratio analysis, Expand computes:

(i)   Capital employed as capital and reserves plus borrowings
(ii) Borrowings as interest –bearing borrowings plus short-term borrowings

Your assistant has computed the four key ratios for the two entities from the financial statements provided and the results are summarised below.

Ratio	A	B
Return on capital employed	18.4%	13.1%
Gross profit margin	38.2%	30.4%
Turnover of capital employed	1.6	1.4
Leverage	46.0%	52.1%

Your assistant has informed you that, on the basis of the ratios calculated, the performance of A is superior to that of B in all respects. Therefore, Expand should carry out a more detailed review of A with a view to making a bid to acquire it. However, you are unsure whether this is necessarily the correct conclusion given the information provided in Notes 1 and 2.

Required

(a) Explain and compute the adjustments that would be appropriate in respect of Notes 1 and 2 so as to make the financial statements of A and B comparable for analysis.

(b) Recalculate the four key ratios mentioned in the question for both A and B after making the adjustments you have recommended in your answer to part (a). You should provide appropriate workings to support your calculations.

(c) In the light of the work that you have carried out in answer to parts (a) and (b), evaluate your assistant's conclusion that a more detailed review of A should be carried out, with a view to making a bid to acquire it.

22 German competitor (25 marks)   45 mins

You are the chief accountant of Tone plc, a UK company. The managing director has provided you with the financial statements of Tone plc's main competitor, Hilde GmbH, a German company. He finds difficulty in reviewing these statements in their non-UK format, presented below.

HILDE GmbH
BALANCE SHEET AS AT 31 MARCH 20X5 (in □ million)

ASSETS	31.3.X5	31.3.X4	CAPITAL AND LIABILITIES	31.3.X5	31.3.X4
Tangible non-current assets			Capital and reserves		
Land	1,000	750	Share capital	850	750
Buildings	750	500	Share premium	100	–
Plant	200	150	Legal reserve	200	200
	1,950	1,400	Profit & loss b/fwd	590	300
			Profit & loss for year	185	290
Current assets			NET WORTH	1,925	1,540
Inventory	150	120			
Trade receivables	180	100	Payables		
Cash	20	200	Trade payables	170	150
	350	420	Taxation	180	150
			Other payables	75	50
Prepayments and accrued income				425	350
Prepayments	50	70			
	2,350	1,890		2,350	1,890

HILDE GmbH

STATEMENT OF COMPREHENSIVE INCOME FOR THE YEAR ENDED 31 MARCH 20X5 (in E million)

EXPENSES	20X5	20X4	INCOME	20X5	20X4
Operating expenses:			Operating income:		
Purchase of raw materials	740	400	Sale of goods produced	1,890	1,270
Variation in inventories thereof	90	40	Variation in inventory of finished goods and WIP	120	80
Taxation	190	125	Other operating income	75	50
Wages	500	285	Total operating income	2,085	1,400
Valuation adjustment on non-current assets: depreciation	200	150			
Valuation adjustment on current assets: amounts written off	30	20			
Other operating expenses	50	40			
Total operating expenses	1,800	1,060			
Financial expenses Interest	100	50			
Total financial expenses	100	50			
TOTAL EXPENSES	1,900	1,110	TOTAL INCOME	2,085	1,400
Balance: PROFIT	185	290			
SUM TOTAL	2,085	1,400		2,085	1,400

Required

Prepare a report for the managing director:

(a) Analysing the performance of Hilde GmbH using the financial statements provided **(18 marks)**

(b) Explaining why a direct comparison of the results of Tone plc and Hilde GmbH may be misleading **(7 marks)**

23 Public sector organisations

The laws, regulations and guidelines relating to public sector accounts are rather different from those which apply to private sector organisations. As far as public sector organisations are concerned:

(a) State why these differences exist

(b) Explain the main differences

(c) Outline the consequences for public sector accounts

24 Small and medium-sized entities (25 marks)   45 mins

On 15 February 2007, the IASB issued the Exposure Draft of its *International Financial Reporting Standard for Small and Medium-sized Entities (IFRS for SMEs)*. The aim of the proposed standard is to provide a simplified, self-contained set of accounting principles for smaller non-listed companies. The resulting draft standard reduces the volume of accounting guidance applicable to SMEs by more than 85% when compared to a full set of IFRS. After 'field testing' by 116 SMEs in 20 different countries, the IASB plan to vote to approve a final IFRS for SME in the final quarter of 2008.

(a)   Discuss the advantages and disadvantages of SMEs a separate IFRS for SMEs as opposed to full
         IFRS.   **10 marks**

The Exposure Draft of *IFRS for SMEs* removes choice for accounting treatment, eliminates topics that are
not generally relevant to SMEs, simplifies methods for recognition and measurement and reduces the
disclosure requirements of full IFRSs.

Required

(b)   Give some examples of full IFRSs which have complex recognition or measurement requirements
         and/or offer a choice of accounting treatment. Explain these complexities and how they might be
         simplified for SMEs.   **13 marks**

         Appropriateness and quality of discussion   **2 marks**

                                                                                          (Total = 25 marks)

25 Peter Holdings

Peter Holdings is a large investment conglomerate.

Required

Explain how divisional performance should be measured in the interest of the group's shareholders.

26 Planet (25 marks)   **45 mins**

Planet has provided the following draft consolidated statement of financial position as at 30 November
20X2.

PLANET
GROUP STATEMENT OF FINANCIAL POSITION AS AT 30 NOVEMBER 20X2

	$'000
Non-current assets	
Property, plant and equipment	76,240
Intangible assets	10,360
	86,600
Net current assets	55,800
Total assets less current liabilities	142,400
Equity	
Share capital	32,200
Share premium account	10,000
Retained earnings	54,800
	97,000
Non-controlling interest	18,200
Non-current liabilities	
Long term borrowings	25,400
Provisions	1,800
	142,400

The group accountant has asked your advice on several matters. These issues are set out below and have
not been dealt with in the draft group financial statements.

(i)   Planet purchased a wholly owned subsidiary company, Moon, on 1 December 20X0. The purchase consideration was based on the performance of the subsidiary. The vendors commenced a legal action on 31 March 20X2 over the amount of the purchase consideration. An amount had been paid to the vendors and included in the calculation of goodwill but the vendors disputed the amount of this payment. On 30 November 20X2 the court ruled that Planet should pay an additional $16 million to the vendors. The directors do not know how to treat the additional purchase consideration and have not accounted for the item.

Note. Ignore the effect of the time value of money.

(ii)   Planet has corporate offices under an operating lease. A requirement of the operating lease for the buildings is that the asset is returned in good condition. The operating lease was signed in the current year and lasts for six years. Planet intends to refurbish the building in six years time at a cost of $12 million in order to meet the requirements of the lease. This amount includes the renovation of the exterior of the building and is based on current price levels. Currently there is evidence that due to exceptionally severe weather damage the company will have to spend $2.4 million in the next year on having the exterior of the building renovated. The company feels that this expenditure will reduce the refurbishment cost at the end of the lease by an equivalent amount. There is no provision for the above expenditure in the financial statements.

An 80% owned subsidiary company, Galaxy, has a leasehold property (depreciated historical cost $16 million). It has been modified to include a swimming pool for the employees. Under the terms of the lease, the property must be restored to its original state when the lease expires in ten years' time or earlier termination. The present value of the costs of reinstatement are likely to be $4 million and the directors wish to provide for $400,000 per annum for ten years. The lease was signed and operated from 1 December 20X1. The directors estimate that the lease has a recoverable value of $19 million at 30 November 20X2 and have not provided for any of the above amounts.

Additionally Planet owns buildings at a carrying value of $40 million which will require repair expenditure of approximately $12 million over the next five years. There is no provision for this amount in the financial statements. Depreciation is charged on owned buildings at 5% per annum and on leasehold buildings at 10% per annum on the straight line basis.

(iii)   On 1 December 20X1, Planet entered into an agreement with a wholly owned overseas subsidiary, Dimanche, to purchase components at a value of 4.2 million krona on which Dimanche made a profit of 20% on selling price. The goods were to be delivered on 31 January 20X2 with the payment due on 31 March 20X2. Planet took out a foreign currency contract on 1 December 20X0 to buy 4.2 million krona on 31 March 20X1 at the forward rate of $1 = 1.4 krona.

At 30 November 20X2, Planet had two-thirds of the components in inventory. The spot rates were as follows.

$1 equivalent

1 December 20X1	1.3 krona
31 January 20X2	1.46 krona
31 March 20X2	1.45 krona
30 November 20X2	1.35 krona

The initial purchase of the inventory had been recorded on receipt at the forward rate and the forward rate had been used for the year end valuation of inventory. The directors are unsure as to how to treat the items above both for accounting and disclosure purposes but they have heard that the simplest method is to translate the asset and liability at the forward rate and they wish to use this method.

(iv)   Galaxy has developed a database during the year to 30 November 20X2 and it is included in intangible non-current assets at a cost of $6 million. The asset comprises the internal and external costs of developing the database. The database is used to produce a technical computing manual which is used by the whole group and sold to other parties. It has quickly become a market leader in this field. Any costs of maintaining the database and the computing manual are written off as incurred. Sales of the manual are expected to general net revenue of $4m. The computing manual requires substantial revision every four years.

Required

(a) Explain how the above four issues should be dealt with in the consolidated financial statements of Planet. Show the accounting entries that need to be made. **(19 marks)**

(b) Prepare a revised group statement of financial position at 30 November 20X2 taking into account the four issues discussed in part (a). **(6 marks)**

27 Wingit (50 marks)   90 mins

The following draft financial statements relate to the Wingit Group, a public limited company.

WINGIT GROUP
DRAFT GROUP STATEMENT OF FINANCIAL POSITION AT 31 MAY 20X3

	20X3 $m	20X2 $m
Assets		
Non-current assets		
Property, plant and equipment	1,239	1,010
Goodwill	100	83
Investments	780	270
	2,119	1,363
Current assets		
Inventories	750	588
Trade receivables	660	530
Cash and cash equivalents	45	140
	1,455	1,258
Total assets	3,574	2,621
Equity and liabilities		
Equity attributable to owners of the parent:		
Share capital: ordinary shares of $1	100	70
Share premium account	85	15
Revaluation surplus	30	10
Retained earnings	405	103
Translation of foreign operations	(195)	
	425	198
Non-controlling interest	250	150
Total equity	675	348
Non-current liabilities		
Redeemable preference shares		
($130m at an interest rate of 7% pa)	136	130
Long term borrowings	1,262	930
	1,398	1,060
Current liabilities	1,501	1,213
Total liabilities	2,899	2,273
Total equity and liabilities	3,574	2,621

DRAFT GROUP STATEMENT OF COMPREHENSIVE INCOME FOR THE YEAR ENDED 31 MAY 20X3

	$m	$m
Revenue		7,310
Cost of sales		(5,920)
Gross profit		1,390
Distribution and administrative expenses		(762)
Profit on sale of property, plant and equipment		15
Interest receivable	34	
Interest payable	(37)	
		(3)
Share of profit of associates		83
Profit before tax		723
Income tax expense		(198)
Profit for the year		525
Profit attributable to:		
Owners of the parent		428
Non-controlling interest		97
		525

OTHER COMPREHENSIVE INCOME
FOR THE YEAR ENDED 31 MAY 20X3

	$m
Surplus on revaluation of property (Wingit)	20
Exchange difference on retranslation of foreign operation (100% sub)	(195)
Other comprehensive income (525 – 375) for the year	(175)
	350
Total comprehensive income for the year	
Attributable to: owners of the parent	253
non-controlling interest	97
	350

STATEMENT OF CHANGES IN EQUITY FOR THE YEAR ENDED 31 MAY 20X3

	Share capital	Share premium	Revaluation surplus	Retained earnings	Translation of foreign operations	Parent equity	Non-controlling interest	Total
	$m	$m	$m	$m	$m	$m	$m	$m
Balance at 31 May 20X2	70	15	10	103		198	150	348
On acquisition of subsidiary							20	20
Total comprehensive income for the year			20	428	(195)	253	97	350
Dividends				(126)		(126)	(17)	(143)
Issue of share capital	3	70				100		100
	100	85	30	405	(195)	425	250	675

The following information is relevant to the Wingit Group.

(i)   Wingit acquired an eighty per cent holding in Regent on 1 June 20X2. The fair values of the assets of Regent on 1 June 20X2 were as follows:

	$m
Property, plant and equipment	60
Inventories	30
Trade receivables	25
Cash and cash equivalents	35
Trade payables	(20)
Taxation	(30)
	100

The purchase consideration was $97 million and comprised 20 million ordinary shares of $1 in Wingit, valued at $4 and $17 million in cash.

(ii) The movement of property, plant and equipment for the period comprised the following amounts at net book value:

	$m
Balance at 1 June 20X2	1,010
Additions (including Regent)	278
Revaluations of properties (Wingit)	20
Disposals	(30)
Depreciation	(39)
Balance at 31 May 20X3	1,239

(iii) There have been no sales of non-current asset investments in the year. The investments included under non-current assets comprised the following items.

	20X3	20X2
	$m	$m
Investment in associate	300	220
Trade investment (including foreign operation of $400m		
acquired during year to 31 May 20X3)	480	50
	780	270

(iv) Interest receivable included in trade receivables was $15 m as at 31 May 20X2 and $17 m as at 31 May 20X3.

(v) Current liabilities comprises the following items:

	20X3	20X2
	$m	$m
Trade payables (including interest payable $9m 20X3, Nil 20X2)	1,193	913
Taxation	203	200
Dividends	105	100
	1,501	1,213

(vi) Wingit had allotted 10 million ordinary shares of $1 at a price of $2 upon the exercise of directors options during the year.

(vii) Included in non-current liabilities is a bill of exchange for $100 million (raised 30 June 20X2) which was given to a supplier on the purchase of property, plant and equipment which is payable on 1 July 20X3.

(viii) The exchange difference included in 'other comprehensive income' relates to a translation involving a foreign equity investment in Peer of $400 million. A loan of $300 million was taken out during the year to finance the foreign country investment. (Both amounts are after re-translation at the year end.)

(ix) The preference share dividends are always paid in full on 1 July each year, and are included in interest payable in the income statement. Additionally a charge of $6 million has been made in the interest payable figure to provide for a premium payable on the preference shares on redemption.

(a) Prepare a group statement of cash flows using the indirect method for the Wingit Group plc for the year ended 31 May 20X3 in accordance with the requirements of IAS 7 *Statement of cash flows*.

The notes to the statement of cash flows are not required. **(27 marks)**

Wingit has a subsidiary, Springit. On 1 June 20X3, the chief executive of Springit, Mr Springer, retired from the company. The ordinary share capital at the time of his retirement was six million shares of $1. Mr Springer owns 52% of the ordinary shares of Springit and the remainder is owned by employees. As an incentive to the new management, Mr Springer agreed to a new executive compensation plan which commenced after his retirement. The plan provides cash bonuses to the board of directors when the company's earnings per share exceeds the 'normal' earnings per share which has been agreed at $0.50 per share. The cash bonuses are calculated as being 20% of the profit generated in excess of that required to give an earnings per share figure of $0.50.

The new board of directors has reported that the compensation to be paid is $360,000 based on earnings per share of $0.80 for the year ended 31 May 20X4. However, Mr Springer is surprised at the size of the compensation as other companies in the same industry were either breaking even or making losses in the period. He was anticipating that no bonus would be paid during the year as he felt that the company would not be able to earn the equivalent of the normal earnings per share figure of $0.50.

Mr Springer, who had taken no active part in management decisions, decided to take advantage of his role as non-executive director and demanded an explanation of how the earnings per share figure of $0.80 had been calculated. His investigations revealed the following information.

(i)   The company received a grant from the government of $5 million towards the cost of purchasing a non-current asset of $15 million. The grant had been credited to profit or loss in total and the non-current asset had been recognised at $15 million in the statement of financial position and depreciated at a rate of 10% per annum on the straight line basis. The directors explained that current thinking by the International Accounting Standards Board was that the accounting standard on government grants was conceptually wrong because it misstates the assets and liabilities of the company and hence they were following the approach which has recently been advocated in a recent discussion paper.

(ii)   Shortly after Mr Springer had retired from the company, Springit made an initial public offering of its shares. The sponsor of the issue charged a fee of $300,000. The fee on 1 August 20X3 was paid by issuing one hundred thousand $1 ordinary shares at a market value of $120,000 and by cash of $180,000. The directors had charged the cash paid as an expense in profit or loss. Further, they had credited the value of the shares issued to the sponsor in the profit or loss for the year as they felt that the shares were issued for no consideration and that, therefore, they should offset the cash paid by the company. The public offering was made on 1 August 20X3 and involved vesting four million ordinary (exclusive of the sponsor's shares) shares of $1 at a market price of $1.20. Mr Springer and other current shareholders decided to sell three million of their shares as part of the offer, leaving one million new shares to be issued. The cost of issuing shares are to be regarded as an element of the net consideration.

(iii)   The directors sold on 1 June 20X3 a property under a twenty year lease to a company, Highball, which the bank had set up to act as a vehicle for investments and special projects. The consideration for the lease is $4.5 million. Springit has signed an unconditional agreement to repurchase the lease of the property after four years for a fixed amount of $5.5 million. The property has been taken off the statement of financial position and the profit on the transaction, which has been included in profit or loss, is $500,000. The profit has been calculated by comparing the value of the property with the consideration received.

Depreciation on the property is charged at 5% per annum on the carrying value of the asset. The effective interest rate is 5.14%.

(iv)   Springit had made a 1 for 4 rights issue on 30 June 20X4. The cost of the shares was $1.60 per share and the market price was $2.00 per share before the rights issue. The directors had ignored this transaction because it occurred after the year end but they intend to capitalise retained earnings to reflect the bonus element of the rights issue in the financial statements for the year ending 31 May 20X5. The financial statements are not yet approved for the current year.

(v)   The directors had calculated earnings per share for the year ended 31 May 20X4 as follows.

Profit after tax	$4.8 million
Ordinary shares of $1	6,000,000
Earnings per share	$0.80

Mr Springer was concerned over the way that earnings per share had been calculated by the directors and also he felt that some of the above accounting practices were at best unethical and at worst fraudulent. He, therefore, asked your technical and ethical advice on the practices of the directors.

Required

(b)   Advise Mr Springer as to whether earnings per share has been accurately calculated by the directors showing a revised calculation of earnings per share.   **(16 marks)**

(c)   Discuss whether the directors may have acted unethically in the way they have calculated earnings per share.   **(7 marks)**

Exam answer bank

1 Framework

(a)   The stated **purposes** of the *Framework* are as follows.

    (i)   To assist the IASB in developing IASs and reviewing existing standards.

    (ii)   To assist the IASB in harmonising regulations and accounting standards by reducing alternative treatments.

    (iii)   To assist national bodies in developing their own standards.

    (iv)   To assist preparers of financial statements in applying IASs and to deal with topics not yet covered by IASs.

    (v)   To assist users of financial statements by ensuring statements comply with IASs.

    (vi)   To assist users in interpreting financial statements.

    (vii)   To assist those interested in the work of the IASB by giving them information as to how IASs are formulated.

(b)   The people who might be **interested** in financial information about the company may be classified as follows.

    (i)   **Shareholders in the company.** They will be interested in the company's profitability and its ability to pay dividends. They will also be interested in the company's long term prospects

    (ii)   **Managers of the company**. These are people appointed by the company's owners to supervise the day-to-day activities of the company. They need information about the company's financial situation as it is currently and as it is expected to be in the future. This is to enable them to manage the business efficiently and to take effective control and planning decisions.

    (iii)   **Trade contacts**, including suppliers who provide goods to the company on credit and customers who purchase the goods or services provided by the company. Suppliers will want to know about the company's ability to pay its debts; customers need to know that the company is a secure source of supply and is in no danger of having to close down.

    (iv)   **Providers of finance to the company**. These might include a bank which permits the company to operate an overdraft, or provides longer-term finance by granting a loan. The bank will want to ensure that the company is able to keep up with interest payments, and eventually to repay the amounts advanced.

    (v)   **The taxation authorities**, who will want to know about business profits in order to assess the tax payable by the company on its profits and any sales taxes.

    (vi)   **Employees of the company**. These should have a right to information about the company's financial situation, because their future careers and the size of their wages and salaries depend on it.

2 Fundamental principles

Tutorial note. Don't let this scenario panic you in the long list of details it gives you. Deal with each point as it arises. Also, don't be afraid to draw a conclusion about the facts given to you, but remember to back your opinions up with justification. Consider what the fundamental principles and general guidance of the ACCA say, but also think about practical issues, such as ease of modern communication. Deal with the two issues raised in the scenario (the individual partner issue and the firm split) separately, there is no need to assume any connection between them. However, you may feel there is a point to be made about the juxtaposition of the two events.

Independence

It is important that auditors are, and are seen to be, independent. **Independence** is at the heart of the auditing profession as auditors claim to give an **impartial, objective** opinion on the truth and fairness of the financial statements.

Objectivity

A **family relationship** between an auditor and the client **can substantially affect the objectivity** of the audit, so auditors are advised not to build close personal relationships with audit clients and should not audit a company where family are employed in a capacity which is sensitive to the accounts, for example, in the finance department, although this is **not prohibited by law**.

In this instance, the **partner was not the reporting partner** for the audit client in which his brother-in-law was a financial controller. According to generally accepted ethical practice then, the firm appeared to be independent of the audit client if the related partner did not have anything to do with the audit.

Resolution?

The regulatory body required the audit partner to move 400 miles. This presumably implies that the partner was requested to change offices within the firm by which he was employed. Given current levels of computer networking and other **communications** common in business, this would appear to be an **arbitrary distinction**, as a partner in an office 400 miles away could have similar access and influence over a single audit carried out by the firm as a partner in the locality.

Independence in appearance

However, in this situation, the regulatory body appear to be concerned about the appearance of independence. They appear to be concerned that the public will not perceive the distinction between a partner and a partner who reports on a specific engagement. This may or may not be fair. Arguably, it is only in publicising the problem that the public are likely to have a perception at all.

Also, given the comments made about modern communications above, the public are unlikely to be convinced that moving a member of staff to a different office will solve this independence problem, if they perceive that there is one.

Split of audit firm

The decision of the firm to split into three divisions could **enhance the public perception of the independence of the audit department**. While there might be **underlying scepticism** relating to the reasons behind the split (which could merely be for marketing purposes or to enable non-audit divisions to raise capital more easily), the **underlying benefit for objectivity still exists**.

However, some audit clients will be unhappy with the move of the firm as it will entail their appointing several different service providers to gain the services they previously got from the one audit firm.

3 Tree

(a)   IAS 18 *Revenue* states that the following conditions must be satisfied before revenue from the sale of goods can be recognised.

(i)   The entity **has transferred to the buyer the significant risks and reward** of ownership of the goods. In most cases, transfer of the risks and rewards of ownership coincides with the transfer of legal title or the passing of possession to the buyer, but **this is not always the case**. If the entity retains significant risk of ownership, the transaction is not a sale and revenue cannot be recognised. For example, the entity might retain an obligation for unsatisfactory performance not covered by normal warranty provisions. However, if the risk retained is insignificant, the transaction is a sale and revenue is recognised. For example, a retail sale is recognised where a refund is offered if the customer is not satisfied, provided that the seller can reliably estimate future returns and recognises a liability based on previous experience and other relevant factors.

(ii) The entity retains **neither continuing managerial involvement** to the degree usually associated with ownership **nor effective control** over the goods sold.

(iii) The amount of revenue can be **measured reliably**.

(iv) It is **probable** that the economic benefits associated with the transaction will flow to the entity. For example, it may be uncertain that a foreign government will grant permission to remit consideration from a sale in a foreign country. Revenue cannot be recognised until the uncertainty is removed.

(v) The costs incurred or to be incurred in respect of the transaction can be **measured reliably**.

(b) **Transaction 1**

The key issue here is whether Tree has retained the risks inherent in owning the property. This depends on whether Tree is likely to exercise its option to repurchase the property in practice.

(i) Tree can repurchase the property at any time until 28 February 20X6, but the bank cannot require repurchase. This means that Tree is **protected against any fall in the value of the property** below $5 million. This suggests that **some risk** has been **transferred to the bank**.

(ii) In practice, the value of the property is expected to rise by 5% each year for the foreseeable future. Therefore it is **extremely unlikely** that the value of the property will fall below $5 million.

(iii) Tree **can benefit from the expected rise** in the value of the property by buying it back at a price that is well below its anticipated market value.

In conclusion, Tree is **likely to exercise the option** and therefore has **retained the risk of changes** in the property's market value. Other important aspects of the transaction are:

(i) The 'sale' price of the property was **only 50% of its market value**.

(ii) Tree occupies the **property rent-free** (a reward of ownership).

(iii) The repurchase price depends on the **length of time that elapses** between the date of the agreement and the date of repurchase, **rather than on the market value** of the property.

Therefore, the transaction is essentially a **loan secured on the property**, rather than an outright sale. The $50,000 payable for each month that the bank holds the property is **interest** on the loan.

The property **remains in the consolidated statement of financial position** at its cost or market value (depending on the accounting policy adopted by Tree). The **loan** of $5 million and **accrued interest** of $300,000 (6 × 50,000) are reported under **non-current liabilities**. Interest of $300,000 is recognised in consolidated profit or loss.

Transaction 2

The key issue is whether Tree **retains the risks associated** with the ownership of the branch.

Tree **continues to control the operations** of the branch and the amount that it receives from Vehicle is the operating profit of the branch less the interest payable on the loan. Tree also suffers the effect of any operating losses made by the branch. Therefore the **position is essentially the same as before** the 'sale'.

Although Vehicle is not a subsidiary of Tree plc as defined by IAS 27 *Consolidated and separate financial statements,* it is a special purpose entity (**quasi-subsidiary**). It gives rise to benefits for Tree that are in substance no different from those that would arise if it were a subsidiary. Its assets, liabilities, income and expenses **must be included** in the consolidated financial statements.

The assets and liabilities of Vehicle are included in the consolidated statement of financial position at $7 million (their original value to the group). The loan of $8 million is recognised as a non-current liability. The profit on disposal of $1 million and the operating fee of $1,200,000 are cancelled as intra-group transactions. The operating profit of $2,000,000 is included in consolidated profit or loss as is the loan interest of $800,000.

4 Greensmith

Memorandum

The need for and impact of possible revaluations of assets by Greensmith Co

To: FD, Greensmith Co
From: Accountant

For the private use of the company

I have considered the issues you raised and would advise you of the following matters:

(a)   **Need to revalue**

- IAS 36 *Impairment of Assets* indicates that impairments losses such as that for Conway Square must be reflected in the financial statements in the year that they occur.

- There is no need to revalue the Berkshire Training Centre if you do not wish to, but if you were to revalue this asset, all assets of the same class would need to be revalued, per IAS 16 *Property, Plant and Equipment*. Furthermore, the revaluations need to be kept up to date so that the carrying amount is not materially different to the asset's fair value at the year end. IAS 16 suggests that every three to five years may be sufficient if prices are not too volatile.

(b)   **Pooling/Accounting Treatment**

- When you take account of the impairment of Conway Square and if you revalue the Training Centre they will have to be accounted for separately. You could not pool the net movement.

- The fall in the value of Conway Square of $0.7 million would go through profit or loss as it has not been previously revalued.

- The $3.5 million increase in the Training Centre's value would go through the revaluation surplus and it would therefore be reflected in other comprehensive income.

(c)   **Effect on profit or loss of future disposals**

The reported profit sale would be lower if an upward revaluation had occurred as the profit on disposal is calculated as proceeds less book value as it must be calculated by reference to the new carrying value.

The previously recognised revaluation surplus, would be credited directly to retained earnings.

The profit on any disposal of Conway Square would conversely be higher (or any loss lower).

(d)   **Effect on EPS, ROCE and NAPS**

(i)   *EPS*

- reflecting the impairment of Conway Square would almost certainly need to be disclosed (under IAS 1) given its size and would reduce earnings and therefore EPS.

- Revaluing the Training Centre will lead to an increased amortisation charge

$$\$'000$$

$$- \text{new} \quad \frac{8m}{18} \quad\quad 444 \quad \text{per annum}$$

$$- \text{existing} \quad \frac{5m}{20} \quad\quad 250 \quad \text{per annum}$$

This will obviously lower EPS for the remainder of the lease term.

(ii) *ROCE*

- The revaluation upwards would worsen ROCE by increasing capital employed. Additionally, the revaluation will increase the amortisation and thus reduce the return.

- Reflecting the impairment of Conway Square would reduce the return in the year in question but would also reduce capital employed for the indefinite future.

(iii) *NAPS*

- The revaluations upwards would strengthen NAPS.
- The impairment in Conway Square would weaken it.

(e) **Summary and recommendations**

- Conway Square must be reduced in value to reflect its impairment in value. This will have the effect of making all of the measures of concern look worse this year. ROCE will be improved in the future.

- The Training Centre should not be revalued upwards. It will reduce EPS for the next 18 years and worsen ROCE. The increase in NAPS does not seem a reasonable trade-off as it is likely to be the least used of the three measures.

(f) **Advice on accounting for franchise and brand valuation**

(i) *Purchase of a franchise*

IAS 38 *Intangible Assets* states that an intangible asset acquired separately from a business should be capitalised at its cost, which in this case is $500,000. Given that the franchise is for a fixed period, it should be amortised on a systematic basis over its 15-year useful life.

(ii) *Brand value*

The Standard is clear on this area and states that internally generated brands should not be recognised as intangible assets. This is because expenditure on internally generated brands cannot be distinguished from the cost of developing the business as a whole. Costs of developing the business as a whole represent internally generated goodwill which is also not capitalised as it is not an identifiable resource that can be measured reliably at cost. The brand value cannot therefore be recognised in the statement of financial position.

I hope this assists you in your decision taking. These are complex issues so please contact me if any points in my report need clarifying or if there is any other way I can help out.

T Brown
1 December 20X2

5 Acquirer

> **Tutorial note.** This question tests students' ability to apply the principles of IFRS 3 and IAS 36. In Part (d) you should have computed the value in use of the relevant net assets. This involved allocating assets into cash generating units. In Part (e) you needed to allocate this impairment loss by computing the carrying value of the goodwill and therefore of the total carrying value of the individual subsidiary. The whole impairment loss was allocated to goodwill. Remember that the impairment review has to be done in two stages.

(a) To determine whether impairment of a non-current asset has occurred, it is necessary to compare the carrying amount of the asset with its **recoverable amount.** The recoverable amount is the **higher of fair value less costs to sell and value in use.** It is not always easy to estimate value in use. In particular, it is not always practicable to identify cash flows arising from an individual non-current asset. If this is the case, value in use should be calculated at the level of **cash generating units.**

A **cash generating unit** is defined as a group of assets, liabilities and associated goodwill that generates income that is **largely independent of the reporting entity's other income streams.** The assets and liabilities include those already involved in generating the income and an appropriate portion of those used to generate more than one income stream.

(b)   IAS 36 *Impairment of assets* requires that there should be some indication of impairment of a non-current asset before an impairment review is carried out. However, IFRS 3 *Business Combinations* sets out different requirements for the special case of goodwill.

IFRS 3 states that goodwill resulting from a business combination should be recognised in the statement of financial position and measured at cost. Goodwill is **not amortised.** Instead, it should be **reviewed for impairment annually** and written down to its recoverable amount where necessary. Where goodwill is acquired in a business combination during the current annual period, it should be tested for impairment before the end of the current annual period. Prospects was acquired on 30 June 20X0, so the impairment review should be carried out by 31 December 20X0.

(c)   An impairment review involves a **comparison of the carrying value of a non-current asset or goodwill with its recoverable amount.** To the extent that the carrying amount exceeds the recoverable amount, the non-current asset or goodwill is impaired and needs to be written down.

Recoverable amount is the higher of fair value less costs to sell and value in use. Generally, recoverable amount is taken to be **value in use.** This is because fair value less costs to sell may be difficult to determine, and may in any case be very low, because the asset is only of use in the business rather than of value in the open market. This means that an impairment review usually involves computing value in use, particularly in the case of goodwill.

It is not always easy to estimate value in use. In particular, it is not always practicable to identify cash flows arising from an individual non-current asset. This is certainly true of goodwill, which cannot generate cash flows in isolation from other assets. If this is the case, value in use should be calculated at the level of **cash generating units.** A cash generating unit is the smallest grouping of assets that can be said to generate cash flows that are independent of those generated by other units. To calculate value in use, we therefore need to **identify the cash generating units and the cash flows attributable to them.**

(d)   The value in use of the assets of Unit A is $72m, which is less than the carrying value of $85m. There is therefore an **impairment loss of $13m.** This must be allocated as follows.

    (i)   To any **assets** which have suffered **obvious impairment.** We are not given any indication that there are any such assets here.

    (ii)   To **goodwill** in the unit. We are not told that there is any.

    (iii)   To **other assets** in the unit, ie the patents of $5 and tangible non-current assets of $60m.

    (iv)   Therefore the $13m is written off in proportion against patents (5/65 × $13m = $1m) and tangible non-current assets (60/65 × $13m = $12m).

(e)   The goodwill on consolidation is:

	$m
Cost of investment	260
Net assets acquired	180
	80

This goodwill cannot be allocated to individual units, so the impairment review must be carried out in two stages.

Stage 1: Review individual units for impairment.

It is clear that the assets of unit A have suffered impairment, since the value in use of $72m is less than the carrying value of $85m. The assets of unit A must therefore be written down to $72m.

Stage 2: Compare the adjusted carrying value of the net assets of Prospects, including goodwill, with the value in use of the whole business.

The carrying value is as follows.

	£m
Goodwill	80
Unit A	72
Unit B	55
Unit C	60
Total	267

The value in use of the whole business is $205m, so an additional impairment loss of $267m – $205m = $62m must be provided for. This is allocated first to goodwill, reducing the goodwill to $80m – $62m = $18m.

6 Investor

(a) The recognition and measurement of goodwill on acquisition is governed by IFRS 3. Where the purchase price is paid in instalments, the cost of the investment is calculated on a discounted cash basis and the fair value is based on present values.

Goodwill arising on acquisitions

	$m	$m
Cost of Cornwall $\left(30m + \dfrac{30m}{1.10^2}\right)$		54.793
Net assets	55	
Add back pension provision	6	
Deduct pension scheme deficit	(11)	
	50	
Fair value of assets acquired (80% × $50m)		40.000
Goodwill		14.793

Goodwill recognised in a business acquisition is not amortised, but reviewed for impairment annually.

(b) **MEMORANDUM**

To: The financial director
From: The accountant
Subject: Intangible assets

1   Introduction

1.1   It is group policy to write off all intangible assets over twenty years. This complies with the requirements of IAS 38.

1.2   However it is possible to select a longer period.

2   Determining the useful life of an intangible asset

2.1   IAS 38 states that an entity should assess the useful life of its intangible assets. Assets with a finite useful life are amortised over that useful life.

2.2   The useful life of an intangible asset depends on many factors. For example, many computer related assets have short lives because they are susceptible to technological obsolescence. Where an asset arises from contractual or legal rights, the period of the rights normally determines the useful life. However, some types of asset, such as brand names, may have very long lives or indefinite lives.

2.3   An intangible asset has an indefinite useful life when there is **no foreseeable limit** to the period over which the asset is expected to generate net cash inflows for the entity.

2.4   IAS 38 allows intangible assets to be treated as having indefinite lives. An intangible asset with an indefinite life is not amortised.

2.5   However, it is clearly not appropriate to treat assets as having an indefinite useful life unless this can be demonstrated to be the case. IAS 38 requires that the useful life of an asset should be realistic; it is not acceptable to select a useful life simply on the basis of practical simplicity or expediency.

2.6   Therefore, it is possible to avoid amortising intangible assets in theory; but the intangible assets needs to be able to be continually measured, so that impairment reviews can be carried out.

3   Future implications

3.1   Where an intangible asset is assessed as having an indefinite useful life, IAS 38 requires an impairment review to be carried out annually. In addition, the useful life of the asset should be reviewed each period to determine whether events and circumstances continue to support this assessment.

3.2   If an asset is assessed as having a finite useful life, then an impairment review is only required if there are indications that the carrying value is not recoverable.

3.3   Therefore adopting your proposals would mean carrying out an annual impairment review, which could be costly both in time and staff.

(c)   **Arguments for capitalisation**

(i)   The statement of financial position reflects commercial reality if brands are included, provided they meet fully the IAS 38 definition of a purchased intangible asset.

(ii)   IAS 38 does not permit non purchased or internally generated brands to be recognised. This may be unfair since predator entities could acquire entities with valuable brand names at less than true value.

(iii)   Many entities would argue that the inclusion of non-purchased brands might provide valuable information to users. However, the difficulties associated with revaluation and assigning an appropriate amortisation period may negate these benefits.

7 Radost

(a)   **Note to the statement of comprehensive income**

Defined benefit expense recognised in profit or loss

	$'000
Current service cost	3,750
Interest cost (10% × 45,000)	4,500
Expected return on plan assets (11% × 52,000)	(5,720)
Recognised actuarial gains (W1)	(40)
Profit or loss expense	2,490

Notes to the statement of financial position

Net defined benefit asset recognised in the statement of financial position

	$'000
Present value of defined benefit obligation	44,000
Fair value of plan assets	(64,170)
	(20,170)
Unrecognised actuarial gains (W1)	9,660
Net asset	(10,510)

Changes in the present value of the benefit obligation

	$'000
Opening defined benefit obligation	45,000
Interest cost (10% × 45,000)	4,500
Current service cost	3,750
Benefits paid	(8,000)
Actuarial gain (balancing figure)	(1,250)
Closing defined benefit obligation – per actuary	44,000

Changes in the fair value of plan assets

	$'000
Opening fair value of plan assets	52,000
Expected return on plan assets (11% × 52,000)	5,720
Contributions	12,000
Benefits paid	(8,000)
Actuarial gain (balancing figure)	2,450
Closing fair value of plan assets – per actuary	64,170

Working: Recognised/unrecognised gains and losses

	$'000	$'000
Corridor limits, higher of		
10% of b/d obligation (10% × 45,000)	4,500	
10% of b/d obligation assets (10% × 52,000)	5,200	
Corridor limit	5,200	
Unrecognised actuarial gains/losses b/d		6,000
Gain recognised in profit or loss (6,000 – 5,200)/20 years		(40)
Gain on obligation in the year		1,250
Gain on assets in the year		2,450
Unrecognised gains c/d		9,660

(b)   Legally the assets of the Radost pension scheme do not belong to Radost once the contributions are made. This is because to meet the definition of plan assets of a post-employment benefit scheme under IAS 19 *Employee benefits* they must be held by an entity/fund that is legally separate from the reporting entity. This provides the employees with a measure of protection should the entity go bankrupt or should the directors fraudulently attempt to plunder the assets of the pension scheme. Nevertheless, the substance of the arrangement is that the assets are held exclusively to pay the company's future defined benefit obligation and it is therefore logical that they should be shown in the company's statement of financial position reducing that liability. In the case of plan assets that exceed the value of the associated obligation (as in Radost's case), a net asset would normally be recognised in the company's statement of financial position on the grounds that the definition of an asset ('a resource controlled by the entity as a result of past events and from which future economic benefits are expected to flow to the entity') is met. In this case the 'benefits' are reduced future contributions as the scheme is in surplus.

8 DT Group

(a)   (i)   IAS 12 focuses on the statement of financial position in accounting for deferred taxation. It is based on the principle that a deferred tax liability or asset should be recognised if the recovery of the carrying amount of the asset or the settlement of the liability will result in higher or lower tax payments in the future than would be the case if that recovery or settlement were to have no tax consequences. Future tax consequences of past events determine the deferred tax liabilities or assets. (IAS 12 gives certain exceptions to this general rule, eg deferred tax is not provided on goodwill). The calculation of deferred tax balances is determined by looking at the difference between the tax base of an asset and its statement of financial position carrying value. Thus the calculation is focused on the statement of financial position.

Differences between the carrying amount of the asset and liability and its tax base are called 'temporary differences'. The word 'temporary' is used because it is a fundamental proposition in the IAS framework that an enterprise will realise its assets and settle its liabilities over time at which point the tax consequences will crystallise.

The objective of the temporary difference approach is to recognise the future tax consequences inherent in the carrying amounts of assets and liabilities in the statement of financial position. The approach looks at the tax payable if the assets and liabilities were realised for the pre tax amounts recorded in the statement of financial position. The presumption is that there will be recovery of statement of financial position items out of future revenues and tax needs to be provided in relation to such a recovery. This involves looking at temporary differences between the carrying values of the assets and liabilities and the tax base of the elements. The standard recognises two types of temporary differences, which are described as 'taxable' and 'deductible' temporary differences.)

(ii)   By definition, deferred tax involves the postponement of the tax liability and it is possible, therefore, to regard the deferred liability as equivalent to an interest free loan from the tax authorities. Thus it could be argued that it is appropriate to reflect this benefit of postponement by discounting the liability and recording a lower tax charge. This discount is then amortised over the period of deferment. The purpose of discounting is to measure future cash flows at their present value and, therefore, deferred tax balances can only be discounted if they can be viewed as future cash flows that are not already measured at their present value.

Some temporary differences clearly represent future tax cash flows. For example, where there is an accrual for an expense that is to be paid in the future and tax relief will only be given when the expense is paid. Some expenses are already measured on a discounted basis (eg retirement benefits), and it is not appropriate to discount the resulting deferred tax. However, there is controversy over whether it is valid to discount deferred tax when tax cash flows have already occurred as in the case of accelerated tax depreciation. It is argued that this temporary difference does not give rise to a future cash flow and there is no basis for discounting. An alternative view is that accelerated tax depreciation is a liability that will be repaid in the form of higher tax assessments in the future. It can be argued that there are two cash flows, with the second cash flow occurring on the reversal of the temporary difference, as the tax payment will be higher.

Discounting, however, makes the deferred tax computation more difficult to calculate and more subjective. Also there will be an additional cost in scheduling and calculating deferred taxation, as well as the problem of the determination of the discount rate. IAS12 specifically prohibits discounting.

(b)   **Calculation of deferred tax liability**

		Carrying amount $m	Tax base $m	Temporary differences $m
Goodwill (note 1)		14	–	–
Subsidiary (note 1)		76	60	16
Inventories (note 2)		24	30	(6)
Property, plant and equipment (note 3)		2,600	1,920	680
Other temporary differences				90
Liability for health care benefits		(100)	0	(100)
Unrelieved tax losses (note 4)				(100)
Property sold – tax due 30.11.20X4 (165/30%)				550
Temporary differences				1,130
Deferred tax liability	1,320	at 30%		396
(680 + 90 + 550)				
Deferred tax liability	16	at 25%		4
Deferred tax asset	(200)	at 30%		(60)
Deferred tax asset	(6)	at 25%		(1.5)
	1,130			338.5

Deferred tax liability b/d (given)	280
Deferred tax attributable to subsidiary to goodwill (76 – 60) × 25%	4
∴ Deferred tax expense for the year charged to P/L (balance)	54.5
Deferred tax liability c/d (from above)	338.5

Notes

1   As no deduction is available for the cost of goodwill in the subsidiary's tax jurisdiction, then the tax base of goodwill is zero. Paragraph 15(a) of IAS 12, states that DT Group should not recognise a deferred tax liability of the temporary difference associated in B's jurisdiction with the goodwill. Goodwill will be increased by the amount of the deferred tax liability of the subsidiary ie $4 million.

2   Unrealised group profit eliminated on consolidation are provided for at the receiving company's rate of tax (ie at 25%).

3   The tax that would arise if the properties were disposed of at their revalued amounts which was provided at the beginning of the year will be included in the temporary difference arising on the property, plant and equipment at 30 November 20X1.

4   DT Group has unrelieved tax losses of $300m. This will be available for offset against current year's profits ($110m) and against profits for the year ending 30 November 20X2 ($100m). Because of the uncertainty about the availability of taxable profits in 20X3, no deferred tax asset can be recognised for any losses which may be offset against this amount. Therefore, a deferred tax asset may be recognised for the losses to be offset against taxable profits in 20X2. That is $100m × 30% ie $30m.

Comment

The deferred tax liability of DT Group will rise in total by $335.5 million ($338.5m – $3m), thus reducing net assets, distributable profits, and post-tax earnings. The profit for the year will be reduced by $54.5 million which would probably be substantially more under IAS 12 than the old method of accounting for deferred tax. A prior period adjustment will occur of $280m – $3m as IAS are being applied for the first time (IFRS 1) ie $277m. The borrowing position of the company may be affected and the directors may decide to cut dividend payments. However, the amount of any unprovided deferred tax may have been disclosed under the previous GAAP standard used. IAS 12 brings this liability into the statement of financial position but if the bulk of the liability had already been disclosed the impact on the share price should be minimal.

9 PQR

Investment in debentures

Given that these debentures are planned to be held until redemption, they would be classed as a financial asset – investment held to maturity – held at amortised cost. This means that they are initially shown at their cost (including any transaction costs) and their value increased over time to the redemption value by applying a constant effective interest rate which takes into account not only the annual income due from the coupon, but also amortisation of the redemption premium. Their value is reduced by distributions received, ie the coupon.

Consequently the amortised cost valuation of these debentures at the year end would be:

Cost (40,000 – 6,000)	34,000	
Effective interest at 8.6%	2,924	shown as finance income
Coupon received (4% × 40,000)	(1,600)	Debited to cash
	35,324	

The debentures are an asset belonging to the equity holders and so as the increase in value is recognised until redemption, the equity of the business will increase, marginally reducing gearing.

Forward contract

Providing the forward meets the following criteria it qualifies for hedge accounting:

- Designated as a hedge on entering into the contract (including documentation of company's strategy)
- Expected to be 'highly effective' during its whole life (ie gains/losses on the hedging instrument vs losses/gains on the hedged item or *vice versa* fall within the ratio 80% to 125% – this is likely to be the case with a foreign currency forward contract, IAS 39, para AG108)
- The hedge effectiveness can be reliably measured.

A foreign currency forward contract can be argued to be either a hedge of the future cash flow or a hedge of the fair value of the machine to be purchased. IAS 39 *Financial Instruments: Recognition and Measurement* therefore allows foreign currency hedges of firm commitments to be classed as either a cash flow hedge or a fair value hedge.

If the contract is classed as a cash flow hedge, given that the machine is not yet recognised in the books, any gain or loss on the hedging instrument is split into two components:

- The effective portion of the hedge (which matches the change in expected cash flow) is recognised initially in other comprehensive income (ie recognised in reserves). It is transferred out of reserves either when the asset is recognised (adjusting the asset base and future depreciation) or when the cash flow is recognised in profit or loss (eg by deprecation) as a reclassification adjustment. Both options therefore apply the accruals concept.
- The ineffective portion of the hedge is recognised in profit or loss immediately as it has not hedged anything.

If the contract is classed as a fair value hedge, all gains and losses on the hedging instrument must be recognised immediately in profit or loss. However, in order to match those against the asset hedged, the gain or loss on the fair value of the asset hedged is also recognised in profit or loss (and as an asset or liability in the statement of financial position). This is arguably less transparent as it results in part of the asset value (the change in fair value) being recognised in the statement of financial position until the purchase actually occurs – consequently, IAS 39 allows the option to treat foreign currency forward contracts as a cash flow hedge.

Gearing will be different depending on whether the forward contract is accounted for as a cash flow hedge or a fair value hedge (and whether a gain or loss on the hedging instrument occurs). Gearing will be less volatile if a fair value hedge is used as the change in fair value of the hedged asset is also recognised offsetting gains or losses on the hedging instrument, whereas this is not the case until the asset is purchased (and recognised) for the cash flow hedge.

Redeemable preference shares

Redeemable preference shares, although called shares, are not, in substance, equity, they are a debt instrument, ie a loan made to the company which receives interest and is paid back at a later date.

Consequently, IAS 32 requires them to be classed as such, ie as a non-current liability in the statement of financial position. The 'dividends' paid will be shown in profit or loss as finance costs and accrued at the end of the year if outstanding, whether declared or not.

The shares are consequently a financial liability held at amortised cost. In this case, given that the shares are issued and redeemed at the same value, the effective interest rate and nominal coupon rate will be the same (6%) and each year $6,000 will be shown as a finance cost in profit or loss and the balance outstanding under non-current liabilities at each year end will be $100,000 as follows:

Cash received/ b/d value	100,000	
Effective interest at 6%	6,000	shown as finance cost
Coupon paid (6% × 100,000)	(6,000)	credited to cash
	100,000	

In the financial statements for the year ending 31 December 20X7, the shares will need to be reclassified as a current liability given that they will be repaid within one year.

Given that these shares are classed as a financial liability, gearing will be higher (as they are treated as debt) than if they were ordinary shares (which would be treated as equity).

10 Hedging

The futures contract was entered into to protect the company from a fall in oil prices and hedge the value of the inventories. It is therefore a fair value hedge.

The inventories are recorded at their cost of $2,600,000 (100,000 barrels at $26.00) on 1 July 20X2.

The futures contract has a zero value at the date it is entered into and so no entry is made in the financial statements.

Tutorial note: however, the existence of the contract and associated risk would be disclosed from that date in accordance with IFRS 7 (detail outside the scope of the syllabus).

At the year end the inventories must be shown at the lower of cost and net realisable value. Hence they will be shown at $2,250,000 (100,000 barrels at $22.50) and a loss of $350,000 recognised in profit or loss.

However, a gain has been made on the futures contract:

	$
The company has a contract to sell on 31 March 20X3 at $27.50	2,750,000
A contract entered into at the year end would sell at $23.25 on 31 March 20X3	2,325,000
Gain (= the value the contract could be sold on for to a third party)	425,000

The gain on the futures contract is also recognised in profit or loss:

		$	$
Dr	Future contract asset	$425,000	
Cr	Profit or loss		$425,000

The net effect on profit or loss is a gain of $75,000 ($425,000 less $350,000) whereas without the hedging contract the whole loss of $350,000 would have been the only impact on profit or loss.

Note

If the inventories had gained in value, this gain would also be recognised in profit or loss as hedge accounting is being applied (normally gains on inventories are not recognised until sale). A loss would have occurred on the futures contract, which would also be recognised in profit or loss.

11 Share-based payment

(a)   **Accounting entries**

31.12.X1

		$	$
DEBIT	Profit or loss (Staff costs)	188,000	
CREDIT	Equity reserve ((800 − 95) × 200 × $4 × 1/3)		188,000

31.12.X2

		$	$
DEBIT	Profit or loss (Staff costs) (W1)	201,333	
CREDIT	Equity reserve		201,333

31.12.X3

		$	$
DEBIT	Profit or loss (Staff costs) (W2)	202,667	
CREDIT	Equity reserve		202,667

Issue of shares:

		$	$
DEBIT	Cash (740 × 200 × $1.50)	222,000	
DEBIT	Equity reserve	592,000	
CREDIT	Share capital (740 × 200 × $1)		148,000
CREDIT	Share premium (balancing figure)		666,000

Workings

1   *Equity reserve at 31.12.X2*

		$
Equity b/d		188,000
∴ P/L charge		201,333
Equity c/d ((800 − 70) × 200 × $4 × 2/3)		389,333

2   *Equity reserve at 31.12.X3*

Equity b/d	389,333
∴ P/L charge	202,667
Equity c/d ((800 − 40 − 20) × 200 × $4 × 3/3)	592,000

(b)   **Cash-settled share-based payment**

If J&B had offered cash payments based on the value of the shares at vesting date rather than options, in each of the three years an accrual would be shown in the statement of financial position representing the expected amount payable based on the following:

No of employees estimated at the year end to be entitled to rights at the vesting date	×	Number of rights each	×	Fair value of each right at year end	×	Cumulative proportion of vesting period elapsed

The movement in the accrual would be charged to profit or loss representing further entitlements received during the year and adjustments to expectations accrued in previous years.

The accrual would continue to be adjusted (resulting in a profit or loss charge) for changes in the fair value of the right over the period between when the rights become fully vested and are subsequently exercised. It would then be reduced for cash payments as the rights are exercised.

12 Clean

(a)   **Why there was a need for an accounting standard dealing with provisions**

IAS 37 *Provisions, contingent liabilities and contingent assets* was issued to prevent entities from using provisions for creative accounting. It was common for entities to recognise material provisions for items such as future losses, restructuring costs or even expected future expenditure on repairs and maintenance of assets. These could be combined in one large provision (sometimes known as the 'big bath'). Although these provisions reduced profits in the period in which they were recognised (and were often separately disclosed on grounds of materiality), they were then released to enhance profits in subsequent periods. To make matters worse, provisions were often recognised where there was no firm commitment to incur expenditure. For example, an entity might set up a provision for restructuring costs and then withdraw from the plan, leaving the provision available for profit smoothing.

The criteria that need to be satisfied before a provision is recognised

IAS 37 states that a provision should not be recognised unless:

- An entity has a present obligation to transfer economic benefits as a result of a past transaction or event; and
- It is probable that a transfer of economic benefits will be required to settle the obligation; and
- A reliable estimate can be made of the amount of the obligation.

An obligation can be legal or constructive. An entity has a constructive obligation if:

- It has indicated to other parties that it will accept certain responsibilities (by an established pattern of past practice or published policies); and

- As a result, it has created a valid expectation on the part of those other parties that it will discharge those responsibilities.

(b) Two of the three conditions in IAS 37 are very clearly met. Clean will **incur expenditure** (transfer of economic benefits is virtually certain) and the directors have prepared **detailed estimates** of the amount.

Although Clean is not legally obliged to carry out the project, it appears that it has a **constructive obligation** to do so. IAS 37 states that an entity has a constructive obligation if both of the following apply.

(i) It has **indicated to other parties** that it will accept certain responsibilities (by an **established pattern** of past practice or published policies).

(ii) As a result, it has created a **valid expectation** on the part of those other parties that it will discharge those responsibilities.

Clean has a reputation of fulfilling its financial commitments once they have been publicly announced. Therefore the obligating event is the announcement of the proposal on 25 June 20X0, the obligation exists at 30 June 20X0 (the year end) and Clean is **required to recognise a provision**.

(c) Provision at 30 June 20X0:

		$'000
Expenditure on:		
30 June 20X1	30,000 × 0.926	27,780
30 June 20X2	30,000 × 0.857	25,710
30 June 20X3	40,000 × 0.794	31,760
		85,250

Provision at 30 June 20X1:

		$'000
Expenditure on:		
30 June 20X2	30,000 × 0.926	27,780
30 June 20X3	40,000 × 0.857	34,280
		62,060

(d) The charge to profit or loss for the year ended 30 June 20X1 consists of:

(i) Depreciation (85,250,000 ÷ 20) $ 4,262,500

This is reported in cost of sales.

The provision of $85,250,000 also represents an **asset** as it gives rise to future economic benefits (it enhances the performance of the factories). This is **capitalised and depreciated over 20 years** (the average useful life of the factories).

(ii) Unwinding of the discount (see working) $ 6,810,000

This is reported as a **finance cost**.

Working

	$'000
Provision at 1 July 20X0	85,250
Expenditure on 30 June 20X1	(30,000)
Unwinding of discount (balancing figure)	6,810
Provision at 30 June 20X1	62,060

Alternative calculation

	$'000
Expenditure on:	
30 June 20X1 (30,000 – 27,780)	2,220
30 June 20X2 (27,780 – 25,710)	2,070
30 June 20X3 (34,280 – 31,760)	2,520
	6,810

13 Ace

Year ended 31 March 20X2

Relationship

Ace Co has a 75% subsidiary (Deuce Co) and an 80% subsidiary (Trey Co).

Ace is a related party of Deuce and Trey and *vice versa*.

Deuce and Trey are also related parties because they are subject to 'common control'. Any transactions between Ace, Deuce and Trey need not be disclosed in Ace's *consolidated* accounts as they are eliminated.

Disclosures

Ace Co

- Intragroup sale of machine for $25,000 at profit of $5,000. No balances outstanding.
- Management services provided to Deuce (nil charge) and Trey (nil charge)

No disclosure is required in the group accounts of Ace of these items as they are eliminated.

Deuce

- Parent (and ultimate controlling party) is Ace Co
- Machine purchased from parent $25,000 (original cost $20,000) and depreciation charge $5,000. No amounts outstanding at year end.
- Purchase of management services from Ace (nil charge)

Trey

- Parent (and ultimate controlling party) is Ace Co
- Purchase of management services from Ace (nil charge)

For all transactions the nature of the related party relationship (ie parent, subsidiary, fellow subsidiary) should be disclosed.

Year ended 31 March 20X3

Relationship

Ace Co has a 100% subsidiary (Deuce Co) and an 80% subsidiary (Trey Co).

Ace is a related party of Deuce and Trey and *vice versa*. Deuce and Trey are related because they remain under common control. Any transactions between Ace, Deuce and Trey need not be disclosed in Ace's *consolidated* accounts as they are eliminated.

Disclosures

Ace Co

- Management services provided to Deuce (nil charge) and Trey ($10,000 outstanding)

No disclosure is required in the group accounts of Ace of these items as they are eliminated.

Deuce

- Parent (and ultimate controlling party) is Ace Co

Disclosures of intragroup transactions is still required even though Deuce is a wholly-owned subsidiary:

- Sale of inventories to Trey for $15,000 (original cost $12,000) all sold on, no amounts outstanding at year end
- Purchase of management services from Ace (nil charge)

Trey

- Parent (and ultimate controlling party) is Ace Co
- Purchase of inventories from Deuce $15,000 (original cost $12,000) all sold, no amounts outstanding at year end
- Purchase of management services from Ace costing $10,000. All outstanding at year end

For all transactions the nature of the related party relationship (ie parent, subsidiary, fellow subsidiary) should be disclosed.

14 Able

(a)   (i)   IAS 17 *Leases* differentiates between operating and finance leases.

A finance lease:

(1)   Substantially transfers all of the risks and rewards incident to ownership of an asset to a lessee.

(2)   Should be capitalised in the accounts at the fair value of the leased asset or, if lower, the present value of minimum lease payments over the lease term using the interest rate implicit in the lease (otherwise the lessee's marginal borrowing rate may be used). Any residual payments guaranteed by the lessee should also be included.

(3)   The capitalised asset is depreciated over the shorter of the lease term or useful life.

(4)   Interest and principal components of each payment must be identified and allocated to accounting periods, thus reducing the lease liability.

(5)   Finance charges are calculated as the difference between the total of the minimum lease payments and value of the liability to the lessor. Finance charges are applied to produce a constant periodic rate of charge on the liability in profit or loss.

An operating lease:

(1)   Is any lease which is not a finance lease.

(2)   Lease rentals are charged to profit or loss on a systematic basis which represents the pattern of the benefits derived by the users from the leased asset.

(ii)   **Current standards do not adequately deal with leases. The problems are as follows.**

(1)   The rights and obligations under operating leases are not recognised in the lessee's accounts. IAS 17 takes the view that if risks and rewards of ownership are *not* substantially transferred to a lessee then the lease is classified as an operating lease.

(2)   The issue lies with the definition of 'substantial', which has been judged against quantitative not qualitative factors. If a lease is non-cancellable and the present value of the minimum lease payments is greater than or substantially equal to the asset's fair value or the lease term covers the major part of the asset's life, then the lease is usually treated as a finance lease.

(3)   'Substantially equal' has been taken to be in excess of 90% of the fair value of the leased asset and the figure of 75% of the life has typically been used, but these terms are not defined in IAS 17.

(4)   However, many leases have been designed which are in *substance* finance leases but, when judged in quantitative terms, are classified as operating leases.

(5)   Factors such as relative responsibilities of lessor/lessee for maintenance, insurance and bearing losses have also blurred the distinction and classification of leases.

(6)   Long term finance leases have often been packaged as operating leases in order to represent a source of 'off balance sheet finance'.

(7)   Specific measures used to enable classification as operating leases include:

- Contingent rentals which are excluded from the calculation of minimum lease payments
- Making the implicit interest rate impossible to calculate, so the lessee uses an estimated rate which could reduce the present value of minimum lease payments
- For leases of land and buildings, it is expected that the risks and rewards of ownership of land cannot pass without legal transfer of ownership. Companies may allocate as much as possible to the land element, thus ensuring the buildings element is also treated as an operating lease by reducing the present value of the minimum lease payments.

(b)   (i)   **Electrical distribution system**

Where a lessee enters a sale and leaseback transaction resulting in an operating lease, then the original asset should be treated as sold. If the transaction is at fair value then immediate recognition of the profit/loss should occur.

If the transaction is above fair value, then the profit based on fair value of $65m should be recognised. The balance in excess of fair value of $100m (198 – 98) should be deferred and amortised over the period for which the asset is expected to be used (10 years) ie $10m pa.

If the sales value is not at fair value, the operating lease rentals of $24m are likely to have been adjusted for the excess price paid. For Able the sales value is more than twice the fair value and the use of the *Framework* and standards dictate the substance of a transaction is essentially one of sale and a loan back equal to the deferred income element. The entity may have shown the excess over fair value as a loan and part of the costs of the operating lease will essentially be repayment of capital and interest ($12m pa).

(ii)   **Sale and leaseback of plant**

This appears to create a finance lease because the lease term is for the major part of the asset's remaining economic life and the present value of the minimum lease payments is substantially equal to the fair value ($43.5 + ($43.5m × 2.49))= $151.82m, compared to fair value $152m). The lease also contains a bargain purchase option. Able seems to enjoy all the risks and rewards of ownership.

Under IAS 17, where a sale and leaseback transaction results in a finance lease, any excess of sale proceeds over the carrying amount should be deferred and recognised over the lease term. Therefore the excess proceeds over $100m ($52m) will be amortised over four years at $13m pa. The asset and the lease obligation are recorded at the sale value of $152m. Depreciation is charged on the new asset value and if the revaluation reserve is transferred to revenue reserves, this will also occur over the four year lease term.

15 Highland

HIGHLAND GROUP
CONSOLIDATED STATEMENT OF COMPREHENSIVE INCOME FOR THE YEAR ENDED 31 MARCH 20X8

	$'000
Revenue $(5,000 + 3,000 + (2,910 \times {}^4/_{12}))$	8,970
Cost of sales $(3,000 + 2,300 + (2,820 \times {}^4/_{12}))$	(6,240)
Gross profit	2,730
Administrative expenses $(1,000 + 500 + (150 \times {}^4/_{12}) + (W4) 63.5 + (W5) 5 -$ (W6) 85 + (W8) 65)	(1,599)
Finance income* $(230 + (W3) 35 - (W6) 85 - (W6) 40)$	140
Finance costs $(50 + (210 \times {}^4/_{12}) - (W3) 70)$	(50)
Profit before tax	1,221
Income tax expense $(300 + 50)$	(350)
Profit for the year	871
Other comprehensive income, net of tax $(130 + 40 + (120 \times {}^4/_{12}))$	210
total comprehensive income for the year	1,081

	$'000
Profit attributable to:	
Owners of the parent $(871 + 26)$	897
Non-controlling interests (W2)	(26)
	871
Total comprehensive income attributable to:	
Owners of the parent $(1,081 + 4)$	1,085
Non-controlling interests (W2)	(4)
	1,081

* Other income becomes finance income as only interest income from Buchan remains

Workings

1   *Group structure*

```
              Highland
             /        \
      Aviemore         Buchan
        80%            65%  (owned for 4 months)
```

2   *Non-controlling interests*

	Aviemore $'000	Buchan $'000	Aviemore $'000	Buchan $'000
Profit/(loss) for the year (B: 270 loss $\times {}^4/_{12}$)	100	(90)		
Total comp income for the year (B: 150 loss $\times {}^4/_{12}$)			140	(50)
Unrealised profit on disposal (W4)	(63.5)		(63.5)	
FV depreciation (W5)		(5)		(5)
	36.5	(95)	76.5	(55)
NCI share (20%/35%/20%/35%)	7.3 DR	(33.3) CR	15.3 DR	(19.3) CR
	\multicolumn{2}{c}{(26.0) CR}		\multicolumn{2}{c}{(4.0) CR}	

Hence, rounding to nearest $'000, NCI *increases* profit/total comprehensive income attributable to owners of the parent.

3   Interest income/payable

$'000

Interest income: $2,100,000 × 10%   × 6/12   105   recorded on 1 October 20X7
                                       × 6/12   105   to be recorded
                                                 210

Pre-acquisition   Post-acquisition
$210 × \frac{8}{12} = 140$ $(210 × \frac{4}{12}) = 70$

Genuine finance income   Cancel on consolidation:
                                       DR Finance income 70
                                       CR Finance costs   70

Overall adjustment to interest income:

	$'000
Interest income from Buchan not yet recorded (210 × 6/12)	105
Less: post acquisition intragroup element (210 × $\frac{4}{12}$)	(70)
	35

4   Unrealised profit on disposal of freehold property

		$'000	$'000
Land	Proceeds	300	
	Net book value	(100)	
	Profit on disposal (in Aviemore)		200
Buildings	Proceeds (800 – 300)	500	
	Net book value (800 × $\frac{40}{50}$)	(640)	
	Loss on disposal (in Aviemore)		(140)
Proportion of loss depreciated (1/40)			3.5
			63.5

5   Fair value depreciation

	At acquisition	Additional depreciation*	At year end
	$'000	$'000	$'000
Property, plant and equipment (500 – 350)	150	(5)	145
	150	(5)	145

* Additional depreciation = $^{150}/_{10}$ = 15 per annum × $^4/_{12}$ = $5,000

6   Intragroup cancellations

Cancel management services:

DR Other income	$85,000
CR Administrative expenses	$85,000

Cancel dividend income from Aviemore:

DR Other income (50 × 80%) $40,000
CR Aviemore's retained earnings $40,000

7 Goodwill

	Aviemore		Buchan	
	$'000	$'000	$'000	$'000
Consideration transferred		5,000		2,600
FV net assets acquired:				
Net book value per question	4,000		3,350	
Fair value adjustment (W5)	-		150	
	4,000		3,500	
Group share	× 80%	(3,200)	× 65%	(2,275)
		1,800		325

8 Impairment losses

	Aviemore	Buchan
	$'000	$'000
Goodwill (W7)	1,800	325
'Notional' goodwill (× 100%/80%) (× 100%/65%)	2,250	500
Net assets at 31 March 20X7	4,450	3,300
	6,700	3,800
Recoverable amount	7,040	3,700
Impairment loss	0	100
Allocated to:		
'Notional' goodwill	–	100
Other assets	–	–
	0	100
Recognised impairment loss:		
Recognised goodwill (100 × 65%)	–	65
Other assets (100%)	–	–

16 Armoury

ARMOURY GROUP
CONSOLIDATED STATEMENT OF FINANCIAL POSITION AS AT 31 DECEMBER 20X9

	$'000
Non-current assets	
Property, plant and equipment (14,500 + 12,140 + 17,500)	44,140
Goodwill (W2)	3,580
	47,720
Current assets	
Inventories (6,300 + 2,100 + 450)	8,850
Trade receivables (4,900 + 2,000 + 2,320)	9,220
Cash (500 + 1,440 + 515)	2,455
	20,525
	68,245

Equity attributable to owners of the parent
Share capital – 50c ordinary shares | 5,000
Retained earnings (W4) | 40,680
| 45,680

Non-controlling interests (W4) | 12,600
| 58,280

Current liabilities (5,700 + 2,280 + 1,985) | 9,965
| 68,245

Workings

1 *Group structure*

B

1.1.X5
$\frac{6,000}{8,000} = 75\%$ ∴ NCI: 25%

R

$\frac{4,000}{5,000} = 80\%$

31.12.X2

P   Effective interest in P (75% × 80%)   60%
∴ NCI   40%
   100%

2 *Goodwill*

	$'000	Group $'000	NCI in Rifle $'000	NCI in Pistol $'000
Consideration transferred		10,000		
FV of non-controlling interests			980	4,600
Fair value of identifiable net assets acquired:				
Rifle Share capital	4,000			
Pre-acquisition retained earnings	8,000			
Investment in Pistol	(9,000)			
	3,000 × 75%	(2,250) × 25%	(750)	
Pistol Share capital	2,500			
Pre-acquisition retained earnings	6,500			
	9,000 × 60%	(5,400) × 40%		(3,600)
		2,350	230	1,000

3,580

3 *Retained earnings*

	Bayonet $'000	Rifle $'000	Pistol $'000
Per question	25,500	20,400	16,300
Retained earnings at acquisition		(8,000)	(6,500)
	25,500	12,400	9,800
Rifle– share of post acquisition earnings (12,400 × 75%)	9,300		
Pistol– share of post acquisition earnings (9,800 × 60%)	5,880		
	40,680		

4   *Non-controlling interests*

	Rifle	Pistol
	$'000	$'000
Net assets at year end per question	24,400	18,800
Less: cost of investment in Pistol	(9,000)	
	15,400	18,800
Non-controlling interest share	× 25%	× 40%
	3,850	7,520
Non-controlling interests in goodwill (W2)	230	1,000
	4,080	8,520
		12,600

17 Murder, Mystery and Suspense

MURDER GROUP
CONSOLIDATED STATEMENT OF FINANCIAL POSITION AS AT 31 DECEMBER 20X7

	$'m
Non-current assets	
Property, plant and equipment (2,458 + 1,410 + 870)	4,738
Goodwill (W2)	320
	5,058
Current assets	
Inventories (450 + 200 + 260 – (W5) 52)	858
Trade receivables (610 + 365 + 139)	1,114
Cash (240 + 95 + 116)	451
	2,423
	7,481
Equity attributable to owners of the parent	
Ordinary share capital	500
Share premium	250
Retained earnings (W3)	3,605
	4,355
Non-controlling interests (W4)	1,193
	5,548
Current liabilities	
Trade payables (1,130 + 418 + 385)	1,933
	7,481

Workings

1   *Group structure*

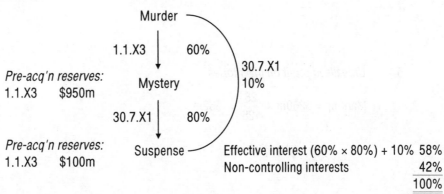

2   *Goodwill (including step acquisition of Suspense)*

	Murder in Mystery			Mystery in Suspense		Murder in Suspense	NCI in Suspense
	Group		NCI				
	$m	$m	$m	$m	$m	$m	$m
Consideration transferred		900		(240 × 60%)	144	50	
Fair value NCI			536				210
Fair value of NA acquired							
Share capital	200			100			
Share premium	120			50			
Pre-acq retained earnings	950			100			
	1,270	60%	40%	250	48%	10%	42%
Group/NCI share		(762)	(508)		(120)	(25)	(105)
		138	28		24	25	105

320

3   *Retained earnings*

	Murder	Mystery	Suspense
	$m	$m	$m
Per question	2,805	1,572	850
P/L gain on investment in Suspense (50 – 27)	23		
Less: unrealised profit (W5)		(52)	
Retained earnings at acq'n		(950)	(100)
		570	750
Mystery – share of post acq'n earnings (570 × 60%)	342		
Suspense – share of post acq'n earnings (750 × 58%)	435		
Impairment losses to date	(0)		
	3,605		

4   *Non-controlling interests*

	Mystery	Suspense
	$m	$m
Net assets at year end per question	1,892	1,000
PUP (W2)	(52)	
Less: cost of investment in Suspense	(240)	
	1,600	1,000
Non-controlling interests	× 40%	× 42%
	640	420
Non-controlling interests in goodwill (W3)	28	105
	668	525

1,193

5   *Unrealised profit on inventories*

Mark-up = $260m × $\frac{25}{125}$ = $52m

18 Holmes & Deakin

(a)   HOLMES
STATEMENT OF COMPREHENSIVE INCOME FOR THE YEAR ENDED 31 MAY 20X3

	$'000
Profit before gain on disposal of shares in subsidiary	130
Gain on disposal of shares in subsidiary (W5)	100
Profit before tax	230
Income tax expense (40 + (W5) 30)	(70)
Profit for the year	160
Other comprehensive income, net of tax	20
Total comprehensive income for the year	180

STATEMENT OF CHANGES IN EQUITY (TOTAL)	$m
Balance at 1 June 20X2 (810 – 110)	700
Total comprehensive income for the year	180
Balance at 31 May 20X3	880

(b)   HOLMES GROUP CONSOLIDATED STATEMENT OF COMPREHENSIVE INCOME
FOR THE YEAR ENDED 31 MAY 20X3

	$m
Profit before tax (130 + 60)	190
Income tax expense (40 + 20)	(60)
Profit/ for the year	130
Other comprehensive income, net of tax (20 + 10)	30
Total comprehensive income for the year	160

Profit attributable to:	
Owners of the parent	122
Non-controlling interests $(40 \times \frac{9}{12} \times 15\%) + (40 \times \frac{3}{12} \times 35\%)$	8
	130

Total comprehensive income attributable to:	
Owners of the parent	150
Non-controlling interests $(50 \times \frac{9}{12} \times 15\%) + (50 \times \frac{3}{12} \times 35\%)$	10
	160

(c)   HOLMES GROUP
CONSOLIDATED STATEMENT OF FINANCIAL POSITION AS AT 31.5.X3

	$m
Non-current assets	
Property, plant and equipment (535 + 178)	713
Goodwill (W2)	80
	793
Current assets	
Inventories (320 + 190)	510
Trade receivables (250 + 175)	425
Cash (80 + 89)	169
	1,104
	1,897

Equity atttributable to owners of the parent				
Share capital $1 ordinary shares				500
Reserves (W3)				477.5
				977.5
Non-controlling interests (W4)				157.5
				1,135.0
Current liabilities				
Trade payables (295 + 171)				466
Income tax payable (80 + 60 + (W5) 30)				170
Provisions (95 + 31)				126
				762
				1,897

(d) STATEMENT OF CHANGES IN EQUITY (TOTAL COLUMN)

	Group	NCI	Total
	$m	$m	$m
Balance at 1 June 20X2 (500 + (W7) 285)/((370 – 50) × 15%)+ (W2) 12)	785	60	845
Adjustment to parent's equity on sale of non-controlling interests ((W6) 72.5 – (W5) 30)	42.5		42.5
Increase in non-controlling interests (71.5(W6) + 16)		87.5	87.5
Total comprehensive income for the year	150	10	160.0
Balance at 31 May 20X3 (from SOFP)	977.5	157.5	1,135.0

Shown for clarity
(not required)

Workings

1   *Timeline*

2   *Goodwill*

	$m	Group $m	NCI $m
Consideration transferred/FV of non-controlling interests		255	45
Fair value of identifiable net assets acquired:			
Share capital	200		
Pre-acquisition reserves	20		
	220 × 85%	(187) × 15%	(33)
		68	12
Increase in NCI in goodwill (W6)		(16)	16
		52	28

80

3   Group reserves at 31 May 20X3

	Holmes $m	Deakin 85% $m	Deakin 65% ret'd $m
Per question/at date of disposal (170 – (50 × 3/12))	310	157.5	170
Adjustment to parent's equity on disposal (W6)	72.5		
Tax on parent's gain (W5)	(30)		
Reserves at acquisition/date of disposal (as above)		(20)	(157.5)
		137.5	12.5
Share of post acquisition reserves:			
Deakin – 85% (137.5 × 85%)	116.9		
Deakin – 65% (12.5 × 65%)	8.1		
	477.5		

4   Non-controlling interests (SOFP)

	$m	$m
Net assets per question at year end	370	
NCI share (35%)		129.5
NCI in goodwill (W2)		28.0
		157.5

5   Gain on disposal of shares in parent's separate financial statements

	$m
Fair value of consideration received	160
Less: original cost of shares (255 × 20%/85%)	(60)
Parent gain	100
Less: tax on parent's gain (30%)	(30)
	70

6   Adjustment to parent's equity on disposal of shares in group financial statements

	$m
Fair value of consideration received	160
Increase in NCI in net assets at disposal [(370 – (50 × $\frac{3}{12}$)) × 20%]	(71.5)
Increase in NCI in goodwill ((W2) 12 × 20%/15%)	(16)
	72.5

7   Reserves brought forward

	Holmes $m	Deakin $m
Per question (31.5.X3)	310	170
Less: comprehensive income for the year	(110)	(50)
Reserves at acquisition		(20)
	200	100
Deakin – share of post acquisition reserves (100 × 85%)	85	
	285	

19 Harvard

(a)   HARVARD GROUP
CONSOLIDATED STATEMENT OF FINANCIAL POSITION AT 31 DECEMBER 20X5

	$'000
Non-current assets	
Property, plant and equipment (2,870 + (W2) 1,350)	4,220
Goodwill (W4)	184
	4,404
Current assets	
Inventories (1,990 + (W2) 2,310)	4,300
Trade receivables (1,630 + (W2) 1,270)	2,900
Cash at bank and in hand (240 + (W2) 560)	800
	8,000
	12,404
Equity attributable to owners of the parent	
Share capital ($1)	118
Retained reserves (W5)	3,019
	3,137
Non-controlling interests ((W2) 4,280 × 25%) + (W4) 37)	1,107
	4,244
Non-current liabilities	
Loans	1,920
Current liabilities	
Trade payables (5,030 + (W2) 1,210)	6,240
	12,404

(b)   CONSOLIDATED STATEMENT OF COMPREHENSIVE INCOME FOR YEAR ENDED 31 DECEMBER 20X5

	$'000
Revenue (40,425 + (W3) 25,900)	66,325
Cost of sales (35,500 + (W3) 20,680)	(56,180)
Gross profit	10,145
Distribution and administrative expenses (4,400 + (W3) 1,560)	(5,960)
Profit before tax	4,185
Income tax expense (300 + (W3) 1,260)	(1,560)
Profit for the year	2,625
Other comprehensive income:	
Exchange differences on translating foreign operations (W6)	316
Total comprehensive income for the year	2,941
Profit attributable to:	
Owners of the parent (2,625 – 600)	2,025
Non-controlling interests ((W3) 2,400 × 25%)	600
	2,625
Total comprehensive income attributable to:	
Owners of the parent (2,941 – 678.25)	2,262.75
Non-controlling interests [((W3) 2,400 + (W7) 297) × 25%] + (W4) 4]	678.25
	2,941.00

STATEMENT OF CHANGES IN EQUITY FOR THE YEAR ENDED 31 DECEMBER 20X5 (EXTRACT)

	$'000 Retained Reserves
Balance at 1 January 20X5 (W5)	1,456
Dividends	(700)
Total comprehensive income for the year (per SOCI)	2,263
Balance at 31 December 20X5 (W5)	3,019

Workings

1   *Group structure*

Harvard

31.12.X2 $\dfrac{1,011}{1,348}$ = 75%

Pre-acq'n ret'd earnings = PLN 2,876,000

Krakow

2   *Translation of Krakow – statement of financial position*

	PLN '000	Rate	$'000
Property, plant and equipment	4,860	3.6	1,350
Inventories	8,316	3.6	2,310
Trade receivables	4,572	3.6	1,270
Cash	2,016	3.6	560
	19,764		5,490
Share capital	1,348	4.4	306
Retained reserves			
– pre-acquisition	2,876	4.4	654 ⎫ 3,974
– post-acquisition	11,184	β	3,320 ⎭
	15,408		4,280
Trade payables	4,356	3.6	1,210
	19,764		5,490

3   *Translation of Krakow – statement of comprehensive income*

	PLN '000	Rate	$'000
Revenue	97,125	3.75	25,900
Cost of sales	(77,550)	3.75	(20,680)
Gross profit	19,575		5,220
Distribution and administrative expenses	(5,850)	3.75	(1,560)
Profit before tax	13,725		3,660
Income tax expense	(4,725)	3.75	(1,260)
Profit for the year	9,000		2,400

4 Goodwill

	Group PLN '000	NCI PLN '000	NCI PLN '000	Rate	Group $'000	NCI $'000	Total $'000
Consideration transferred/FV NCI (840/270 × 4.4)		3,696	1,188				
Less: Share of net assets acquired							
Share capital	1,348						
Retained earnings	2,876						
	4,224						
Group/NCI share (75%/25%)		(3,168)	(1,056)				
Goodwill at acquisition		528	132	4.4	120	30	150
Exchange gain 20X3 – 20X4		-	-	β	12	3	15
Goodwill at 31 December 20X4		528	132	4.0	132	33	165
Exchange gain 20X5		-	-	β	15	4	19
Goodwill at year end		528	132	3.6	147	37	184

5 Proof of retained reserves

	$'000
(i) **At 31 December 20X5**	
Harvard	502
Add: post-acquisition retained reserves of Krakow*	2,490
((W2) 3,320 × 75%)	
Goodwill impairment losses to date	(0)
Exchange differences on goodwill ((W4) 12 + 15)	27
	3,019

* **Note**. This is calculated by comparing the net assets at the two dates.

	$'000
(ii) **At 31 December 20X4**	
Harvard (502 – (943 – 700))	259
Add: post-acquisition retained earnings of Krakow	1,185
((PLN15,408 – 9,000 + 3,752)/4) – (PLN4,224/4.4) × 75%)	
Goodwill impairment losses to 31.12.X4	(0)
Exchange differences on goodwill (W4)	12
	1,456

6 Exchange differences arising during the year

	SOCI $'000
On translation of net assets of Krakow:	
Closing NA at CR (W2)	4,280
Opening NA @ OR [(15,408 – 9,000 + 3,752)/4.0]	(2,540)
	1,740
Less: retained profit as translated ((W3) 2,400 – 3,752/3.92)	(1,443)
	297
On goodwill (W4)	19
	316

20 Porter

PORTER GROUP
STATEMENT OF CASH FLOWS FOR THE YEAR ENDED 31 MAY 20X6

	$'m	$'m
Cash flows from operating activities		
Profit before taxation	112	
Adjustments for:		
Depreciation	44	
Impairment losses on goodwill (W2)	3	
Foreign exchange loss (W8)	2	
Investment income – share of profit of associate	(12)	
Investment income – gains on financial assets at fair value through profit or loss	(6)	
Interest expense	16	
	159	
Increase in trade receivables (132 – 112 – 16)	(4)	
Decrease in inventories (154 – 168 – 20)	34	
Decrease in trade payables (110 – 98 – 12 – (W8) 17 PPE payable)	(17)	
Cash generated from operations	172	
Interest paid (W7)	(12)	
Income taxes paid (W6)	(37)	
Net cash from operating activities		123
Cash flows from investing activities		
Acquisition of subsidiary, net of cash acquired (26 – 8)	(18)	
Purchase of property, plant and equipment (W1)	(25)	
Purchase of financial assets (W4)	(10)	
Dividend received from associate (W3)	11	
Net cash used in investing activities		(42)
Cash flows from financing activities		
Proceeds from issuance of share capital	18	
(332 + 212 – 300 – 172 – (80 × 60%/2 × $2.25))		
Proceeds from long-term borrowings (380 – 320)	60	
Dividend paid	(45)	
Dividends paid to non-controlling interests (W5)	(4)	
Net cash from financing activities		29
Net decrease in cash and cash equivalents		110
Cash and cash equivalents at the beginning of the year		48
Cash and cash equivalents at the end of the year		158

Workings

1   *Additions to property, plant and equipment*

PROPERTY, PLANT AND EQUIPMENT

	$'m		$'m
b/d	812		
Revaluation	58	Depreciation	44
Acquisition of subsidiary	92		
Additions on credit (W8)	15		
∴ Additions for cash	25	c/d	958
	1,002		1,002

2 *Impairment losses on goodwill*

GOODWILL

	$'m		$'m
b/d	10		
Acq'n of subsidiary		∴ Impairment losses	3
[(80 × 60%/2 x 2.25) + 26 − (120 × 60%)]	8		
		c/d	15
	18		18

3 *Dividends received from associate*

INVESTMENT IN ASSOCIATE

	$'m		$'m
b/d	39		
P/L	12	∴ Dividends received	11
OCI	8		
		c/d	48
	59		59

4 *Purchase of financial assets*

FINANCIAL ASSETS AT FAIR VALUE THROUGH PROFIT OR LOSS

	$'m		$'m
b/d	0		
P/L	6		
∴ Additions	10		
		c/d	16
	16		16

5 *Dividends paid to non-controlling interests*

NON-CONTROLLING INTERESTS

	$'m		$'m
		b/d	28
∴ Dividends paid	4	TCI	12
c/d	84	Acquisition of subsidiary (120 × 40%)	48
			88
	88		

6 *Income taxes paid*

INCOME TAX PAYABLE

	$'m		$'m
		b/d (deferred tax)	26
		b/d (current tax)	22
		P/L	34
∴ Income taxes paid	37	OCI	17
c/d (deferred tax)	38	Acquisition of subsidiary	4
c/d (current tax)	28		
	103		103

7   Interest paid

INTEREST PAYABLE

	$'m		$'m
		b/d	4
		P/L	16
∴ Interest paid	12		
c/d	8		
	20		20

8   Foreign currency transaction

Transactions recorded on: $'m

1) 5 March   DEBIT Property, plant and equipment (102m/6.8)   15
                CREDIT Payables   15

2) 31 May   Payable = 102m/6.0 = $17m

                DEBIT P/L (Admin expenses)   2

                CREDIT Payables (17 – 15)   2

21 Grow by acquisition

(a)   **Note 1**

The substance of this transaction is that X has made a loan of $2.4m to A. All aspects of the 'sale' should be eliminated, as follows.

(i)   Reduce revenue by $2,400,000.
(ii)   Reduce cost of sales by $2,400,000 × 100/160 = $1,500,000.
(iii)   Reduce gross profit by ($2,400,000 – $1,500,000) = $900,000.
(iv)   Increase loans by $2,400,000.

Note 2

To be comparable, the non-current assets of A and B should either both be shown at cost or both at a revalued amount, with the revaluation done on the same basis. It is not feasible to 'revalue' A's non-current assets for purposes of comparison. However, B's non-current assets can be shown at cost by reversing out the revaluation, as follows.

(i)   Reduce non-current assets by $5,000,000.
(ii)   Reduce the revaluation reserve to nil.
(iii)   Reduce cost of sales by $1,000,000. This is the excess depreciation no longer required.
(iv)   Increase gross profit by $1,000,000.

Summary

A

Item	Per original f/s	Adjustment	New figure
	$'000	$'000	$'000
Revenue	68,000	(2,400)	65,600
Cost of sales	42,000	(1,500)	40,500
Gross profit	26,000	(900)	25,100
Profit from operations	8,000	(900)	7,100
Inventory	6,000	1,500	7,500
Short term borrowing	–	2,400	2,400
Total borrowings (4,000 + 16,000)	20,000	2,400	22,400
Shareholders' funds	23,500	900	22,600

B

Item	Per original f/s	Adjustment	New figure
Non-current assets	35,050	(5,000)	30,050
Revaluation reserve	5,000	(5,000)	Nil
Cost of sales	45,950	(1,000)	44,950
Gross profit	20,050	1,000	21,050
Profit from operations	6,050	1,000	7,050
Shareholders' funds	22,050	(5,000)	17,050

(b) All monetary amounts in $'000

Ratio	A		B	
Return on capital employed	$\dfrac{7,100}{22,600 + 22,400}$	= 15.8%	$\dfrac{7,050}{17,050 + 6,000 + 18,000}$	= 17.2%
Gross profit margin	$\dfrac{25,100}{65,600}$	= 38.3%	$\dfrac{21,050}{66,000}$	= 31.9%
Turnover of capital employed	$\dfrac{65,600}{45,000}$	= 1.5	$\dfrac{66,000}{41,050}$	= 1.6
Leverage	$\dfrac{22,400}{45,000}$	= 49.8%	$\dfrac{24,000}{41,050}$	= 58.5%

BPP note. The effective loan of $2.4m could arguably be excluded from borrowings as it is short term.

(c) The adjustments carried out to make the financial statements of the two entities comparable make it **far less easy to decide** which entity to target. The ratios are now far more similar. **A** has a **higher gross profit and gross profit margin**. However, the **return on capital employed is lower.** The main reason for this is that A's other operating expenses are higher than B's. The revenue figures are now nearly identical due to the elimination of the 'sale' from the accounts of A. The asset turnover ratios, both before and after adjustments, do not show significant differences.

Where **A** has an **advantage** over B is in **the leverage ratio**. Leverage of both entities has increased, but more so in the case of B. Whether this influences the directors' decision depends on whether they intend to change the financial structure of the company.

Overall it would appear that **B** would be a **better investment**. However, there is not a great deal to choose between the two entities, and this exercise shows the importance of adjusting financial statements to achieve uniform accounting policies when making this kind of decision. It is notable that the 'sale' by A was **incorrectly** accounted for, while B's revaluation is **permissible**.

22 German competitor

> **Tutorial note.** You do not need to know about German accounting practice to answer this question, just a basic knowledge of the differences between the European and UK models and your common sense! Think of this as an interpretation of accounts questions.

To: Managing Director
From: An Accountant
Date: xx.xx.xx
Re: *Hilde GmbH*

(a) *Analysis of performance plus commentary (□ million)*

Income statement	20X4	20X5	% Increase (decrease)
Sales	1,270	1,890	49
Cost of sales			
Material purchased	400	740	
De-stocking of materials	40	90	
Material cost	440	830	89
Labour cost	285	500	75
Depreciation	150	200	33
Current assets written off	20	30	50
Other operating expenses	40	50	25
Finished goods inventory increase	(80)	(120)	50
	855	1,490	
Operating profit before other income	415	400	(4)
Profit rate on revenue	32%	21%	
Other operating income	50	75	50

Cash flows

	E million
Share capital issued	200
Increased payables	75
Increased accruals	20
Profit ploughed back (185 + 200)	385
	680
These flows were used to finance:	
Purchases of plant (550 + 200)	750
Net inventory	30
More credit to customers	80
	860
Difference: reduction in cash reserves	180

Other relevant performance measures

	20X4	20X5

Receivables turnover

$$= \frac{\text{Trade receivables}}{\text{Sales}} \times 365$$

$20X4$: $\frac{100}{1,270} \times 365 = 29$ days

$20X5$: $\frac{180}{1,890} \times 365 = 35$ days

Current ratio

$$= \frac{\text{Current assets}}{\text{Current liabilities}}$$

$20X4$: $\frac{420+70}{350} = 1.4$

$20X5$: $\frac{350+50}{425} = 0.94$

Quick ratio

$$= \frac{\text{Current assets} - \text{Inventory}}{\text{Current liabilities}}$$

$20X4$: $\frac{100+200+70}{350} = 1.06$

$20X5$: $\frac{180+20+50}{425} = 0.59$

Commentary

(i) Material costs and labour costs have risen at an alarming rate in 20X5 and to a certain extent other costs have also increased substantially. These increases are far greater than the increase in revenue. A lack of co-ordination of production to sales has created a substantial build up of finished goods in inventory.

(ii) Interest costs and other operating income have both increased substantially, but because debt and investments (respectively) are not shown on the statement of financial position it is not possible to judge why these rises have taken place. One possibility is that the increases in the value of land and buildings represent additions which are being rented out.

(iii) Payables have increased only slightly considering the increases in purchases during the year. This may indicate that the company's trade payables are taking a very firm line with the company and thus the trade payables balance is being held firm.

(iv) Although shares were issued during the year, at a premium of 100%, the fact that appropriations are not disclosed in the income statement makes it very difficult to determine what type of dividend policy the company is following, and hence what kind of return shareholders have received over the two years.

(v) The length of credit period given to customers has increased (if all sales are on credit). While trading conditions may make this slip in credit control a necessity, it is regrettable that the company cannot obtain the same more relaxed terms from its suppliers; this would balance out working capital requirements, at least to some extent.

(vi) The inventory situation is what has changed most dramatically between 20X4 and 20X5. The rise in position statement inventories of E 30m may appear moderate, but it represents a rise of E 120m in finished goods and a fall of E 90 m in raw materials. It may be the case that the company is manufacturing less and buying in more finished goods, but the increase in labour costs would tend to negate this. It seems more likely that the company has greatly over-estimated the level of sales for 20X5, and has therefore ended 20X5 with an anomalous inventory position.

(vii) The cash levels held by the business, while perhaps on the high side at the beginning of the year, now appear far too low. The company is verging on an overdraft situation, in spite of receiving cash from a share issue during the year. The working capital situation, and in particular the inventory levels, must be resolved in order to recover the liquidity position of the business. If not, then there will be some difficulty in paying suppliers and taxes in the near future.

(b) A direct comparison of the results of Tone and Hilde GmbH may be misleading for the following reasons.

(i) It is unlikely that the two companies follow the same, or even similar, accounting policies, for example on inventory valuation, depreciation, valuation of land and buildings etc. Also, the general approach to receivables recoverability may be more or less prudent in the UK than under Tone's approach. These policies would have to be investigated to discover whether comparison is really feasible.

(ii) Hilde GmbH's payables are not split between short and long term, ie those due within one year and in more than one year (if any). Gearing ratios cannot be calculated, and the current and quick ratios calculated in (a) are of limited value.

(iii) There may be local or country-specific types of relationships between customers and suppliers which are different from the UK methods of doing business.

(iv) There is an interest charge shown in the statement of comprehensive income but the statement of financial position shows no separate disclosure of loans. The explanation may be that an interest charge is payable on the share capital in place of dividends.

(v) A legal reserve is shown. There is no indication of what type of reserve this may be comparable with (if any) in UK financial statements.

(vi) The statement of comprehensive income does not show a figure of gross profit making it difficult to compare margins.

(vii) The expenses include valuation adjustments for depreciation and current assets. It is not clear how these arise. They may simply comprise the normal depreciation charge and, say, a provision against doubtful receivables and obsolete inventory. It is true of many of the income statement figures, that a lack of knowledge about how, say, 'cost of sales' is computed, prevents comparison with UK accounts.

23 Public sector organisations

(a) The principal reason for the differences stem from the different way in which the organisations receive their funding and how they are controlled.

In the private sector capital funds are generally provided by means of the issue of shares or by the owners. From the point of view of the company, accounts are necessary initially to report to the shareholders or owners. Since shareholders will be interested in comparing investment prospects of different companies it is necessary that accounts are prepared using standard accounting principles.

Private sector accounts are also used by potential lenders and creditors to determine the credit worthiness of companies so the accounts need to be prepared in such a way that this can be determined.

In the private sector, revenue income is derived from the customers but this does not result in any accounting obligation because customers are free to use other suppliers if the service provided is unsatisfactory.

In the public sector, the sources of funds both capital and revenue are ultimately from the public in the form of taxation, council tax and charges for services. These are controlled by central government and local authorities. Since there is no choice on behalf of the providers of these funds the function of the accounts is rather different to those of the private sector and more rigorously controlled.

(b) The main differences between the laws regulations and guidelines are as follows.

(i) *Laws*. In the private sector the accounts are governed by statute. These specify the items which must be included in the accounts and the general format. The purpose of the provisions in these acts is to ensure the accounts give a 'true and fair' view of the financial position and performance of the company for the shareholders, lenders and creditors.

In the public sector there are separate laws for each service requiring them to produce accounts. Some of these services, such as the healthcare, are funded by central government and in these cases the laws generally state simply that accounts must be prepared. The relevant government department is responsible for the format in which the accounts are to be prepared for the purpose of reporting to Government.

In the case of local authorities, funds come from central government in the form of the revenue support grant, from the local population in the form of local taxes and from the users of services in the form of charges. The laws relating to the accounts of local authorities require the accounts to be prepared in such a way as to account to each of these groups.

(ii) *Regulations.* Although the laws indicate the general way in which accounts are to be prepared, not all eventualities can be covered and there is much room for variation in the way particular financial transactions can be accounted for. As a consequence of this, International Financial Reporting Standards have been produced by the accounting profession specifying in more detail how items are to be treated in the accounts with a view to producing accounts which are more comparable and reliable.

However, these standards are written primarily with the private sector in mind and under certain circumstances the requirements of central government regarding the accounts in some public sector organisations will override these.

(iii) *Guidelines.* In the public sector the purpose of the accounts is to report to central government, local tax payers and users of the services. As a consequence it is often necessary that the accounts be produced in a particular format to provide the necessary information, or to include details of particular aspects of the financial transactions. Consequently, Government has considerable powers under the law to issue detailed guideline on how the accounts are to be prepared. An example of this is the Manual of Accounts produced by the Department of Health. This gives the precise format of the accounts together with great detail of accounting procedures to be adopted. In some cases these powers have been delegated to Standard Setting bodies, for example for local authority accounts.

(c) The consequences for the public accounts in the public sector is that, although the accounts are produced using generally the same principles as the private sector, their details are often quite different depending on the bodies to be reported to.

In central government departments, such as the Health Service, the accounts are produced fundamentally to account to Government for the funds voted to the Health Service. Consequently they are produced in an absolutely prescribed form so that they can be easily consolidated. The reporting to the general public on the use of funds is a secondary consideration as it is assumed that parliament are responsible for the use of the funds on behalf of the taxpayers.

In case of local government, the annual report which they are required to produce includes comparative statistics and information about the council's policies which are intended to inform the general public about the activities of the council. This is necessary because the council which is responsible for the expenditure is elected by the residents of the area.

24 Small and medium-sized entities

(a) **Advantages**

Although International Accounting Standards (IAS) issued by the International Accounting Standards Committee (IASC) were originally designed to be suitable for all types of entity, in recent years, IAS and IFRS have come increasingly complex. They are now designed primarily to meet the information needs of **institutional investors in large listed entities**.

Shareholders of SMEs are often also directors. Therefore, through managing the company and maintaining the financial records, they are already aware of the company's financial performance and position and so do not need the level of detail in financial statements required by external institutional investors of larger companies.

The main external **users of SMEs tend to be lenders, trade suppliers and the tax authorities**. They have **different needs** from institutional investors and are more likely to focus on shorter-term cash flows, liquidity and solvency.

The full IFRSs cover a wide range of issues, contain a sizeable amount of implementation guidance and include disclosure requirements appropriate for public companies. This can make them **too complex for users of SMEs to understand**.

Many SMEs now feel that following full IFRSs places an unacceptable burden on preparers of SME accounts – a burden that has been growing as IFRSs become more detailed and more countries adopt them. The **cost of following full IFRSs often appears to outweigh the benefits**.

The **disclosure** requirements of full IFRSs are very **extensive** and as such, can result in **information overload** for the users of SME accounts, reducing the understandability of financial statements.

Some IFRS still offer **choice of accounting treatments**, leading to **lack of comparability** between different companies adopting different accounting standards.

Disadvantages

If SMEs follow their own simplified IFRS, their accounts will **no longer be comparable** with larger companies following full IFRSs or SMEs choosing to follow full IFRSs. This may make it harder to attract investors.

The changeover from full IFRSs to the simplified IFRS for SMEs, will require training and possible changes in systems. This will place both a **time and cost** burden on the company.

Full IFRSs are now well established and respected and act as a form of **quality control** on financial statements which comply with them. It could be argued therefore that financial statements which no longer comply with full IFRSs will **lose their credibility**. This is often called the 'Big GAAP, Little GAAP divide'.

The new IFRS for SMEs proposes to **reduce disclosures** required by full IFRSs. Omission of certain key information might actually make the financial statements **harder to understand**.

Conclusion

The advantages for SMEs of having a separate simplified IFRS outweigh the disadvantages. Once the Exposure Draft becomes an IFRS, both preparers and users of SME accounts will benefit.

(b)   The following standards are examples of IFRS with complex recognition, measurement and disclosure requirements and/or areas of choice.

Financial instruments

IAS 39 *Financial Instruments: Recognition and Measurement* is such a complex accounting standard that it has extensive implementation guidance. Examples of such complexities are as follows:

Recognition

IAS 39 requires financial instruments to be recognised when the entity becomes party to the contractual provisions of the instrument. To ascertain this point in time requires significant professional judgement, particularly for complex transactions such as consignment inventories.

Measurement

There are four categories of financial assets and two categories of financial liabilities. It is not always clear cut as to which category a financial instrument should belong. For example, financial assets 'held for trading' are defined as being 'acquired for the purposed of selling…. in the near term', yet the 'near term' is not defined.

Once the instrument is classified, it is measured either at fair value or amortised cost. Fair value can be very difficult to ascertain particularly where there is no active market for that instrument.

It would be easier if SMEs were just given a list of types of financial instruments which should be measured at amortised cost and types which should be measured at fair value. That way, the entity would not have to worry which class of asset or liability the financial instrument belongs to.

Deferred tax

IAS 12 *Income Taxes* covers both current and deferred tax. Many companies struggle to understand the requirements for deferred tax.

Deferred tax is defined as the amount of tax payable or recoverable in respect of temporary differences. A temporary difference is the difference between the carrying amount of an asset or liability and its tax base. Whilst the carrying amount is easy to ascertain as it can be lifted from the statement of financial position, the tax base is harder to identify. This is because it is a purely notional amount that would be found in the theoretical statement of financial position relating to the tax computation prepared for the tax authorities.

It would be simpler for SMEs if they were given a list of the most typical types of temporary difference with the relevant tax base.

Employee benefits

IAS 19 *Employee Benefits* has complex accounting requirements for defined benefit pension schemes. It requires the pension scheme's assets and obligations to be shown net in the company's statement of financial position.

Pension assets should be measured at fair value which again can be hard to ascertain where there is no active market. Pension obligations should be measured at present value. This can also be hard to ascertain as there are many elements of judgement required, for example:

- The relevant discount factor
- What the final salary of the employee might be
- How many years the employee might work/live for

Also, there is significant choice in how the company may recognised actuarial gains or losses:

- In profit or loss in the period in which they occur, or
- Deferred on a systematic basis, eg 10% corridor, or
- In retained earnings in the period in which they occur

It would be easier for SMEs to just be given one of the above options to avoid the need for choice. Immediate recognition would be simpler than deferral using the 10% corridor method.

Share-based payment

IFRS 2 *Share-based Payment* requires equity settled share-based payments to be measure either at the fair value of the goods or services received or if that fair value cannot be estimated reliably, at the fair value of the equity instruments granted.

The fair value of equity instruments can be particularly complex to ascertain especially in the case of share options where an option pricing model will need to be used.

The expense relating to share-based payments must be spread over the vesting period. If there are performance-related conditions, management must assess the likelihood of them being met. This is a complex area of judgement.

The standard could be simplified for SMEs by allowing them to use the 'intrinsic value' to value options rather than the fair value.

Leases

IAS 17 *Leases* requires leases to be classified as finance or operating leases depending on whether the lessee or lessor bear the risks and rewards incidental to ownership. This is not always clear cut.

Also, the treatment of the profit or loss on disposal in the case of a sale and operating leaseback is particularly complex.

The IAS could be simplified for SMEs by giving numerical guidance to distinguish between the types of lease. For example, UK GAAP deems leases where the present value of minimum lease payments is greater than or equal to 90% of the leased property's fair value at inception to be finance leases, in the absence of information to the contrary.

Choice in accounting treatment

IAS 31 *Interests in Joint Ventures* allows jointly controlled entities to be accounted for using either equity accounting or proportionate consolidation.

IAS 40 *Investment Property* allows a company to adopt either the cost or fair value model.

IAS 16 *Property, Plant and Equipment* allows a company to hold their assets at historical cost or fair value. Also, the entity may choose their own depreciation method as long as they depreciate the asset on a systematic basis over its useful life.

It would be simpler for SMEs if all areas of choice were removed and for only one option to be offered.

25 Peter Holdings

Divisional performance should be measured, in the interests of the group's shareholders, in such a way as to indicate what sort of return each subsidiary is making on the **shareholder's investment**. Shareholders themselves are likely to be interested in the performance of the group as a whole, measured in terms of return on shareholders' capital, earnings per share, dividend yield, and growth in earnings and dividends. These performance ratios cannot be used for subsidiaries in the group, and so an alternative measure has to be selected, which compares the return from the subsidiary with the value of the investment in the subsidiary.

Two performance measures could be used. Both would provide a suitable indication of performance from the point of view of the group's shareholders.

(a)   Return on capital employed, which from the shareholders' point of view would be:

$$\frac{\text{Profit after interest}}{\text{Net assets at current valuation minus non-current liabilities (eg long-term borrowings)}}$$

(b)   Alternatively, residual income could be used. This might be:

	Profit after debt interest
Minus	A notional interest charge on the value of assets financed by shareholders' capital
Equals	Residual income.

Residual income might be measured instead as:

	Profit before interest (controllable by the subsidiary's management)
Minus	A notional interest charge on the controllable investments of the subsidiary
Equals	Residual income.

Each subsidiary would be able to increase its residual income if it earned an incremental profit in excess of the notional interest charges on its incremental investments – ie in effect, if it added to the value of the group's equity.

26 Planet

Tutorial note. A typical multi-standard question, requiring advice to a client.

(a)   (i)   **Additional purchase consideration**

The company should **recognise a liability of $16 million and additional goodwill of $16 million**. Although IFRS 3 *Business combinations* sets a time limit for recognition of fair value adjustments this applies only to the acquired assets and liabilities. There is **no time limit** for the recognition of **goodwill relating to contingent consideration**.

The accounting entries required are:

		$'000	$'000
DEBIT	Intangible assets (goodwill)	16,000	
CREDIT	Current liabilities		16,000

(ii)   **Buildings**

In each case the main issue is whether Planet should recognise a provision for future repair and refurbishment expenditure.

Operating lease

IAS 37 *Provisions, contingent liabilities and contingent assets* states that a provision should only be recognised if there is **a present obligation resulting from a past event.** The terms of the lease contract mean that Planet has an obligation to incur expenditure in order to return the buildings to the lessee in good condition. The past obligating event appears to be the signing of the lease.

However, **future repairs and maintenance costs** relate to the future operation of the business. They are **not present obligations** resulting from past events. If IAS 37 is interpreted strictly, no provision should be recognised. The repair costs should either be charged as operating expenses in the period in which they occur or capitalised as assets.

Despite this, there is a strong case for recognising a provision for at least some of the expenditure. A lessee may be required to incur periodic charges to **make good dilapidations** or other damage occurring during the rental period. These liabilities **may be recognised, provided that the event giving rise to the obligation** under the lease **has occurred**. Damage to the building has occurred because of the severe weather and therefore a provision should be recognised for the $2.4 million needed to rectify this damage.

Whether any further amounts should be provided depends on the event that gives rise to the present obligation. It is possible to argue that the obligating event is the occurrence of specific damage to the building, but the cost of repairing actual dilapidation to the building during the year would be **difficult to estimate accurately**. It could also be argued that the obligating event is the passage of time, because some expenditure would be necessary if the lease were terminated immediately. Therefore a further $1,600,000 should be provided ($12 million less $2.4 million divided by six). The total provision is $4 million.

The accounting entries required are:

		$'000	$'000
DEBIT	Retained earnings	4,000	
CREDIT	Provisions		4,000

Leasehold property

In this case the company has a present obligation to incur expenditure as a result of a past event (the creation of the swimming pool). Under IAS 37 **a provision should be recognised for the full restoration cost** of $4 million. It is not possible to build up the provision over ten years as the directors propose.

Because the swimming pool represents access to future economic benefits, the future cost also represents an **asset** and this **should be recognised**. The asset will be depreciated at 10% per annum.

The carrying value of the leased building is $19.6 million ($16 million + $4 million – $400,000). This is above the recoverable amount of $19 million and therefore an impairment loss of $600,000 should be recognised.

The accounting entries required are:

		$'000	$'000
DEBIT	Non-current assets	4,000	
CREDIT	Provisions		4,000
DEBIT	Retained earnings (group retained profits)	320	
DEBIT	Non-controlling interest	80	
CREDIT	Depreciation (4,000 × 10%)		400
DEBIT	Retained earnings (group retained profits)	480	
DEBIT	Non-controlling interest	120	
CREDIT	Non-current assets		600

Owned buildings

Future repair expenditure does **not** represent a **present obligation** of the company because there has been **no past obligating event**. The repairs relate to the future operations of the company and in theory the expenditure **could be avoided** by selling the buildings. Under IAS 37 no provision can be recognised.

Any loss in service potential of the asset should be reflected in the depreciation charge. If the repairs are necessary to restore the service potential of the asset the expenditure should be capitalised.

(iii) **Agreement with subsidiary**

This has several implications for the financial statements. Because two thirds of the inventory remains unsold, the **unrealised intra-group profit** of $400,000 (2/3 × 4.2 million krona ÷ 1.4 × 20%) **must be eliminated**.

The accounting entries required are:

		$'000	$'000
DEBIT	Retained earnings (group retained profit)	400	
CREDIT	Inventory		400

In addition, because Planet is a listed company it must comply with the requirements of IAS 32 *Financial instruments: disclosure and presentation* and IAS 39 *Financial instruments: recognition and measurement*. The **forward contract is a derivative financial instrument**. By entering into the contract the company has fixed the price of the inventory and has avoided the effect of changes in the exchange rate. **No exchange gain or loss is recognised** on the transaction. The company is required to **disclose its accounting policy** in respect of hedge accounting, which is to translate its foreign currency assets and liabilities at the forward rate at the date of delivery. It is also required to disclose certain information about the contract, including details of any gains and losses carried forward in the statement of financial position at the year end and the extent to which these are expected to be recognised in the profit or loss in the next accounting period.

Because Planet entered into the contract without incurring any costs, the **book value** and the **fair value** of the forward contract were nil at its inception date. The cost of the inventory to the company was $3 million (4.2 million ÷ 1.4) but by 31 March 20X0 (the settlement date), exchange rates had moved so that the company would only have paid $2,896,552 for the inventory at the spot rate of 1.45. Therefore the company has made a **loss** of $103,448. **One third** of this ($34,482) relates to the **inventory sold** and has effectively been **recognised in the profit or loss for the year**. The **remainder** ($68,966) is **carried forward in the value of inventory** and will be recognised in the profit or loss in the next accounting period. There is an argument for **reducing this figure by 20%** as this is the amount of the intra-company profit which is eliminated on consolidation. The amount of the loss to be disclosed is therefore $55,173.

(iv) **Database**

The issue here is whether the cost of developing the database can be capitalised as an intangible asset. IAS 38 *Intangible assets* **prohibits the recognition** of internally generated brands, mastheads, publishing titles, customer lists and items similar in substance as assets. It could be argued that the database is similar to these items.

However, the expenditure has resulted in a new product which is now generating income for the group. IAS 38 **permits the capitalisation of development costs**, provided that the project meets **certain criteria**. The company must be able to demonstrate the technical feasibility of completing the asset, and the intention and ability to complete the asset and to use or sell it. The company must also be able to demonstrate that the asset will generate probable future economic benefits and that adequate technical, financial and other resources are available to complete the development. It must be possible to measure the expenditure attributable to the asset reliably.

Although the cost of the database is $6 million, sales of the manual are only expected to generate net revenue of $4 million. Therefore $4 million is **the amount of the future economic benefits that will flow to the company** and this is the amount that should be **recognised as an intangible asset**. Because the manual will require substantial revision every four years the development costs should be **amortised over this period**.

The accounting entries required are:

		$'000	$'000
DEBIT	Retained earnings	1,600	
DEBIT	Non-controlling interest	400	
CREDIT	Intangible assets (6,000 – 4,000)		2,000

To write down the development costs to $4,000

		$'000	$'000
DEBIT	Retained earnings	800	
DEBIT	Non-controlling interest	200	
CREDIT	Intangible assets		1,000

To amortise the asset over four years (4,000 ÷ 4)

(b)   PLANET
REVISED GROUP STATEMENT OF FINANCIAL POSITION AT 30 NOVEMBER 20X2

	$'000
Non-current assets	
Property, plant and equipment (76,240 + 4,000 – 600 – 400)	79,240
Intangible assets (10,360 + 16,000 – 2,000 – 1,000)	23,360
	102,600
Net current assets (55,800 – 16,000 – 400)	39,400
Total assets less current liabilities	142,000
Equity attributable to owners of the parent	
Share capital	32,200
Share premium	10,000
Retained earnings (W)	47,200
	89,400
Non-controlling interest (18,200 – 80 – 120 – 400 – 200)	17,400
	106,800
Non-current liabilities:	
Long term borrowings	25,400
Provisions (1,800 + 4,000 + 4,000)	9,800
	142,000

Working: retained earnings

	$'000
Draft	54,800
Provision for repairs (operating lease)	(4,000)
Additional depreciation (leased property)	(320)
Impairment loss (leased property)	(480)
Unrealised profit (intra-company sales)	(400)
Impairment loss (database)	(1,600)
Amortisation of development expenditure (database)	(800)
	47,200

27 Wingit

(a)   WINGIT GROUP
STATEMENT OF CASH FLOWS FOR THE YEAR ENDING 31 MAY 20X3

	$m	$m
Cash flow from operating activities		
Profit before taxation	723	
Adjustments for		
Depreciation	39	
Profit on sale of property, plant and equipment	(15)	
Net interest payable	3	
Share of profit of associate	(83)	
	667	
Increase in inventories (750 – 30 – 588)	(132)	
Increase in trade receivables (660 – 25 – 530 – 17 + 15)	(103)	
Increase in trade payables (1,193 – 20 – 913 – 9)	251	
Cash generated from operations	683	
Interest paid (37 – 6 – 9)	(22)	
Income taxes paid (W2)	(225)	
Net cash from operating activities c/f		436

	$m
Net cash from operating activities b/f	436
Cash flows from investing activities	

	$m	$m
Interest received (34 + 15 – 17)	32	
Dividend from associate (W3)	3	
Acquisition of subsidiary net of cash (17 – 35)	18	
Purchase of property, plant and equipment (278 – 60 – 100)	(118)	
Proceeds of sale of property, plant and equipment (30 + 15)	45	
Purchase of trade investments (W4)	(625)	
Net cash used in investing activities		(645)
Cash flows from financing activities		
Dividends paid (W5)	(121)	
Dividends paid to non-controlling interest (W6)	(17)	
Proceeds from exercise of options	20	
Proceeds from long term borrowing (W7)	232	
Net cash from financing activities		114
Net decrease in cash and cash equivalents		(95)
Cash and cash equivalents at start of period		140
Cash and cash equivalents at end of period		45

Workings

1   *Purchase of subsidiary (proof)*

	$m
Purchase consideration	97
Group share of net asset acquired (100 m × 80%)	80
Goodwill on acquisition	17

2   *Income taxes paid*

INCOME TAXES

	$m		$m
Cash paid (bal fig)	225	Opening balance	200
Closing balance	203	Tax payable in Regent	30
		P/L	198
	428		428

3   *Associate*

ASSOCIATE

	$m		$m
Opening balance	220	Cash received (bal fig)	3
P/L – profit	83	Closing balance	300
	303		303

4   *Trade investments*

TRADE INVESTMENTS

	$m		$m
Opening balance	50		
Other investments purchased (bal fig)	30		
Foreign equity investment	400	Closing balance	480
	480		480

	$m
Foreign operation – value	400
Exchange difference	195
Cash paid	595

Total purchases of investments (30 + 595) = 625

5   *Dividends paid*

DIVIDENDS

	$m		$m
Cash paid (bal fig)	121	Opening balance	100
Closing balance	105	Changes in equity	126
	226		226

6   *Non-controlling interest*

NON-CONTROLLING INTEREST

	$m		$m
Cash paid (bal fig)	17	Opening balance	150
		Regent (100 × 20%)	20
Closing balance	250	P/L	97
	267		267

7   *Long term borrowings*

LONG TERM BORROWINGS

	$m		$m
Cash paid	68	Opening balance	930
		Loan taken out	300
Closing balance	1,262	Bill of exchange	100
	1,330		1,330

	$m
Loan to finance foreign operation	300
Less loans repaid	(68)
Cash received	232

(b)   **Basis of calculating EPS**

Earnings per share is a widely used measure of financial performance. Detailed guidance on its calculation and on presentation and disclosure issues is given in IAS 33 *Earnings per share*.

IAS 33 does not address the issue of **manipulation of the numerator** in the calculation, that is the profit attributable to ordinary shareholders. The directors may manipulate it by **selecting accounting policies** designed generally to boost the earnings figure, and hence the earnings per share.

The **denominator** in the calculation is the number of shares by which the earnings figure is divided. It is defined as the weighted average number of ordinary shares outstanding during the period and is **more difficult to manipulate**, although the directors may try, as explained below.

(i) **Government grant**

IAS 20 *Accounting for government grants and disclosure of government assistance* allows two methods of accounting for government grants.

(1) Net the grant off against the cost of the asset and depreciate the net figure.

(2) Carry the grant as a **deferred credit** and release it to income over the life of the asset to offset the depreciation charge.

The **directors** justify their treatment of the government grant by reference to a past IASB Discussion Paper. This considered whether a grant should be **credited to income in the period in which it is made** rather than over several periods. However, there has been no discernable progress on that discussion paper and hence we have to apply IAS 20 as it stands.

The grant should therefore be removed from the statement of comprehensive income. Only $500,000 ($5m ÷ 10 years) should be credited to income; the balance of $4.5m should be shown as a deferred credit or deducted from the cost of the asset.

(ii) **Share issue**

In the calculation of EPS, the directors have used the number of shares in issue when Mr Springer retired from the company (6 million). They have **not taken into account the new issue of shares** made at the initial public offering.

The **number of new shares issued** is one million **plus** the **sponsor's shares** of 100,000. This needs to be **time apportioned** (the shares were in issue for ten months) and **added** to the **denominator** of the EPS calculation.

The treatment of the **issue costs is also incorrect**. IAS 39 states that **transaction costs**, defined as **incremental external costs** directly attributable to an equity transaction, should be **accounted for** as a **deduction from equity**. It was therefore incorrect to credit the value of the shares to profit or loss and likewise incorrect to charge the cash paid as an expense in profit or loss.

The **accounting entries** should have been as follows.

DEBIT	Retained earnings/share premium	$300,000	
CREDIT	Cash		$180,000
	Share capital		$100,000
	Share premium		$20,000

(iii) **Lease**

The lease arrangement includes an unconditional agreement to repurchase the lease. The substance of the transaction is therefore that of a loan secured on the property, rather than a genuine sale. Lease accounting is generally governed by IAS 17 *Leases,* but the *Framework* document and IAS 1 *Presentation of financial statements* stipulate the importance of substance over form.

(1) The **asset must be shown on the statement of financial position** and the 'sale proceeds' must be shown as a **finance liability**.

(2) The **profit** on the transaction ($500,000) needs to be eliminated from the **profit or loss for the year**.

(3) **Depreciation needs to be charged** on the carrying value.

(4) The carrying value of the property is the lease consideration of $4.5m less the profit, ie $4m.

(5) Depreciation at 5% per annum is therefore $200,000.

(6) **Interest needs to be charged** to the profit or loss, as we have concluded that this is in substance a loan.

(7) With an effective interest rate of 5.14%, the interest charge is $4.5m × 5.14% = $231,300.

(iv) **Rights issue**

The **rights issue** took place **after the company's year end**. The **proceeds** of the rights issue were **not available** for use **during the accounting period**. It would not therefore be appropriate to adjust EPS to reflect any part of the rights issue.

However, **an adjustment needs to be made for the bonus element** in the **rights issue**, since this is deemed to **affect** the **number of shares**, and hence **EPS** for **all accounting periods**.

The bonus element is $\dfrac{\text{fair value of share before rights issue}}{\text{theoretical ex rights price}}$

The theoretical ex rights price is:

			c
Initial holding	4	× 200c	800
Rights issue	1	× 160c	160
	5		960

$\therefore$ TERP = $\dfrac{960}{5}$ = $1.92

The fair value of the share is $2.00, therefore the bonus element is:

$$\dfrac{2.00}{1.92} = \dfrac{25}{24}$$

The number of shares in the EPS calculation needs to be increased by $^1/_{24}$.

Revised EPS calculation

Revised earnings

		$'000
	Profit per directors	4,800
(1)	Government grant taken to deferred income	(5,000)
	Credited to income in year	500
(2)	Cash paid	180
	Shares issued to sponsor	(120)
(3)	Profit on 'sale' eliminated	(500)
	Depreciation	(200)
	Interest charge	(231)
		(571)

Revised number of shares

Per directors	6,000,000
Additional shares issued	
$1,100,000 \times \dfrac{10}{12}$	916,667
	6,916,667
Bonus element: $6,916,667 \times \dfrac{1}{24}$	288,194
	7,204,861

$\therefore$ Loss per share $\dfrac{(571,000)}{7,204,861}$ = (7.9c)

(c) **Ethical matters**

(i) It is not always easy to determine whether creative accounting of this kind is **deliberate or whether it arises from ignorance or oversight**. The **assessment** of whether directors have acted **ethically** is often a matter of the exercise of **professional** judgement. In **practice**, it is important to act **fairly** and **tactfully** and not jump to unwarranted conclusions.

(ii) In factual terms when the correct accounting treatment is used, an earnings per share of **80c is converted into a loss per share of 7.9c**. Since the directors are entitled to a **cash bonus** for an EPS of above 50c, there would appear to be a strong **incentive** for them to select **accounting policies** designed to **boost it**.

(iii) The directors' explanation for their treatment of the **government grant** does **not stand up to scrutiny**. IAS 20 is not a complicated accounting standard and has been in force for many years. The treatment proposed in the Discussion Paper stage has not been driven forward by the IASB.

(iv) The treatment of the **issue of shares** may simply reflect **lack of knowledge** on the part of directors, rather than unethical accounting. **When corrected**, the **earnings figure** is **actually increased**, although the **number** of **shares** is **also increased**.

(v) The treatment of **issue costs** is a **complex** area and can often be **misunderstood**. It is more likely, therefore, that the **directors** were **confused** about the appropriate treatment and should be allowed the benefit of any doubt.

(vi) Regarding the **sale and repurchase agreement**, again it is difficult to assess whether this off balance sheet scheme was deliberate. Whether it was or not, the requirements of *Framework* document have been extant for some time, and the directors would reasonably be expected to be aware of the importance of **substance over form**.

(vii) The **failure to include the bonus element** of the rights issue after the reporting period in the calculation of the number of shares may be deliberate, but it is more likely to be an **error** or oversight.

Conclusion

(a) In practice unethical intent is difficult to prove. The best approach should be a proactive, preventative one, rather than letting matters get out of hand.

(b) On the facts of the case, **accounting standards have not been followed**, and generally in a manner **likely to boost EPS**.

(c) Accusations of fraud should not be made hastily without taking legal advice.

(d) As suggested in (i) above, in practice there should be internal controls to ensure that the **directors should be made aware** of their **responsibility** for the accuracy and fairness of the financial statements and their **obligation to apply accounting standards**.

Index

Review Form & Free Prize Draw – Paper P2 Corporate Reporting (INT) (6/09)

All original review forms from the entire BPP range, completed with genuine comments, will be entered into one of two draws on 31 July 2009 and 31 January 2010. The names on the first four forms picked out on each occasion will be sent a cheque for £50.

Name: _____

Address: _____

_____

_____

How have you used this Text?
(Tick one box only)

☐ Home study (book only)

☐ On a course: college _____

☐ With 'correspondence' package

☐ Other _____

Why did you decide to purchase this Text? *(Tick one box only)*

☐ Have used BPP Texts in the past

☐ Recommendation by friend/colleague

☐ Recommendation by a lecturer at college

☐ Saw information on BPP website

☐ Saw advertising

☐ Other _____

During the past six months do you recall seeing/receiving any of the following?
(Tick as many boxes as are relevant)

☐ Our advertisement in *Financial Management*

☐ Our advertisement in *Pass*

☐ Our advertisement in *PQ*

☐ Our brochure with a letter through the post

☐ Our website www.bpp.com

Which (if any) aspects of our advertising do you find useful?
(Tick as many boxes as are relevant)

☐ Prices and publication dates of new editions

☐ Information on Text content

☐ Facility to order books off-the-page

☐ None of the above

Which BPP products have you used?

Text	☑	Success CD	☐	Learn Online	☐
Kit	☐	i-Learn	☐	Home Study Package	☐
Passcard	☐	i-Pass	☐	Home Study PLUS	☐
MCQ cards	☐				

Your ratings, comments and suggestions would be appreciated on the following areas.

	Very useful	Useful	Not useful
Introductory section (Key study steps, personal study)	☐	☐	☐
Chapter introductions	☐	☐	☐
Key terms	☐	☐	☐
Quality of explanations	☐	☐	☐
Case studies and other examples	☐	☐	☐
Assessment focus points	☐	☐	☐
Questions and answers in each chapter	☐	☐	☐
Fast forwards and chapter roundups	☐	☐	☐
Quick quizzes	☐	☐	☐
Question Bank	☐	☐	☐
Answer Bank	☐	☐	☐
Index	☐	☐	☐

Overall opinion of this Study Text   Excellent ☐   Good ☐   Adequate ☐   Poor ☐

Do you intend to continue using BPP products?   Yes ☐   No ☐

On the reverse of this page are noted particular areas of the text about which we would welcome your feedback.

The BPP author of this edition can be e-mailed at: katyhibbert @bpp.com

Please return this form to: Lesley Buick, ACCA Publishing Manager, BPP Learning Media Ltd, FREEPOST, London, W12 8BR

Review Form & Free Prize Draw (continued)

TELL US WHAT YOU THINK

Please note any further comments and suggestions/errors below

Free Prize Draw Rules

1. Closing date for 31 July 2009 draw is 30 June 2009. Closing date for 31 January 2010 draw is 31 December 2009.

2. Restricted to entries with UK and Eire addresses only. BPP employees, their families and business associates are excluded.

3. No purchase necessary. Entry forms are available upon request from BPP Learning Media Ltd. No more than one entry per title, per person. Draw restricted to persons aged 16 and over.

4. Winners will be notified by post and receive their cheques not later than 6 weeks after the relevant draw date.

5. The decision of the promoter in all matters is final and binding. No correspondence will be entered into.